Indonesia Update Series

Regional Dynamics in a Decentralized Indonesia

EDITED BY

HAL HILL

ISEAS

INSTITUTE OF SOUTHEAST ASIAN STUDIES

Singapore

First published in Singapore in 2014 by
ISEAS Publishing
Institute of Southeast Asian Studies
30 Heng Mui Keng Terrace
Pasir Panjang
Singapore 119614

E-mail: publish@iseas.edu.sg
Website: http://bookshop.iseas.edu.sg

The responsibility for facts and opinions in this publication rests exclusively with the authors and their interpretations do not necessarily reflect the views or the policy of the Institute or its supporters.

ISEAS Library Cataloguing-in-Publication Data

Regional dynamics in a decentralized Indonesia / edited by Hal Hill.
    This book emanates from the Indonesia Update 2013 Conference presented by the Indonesia Project at Crawford School of Public Policy, The Australian National University and held on 21-22 September 2013.
1.   Decentralization in government—Indonesia—Congresses.
2.   Regional planning—Indonesia—Congresses.
3.   Local government—Indonesia—Congresses.
4.   Poverty—Indonesia—Congresses.
5.   Migration, Internal—Indonesia—Congresses.
I.   Hill, Hal, 1948-
II.   Australian National University. Indonesia Project.
III.   Indonesia Update Conference (31st : 2013 : Australian National University)
DS644.4 I41 2013   2014

ISBN 978-981-4459-84-6 (soft cover)
ISBN 978-981-4459-85-3 (hard cover)
ISBN 978-981-4519-17-5 (e-book, PDF)

Edited and typeset by Beth Thomson, Japan Online, Canberra
Indexed by Angela Grant, Sydney
Printed in Singapore by Markono Print Media Pte Ltd

In memory of Dr Thee Kian Wie

As this book was in preparation, one of Indonesia's most remarkable intellectuals, Dr Thee Kian Wie, passed away.

Kian Wie was a close friend of and mentor to many of the contributors to this volume. We therefore dedicate this volume to his memory, acknowledging his generous friendship, his boundless enthusiasm, his outstanding contribution to the Indonesian research and policy communities, and his commitment to public service. We will miss him.

Contents

Tables

Figures

Contributors

Greg Acciaioli, University of Western Australia, Perth

Edward Aspinall, Australian National University, Canberra

Geoff Baker, Murdoch University, Perth

Anne Booth, SOAS, University of London, London

Mohamad Adhi Prakoso Dipo, World Bank, Jakarta

Tommy Firman, Institute of Technology, Bandung

Hal Hill, Australian National University, Canberra

Amri Ilmma, World Bank, Jakarta

Sidney Jones, Institute for Policy Analysis of Conflict, Jakarta

Hans Kaiwai, Cenderawasih University, Jayapura

Blane D. Lewis, International Consultant, Jakarta

Anton Lucas, Flinders University, Adelaide

Edmund Malesky, Duke University, Durham

Chris Manning, Australian National University, Canberra

Sofi Mardiah, Center for International Forestry Research, Bogor

John F. McCarthy, Australian National University, Canberra

Peter McCawley, Australian National University, Canberra

Neil McCulloch, Australian Department of Foreign Affairs and Trade, Jakarta

Marcus Mietzner, Australian National University, Canberra

Julius A. Mollet, Cenderawasih University, Jayapura

Salut Muhidin, Macquarie University, Sydney

Cillian Nolan, Institute for Policy Analysis of Conflict, Jakarta

Nanda Nurridzki, World Bank, Jakarta

Ngakan Putu Oka, Hasanuddin University, Ujungpandang

Arianto A. Patunru, Australian National University, Canberra

Raden Muhamad Purnagunawan, Padjadjaran University, Bandung

Erman A. Rahman, The Asia Foundation, Jakarta

Vivianti Rambe, Murdoch University, Perth

Umbu R. Raya, Australian National University, Canberra, and Nusa Cendana University, Kupang

Budy P. Resosudarmo, Australian National University, Canberra

Ida Aju Pradnja Resosudarmo, Center for International Forestry Research, Bogor

Henry Sandee, World Bank, Jakarta

Günther G. Schulze, University of Freiburg, Freiburg, and Australian National University, Canberra

Bambang Suharnoko Sjahrir, University of Freiburg, Freiburg

Solahudin, Institute for Policy Analysis of Conflict, Jakarta

Dirk Steenbergen, Murdoch University, Perth

Sudarno Sumarto, SMERU Research Institute and National Team for the Acceleration of Poverty Reduction (TNP2K), Jakarta

Nugroho Adi Utomo, Center for International Forestry Research, Bogor

Yogi Vidyattama, University of Canberra, Canberra

Marc Vothknecht, European Commission, Brussels

Matthew Wai-Poi, World Bank, Jakarta

Carol Warren, Murdoch University, Perth

Laura Wijaya, World Bank, Jakarta

Acknowledgments

This volume is based on the papers presented and discussed at the thirty-first Indonesia Update conference held at the Australian National University (ANU), Canberra, on 20–21 September 2013.

It is a pleasure to thank the many institutions and people who contributed to the success of the conference, and to this book. Our biggest debt goes to the contributors, for their papers, for making the trip to Canberra and for replying promptly to numerous editorial queries.

The wonderful staff of the ANU's Indonesia Project, ably led by Budy Resosudarmo, ensured that the huge logistical effort of coordinating the event ran very smoothly. Special thanks go to the core Project staff, Cathy Haberle and Nurkemala Muliani, who went way beyond the course of normal duties. They were supported by many other colleagues, including Allison Ley, Kiki Verico, Trish van der Hoek, Thuy Thu Pham and a team of volunteers, many from the ANU Indonesian student community.

The Update continues to receive strong support from the ANU's College of Asia and the Pacific. The College's then Dean, Andrew MacIntyre, opened the event. Academic colleagues in the Indonesia Project, the Arndt-Corden Department of Economics and the Department of Political and Social Change contributed to the success of the event, as informal advisors and as session chairs.

The Department of Foreign Affairs and Trade has been a long-term supporter of the Update, through its grant to the Indonesia Project. We gratefully acknowledge that support, without which the event would not be possible. We also thank the ANU Department of Political and Social Change, the World Bank Jakarta office and the Asia Foundation, Jakarta, for sponsoring speakers and contributors.

The production of a very large, high-quality manuscript at breakneck speed would only be possible with the remarkable editorial work of Beth Thomson. Beth has been involved with all aspects of the production of the Update volume since 1994. We are indebted to her for her diligence, professionalism and collegiality. Liz Drysdale, another long-term Indonesia Project staffer, assisted Beth with some of the editing, and Angela Grant prepared the index.

As has been the case continuously since 1994, this volume is published by the Institute of Southeast Asian Studies (ISEAS), Singapore, under an arrangement established with the Institute's remarkable long-time Managing Editor, Triena Ong. In 2013 Triena resigned from ISEAS, and we thank Senior Editor Rahilah Yusuf for efficiently overseeing the production of this volume.

Hal Hill
Canberra, March 2014

Glossary

adat	custom or tradition, customary or traditional law
APBD	*anggaran pendapatan dan belanja daerah* (subnational government budget)
Apindo	Asosiasi Pengusaha Indonesia (Indonesian Employers Association)
Bappenas	Badan Perencanaan Pembangunan Nasional (National Development Planning Agency)
BKN	Badan Kepegawaian Negara (State Civil Service Agency)
BKSP	Badan Kerjasama Pembangunan (Development Cooperation Agency)
BOT	build–operate–transfer
BPD	Badan Perwakilan Desa, renamed Badan Permusyawaratan Desa in 2004 (Village Deliberative Council)
BPK	Badan Pemeriksa Keuangan (State Audit Agency)
BPN	Badan Pertanahan Nasional (National Land Agency)
BPS	Badan Pusat Statistik (Statistics Indonesia)
BRR	Badan Rehabilitasi dan Rekonstruksi (Aceh-Nias Rehabilitation and Reconstruction Agency)
bupati	district head
camat	subdistrict head
CDD	community-driven development
D&D	decentralization and democratization
Daerah Istimewa	Special Territory
DAK	Dana Alokasi Khusus (Special Purpose Fund)
dana otsus	special autonomy funds
dapil	*daerah pemilihan* (voting district)
DAU	Dana Alokasi Umum (General Purpose Fund)
DBH	Dana Bagi Hasil (Revenue Sharing Fund)
DFID	Department for International Development
distrik	subdistrict (Papua)

DKI	Daerah Khusus Ibukota (Special Capital Region)
DPD	Dewan Perwakilan Daerah (Regional Representative Council)
DPR	Dewan Perwakilan Rakyat (People's Representative Council), the national parliament
DPRD	Dewan Perwakilan Rakyat Daerah (Regional People's Representative Council), regional parliament
EGI	Economic Governance Index
ESRC	Economic and Social Research Council
FE	fixed effects
Fitra	Forum Indonesia untuk Transparansi Anggaran (Indonesian Forum for Budget Transparency)
GAM	Gerakan Aceh Merdeka (Free Aceh Movement)
GDP	gross domestic product
GeRAK	Gerakan Rakyat Anti Korupsi (Movement against Corruption)
Gerindra	Gerakan Indonesia Raya (Greater Indonesia Movement Party)
Golkar	Golongan Karya (the state political party under the New Order, and one of the major post-New Order parties)
gotong royong	mutual assistance
GRP	gross regional product
HDI	Human Development Index
hibah	grant
Inpres	Instruksi Presiden (Presidential Instruction), a program of special grants from the central government
Inpres Desa Tertinggal	Special Presidential Program for Poor Villages
Inpres Kabupaten	Special Presidential Program for Districts
Inpres Sekolah Dasar	Special Presidential Program for Primary Schools
IPAC	Institute for Policy Analysis of Conflict
Ipeda	land tax
Jabodetabek	Jakarta and the surrounding metropolitan area, including Bogor, Depok, Tangerang and Bekasi
Jamkesda	Jaminan Kesehatan Daerah (Regional Health Insurance for the Poor)
Jamkesmas	Jaminan Kesehatan Masyarakat (National Health Insurance for the Poor)
JICA	Japan International Cooperation Agency
kabupaten	district
Kadin	Kamar Dagang dan Industri (Chamber of Commerce and Industry)
kampung	village
kawasan hutan	forest lands, the Indonesian forest estate
kawedanan	administrative unit between a district (*kabupaten*) and a subdistrict (*kecamatan*)

KDP	Kecamatan Development Program
kecamatan	subdistrict
kelurahan	village
kepala daerah	regional head
kepala desa	village head
KHL	Kebutuhan Hidup Layak (Workers Decent Basic Needs Index)
Kopassus	Komando Pasukan Khusus (Special Forces Command)
kota	city, municipality
KPA	Komite Peralihan Aceh (Aceh Transitional Committee)
KPK	Komisi Pemberantasan Korupsi (Corruption Eradication Commission)
KPPOD	Komite Pemantauan Pelaksanaan Otonomi Daerah (Regional Autonomy Watch)
KPU	Komisi Pemilihan Umum (General Elections Commission)
KPUD	Komisi Pemilihan Umum Daerah (Regional Elections Commission)
LPI	Logistics Performance Index
LRRD	linking relief, rehabilitation and development
lurah	village head (appointed civil servant)
Masyumi	Majelis Syuro Muslimin Indonesia (Indonesian Muslim Consultative Council)
merdeka	independence
MOU	memorandum of understanding
MP3EI	Masterplan Percepatan dan Perluasan Pembangunan Ekonomi Indonesia (Masterplan for the Acceleration and Expansion of Indonesia's Economic Development)
MPR	Majelis Permusyawaratan Rakyat (People's Consultative Assembly)
MRP	Majelis Rakyat Papua (Papuan People's Council)
musrenbang	*musyawarah perencanaan pembangunan* (development planning meeting)
musyawarah	consensus
nagari	village community (Minangkabau, West Sumatra)
NER	net enrolment rate
noken	traditional bag woven from bark that Papuan highlanders use as a carry-all; also refers to a diverse range of largely unregulated voting practices that share two features: voting by consensus, in which communities (or community leaders) come to an agreement before the poll on how everyone will vote, and an absence of any marking of ballots
OECD	Organisation for Economic Co-operation and Development
OLS	ordinary least squares

OPM	Organisasi Papua Merdeka (Free Papua Movement)
PAD	*pendapatan asli daerah* (own-source revenue, locally generated revenue)
PBB	*pajak bumi dan bangunan* (land and buildings tax)
PCI	Provincial Competitiveness Index
PD	Partai Demokrat (Democrat Party), the party led by President Susilo Bambang Yudhoyono
PDAM	*perusahaan daerah air minum* (local water enterprise)
PDIP	Partai Demokrasi Indonesia Perjuangan (Indonesian Democratic Party of Struggle), the party led by former president Megawati Sukarnoputri
pemekaran	'blossoming', referring to the process of subdivision of administrative units
Perdasus	Peraturan Daerah Khusus (Special Regional Regulation)
pilkada	*pemilihan kepala daerah* (elections for regional heads of government)
PISA	Programme for International Student Assessment
PNPM	Program Nasional Pemberdayaan Masyarakat (National Community Empowerment Program)
Podes	Potensi Desa (Village Potential), a BPS survey of village economic status
PP	*peraturan presiden* (presidential regulation)
PPIP	Program Pembangunan Infrastruktur Perdesaan (Rural Infrastructure Development Program)
PPP	Partai Persatuan Pembangunan (United Development Party)
PPP	purchasing power parity
Prospek	Program Strategis Pembangunan Ekonomi dan Kelembagaan Kampung (Strategic Village Economic and Institutional Development Program), Papua
puskesmas	*pusat kesehatan masyarakat* (community health centre, local public clinic)
qanun	regulation passed by the Aceh provincial parliament or one of the Aceh district parliaments
REDD+	Reducing Emissions from Deforestation and Degradation
reformasi	reform (used to characterize post-New Order Indonesian society and politics)
Respek	Rencana Strategis Pembangunan Kampung (Strategic Village Development Plan), Papua
RTRW	*rencana tata ruang wilayah* (regional spatial plan)
Sakernas	Survei Angkatan Kerja Nasional (National Labour Force Survey)
SD	Sekolah Dasar (primary school)
SDO	Subsidi Daerah Otonom (Autonomous Regional Subsidy)

Seknas Fitra	Sekretariat Nasional Forum Indonesia untuk Transparansi Anggaran (National Secretariat of the Indonesian Forum for Budget Transparency)
shariah	Islamic law
SIKD	Sistem Informasi Keuangan Daerah (Regional Financial Information System), Ministry of Finance
SILPA	*sisa lebih pembayaran anggaran* (unspent budget funds)
SIUP	*surat izin usaha perdagangan* (trading permit)
SMP	Sekolah Menengah Pertama (junior secondary school)
SPP	Simpan Pinjam Perempuan (Savings and Credit for Women)
suku	clan (Papua)
Supas	Survei Penduduk antar Sensus (inter-censal survey)
Susenas	Survei Sosio-Ekonomi Nasional (National Socio-Economic Survey)
TDP	*tanda daftar perusahaan* (company registration certificate)
TGHK	*tata guna hutan kesepakatan* (forest land-use map based on consensus)
TKPKD	Tim Koordinasi Penanggulangan Kemiskinan Daerah (Local Coordinating Team for Poverty Reduction)
TNP2K	Tim Nasional Percepatan Penanggulangan Kemiskinan (National Team for the Acceleration of Poverty Reduction)
TPNPB	Tentara Pembebasan Nasional Papua Barat (West Papua National Liberation Army)
ulama	Islamic teacher or cleric
USAID	United States Agency for International Development
VCP	Vietnamese Communist Party
Wali Nanggroe	Guardian of the State (Aceh)
walikota	mayor
warung	roadside food kiosk

Currencies

$	US dollar
Rp	Indonesian rupiah

Map of Indonesia

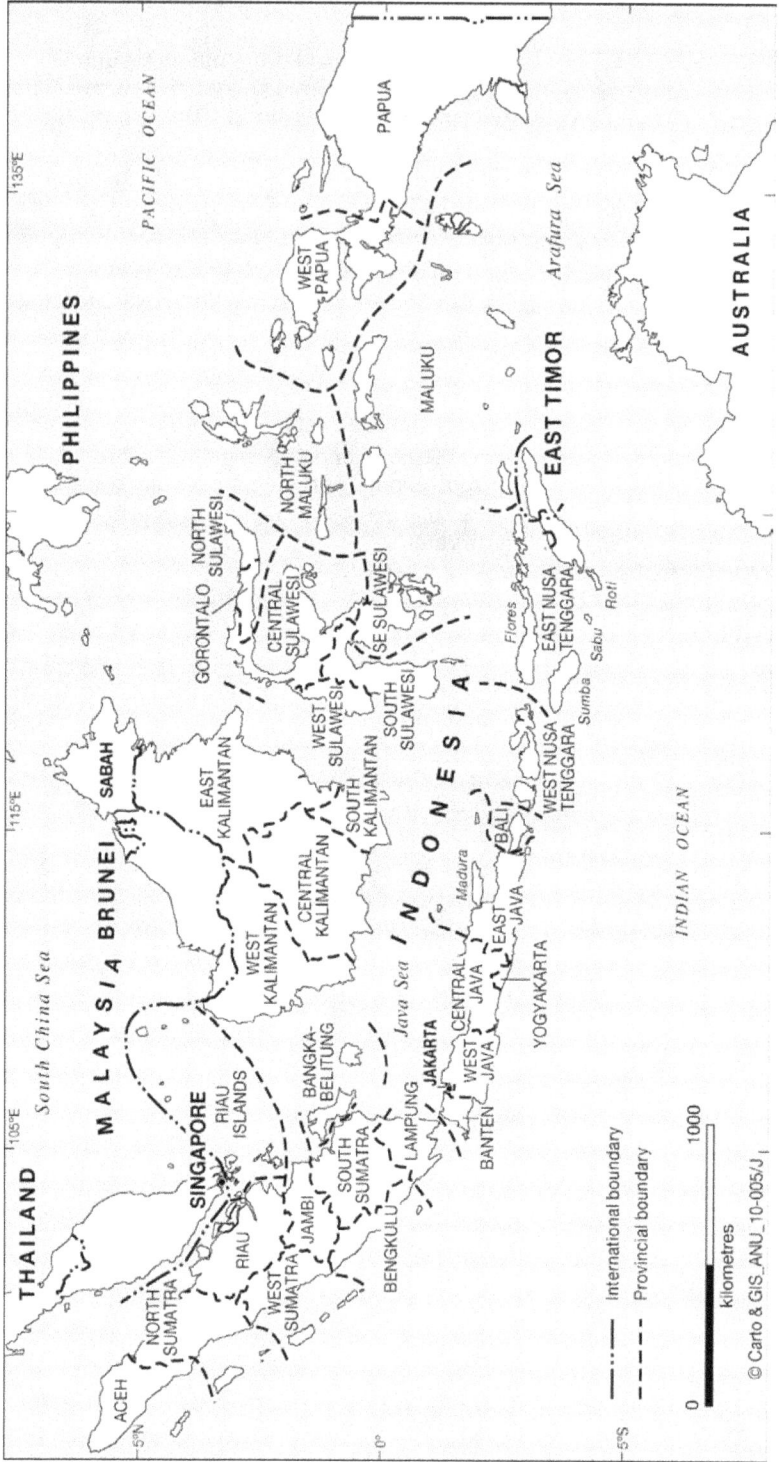

THAILAND

PHILIPPINES

South China Sea

PACIFIC OCEAN

MALAYSIA

BRUNEI

SABAH

SINGAPORE

RIAU
ISLANDS

ACEH

NORTH
SUMATRA

RIAU

WEST
SUMATRA

JAMBI

BANGKA-
BELITUNG

BENGKULU

SOUTH
SUMATRA

LAMPUNG

WEST
KALIMANTAN

CENTRAL
KALIMANTAN

EAST
KALIMANTAN

SOUTH
KALIMANTAN

WEST
SULAWESI

CENTRAL
SULAWESI

GORONTALO

NORTH
SULAWESI

NORTH
MALUKU

WEST
PAPUA

PAPUA

SE SULAWESI

SOUTH
SULAWESI

MALUKU

Java Sea

JAKARTA

BANTEN

WEST
JAVA

CENTRAL
JAVA

EAST
JAVA

Madura

YOGYAKARTA

INDONESIA

BALI

WEST NUSA
TENGGARA

EAST NUSA
TENGGARA

Sumba

Sabu

Roti

Flores

EAST TIMOR

Arafura Sea

INDIAN OCEAN

AUSTRALIA

International boundary

Provincial boundary

kilometres

0   1000

© Carto & GIS_ANU_10-005/J

135°E

115°E

105°E

5°N

0°

5°S

1 An introduction to the issues

Hal Hill

1.1 THE ISSUES

In 2001, Indonesia embarked on a 'big bang' decentralization involving a major transfer of administrative, political and financial authority primarily to the district/municipality (*kabupaten/kota*) level of government.[1] Together with the rapid transition from authoritarian to democratic rule in the late 1990s, this initiative has transformed the country's political, social and business life. While national government remains the major area of contestation, power has shifted irreversibly away from the centre. How this significantly increased regional autonomy works will have a crucial bearing on the future of the Indonesian nation-state. This volume, featuring contributions by 43 authors, provides a timely, comprehensive and analytical assessment of the country's regional development dynamics in the post-decentralization environment.

The regions (*daerah*) are central to an understanding of modern Indonesia. With its 17,000 islands stretching across three time zones, Indonesia is the world's largest archipelagic state. It features enormous diversity in its economy, ecology, ethnography, demography and much else. At the district level, for example, the richest region has a per capita income more than 50 times that of the poorest. Were they independent states, some parts of Indonesia would be classified as upper middle-income states, comparable to much richer Malaysia and Thailand, while other regions would be in the least developed group of extremely poor states.

The policy and intellectual paradigms in and on Indonesia reflect this diversity. It is the key sentiment in the national motto, 'Unity in diversity'

---

1 Except where indicated otherwise, I refer to the second tier of subnational governments (*kabupaten/kota*) collectively as 'districts'.

(*'Bhinneka tunggal ika'*). Indonesians worry about the preservation of territorial integrity and national unity to an extent that may surprise outsiders unfamiliar with the country's struggle to create a new nation-state. After all, Indonesia did not formally exist as an entity until 1945, or even in the imagination of the nation's independence leaders until the early twentieth century. In fact, it came into existence in part as a result of lines drawn arbitrarily on a map in far-off European metropolitan capitals. Given the colonial history of divide-and-rule tactics, Indonesians are often shocked by the seemingly innocuous observation to the effect that 'A glance at a map might seem enough to suggest the improbability of Indonesia' (Cribb 1999: 3). This sensitivity about territorial integrity is heightened by the fact that Indonesia's international boundaries have changed twice, first with the entry of what is now the two Papua provinces following an 'Act of Free Choice' in 1969, and then with the entry – in Indonesian if not international eyes – of East Timor in 1975 and its exit in 1999. In addition, there have been periodic secessionist movements, most notably the Permesta Revolt of 1957–58, when several regions attempted to leave the Republic. Unhappiness with Jakarta's authority has been present for much of Indonesia's history as a nation-state, with the peripheral regions of Aceh and Papua the most prominent examples.

Like all large nation-states, Indonesia has had to forge a workable set of arrangements governing administrative, political and financial relations between the central government and its subnational authorities. Although the country has always been a unitary state, in practice these arrangements have varied from strongly centralist to de facto federalist, as at present (Booth, Chapter 2; see also Mackie 1980). Although the Suharto regime (1966–98) was strongly centralist, in later years even it recognized the impracticability of concentrating so much administrative and financial power in the capital. Intellectually, the case for a more decentralized state was put eloquently by Clifford Geertz (1971: 19), arguably the most famous foreign researcher of Indonesia:

> Archipelagic in geography, eclectic in civilization, and heterogeneous in culture, Indonesia flourishes when it accepts and capitalizes on its diversity, and disintegrates when it denies and suppresses it …

The 1999 decentralization laws, Law 22/1999 on Regional Government and Law 25/1999 on the Fiscal Balance between the Central Government and the Regions (since revised as Law 32/2004 and Law 33/2004), define the current arrangements. They took effect from the beginning of 2001 and are regarded in the comparative literature on decentralization as substantial. The number of subnational administrative units is large and increasing rapidly. According to the central statistical agency, Badan Pusat Statistik (BPS), over the period 1998–2012 the number of provinces rose from 27 to 34,[2] the number of districts (*kabupaten*) from 249 to 399, the number of municipalities (*kota*) from 65 to 98, the number of subdistricts (*kecamatan*) from 4,028 to 6,793, and the number of villages (*kelurahan*) from 67,925 to 79,075. As a result of these increases, subnational expenditure now makes up about half of consolidated government expenditure, net of interest payments and subsidies. Not only is the flow of funds to subnational governments large, but the use of these funds is mostly unrestricted. Over 90 per cent of subnational government revenue comes from central government transfers, with the General Purpose Fund (Dana Alokasi Umum, DAU) providing about 60 per cent of the total.

Combined with the equally abrupt transition from authoritarian to democratic rule, decentralization has transformed the Indonesian nation-state. More than a decade after the introduction of this reform, it is therefore timely to examine how effective the changes have been, and how they have affected Indonesian development. Theory suggests that decentralized governance is likely to produce superior governance outcomes, since policy makers will be closer and more directly accountable to local communities, and since competition among local governments for scarce mobile factors of capital and skills will lift general governance quality. A major issue to be addressed in this volume is whether the Indonesian experience confirms this a priori expectation.

Among the questions the contributors to this volume address are the following. First, how have Indonesia's regional development dynamics changed since the reforms? Second, how closely do social outcomes, including poverty incidence and environmental management, correlate with these development dynamics over this period, and have the poorer regions been protected by the decentralization reforms? Third, among the many factors shaping regional socio-economic outcomes – from the provision of infrastructure to the China-induced commodity boom – how important has decentralization been? Fourth, has decentralization contributed to the strategically important goal of preserving the country's territorial integrity, especially in the sometimes troubled peripheral regions? Fifth, how have population mobility, labour market integration and urbanization been affected by the changes?

More generally, the authors in this book are interested in finding out how the reforms are working in practice. Can one conclude that Indonesia is better governed as a result of decentralization? Are the better-governed regions being 'rewarded' with more investment and better amenities, suggesting that the reforms have contributed to faster socio-

---

2 This has involved the creation of eight new provinces, since East Timor was counted as one of the 27 provinces.

economic development? Or has the continued splitting (*pemekaran*) of administrative units to create new ones introduced a permanent, deep, institutionalized instability that is likely to retard the country's development progress?

1.2   MAJOR FINDINGS

The chapters that follow address these and related issues. They are based primarily on presentations delivered and discussed at the 2013 Indonesia Update Conference, held annually at the Australian National University, Canberra, in September. The organization of the book follows the conference structure, with contributions grouped under five headings: an overview of historical, economic, political and social patterns; decentralization and governance; local-level perspectives; migration, cities and connectivity; and challenges for Indonesia's periphery, with special reference to Aceh and Papua. I now briefly summarize the key findings of each chapter.

Historical, economic, political and social patterns

The four chapters in Part 1 provide an entrée to the issues.

In Chapter 2, Anne Booth examines the state of centre–region relations in 1949–99, before Indonesia's 'big bang' decentralization. She points out that much of the considerable literature on the decentralization reforms assumes that Indonesia's system of government was highly centralized from the time of the transfer of power from the Dutch in 1949 until the end of the Suharto era in 1998. She commences by examining the debates of the early 1950s about the optimal economic and political structure of the newly independent republic. These culminated in the Nasroen proposals to give some revenue-raising powers to local governments. Booth argues that, had the proposals been implemented, they would have made a considerable difference to the future course of central–regional relations. However, they turned out to be the road not followed. Instead, and especially after the regional revolts of the late 1950s, 'A system of "de facto federalism" came to apply, in which compromise and ad hocery affected economic as well as political aspects of the relationship between the centre and the regions' (p. 32).

After Suharto took power from Sukarno in 1966, 'an inexorable trend towards re-centralization' of both economic and political power took place (Mackie 1980: x). The second part of Chapter 2 therefore examines the consequences of the Suharto-era policies for regional development in Java and elsewhere. Law 5/1974 on Basic Principles of Regional Government provided the guiding framework, placing regional governors, many of them military officers, under the direct control of Jakarta. Large funds began to flow to the regions, especially during the oil boom period, thus assuaging local discontent to some extent. Greatly improved transport networks facilitated large-scale mobility, some of it officially supported through the national government's transmigration program.

There was little attempt, however, to encourage greater local resource mobilization, apart from some marginal attempts to reform the regional finance system in the 1990s. Hence, 'By the early 1990s, it was clear that there was considerable unrest in many parts of the country over the system of regional and local government that had grown up under Suharto' (p. 40). A major problem was that of 'rich provinces, poor people', with resource-rich regions receiving little revenue from the resource-based activities within their jurisdictions. Moreover, centralized controls remained cumbersome, leaving little scope for local initiative. The 1999 regional autonomy laws, which were in preparation prior to the Asian financial crisis, were thus a major advance. However, a key limitation was that 'they did not tackle the issue of devolving greater revenue-raising powers to either provinces or districts' (p. 41).

In Chapter 3, Marcus Mietzner provides a comprehensive yet nuanced overview of local-level politics since decentralization. He argues that it would be a mistake to focus solely on the myriad problems associated with the decentralization initiative, evaluated according to textbook principles of federal fiscal relations. It is not that these issues are unimportant, as the public's dismay over the seemingly endless cases of corruption at all levels of government attests. What is more important, however, is that the Indonesian nation-state has survived a traumatic episode in its history, despite 'Yugoslav'-type predictions of territorial disintegration. In fact, it is probably stronger now than at any point in its history: 'the really astonishing feature of decentralization 13 years after it was launched is how stable centre–periphery relations have become' (p. 62). From this perspective, the reform has achieved its main objective. In this respect, 'Indonesia seems to have made the right call on the project's fundamentals' (p. 64).

Mietzner develops this thesis with reference to five factors that explain the new system's strength and durability. These are the strong public satisfaction with decentralization; the flourishing of local identities after decades of attempts to impose uniformity; the increased level of state penetration and thus greater capacity of the civilian bureaucracy; the effective design of local elections that has avoided the dangers of ethno-political mobilization; and the emergence of new, popular leaders at the local level who – in some cases at least – have broken the monopolistic grip of established elites on positions of political power.

Together, the country's democratization and decentralization reforms have forged a radically different system of governance in Indonesia. Power has been devolved from the centre, yet the state as a whole has not been weakened, but rather strengthened. No longer are regional heads imposed by Jakarta. Electoral rights have been massively expanded, with the citizenry now electing personnel for 11 political institutions. The country now ranks highest in Southeast Asia in terms of electoral freedom. Long-suppressed local identities have been allowed to flourish, but this has not come at the cost of heightened inter-ethnic tensions. In fact, these are now better managed: 'decentralization and the renaissance of local identities [have] curtailed rather than catalysed centrifugal tendencies and major communal tensions' (p. 54). In addition, the focus on subprovincial units of administration, careful electoral design and the substantial, formula-driven injection of central government funds into the regions have all ensured that the major political parties have a national rather than a parochial orientation. There has also been a rapid civilianization of Indonesian politics. In the early Suharto era, 80 per cent of provincial governors had a military background. By the end of his rule the percentage had halved, and it has now fallen to just 6 per cent. Another important point to note is that local elections offer pathways to the national level, as illustrated by the dramatic rise of the leading contender in the 2014 presidential elections, Joko Widodo, from mayor of a small central Javanese city to governor of Jakarta.

Hal Hill and Yogi Vidyattama provide the first of the quantitative investigations of regional development outcomes in Chapter 4. Indonesia's subnational socio-economic statistics are reasonably well developed, with provincial accounts reliably available since the mid-1970s and district data since the mid-1990s. It is therefore possible to examine subnational dynamics for over four decades at the provincial level, and for almost two decades at the district level. A major empirical challenge is the frequent splitting (*pemekaran*) of administrative units since the late 1990s, especially at the district level. To prepare consistent estimates over time, the regional data have to be consolidated back to the boundaries that applied before these changes occurred.

The authors find evidence of both continuity and change in regional development outcomes. With regard to the continuities, they find that inter-regional differences in incomes and social indicators remain large, that inter-regional rankings have remained reasonably stable over time, that the east–west divide remains pronounced, that the provinces of Jakarta and East Kalimantan are still by far the two richest in the country, and that, among the major island groupings, Java continues to be the dominant regional economy. With regard to the changes, the authors find that the earlier and more recent commodity booms have lifted the economic position of Kalimantan, and that the adverse effects of conflict are clearly evident, notably in Aceh and Maluku. The correlation between economic and social indicators at the subnational level is generally quite strong, with Papua being a major exception. Overall interregional inequality remains high, but stable, and is not greatly sensitive to the choice of indicators or administrative classifications. As would be expected, at the finer (that is, district) level of disaggregation there are greater inter-regional disparities and more fluid rankings. Perhaps surprisingly, however, the 2001 decentralization reforms do not appear to have had a significant impact on the underlying patterns of socioeconomic inequality.

In Chapter 5, Amri Ilmma and Matthew Wai-Poi comprehensively examine regional social outcomes at both the provincial and district levels, with attention to what they term 'uneven' progress. The central question they ask is whether patterns of provincial poverty reduction have changed during the decentralization era. They commence with the observation that, putting aside the slowdown in poverty reduction in 2005–06 caused by food and fuel price increases, 'At first glance, ... it would seem that poverty has fallen neither faster nor slower under decentralization than in the pre-*reformasi* period, whether in annualized percentage point terms or with reference to growth elasticities' (p. 100). Poverty rates in Eastern Indonesia are about double the national average, while those in the three large Java provinces are close to the national average. Owing to Java's large population, however, about 52 per cent of the poor reside there. Focusing on the period 1993–2012, Ilmma and Wai-Poi identify two subperiods, of economic and political crisis and recovery (1996–2003) and of a return to growth (2003–13). For the period as a whole, their two main conclusions are that poverty fell, except in the two special cases of Papua and conflict-affected Aceh, and that there was clear inter-regional convergence, in the sense that poverty fell more quickly in the poorer regions. In general, the provincial poverty rankings remained stable after 2002.

Turning to the district story, the authors examine the effects of *pemekaran* using a panel regression approach, and dividing the splitting (that is, newly created) districts into those that split early (up to 2005) and those that split late (after 2005). Noting that the districts that would later split were considerably poorer than those that would not, they find that 'Districts that have split have enjoyed better socio-economic outcomes than those that have not' (p. 125). These outcomes include greater poverty reduction, faster economic growth and better education indicators. In addition, they confirm convergence among districts, and highlight the effects of the natural resource boom, with commodity-intensive districts performing better than the average.

Decentralization and governance

The four chapters in Part 2 examine various aspects of the evolving system of local government, centre–region relations and the quality of local governance.

In Chapter 6, Blane Lewis provides a comprehensive balance sheet of the record since 2001. The expected outcomes from the decentralization reforms included better-quality services, as legislators would be closer to their constituents. Yet there is little evidence for this, as indicated, for example, by the deteriorating quality of local roads. Funding does not appear to be the main explanation: 'The argument that regions ... lack sufficient funds to deliver improved public services seems implausible. ... It is hard to see how central–local transfers could be much larger than they are given the country's current fiscal circumstances' (p. 145). In fact, the problem seems to have more to do with efficiency: subnational governments 'spend too much on administration and personnel ... and not enough on actual service delivery. ... More broadly, the general level of spending appears to have little or no effect on a wide range of service outcomes' (pp. 145–6). Lewis also notes other features of the decentralization initiative, including the variable quality of local governments, the rigidity of the central government's funding formulas and some promising, albeit tentative, results from two experiments with inter-governmental performance grants.

Notwithstanding the significant transfer of funds to provinces and districts since 2001, Lewis concludes that service delivery outcomes have improved little if at all. Theories abound as to why this is the case. The most frequently voiced explanations concern insufficient funding of provincial and local governments, weak subnational implementation capacity and improper design of intergovernmental fiscal relations. While all of these may be legitimate to a certain extent, taken together they are insufficient to explain the poor results. Arguably, the most binding constraint to successful decentralization in Indonesia is weak accountability at the local level. And this lack of accountability is to a large extent a function of insufficient demand from citizens for improvements to services.

The next three chapters probe various aspects of local-level governance in more detail. In Chapter 7, Arianto Patunru and Erman Rahman focus on the quality of local governance and development outcomes. Taking advantage of datasets on local economic governance covering more than 400 districts in the period 2007–11 and auditor opinions issued by the State Audit Agency (Badan Pemeriksa Keuangan, BPK), they explore the correlation between governance indicators and social and economic outcomes. They also relate these factors to budget policy as revealed by a dataset on local budget allocations. In doing so they are able to control for whether the districts have or have not split. Thus, they are able to examine whether good governance leads to better economic and social outcomes, whether good budget allocation leads to better development outcomes, and whether good governance leads to better budget allocations.

Among other things, they find that better governance is associated with higher economic growth. Governance in infrastructure issues (for example, quality of infrastructure, time needed to repair damage) matters the most, while a higher proportion of personnel expenditure in total expenditure is associated with poorer outcomes. In fact, while business licensing procedures and audit outcomes appear to be improving, infrastructure provision is highlighted as a consistently serious problem. The authors also observe that newly established districts are less likely to receive a positive auditor report from BPK, suggesting that the formation of new districts does not necessarily lead to good governance and hence to better development outcomes. This conclusion adds weight to the case for tightening the *pemekaran* processes. The diversity of the provinces surveyed – Aceh, East Java and West Nusa Tenggara – adds plausibility to the authors' results.

Complementing this analysis, in Chapter 8 Günther Schulze and Bambang Sjahrir examine the effects of decentralization on the quality of local governance and public service delivery. The chapter is premised on the notion that theory does not provide clear guidance on the expected effects: decentralized public service delivery may better cater to regionally differentiated preferences and allow for greater transparency because decisions are closer to the people; or powerful local elites may capture the process of public service delivery, thereby negating the positive effects of decentralization. The authors attempt to resolve this issue empirically, through econometric evidence (not reported in detail) derived from large panel datasets of Indonesian districts.

Specifically, the authors investigate the process of public service delivery from three perspectives, the input stage, the production stage and the output stage. First, the input perspective concentrates on whether the spending patterns of districts have become more 'needs-oriented', and thus better reflect the preferences of the constituency. Schulze and Sjahrir conclude that decentralization has led to more needs-based spending patterns in district budgets, but that the steps towards deepened democratization at the district level – the progression from appointed to indirectly elected to directly elected district heads – has had no statistically significant effect.

Second, the authors analyse public service delivery from the production (technology/governance) perspective, asking how efficiently local government resources have been used. They take as a proxy for waste the extent of local government spending on administration. Controlling for the emergence of new districts (*pemekaran*), they show that a lack of political accountability is responsible for administrative overspending of districts. The extent of this overspending is significantly higher in districts with lower political competition; the transition to direct elections of district heads, however, did not curtail the waste.

Third, the authors look at public service delivery from an output perspective, comparing service delivery patterns in health, education and infrastructure before and after decentralization. They conclude that districts with relatively low levels of public service provision raised their service levels faster than well-performing districts, thereby leading to convergence of service delivery levels. Decentralization had positive effects on public service delivery levels but democratization has not yet had a significant effect on budget composition and the efficiency of local government spending.

Chapter 9, by Neil McCulloch and Edmund Malesky, investigates the determinants of the large variations in the quality of local economic governance in Indonesia and Vietnam. The differences between the two countries are of course significant: Indonesia is significantly larger with respect to both population and geography, it is more democratic, and its decentralization was both quicker and more comprehensive. But the comparative dimension is nevertheless important as a means of benchmarking the Indonesian record against that of a dynamic neighbouring economy.

The authors explore the empirical relationship between structural characteristics and economic governance in both countries; that is, they seek answers in the realm of structural determinants rather than simply the quality of political leadership. They find that GDP per capita, population and location have a significant impact on the quality of local economic governance in Indonesia, but not in Vietnam. They also find evidence that regions with greater policy autonomy have better governance in both countries. In the case of Indonesia, they find that districts with larger economies, and larger populations, have worse governance; that being a city has no impact on governance; and that there is no relationship between governance quality and the share of mining in the local economy. Surprisingly, however, ethno-linguistic fragmentation did appear to have a positive influence on the overall governance measure. A concluding section advances a hypothesis for how the two countries' different political institutions might explain the observed differences. As in the cross-country literature on this subject, the direction of causality between the quality of governance and economic performance remains controversial.

Local-level perspectives

Much of the analysis of decentralization has focused on national perspectives, and how the system works as seen from Jakarta. The three
papers in Part 3 take as their starting point various local-level perspectives, including community empowerment, ecological management and
poverty outcomes.

In Chapter 10, John McCarthy and colleagues draw attention to an
important subnational initiative that is formally outside the decentralization reform program, the National Community Empowerment Program
(Program Nasional Pemberdayaan Masyarakat, PNPM). Scaling up a
program pioneered by the World Bank, in 2006 the Indonesian government began to roll out this community-driven development program
on a nationwide scale, across nearly 70,000 villages in 6,681 subdistricts.
Now one of the largest and best-known examples of its kind, the PNPM
program focuses on improving participation in the allocation and management of block-grant community development funds. By strengthening the role of local communities in this way, it seeks to harness the
energies of civil society to improve the transparency and accountability
of local development projects, and to stimulate community ownership of
development goals.

The authors note that, for all its lofty rhetoric, the PNPM suite of
programs has attracted mixed reviews. They conclude that, 'compared
with state-level planning processes, PNPM offers a more effective means
of channelling central government funds to the village level and an
improved approach to planning and delivering local infrastructure, by
providing mechanisms for increased participation' (pp. 252–3). It also
gives villagers the opportunity to acquire knowledge and skills, by participating in planning meetings for several years. However, the authors
conclude that the potential for PNPM to address poverty remains a vexed
question. The program involves lengthy and complicated planning and
implementation procedures with considerable transaction and opportunity costs, which in turn constitute a disincentive for the involvement of
the poor. The 2004 revisions of the 1999 regional autonomy laws were
clearly aimed at restoring executive over legislative authority at the village level. McCarthy and colleagues contend that the revived constraints
on the authority of village councils in this legislation, and the fact that
PNPM processes ignore them, 'has to be considered one of the serious
structural problems that must be addressed in order to overcome deficiencies in achieving the program's objectives' (p. 256).

In Chapter 11, Ida Aju Pradnja Resosudarmo, Ngakan Putu Oka, Sofi
Mardiah and Nugroho Adi Utomo switch the focus to the management
of forest lands in Indonesia's Outer Islands. Decentralization has shifted
authority over most natural resources to subnational governments,

with analysts arguing that bringing decision making closer to the people should improve the management of resources because 'locals know best'. As part of the reforms, land use was decentralized but forest management was not. More than a decade on, the authors pose the following questions. Is improved management evident in the forest sector? What factors have contributed to this outcome? Can the most recent initiatives to improve the management and governance of forest lands work?

The authors also examine whether decentralization has fundamentally changed the ways in which the fragile ecologies outside Java are managed, focusing on the Indonesian forest estate (*kawasan hutan*). They investigate regional and national spatial planning processes, oil palm and mining developments as these relate to forest lands, and the programs currently being implemented under the United Nations' Reducing Emissions from Deforestation and Degradation (REDD+) scheme. They find that the impetus for local development continues to outweigh longer-term ecological considerations and thus affects the ways in which forests are managed. REDD+ has been put forward as one option to reconcile the competing livelihood and environmental goals held for Indonesia's forests. The scheme is still in the initial phase and is being implemented within a context of complex governance challenges, so it remains to be seen whether it can help reshape the current development agendas in the regions in a more environment-friendly manner. The presidential instruction (Inpres) placing a moratorium on the conversion of primary forests and peatland is proving effective and is a step in the right direction.

In Chapter 12, Sudarno Sumarto, Marc Vothknecht and Laura Wijaya return to the issue of poverty, asking how economic growth has contributed to poverty reduction at the regional level, with particular emphasis on the role of decentralization. Although poverty incidence at the national level almost halved between 1999 and 2013, the regional patterns are uneven. The authors examine the factors that have driven the evolution of poverty since 2001, and relate district performance in poverty reduction to a wide range of social, economic and political characteristics. They find, as expected, that GDP per capita is one of the major driving forces behind the decline in regional poverty. Results from a panel data analysis covering the period 2005–10 show that poverty has decreased in particular in those districts with a larger share of local leaders with secondary education; higher overall average educational attainment; an established local office for the coordination of poverty reduction initiatives (Tim Koordinasi Penanggulangan Kemiskinan Daerah,TKPKD); a higher share of fiscal revenues; and a more urbanized population. Moroever, there appears to be a link between income inequality and poverty, suggesting that a successful poverty reduction strategy requires both economic growth and sound social policies.

The authors make some pertinent general observations on the decentralization process and regional social outcomes. A key point is that the revised administrative and political systems are still in transition – that decentralization 'occurred too quickly and therefore lacks a comprehensive policy framework' (p. 310) – so definitive judgements may be premature. Local-level violence and *pemekaran* are still seen as major problems, and help to explain the uneven reductions in poverty across regions. Unobserved variables also account for some of these variations. For example, the authors conclude that: 'Beyond the socio-economic factors controlled for, districts in Kalimantan appear particularly successful in reducing poverty, while the opposite is observed for districts in Papua' (p. 308).

Migration, cities and connectivity

The regional components of a nation-state connect through the movement of people, through commerce and through various forms of media. Rapidly increasing urbanization is one manifestation of these developments. Hard and soft infrastructure is the glue that binds a nation together. The four chapters in Part 4 examine various aspects of these issues, including migration, labour market structure and adjustment, the state of logistics and the challenges of managing the urban colossus of greater Jakarta.

First, Chapter 13 by Salut Muhidin looks at 'people on the move'. The author documents population mobility from the 1970s through to 2010, drawing on both lifetime and recent migration data from the decennial population censuses and survey data. A major focus is the effect of migration on settlement patterns, that is, the relationship between internal migration streams and regional development, including urbanization, economic indicators (GDP and employment rates) and measures of human capital (life expectancy and the proportion of the population with a secondary education). The results demonstrate that migration has been an important cause of the complex transformations in the patterns of human settlement in Indonesia.

The analysis highlights both continuity and change in these patterns. There are the established patterns of out-migration from regions such as West Sumatra, and from the conflict zones, Aceh and Maluku, in contrast to the major inward flows to the strong regional economies of East Kalimantan and Riau. Some regions, most clearly Bali, have switched their migration status from net out-migration to net in-migration. It is also important to distinguish between intra-provincial, inter-provincial and inter-island movements of people. Whereas intra-provincial migration appears to be rising over time, the other two forms are relatively stable.

Some migration takes place in steps, with the ultimate target destination of many migrants to West Java, for example, being Jakarta. The age profile of migrants is clear, with a peak in the 20–24 age group. Aside from the usual employment and family explanations, education is an important motive for people in this younger age group to migrate to Java, and to particular regions within Java, most notably Yogyakarta.

Migration is also central to an understanding of regional labour market outcomes and patterns, as analysed in Chapter 14 by Chris Manning and Raden Muhamad Purnagunawan. They commence with the observation that the Indonesian labour market is fragmented geographically and still bears the signs of the dualistic division dating from colonial times between densely populated Java–Bali and most of the more land-abundant Outer Islands. Rapid national economic growth based on both export-oriented industrialization and resource booms began to alter that historical pattern during the Suharto years. Labour market patterns have become more complicated since decentralization. Manufacturing has stagnated in Java, while the commodity boom and increased local revenues from natural resources have provided opportunities for human resource development and economic diversification outside Java.

The large inter-regional differences in income are reflected in labour productivity patterns, with output in Jakarta and East Kalimantan, for example, being at least three to four times the national average, and the proportion of the workforce in formal sector employment being higher. Manning and Purnagunawan observe that there are some signs of convergence between provinces, with several poorer provinces shedding some of their agricultural workers. In others, however, high rates of population growth, low levels of education and low levels of out-migration mean that much of the workforce continues to be trapped in low-productivity agriculture. Still, there are remarkable similarities in the trends towards greater formalization of the workforce and improvements in unemployment rates and wages across Indonesia, indicating that the worse-off provinces have not been left seriously behind.

While forces outside the labour market have contributed most to inter-provincial differences in employment and wages, the authors note that government regulation of wages has had an impact on manufacturing employment growth across the country, and especially in Java. They single out the dampening effect of national legislation (Law 13/2003 on Labour), regional variations in wages, and union and political party alliances to push up wages in manufacturing around the national capital.

Nowhere are migration and labour market patterns more pronounced than in the national capital, Jakarta, the subject of Chapter 15 by Tommy Firman. Appropriately, the author focuses on the greater Jakarta region, termed Jabodetabek, which not only comprises the urban area within the city's administrative boundaries but also extends across three provinces (Jakarta, West Java and Banten), and includes five municipalities (Bogor, Depok, Tangerang, South Tangerang and Bekasi) and three districts (Bogor, Tangerang and Bekasi). This region accounts for about one-quarter of Indonesia's non-oil GDP, a much larger share than the next group of major cities (Surabaya, Bandung, Semarang, Medan and Makassar) or the remaining, smaller group of urban areas, which each contributes about 15 per cent of the national economy. Most of the population growth in greater Jakarta is in fact occurring outside the city boundaries, reflected in the fact that Jakarta city's share of the total population of Jabodetabek declined from 55 per cent in 2000 to 36 per cent in 2010. The greater Jakarta region had a population of about 28 million people in 2010.

The rate of what the author terms 'mega-urbanization' in Jabodetabek appears to be accelerating, but the process is largely uncontrolled. There is intensifying land-use conversion, growing numbers of condominium and infrastructure projects in the city centre, and a proliferation of new towns, large-scale residential areas and industrial estate developments in the fringe areas. The challenges are therefore daunting and complex. They include increased vulnerability to natural disasters such as floods and rising seawater, and actual and potential human-induced calamities caused by excessive groundwater extraction and air and water pollution. Overall, the recent development of Jabodetabek reflects the impact of liberalization of the economy on mega-urban development, and demonstrates how the new decentralization policy has resulted in further fragmentation of administrative authority in the region.

The key challenges for policy makers are to improve governance, to enhance the city's competitiveness and to improve its citizens' quality of life. Urban settlements are spreading into areas set aside for conservation and water supply or as water recharge areas. Land-use planning arrangements are weak. Transport is a huge concern, contributing to onerous commuting times and very high levels of air pollution. Mass transit schemes have been proposed for over a third of a century but only now appear to be under way. Flooding is becoming an ever more serious problem, especially for the poor; in 2007, 40 per cent of the capital was under water for several days. Governance is complicated by split jurisdictions, with the role of the coordinating agency headed by the three provincial governors seen as 'ineffective and powerless' (p. 380).

The processes of migration, labour market integration and urbanization work effectively only if there is an efficient transport network that glues the country together. This is the subject of Chapter 16 by Henry Sandee, Nanda Nurridzki and Mohamad Adhi Prakoso Dipo. They note that intra-island, inter-island and international transport connectivity has received ample attention in recent years, with the formulation of master plans and logistics blueprints to reduce transport costs and increase reliability. However, the challenges remain great, as indicated by the high cost of inter-island transport and consequent large inter-regional price differences. The authors present ample comparative data demonstrating that logistics costs are considerably higher – sometimes by a very large margin – in Indonesia than in its more efficient neighbours. They draw attention to the problems at the country's major port, Tanjung Priok, where throughput doubled between 2007 and 2013 but 'no substantial investments to improve productivity and to start planning for an extension were made for many years' (p. 394).

The problems derive from both limited infrastructure investment and regulatory barriers. Underinvestment in infrastructure since the late 1990s has contributed to the low quality and quantity of roads, ports and railways. As a percentage of GDP, Indonesia's infrastructure expenditure is currently about half that in the Suharto era. Regulated constraints on competition and on efficient service provision compound the problems. The contrast between the successful deregulation of air transport and the lack of reform in shipping is striking. In fact, Law 17/2008 on Shipping introduced cabotage principles that limit the movement of cargo between domestic ports to Indonesia-flag vessels. The government has recently released master plans and blueprints laying out a strategy to improve connectivity. The question is whether they will be able to address crucial bottlenecks, such as the lack of coordination between the central and local governments and the uncertain commercial environment for potential private sector providers.

Challenges for Indonesia's periphery

The challenges of managing the immensely complicated Indonesian nation-state are nowhere better illustrated than in the peripheral regions. These are examined in Part 5 of this volume through detailed economic and political analyses of the far eastern region of Papua and the northwestern region of Aceh. Both have turbulent histories, have experienced episodes of serious conflict and have uneasy relationships with Jakarta. Living standards have also risen more slowly in these provinces than elsewhere, a situation exacerbated in Papua's case by its isolation, and in Aceh's case by Indonesia's worst natural disaster in modern times.

The first two chapters in Part 5 examine Papua. In Chapter 17, Cillian Nolan, Sidney Jones and Solahudin explore the connections between *pemekaran*, local elections and conflict. Using Nduga district as a case study, the authors examine how the redrawing of administrative boundaries in the Papuan central highlands is frequently based on highly dubious population data, and how it creates entities that too often result in more corruption and worse governance. The creation of dozens of new districts in the last few years is changing the political face of Papua, reducing the long-term dominance of coastal elites in favour of highlanders. The authors maintain that Jakarta initially saw *pemekaran* as a divide-and-rule strategy to ensure that no region in Papua became too powerful. But the result has been to create a 'gigantic headache for Jakarta'. Moreover, they assert, bringing government closer to the people is a smokescreen: '*Pemekaran* appears largely to be about gaining access to resources – especially central government revenue streams – but it is also about promoting the interests of clans (*suku*) and subclans' (p. 413).

All governance indicators look discouraging. The number of civil servants has risen dramatically, from 37,000 in 2000 to 114,000 in 2011. The number of villages has also risen very quickly, induced by the prospect of block grant payments to each village of about Rp 100 million. There are persistent auditing problems at the provincial and district levels, and many of the Papuan districts rank poorly on the central government's governance quality indicators. Although there is increased 'Papuanization' of local governments, there has also been a rise in local electoral conflict, prompting the Ministry of Home Affairs and the current Papuan governor, himself a highlander, to suggest that direct local elections be abolished in Papua. The authors argue that it would be better to reform the *pemekaran* process than to stop local elections, but that this may now be politically impossible.

Complementing this analysis, Budy Resosudarmo, Julius Mollet, Umbu Raya and Hans Kaiwai investigate Papua's development challenges in Chapter 18. Their starting point is the observation that, notwithstanding the implementation of Law 21/2001 on Special Autonomy for Papua, there is a common perception that Papuan development is a failed process. In particular, development has so far been limited to extractive industries and has not been inclusive, marginalizing indigenous Papuans. Like other authors in this book, Resosudarmo and co-authors highlight Papua's very high poverty incidence and lagging social indicators, especially in rural areas, the urban bias in much government spending, the region's very poor rural infrastructure and the enclave nature of its natural resource developments. In passing, and as a further reminder of the region's complexities, it could be noted that these are very similar to the problems facing neighbouring Papua New Guinea.

Each of the Papua provinces is highly dependent on a single, very large natural resource project: Freeport accounts for about 47 per cent of the GDP of Papua province, and BP Indonesia's Tangguh gas project accounts for about 54 per cent of the GDP of West Papua province. The economic fortunes of both provinces therefore depend on these volatile

natural resource activities. More generally, the authors seek to understand the factors behind the failure of development in Papua over the
past 10 years. Particular attention is given to describing demographic,
social and regional economic changes; agglomeration and resource-
based industries; poverty and equality; and some key regional government policies.

Turning to Aceh, in Chapter 19 Edward Aspinall examines political developments since the August 2005 peace settlement and the local
autonomy package embodied in Law 11/2006 on the Governing of Aceh.
The author cautions against overstating the importance of the latter: the
law's provisions either do not exceed those granted to other provinces,
or go no further than those of the previous, unsuccessful, 2001 special
autonomy law (Law 18/2001 on Special Autonomy for Nanggroe Aceh
Darussalam). Moreover, several important implementing regulations for
the 2006 law have not yet been issued.

Nevertheless, special autonomy has been critical to securing peace.
Above all, two sets of provisions have helped prevent a return to conflict.
First are the provisions allowing former combatants of the Free Aceh
Movement (Gerakan Aceh Merdeka, GAM) to contest elections in Aceh,
and thus to occupy a dominant position in local government. Second
are provisions that have significantly boosted Aceh's revenues, providing increased funds for patronage as well as development. This combination has fostered an environment characterized by what the author
terms 'predatory peace', in which former rebels have been persuaded to
accept the authority of the Indonesian state as much by the opportunities for self-enrichment peace has afforded them as by their willingness
to find a new modus vivendi in relations between Aceh and the rest of
Indonesia. The challenge now is to convert the peace into development
through improved governance, and to overcome the widespread perception of, in the author's words, 'the enrichment of a whole layer of former
GAM commanders and leaders ... which is everywhere visible in the
fancy houses, cars, second and third wives, and other symbols of wealth
now possessed by many former insurgents' (p. 478).

In Chapter 20, Peter McCawley observes that sustained economic
development in Aceh was held back by local conflict and dissent for over
three decades from the mid-1970s. This changed following the dramatic
events of 2004 and 2005 – the tsunami of 26 December 2004 and the Helsinki peace accord of 2005 – which created opportunities for progress and
development. The return to 'normal times' since 2009 has given policy
makers an opportunity to devise an effective development strategy for
the province.

McCawley concludes that the huge aid flows to Aceh have had the
desired effect of rebuilding shattered coastal infrastructure and provid-

ing local livelihoods. But there have also been local 'Dutch disease' effects resulting from the large-scale importation of relatively high-cost equipment and labour. One symptom of this problem is that per capita income is below the national average but minimum wages are above it. Such a divergence also reflects the dualistic features of the local economy, with a large natural resource sector existing alongside the major employment sectors of agriculture and services. Poverty remains above the national average, while governance quality is indifferent. The author argues that the province's relatively small size and its comparatively isolated location may constrain future development.

1.3   SUMMING UP

Distilling these findings, several major conclusions emerge from the book.

First, the decentralization reforms have 'worked' in the sense that Indonesia is by and large an increasingly prosperous, functional nation-state, with high levels of democratic participation and no serious threats to its territorial integrity. Given the record of territorial disintegration in several other ethnically and geographically diverse countries since 1970, and the periodic threats to Indonesia's own national unity and prosperity during its nearly seven decades of independence, this must be counted as an impressive, indeed remarkable, achievement.

Second, it comes as no surprise to find that, thus far, the operation of centre–region arrangements and local government administration has been uneven, and generally does not accord with textbook theories of federal fiscalism. There is little evidence of significantly improved public services; resource-rich areas have had much higher growth rates than poorer districts; government spending on salaries and buildings has ballooned; powerful elites have become the main players in local elections; and corruption is rampant, not least because of the rising costs of local political campaigns. The proliferation of new districts is proving to be a major headache for the central government. Infrastructure provision is a serious problem practically everywhere.

These two observations might appear to be mutually contradictory, but they are not. The decentralization system is still in its infancy, and the reforms are a work in progress. Voters relish the opportunity to punish poorly performing governments, and do so regularly. Moreover, Indonesia is hardly the only country in the world to experience poor standards of local governance. The key test will come in another decade or so, when the novelty of democratic freedoms will perhaps wane, and voters will be looking for institutionalized reform mechanisms that lock in better standards of governance.

Third, Indonesia's regional development patterns have changed less than might have been expected on the basis of these far-reaching reforms. Except for a small number of special cases, all regions have participated in the moderately high rates of economic growth enjoyed by Indonesia in the twenty-first century. The western region continues to be more dynamic than the poorer east, but there has been a slight convergence between regions on most economic and social indicators. At the very least, it can safely be concluded that inter-regional inequality in aggregate has not increased with the advent of greater regional autonomy.[3] These conclusions apply regardless of the units of observation and the methodologies applied. In particular, the fear that the poor eastern regions would fall further behind as the fiscal equalization mechanisms embodied in the former centralized system were modified has not materialized.

Fourth, it is important to emphasize that the regional development agenda extends well beyond the decentralization reforms, and it is therefore unrealistic to expect these reforms to be able to address many local-level issues. For example, the country faces a serious infrastructure deficit. Decentralization has contributed to the problem, to the extent that there are greater inter-jurisdictional coordination issues, and the short horizons of many local governments have resulted in infrastructure investments receiving a lower priority. But the analysis in this volume indicates that much of the problem resides with the central government, including its inability to allocate sufficient resources and to create at the national level a regulatory and investment climate conducive to private investors. Another example concerns the management of the troubled peripheral regions, particularly Aceh and Papua. Democratic local governance has at least diffused the potent anti-Jakarta sentiment that used to exist in some regions, and the central government's management of its relations with Aceh in particular is generally seen as adroit. However, Papua remains the country's major regional development challenge, with seemingly the most intractable poverty problems. At the other extreme on the spatial continuum, there is no evidence that decentralization has facilitated the task of managing the mega-urban complex of Jakarta. Here too, the problems are to some extent beyond the remit of the regional autonomy legislation, to the extent that they reside in the national government's failure to keep up with the capital's need for infrastructure,

---

3 Kanbur, Rhee and Zhuang (2014) estimate the contribution of spatial inequality to total inequality in several developing Asian economies. Among the populous countries, Indonesia adopts an intermediate position in these estimates, with the spatial component contributing about one-quarter of total inequality, much lower than in China (over 50 per cent) and in India and Vietnam (in excess of 30 per cent), but slightly higher than in Pakistan and the Philippines.

and the historical lack of inter-jurisdictional cooperation between the leaders of the greater Jakarta area.

The chapters in this volume focus on both national and local development challenges. But one volume on such a vast topic cannot be the last word on the subject. In particular, the country's diversity and vast geographic spread dictate that the 'binding constraints' to development will vary enormously, and thus national development blueprints will have to be more sensitive to local conditions than they have in the past.[4]

A few brief local snapshots illustrate this proposition. First, for Jakarta, transport and environmental amenity are arguably the key preoccupations of local officials as the city struggles to cope with substandard infrastructure, deteriorating air quality and shrinking green space. As most of the growth in greater Jakarta now takes place beyond its formal administrative borders, inter-jurisdictional coordination and cooperation is a major challenge.

A second example is Papua, where the priorities are radically different: how to ensure the 'unity of the dual economy', so that the benefits of huge enclave mining projects are distributed more evenly to the local population. This must take place in the context of an uneasy relationship with Jakarta, pockets of extreme physical isolation, and very large socio-economic development gaps between urban and remote regions and between commercially aggressive migrants and a less sophisticated local populace.

A third illustration concerns the country's major export-oriented industrial regions, principally West Java, but also East Java and the Riau Islands adjacent to Singapore. For these provinces, a major challenge is to maintain their competitive positions in global production and buying networks, such as electronics, automobiles, garments and footwear, and to ensure that they continue to be major engines of broad-based employment growth. To achieve this, they need efficient, internationally oriented infrastructure, smart, simple regulatory regimes and access to high-quality, internationally competitive labour markets.

Most of Indonesia's natural resource endowments are located outside Java, with Kalimantan having the fastest-growing economy among the major island groups. These regions illustrate a fourth type of development challenge, with a focus on environmental sustainability. In mining and cash crops – with coal and palm oil the most profitable – local governments have to ensure that the proceeds of the boom are broadly

---

4 Some of these local development issues were examined in detail in the set of provincial economic surveys contained in Hill (1989), in an era when Indonesia was a more centralized, authoritarian state, and had a smaller, less complex economy. This is a volume that is greatly in need of an update.

distributed, both within and between generations. This in turn entails embedding efficient tax arrangements, strong environmental safeguards and the equitable and transparent allocation of resource rents, in what are inherently corruption-prone industries. Weak local institutions and infant democracies compound these challenges.

A final illustration comes from Indonesia's vast eastern islands. These are typically poor, remote, bypassed regions, in which the maritime economy is significant. Historically they have been regions of out-migration, and this could indeed continue to be a major pathway out of poverty for the inhabitants. But more could be done to raise living standards in situ. The maritime resources of the poorer regions could be used more effectively to benefit local communities. Tourism and dry-land agriculture also have potential in these regions.

The reader is invited to explore these and other issues in the rich and diverse set of chapters that follows.

REFERENCES

Cribb, R. (1999) 'Nation: making Indonesia', in D.K. Emmerson (ed.) *Beyond Suharto: Polity, Economy, Society, Transition*, M.E. Sharpe, Inc., New York.

Geertz, C. (1971) 'A program for the stimulation of the social sciences in Indonesia', report to the Ford Foundation, Jakarta.

Hill, H. (ed.) (1989) *Unity and Diversity: Regional Economic Development in Indonesia since 1970*, Oxford University Press, Singapore.

Kanbur, R., C. Rhee and J. Zhuang (2014) *Inequality in Asia and the Pacific: Trends, Drivers, and Policy Implications*, Routledge, London.

Mackie, J.A.C. (1980) 'Integrating and centrifugal factors in Indonesian politics since 1945', in J.A.C Mackie (ed.) *Indonesia: The Making of a Nation*, Research School of Pacific and Asian Studies, Australian National University, Canberra.

PART 1

Historical, economic, political and social patterns

2 Before the 'big bang': decentralization debates and practice in Indonesia, 1949–99

Anne Booth

2.1 INTRODUCTION

Indonesia's 'big bang' decentralization program has already generated a considerable literature, although few of the published studies examine the post-2001 changes in light of previous debates on central–regional political and economic relations in Indonesia. A common assumption appears to be that the system in place from the transfer of power from the Dutch in 1949 until the end of the Suharto era in 1998 was highly centralized. Section 2.2 of this chapter reviews the changes in the structure and role of provincial and subprovincial governments in Indonesia after independence, and examines the debates in the early 1950s culminating in the Nasroen proposals for reforming central–regional fiscal relations. Had the proposals been properly implemented, they would have made a considerable difference to the future course of central–regional relations. But they turned out to be the road not followed; instead, after Suharto took power in 1966, a process of recentralization of economic and political power took place. Section 2.3 examines the consequences of the Suharto-era policies for regional development in Java and elsewhere.

2.2 DEVELOPMENT OF REGIONAL GOVERNMENT AFTER 1950

Federalism: the path not taken

To many observers both at the time and later, it would have seemed logical for the newly independent Indonesian republic to choose a federal constitutional structure in 1949. Indeed, as Feith (1962: 72) has claimed, there were some convinced advocates of a federal structure within the republican leadership, 'and Prime Minister Hatta appeared at times to be one of them'. In an interview after Suharto had left office, Feith pointed out that Hatta, 'who played the central role in dissolving that federal structure, was actually a federalist' (*Jakarta Post*, 18 November 1999). Hatta became Indonesia's first prime minister after the Dutch finally conceded sovereignty in 1949. He wanted to hold an election immediately so that an elected body could decide between a federal and a unitary state. But this did not happen; instead, general elections were held only in September 1955. Elections for a Constituent Assembly (Konstituante), which was to decide on a constitution, followed in December 1955. Voter turnout for both elections was high (Nasution 1992: 30).

We can only speculate on what kind of constitution might have emerged in Indonesia had the processes set in train in 1955 been allowed to run their course. Certainly the forces opposed to a federal constitution were considerable. During the Japanese occupation, Raden Supomo and Mohammad Yamin had already begun to debate the form of a post-war constitution. A product of the Leiden *adatrecht* school,[1] and under the influence of the Japanese, Supomo wanted an 'integralistic' state; Yamin, on the other hand, inclined more towards the American model, with a clear separation of powers between the legislative, executive and judicial functions. Lev (1996: 149) has argued that, among the small group of Indonesian lawyers trained under the Dutch (numbering around 400 when the Japanese arrived in 1942), the majority supported 'a powerful state in control of a submissive society'. Supomo's main criticism of the Yamin proposals was that virtually no Indonesian lawyer had any experience of an American-style constitution, which was based on liberal individualism rather than the 'family principles' that would be enshrined in the 1945 document.[2]

It has also been argued that the Dutch stratagem of creating a federal Indonesian state in 1945–46 effectively discredited the concept of federalism in the eyes of many in the nationalist leadership. Legge (1961: 7) pointed out that 'in developing their proposals for a federal Indonesia after 1945 the Dutch were not building on pre-war foundations'. In spite of some devolution of powers to the provincial administrations in Java in the years from 1900 to 1930, the colonial government had certainly

---

1 The Leiden *adatrecht* school advocated a dual legal system in which Dutch law (*recht*) would apply only to Dutch and other foreign individuals and companies, and customary law (*adat*) to the indigenous populations of the archipelago.

2 For more on Supomo's ideas, see Nasution (1992: 90–103).

never been federal in concept or in practice. Rather, particularly in Java, it had been based on a highly centralist hierarchical system whereby the heads of each level of government were accountable to those above, and where elected councils played only a very weak role, both in the selection of these heads and in monitoring their behaviour (Maryanov 1959: 140–52). Outside Java, the various 'native states' had greater autonomy to levy taxes in labour and in kind, and to implement a range of investment projects.

The newfound Dutch enthusiasm for federalism after 1945 rested not on any explicit plan to devolve more fiscal powers to the regions, but rather on the adoption of 'divide-and-rule tactics' (Taylor 1960: 330). By far the largest of the federal units created by the Dutch was the state of East Indonesia. By the end of 1947 responsibility for finance, justice, general economic affairs, police, education, information, health, social affairs, industry, shipping, forestry, irrigation and agrarian affairs had all been delegated to the regional government, although in practice, as Kahin (1952: 60) has stressed, the exercise of all these powers was greatly vitiated by the numerous general and specific powers reserved to the central government in Batavia. It was not by accident that eastern Indonesia was chosen as the model for the Dutch experiment in federalism. As Kahin has shown in his classic study, the Dutch found it easier to deal with the nationalist movement there than in Java or Sumatra. Although some traditional leaders in Sulawesi supported the republic, the Dutch were able to muster sufficient force to overcome their resistance, sometimes by replacing leaders sympathetic to the republic with more pliant people.

In his study of the formation and subsequent history of the state of East Indonesia, Agung (1996: 798) states that the behaviour of the Dutch postwar administrator, Hubertus van Mook, in creating states and regions within the territory of the Republic of Indonesia 'sounded the death knell for the concept of a federation in Indonesia'.[3] Indeed, so cynical were the means used by the Dutch to establish a federal state in eastern Indonesia and elsewhere that the nationalists, not surprisingly, equated federalism with collaboration. As Feith (1962: 71) has argued, when the form of the independent state came to be finalized in 1949, the issue was not one of a federal versus a unitary constitutional form. Rather, it became one of

---

3 See also Chauvel (1997) and Kahin (2012: 64–5) for a discussion of the failure of the Dutch attempt to create a federal state in the years from 1946 to 1949, and the reaction of Hatta and others in 1949–50. That some politicians from the Suharto era had an interest in the van Mook proposals is confirmed by Mboi (2009: 42). He writes that when he went to the Netherlands in 1989 after a period as governor of East Nusa Tenggara, he was asked by Soepardjo Rustam, then the Minister of Home Affairs, to look again at the van Mook proposals and report on their relevance for contemporary Indonesia.

support for an independent republic versus cooperation with Dutch policies of divide and rule. However, Feith also pointed out that the appeal of the anti-federalist case was 'undoubtedly greatest in Java'. This was because the federal units established by the Dutch in Java were transparently artificial, and also because the independence struggle had generally come to take on a deeper importance in Java than elsewhere.

The creation of provinces after 1950

A provisional unitary constitution was adopted in 1950. Maryanov (1958: 31) argued that 'the spirit of 1950 was to make the unitary state work' while discussion continued about a permanent constitutional framework for the new state of Indonesia. In practice, making the system work involved some pressing decisions about appropriate administrative structures for the new nation. Most of the subprovincial units in Java – districts/municipalities (*kabupaten/kota*), units below the districts (*kawedanan*), subdistricts (*kecamatan*) and villages (*kelurahan*) – were held over from the colonial era with few alterations, although there was a trend towards amalgamation of the villages.[4] But outside Java the problems were more difficult, as provinces had not been formed in the colonial era, and boundaries were often more contested. It was decided to carve Sumatra into three provinces (North, Central and South), while Kalimantan, Sulawesi, the Moluccas and the Lesser Sundas (Bali and Nusa Tenggara) each became one province. As Feith (1962: 99) has pointed out, this arrangement 'paid little heed to regional or ethnic group feeling' and soon provoked strong reactions. In Aceh there was particular resentment among the leaders who had sided with the republican forces from 1945 to 1949; they felt betrayed when the promise of provincial status made to them in the late 1940s was withdrawn (Miller 2006: 293). Other parts of Sumatra feared domination by particular ethnic groups, and those regions that produced substantial export surpluses wanted more control over their export revenues.

In response to these demands, several new provinces were created in the late 1950s; by the time of the first post-independence population census in 1961, Indonesia had 22 provinces, although one was still under

---

4 This amalgamation was accompanied by the introduction of elections for all village officials on the basis of universal adult suffrage (Kahin 1952: 472). Outside Java the pace of change was slower, although some amalgamation of small villages into larger units probably took place during the first two decades of independence. In colonial Java there was also a further layer of government between the province and the district, called the residency. This layer survived into the post-independence era; its head was usually referred to as an 'assistant governor'.

Dutch control (West Irian as it was then known). By 1961 Aceh had been awarded provincial status[5] and the original province of Central Sumatra had been split into three (West Sumatra, Jambi and Riau). Sulawesi was divided into two and Kalimantan into four provinces.[6] The Lesser Sundas became three provinces (Bali, West Nusa Tenggara and East Nusa Tenggara). More divisions took place in the early 1960s, when the two provinces in Sulawesi were divided into four, and Lampung and Bengkulu were split off from South Sumatra.[7]

Each of the provinces was divided into districts and municipalities, and these in turn were divided into subdistricts and villages. Boundaries in Java remained largely unchanged, and because the populations of its three provinces were so much larger than those of any province outside Java, the populations of its districts and municipalities were also on average much larger. In 1961, the average population of a district-level government in Java was 618,000, compared with around 250,000 in Sumatra and an even lower average elsewhere (Table 2.1).

But creating more provinces and districts did little to remove the grievances felt by many outside Java towards the central government. The main resentments have been well summarized by Feith (1962: 487–8). The provinces outside Java resented the imposition of cumbersome administrative procedures that meant that senior officials often had to fly to Jakarta for approval of quite minor policy decisions. From an economic point of view, their main grievance was that by the mid-1950s only around 14 per cent of exports were being produced in Java, but 68 per cent of imports were arriving at Javanese ports. Comparable figures for the late 1930s were 35 per cent of exports and 65 per cent of imports (Lindblad 1992: 21). The main reason for the decline in exports from Java

---

5 Reid (2007: 153) has argued that one of the key Acehnese leaders, Daud Beureu'eh, was never reconciled to Aceh becoming a mere province in a unitary state, and continued to push for a federal Indonesia.

6 For a discussion of the splitting of Kalimantan into four provinces, see Mubyarto and Baswir (1989: 503). Central Kalimantan was formed a few months after the other three in 1957; the main reason for separate provincial status for this isolated and lightly populated region appears to have been the fact that the population was mainly Dyak, rather than Banjarese.

7 See the relevant chapters in Hill (1989) for a discussion of the reasons for the formation of these provinces. The splitting of Sulawesi into four provinces had been preceded by the formation of several new districts in both Central and Southeast Sulawesi in the latter part of the 1950s. Southeast Sulawesi had been a single district after independence; it was split into four districts in 1959 and the new province was created in 1964. Bengkulu, which had the smallest population of any province in 1971, appears to have been given provincial status because of pressure from Sukarno's second wife, Fatmawati – a native of Bengkulu whom Sukarno had met during his exile there in the late 1930s.

Table 2.1   Average population size of districts, 1961–2007 (thousand)

Region	1961	1995	2007
Java	618	1,072	1,121
Sumatra	246	559	350
Kalimantan	158	374	233
Sulawesi	191	352	223
Bali/Nusa Tenggara	214	361	326
Maluku	197	417	129
Papua	n.a.	194	72
Indonesia	**372**[a]	**669**	**477**

a   Excludes Irian Jaya/Papua.
Source: BPS (1963, 1996, 1997, 2006, 2007).

after 1950 was the fall in exportable surpluses of sugar. While some of the imports arriving at Javanese ports were transhipped to smaller ports outside Java, most stayed in Java, fuelling particular resentment in the provinces that produced the most exports but received only a small share of total imports. Their citizens complained, with some justification, that it was their export production that generated a large part of government revenue, but that they were neglected when decisions were made about government expenditures.

The Nasroen proposals and the legislation of 1956–57

What was to be done? In the mid-1950s the whole issue of regional finance was subjected to a detailed investigation by a committee headed by M. Nasroen, a senior civil servant in the Ministry of Home Affairs, and composed of fiscal experts from various government agencies. The committee's report proposed a complex system whereby local governments would be funded through two streams, one exclusively local and the other composed of a share of central government revenues from income, company and wage taxes, stamp taxes, property taxes and customs and excise duties (Paauw 1960: appendix D; Legge 1961: 189–200). Paauw (1960: 411) criticized the Nasroen proposals on the grounds that they neither simplified the tax structure nor attacked the problem of an extremely complex administrative system. He pointed out that most of the taxes assigned to local governments were never going to yield much revenue. This was a criticism that was to recur in most assessments of regional finance in Indonesia through to the present day.

Paauw also argued that there were some taxes that could have yielded substantial revenue to local governments, but that the latter lacked the incentives to assess and collect them effectively, because the revenues had to be sent on to Jakarta. Moreover, the formulas suggested in the Nasroen proposals for distributing central revenues did not appear to be based on either the needs or the capacity of the local governments. In spite of these criticisms, many of the findings of the committee were incorporated in Law 32/1956, concerning financial relations between the centre and the autonomous regions. The law made some important concessions to the regions in that it allowed the proceeds of both income taxes and foreign trade taxes to be shared between the provinces where the tax revenues originated and the centre. But as Legge (1961: 193) pointed out, implementation of the law was slow. In particular, little progress was made in laying down rules for the sharing of the most important taxes between the centre and the regions.

Local government finance in the 1950s

While debate was continuing at the centre about the appropriate form of government for an independent Indonesia, the provinces, districts/ municipalities and villages across the archipelago were beginning to take responsibility for providing a range of services to an increasingly assertive population. Many millions of Indonesians expected that independence (*merdeka*) would bring with it greatly increased access to education and health care and provide opportunities for better and more lucrative employment. One way or another, local governments had to respond to these demands. At the same time, as Paauw (1960: 273) has argued, 'the operating assumption in Djakarta had been that local finance ... had been almost completely inoperative after the Dutch relinquished control'. This assumption was reflected in various official reports, including the influential annual reports of Bank Indonesia.

But Paauw's own fieldwork told a different story. Especially in Central Sumatra, districts and villages were heavily involved in a range of projects, including the building and repair of roads and bridges and the erection of school buildings, clinics and other public facilities. At the provincial level, investment expenditure comprised 40 per cent of total expenditure in Central Sumatra; according to Paauw (1960: 283), this was a consequence of the 'force of historical precedent'. Where there had been a tradition of local autonomy, especially outside Java, local governments were better able to raise taxes in both labour and kind. But Paauw also argued that the diversity of central government taxes interfered with the 'effective administration' of important revenue streams. Complex central taxes inevitably took time to assess and collect; in addition, it was often the case that central tax officials lacked the ability to supervise collections beyond the large cities, especially outside Java. This especially affected the collection of rural taxes. These problems remained to be tackled in the post-Sukarno era.

The Guided Democracy years

The regional rebellions of the late 1950s were triggered by several factors, but the problem of an appropriate division of powers, both economic and political, between the centre and the regions was certainly one important cause.[8] Whatever their aims, the rebellions failed, and by the early 1960s the army had demonstrated its capacity to impose the rule of the central government in most parts of the archipelago. But this rule became increasingly tenuous as inflation and a hugely overvalued exchange rate led to growth in smuggling, much of it carried on with army connivance. Increasingly the dissident regions found that they could make common cause with the anti-communist military (in whose senior ranks there were, after all, a fair sprinkling of non-Javanese) in their continuing struggles with the centre. As Mackie (1980: 674–5) summed up the situation, a politics of manipulation and compromise replaced the earlier confrontational pattern. A system of 'de facto federalism' came to apply, in which compromise and ad hocery affected economic as well as political aspects of the relationship between the centre and the regions.

Local officials, the military and civilian representatives of the central government struck bargains over the imposition of illegal taxes and imposts, and the sharing of revenues from smuggling, with the central government officials usually being by far the weakest partner. The centre, indeed, had little option but to turn a blind eye to much of what was going on, because it had no effective means of enforcing central government laws and regulations even where its official representatives – in the form of governors, district heads (*bupati*), subdistrict heads (*camat*) and so on – might have wished to do so. In many regions outside Java, it is probable that district and village governments continued to assess

---

8 With the exception of an early attempt to establish an independent republic in the southern part of Maluku, these rebellions were not secessionist in nature. The rebels in both Sumatra and Sulawesi wanted their regions to remain part of Indonesia but with far greater autonomy than the central government was prepared to concede. Apart from grievances over their share of export revenues, they objected especially to the imposition of Javanese in senior positions rather than local people; see Holland (1999: 204). Most of those supporting the rebellions wanted Indonesia to adopt a more explicitly federalist constitution. Kahin (2012: 136–7) claims that, while in West Sumatra, Natsir and other Masyumi leaders drew up a new federal constitution comprising 113 single-spaced pages and a further 41 pages of appendices. But other participants in the rebellion, including Sumitro, wanted to keep the unitary state.

and collect taxes in labour, kind and cash to repair infrastructure. But economic stagnation and mounting inflation made it more difficult for governments at any level to collect revenue and carry out much needed maintenance projects. Everywhere in the country infrastructure deteriorated, often to a point where roads became impassable and irrigation systems ceased to function.

2.3   THE SUHARTO ERA

A recentralization of power

There is universal agreement that the Suharto years were marked by 'an inexorable trend towards re-centralization of power' (Mackie 1980: 676). In the early years of his long period in power, Suharto was most concerned with curbing the power of regional army commanders, but by 1974 his control over the parliament was strong enough to ensure the passage of Law 5/1974 on Basic Principles on Administration in the Regions, which remained in force until 1999. Some observers have seen this legislation as a return to the highly centralized model of the Dutch colonial era (Malley 1999: 81). Certainly there were few concessions to any real regional autonomy, and both provincial and subprovincial levels of government were placed under strong central control. The 1974 law vested power in the regional head (*kepala daerah*), who was under the direct control of the central government (Holland 1999: 210–11). Regional parliaments had few powers. Many governors and *bupati* were from the military, although Suharto was also astute enough to appoint some respected civilians as provincial governors, including M. Noer in East Java and Harun Zain in West Sumatra, both provinces where Islamic political parties had commanded strong support in the 1950s. But elsewhere, unpopular governors were often 'dropped in' from the centre, especially in provinces that were rich in natural resources (Malley 1999).

Mackie (1980: 677) has identified a number of other factors that enhanced Suharto's control over the regions during the 1970s. The one that is perhaps the most important, the centre's much greater budgetary resources, will be examined in more detail below. In addition, Suharto tightened central control over the military, eliminating most of the warlordism of the years from 1957 to 1966. Political activity was also tightly controlled. Another factor was the greatly improved transport network, which permitted more movement of Indonesians around the country for education and employment. With substantial assistance from the World Bank and other donors, the program of land settlement outside Java was also greatly expanded, leading to millions of Javanese and Balinese settling on land outside Java between 1969 and 1997.

Inpres grants

The system of central grants to the regions played a crucial role in the recentralization process. During the 1960s the value of such grants had been eroded by inflation, and by 1968 they were virtually worthless. Beginning in 1969, the central government introduced a series of programs whose purpose was to enable provincial, district and village administrations to carry out much needed rehabilitation of infrastructure (roads, bridges, irrigation facilities, village halls and so on) using earmarked grants from the centre. It was envisaged that labour-intensive construction techniques would be used, and that much of the work would be carried out during the agricultural slack season.[9] From the outset it was made clear that the grants were not to be used for office buildings or vehicles, although other funds at the disposal of district/municipality governments, including revenue from the land tax (Ipeda), were used for office buildings in many cases.[10]

These programs – which became known as the Presidential Instruction (Instruksi President, Inpres) programs – were important not just because they demonstrated the concern of the centre for the parlous state of local infrastructure, especially in rural areas, but also because they attempted to address the problem of rural underemployment. It was argued that there was considerable capacity at the subprovincial levels of government to implement a range of labour-intensive projects that would use local materials and employ local people. In the early years, almost 70 per cent of District Inpres (Inpres Kabupaten) funds were spent on wages and local materials; in 1972/73 it was estimated that 435,000 men were employed for an average of 100 days (Patten, Dapice and Falcon 1980: 170). After the first oil shock in 1973–74, which coincided with the drafting of the second five-year plan of the Suharto era, new Inpres programs were initiated that were directed to specific types of infrastructure.

The largest was the presidential program to build primary schools (Inpres Sekolah Dasar), which provided funding for the construction of a simple three-room schoolhouse in every village unit in the country, using a plan drawn up by the Ministries of Education and Public Works in Jakarta, and sent to every province in the country. A parallel program provided funds for the construction of primary health care cen-

---

9   See de Wit (1973) and Patten, Dapice and Falcon (1980) for a discussion of the aims and implementation of the original Inpres Kabupaten program. These papers were written by advisers who were closely connected with the original Inpres programs and give an outline of the way the projects were implemented, at least in the early years.

10   Booth (1974) discusses the use of Ipeda funds by district/municipality governments in the early 1970s.

tres. Again, clear guidelines were laid down on the allocation of funds and the construction of facilities, supposedly to minimize corruption and waste. As these programs accelerated, together with expenditure on development projects implemented by central government agencies, people everywhere in the archipelago began to see some evidence that the country's oil wealth was being used on facilities that would directly benefit them and their families. But the grant allocation system remained highly centralized, with the central government maintaining tight control over grant allocations, and also over how the money was spent.

It is perhaps surprising that the oil boom of the 1970s did not bring with it any demand on the part of the producing provinces to retain a larger share of the profits. In fact, during the oil boom period (1973–81) most of the oil came from just two provinces, Riau in central Sumatra, and East Kalimantan. Both were small and lacking in strong regional identities or in much tradition of regional nationalism, although the local population in Riau did show resentment towards a Javanese governor who was considered arrogant in his attitudes to local people and local customs (Malley 1999: 87–9). In both provinces, but especially in East Kalimantan, a large number of migrants from other parts of the country were drawn into the oil and logging sectors and related activities, and in both provinces ethnic Javanese held key positions in the civilian and military bureaucracies.[11] Although there was debate about the extent to which the benefits of the oil boom spilled over to the local populations in both these provinces, there were sufficient signs of improvement in infrastructure and living standards to convince the majority of the indigenous populations that they were benefiting from the exploitation of their provinces' natural resources, even if these benefits were modest in comparison with the total value of their oil exports.[12]

As world oil prices began to fall in the early 1980s, the Indonesian government was forced to make cuts in its budgetary expenditures to

---

11 From the 1960s through to the end of the century, the demographic structure of East Kalimantan evolved in a very different way from that of other provinces in Indonesia. By 2000, 70 per cent of the province's population was living in the four main cities, and the urban populations were mainly of Javanese, Buginese and Banjarese origin (Morishita 2008: 89–90). In Riau, large numbers of migrants from Java and other parts of Sumatra also flooded in, giving rise to a continuing debate in the post-Suharto era as to who exactly was an 'Orang Riau' (Ford 2003).

12 For a more detailed discussion of economic development in the resource-rich provinces until the mid-1980s, see Chapters 3–6 in Hill (1989). Although written by Indonesians, these chapters demonstrate a remarkable lack of concern over the issue of sharing of resource rents. This suggests that the provincial elites in provinces such as Riau were not unhappy with the system prevailing at the time.

compensate for falling oil revenues. In the early 1980s, fiscal austerity particularly affected the routine budget (excluding the debt service component), leading to a freezing in nominal terms of the salaries and perquisites of the military and civilian bureaucracies and to a drastic curtailment in other types of routine expenditure (for example, on maintenance of buildings, equipment and infrastructure). In fiscal year 1986/87, foreign debt service obligations increased substantially in rupiah terms as a result of a rupiah devaluation and a yen revaluation. To maintain the budget balance, the government had little choice but to make deep cuts in the development budget, which fell from 11 per cent to 8 per cent of GDP in a single year (Asher and Booth 1992: Table 2.6). Although these cuts had a more drastic effect on the development budgets of departments (especially industry, energy, transmigration and environment) than on regional development grants, these grants also declined in real terms, and by 1989/90 were only 3.4 per cent of total budgetary expenditures, compared with 7.2 per cent two years earlier (Asher and Booth 1992: Table 2.11).

The period of the fifth five-year plan (1989–94) saw considerable growth in Inpres expenditures relative to both total domestic revenues and total government development expenditures. By 1995/96, they accounted for over 25 per cent of the development budget (Table 2.2). There was also considerable growth in revenue accruing to provincial and district/municipality governments from the land and buildings tax (*pajak bumi dan bangunan*, PBB), which replaced the Ipeda after the tax reforms of the mid-1980s (Kelly 2004).[13] Most categories of Inpres expenditures shared in the growth over these five years, although the program targeting the rehabilitation and extension of the road network experienced the fastest growth (Shah and Qureshi 1994: Ch. 4; Booth 1996: Table 11.1). In 1994/95, a new Inpres program was introduced for villages that were considered to have been 'left behind', that is, those that had not benefited from the rapid economic growth of the previous two decades.[14] This new program reflected growing official concern with

---

13 These reforms involved the introduction of a value-added tax and substantial reform of the personal and corporate income tax systems. These taxes accrued to the central government; apart from the reforms to the PBB, there was no attempt to give regional governments further taxing powers. By 1999/2000 the PBB accounted for a much greater proportion of non-grant revenues for both provinces and districts/municipalities than in 1987/88 (Kelly 2004: Table 9.1). Lewis (2003) points out that much of the growth in PBB revenues in the 15 years after the reform came from the mining sector, and to a lesser extent from urban property taxes.

14 For a discussion of the Inpres program for poor villages (Inpres Desa Tertinggal), see Pangestu and Azis (1994: 32ff).

Table 2.2   Trends in Inpres and routine (SDO) grants from the central
budget to the regions, 1984/85–1998/99 (%)[a]

Fiscal year	Inpres as a share of total domestic revenue	SDO + Inpres as a share of total domestic revenue	Inpres as a share of total development spending
1984/85	9.6	20.8	18.2
1985/86	6.9	18.8	12.2
1986/87	8.9	24.8	14.2
1987/88	7.6	20.5	14.4
1988/89	7.1	19.9	11.0
1989/90	5.6	17.0	10.8
1990/91	7.1	16.3	15.3
1991/92	9.7	19.9	16.8
1992/93	10.3	21.3	18.4
1993/94	9.8	22.1	19.4
1994/95	10.8	21.7	24.9
1995/96	10.0	21.2	25.3
1996/97	10.0	21.6	24.9
1997/98	8.4	17.5	19.8
1998/99	8.4	16.6	20.2

a   'Inpres' refers to all Inpres grants, including those to provinces, districts and villages as well as sectoral grants for health and education; revenue from the land and buildings tax (PBB) is also included. Routine grants from the central government to the regions (Subsidi Daerah Otonom, SDO) mainly cover the salaries and wages of regional employees. Total domestic revenue in the central budget includes revenue from oil and gas, but excludes that from aid and borrowing.

Source: World Bank (1999: appendix tables).

spatial inequities in economic development, and especially with what was seen as the 'problem' of eastern Indonesia. By the early 1990s many of the Inpres grants were skewed to regions outside Java. The majority of funds were spent in Java only in the case of the Inpres Kabupaten, whose main criterion for allocating funds remained population (Booth 2011: Table 4).[15]

---

15 Already by the 1980s there was a tendency for the smaller, less densely settled provinces to receive higher Inpres grants both in per capita terms and relative to GDP. See Booth (2003: 189–90) and Silver, Azis and Schroeder (2001: 354–6) for evidence that there was no 'Java bias' in the allocation of Inpres grants. The evidence does not support the claim of Horowitz (2013: 71) that the grant system favoured Java.

Population growth and the numbers of regional and local governments

Between 1961 and 1995, Indonesia's population doubled from 97 million to 195 million. Given that there were only modest increases in the number of provinces and districts/municipalities during these years, the average size of provincial and district/municipality populations also grew. By 1995, the three large provinces in Java had populations of close to or over 30 million, while several others had populations in excess of 5 million. The average size of a district in Java was over 1 million in 1995, and around 560,000 in Sumatra. Rapid increases in the average population of districts also occurred in other regions (Table 2.1). The most dramatic changes in the numbers of local government units during the Suharto era, however, occurred at the village level. In 1969/70 Indonesia had around 44,500 villages according to the official definition (Booth 2011: Table 3). By 1983/84 this had increased to 66,000, although there was some decline after 1988/89. The creation of new 'villages', especially outside Java, was sometimes controversial in that it was viewed as a deliberate attempt by the central government to impose an essentially Javanese construct on indigenous systems in other regions.[16]

Other sources of regional government revenue

Given the increasing populations of local government units, together with the growth in real income that undoubtedly occurred in the three decades from 1967 to 1997, it might have been expected that the central government would have tried to increase revenue mobilization at the regional level, either through some form of tax sharing with the provinces or by giving provincial and district-level governments some potentially lucrative revenue instruments. The main tax instruments assigned to the provinces were the taxes on registration and change of ownership of motor vehicles, which for the larger and richer provinces were quite buoyant sources of revenue. But the other taxes assigned to provinces were generally less lucrative, so that motor vehicle taxes accounted for a high proportion of all own-source revenues in most provinces throughout the Suharto era. In East Java, for example, they comprised over 80 per

---

16 Law 5/1979 on Village Administration set out the principles of the New Order regarding village government; Antlöv (2003: 195) argues that with the passage of the law, 'village affairs were brought firmly under the supervision and control of higher authorities, and village structures were recast within a single homogeneous mould' (see also Holland 1999: 208–10). Although most village heads continued to be elected, the elections were supervised by higher levels in the administration.

cent of own-source revenues during the 1980s. Most provinces depended on central grants for around 80 per cent of their total revenues (Booth 1993: Tables 14.1 and 14.2).

The district-level governments were also very dependent on grants and on the land tax, which was centrally assessed, although most of the revenue was assigned to the districts (Booth 1974). Only small amounts of revenue could be collected through most of the taxes assigned to the districts (radio tax, dog tax, tax on non-motor vehicles); the main exception was the tax on hotels and restaurants, which was quite an important source of revenue for some urban districts, and for districts in Bali, which had a well-developed tourist sector. Fieldwork I carried out in the early 1970s showed that the land tax was the most important source of revenue for many districts in Java, although in South Sulawesi a number were levying a tax on motor vehicles using particular roads, supposedly to fund road rehabilitation (*pajak rehabilitasi jalan*). In some provinces this tax was an important source of revenue (Booth 1974: Table 3). But it was in effect a levy on buses and on trucks carrying goods, which added to the cost of transporting agricultural and other produce along rural roads.[17]

Village governments tended to be less dependent than other levels of government on grants from above, although the amount collected in local taxes (including requirements to provide labour) fell as a proportion of the total funds available to village governments during the 1970s and 1980s. Officials at higher levels of government tended to regard village people as willing to engage in local projects on a mutual self-help (*gotong royong*) basis, which in effect meant they were willing to contribute their labour without payment. Whether this was really the case has often been disputed.[18] Certainly there was considerable criticism by many people in both rural and urban areas that district and village governments often spent the discretionary funds at their disposal on lavish office buildings rather than on the services people wanted and needed, such as infrastructure, health and education. The evidence suggests that these criticisms have not gone away in the post-Suharto era.

Some tentative reforms of the system of regional finance occurred during the 1990s. But the approach of the central government was to move very cautiously, and to make no meaningful transfer of power, whether political or financial, to provincial and local governments. As

---

17 Such taxes are still levied in some areas, in spite of official attempts to eliminate them.

18 Devas (1989: 35–8) discusses village finances in the 1970s and 1980s. His estimates suggest that self-help contributions from within the village were of roughly the same magnitude as the Inpres grants from the central government, although he thinks that the size of such contributions may have been exaggerated in some official data.

Devas (1997: 364) has argued, this caution was motivated by the centre's continuing belief that the regions lacked the skills and capacity to carry out important government functions. But more cynical observers considered that this belief was underpinned by a desire on the part of powerful central bureaucrats to keep all opportunities for rent seeking firmly under their control. A law passed in 1997 tried to ban some of the taxes and levies that provincial and local governments had imposed on the transit of goods, and which were deemed to impede the marketing of agricultural produce. An analysis of the impact of this law on district budgets found that removing the taxes had only a minor effect, mainly because compensating grants were given from the centre (Montgomery et al. 2002: 112). But there was no attempt to give provinces, districts or villages any other taxes that they could assess and collect themselves. Unsurprisingly, when the districts were given greater autonomy after 2001, they reimposed some of the taxes and levies that had been abolished in 1997, and paid little attention to the attempts by the centre to stop them.

2.4   FRUSTRATIONS AT THE END OF THE SUHARTO ERA

By the early 1990s, it was clear that there was considerable unrest in many parts of the country over the system of regional and local government that had grown up under Suharto (Booth 2003: 185–94). In the resource-rich parts of the country, the old grievances about Javanese exploitation had not gone away, and when provincial poverty estimates were published in the early 1990s, the problem of 'rich provinces and poor people' became more obvious. Although the headcount measure of poverty in 1996 was lower than the national average in Aceh, Riau and East Kalimantan, it was much higher in Irian Jaya (Booth 2004: Table 4). And in East Kalimantan, which shared a long border with East Malaysia, differences in poverty levels between East Kalimantan and the states of East Malaysia were considerable, in spite of the fact that per capita gross regional product (in US dollar terms) was higher in East Kalimantan than in either Sabah or Sarawak (Booth 2003: Table 6). These differences might not have mattered very much if Indonesians in Kalimantan, and in many other provinces, were ignorant of conditions in neighbouring Malaysia. But by the early 1990s well over 1 million Indonesians were working in Malaysia, and to them at least the gap in living standards was all too obvious.

But the criticisms were not confined to the resource-rich provinces outside Java. Many officials at the provincial and district levels considered that the system of central grants to the regions had become cumbersome and inequitable and that the allocation criteria were increasingly opaque. The lower per capita allocations to the more densely settled regions, especially in Java, were leading to grievances there. Many in Java felt that the three provinces of West, Central and East Java, whose populations were larger than several independent countries elsewhere in Asia, had reached the stage where they could organize their own finances with minimal interference from the centre. The larger provinces in Sumatra and Sulawesi shared these views, even where they were not well endowed with natural resources. Senior civil servants in the provincial bureaucracies resented the attitude of the centre that they were incapable of assessing taxes, or of making decisions on expenditure, especially as evidence of mounting corruption at the centre became too obvious to disguise. Resentment was even stronger in those provinces that possessed oil, gas, forests and minerals such as coal. Many in the regions that were well endowed with natural resources considered that the main beneficiaries from their exploitation were the large conglomerates controlled by the presidential family and its business partners, most of whom were Chinese.

These perceived injustices were building into demands for change when the economic crisis erupted in late 1997. The resignation of Suharto in May 1998, after 32 years in power, presented an opportunity for reform, culminating in the passage of two decentralization laws in 1999[19] and the implementation of the decentralization legislation in 2001. While these reforms gave resource-rich regions a greater share in resource revenues, and much greater autonomy to all district-level governments in the allocation of expenditures, they did not tackle the issue of devolving greater revenue-raising powers to either provinces or districts (Alm, Aten and Bahl 2001: 88–9). Thus, one of the key problems that had been highlighted in the 1950s remained unresolved.[20] However radical the reforms may appear to contemporary observers, both Indonesian and foreign, one suspects that many of those who fought for a more decentralized system in the early post-independence years would be disappointed with the changes that have taken place since Suharto's departure.

---

19 Law 22/1999 on Regional Government and Law 25/1999 on the Fiscal Balance between the Central Government and the Regions.
20 According to Horowitz (2013: 73–4), a survey of members of the People's Consultative Assembly (Majelis Permusyawaratan Rakyat, MPR) in 1999–2000 found that 65 per cent of them approved of the regional autonomy legislation, and almost 22 per cent thought it did not go far enough. But only 11.5 per cent were reported as favouring federalism.

REFERENCES

Agung, I.A.A. (1996) *From the Formation of the State of East Indonesia towards the Establishment of the United States of Indonesia*, Yayasan Obor Indonesia, Jakarta.

Alm, J., R. Aten and R. Bahl (2001) 'Can Indonesia decentralise successfully? Plans, problems and prospects', *Bulletin of Indonesian Economic Studies*, 37(1): 83–102.

Antlöv, H. (2003) 'Village government and rural development in Indonesia: the new democratic framework', *Bulletin of Indonesian Economic Studies*, 39(2): 193–214.

Asher, M. and A. Booth (1992) 'Fiscal policy', in A. Booth (ed.) *The Oil Boom and After: Indonesian Economic Policy and Performance in the Soeharto Era*, Oxford University Press, Singapore.

Booth, A. (1974) 'Ipeda – Indonesia's land tax', *Bulletin of Indonesian Economic Studies*, 10(1): 55–81.

Booth, A. (1993) 'Regional finance in Indonesia: an East Java case study', in H. Dick, J. Fox and J. Mackie (eds) *Balanced Development: East Java in the New Order*, Oxford University Press, Singapore.

Booth, A. (1996) 'Intergovernmental relations and fiscal policy in Indonesia: the national impact of equity and inequity in the provinces', in C. Fletcher (ed.) *Equity and Development across Nations*, Allen & Unwin, Sydney.

Booth, A. (2003) 'Decentralisation and poverty alleviation in Indonesia', *Environment and Planning C: Government and Policy*, 21: 181–202.

Booth, A. (2004) 'Africa in Asia? The development challenges facing Eastern Indonesia and East Timor', *Oxford Development Studies*, 32(1): 19–36.

Booth, A. (2011) 'Splitting, splitting and splitting again: a brief history of the development of regional government in Indonesia since independence', *Bijdragen tot de Taal-, Land- en Volkenkunde*, 167(1): 31–59.

BPS (Badan Pusat Statistik) (1963) *Sensus Penduduk 1961 Republik Indonesia Angka2 Sementara* [Population Census 1961 of the Republic of Indonesia: Preliminary Figures], BPS, Jakarta.

BPS (Badan Pusat Statistik) (1996) *Produk Domestik Regional Bruto Kabupaten/ Kotamadya 1993–95* [Gross Regional Domestic Product of Districts/Municipalities, 1993–95], BPS, Jakarta.

BPS (Badan Pusat Statistik) (1997) *Penduduk Indonesia: Hasil Survei Penduduk Antar Sensus 1995* [Population of Indonesia: Results of the 1995 Inter-censal Survey], BPS, Jakarta.

BPS (Badan Pusat Statistik) (2006) 'Key indicators of Indonesia 2006', BPS, Jakarta, available at ww.bps.go.id.

BPS (Badan Pusat Statistik) (2007) 'Daftar nama provinsi/kapupaten/kota menurut dasar hukum pembentukan wilayah' [List of names of provinces/ districts/municipalities according to regional legal status], BPS, Jakarta, available at ww.bps.go.id.

Chauvel, R. (1997) 'Tarred with the Dutch brush: the fate of federalism in Indonesia', in P.J. Drooglever and M. Schouten (eds) *De Leeuw en de Banteng* [The Lion and the Wild Ox], Instituut voor Nederlandse Geschiedenis, The Hague.

de Wit, Y.B. (1973) 'The Kabupaten Programme', *Bulletin of Indonesian Economic Studies*, 9(1): 65–85.

Devas, N. (1989) 'Local government finance in Indonesia: an overview', in N. Devas et al. (eds) *Financing Local Government in Indonesia*, Southeast Asia Series No. 84, Ohio University Center for International Studies, Athens.

Devas, N. (1997) 'What do we mean by decentralization? The Indonesian case', *Public Administration and Development*, 17(3): 351–67.

Feith, H. (1962) *The Decline of Constitutional Democracy in Indonesia*, Cornell University Press, Ithaca.

Ford, M. (2003) 'Who are the Orang Riau? Negotiating identity across geographic and ethnic divides', in E. Aspinall and G. Fealy (eds) *Local Power and Politics in Indonesia*, Institute of Southeast Asian Studies, Singapore.

Hill, H. (1989) (ed.) *Unity and Diversity: Regional Economic Development in Indonesia since 1970*, Oxford University Press, Singapore.

Holland, P. (1999) 'Regional government and central authority in Indonesia', in T. Lindsey (ed.) *Indonesia: Law and Society*, Federation Press, Sydney.

Horowitz, D.L. (2013) *Constitutional Change and Democracy in Indonesia*, Cambridge University Press, Cambridge.

Kahin, G.M. (1952) *Nationalism and Revolution in Indonesia*, Cornell University Press, Ithaca.

Kahin, A.R. (2012) *Islam, Nationalism and Democracy: A Political Biography of Mohammad Natsir*, NUS Press, Singapore.

Kelly, R. (2004) 'Property taxation in Indonesia', in R.M. Bird and E. Slack (eds) *International Handbook of Land and Property Taxation*, Edward Elgar, Cheltenham.

Legge. J.D. (1961) *Central Authority and Regional Autonomy in Indonesia: A Study in Local Administration 1950–1960*, Cornell University Press, Ithaca.

Lev, D. (1996) 'Between state and society: professional lawyers and reform in Indonesia', in D.S. Lev and R. McVey (eds) *Making Indonesia: Essays on Modern Indonesia in Honor of George McT. Kahin*, Southeast Asia Program, Cornell University, Ithaca.

Lewis, B.D. (2003) 'Property tax in Indonesia: measuring and explaining administrative (under-) performance', *Public Administration and Development*, 23: 227–39.

Lindblad, J.T. (1992) 'Regional patterns in the foreign trade of Java, 1911–1940', in A. Clemens, J.T. Lindblad and J. Touwen (eds) *Changing Economy of Indonesia. Volume 12b: Regional Patterns of Foreign Trade 1911–1940*, Royal Tropical Institute, Amsterdam.

Mackie, J.A.C. (1980) 'Integrating and centrifugal factors in Indonesian politics since 1945', in J.A.C. Mackie (ed.) *Indonesia: The Making of a Nation*, Research School of Pacific Studies, Australian National University, Canberra.

Malley, M.S. (1999) 'Regions: centralization and resistance', in D.K. Emmerson (ed.) *Indonesia beyond Suharto*, M.E. Sharpe, Armonk.

Maryanov, G.S. (1958) *Decentralization in Indonesia as a Political Problem*, Interim Report Series, Modern Indonesia Project, Southeast Asia Program, Cornell University, Ithaca.

Maryanov, G.S. (1959) 'The establishment of regional government in the Republic of Indonesia', PhD dissertation, Department of Government, Indiana University, Bloomington.

Mboi, A.B. (2009) 'The first step on the long road to a dualistic provincial and district government', in M. Erb and P. Sulistiyanto (eds) *Deepening Democracy in Indonesia, Direct Elections for Local Leaders (Pilkada)*, Institute of Southeast Asian Studies, Singapore.

Miller, M.A. (2006) 'What's special about special autonomy in Indonesia?', in A. Reid (ed.) *Verandah of Violence: The Background to the Aceh Problem*, Singapore University Press, Singapore.

Montgomery, R. et al. (2002) 'Deregulation of Indonesia's agricultural trade', *Bulletin of Indonesian Economic Studies*, 38(1): 93–117.

Morishita, A. (2008) 'Contesting power in Indonesia's resource-rich regions in the era of decentralization: new strategy for central control over the regions', *Indonesia*, 86(October): 81–107.

Mubyarto and R. Baswir (1989) 'Central Kalimantan: the Dayak heartland', in H. Hill (ed.) *Unity and Diversity: Regional Economic Development in Indonesia since 1970*, Oxford University Press, Singapore.

Nasution, A.B. (1992) *The Aspiration for Constitutional Government in Indonesia: A Socio-legal Study of the Indonesian Konstituante 1956–1959*, Sinar Harapan, Jakarta.

Paauw, D. (1960) *Financing Economic Development: The Indonesian Case*, Free Press, Glencoe.

Pangestu, M. and I.J. Azis (1994) 'Survey of recent developments', *Bulletin of Indonesian Economic Studies*, 30(2): 3–47.

Patten, R.H., B. Dapice and W. Falcon (1980) 'An experiment in rural employment creation: the early history of Indonesia's Kabupaten Development Programme', in G.F. Papanek (ed.) *The Indonesian Economy*, Praeger, New York.

Reid, A. (2007) 'Indonesia's post-revolutionary aversion to federalism', in B. He, B. Galligan and Y. Inoguchi (eds) *Federalism in Asia*, Edward Elgar, Cheltenham.

Shah, A. and Z. Qureshi (1994) 'Inter-governmental fiscal relations in Indonesia: issues and reform options', World Bank Discussion Paper No. 239, World Bank, Washington DC.

Silver, C., I.J. Azis and L. Schroeder (2001) 'Intergovernmental transfers and decentralisation in Indonesia', *Bulletin of Indonesian Economic Studies*, 37(3): 345–62.

Taylor, A.D. (1960) *Indonesian Independence and the United Nations*, Stephens and Sons, London.

World Bank (1999) *Indonesia: From Crisis to Opportunity*, World Bank, Washington DC, 21 July.

3 Indonesia's decentralization: the rise of local identities and the survival of the nation-state

Marcus Mietzner

3.1 INTRODUCTION

Nation-states launch decentralization programs in highly different historical contexts and for a wide variety of reasons (Eaton, Kaiser and Smoke 2010: 8–9). China and Vietnam, for example, have pursued moderate decentralization policies in order to respond to economic modernization pressures. Brazil, South Africa and Mexico introduced decentralization as part of their post-authoritarian transitions, while Cambodia, Rwanda and Uganda gave more power to the local level to heal post-conflict traumas. Most importantly, many developing countries use decentralization as a tool to improve government effectiveness, responsiveness and accountability (Asante and Ayee 2004: 3). Few states, however, implement decentralization as an urgent measure to prevent the disintegration of the state in the middle of a severe political crisis. Arguably, Indonesia in 1999 was such a state: many observers were concerned that, having emerged from 40 years of centralist authoritarianism, post-Suharto Indonesia could become the next Yugoslavia or Soviet Union. Fuelled by the secession of East Timor in 1999, anxiety spread within Indonesia that other parts of the archipelago could also demand independence. While most serious foreign scholars believed that a territorial break-up was unlikely (Cribb 1999; Emmerson 2000; Aspinall and Berger 2001), they nevertheless devoted much time to discussing such a probability. This, in turn, did little to reassure Indonesian policy makers.

Faced with the threat of territorial disintegration, the Indonesian elite turned to decentralization. First designed in 1999 and implemented since 2001, decentralization transformed Indonesia from one of the most centralist nations in the world into a polity with near-federal structures. As a result, the share of regional spending in total government expenditure increased from 17 per cent in 2000 to 40 per cent in 2009 (World Bank 2002, 2009: 65). This reform was implemented despite a number of well-documented risks inherent in decentralization. First, the empirical record of decentralization around the globe is 'mixed at best in terms of realizing many of the stated objectives of reform' (Eaton, Kaiser and Smoke 2010: xi), providing no 'unambiguous proof of its desirability' (Smoke 2003: 7). Second, 'decentralization is likely to accentuate the already precarious imbalance within the state' because it often favours already rich districts over poorer ones (Asante and Ayee 2004: 2). Third, decentralization frequently leads to wasteful spending on bureaucratic apparatuses (Mawhood 1993). Fourth, political decentralization does not automatically produce improved democratic quality, as 'the devolution of power may help to augment the dominance of those who, because of their wealth or status, are already powerful at the local level' (Asante and Ayee 2004: 2). Finally, decentralization can increase rather than reduce the levels of corruption (Prud'homme 1995).

Most studies of Indonesia's decentralization process have found that the country has fallen victim to most of the phenomena outlined above.[1] There is little evidence of significantly improved public services; resource-rich areas have seen higher growth rates than poorer districts; government spending on salaries and buildings has ballooned; elites have become the main players in local elections; and corruption is rampant. Yet, despite these deficiencies, the Indonesian nation-state not only has survived, but is probably stronger today than at any other point in its history. As Aspinall (2013: 132) has pointed out, the 'execution of decentralization policies played a major role in heading off severe state crisis in Indonesia', mostly through its 'immediate taming effects' on separatist sentiment in some regions.

While Aspinall focuses on the elites and their endorsement of policies that gave them more resources, there are at least four additional factors behind the consolidation of centre–periphery relations in Indonesia. These are the strong public satisfaction with decentralization; the non-violent flourishing of local identities; the increased level of state penetration; and the effective design of local elections as a channel for cross-constituency cooperation and the rise of alternative leaders. This chapter explores the role of each of these factors in turn (sections 3.2–3.5).

---

1 See, for example, Hofman and Kaiser (2004), Aspinall and Fealy (2003), Malley (2003), Schulte Northolt and van Klinken (2007), Bünte (2009) and Hadiz (2010).

Through a discussion of the ways in which decentralization has reduced tensions and stabilized the state, the chapter confirms that effectively designed policies can help heterogeneous states to decentralize without risking disintegration (Falleti 2005; Miodownik and Cartrite 2009).

3.2   MESSY BUT POPULAR: DECENTRALIZATION IN OPINION POLLS

While the popularity of decentralization among local elites is important for its success (Aspinall 2013), sufficient levels of popular support are equally critical. The degree of this support, in turn, can be assessed through public opinion polls. Until the early 2000s, most political scientists were reluctant to use opinion surveys to gauge the views of citizenries in new democracies. This scepticism was only partly related to questions of methodology; more importantly, it was based on the dominant view among theorists that most polities in Asia, Africa and Latin America were inevitably elite driven (Linz and Stepan 1996). It was only with the emergence of multi-country opinion survey projects such as Asian Barometer (which started in 2001) that senior political scientists began to take a closer look at public opinion as a determinant of political processes (Diamond 2010).

In Indonesia, for instance, the study of public opinion has been crucial in explaining the surprising stability of post-Suharto democracy despite the endemic corruption, weak rule of law and complaints about government effectiveness (Aspinall and Mietzner 2010). While some analysts have traced this stability to concessions made to potential spoilers such as the military (Aspinall 2010), a more compelling answer is hidden in opinion polls: since 1998, between 71 and 90 per cent of Indonesians have consistently supported democracy. Regardless of whether this support is deserved or not, the fact that it exists is politically relevant in itself. In essence, it means that there is no public pressure to adopt a different system – much in contrast to Russia, for example, where the authoritarian leadership can operate in the knowledge that only 29 per cent of its citizens support democracy (Pew Research Center 2009: 26).

A similar pattern marks the study of Indonesia's decentralization. At first glance it seems peculiar that amidst questionable performance indicators and continued corruption, decentralization should have stabilized the relationship between the capital and the periphery. But as in the case of democracy, opinion polls can shed a different light on the way decentralization has played out in post-Suharto Indonesia. In a 2007 poll, 73 per cent of respondents supported decentralization and only 27 per cent rejected it (LSI 2007). More specifically, 61 per cent of Indonesians

Table 3.1   Views on education and health services after decentralization, 2007[a]

	Better	Same	Worse	Don't know
Education	61	25	9	5
Health	54	29	12	4

a Respondents were asked whether the quality of education and health services had improved, stayed the same or declined after decentralization.
Source: LSI (2007).

believed that education services had become better under decentralization than they had been under centralist rule, while only 9 per cent thought they had become worse (Table 3.1). In the area of health, 54 per cent of respondents saw improvements, while 12 per cent thought that the quality of services had declined. Indonesians were less enthusiastic, however, about the impact of decentralization on the fight against poverty and unemployment: 34 per cent believed that poverty had become worse under decentralization (27 per cent thought that it had been reduced); and 40 per cent felt that unemployment had increased, while 23 per cent thought it had declined. The high level of overall support for decentralization has been confirmed by polls conducted by the World Bank, in which around 70 per cent of respondents testified to improved quality of health and education services and about 56 per cent to improved administrative services (World Bank 2009: 66).

Other opinion polls show consistently high levels of satisfaction with local government officials. In fact, with the exception of the presidency and the military, the popularity of government institutions increases inversely to administrative level. In other words, satisfaction levels are highest for the lowest level of state administration (village leaders), second highest for subdistrict offices and so forth (Figure 3.1). In a 2008 poll (Democracy International 2008: 19), village administrations received a net satisfaction rating of 61 percentage points, followed by subdistrict offices (57 per cent), district heads and mayors (38 per cent) and governors (31 per cent). This pattern is even reflected in the hierarchy of the least popular political institution in Indonesia, the legislature. While the national parliament received a negative net satisfaction rating of minus 16 per cent, its provincial pendant enjoyed a positive rating of 6 percentage points, and the district-level legislature of 11 points. In the same poll, 70 per cent of respondents described local government leaders as 'accountable', 67 per cent thought that local government services were of 'good quality' and 56 per cent said they had more confidence in local

Figure 3.1   Net satisfaction with political administrations and institutions, 2008 (%)[a]

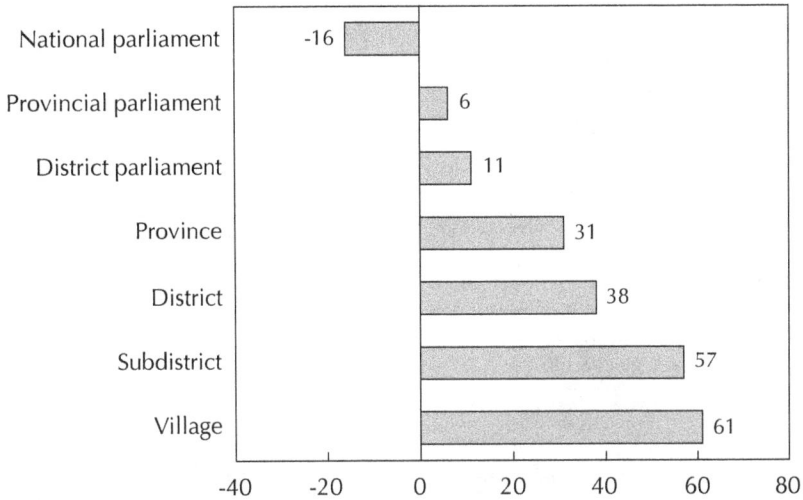

a   Net satisfaction is calculated by subtracting the percentage of respondents dissatisfied with a particular administration or institution from the percentage of satisfied respondents.

Source: Democracy International (2008: 19).

administrations than in national government (Democracy International 2008: 29).

As indicated above, the message of these opinion poll numbers stands in stark contrast to the often unflattering accounts of decentralization by scholars. In one of the most striking examples of the large gap between scholarship and opinion surveys, Kristiansen and Santoso (2006: 247) have described health services under decentralization as non-transparent, profit oriented and disadvantageous for the poor. However, their own survey data showed that 75 per cent of respondents thought the quality of health services was better today than before decentralization. Puzzled by this result, the authors dismissed their own survey as 'weak', 'remarkable' and having 'limited reliability' (Kristiansen and Santoso 2006: 255).

What, then, accounts for this discrepancy between scholarly assessments of performance indicators and the 'remarkable' levels of satisfaction among Indonesians with decentralization? To begin with, there are many statistics that would confirm the general sentiments of the citizenry. For example, Indonesia's score on the Human Development Index (HDI, a composite of life expectancy, literacy, education and living standards) has consistently increased since decentralization. According to the

Table 3.2   Human Development Index, selected Indonesian provinces, 1996–2010[a]

	1996	1999	2002	2004	2005	2006	2007	2008	2009	2010
West Nusa Tenggara	56.7	54.2	57.8	60.6	62.4	63.0	63.7	64.1	64.6	65.2
West Kalimantan	63.6	60.6	62.9	65.4	66.2	67.1	67.5	68.2	68.8	69.2
West Sulawesi	–	–	–	64.4	65.2	67.1	67.7	68.6	69.2	69.6
Gorontalo	–	–	64.1	65.4	67.5	68.0	68.8	69.3	69.8	70.3
Jakarta	76.1	72.5	75.6	75.8	76.1	76.3	76.6	77.0	77.4	77.6
National	**67.7**	**64.3**	**65.8**	**68.7**	**69.6**	**70.1**	**70.6**	**71.2**	**71.8**	**72.3**

a   The numbers in the table differ slightly from those in the Human Development Index calculated by the United Nations.
Source: BPS (2012).

calculations of Indonesia's central statistics agency, Badan Pusat Statistik (BPS), Indonesia's HDI score was 67.7 in 1996, declining to 64.3 in 1999 as a result of the Asian financial crisis. By 2010, however, it had risen to 72.3. Even more importantly, the provinces with the highest HDI growth rates have all been areas in the Outer Islands: West Nusa Tenggara, West Kalimantan, West Sulawesi and Gorontalo. The capital, Jakarta, by contrast, has recorded below-average growth in its HDI score (Table 3.2).

But the discrepancy between scholarly assessments and public views of decentralization has its roots not only in different readings of statistics; it also points to the fact that Indonesians base their evaluations of decentralization on factors other than just government services. Significantly, Thomas Carothers has applied a similar argument to refute Larry Diamond's notion of an inseparable link between government effectiveness and the level of support for democracy. For Diamond, dissatisfaction with the performance of government is the main factor causing support for democracy to decline and democratic reversals to occur (Diamond 2008). While acknowledging the 'powerful intuitive logic' of Diamond's approach, Carothers nevertheless believes that it misses a large part of citizens' motivations to support a particular polity. For Carothers (2009: 12), people's attachment to ideals such as democracy or decentralized governance 'does not necessarily rest solely on the socioeconomic performance of their government'.

The survey data certainly endorse Carother's point. Most Indonesians are disappointed with the lack of improvements in poverty alleviation and unemployment, and they believe that local governments fail to inform the citizenry about their activities (Democracy International

2008: 29). Yet, three-quarters of the Indonesian population still supports decentralization. This indicates that public backing for decentralization – and the stability of centre–periphery relations that results from it – are due to factors that go beyond bureaucratic performance. The following sections look at these factors in detail.

3.3   THE NON-VIOLENT RENAISSANCE OF LOCAL IDENTITIES

Arguably, one of the reasons that the majority of Indonesians support decentralization despite its many deficiencies concerns the renaissance of local identities after 2001. To grasp the dimensions of this revival, one needs to recall the tight management of nation building under Suharto's centralist regime. Despite the New Order's slogan of 'unity in diversity', at the core of its policies towards the regions was an aggressive push for uniformization. Politically, Law 5/1974 on Basic Principles of Regional Government led to the de facto appointment of district heads, mayors and governors by the central government, and Law 5/1979 on Village Government standardized previously heterogeneous forms of village administration. Culturally, the regime unashamedly promoted its Javanese values as the nucleus of Indonesian nationhood. As Hatley (1993: 50) has observed, the regime celebrated

> … conservative, hierarchical values. The central state – Java-based and Javanese-dominated – supports Javanese culture of a particular type, that of court tradition. Images of noble grandeur and hierarchical social order serve to display and confirm the authority of the contemporary state.

In this regime, the government tolerated alternative expressions of local identity as long as they came in the form of folklore, but cracked down on them if they turned political.

The regime party, Golkar, and the military also drove this standardization, spreading their symbols, colours and rhetoric throughout the archipelago. The archetypical small town in New Order Indonesia would have as its power centres the local military command, the Golkar building (usually painted in yellow) and the district head's office (run by either a military officer or a bureaucrat). Importantly, most military officers and senior bureaucrats stationed in the Outer Islands were from Java. Indeed, it was a declared policy by army headquarters to keep non-Javanese officers out of their home areas – a response to the involvement of local military officers in the regional rebellions of the late 1950s. Similarly, between 1965 and 1998, 73 per cent of all provinces outside Java were ruled by Javanese or Sundanese governors for at least one term. Half the provinces experienced more than 10 years of government by

Javanese and Sundanese officials, and 23 per cent witnessed more than 15 years of external rule. In the province of West Nusa Tenggara, Javanese leaders ruled continuously between 1958 and 1998.

But decentralization turned Indonesia into a very different place. The 1999 decentralization laws abolished the right of the central government effectively to appoint local government heads, which put an almost immediate end to the dominance of Javanese and Sundanese bureaucrats in the Outer Islands. The 2005 introduction of direct local elections strengthened that trend, and by 2013 only one province outside Java (North Sumatra) was ruled by a Javanese or Sundanese. Political liberalization and decentralization also terminated Golkar's uniform hegemony across the archipelago. In today's polity, the political affiliations of areas differ not only from district to district, but often from village to village (Jones 2010). Indeed, the electoral rights of Indonesians have been massively expanded: since 2005, citizens have been able to elect personnel for 11 political institutions in up to seven different polls within a five-year cycle. This in turn has encouraged democracy indexes such as Freedom in the World to grant Indonesia the highest score in political rights in Southeast Asia (Freedom House 2013).

This electoral liberalization and decentralization has resulted in a renaissance of long-suppressed local identities. In fact, appealing to specific local identities is now a prerequisite for political leaders to compete in local elections. In her ethnographic study of post-decentralization politics in West Sumba in East Nusa Tenggara, Jacqueline Veil (2008) described how local politicians had to command extensive knowledge of local customs and participate regularly in rituals in order to get elected. In contrast, outsiders who concentrated their campaign efforts on distributing money in a short period of time generally failed. Most importantly, the post-2001 localization of politics has not only strengthened existing identities, but also created new ones. In many cases, citizens located far from the main administrative centres of their localities began to organise around their collective feelings of marginalization, and to ask for the division (*pemekaran*) of the original district or province. Local elites in the western part of West Sumba, for instance, pushed for the creation of a new district of Central Sumba, arguing that they no longer wanted to be dominated by the West Sumbanese capital, Waikabukak. The split was formalized in 2007, defining a new Central Sumbanese identity for a population that now viewed itself as a distinct politico-cultural community.

This pattern of diversification is also mirrored in the 'new pluriformity of village governance' (Henley and Davidson 2008: 852), which removed the institutional standardization imposed by Law 5/1979 on Village Government. The new Law 22/1999 on Regional Government explicitly stated that 'Law 5/1979 … which made the name, shape, organization and position of village administration uniform, was not in line with ... the need to acknowledge and respect the special customary rights of the regions, and thus had to be replaced'. The cancellation of Law 5/1979 eventually led to the re-emergence of traditional forms of village management. In West Sumatra, for example, the customary forms of administering villages (*nagari*) made a comeback after decentralization (Biezefeld 2007). At the same time, there was a revitalization of *adat* (customary law), which had been recognized by the Dutch but had experienced a process of constant erosion under the New Order. Among others, many marginalized ethnic minorities used the new emphasis on *adat* to defend their land and resource exploitation rights. Law 32/2004 on Regional Government, which replaced Law 22/1999, clarified that the state 'respects units of customary societies and their traditional rights'. While some have argued that the revival of *adat* played a role in the ethnic strife that marred Indonesia in the early 2000s, there is also little doubt that it has increased the 'protection, empowerment, and mobilization of underprivileged groups' (Henley and Davidson 2008: 815).

Beyond the localization of political institutions, the media and civil society have also contributed to the strengthening of localist identities. The number of Indonesian newspapers grew from 250 in 1998 to 900 in 2010 (many of them local), while 274 regional television stations emerged, many delivering news in local languages.[2] Bali TV, for example, commenced regular programming in Balinese in 2002. Similarly, the Pekanbaru-based station Radio Soreram Indah devotes 60 per cent of its schedule to programs that 'express a distinct feeling of locality and ethnicity' (Suryadi 2005: 144). The number of local civil society organizations has also exploded. Where there were around 6,000 tightly controlled NGOs in 1996, there are now tens of thousands of such groups operating freely. To be sure, not all of these groups are benign. A not-insignificant percentage of them serve the interests of predatory elites, and some have exclusive ethnic or religious platforms. Most notably, the small-scale but increasingly violent attacks on religious minorities and Muslim sects in several regions since 2005 have generally involved militias hiding behind the mask of civil society activism.

Overall, however, decentralization and the increased opportunities for the expression of local interests have reduced the potential for conflict inherent in centre–periphery relations. In fact, the majority of the ethnic and religious clashes often blamed on decentralization (such as the violence in Maluku, North Maluku and Central Sulawesi) erupted *before* the 1999 decentralization laws were passed and ended shortly after the legislation came into effect. Varshney, Tadjoeddin and Panggabean (2010:

---

2   I am grateful to Bram Hendrawan for providing these numbers.

Figure 3.2   Incidence of communal violence in Indonesia, 1990–2003

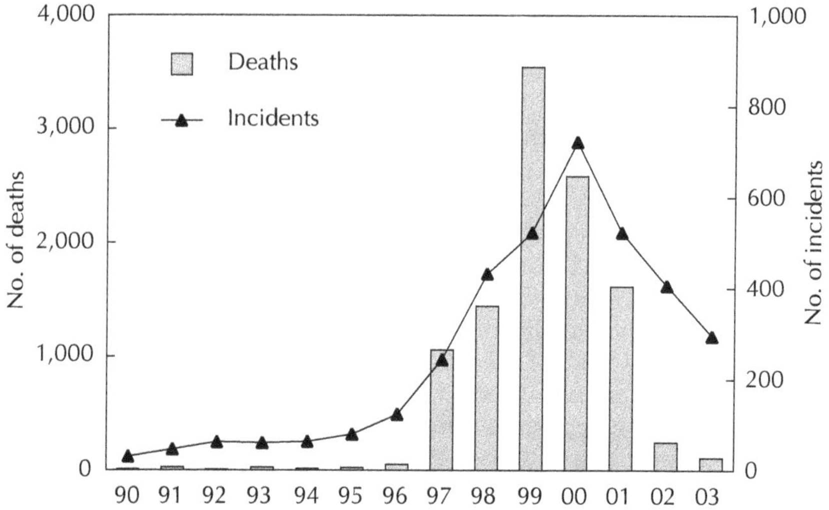

	90	91	92	93	94	95	96	97	98	99	00	01	02	03
Deaths	10	25	7	25	14	23	51	1,059	1,442	3,546	2,585	1,615	245	111
Incidents	30	46	62	60	63	79	123	244	432	523	722	523	406	295

Source: Varshney, Tadjoeddin and Panggabean (2010: 35).

35) have shown that the local violence surrounding Suharto's fall peaked in the volatile post-transition year of 1999 and declined sharply in 2001 when the decentralization regulations became operational (Figure 3.2). By 2002–03, the number of violent incidents had returned to unremarkable levels, except in Aceh, where the separatist conflict was resolved in 2005 through a separate peace agreement. Since then, large-scale communal violence has largely dissipated. Thus, while uncertainty over the specifics of decentralization may have contributed to the unrest in some areas (particularly, it seems, to the 2001 violence in Central and West Kalimantan), the full implementation of decentralization in the post-2001 period not only prevented the outbreak of further mass violence, but also helped to end existing conflicts.

There are three reasons why decentralization and the renaissance of local identities curtailed rather than catalysed centrifugal tendencies and major communal tensions. First, the Indonesian elite decided in 1999 that power and resources would be delegated not to the provincial but to the district and municipality level of government (Crouch 2010: 94). This was done to prevent the emergence of separatist movements in territories large enough to stake a credible claim to nationhood. In other words, while provinces like Riau or Bali might have felt encouraged by greater political and financial powers to secede from Indonesia, districts within those provinces had no realistic prospect of establishing their own micro-states. Significantly, the state's concentration on the district and munici-pality level of government fuelled the previously mentioned process of *pemekaran*, leading to the creation of more than 200 new subprovincial units between 1999 and 2013. While often criticized as wasteful and bureaucratically ineffective, this increasing fragmentation of the admin-istrative map has pre-empted centrifugal ambitions. As Indonesia's ter-ritorial units have become smaller, so have the chances of serious threats to the unitary state. Not coincidentally, the Soviet Union and Yugoslavia disintegrated largely because they had decentralized power to the state rather than to the district level – Jakarta not only avoided this mistake, but has shifted the focus of local politics from centre–periphery power struggles to competition within and between districts.

The second explanation for the non-violent consolidation of Jakarta's relationship with the regions despite the greater assertiveness of local-ist interests lies in the equalizing effect of fiscal decentralization policies. While the decentralization laws have ensured that resource-rich regions retain more of their locally generated revenues, Jakarta continues to con-trol how the bulk of nationally raised tax income is distributed to the regions as general purpose grants (Dana Alokasi Umum, DAU). Since the vast majority of districts are still dependent on these funds, the system through which they are apportioned is crucial to maintaining the balance between rich and poor regions. For the most part, the DAU mechanism has compensated poorer districts generously (Hofman and Guerra 2007; Fengler 2009), to the point where some economists believe that the system now serves as a disincentive to raising local revenues (Lewis and Smoke 2009: 423; Fadliya and McLeod 2011: 20). Politically, however, the DAU payments have prevented the emergence of serious conflicts between resource-rich and low-income regions. According to the World Bank (2009: 66), the 'regions, even the poorest, have received large increases in transfers in recent years (most now have surpluses) and the challenge has moved [from financial shortages] to spending wisely'. Unquestion-ably, without this equalizing impact of fiscal decentralization, the rise of political localism would have created much more inter-regional friction.

The third factor ensuring that the rise of local identities did not erode the nation-state was careful electoral engineering. Despite its empha-sis on decentralization, the Habibie government designed an electoral framework aimed at building national rather than local political parties. The political party and electoral laws demand that all parties develop a nationwide network of branches, effectively ruling out the possibility of locally or ethnically defined parties. These regulations have been tight-ened over the years, with the latest incarnation in 2011 requiring parties to have representation in all 34 provinces, 75 per cent of all districts and 50 per cent of the subdistricts in those districts in order to contest national elections (Law 2/2011 on Political Parties, article 3.2(c)). Moreover, the electoral laws do not allow independents to nominate for the national or local legislatures. In the same vein, candidates in executive local elections initially had to be nominated exclusively by national parties. Although this regulation has since been changed and independent candidacies are now possible, the laws continue to privilege national parties. While some pro-democracy activists have criticized the de facto ban on local parties and candidates as an impediment to democratic consolidation, it has provided an important counterbalance to the localization of politics since 2001.

The expanded space for the expression of local identities and interests is one of the main reasons for the popularity of decentralization among elites and ordinary citizens. The New Order's artificial imposition of standardized forms of local governance and state-approved concepts of culture was replaced by a new pluralism that allowed citizens to adhere to local customs *and* to be proud Indonesians at the same time. Furthermore, the delegation of powers to the district level, an equalizing fiscal system and the maintenance of national parties guaranteed that this explosion of localisms did not undermine the notion of Indonesian nationhood. However, there was another important factor that protected Indonesia from the potential risks of decentralization: contrary to widespread perceptions, decentralization did not lead to a *weakening* of the state; rather, it resulted in an unprecedented *expansion* of the state's infrastructure. This state expansion is the subject of the next section.

3.4   DECENTRALIZATION AND THE EXPANSION OF THE STATE

One of the main arguments against decentralization has been that it weakens the authority of the state and thus could lead to its disintegration (Asante and Ayee 2004: 2; Miodownik and Cartite 2009). In Indonesia, this fear was the main driver of opposition to decentralization in conservative circles (Bünte 2009: 118). But in many of the critiques, the term 'state' is confused with 'central government'. Obviously, decentralization takes some powers away from the *central government*, but that does not mean that the *state* is necessarily weakened. The state, according to Migdal (2001: 15–16), is

> ... a field of power marked by the use and threat of violence and shaped by (1) the image of a coherent, controlling organization in a territory, which is a representation of the people bounded by that territory, and (2) the actual practices of its multiple parts.

Based on this definition, the Indonesian state today is stronger, more visible and more deeply engrained in society than ever before. Among others, this consolidated state capacity is evidenced by the effective use of coercive force against regions that, despite the concessions offered by decentralization, sought to secede from the unitary state (Aspinall 2013).

In contrast to many other Southeast Asian countries (Burma, the Philippines, Laos), Indonesia has had a relatively strong state (Crouch 1998). This was partly due to the Dutch colonial heritage, but also to the efficacy of the New Order bureaucracy. Even under Suharto, however, many remote areas outside Java, Bali and Sumatra had never been touched by the state's administrative infrastructure. Post-authoritarian Indonesia, by contrast, has seen a massive expansion of the state apparatus into isolated areas in the Outer Islands. The main catalyst for this development has been the much criticized process of *pemekaran*, which has led to the establishment of new provinces, districts and municipalities. Many economists have dismissed these new creations as patronage fiefdoms. According to the World Bank (2009: 66), 30 per cent of the budgets of subnational governments is swallowed by administrative spending benefiting the elite, whereas 'best practice is usually closer to 5 per cent'. In political terms, however, the increased presence of the state in remote territories has moderated concerns that decentralization could create a power vacuum in many parts of the archipelago. While the communal conflicts of 1999, 2000 and 2001 initially suggested that this fear could become a reality, the subsequent proliferation of state bureaucracies has filled the void.

The statistics on *pemekaran* reflect the deepening and broadening of the state in the Outer Islands. Of the eight new provinces created since decentralization, only one is in Java; the other six are located in Papua, Maluku, Sulawesi, Kalimantan and Sumatra. At the district and municipality level the trend is even more evident: there, 95 per cent of all new territories are outside Java – the majority of them in Sumatra (77), followed by Sulawesi (35), Papua (31), Kalimantan (25), Maluku (13) and Nusa Tenggara (11). Overall, the figures show a gradual but strong growth of state institutions since decentralization – not only at the provincial and district levels, but also at the subdistrict and village levels (Table 3.3). Importantly, this development is likely to continue, albeit at a slower pace. In 2011, the Yudhoyono government's new 'Grand Design for the Structuring of Regions' predicted that Indonesia would have 44 provinces and 545 districts and municipalities by 2025.[3]

The post-decentralization expansion of state institutions has also accelerated the 'civilianization' of Indonesian local politics. In 1998,

---

3 'Govt unveils new autonomy design', *Jakarta Post*, 21 April 2011.

Table 3.3   Number of provinces, districts, municipalities, subdistricts and villages, 1998–2010

	1998	2000	2002	2004	2006	2008	2010	2012
Provinces	27	30	31	33	33	33	33	34
Districts	249	268	302	349	349	370	399	399
Municipalities	65	73	89	91	91	95	98	98
Subdistricts	4,028	4,049	4,918	5,277	5,656	6,425	6,699	6,793
Villages/*kelurahan*	67,925	69,050	70,460	69,858	71,563	75,410	77,548	79,075

Source: BPS (2012).

many observers had not only predicted, but even *demanded*, a continued role for the armed forces in politics because it was supposedly the only institution that could keep the vast archipelago together (Walters 1999: 59–60). Of course, this perception echoed conventional wisdom that had dominated studies of Indonesia since the 1940s. But the reality of today's decentralized Indonesia is vastly different. The new districts, subdistricts and villages embedded civilian governance in far-flung regions and replaced military units as the main representatives of state authority. District heads, subdistrict chiefs (*camat*) and village leaders (*kepala desa* or *lurah*) gradually took the place of army commanders who had owed their prominence at the grassroots to the military's territorial structure. The command system established in the 1950s to counter unrest in the Outer Islands still exists today, but it now plays second fiddle to local government authorities.

Significantly, military officers were also unable to take advantage of electoral reforms at the local level. When direct elections for local government heads were introduced in 2005, some observers believed this would allow the military to stage a political comeback. But the results were disillusioning for the armed forces: many governorships and district head positions previously held by ex-military personnel fell into the hands of civilians. Well-connected bureaucrats, cashed-up entrepreneurs and politically savvy party leaders understood the electoral dynamics of a decentralized Indonesia much better than the retired officers, who often relied on simplistic law and order platforms. As a result, the number of retired military personnel holding leading positions in local government declined drastically. In 2013, only two of 34, or 6 per cent, of governors in Indonesia had a military background – down from 80 per cent at the beginning of the New Order's rule and 40 per cent at the time of Suharto's fall (Mietzner 2009: 347). The pattern at the district level was similar. Clearly, this new competitiveness and dynamism of local elections has been one of the main factors helping to consolidate public support for decentralization. In the next section, therefore, I discuss why these elections have had a stabilizing effect on centre–periphery relations, and why they have *not* led to ethno-political mobilization.

3.5   LOCAL ELECTIONS, INTER-ETHNIC COOPERATION AND NEW LEADERSHIP

The introduction of direct elections of governors, district heads and mayors in 2005 added a significant political element to the administrative and fiscal decentralization launched in 1999. By putting political decentralization last, Indonesia stood somewhat outside the international norm. Falleti (2005: 329) has shown that most successful decentralization processes begin with the devolution of 'electoral capacities to subnational actors'. According to him, political decentralization 'early in the sequence is likely to produce coordination among the beneficiaries of this policy who will push forward in the direction of further decentralization' (p. 343). Indonesia, in contrast, prioritized administrative and fiscal decentralization, and delayed electoral devolution. The 1999 decentralization laws provided only for the election of local government heads by their respective legislatures. These 'elections' witnessed widespread vote buying, and there was generally no relationship between the result of the parliamentary elections and the outcome of the vote in the legislature. Accordingly, the 2004 revisions to the decentralization laws stipulated that from 2005 onward, all governors, district heads and mayors would be elected through popular ballots.

To be sure, the post-2005 local elections have run into a myriad of problems. First, the rising cost of modern campaigns and the absence of meaningful state funding for parties and candidates have limited the pool of nominees to those who have the necessary financial resources to run (Buehler and Tan 2007; Erb and Sulistiyanto 2009; Hadiz 2010). While less well-off candidates can be competitive if they are strongly rooted in their electoral areas, money has been an indispensible tool for the vast majority of nominees (Mietzner 2011). As a result, many candidates become dependent on the oligarchic interests that sponsor them. In addition, there have been many logistic difficulties in local elections. Voter registration has often been chaotic, and many areas have used manual rather than computerized tabulation mechanisms. While systematic fraud has been rare, the weaknesses in electoral management have led to imprecise results and contested outcomes. Despite these shortcomings, however, the direct local elections have proved popular with the citizenry; they

Figure 3.3   Popular support for different systems of installing governors, 2010

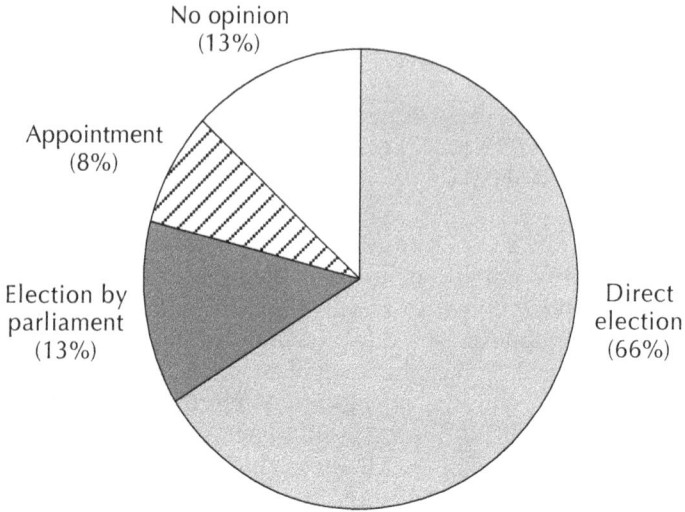

No opinion (13%)

Appointment (8%)

Election by parliament (13%)

Direct election (66%)

Source: Data provided by Lembaga Survei Indonesia (LSI), 24 November 2010.

have provided voters with an instrument to decide the outcome of elite contests, and they have given the electorate a stake in decentralization. This became clear when conservative circles in Jakarta's elite tried to abolish direct gubernatorial ballots (Mietzner 2012). The response by the electorate to this attempt was unambiguous: in an opinion survey held in November 2010, 66 per cent of respondents defended the popular election of governors (Figure 3.3).

The attempt to abolish gubernatorial elections was all the more surprising because the post-2005 regime of direct local ballots had successfully facilitated political cooperation between different ethnic and religious groups. This was achieved by requiring candidates for governor, district head and mayor to team up with a deputy nominee on a single ticket. Had the law provided for individual rather than joint nominations, many candidates would have chosen to appeal to the majority ethnic or religious group in their area. The rules demanding a joint ticket, by contrast, made coalition building between candidates from different backgrounds an electoral necessity. In their study of the 2010 mayoral elections in Medan, Aspinall, Dettman and Warburton (2011: 53) highlighted the 'central role played by cross-ethnic coalition building'. Their analysis showed 'how, at every stage of the election ... candidates were acutely conscious that appealing beyond one's own ethnic group was essential to electoral success'. The same was true for cross-religious coop-

Figure 3.4   *Coalition building between parties in local elections, 2005–07*

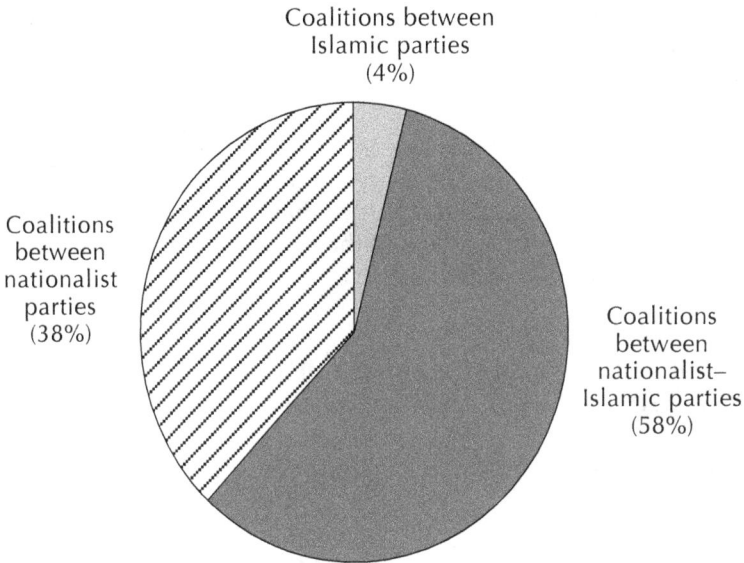

Coalitions between
Islamic parties
(4%)

Coalitions
between
nationalist
parties
(38%)

Coalitions
between
nationalist–
Islamic parties
(58%)

Source: Data provided by Jeremy Gross, Asia Foundation, Jakarta, June 2007.

eration, as reflected in the statistics related to coalition building between nominating parties. For instance, only 4 per cent of all coalitions in elections held between 2005 and 2007 were forged between Islamic parties. By contrast, 58 per cent of the alliances involved secular-nationalist *and* Islamic parties, while 38 per cent were secular-nationalist in character (Figure 3.4).

The direct local elections also facilitated the rise of fresh, alternative political leadership. Indeed, the ascent of Joko Widodo (popularly called Jokowi) to become Indonesia's most popular politician and a presidential front-runner was made possible only by the direct ballots introduced in 2005. A forestry expert and small-scale furniture entrepreneur, Jokowi was not part of the traditional elite networks that dominated pre-2005 local politics. His electoral victories in Solo in 2005 and 2010 made him known to a regional audience in Java, and his triumph in Jakarta's gubernatorial election in 2012 ultimately propelled him to the national stage. His popular deputy, Basuki Tjahaja Purnama (known as Ahok), had also climbed his way up from the depths of Bangka Belitung electoral politics to the heights of national significance. Obviously, there is much evidence of rent seekers and opportunists coming to power as well, but the rise of reformist figures provides a vital counterbalance. Significantly, local elections also offer a mechanism through which aspiring national politicians can gain executive experience. For instance, Ganjar Pranowo – a politician from the Indonesian Democratic Party of Struggle (Partai Demokrasi Indonesia Perjuangan, PDIP) – moved from the national legislature to Central Java politics in 2013, winning the gubernatorial elections there in a landslide. Clearly he'll return to Jakarta a much more seasoned politician.

In short, the direct elections are crucial to understanding the popularity of decentralization: they have given Indonesian voters a say in local affairs; they have strengthened rather than eroded inter-constituency relations; and they have accelerated the regeneration and broadening of political leadership personnel.

3.6   CONCLUSION: DECENTRALIZATION AND THE SURVIVAL OF THE INDONESIAN NATION-STATE

Indonesia's decentralization process has been plagued by many problems, ranging from corruption to chaotic implementation. These weaknesses have been extensively documented, and decentralization critics are unlikely to run out of subjects to study any time soon. But the surprising thing about post-Suharto decentralization is not that it has faced seemingly overwhelming difficulties; this was always to be expected in a country with a per capita income of below $1,000 (in 2001) and a long history of patrimonialism. From a historical perspective, the really astonishing feature of decentralization 13 years after it was launched is how stable centre–periphery relations have become. It is worth remembering that when Indonesia's democratic system of the 1950s issued a major decentralization law in December 1956, the country saw a wave of regional rebellions for two years after that (Legge 1961). By the time the uprisings in Sulawesi, Sumatra and Maluku were over, democracy had collapsed. For the next 40 years, Indonesia was ruled by military-backed regimes that managed the relationship between the capital and the regions through force and centrally planned development programs.

Viewed through this macroscopic lens, post-Suharto decentralization has achieved what it set out to do. The devolution of central power amidst a messy democratic transition was never primarily about introducing good governance to a patronage-driven polity. Rather, it was designed to secure the long-term survival of the nation-state by reconciling the regions with a capital that had systematically undermined their local identities since the 1950s. The post-1999 decentralization has allowed the regions to recapture their traditions and advance their material interests *vis-à-vis* the centre. Apparently, these concessions have been

sufficient for the periphery to settle back into a stable working relationship with the centre. This is demonstrated by the current absence of any
seriously disruptive dispute between Jakarta and the Outer Islands. Such
centre–periphery conflicts were commonplace not only in Indonesia in
the 1950s; more recently, they have torn apart the highly heterogeneous
state of Sudan and continue to threaten similarly structured nations such
as Nigeria, Burma, Ukraine and even Belgium.

Decentralization has worked in Indonesia because both local elites
and the broader citizenry support it. Obviously, local elites have enjoyed
the vastly increased money flows and the expanded patronage opportunities. While many observers point to the benefits reaped by the elite
as an indicator of the shortcomings of decentralization, the accommodation of local elite interests was a necessary precondition for its success.
In order to reduce anti-centralist or even secessionist sentiment in the
regions, central governments have to satisfy at least some of the material demands of the elites that fuel them. Separatist groups are rarely
grassroots movements for clean government – they mainly consist of
elites who feel marginalized from the process of resource distribution
controlled by the centre. Acknowledging this fact, Indonesia resolved the
Aceh conflict in 2005 by offering the leadership of the Free Aceh Movement (Gerakan Aceh Merdeka, GAM) the political and economic opportunities it had been denied for decades (Aspinall 2009). To some extent,
the decentralization strategy followed the same principle: it pre-empted
potential local demands for fairer resource sharing through an immediate and unprecedented transfer of money to the regions. In Falleti's
terminology, Indonesia ensured the success of its decentralization program by offering fiscal devolution parallel to the delegation of administrative powers. With this sequencing, Indonesia avoided the risk of elites
becoming disillusioned with an 'unfunded' delegation of powers (Falleti
2005: 331).

While elite support has been crucial, decentralization would not
have been sustainable without continued backing from the citizenry.
Strong public frustration with decentralization over an extended period
of time would certainly have led to its reversal. But opinion polls show
a consistent pattern of support for decentralization, making it difficult
for national leaders to even consider aborting it. For ordinary citizens,
the increased emphasis on local traditions, the end of the dominance of
Javanese officials in the Outer Islands and the flourishing of local media
and NGOs have been welcome breaks with the centralist, authoritarian
past. Contrary to widespread perceptions, Indonesians are also not dissatisfied with local public services, with the exception of unemployment
and anti-poverty programs. Finally, Indonesians appreciate the opportunities for political participation delivered by the post-2005 electoral

decentralization. The importance of these public perceptions has often been overlooked by scholars – the majority of whom have measured the effectiveness of decentralization by looking at school enrolment numbers, economic statistics and health indicators. These statistics are important, but they show only one side of the coin. Evidently, Indonesians assess decentralization not only by its ability to increase government effectiveness, but also by the extent to which it opens democratic space for them.

Despite heavy criticism directed towards some of the details of the decentralization program, Indonesia seems to have made the right call on the project's fundamentals. To begin with, the decision to delegate fiscal, administrative and political powers to the districts and municipalities rather than the provinces has prevented the emergence of large subnational entities with potentially secessionist ambitions. Similarly, the design of DAU payments has mitigated the regional inequality and interdistrict rivalry inherent in decentralization processes. Indeed, studies have shown that Indonesia's fiscal equalization system reduces regional disparities more effectively than that used by China or the Philippines (Hofman and Guerra 2007). Moreover, sensible electoral engineering has pre-empted both the rise of locally oriented parties *and* the risk of primordially divisive campaigning. The emphasis on national political parties enshrined in the electoral laws has ensured that the nation-state remains the main frame of reference even in local politics, and the regulations on direct local polls have fostered cross-ethnic and inter-religious cooperation. Less planned was the post-decentralization proliferation of provinces, districts, municipalities, subdistricts and villages, but its effect has been to increase the level of state penetration into previously untouched areas in Indonesia's periphery. As a result, the Indonesian state is arguably more robust today than it was even under Suharto, and it has acquired a much more civilian face.

The case of Indonesia, then, confirms studies that link the success of decentralization to the sequencing and extent of the devolution that takes place. Miodownik and Cartrite (2009: 743) have argued that 'half-hearted reforms may in fact produce the most extreme ethno-political mobilization'. In other words, if decentralization is launched but fails to address the demands of the regions, it can aggravate the situation instead of mitigating it. For Falleti (2005: 327), such scenarios are mostly the result of wrong sequencing or incomplete design of decentralization initiatives, with some governments devolving duties but not funds. As explained above, Indonesia did not make the error of offering 'unfunded' decentralization, and has in fact constantly increased payments rather than rolling them back. As a result, the interests of regional elites and societies were effectively accommodated. Miodownik and Cartrite (2009: 743) thus found that 'accommodation, rather than suppression or control, of the diverse interests of regions and groups will protect the integrity of the state' – an insight clearly underlined by the consolidation of the Indonesian nation-state a decade after decentralization.

REFERENCES

Asante, F.A. and J.R.A. Ayee (2004) 'Decentralization and poverty reduction', Institute of Statistical, Social and Economic Research (ISSER), University of Ghana, Accra.

Aspinall, E. (2009) *Islam and Nation: Separatist Rebellion in Aceh, Indonesia,* Stanford University Press, Stanford.

Aspinall, E. (2010) 'Indonesia: the irony of success', *Journal of Democracy,* 21(2): 20–34.

Aspinall, E. (2013) 'How Indonesia survived: comparative perspectives on state disintegration and endurance', in A. Stepan and M. Kunkler (eds) *Indonesia, Islam, and Democracy: Comparative Perspectives,* Columbia University Press, New York.

Aspinall, E. and M.T. Berger (2001) 'The breakup of Indonesia? Nationalism after decolonisation and the contradictions of modernity in post-Cold War Southeast Asia', *Third World Quarterly,* 22(6): 1,003–24.

Aspinall, E. and G. Fealy (eds) (2003) *Local Power and Politics in Indonesia: Decentralisation and Democratisation,* Institute of Southeast Asian Studies, Singapore.

Aspinall, E. and M. Mietzner (eds) (2010) *Problems of Democratisation in Indonesia: Elections, Institutions and Society,* Institute of Southeast Asian Studies, Singapore.

Aspinall, E., S. Dettman and E. Warburton (2011) 'When religion trumps ethnicity: a regional election case study from Indonesia', *South East Asia Research,* 19(1): 27–58.

Biezefeld, R. (2007) 'The many roles of *adat* in West Sumatra', in J. Davidson and D. Henley (eds) *The Revival of Tradition in Indonesian Politics: The Deployment of Adat from Colonialism to Indigenism,* Routledge, London.

BPS (Badan Pusat Statistik) (2012) *Statistik Indonesia, 2012* [Indonesian Statistics, 2012], BPS, Jakarta.

Buehler, M. and P. Tan (2007) 'Party–candidate relationships in Indonesian local politics: a case study of the 2005 regional elections in Gowa, South Sulawesi province', *Indonesia,* 84: 41–69.

Bünte, M. (2009) 'Indonesia's protracted decentralization: contested reforms and their unintended consequences', in M. Bünte and A. Ufen (eds) *Democratization in Post-Suharto Indonesia,* Routledge, London.

Carothers, T. (2009) *Stepping Back from Democratic Pessimism,* Carnegie Endowment for International Peace, Washington DC.

Cribb, R. (1999) 'Not the next Yugoslavia: prospects for the disintegration of Indonesia', *Australian Journal of International Affairs,* 53(2): 169–78.

Crouch, H. (1998) 'Indonesia's "strong" state', in P. Dauvergne (ed.) *Weak and Strong States in Asia-Pacific Societies,* Allen & Unwin, Sydney.

Crouch, H. (2010) *Political Reform in Post-Suharto Indonesia,* Institute of Southeast Asian Studies, Singapore.

Democracy International (2008) *Indonesia Annual Public Opinion Surveys: 2008 Report,* Democracy International, Bethesda.

Diamond, L. (2008) 'The democratic rollback', *Foreign Affairs*, 87(2): 17–22.

Diamond, L. (2010) 'Indonesia's place in global democracy', in E. Aspinall and M. Mietzner (eds) *Problems of Democratisation in Indonesia: Elections, Institutions and Society*, Institute of Southeast Asian Studies, Singapore.

Eaton, K., K. Kaiser and P. Smoke (2010) *The Political Economy of Decentralization Reforms: Implications for Aid Effectiveness*, World Bank, Washington DC.

Emmerson, D. (2000) 'Will Indonesia survive?', *Foreign Affairs*, 79(3): 95–106.

Erb, M. and P. Sulistiyanto (eds) (2009) *Deepening Democracy in Indonesia? Direct Elections for Local Leaders (Pilkada)*, Institute of Southeast Asian Studies, Singapore.

Fadliya and R.H. McLeod (2011) 'Fiscal transfers to regional governments in Indonesia', working paper, Arndt-Corden Department of Economics, Australian National University, Canberra.

Falleti, T. (2005) 'A sequential theory of decentralization: Latin American cases in comparative perspective', *American Political Science Review*, 99(3): 327–46.

Fengler, W. (2009) 'Indonesia's economic geography and fiscal decentralization 10 years after designing the big bang', paper presented at the Indonesian Regional Science Association Conference, IRSA Institute, Bogor, 23 July.

Freedom House (2013) *Freedom in the World*, Freedom House, Washington DC.

Hadiz, V.R. (2010) *Localising Power in Post-authoritarian Indonesia: A Southeast Asia Perspective*, Stanford University Press, Stanford.

Hatley, B. (1993) 'Constructions of "tradition" in New Order Indonesian theatre', in V.M. Hooker (ed.) *Culture and Society in New Order Indonesia*, Oxford University Press, Oxford.

Henley, D. and J. Davidson (2008) 'In the name of *adat*: regional perspectives on reform, tradition, and democracy in Indonesia', *Modern Asian Studies*, 42(4): 815–52.

Hofman, B. and S.C. Guerra (2007) 'Ensuring inter-regional equity and poverty reduction', in J. Martinez-Vazquez and B. Searle (eds) *Fiscal Equalisation: Challenges in the Design of Intergovernmental Transfers*, Springer, New York.

Hofman, B. and K. Kaiser (2004) 'The making of the big bang and its aftermath: a political economy perspective', in J. Alm, J. Martinez-Vazquez and S.M. Indrawati (eds) *Reforming Intergovernmental Fiscal Relations and the Rebuilding of Indonesia*, Edward Elgar, Cheltenham.

Jones, S. (2010) 'The normalisation of local politics? Watching the presidential elections in Morotai, North Maluku', in E. Aspinall and M. Mietzner (eds) *Problems of Democratisation in Indonesia: Elections, Institutions and Society*, Institute of Southeast Asian Studies, Singapore.

Kristiansen, S. and P. Santoso (2006) 'Surviving decentralisation? Impacts of regional autonomy on health service provision in Indonesia', *Health Policy*, 77: 247–59.

Legge, J.D. (1961) *Central Authority and Regional Autonomy in Indonesia: A Study in Local Administration 1950–1960*, Cornell University Press, Ithaca.

Lewis, B.D. and P. Smoke (2009) 'Incorporating subnational performance incentives in the Indonesian intergovernmental framework', in National Tax Association (ed.), *NTA Proceedings from the 101st Annual Conference in Philadelphia, PA*, National Tax Association, Washington DC.

Linz, J.J. and A. Stepan (1996) *Problems of Democratic Transition and Consolidation: Southern Europe, South America and Post-communist Europe*, Johns Hopkins University Press, Baltimore and London.

LSI (Lembaga Survei Indonesia) (2007) *Dukungan terhadap Otonomi Daerah* [Support for Regional Autonomy], LSI, Jakarta.

Malley, M.S. (2003) 'New rules, old structures and the limits of democratic decentralization', in E. Aspinall and G. Fealy (eds) *Local Power and Politics in Indonesia: Decentralisation and Democratisation*, Institute of Southeast Asian Studies, Singapore.

Mawhood, P. (ed.) (1993) *Local Government in the Third World: The Experience of Tropical Africa*, Africa Institute of South Africa, Pretoria.

Mietzner, M. (2006) 'Local democracy', *Inside Indonesia*, 85: 17–18.

Mietzner, M. (2009) *Military Politics, Islam and the State in Indonesia: From Turbulent Transition to Democratic Consolidation*, Institute of Southeast Asian Studies, Singapore.

Mietzner, M. (2011) 'Funding *pilkada*: illegal campaign financing in Indonesia's local elections', in E. Aspinall and G. van Klinken (eds) *The State and Illegality in Indonesia*, KITLV Press, Leiden.

Mietzner, M. (2012) 'Indonesia's democratic stagnation: anti-reformist elites and resilient civil society', *Democratization*, 19(2): 209–29.

Migdal, J. (2001) *State in Society: Studying How States and Societies Transform and Constitute One Another*, Cambridge University Press, Cambridge.

Miodownik, D. and B. Cartrite (2009) 'Does political decentralization exacerbate or ameliorate ethnopolitical mobilization? A test of contesting propositions', *Political Research Quarterly*, 63(4): 731–46.

Pew Research Center (2009) 'The pulse of Europe 2009: 20 years after the fall of the Berlin Wall', Pew Research Center, Washington DC.

Prud'homme, R. (1995) 'The dangers of decentralization', *World Bank Observer*, 10(2): 201–20.

Schulte Northolt, H. and G. van Klinken (2007) *Renegotiating Boundaries: Local Politics in Post-Suharto Indonesia*, KITLV Press, Leiden.

Smoke, P. (2003) 'Decentralisation in Africa: goals, dimensions, myths and challenges', *Public Administration and Development*, 23: 7–16.

Suryadi (2005) 'Identity, media and the margins: radio in Pekanbaru, Riau (Indonesia)', *Journal of Southeast Asian Studies*, 36(1): 131–51.

Varshney, A., M.Z. Tadjoeddin and R. Panggabean (2010) 'Patterns of collective violence in Indonesia', in A. Varshney (ed.) *Collective Violence in Indonesia*, Lynne Rienner Publishers, Boulder and London.

Veil, J. (2008) *Uma politics: an ethnography of democratization in West Sumba, Indonesia, 1986–2006*, KITLV Press, Leiden.

Walters, P. (1999) 'The Indonesian armed forces in the post-Soeharto era', in G. Forrester (ed.) *Post-Soeharto Indonesia: Renewal or Chaos?* Institute of Southeast Asian Studies, Singapore.

World Bank (2002) 'Observations on Indonesia's fiscal decentralization from a panel of international experts', World Bank, Jakarta, available at http://site resources.worldbank.org/INTINDONESIA/Resources/Decentralization/Panel_thoughts_on_IndonesiaII.pdf.

World Bank (2009) *Indonesia Development Policy Review: Enhancing Government Effectiveness in a Democratic and Decentralized Indonesia*, World Bank, Washington DC.

4 Hares and tortoises: regional development dynamics in Indonesia

Hal Hill and Yogi Vidyattama

4.1 INTRODUCTION

This chapter examines regional development patterns in Indonesia since the 1970s. In earlier work (Hill, Resosudarmo and Vidyattama 2008; Vidyattama 2008) we concluded that, although inter-regional inequality was high, growth during the period 1975–2005 was spatially quite broadly distributed. A very gradual convergence in provincial per capita income levels was discernible according to the two most widely used economic indicators (discussed below), suggesting some catch-up among the poorest regions. The precise magnitudes depended on which concept of inequality and which income series were used. Few provinces performed consistently poorly and, apart from the special cases related to conflict, very few grew significantly more slowly than the national average. Greater Jakarta became ever more dominant during the period. Together with East Kalimantan, it continued to be the richest province from the 1980s. In general, the better-performing regions were those that were more connected to the global economy, through commodity exports, tourism or the modern industrial–service economy.

However, the unit of analysis in our earlier work was confined to the provinces, as the district (*kabupaten/kota*) dataset was still in its infancy, covering a relatively short time span of about a decade. Moreover, we were able to draw only limited inferences about the effects of decentralization, both because the analysis was conducted at the provincial level and because the regional accounts data were then available only through to 2005. The purpose of this chapter is to extend this research in two directions. First, we pay greater attention to the district as the unit of analysis, consistent with the longer and better data series now available, and with the fact that districts have been the focus of the decentralization measures legislated in 1999 and implemented since 2001. Second, as we now have data for the decade since decentralization commenced, we are able to examine the effects of these reforms on regional development outcomes.

The chapter is organized as follows. In section 4.2 we provide a broad overview of regional development dynamics, among the major island groupings and at the provincial level, extending and updating our earlier research. We also examine the correlations between economic and social indicators, and trends in inequality. Section 4.3 repeats this analysis at the district level, examining in particular whether the broad regional mosaic at the provincial level holds at the more disaggregated district level of analysis. We summarize our major findings in section 4.4.

At the outset, it is useful to keep in mind some qualifications that are an inevitable feature of such analysis. First, and most important, this is a case of 'two-variable analysis'. We make inferences about the effects of decentralization on subnational development dynamics, but we caution against stronger assertions of causality. Indonesia is such a heterogeneous economy that one simply cannot conclude that development outcomes at the regional level are the result just of a single factor such as decentralization. Many other factors have affected regional development outcomes since 2001: Indonesia has experienced a major commodity boom; its real exchange rate has fluctuated considerably; there has been a global economic recession; and the infrastructure deficit – so crucial for regional socio-economic integration – has become more serious. Each of these factors has had substantial micro-level effects; to take the most obvious example, the commodity boom has primarily benefited the resource-rich regions outside Java. It is not possible to separate out, and quantify, the impacts of each factor across all regions. But even if such an analysis were possible, the effects of decentralization would be muted by the fact that the implementation process was far from clean and decisive. Since the 'big bang' reforms of 2001, the administrative and financial arrangements between the centre and the regions have been the subject of constant tinkering, modification and refinement, especially as both the central and provincial tiers of government have sought to reclaim some of the powers lost in 2001 (see Lewis, Chapter 6). Moreover, such a major change to the system of government takes time to implement. Most of the newly powerful local governments have weak administrative capacity, in all manner of service provision, in drawing up budgets and in running education, health and infrastructure services, not to mention dealing with the sometimes recalcitrant bureaucracies above them.

Two additional caveats are important. One is that the subdivision of provinces, districts and smaller administrative units – known in Indonesia as *pemekaran* (fragmentation) – has continued unabated. The number of districts rose from 294 at the end of the Soeharto era to 510 in mid-2013. The increase in the number of provinces, from 26 to 34,[1] has been less rapid, precisely because the incentives and scope for the creation of new regions have been greater at the district level. These frequent and large boundary changes have greatly complicated not only the task of governing the country, but also the analysis of trends in subnational socio-economic development. Our analysis requires a consistent set of boundaries, and this is feasible only with reference to the set of 26 provinces and 294 districts applying immediately before decentralization. Ideally, Indonesia's contemporary regional mosaic would be portrayed with reference to the current administrative boundaries, but the socio-economic statistics are not available on a longitudinal basis, so the analysis has to be undertaken with reference to the earlier boundaries.

The final caveat concerns data quality. We rely on the central statistics agency, Badan Pusat Statistik (BPS), for all our data, and the analysis is only as good as the data. BPS is known as an independent agency of strong analytical quality. It has produced regional economic accounts at the provincial level since the early 1970s, and at the district level since the early 1990s. The economic crisis of 1997–98 and the major political changes over the past decade and a half have presented many tests for BPS, but the quality of its data is well regarded. It is likely, however, that data quality for the smaller, more remote regions is not as good as that for Java–Bali, with its better-established statistics infrastructure.

4.2   AN OVERVIEW OF REGIONAL DYNAMICS

Trends for the major island groups

We first examine long-term trends in regional dynamics among the major island groups, asking where the main economic activity is located, and if it is changing over time. We follow the conventional classification of five island groups: Sumatra, Java–Bali, Kalimantan, Sulawesi and Eastern Indonesia (the latter comprising Maluku, Papua and Nusa Tenggara).[2]

---

1   There were of course 27 provinces in 1996, including East Timor, now the independent nation of Timor Leste. We have excluded the former province from our pre-2000 data; its contribution to the national economy was in any case very small – about 0.25 per cent of GDP.

2   'Eastern Indonesia' is an elusive concept. In official circles, it also includes Sulawesi, and sometimes parts of Kalimantan. However, unless otherwise

Table 4.1   GRP and GRP per capita by island group, 1975–2010[a]

	1975	1990	2000	2010
Share of total GRP (%)				
Sumatra	35.8	26.1	23.2	23.1
Java–Bali excluding Jakarta	38.2	42.6	43.0	43.0
Jakarta	10.8	15.5	16.5	16.3
Kalimantan	6.5	8.6	9.8	9.2
Sulawesi	4.7	3.9	4.2	4.5
Eastern Indonesia	4.1	3.2	3.4	3.9
Relative GRP per capita (national average = 100)				
Sumatra	197.1	127.8	110.3	108.4
Java–Bali excluding Jakarta	62.9	74.6	76.3	78.2
Jakarta	262.3	335.3	405.2	402.8
Kalimantan	145.9	168.9	177.7	157.9
Sulawesi	65.4	55.6	58.0	61.9
Eastern Indonesia	75.0	56.9	58.1	60.1

a   GRP per capita is measured in current prices relative to the national average.
Source: BPS.

Because Jakarta is so atypical, we exclude it from Java–Bali and put it in a category of its own. We present trends in gross regional product (GRP) for the island groups across four points in time: 1975, when the first set of comprehensive and reasonably reliable regional accounts was prepared;[3] 1990, after over two decades of rapid growth during the Soeharto era; 2000, immediately after the Asian financial crisis and before decentralization; and 2010, a decade after decentralization (Table 4.1).[4]

---

indicated, in this chapter we will use the term to refer just to Maluku, Papua and Nusa Tenggara.

3 Note that the 1975 data for Papua (then referred to as Irian Jaya) are very approximate.

4 For reasons of space, we focus only on GRP. This inflates the figures for commodity-rich provinces, providing an exaggerated picture of their living standards. Two alternative series could be provided: non-mining GRP, that is, GRP after removing the output of the mining sector, which is typically enclave in nature; and aggregate household expenditure, using data that have been available since 1984. We undertook this analysis in Hill, Resosudarmo and Vidyattama (2008), concluding that there were considerable, though narrowing,

The major conclusion is the stability of the patterns over this 35-year period. Java–Bali was by far the largest regional economy in 1975, a feature that has since become even more pronounced. Together, Sulawesi and the rest of Eastern Indonesia continue to be a small proportion of the national economy, always less than one-tenth. Kalimantan's share has been rising steadily, and is now similar to the combined total for Sulawesi and Eastern Indonesia.

There are, however, two exceptions to the more general pattern of stability. The first is Jakarta, whose share of total GRP rose significantly from 11 per cent in 1975 to more than 16 per cent in 2010. It accounts for about two-thirds of the rise in the share of Java–Bali (including Jakarta). Its real share is of course greater still, given that the capital is now spilling across its borders into neighbouring West Java and Banten. Depending on exactly where its boundaries are drawn, Greater Jakarta now comprises about one-quarter of Indonesia's total economy (see Firman, Chapter 15). All the increase within the official boundaries occurred in the period 1975–2000, so it might be tempting to conclude that decentralization has stemmed the growth of Jakarta. However, the fact that most of the growth now effectively occurs just outside its borders is a more likely explanation for the stability of its share since 2000.

The other major exception is Sumatra, whose share of national output declined from about one-third in 1975 to less than one-quarter in 2010. Almost all the decline occurred between 1975 and 1990 and, as we will see below, much of it was concentrated in the oil-rich province of Riau. Perhaps surprisingly, the share of the resource-rich regions, particularly Kalimantan but also Sumatra, did not increase in the decade from 2000 to 2010, in spite of the commodity boom and the greatly increased revenue flowing to local governments there.

The patterns for relative income have also been fairly stable, with the same two principal exceptions (Table 4.1). Jakarta has always been richer than the rest of the country, with the gap in income progressively widening from over double the national average in 1975 to more than quadruple in 2000 and 2010, with only a slight tapering-off over the past decade. Kalimantan has consistently been about 50 per cent above the national average, with higher relative per capita GRP in 1990 and 2000 but (surprisingly) slightly lower relative income in 2010. Sumatra has slipped from being well above the average in 1975 to about 10 per cent above it in 2000 and 2010. Java–Bali excluding Jakarta remains below the national average, although its relative income has risen somewhat, with most of the increase occurring before 1990. Sulawesi and the rest of

---

differences in inter-provincial inequality between the series. However, there was very little change in the provincial rankings.

Eastern Indonesia have also been slipping behind, losing most ground during the period 1975–90. Since then, the per capita income of both has been about 60 per cent the national average.[5]

Provincial-level perspectives

We turn now to long-term trends in regional development among the provinces. Once again, we present per capita income relative to the national average for the years 1975, 1990, 2000 and 2010 (Table 4.2). We do this for 26 provinces, that is, using the late Soeharto-era provincial boundaries, and excluding East Timor. Where new provinces have been created subsequently, for this longer-term comparative exercise they have been merged back into their former provinces. Thus, Riau includes Riau Islands; South Sumatra includes Bangka Belitung; West Java includes Banten; North Sulawesi includes Gorontalo; South Sulawesi includes West Sulawesi; Maluku includes North Maluku; and Papua includes West Papua. As one would expect, the provincial patterns exhibit much greater diversity than those for the island groupings. For expositional purposes, and following Hill, Resosudarmo and Vidyattama (2008), we classify provinces into four main groups: the 'consistently wealthy', 'consistently non-poor', 'very poor' and 'slipping behind' provinces.

The four 'consistently wealthy' provinces – Jakarta, East Kalimantan, Riau and Papua – always perform above the national average. As noted, Jakarta has risen dramatically compared to the rest of the country. Riau has experienced the sharpest decline, from 10 times to still 2.5 times the national average. East Kalimantan's income has consistently been four to five times the national average; it has occupied the top spot since at least 2000. The fourth province, Papua, may seem to be a controversial inclusion in this group, as it has the most pronounced enclave development model and the poorest social indicators. But its recorded per capita income has always been well above the national average, by 40–50 per cent in 1990, 2000 and 2010, and by more than double in 1975.

The second group consists of 10 'consistently non-poor' provinces that have per capita incomes around one-quarter above or below the national average for all or most of the time. This is also a very diverse group. It includes the other three Kalimantan provinces, all frontier,

---

5 Among the several caveats to be attached to these figures, one in particular deserves emphasis. The figures are current price estimates that are unadjusted for regional price differentials. Prices are higher in Jakarta, while high terms of trade during commodity booms inflate the relativities for resource-rich regions. It is therefore possible that a region could have a similar real growth rate to the national average, but be slipping behind in the rankings owing to relative price effects.

Table 4.2   Provincial GRP per capita, 1975–2010[a]

	1975	1990	2000	2010
Sumatra				
Aceh	98.4	219.2	168.0	77.9
North Sumatra	86.7	87.7	90.8	95.3
West Sumatra	70.8	72.4	80.8	80.8
Riau	1,504.4	514.0	286.9	259.5
Jambi	74.8	58.2	59.5	78.1
South Sumatra	123.1	94.1	92.0	95.3
Bengkulu	52.4	56.9	47.2	48.8
Lampung	57.6	41.5	53.1	63.9
Java–Bali				
Jakarta	262.3	335.3	405.2	402.8
West Java	73.9	82.6	83.0	78.9
Central Java	39.0	52.4	55.1	61.6
Yogyakarta	64.5	67.0	65.0	59.2
East Java	72.9	84.0	87.5	93.3
Bali	72.3	99.4	82.2	76.9
Kalimantan				
West Kalimantan	78.7	77.9	72.1	61.8
Central Kalimantan	85.9	94.8	88.6	86.5
South Kalimantan	72.8	89.0	94.9	74.0
East Kalimantan	507.1	491.3	519.2	406.7
Sulawesi				
North Sulawesi	92.0	63.2	67.3	61.0
Central Sulawesi	51.6	51.4	58.6	63.6
South Sulawesi	62.4	55.5	57.0	62.9
Southeast Sulawesi	42.3	48.0	47.6	57.0
Eastern Indonesia				
West Nusa Tenggara	38.9	33.1	45.5	49.4
East Nusa Tenggara	41.1	35.6	30.2	26.6
Maluku	75.5	65.1	35.0	23.5
Papua	241.2	138.2	150.9	143.2

a   GRP per capita is measured in current prices relative to the national average (= 100).
Source: BPS.

relatively resource-rich regions with per capita incomes typically in the range 70–90 per cent of the national figure. West Kalimantan now has the lowest income of the three, after slipping sharply since 1990. Two provinces in Java, East Java and West Java, are also in this group, together with Bali. West Java and Bali had almost identical relative incomes in 1975 and 2010; the incomes of both were also higher in 1990, at the height of the booms in export-oriented industrialization (in West Java) and tourism (in Bali). The relative position of Bali, the most dynamic regional economy during the Soeharto era, has declined considerably since the 1990s. Although domestic tourism has remained buoyant, international tourism has been adversely affected by the terrorism incidents in the province in the early 2000s, Indonesia's general political instability during the early *reformasi* period, some regional health pandemics and the global financial crisis.

East Java stands out as a success story, with its relative income rising by over 20 percentage points in the period 1975–2010. In fact, it is the most dynamic regional economy apart from Jakarta and the very resource-rich provinces. The other provinces in this category are all in Sumatra. The diversified and dynamic economy of North Sumatra has consistently ranked close to the national average, while West Sumatra has been around 80 per cent throughout the period. The rankings of Jambi and South Sumatra, particularly the latter, have been more volatile. Both have strong agricultural cash crop sectors, and South Sumatra also has mining.

The third group consists of seven 'very poor' provinces, with per capita income 50–70 per cent of the national average. They are distributed across three major island groupings. They include all four Sulawesi provinces, that is, not just the traditionally poorer ones of Central and Southeast Sulawesi but also the more advanced ones of North and South Sulawesi. Per capita incomes in both North and South Sulawesi, but particularly the former, have slipped considerably since the 1970s. Two provinces in Java, Central Java and Yogyakarta, are also in this group. Their per capita incomes have fluctuated around 60 per cent of the national average, with no clear trend. The inclusion of Yogyakarta in this group might seem anomalous given that its social indicators are among the country's best, a point to which we return below. The southern Sumatran province of Lampung is the final province in this group. Originally intended as a destination to relieve poverty and overcrowding in Java–Bali, it is now significantly poorer than the latter region.

The fourth group, numbering four, consists of the poorest – or 'slipping behind' – provinces, with per capita income less than half the national average. East and West Nusa Tenggara have traditionally been the two poorest. Their rankings were similar in 1975, but the per capita income of the West is now almost double that of the East, owing to the spillover of tourism from Bali to Lombok, and some localized mining in Sumbawa. The sharpest decline of all has occurred in Maluku, where per capita income fell from around three-quarters the national average in 1975 to less than one-quarter in 2010. The sharpest decline occurred in the 1990s, when the severe religious conflict in the province and its aftermath saw relative income almost halve, from 65 per cent of the national average to just 35 per cent. The final province in this group, Bengkulu, serves as a reminder that the western region also has low-income provinces. Like Lampung, it has been a traditional recipient of transmigrants, but its income has now slipped even further behind Lampung's.

Finally, it is not possible to categorize one province, Aceh. Traditionally a relatively prosperous province, its relative per capita income began to rise sharply from the late 1970s with the exploitation of its large-scale offshore gas reserves, resulting in a per capita income more than double the national average in 1990. However, its ranking then fell sharply, particularly in 2000–10, owing to declining gas production, the devastating 2004 tsunami and a protracted civil war. The peace settlement and the large-scale rehabilitation effort have partially restored its position (see Chapter 19 by Aspinall and Chapter 20 by McCawley).

A useful analytical tool to summarize these results is to relate initial (that is, 1975) provincial per capita income to subsequent outcomes over the period 1975–2010. These outcomes are represented by the percentage change in the per capita income of each province relative to the national average. The results are presented in Figure 4.1. Provinces located in the top right quadrant are above the national average in both per capita income in 1975 and the change in relative per capita income in 1975–2010. Provinces in the bottom left quadrant are below the national average in both respects. At a broad level, these are the two groups of greatest analytical interest; they constitute respectively the 'hares' and the 'tortoises' among Indonesia's provinces. The top left quadrant contains provinces with below-average per capita income in 1975 but above-average relative movement subsequently, while the bottom right quadrant refers to the opposite case, of initially richer regions that have fallen behind.

We initially present the results for all provinces (Figure 4.1a). The graph is dominated by the extreme outliers, that is, Jakarta in the top right quadrant, pulling further away from the rest of the country, and the resource-rich provinces in the bottom right quadrant slipping back towards the national average, especially Riau. There is also the special case of Maluku in the bottom left quadrant, falling sharply behind the rest of the country. However, these outliers obscure the picture for the majority of provinces, which are clustered closer to the lines representing the national averages. We therefore present the inner segment of the

Figure 4.1   Change in provincial GRP per capita, 1975–2010, relative to initial GRP per capita in 1975

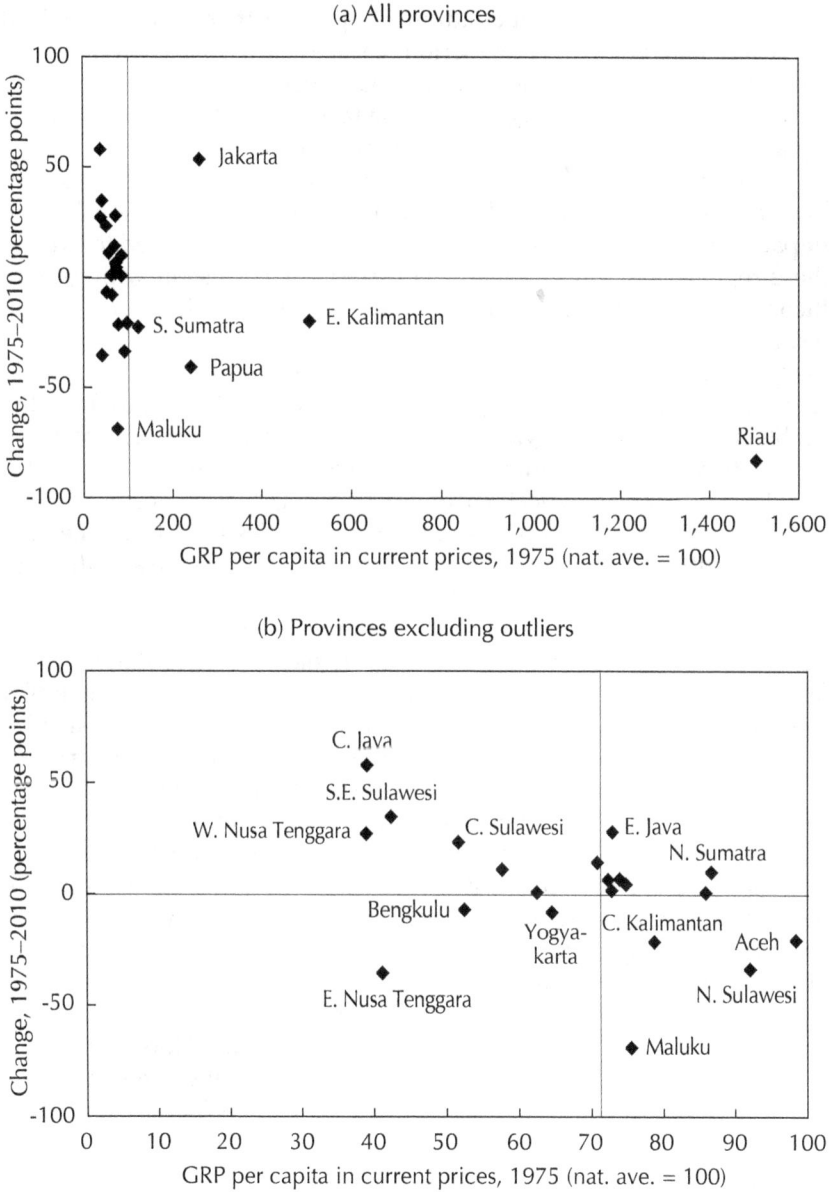

(a) All provinces

(b) Provinces excluding outliers

Source: BPS.

scatter diagram in Figure 4.1b. It is clear from this schema that, in addition to Jakarta, there are just two 'success stories' in the top right quadrant, namely East Java and North Sumatra. There are also three poorer
provinces in the bottom left quadrant slipping further behind, with East
Nusa Tenggara being the most serious case, in terms of both initially low
income and relative decline. The fact that most provinces are located in
the other two quadrants suggests, prima facie, that inter-regional income
equality has not deteriorated to any significant degree.

Are there consistently recurring themes that facilitate an understanding of both dynamism and lethargy, and has decentralization had an
impact? In principle, econometric analysis could be employed to explain
these regional growth variations. For example, consistent with growth
theory, one might hypothesize that provincial size, location, natural
resource and human capital endowments, and institutional quality are
likely to be the major determining factors. However, the small sample
size, the difficulty of obtaining accurate proxies for these variables, the
problem of unobserved variables and the interactive nature of these
explanatory variables render such an exercise hazardous.[6] But it is useful
to at least offer an analytical narrative explaining these outcomes.[7]

First, as in most nation-states, the capital cities tend to be the centres of wealth and economic power. Thus, resources flow to and through
Jakarta, even in the decentralization era. It is the country's major international gateway (even though its airport is now located beyond its
boundaries), and it is also the home to the nation's most skilled workforce, and its highest-value service activities. The other province in this
group, East Java, shares some features with Jakarta, albeit on a smaller
scale. It too is a major gateway, with the nation's second-busiest port, and
it is the de facto capital of Eastern Indonesia. While it is not a major centre of higher education, it hosts many high-value industrial and service
activities. Much of its dynamism is concentrated on the city of Surabaya
and its three surrounding districts (Gresik, Mojokerto and Sidoarjo),
together with the cigarette city of Kediri. An earlier study, by Dick, Fox
and Mackie (1993), maintained that East Java could be considered a case
of 'balanced development' across an array of economic activities, but-
tressed by consistently good-quality governance. In some respects, a
similar observation could be applied to the dynamic North Sumatran
economy, with its estates, manufacturing enterprises and services, building also on its proximity to Malaysia and Singapore (Barlow and Thee

---

6   See Vidyattama (2008: Ch. 6) for a detailed empirical investigation along these
    lines.
7   Some of the themes in the discussion that follows were also identified in the
    1980s by the contributors to Hill (1989).

1989). However, growth in North Sumatra has been more volatile, owing to its larger natural resource sector, and it has traditionally been regarded as beset by high levels of corruption.

International orientation is generally a source of regional dynamism. It boosted the fortunes of Bali as tourism grew rapidly from the 1970s, and promoted growth in the major industrial centres during Indonesia's most successful phase of export-oriented industrialization, the decade from the mid-1980s. This applied particularly to West Java, but also to the rest of Java–Bali (with Bali's exports being concentrated in handicrafts). From the early 1990s, manufacturing and tourism in the Riau Islands – now a separate province – have prospered owing to the region's proximity to Singapore, aided also by special custom zone arrangements.

The other element of this international orientation is of course natural resource abundance. This is most evident in the two extreme cases, East Kalimantan consistently, and Riau earlier. It is also relevant to Papua and Aceh (with major qualifications), and has contributed to the general dynamism of Kalimantan and much of Sumatra. These regions have prospered most during periods of high commodity prices, as in the 1970s and more recently. However, as a group they could hardly be said to be well-governed regions, and thus the local-level impacts of natural resource exploitation have varied considerably. Another key consideration is the nature of the resource activity, including both mining and agriculture – whether, for example, it is enclave in nature, as in Papua, or concentrated in smallholder agriculture, as in much of Kalimantan. We return to this issue shortly.

The common characteristic of the regions that are poor, lagging behind or both is their geographic isolation, and the fact that they do not produce goods or services that are in demand from the rest of the country, or indeed the world. This applies particularly to the two Nusa Tenggara provinces, and to parts of Sulawesi (Resosudarmo and Jotzo 2009). Maluku is a special case owing to conflict, as is Aceh. As well as being afflicted by conflict for extended periods, Aceh also experienced a terrible natural disaster. The explanations for the underperformance of the other less dynamic provinces are less obvious. A particular puzzle is Yogyakarta, whose educational strengths have not yet translated into more robust economic activity. It needs to be remembered, however, that the province includes not only the city but also the surrounding district with its very poor southern regions.

Social trends and inequality

So much for the economic analysis. We now examine trends in interregional inequality, and ask whether economic and social progress is correlated, again at the provincial level. As a measure of inequality, we employ the widely used coefficient of variation, first popularized by Williamson (1965). We use here the population-weighted version of the index, that is:

$$CV_w = \frac{\sqrt{\sum_{i=1}^{n} (Y_i - \bar{Y})^2 \frac{P_i}{P}}}{\bar{Y}}$$

where CV_w is the population-weighted Williamson index; n is the number of regions; Y_i is income in region i; $\bar{Y}$ is average income; P_i is population in region i; and P is total population.

We calculate this measure for the period 1975–2011, for two per capita series: total GRP and non-mining GRP. The premise for including the latter is that much of the return to mining accrues to entities outside the province, that is, to the central government and corporations. The index is calculated using current prices.[8]

Figure 4.2 presents the results. Although the two series converge from the early 1990s, reflecting the declining share of mining in the economy, inequality is moderately high. Whether it has risen or declined depends on which series is used; that is, inequality is lower now than it was in the 1970s if mining is included, but slightly higher if mining is excluded. We prefer the latter series as a more accurate indicator of economic welfare. Focusing on the non-mining series, we see that inequality has been remarkably stable since the late 1970s. It peaked in 2000, and has declined modestly since then. Contrary to popular perceptions, then, decentralization does not appear to have resulted in an increase in inter-regional inequality, at least when measured at the provincial level. This is in spite of the period since decentralization being one of high commodity prices, where the resource-rich regions have received a higher proportion of their locally generated revenues.

With regard to social progress, and the association between economic and social indicators, we first need to decide which social indicators to use. The range of options is large, including poverty incidence, life expectancy, infant mortality and so on, or the composite Human Development Index. Data for most of these are not available at the provincial level for as long a time period as for the income data. Other chapters in

---

8 That is, the various current-price series – for 1975, 1983, 1993, 2000 and 2005 – have been combined, by splicing the figures for the overlapping years. As one would expect given the long time period, the goods and services in the consumption bundle have changed considerably. In principle, the choice of either current or constant prices should not affect the results.

Figure 4.2   Inter-provincial inequality based on GRP per capita and non-mining GRP per capita in current prices, 1975–2011

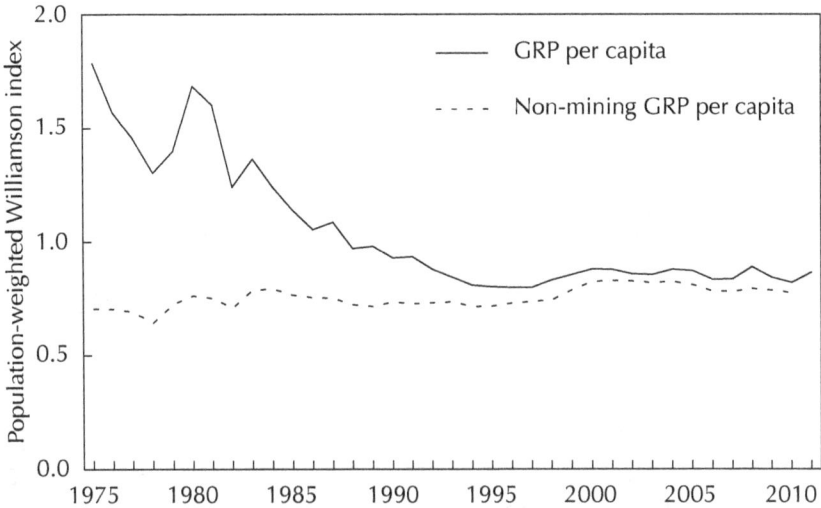

Source: Authors' calculations based on BPS data.

this volume examine regional social outcomes in more detail.[9] The main question we ask here is whether the economic indicators are a reasonably good predictor of social outcomes at the regional level. For our purposes, we proxy social outcomes by the headcount poverty ratio, calculated for each province.

Figure 4.3 presents GRP per capita and headcount poverty ratios for the 26 provinces in 2011. The national averages for the two variables are represented by the vertical and horizontal lines. We would expect most provinces to be located in either the top left quadrant (indicating below-average GRP per capita and above-average poverty) or the bottom right quadrant (above-average GRP per capita and below-average poverty). In general, this is the case. For example, in 2011 the three richest provinces, Jakarta, East Kalimantan and Riau, had among the lowest levels of poverty incidence. By contrast, most of the poorer provinces were in the top left quadrant, with higher poverty incidence. But the relationship is far from uniform. The province with the fourth-highest per capita income, Papua, had the country's highest poverty incidence, reflecting

9 Social progress, in particular poverty, is examined in much greater detail by Ilmma and Wai-Poi (Chapter 5) and Sumarto, Vothknecht and Wijaya (Chapter 12). Our conclusions are generally consistent with their findings, allowing for small differences owing to different concepts, measures and time periods.

Figure 4.3   Provincial GRP per capita and poverty incidence, 2011

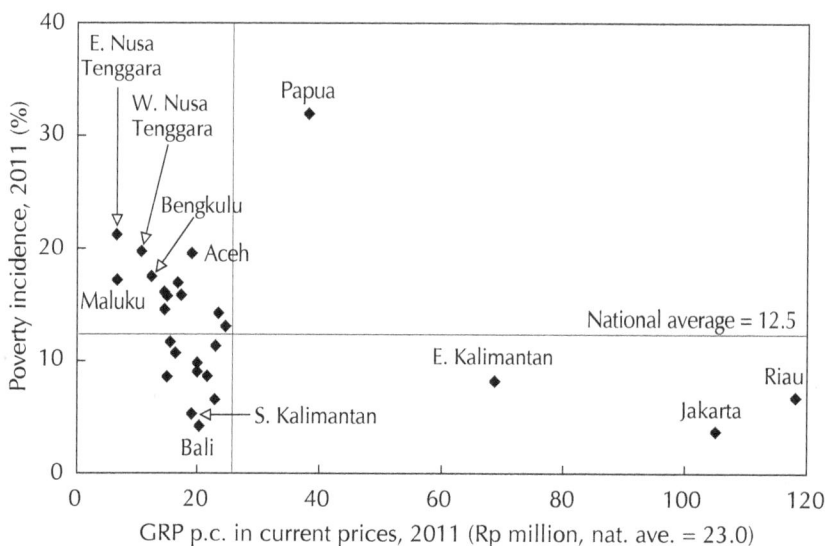

Source: BPS data, amalgamated to 1999 provinces.

the skewed impact of mining. A few other provinces had very low poverty but only moderate incomes, near or below the national average. Bali is one clear example, suggesting that the labour-intensive nature of much of the tourism industry has spread the benefits quite widely. That province's institutions are also regarded as reasonably inclusive.

What of the relationship between per capita income and poverty incidence over time? In Figure 4.4, we examine changes in provincial per capita income and poverty incidence over the period 1996–2011. Both data series are plotted relative to the national averages. Thus, provincial per capita income (in current prices) is normalized, with the national average equal to 100. Therefore, a movement towards the origin (the intersection of the axes) is interpreted as a fall in that province's per capita income relative to the other provinces. The poverty data should be interpreted in a similar fashion. The resulting 'two-dimensional' figure therefore enables us to draw inferences concerning both levels and changes over this period.

Most provinces remain within their initial quadrants. But there are some movements between quadrants, and significant movements within them. Among the richer provinces, both Jakarta and East Kalimantan have become relatively richer, with little change in relative poverty, while Riau's income has slipped back towards the average. Aceh has regressed significantly in both respects, from above average in 1996 to

Figure 4.4   Provincial GRP per capita and poverty incidence, 1996 and 2011

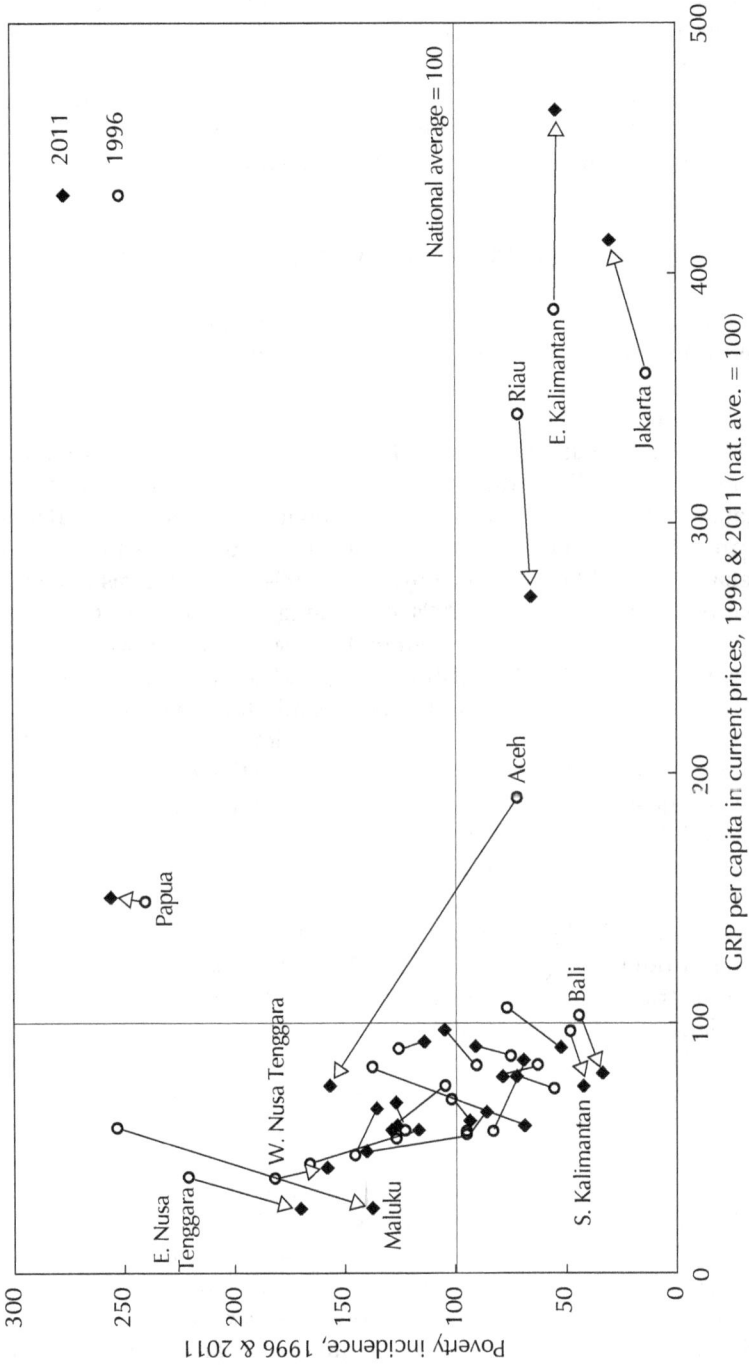

Source: BPS.

below average in 2011. Papua retains its relative income position, but its relative poverty has risen. Maluku has improved its poverty ranking but still remains low on both indicators. Bali and South Kalimantan have also improved their relative poverty positions, with little change in their incomes. All these movements are explicable with reference to the earlier discussion of these provinces and their characteristics.

4.3   DIGGING DEEPER: PERSPECTIVES FROM THE DISTRICT

We now focus on the district as the unit of analysis. As before, we examine economic and social indicators, and their correlation. We would expect there to be greater inequality at the district level, simply because the incomes of more of the very rich and very poor regions are separately identified. The analysis differs from that in the previous section in two main respects. First, the number of districts is too great to present the data for all of them, much less an explanation for each particular circumstance. Second, the time period is shorter, as the district data have been reliably available only since the mid-1990s. Our analysis is confined to the period since the late 1990s, coinciding with the granting of regional autonomy. It is important to remember also that the process of *pemekaran* has been greatest at the district level, and therefore the data should be interpreted with greater caution, especially for the smaller units. As for the provinces, we refer to particular districts by their pre-2000 boundaries and names, not the current ones. We use the term 'district' to refer to all second-level administrative units, so the analysis includes both districts (*kabupaten*) and cities (*kota*).

We first identify the richest and poorest districts as measured by GRP per capita. Table 4.3 presents the results for 1999 and 2011, in current prices. The figures reveal few surprises, with East Kalimantan and Jakarta dominating the list of the 10 richest districts. Four of Jakarta's five districts are represented in 1999, and three in 2011. The ranking of the Jakarta regions is also consistent, with Central Jakarta, in effect the nation's CBD, the richest, followed by North and South Jakarta. Central Jakarta is also becoming richer over time relative to the rest of the city-province. Resource-rich Kutai, the 'Brunei of Indonesia', tops the list in 1999 and is third in 2011, with per capita income 10 times the national average in 1999 and eight times the average in 2011. Also in East Kalimantan, Balikpapan city is ranked seventh in 1999 and ninth in 2011, while the coal region of Berau is ranked fourth in 1999. Other districts to make the list are East Java's Kediri city, ranked second in both years, and the headquarters of the nation's addiction to *kretek* cigarettes; Batam city (in 1999), the commercial–industrial adjunct to nearby Singapore and now

Table 4.3   Districts/municipalities with the highest and lowest GRP per capita, 1999 and 2011 (in current prices, national average = 1)

1999	2011
Highest	**Highest**
1 Kutai, East Kalimantan (10.24)	1 Central Jakarta, DKI Jakarta (11.89)
2 Kediri city, East Java (9.25)	2 Kediri city, East Java (10.13)
3 Central Jakarta, DKI Jakarta (9.11)	3 Kutai, East Kalimantan (8.1)
4 Berau, East Kalimantan (5.14)	4 Fak-Fak, Papua (6.22)
5 North Jakarta, DKI Jakarta (4.25)	5 Bengkalis, Riau (4.96)
6 Batam city, Riau (4.18)	6 North Jakarta, DKI Jakarta (4.68)
7 Balikpapan city, East Kalimantan (3.9)	7 South Jakarta, DKI Jakarta (4.34)
8 North Aceh, Aceh (3.68)	8 Surabaya city, East Java (3.54)
9 South Jakarta, DKI Jakarta (2.87)	9 Balikpapan city, East Kalimantan (3.26)
10 East Jakarta, DKI Jakarta (2.7)	10 Manokwari, Papua (2.87)
Lowest	**Lowest**
1 West Sumba, East Nusa Tenggara (0.23)	1 Central Maluku, Maluku (0.16)
2 Manggarai, East Nusa Tenggara (0.24)	2 Manggarai, East Nusa Tenggara (0.18)
3 South Central Timor, East Nusa Tenggara (0.25)	3 North Central Timor, East Nusa Tenggara (0.18)
4 Grobogan, Central Java (0.26)	4 Jayawijaya, Papua (0.19)
5 Sampang, East Java (0.26)	5 West Sumba, East Nusa Tenggara (0.2)
6 North Central Timor, East Nusa Tenggara (0.26)	6 Alor, East Nusa Tenggara (0.2)
7 Central Maluku, Maluku (0.26)	7 North Maluku, Maluku (0.21)
8 East Flores, East Nusa Tenggara (0.27)	8 Grobogan, Central Java (0.23)
9 Belu, East Nusa Tenggara (0.29)	9 Southeast Maluku, Maluku (0.23)
10 Alor, East Nusa Tenggara (0.29)	10 Belu, East Nusa Tenggara (0.24)

Source: BPS.

a provincial capital in its own right; North Aceh (also in 1999), based on the Lhokseumawe gas fields; Papua's resource-rich Fak-Fak,[10] where the Freeport mine is located, and Manokwari, with its port development and associated industrialization (both in 2011); and Surabaya (in 2011). Thus, there is a consistent picture of wealth generation by capital cities, national or regional, mainly as high-value service providers; and by resource-rich enclaves, generally with limited spillover effects.

At the other end of the spectrum, the results are also more or less as expected. In 1999, East Nusa Tenggara dominated the group, providing seven of the 10 poorest districts, including the three poorest. This indicates that low income is a feature of virtually the entire province. Two of the three remaining districts were in Java, a reminder that this fairly dynamic regional economy still contains some very low-income pockets. (One of them, Sampang, is actually on the island of Madura, off the East Java coast.) Central Maluku, a traditionally poor region that was experiencing serious conflict, was the other district on the list in 1999. The picture had changed by 2011, but not significantly. East Nusa Tenggara was still home to five of the poorest districts, Maluku contributed three, with Central Maluku now the nation's poorest district, and Grobogan in Central Java remained on the list. A district in Papua, Jayawijaya, was also among the 10 poorest. Note also that the range from highest to lowest GRP per capita is extremely large, and has increased over time. In 1999, the per capita income of the richest district, Kutai, was about 40 times that of the poorest, West Sumba, while in 2011 the per capita income of Central Jakarta was almost 70 times that of Central Maluku.

Do these extremes of income broadly correlate with the corresponding extremes of poverty, especially among the low-income regions? Some of the high-income regions are enclaves, with narrowly concentrated incomes and high inequality, and therefore their poverty incidence could still be quite high. In Table 4.4 we identify the districts with the highest and lowest levels of poverty incidence in 1999 and 2011.[11]

Focusing first on the regions with the highest poverty incidence, the major difference from the per capita income listing is that Papua, not East Nusa Tenggara, dominates the picture. It accounts for four of the 10 poorest districts in 1999, and for the five poorest in 2011. This is a stark illustration that the relatively high income ranking for the province is

---

10 Fak-Fak's relative income fluctuates considerably, since it depends not just on a single industry, mining, but on a single firm, Freeport, with its variable production and prices.

11 Note that the poverty data have been adjusted for regional price differences as measured by prices prevailing in provincial capitals. In the more remote and larger provinces, this is at best an approximate adjustment.

Table 4.4   *Districts/municipalities with the highest and lowest poverty incidence, 1999 and 2011 (national average = 1)*

1999	2011
Highest	**Highest**
1 Panial, Papua (3.42)	1 Jayawijaya, Papua (3.13)
2 Jayawijaya, Papua (3.37)	2 Paniai, Papua (2.9)
3 Central Maluku, Maluku (2.75)	3 Manokwari, Papua (2.9)
4 North Central Timor, East Nusa Tenggara (2.75)	4 Yapen Waropen, Papua (2.48)
5 Sikka, East Nusa Tenggara (2.71)	5 Biak Numfor, Papua (2.44)
6 Merauke, Papua (2.48)	6 East Sumba, East Nusa Tenggara (2.35)
7 Nias, North Sumatra (2.43)	7 Southeast Maluku, Maluku (2.32)
8 Fak-Fak, Papua (2.42)	8 Sampang, East Java (2.32)
9 Central Halmahera, Maluku (2.41)	9 West Sumba, East Nusa Tenggara (2.24)
10 Sampang, East Java (2.36)	10 South Central Timor, East Nusa Tenggara (2.08)
Lowest	**Lowest**
1 Denpasar city, Bali (0.05)	1 Denpasar city, Bali (0.14)
2 South Jakarta, DKI Jakarta (0.06)	2 Sawahlunto city, West Sumatra (0.19)
3 Pidie, Aceh (0.11)	3 Badung, Bali (0.2)
4 East Jakarta, DKI Jakarta (0.12)	4 East Jakarta, DKI Jakarta (0.23)
5 Batam city, Riau (0.12)	5 Balikpapan city, East Kalimantan (0.26)
6 Banda Aceh city, Aceh (0.13)	6 South Jakarta, DKI Jakarta (0.26)
7 Bitung city, North Sulawesi (0.14)	7 West Jakarta, DKI Jakarta (0.26)
8 West Jakarta, DKI Jakarta (0.14)	8 Pekanbaru city, Riau (0.27)
9 Pare-Pare city, South Sulawesi (0.14)	9 Central Jakarta, DKI Jakarta (0.27)
10 Badung, Bali (0.14)	10 Banjar, South Kalimantan (0.3)

Source: BPS.

completely misleading as an indicator of socio-economic welfare. Papua is clearly where the nation's most serious poverty incidence is found.[12] However, East Nusa Tenggara scores poorly too, with two districts in the 1999 listing and three in 2011. But the districts are different in each year, suggesting some churn in extreme poverty incidence within the province. The fact that East Nusa Tenggara has fewer districts among the cases of extreme poverty than among the low-income cases suggests that at least its income is distributed reasonably equitably. Maluku provides one district in each year, but not the same one. From western Indonesia, Sampang appears in both years, indicating entrenched poverty, and the Sumatran island of Nias appears in 1999.

Turning to the list of districts with the lowest levels of poverty, we find, as expected, that almost all of the very high-income regions that are also rich in natural resources are *not* among the very low-poverty regions. Jakarta is again well represented, with three districts on the list in 1999 and four in 2011. Confirming anecdotal evidence that the labour-intensive tourism industry has had a major beneficial impact on local living standards, two districts from Bali appear in both years: the capital Denpasar (the district with the lowest poverty in both 1999 and 2011), and the adjacent resort region of Badung. One district from Riau appears in each year: Batam city, a major commercial and industrial city in the new province of Riau Islands, in 1999; and Pekanbaru, the capital of the original province, in 2011. Aceh has two districts on the list in 1999, reflecting its pockets of affluence in the earlier period. The rest are a miscellaneous collection of diverse districts. Typically their income is explained by mining (as, for example, in Sawahlunto) or by other resource activities in the context of relatively small populations.

Figures 4.5 and 4.6 present the full national picture for per capita income and poverty in 1999 and 2011 in map form. The data for each district are grouped into quintiles, from poorest to richest as measured by per capita income (Figure 4.5), and from lowest to highest poverty as measured by poverty incidence (Figure 4.6).

In Figure 4.5, the poorest 20 per cent of districts are represented by the lightest shading, through to the richest 20 per cent, represented by

---

12 The Papua data require more intensive investigation. The poverty data could be understated to the extent that prices are generally higher in the province, with those for Jayapura providing only an approximate guide to prices in the interior. Conversely, it may be that there is more (uncounted) subsistence agriculture in the remote regions that is not recorded in the regional accounts, and therefore actual consumption levels could be higher. For more discussion of these and related development issues, see Chapter 18 of this volume by Resosudarmo, Mollet, Raya and Kaiwai. See also Manning and Rumbiak (1989) for a historical perspective.

the darkest shading. The income patterns are broadly similar in 1999 and 2011. Much of eastern and southern Kalimantan is relatively prosperous in both years, but especially in 2011, suggesting that the resource boom has been reasonably broadly distributed in a spatial sense. By contrast, all five income groups are found within Papua, with extremely wealthy mining and coastal districts existing alongside very poor districts in the highlands. It can be inferred that the spread effects from Papua's resource abundance are very narrowly concentrated, reflecting both geographic and cultural barriers to integration, and limited human capital. Almost all of the rest of Eastern Indonesia is poor, with the two major cities in Sulawesi, Makassar and Manado, being the main exceptions. Most of Sumatra is moderately well-off, except for the southwest coastal region, broadly corresponding to Bengkulu, and pockets of Aceh. Parts of Riau and its islands, and some districts in North and South Sumatra, are among the wealthiest in the country. In Java, the familiar north–south divide, along with urbanization, is the key determinant of affluence, with the most prosperous regions being the cities of Jakarta, Surabaya and Bandung, together with Kediri.

The poverty story is similar in some respects. In Figure 4.6, the lightest shading indicates the lowest incidence of poverty and the darkest shading the highest incidence of poverty. The general trend is for relative poverty to 'migrate' eastward between 1999 and 2011, with the exception of the special case of Aceh with its natural disaster and conflict. Papua stands out as the region of most severe poverty, apart from its enclaves. There can be no doubt that this region is Indonesia's most serious development challenge. There are also very few non-poor regions in the rest of Eastern Indonesia. By contrast, the data suggest very little destitution in Kalimantan, while the relatively few high-poverty regions in Sumatra are concentrated in the north and south of the western coastal regions. Java still has pockets of quite serious poverty, mainly in its southern and central regions, and in Madura.

We now examine movements in relative per capita income among the districts over time, as for the provinces. In this case, we examine outcomes in 1999–2011 with reference to per capita district income in 1999.[13] Both the initial absolute values and the changes are again expressed relative to the national averages. The results essentially capture the changing income relativities in the first decade of the decentralization era. It is not possible to present the data here in graph form because of the very

---

13 For a more detailed discussion of convergence trends at the district level since decentralization, see Vidyattama (2013).

Figure 4.5   District GRP per capita by quintile, 1999 and 2011

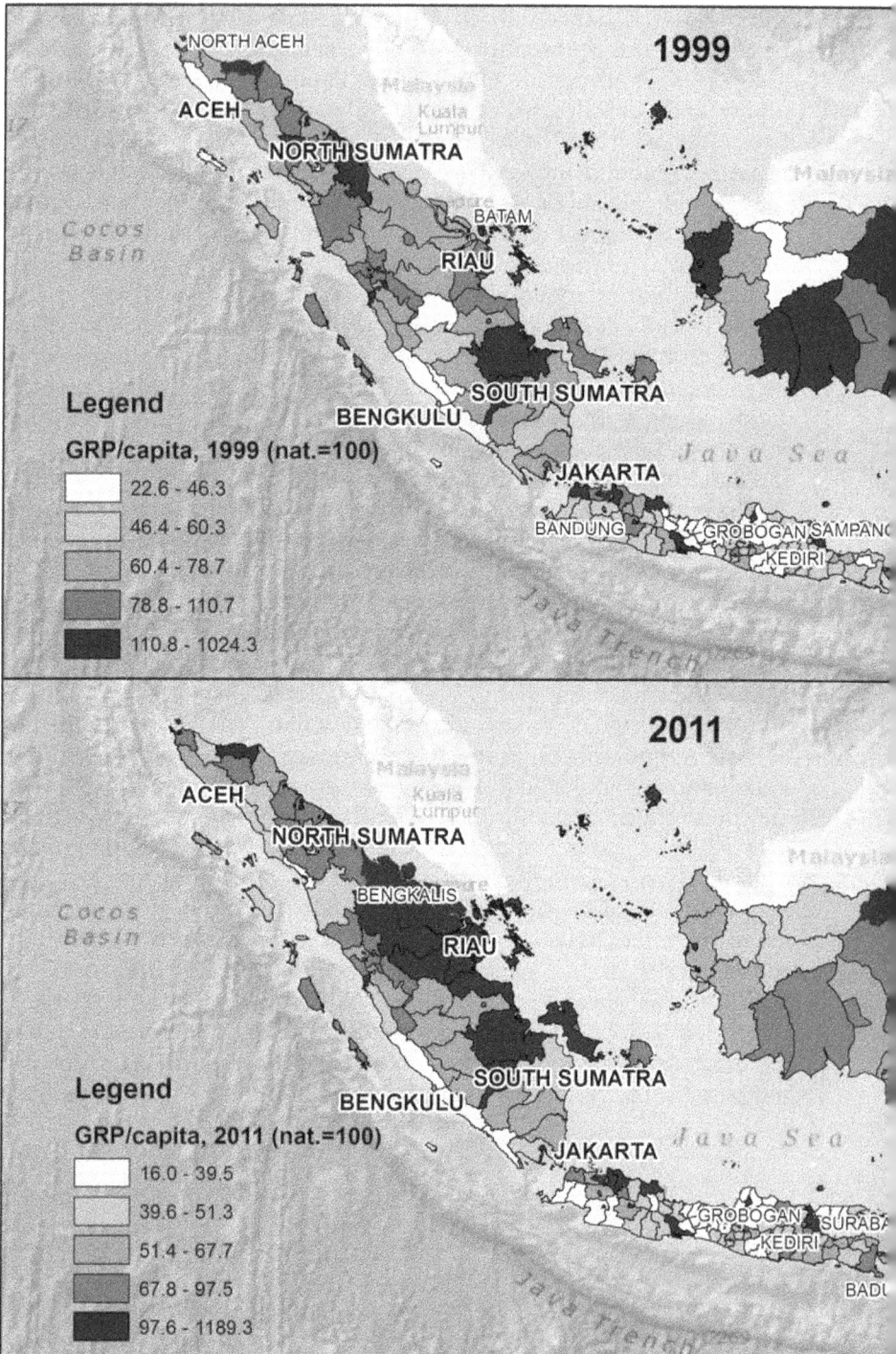

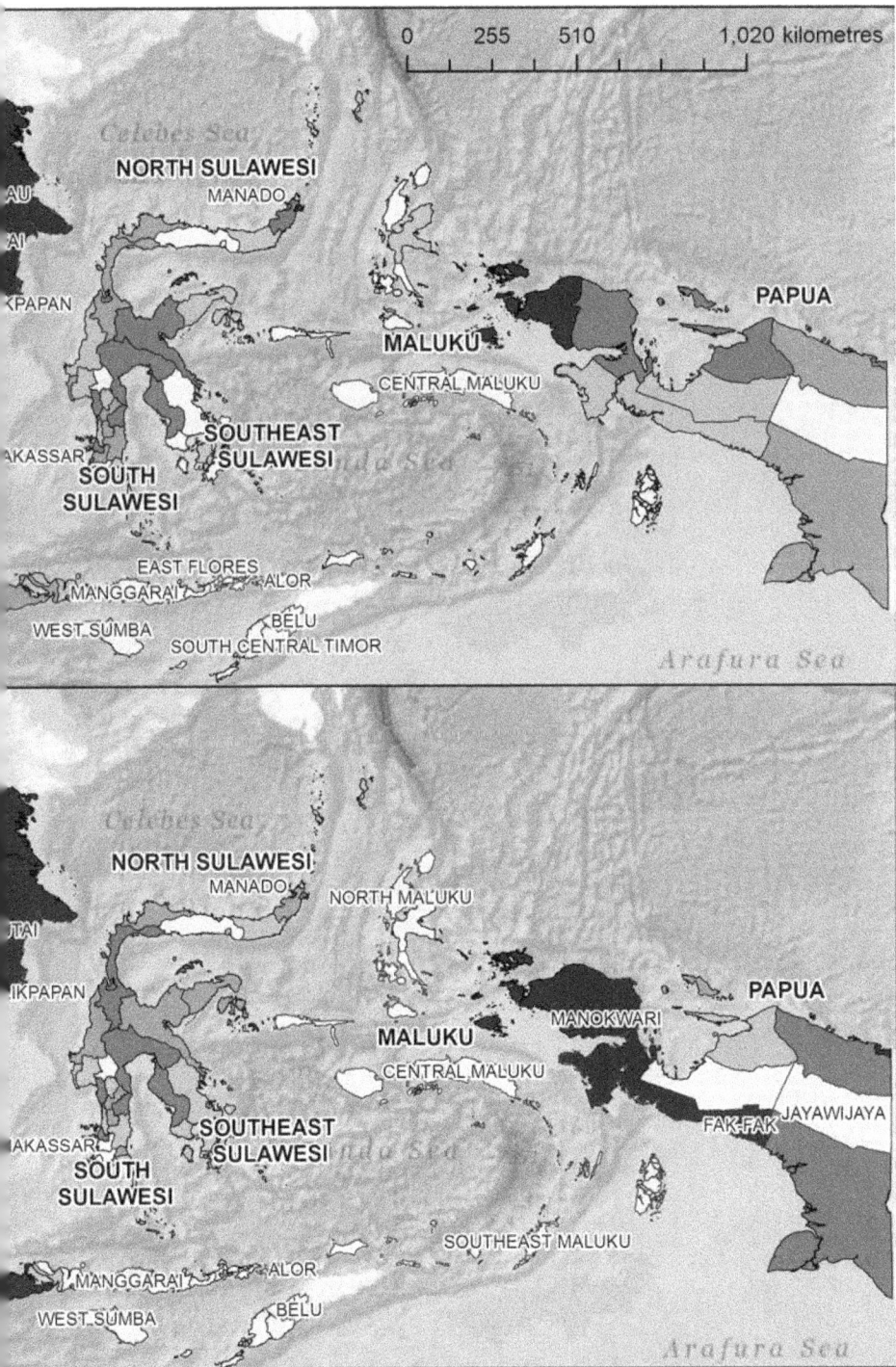

Figure 4.6   District poverty incidence by quintile, 1999 and 2011

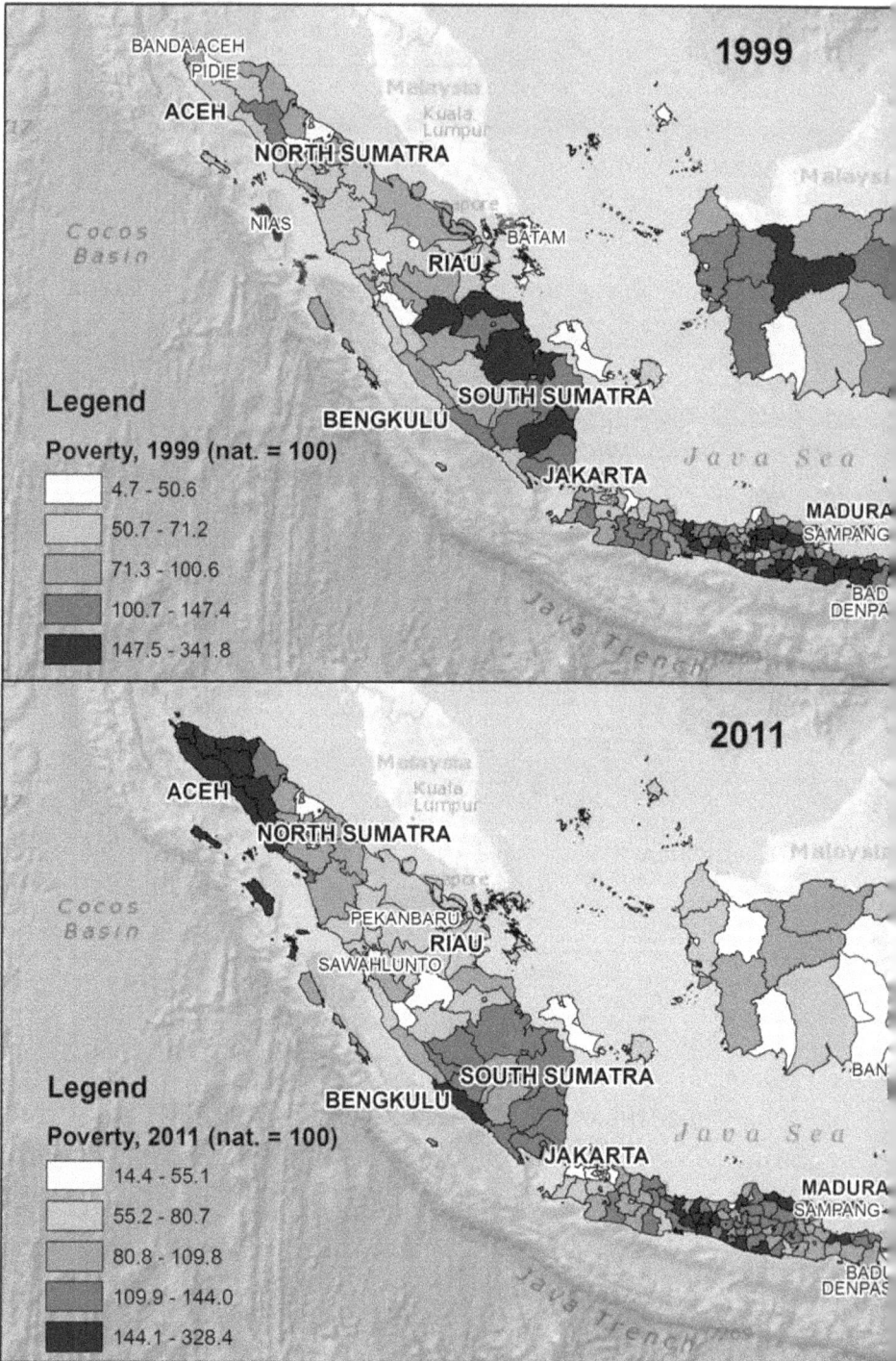

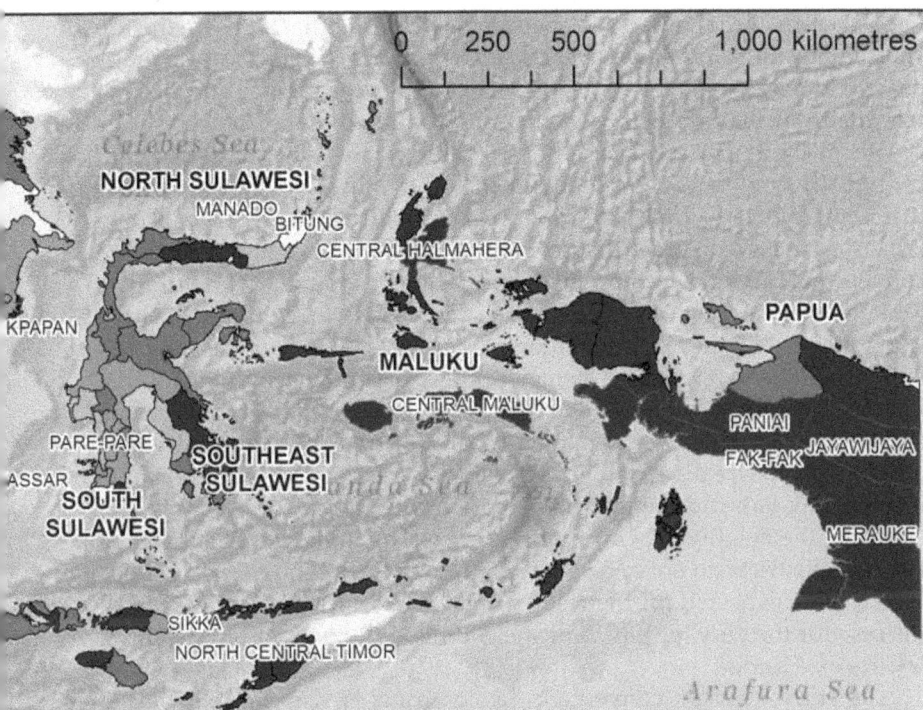

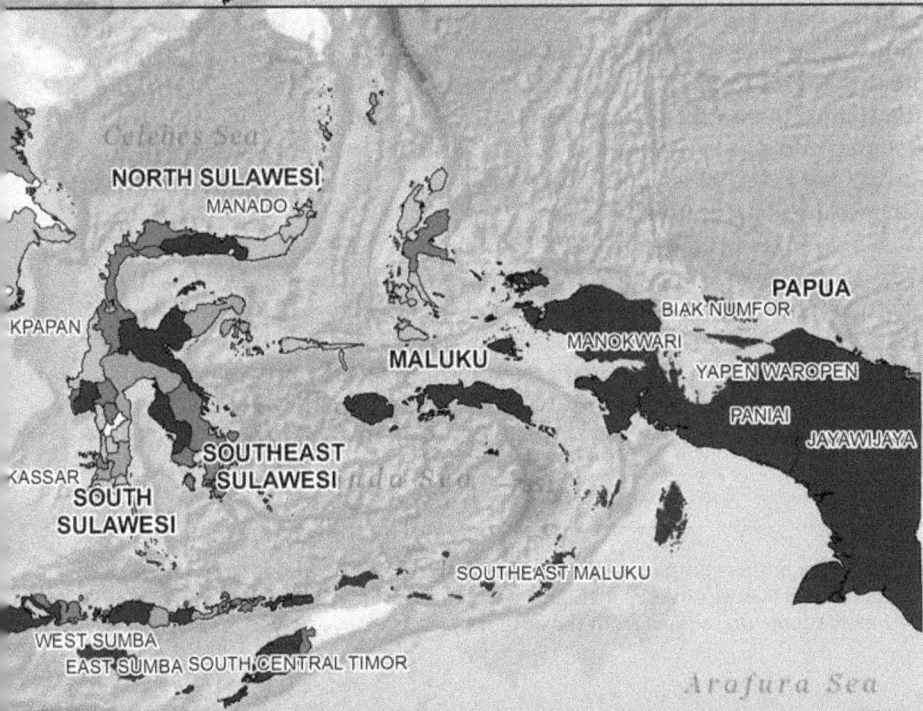

large number of observations, so we confine ourselves to providing a narrative.[14]

As before, we identify four quadrants, including the 'hares' in the top right quadrant with above-average income in 1999 and above-average change in relative income in 1999–2011; and the 'tortoises' in the bottom left quadrant that are below the national average in both respects. The greater the number of observations located in the bottom right quadrant (districts with above-average income but slipping relative to other districts) and the top left quadrant (districts with below-average income but rising relative to other districts), the more likely it is that incomes are converging. We refer to these two cases as the 'convergence quadrants'. Most of the observations are clustered quite close to the origin, with a slight majority in the two convergence quadrants. This suggests the presence of weak convergence. The major outlier exceptions, of high and rising incomes, are all metropolitan districts, in Jakarta as well as Surabaya and Kediri, but the increases in their relative income over time have been quite modest. The districts with the most dramatic increases in relative income, Fak-Fak and Bengkalis, are both resource-rich regions. It is also clear that the neighbourhood spillover effects are limited, that is, that the very rich districts do not necessarily pull along their contiguous districts. This is to be expected for the resource enclaves, but it also appears to be the case for the very high-income metropolitan districts, notably Central Jakarta and Kediri.

The story of weak convergence is confirmed when we remove the outliers, that is, districts with per capita income more than double the national average in 1999, and those whose per capita income rose by more than 1.5 times the national average in 1999–2011. The top right quadrant of high and rising incomes is populated mainly by cities and resource enclaves. Although there are cases of poorer districts falling further behind (that is, located in the bottom left quadrant), the relative declines are comparatively modest.

What of the income–poverty relationship at the district level in 2011? We find that most of the observations are located in the top left quadrant (districts with below-average income and above-average poverty) and the bottom right quadrant (above-average income and below-average poverty). Ignoring minor deviations from the expected relationships, the only significant exceptions are two districts in Papua, Manokwari and Fak-Fak, which combine above-average GRP with above-average pov-

---

14 The data and accompanying charts for both district-level per capita income and district-level poverty incidence, and the relationships between the two, are available on request from the authors.

erty. The high poverty incidence in some of the other districts in Papua is also clearly evident, as noted earlier.

Finally, we examine district-level changes over time in both series, that is, changes in both per capita income and poverty relative to the national averages over the period 1999–2011. Note again that because these are movements relative to the national averages in each case, a movement towards the origin does not signify a decline in absolute income or poverty, but rather a decline relative to other districts. Movements to the right signify increased per capita income relative to the rest of the country. The more these movements slant downward, the more the rising relative incomes are associated with declining relative poverty; that is, the above-average growth has had the expected effect of reducing poverty faster than the national average. Upward-sloping movements in these cases would have the converse interpretation.

The analysis shows that Central Jakarta, for example, behaves in the expected manner, that is, with relative income rising and relative poverty declining, whereas Kediri (with rising income but also rising poverty) does not. Minor movements in the outlier cases of high income/ low poverty are of no great significance, since the identified districts are already well above the national average. However, when we observe major movements in the converse direction in the other quadrants, there is, prima facie, a cause for concern. Thus, for instance, in the top right quadrant, the two already high-income Papua districts record significant increases in relative income. While this has resulted in declining relative poverty for Fak-Fak, Manokwari displays the opposite trend, of rising relative poverty. These data are of course suggestive; they pinpoint potential areas of concern, where the changes in relative income and poverty do not exhibit the expected relationship. They underline the need for greater local research, especially in resource-rich, ethnically fragmented regions such as Papua where there may also be data quality issues.

4.4 CONCLUSIONS

There are elements of both continuity and change in Indonesia's regional development dynamics. The most important continuity is that there remain very large inter-regional differences in living standards and economic structure. The western part of the country is generally more dynamic and richer than the east. The Java–Bali economy continues to prosper, driven by the country's two dominant urban conurbations in Java's northwest and northeast. Jakarta, East Kalimantan and Riau continue to be the richest provinces, while East Nusa Tenggara is consistently poor. Another continuity is that, although inter-provincial inequality is quite high, it is relatively stable. Unlike in some other very large developing countries, regional inequality in Indonesia has not risen over the past three decades, reflecting the fact that growth has been reasonably broad-based across regions.

But these trends mask considerable diversity. Jakarta continues to pull away from the rest of the country, to an extent that could even threaten national cohesion at some point in the future. In some respects Jakarta is becoming 'Bangkok-like', although Indonesia still has a much more spatially diverse economy than either Thailand or the Philippines. Outside the capital, East Java and to a lesser extent North Sumatra emerge as the most dynamic regional economies, in addition to a few special cases of resource abundance. Among the laggards, Maluku has registered the steepest decline in relative income and poverty, owing primarily to conflict. The adverse effects of conflict are also evident in Aceh, while the terrorism incidents in Bali in the early 2000s and the global financial crisis later in the decade are arguably the main reasons why that island is no longer the growth leader it once was.

Economic and social indicators generally move in the same direction, in the sense that richer and faster-growing regions generally have better social indicators. But there are exceptions. The most important is Papua, where the continuing high incidence of poverty clearly demonstrates that the wealth generated in its mining enclaves, and to a lesser extent the major provincial capital of Jayapura, has had limited spillover effects, especially to the more remote and very poor highland region. At the other end of the spectrum, Yogyakarta continues to stand out as having among the best social indicators in the country, even though its per capita income is among the lowest.

These conclusions are based on provincial-level analysis. Inevitably there is greater diversity at the district level, where there is obviously a greater range in per capita incomes, from rich Kutai to some very poor eastern districts, and correspondingly larger variations in social outcomes. Nevertheless, these differences should not be overstated. Income inequality among districts is not significantly different from that among provinces, and the trends in provincial and district-level income inequality are also broadly similar.

Has regional autonomy had a discernible impact? The answer appears to be 'no'. That is, the year 2001 and its aftermath have not introduced a significant discontinuity into any of the series. Of course, the country is now governed in a fundamentally different way, as real resources and authority have been transferred to the regions. But thus far, decentralization has not markedly changed the country's regional growth patterns and social outcomes, or patterns of inter-regional inequality. On reflection, this should not seem so surprising. Decentralization is still in its infancy, and has not been around long enough for the postulates of fiscal federalism – for example, that better-governed regions will be rewarded with higher growth – to take root. Besides, many other factors affect regional growth. The commodity boom of the past decade has been a major factor, and arguably explains much of the dynamism of the progressive regions of Kalimantan and Sumatra. Conversely, the underinvestment in physical infrastructure since the late 1990s has been holding back growth in some of the more remote resource-rich regions, in that it has frustrated their capacity to exploit export market opportunities domestically and abroad.

REFERENCES

Barlow, C. and Thee K.W. (1989) 'North Sumatra: growth with unbalanced development', in H. Hill (ed.) *Unity and Diversity: Regional Economic Development in Indonesia since 1970*, Oxford University Press, Singapore.

Dick, H.W., J.J. Fox and J.A.C Mackie (eds) (1993) *Balanced Development: East Java in the New Order*, Oxford University Press, Singapore.

Hill, H. (ed.) (1989) *Unity and Diversity: Regional Economic Development in Indonesia since 1970*, Oxford University Press, Singapore.

Hill, H., B. Resosudarmo and Y. Vidyattama (2008) 'Indonesia's changing economic geography', *Bulletin of Indonesian Economic Studies*, 44(3): 407–35.

Manning, C. and M. Rumbiak (1989) 'Irian Jaya: economic change, migrants, and indigenous welfare', in H. Hill (ed.) *Unity and Diversity: Regional Economic Development in Indonesia since 1970*, Oxford University Press, Singapore.

Resosudarmo, B.P. and F. Jotzo (eds) (2009) *Working with Nature against Poverty: Development, Resources and the Environment in Eastern Indonesia*, Institute of Southeast Asian Studies, Singapore.

Vidyattama, Y. (2008) 'Patterns of provincial economic growth in Indonesia', PhD dissertation, Australian National University, Canberra.

Vidyattama, Y. (2013) 'Regional convergence and the role of neighbourhood effects in a decentralised Indonesia', *Bulletin of Indonesian Economic Studies*, 49(3): 193–211.

Williamson, J.G. (1965) 'Regional inequality and the process of national development: a description of patterns', *Economic Development and Cultural Change*, 13: 3–45.

5 Patterns of regional poverty in the new Indonesia

*Amri Ilmma and Matthew Wai-Poi**

5.1 INTRODUCTION

Poverty in Indonesia has fallen markedly since 1976, although there have been significant differences in rates of reduction between regions. In the wake of the Asian financial crisis of 1997–98, and the accompanying financial, economic, social and political upheaval, Indonesia entered a new democratic period known as *reformasi*. Shortly afterwards, Indonesia implemented in a relatively short period one of the largest-scale decentralizations ever seen, bypassing the provincial level of government to transfer substantial power and resources to the districts.[1] Since then, the economy has recovered and continues to perform strongly, with average annual growth in GDP of 5.6 per cent, a stable currency and inflation record, and continued reductions in poverty. This new economic expansion has been achieved in part by riding a (largely Chinese-driven) boom in global commodity prices.

As Hill, Resosudarmo and Vidyattama (2008: 408) note, 'Development dynamics are a long-term phenomenon, involving decades rather than years'. It is now over a decade since Indonesia recovered from the crisis, implemented its decentralization reforms and embarked on a period of renewed economic expansion, meaning that only now has sufficient time elapsed for us to take a look at long-run patterns of regional poverty in Indonesia, with a detailed examination of the decentralization period.

---

* Both authors are employed by the World Bank. All views expressed are those of the authors and do not necessarily represent those of the World Bank.

1 In this chapter, we refer to both cities (*kota*) and rural or mixed urban–rural regions (*kabupaten*) as 'districts'.

We update the provincial analysis to cover the two decades from 1993 to 2012, while also offering some initial analysis on district-level poverty performance since decentralization.

We ask two main questions. First, what are the patterns of regional poverty in the periods immediately before and after *reformasi*? Have trends in poverty reduction remained much the same, or did the crisis, *reformasi* and decentralization mark a structural break in patterns of provincial poverty reduction? Second, has decentralization led to faster poverty reduction, as many had hoped? Have the winners and losers with respect to poverty among the districts remained the same, or changed? And what role has the fragmentation of districts – the process of districts splitting to form new ones, known in Indonesia as *pemekaran* – played in poverty reduction and district development?

Section 5.2 provides an overview of poverty at the national level since 1976, along with a brief summary of the literature on regional poverty in Indonesia. Section 5.3 examines provincial poverty trends during three periods: 1993–96, 1996–2003 and 2003–12. It concludes by asking whether the tumultuous changes that occurred in the years of crisis, *reformasi* and decentralization have led to any changes in patterns of poverty reduction. Section 5.4 looks at poverty outcomes among districts. It compares the relative rankings in 2000, before the implementation of decentralization, with the rankings in 2010, to provide a brief and initial exploration of whether patterns have changed since decentralization. In particular, we look at whether districts that have split have performed better or worse with respect to poverty outcomes. We provide some concluding remarks in section 5.5.

5.2   AN OVERVIEW OF POVERTY IN INDONESIA, 1976–2013

National poverty trends

In 1984, the first year for which internationally comparable purchasing power parity (PPP) poverty data are available, 63 per cent of Indonesians lived on less than PPP$1.25 per day, and 88 per cent on less than PPP$2.00.[2] By 2011, these rates had dropped to 16 per cent and 43 per cent respectively. This represented a dramatic fall in poverty over the 27-year period, driven in large part by 5.4 per cent annualized growth in GDP.

---

2   The figures are from the World Development Indicators database. PPP$ are adjusted by relative prices in different countries to represent a similar bundle of goods.

Using Indonesia's official poverty line allows us to look back further (Figure 5.1). In the two decades from 1976 to 1996, the official poverty rate fell by three-quarters, from 40 per cent to just over 10 per cent, that is, by 1.4 percentage points per annum (Figure 5.1(a)).[3] The method of calculating poverty was revised in 1998, resulting in a higher official poverty line, and therefore higher poverty rates. From 11.3 per cent under the old method, poverty in 1996 was revised to 17.3 per cent under the new one. Shortly after the revision, poverty leapt by a third during the Asian financial crisis as Indonesian GDP plunged 13 per cent. By the time the economy recovered to its pre-crisis levels in 2000, the official poverty rate was 19 per cent, and would not fall back to its pre-crisis level until 2002 (Figure 5.1(b)). Since peaking at nearly one in four Indonesians (24 per cent) in 1998, poverty has declined nearly continuously, with the exception of an increase in 2005–06 due to a global food price crisis and domestic fuel price increases. By early 2013, official poverty was just over 11 per cent.[4]

Half of Indonesia's poverty reduction came in the 11 years between 1976 and 1987 alone, when poverty fell from 40 per cent to 17 per cent (old definition), or by 2.1 percentage points annually (Figure 5.2). The speed of decrease has been relatively stable since then (with the exception of the period spanning the Asian financial crisis and the recovery), averaging 0.7 percentage points between 1987 and 1996 and 0.6 percentage points between 2002 and 2012. Since the mid-1980s, the relationship between poverty decline and economic growth has remained relatively constant, despite the effects of the Asian financial crisis and a changing economic structure. Suryahadi, Hadiwidjaja and Sumarto (2012) have estimated the growth elasticity of poverty, that is, how many percentage points of poverty reduction are achieved per percentage point increase in economic growth. They find that, before the Asian financial crisis, poverty fell by 0.30 percentage points per point of rural economic growth, and by an additional 0.20 percentage points per point of urban economic growth. These elasticities remained similar after the crisis (actually increasing slightly to 0.37 and 0.23 respectively).

At first glance, then, it would seem that poverty has fallen neither faster nor slower under decentralization than in the pre-*reformasi* period, whether in annualized percentage point terms or with reference to growth elasticities. Nonetheless, the rate of poverty reduction has been slowing in recent years, with the 0.5 and 0.6 percentage point decreases

---

3 Poverty data are available only for some years before 1996. To make the trends before and after 1996 comparable over time, poverty rates have been interpolated from the last year before, and the first year after, the missing years.

4 The government is targeting a range of 8–10 per cent by 2014 in its Medium Term Development Plan (Rencana Pembangunan Jangka Menengah).

Figure 5.1   Official poverty rate, 1976–96 and 1996–2013[a]

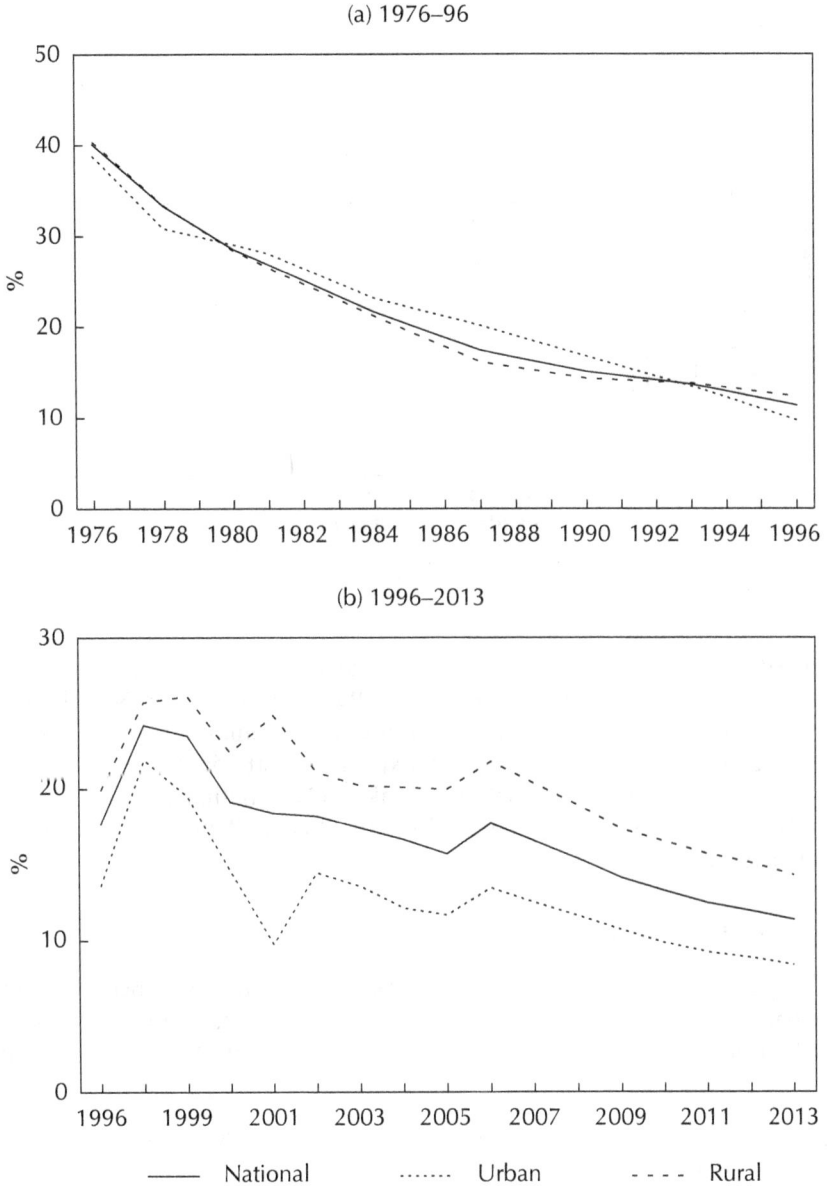

(a) 1976–96

(b) 1996–2013

———— National   ⋯⋯ Urban   - - - - Rural

a   The method of calculating the official poverty line changed in 1998, resulting in a revised estimate for 1996 of 11.3 per cent under the old method (the last year in Figure 5.1(a)) and 17.7 per cent under the new method (the first year in Figure 5.1(b)).

Source: BPS; authors' calculations.

Figure 5.2   Change in poverty rate, 1976–2013

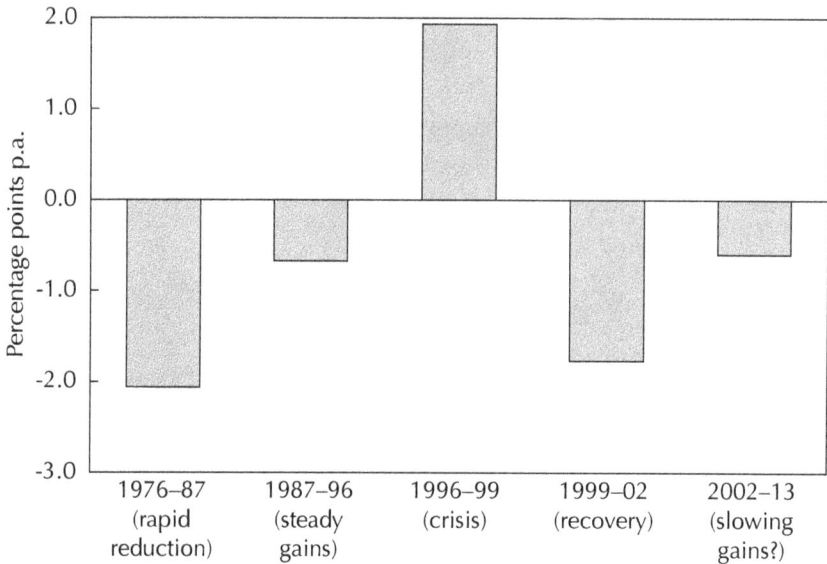

Source: BPS; authors' calculations.

in 2012 and 2013 being the smallest reductions in the last 10 years (and poverty actually increasing during the 2005–06 food price crisis). This is to be expected; as poverty falls to low levels, the remaining poor are situated further below the poverty line, requiring greater increases in income to lift them out of poverty (World Bank 2012). Whether a decentralized Indonesia will be effective in addressing this challenge in the coming years is examined in section 5.3.

Regional poverty trends

The general decline in poverty since 1976 has been experienced in both urban and rural areas, although rural poverty has continued to exceed urban poverty (Figure 5.1).[5] There is significant variation in provincial

---

5   Under the old poverty line methodology, urban poverty was actually higher than rural poverty throughout the 1980s and early 1990s. However, the previous poverty lines have been criticized for representing a higher standard of living in urban areas than in rural ones, and thus greatly overstating urban relative to rural poverty (Ravallion 1992; Ravallion and Bidani 1994; Asra 2000). Interestingly, Figure 5.1(b) shows a sharp divergence in urban and rural poverty in 2001 only. This outcome is difficult to explain, but may be due to the use of a different survey weighting methodology.

Figure 5.3   Provincial poverty, 2012

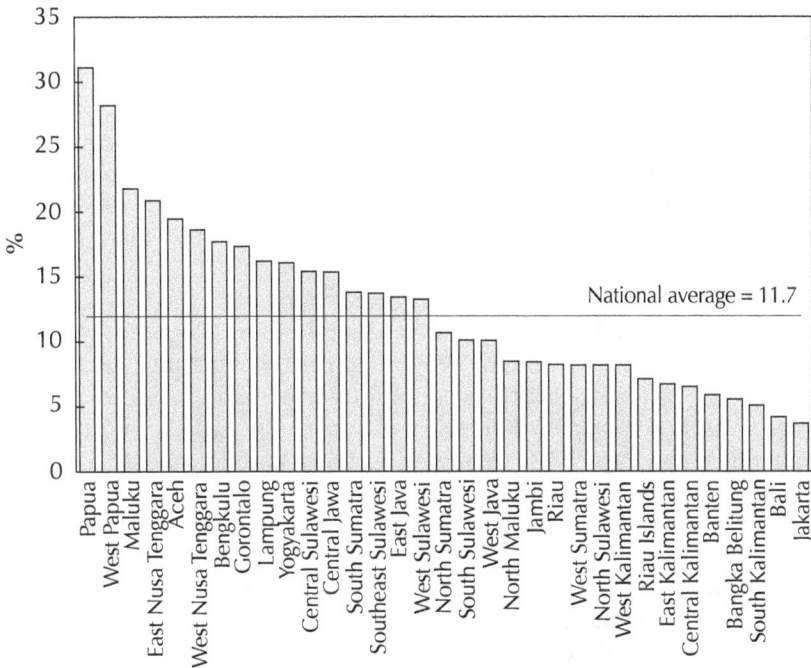

Source: BPS.

poverty rates, however, with those in Eastern Indonesia, and Aceh, being more than double the national average (Figure 5.3). The lowest poverty rates are observed in Jakarta and Bali, now being below 5 per cent. The most heavily populated provinces of East, West and Central Java have poverty rates around the national average; 52 per cent of all poor people live in these three provinces. It is these provincial differences that this chapter wishes to explore. In particular, we are interested in contrasting the poverty outcomes for provinces before and after the Asian financial crisis, to understand whether the fundamental changes that Indonesia has experienced since the crisis – in particular, decentralization – have led to changes in provincial poverty trends and rankings.

Before turning to the updated provincial analysis, extended for the decade after crisis, *reformasi* and decentralization, we briefly review the existing literature on regional poverty in Indonesia.

Previous work has focused mainly on the 1980s and 1990s, through to the recovery from the Asian financial crisis. Hill, Resosudarmo and Vidyattama (2008) examine provincial-level economic growth, inequality, convergence, structural change, demographics and social indicators over the 30-year period to 2004.[6] They argue that differing provincial outcomes are driven in large part by differing responses to international and domestic events. In particular, they highlight the 1970s oil boom, the rapid export-oriented industrialization arising from policy reforms in the 1980s, the Asian financial crisis and decentralization. They emphasise that it is the regions most connected to the global economy that are likely to grow fastest; this holds true now as much as it did in 2004, with Jakarta in particular currently benefiting from its economic geography. Conversely, however, this degree of global integration made Jakarta and Java the most exposed during the Asian financial crisis, as we shall see shortly.

Based on gross regional product (GRP) per capita, Hill, Resosudarmo and Vidyattama (2008) classify provinces into four categories: (1) those that are 'consistently wealthy' (Jakarta, East Kalimantan and Riau); (2) those that are 'consistently non-poor' (North Sumatra, Central Kalimantan, West and East Java, Bali and West Sumatra);[7] (3) those that are 'very poor' (East and West Nusa Tenggara, Maluku and Southeast Sulawesi); and (4) those that are 'slipping behind' (South Sumatra, Jambi, Bengkulu, West and South Kalimantan, North and South Sulawesi, Papua, Lampung, Central Java and Yogyakarta). We return to this classification later to see whether it holds in 2012, and how it fits with provincial poverty rankings. Finally, based on Miranti (2007), Hill, Resosudarmo and Vidyattama (2008) briefly examine provincial poverty trends between 1984 and 2002. They note a broad-based decline in poverty in all provinces except Papua (which suffered from both data weaknesses and unequal development) and Aceh (which had experienced prolonged conflict).

Miranti (2007, 2011) reviews regional poverty outcomes in Indonesia, focusing mostly on the pre-decentralization period 1984–2002, and linking poverty reduction with socio-economic and development indicators.[8] She finds some convergence in poverty rates during the period, with the greatest reductions in poverty occurring in the initially poorest, sparsely populated and isolated provinces, and slight increases occurring in the densely populated provinces that were initially least poor. The latter result may reflect the time period of the analysis, with a number of provinces still just recovering from the Asian financial crisis (which

---

6   Hill and Vidyattama update the end year of this research to 2010 in Chapter 4 of this volume.

7   Aceh would have been included in this group, except for the effects of conflict and the tsunami in the early and mid-2000s.

8   Miranti, extending Hill (1989), uses an alternative classification to that described by Hill, Resosudarmo and Vidyattama (2008) and Hill and Vidyattama (Chapter 4, this volume).

affected urban areas of densely populated provinces the most); in all seven densely populated provinces, poverty declined between 1993 and 1996. The settled Outer Islands, which had initial poverty levels near the national average, experienced declines in poverty during the period that were also in line with the national average. The resource-rich provinces saw relatively little poverty reduction, even though they had relatively large increases in GRP. Despite the convergence in provincial poverty rates, Miranti nonetheless finds persistent poverty patterns, with only three provinces (Bali, West Kalimantan and East Kalimantan) moving from above-average poverty in 1984 to below-average poverty in 2002. She also briefly considers the period since 2002, finding that the patterns of persistence and change under decentralization seem to have remained much the same.

Balisacan, Pernia and Asra (2002) shift the analysis to the district level, conducting panel regressions to examine changes in poverty during the 1990s. They seek to understand the extent to which differences in district-level growth can explain differences in poverty reduction, as well as the role of government policies and programs, geographic attributes and local institutions. They estimate a growth elasticity of poverty of 0.7, and conclude that differences in district consumption growth do indeed drive differences in poverty reduction. However, they find that income growth benefits the richer quintiles more (an issue we discuss later). Among other results, they find that natural resources do not play a role in poverty reduction. This result is discussed by Hill, Resosudarmo and Vidyattama (2008), who note that the indifferent record of the four resource-rich provinces (Aceh, Papua, East Kalimantan and Riau) does not necessarily indicate a resource 'curse' (Sachs and Warner 2001), given that Aceh and Papua have suffered from serious conflict, that most of the resource wealth in the pre-decentralization period did not stay in the province, and that East Kalimantan and Riau have become increasingly prosperous.

Thus, the existing regional poverty literature finds broad-based, growth-driven poverty reduction, with some evidence of convergence in poverty rates between the initially poorest and least poor provinces. A key question we address is whether this convergence has continued in the decentralization period.

We turn now to the impact of the Asian financial crisis. Indonesia was the worst-affected country. The rupiah lost more than 85 per cent of its value against the dollar, GDP contracted by 13 per cent and inflation reached nearly 80 per cent. Nationally, poverty rose six percentage points, from 18 per cent in 1996 to 24 per cent in 1998; the number of poor increased by 43 per cent during this period, from 34.5 million to 49.5 million.

Examining the crisis at a subnational level, Sumarto, Wetterberg and Pritchett (1999) provide results from a qualitative survey of three experts in every subdistrict of Indonesia. They find that urban areas were hit hardest (consistent with Friedman and Levinsohn 2002), but that the effects differed greatly between regions. Some areas were minimally affected by the crisis, or even benefited from the currency devaluation effect on foreign exchange-earning activities (see also Hill, Resosudarmo and Vidyattama 2008). There was little connection between initial poverty level and the extent to which an area was hit by the crisis; the role played by non-crisis-related factors such as drought and fires is also unclear.

Brodjonegoro (2002) provides a detailed examination of the effects of the Asian financial crisis for each province. Overall, he notes that it was a modern sector crisis that affected the more developed and natural resource-rich provinces the most. The rupiah depreciation hurt manufacturing sectors with high import content, as well as the construction and banking sectors, which had significant foreign currency exposures. Falling world oil prices hit the resource-rich provinces. At the same time, other provinces were affected by non-crisis-related factors, such as forest fires and severe drought from the El Niño effect, making it difficult to separate out the direct effects of the crisis. Brodjonegoro (2002: 22) concludes that:

> In summary, Java, most of Nusa Tenggara, Aceh and East Kalimantan were affected by the crisis; North Sumatra, Lampung, most of Kalimantan, and Irian Jaya were moderately hit; [and] Sulawesi, most of Sumatra, Bali and Maluku were slightly hit by the crisis.

Decentralization, *pemekaran* and poverty

Before examining patterns of provincial poverty before and after *reformasi* and decentralization, we briefly discuss decentralization in Indonesia.[9] Here we focus on the expected effects of decentralization on poverty, including the incentive it created for the splitting of districts (*pemekaran*). Sumarto, Suryahadi and Arifianto (2004) review the literature linking good governance to poverty reduction, and Seymour and Turner (2002) summarize the considerable theoretical and empirical global literature on decentralization. Although decentralization can have considerable benefits, Seymour and Turner (2002: 35) conclude that the experience in developing countries to date 'shows that tangible success stories are rare, and that decentralization is seldom an effective poverty-

---

9   The legal framework and other aspects of decentralization are discussed elsewhere in this volume (see Chapter 6 by Lewis).

reducing strategy', and that it 'has actually reduced the quality of service provision in some cases, widened existing regional disparities in others, and may increase corruption'.

Decentralization in Indonesia is underpinned by two laws, Law 32/2004 on Regional Government (revising Law 22/1999) and Law 33/2004 on the Fiscal Balance between the Central Government and the Regions (revising Law 25/1999). The first law provides districts with significant autonomy, although in some areas the division of responsibilities between the provincial and district governments remains unclear (Seymour and Turner 2002: 35). The law also provides for local parliaments (Dewan Perwakilan Rakyat Daerah, DPRD) that are tasked, among other things, with improving people's welfare. The second law allows local governments to generate more own-source revenues (*pendapatan asli daerah*, PAD), and to receive a much greater share of the wealth generated by their natural resources: 80 per cent of net revenue from forestry, mining and fishery; 15 per cent from oil; and 30 per cent from gas.[10] Land and property taxes go mainly to local governments (90 per cent), and income tax mostly to the centre (80 per cent). The law also provides for general funding of local government activities through the national government's General Purpose Fund (Dana Alokasi Umum, DAU), and for funding to achieve specific development objectives in certain locations through the Special Purpose Fund (Dana Alokasi Khusus, DAK). The districts receive 90 per cent of DAU funds, with the remainder going to provincial governments.

From the start, there was considerable concern that decentralization could lead to a number of problems in Indonesia, including fears that hasty implementation and a lack of local government capacity would limit its effectiveness, and that local revenue generation would favour urban and resource-rich districts, leaving others behind.[11] Moreover, with nearly 70 per cent of all local government revenue still derived from transfers from the centre, and all districts entitled to DAU funding, observers were worried that this would provide an incentive for districts to split into smaller areas (Ratnawati 2006).

Indeed, despite the widespread enthusiasm for decentralization, it quickly became clear that hasty implementation had led to a number of short-term problems. These included an initial lack of implementing regulations; insufficient financing for the personnel transferred from central

---

10 In the case of Aceh (due to its special autonomy status) and the two Papuan provinces (for development purposes), this increases to 70 per cent from both oil and gas.

11 See Brodjonegoro and Asanuma (2000), Sadli (2000), Seymour and Turner (2002), Suharyo (2003), Ratnawati (2006) and Ministry of Finance (2012).

government to local government agencies; the tendency for local parliaments to use their new powers to substantially increase members' salaries, and widespread scepticism that they would or could have a positive influence on local administration; increases in taxes as local governments sought to expand their own-source revenues; and increased corruption at the local level (Suharyo 2003). Sumarto, Suryahadi and Arifianto (2004) discuss the failure of decentralization to reduce corruption, arguing that it may in fact have spread it further, from the central to the local level of government. They also identify a number of other failings, including the wide range of new taxes and levies imposed by local governments, leading to higher prices that hurt the poor, and creating distortions in the economy; the reduced amounts of funding available for village development; and reduced spending on health.

Nonetheless, commentators held out hope that in the long term decentralization would facilitate greater local-level participation in governance and development (Seymour and Turner 2002), that it would 'improve the conduciveness of poverty reduction policy' (Sumarto, Suryahadi and Arifianto 2004: 30) and that differences in welfare measures would narrow over time due to greater resource revenue sharing (Hill, Resosudarmo and Vidyattama 2008).

A report by Bappenas and UNDP (2008) includes an early post-decentralization evaluation of poverty outcomes between 2001 and 2005. It finds that levels of poverty are higher in newly autonomous districts (those that have broken away from a parent district) than in the parent districts or in districts that have not split. The report concludes that the higher poverty is explained by several factors: the new regions' limited natural resources, including agricultural resources; their poor infrastructure (roads, schools) and distance to the former district capital, which limit their access to welfare-improving resources; and the lack of access to education, which particularly affects the poor. Consequently, 'it is virtually impossible to bring poverty levels down in a short period of time' (Bappenas and UNDP 2008: 15).

Much of the literature on decentralization in Indonesia was written in the years immediately after its implementation, leaving more questions than answers. This chapter takes advantage of the decade since decentralization to build on those initial conclusions. As we have seen, at an aggregate level, the rate of poverty reduction remained the same before and after the crisis, *reformasi* and decentralization. Later we examine whether there has been divergence or convergence in poverty rates, how district poverty rankings have changed since decentralization, and whether *pemekaran* has been good or bad for poverty reduction. Before doing so, however, we examine provincial-level poverty patterns before and after *reformasi* and decentralization.

5.3 LONG-RUN TRENDS IN REGIONAL POVERTY, 1993–2012

We now examine trends in poverty reduction and development in Indonesian provinces from 1993 until 2012. The data and methodology are discussed in detail in Appendix A5.1. We note two points here. First, we analyse provincial outcomes for the 26 provinces (excluding East Timor) that existed during the Suharto era, aggregating new provinces back into the previous ones for the period after decentralization.[12] Second, we begin in 1993 for reasons of data. The provincial poverty estimates before 1993 are not strictly comparable with those that come afterwards. In 1993 the national statistics agency, Badan Pusat Statistik (BPS), introduced a heavily revised consumption module to its main household socio-economic survey (Survei Sosio-Ekonomi Nasional, Susenas) and expanded the survey's coverage from 65,000 to 200,000 households (Balisacan, Pernia and Asra 2002). Moreover, in the pre-1993 surveys, poverty rates for some provinces were estimated jointly. For example, in 1990 separate poverty rates were estimated for only 18 provinces, with Jambi, Bengkulu, East Timor, Central Kalimantan, East Kalimantan, Central Sulawesi, Southeast Sulawesi, Maluku and Papua having a combined estimate.

In 1993, the provinces in Sumatra, Java and Bali had poverty rates approximately at or below the national average of 13.7 per cent (old poverty line) (Figure 5.4). Rates were also below average in the provinces of Sulawesi, but poverty was high in Eastern Indonesia (Papua, Maluku, East and West Nusa Tenggara), as well as in Kalimantan, other than East Kalimantan.

These patterns of provincial poverty are largely reflected in other development indicators, such as GRP per capita, provincial government revenues and expenditures per capita, school enrolment rates and average household consumption per capita.[13]

1993–96: converging provincial poverty

From 1993 until 1996, shortly before the Asian financial crisis, the poorest half of provinces generally experienced annualized reductions in poverty rates equal to or greater than the national average of 0.8 of a percentage point, with the exception of East and West Nusa Tenggara and

---

12 Thus, Riau includes Riau Islands; South Sumatra includes Bangka Belitung; West Java includes Banten; North Sulawesi includes Gorontalo; South Sulawesi includes West Sulawesi; Maluku includes North Maluku; and Papua includes West Papua.

13 Many of these indicators are in Hill and Vidyattama (Chapter 4, this volume); the others are available from the authors upon request.

Figure 5.4   Provincial poverty, 1993

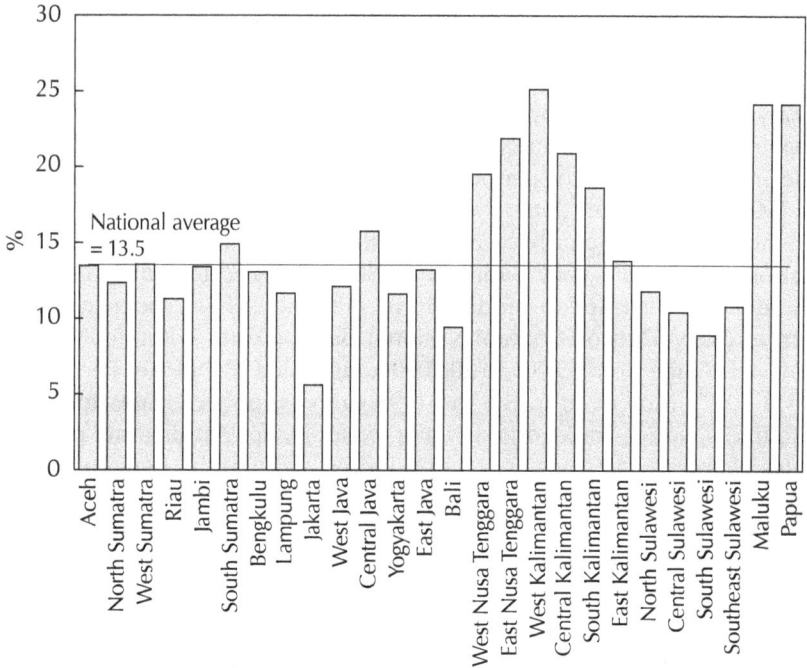

Source: Susenas; authors' calculations.

Central Java (Figure 5.5). Meanwhile, the least poor 50 per cent of provinces generally experienced declines equal to or less than the average,
with the notable exception of Bali, where poverty fell by nearly two percentage points annually. These results are consistent with Miranti (2009),
and confirm that the convergence she finds between 1984 and 2002 was
not simply a product of measuring change in poverty at a point just after
the crisis, nor of the change in poverty measurement methodology.

Interestingly, while the rate of poverty reduction is positively correlated with higher provincial government revenue per capita in 1996 (Figure 5.6(a)),[14] as well as with growth in average household consumption
per capita, it has little correlation with GRP growth per capita (Figure
5.6(b)). The same result holds when we use GRP per capita excluding oil
and gas, or, as Hill, Resosudarmo and Vidyattama (2008) and Balisacan,

---

14 Expenditure data are not available before 2001, but revenues are a reasonable
    proxy for local spending levels. Revenues are calculated as the total of pro-
    vincial and district government revenues.

Figure 5.5   Change in provincial poverty, 1993–96, relative to initial poverty in 1993

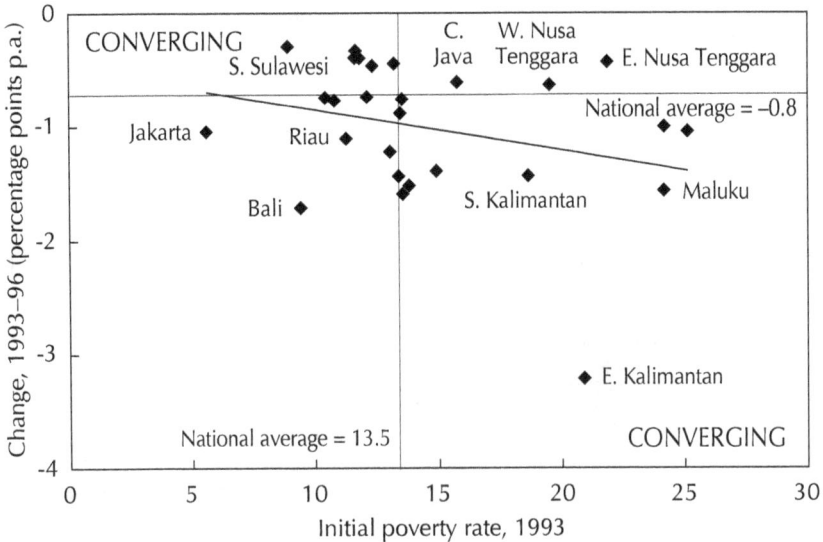

Source: Susenas; authors' calculations.

Pernia and Asra (2002) suggest, household consumption per capita from surveys. This might suggest that while economic growth does indeed drive national poverty reduction in Indonesia, as we see in the growth elasticities and regressions of Balisacan, Pernia and Asra (2002) and Suryahadi, Hadiwidjaja and Sumarto (2012), at the provincial level, this effect can be uneven. However, these are simple two-way correlations, and we return to this more formally in section 5.4.

1996–2003: crisis and recovery

During the Asian financial crisis, all provinces experienced an increase in poverty, but with considerable variation (Figure 5.7). The worst-affected provinces (Papua, Jambi and East Kalimantan) saw increases in the poverty rate of over 10 percentage points – that is, at least an additional 10 per cent of the population in these provinces fell into poverty. The heavily populated provinces in Java suffered increases of six to nine percentage points, except for Jakarta. Despite being one of the most heavily affected in an economic sense, it experienced a rise of less than two percentage points (although this was still an increase of around two-thirds over the non-crisis rate). At the other end of the spectrum, poverty in Bali, Southeast Sulawesi and North Sulawesi rose by less than one percentage point.

Figure 5.6   Correlation of poverty reduction with government revenue and economic growth, 1993–96

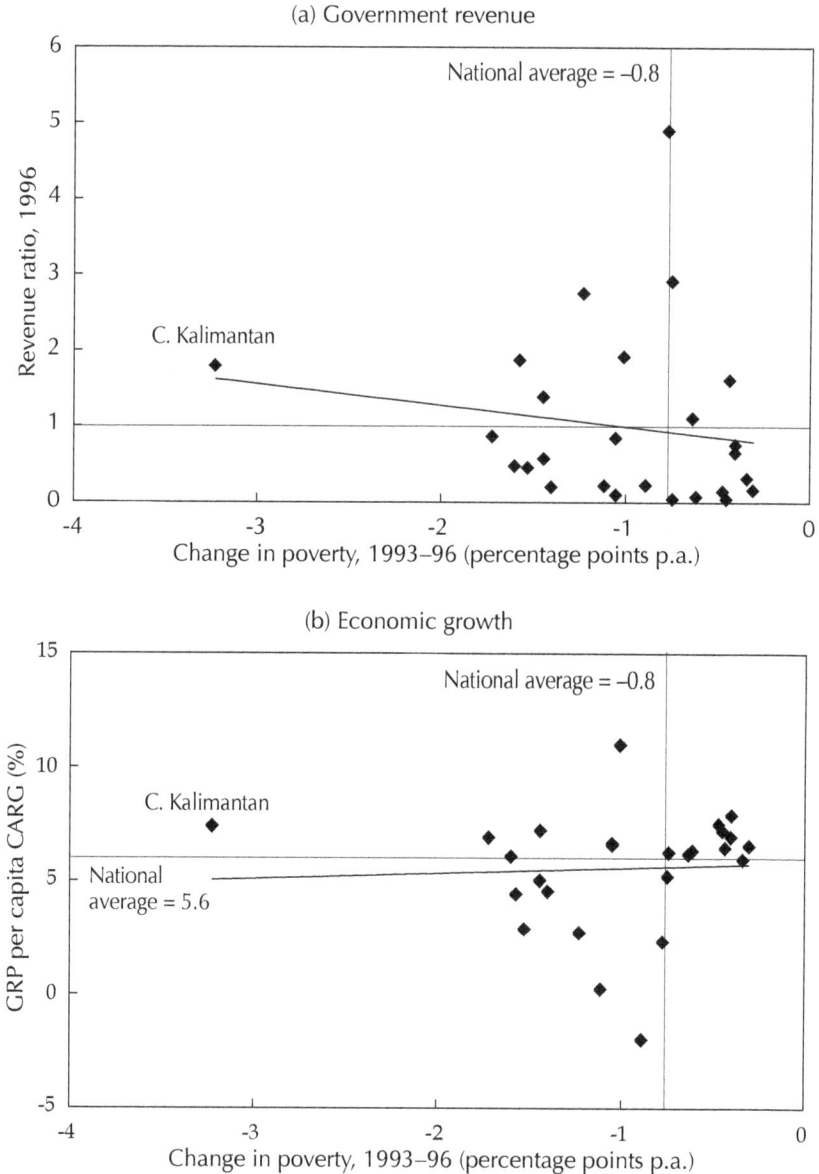

(a) Government revenue

(b) Economic growth

CAGR = compound annual growth rate.
a   Revenue ratio is provincial revenue per capita/provincial GRP per capita, as a ratio of the average over all provinces.

Source: Susenas; Ministry of Finance; national accounts; authors' calculations.

Figure 5.7   Change in provincial poverty, 1996–99

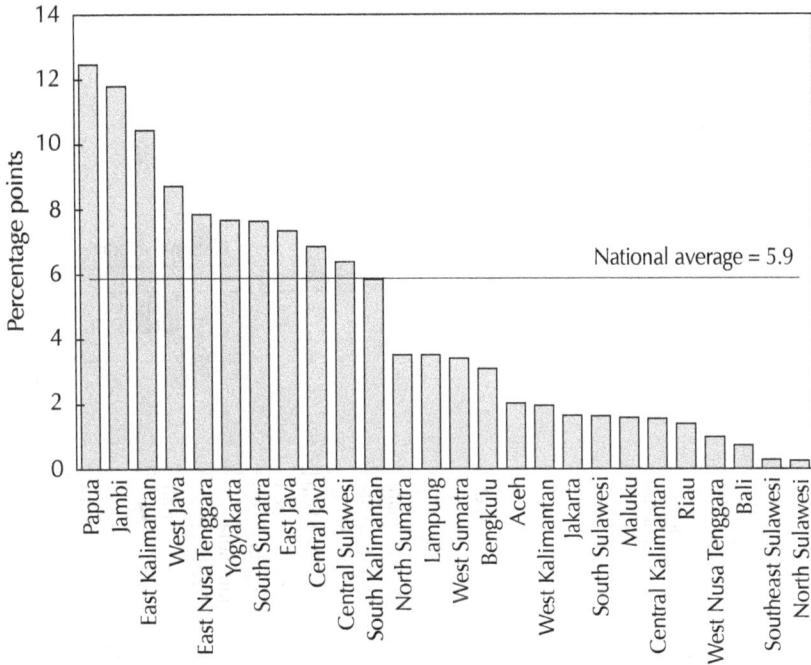

Source: Susenas; authors' calculations.

The increase in poverty was less than two percentage points in 11 provinces, and less than four points in a further four provinces. These results are relatively consistent with the literature on the provincial effects of the crisis, discussed above.

One danger of looking at the poverty impacts of the crisis using the 1999 Susenas data (the first dataset available after the crisis that is comparable at a provincial level to 1996) is that many urban workers moved back to their rural villages of origin, where the ability to produce some of their own food provided some relief (Friedman and Levinsohn 2002). Consequently, by the time poverty was measured at a provincial urban–rural level in 1999, the largest increases were often seen in the rural areas of many provinces (Jambi, Bengkulu, Lampung, Yogyakarta, East Java, East Nusa Tenggara, Central Kalimantan, South Kalimantan, East Kalimantan and Papua). Nonetheless, with the exception of Jakarta, from which many displaced workers probably departed for rural areas of origin, the provincial-level changes are probably fairly accurate, with urban–rural migration more likely to have been within rather than between provinces during the crisis.

Figure 5.8   Change in provincial poverty, 1996–2000

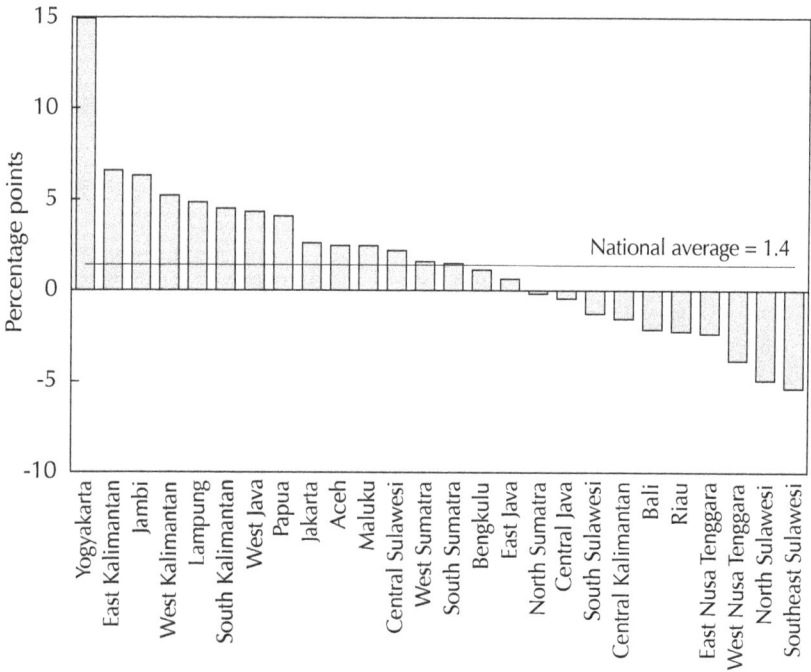

Source: Susenas; authors' calculations.

By the time the economy had recovered to pre-crisis levels in 2000, the national poverty rate had nearly recovered as well, being only 1.4 percentage points higher than in 1996, compared with the six percentage point increase at the height of the crisis. At a provincial level, by 2000 poverty was at or lower than 1996 levels in 10 provinces, and slightly higher, but in line with the national poverty rate, in another eight (Figure 5.8). In the remaining eight provinces poverty was significantly higher than before the crisis, notably in Yogyakarta, where 33 per cent of the population was classified as poor, compared with 18 per cent beforehand. For some of these provinces, poverty rates would not return to their pre-crisis levels until 2001 or 2002, and in three (West Java, Yogyakarta and East Kalimantan) it would take over a decade to return to pre-crisis levels.

2003–12: continued convergence

Since the recovery from the crisis, national poverty has fallen by around 0.6 percentage points per year, roughly the same as during the decade leading up to the crisis, although with signs of poverty reduction having

Figure 5.9   Change in provincial poverty, 2003–12, relative to inital poverty in 2003

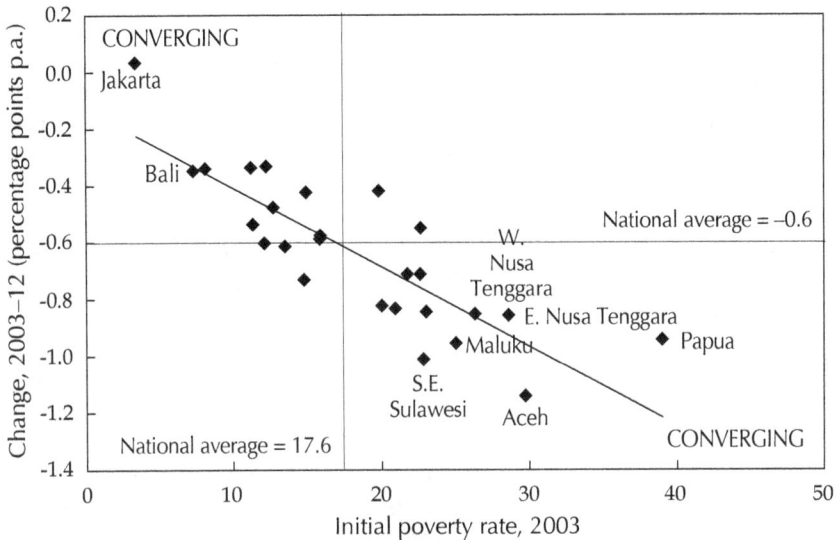

Source: Susenas; authors' calculations.

slowed in the last seven years. Figure 5.9 shows the rate of reduction in each province between 2003 and 2012, plotted against initial poverty. We use a starting year of 2003 rather than 2000 (marking the economic recovery) because of the number of provinces that had not returned to their pre-crisis levels of poverty by 2000; in many ways the 2003–12 changes better represent poverty reduction in the decade since decentralization and the renewal of economic expansion.

The first key result is that convergence clearly continues in the post-decentralization period, with poorer provinces in 2003 enjoying declines in poverty that are greater than the national average, and less poor provinces having declines in line with or less than the national average. Annual reductions of around one percentage point are seen in large parts of Eastern Indonesia (Papua, Maluku, East and West Nusa Tenggara, and Central and Southeast Sulawesi), compared with 0.6 percentage points across Indonesia as a whole. The lowest reductions in poverty are in Bali and Jakarta, where poverty was already very low in 2003 at 7 per cent and 3 per cent respectively, and so had little room to fall further (in fact, it increased slightly in Jakarta).

Poverty trends in Aceh require careful consideration. Over the period 2003–12, Aceh enjoyed one of the highest rates of poverty reduction, of around 1.1 percentage points per year. This was driven in part by the massive amounts of aid and government spending invested in the wake of the 2004 tsunami and the end of the long-running separatist conflict. However, despite the 10 percentage point reduction during this period, the poverty rate of 19.5 per cent in 2012 remains considerably higher than the rate of 14.7 per cent in 1999.[15] As conflict escalated in the early 2000s, poverty increased to as much as 29.8 per cent in 2003. Consequently, Aceh's superior poverty reduction over the last 10 years can be considered a reversion towards the pre-escalation poverty rates.

As in 1993–96, poverty reduction is positively correlated with local government revenue in 2003–09 (Figure 5.10(a)) and negatively correlated with growth in per capita GRP (Figure 5.10(b)).[16] The latter result holds when we use GRP per capita without oil and gas, or slightly different ending points.

1993–2012: provincial conclusions

So what can we conclude about regional poverty outcomes in the two decades spanning the Asian financial crisis, *reformasi* and decentralization? First, despite an economic, political and social crisis that lasted for years, almost all of Indonesia has lower poverty now than it did in 1996, with the notable exception of conflict-affected Aceh.[17] Second, convergence in provincial poverty rates is clear. As Figure 5.11 shows, the ratio of provincial poverty to national poverty has fallen for provinces with the highest ratios in 1993, and risen for those with the lowest ratios.[18] The pattern is even more pronounced if we use initial 1984 poverty ratios (from Miranti 2009) and the change in relative ratios from 1984 to 2012[19] – that is, it is not just the short 1993–96 period driving these results. Further evidence of convergence is provided by the standard deviation across provinces; after increasing during the crisis, it fell to 11.8 in 1999, 8.6 in 2002 and 6.1 in 2012. Certain provinces are exceptions. In particular, relative poverty in Papua has remained high.

---

15 Note that BPS did not conduct a Susenas survey in Aceh in 2000 or 2001 due to the conflict.

16 The World Bank's subnational Database for Policy and Economic Research provides revenue and expenditure data only to 2009, and GRP data until 2010. Using the 2010 GRP data gives qualitatively similar results.

17 Poverty is also slightly higher in Jakarta and Bengkulu, but only by around one percentage point.

18 We use the ratio of provincial poverty rates to the national average because the change in the definition of the poverty line during the period means that poverty rates from 1993 cannot be compared with those after 1996.

19 Available from the authors upon request.

Figure 5.10   Correlation of poverty reduction with government revenue and economic growth, 2003–09

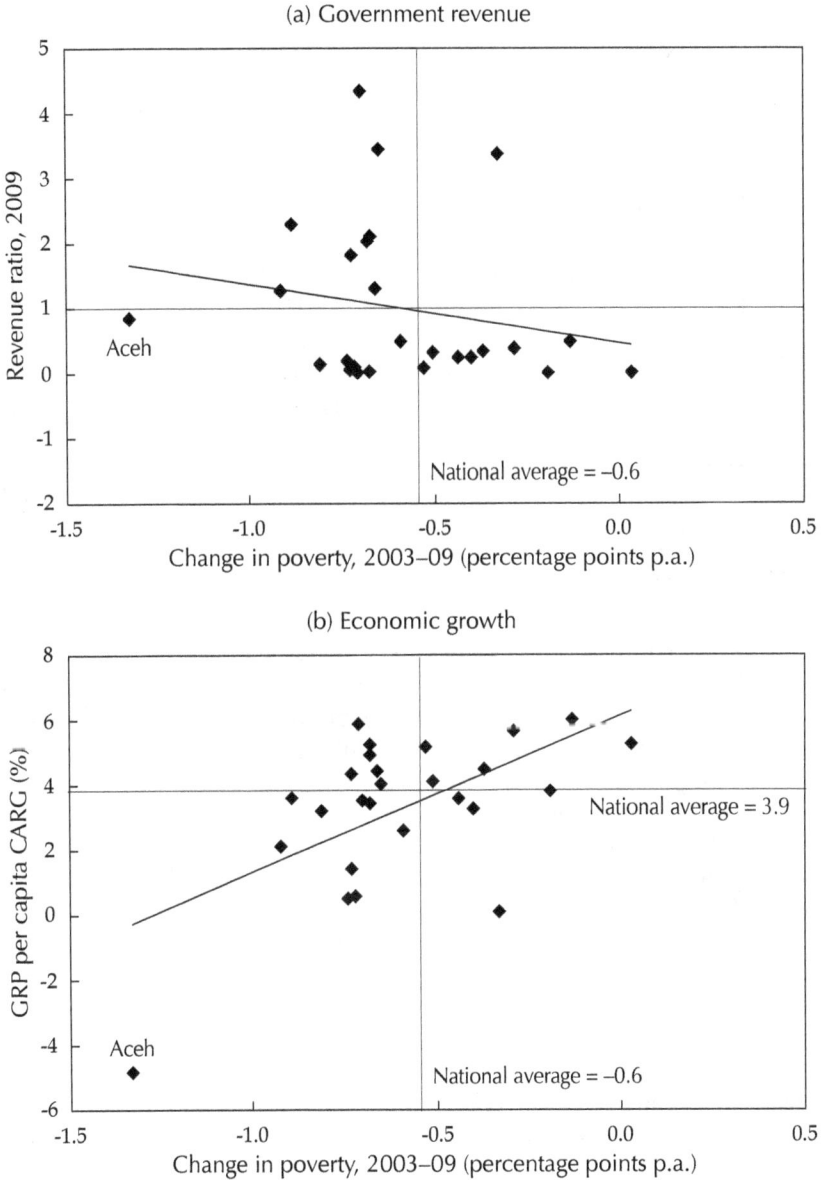

(a) Government revenue

National average = –0.6

(b) Economic growth

National average = 3.9

National average = –0.6

CAGR = compound annual growth rate.
a   Revenue ratio is provincial revenue per capita/provincial GRP per capita, as a ratio of the average over all provinces.

Source: Susenas; Ministry of Finance; national accounts; authors' calculations.

*Figure 5.11   Change in ratio of provincial poverty to national average,
1993–2012, relative to initial poverty ratio in 1993*

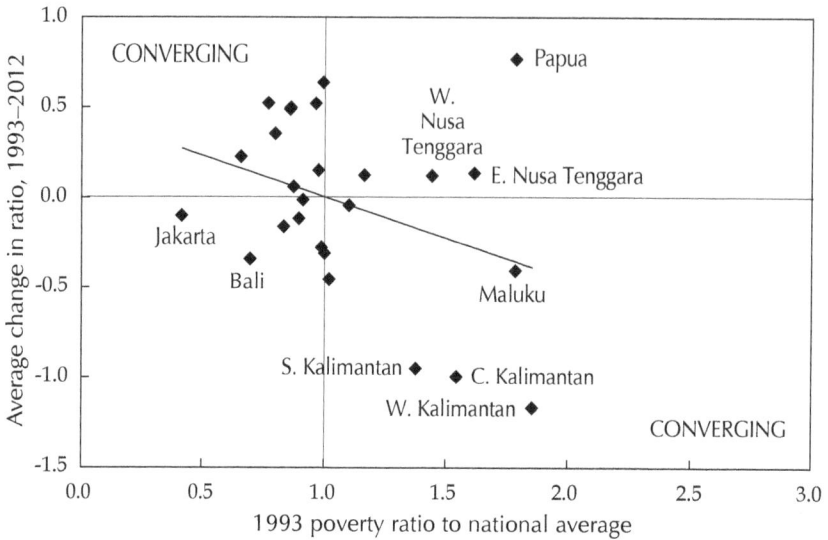

Source: BPS; authors' calculations.

When we compare 1993–96 and 2003–12, we see that the pace of poverty reduction has stayed relatively constant for some provinces, but not for others (Figure 5.12, Table 5.1). However, the data restricts the earlier period to only three years and may not fully represent pre-crisis trends. In Lampung, East Java and East Nusa Tenggara, the speed of poverty reduction increased considerably between 1993–96 and 2003–12. In a number of provinces (West Sumatra, Riau, Jambi, Jakarta, West Java, Bali, and Central, South and East Kalimantan), poverty reduction has slowed, although in most of these poverty is now below 10 per cent, so a slower decline is to be expected. However, the pace of poverty reduction has slowed significantly in two relatively poor provinces: Bengkulu (from 1.2 percentage points per year in 1993–96 to 0.5 points per year in 2003–12) and Maluku (1.6 to 1.0).

Despite the crisis, the convergence of poverty rates and the changes in poverty reduction rates, the relative provincial rankings of poverty have not changed dramatically over the last two decades (Figure 5.13). West Kalimantan is the only province that has significantly improved its ranking, and Aceh the only one whose ranking has significantly declined. Papua, Maluku, and East and West Nusa Tenggara remain consistently poorer, while Jakarta and Bali are consistently the least poor.

Figure 5.12   Change in provincial poverty, 2003–12, relative to change in poverty in 1993–96

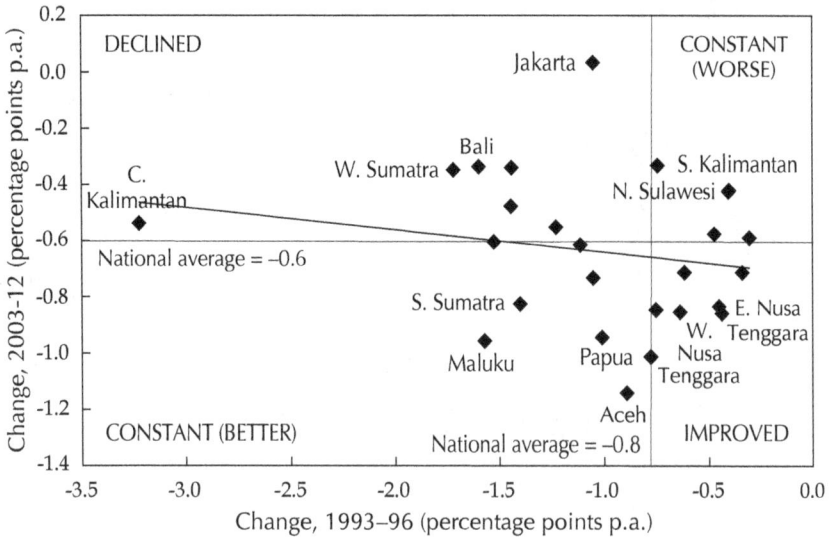

Source: BPS; authors' calculations.

In fact, the thing that has had the greatest impact on relative poverty in Indonesia is the change in poverty line methodology in 1998. Under the new methodology, the national poverty rate for 1996 increased from 11 per cent to 18 per cent; poverty doubled or more than doubled in most of Sulawesi; yet rates remained relatively constant or even fell in Kalimantan.

We now return to the four categories of provinces identified by Hill, Resosudarmo and Vidyattama (2008) on the basis of their per capita GRP: the 'consistently wealthy' provinces, the 'consistently non-poor' provinces, the 'very poor' provinces and the 'slipping behind' provinces.[20] From the poverty ratios for 2012 shown in Table 5.1, we see that the consistently wealthy provinces (Jakarta, East Kalimantan and Riau) also have some of the lowest poverty rates as a ratio to the national average (0.7 or less). Similarly, most of the very poor provinces (East and West Nusa Tenggara and Maluku) also have among the highest poverty ratios (1.4 or higher), the exception being Southeast Sulawesi (1.1). This is despite all four having a degree of exposure to the commodities boom.

---

20 Table 5.1 updates the GRP per capita ratios in Hill, Resosudarmo and Vidyattama (2008) to 2010, but this does not change any province's classification.

Table 5.1 GRP per capita and poverty rankings[a]

District	GRP per capita without oil and gas (ratio)					Poverty ratio					Change in ratio					Change in poverty (ppt p.a.)	
	1993	1996	1999	2003	2010	1993*	1996	1999	2003	2012	1993-96*	1996*-96	1996-99	2003-12	1993-2012	1993-96	2003-12
Aceh	0.8	0.8	0.8	0.8	0.8	1.0	0.7	0.6	1.7	1.6	0.0	-0.2	-0.1	-0.1	0.6	-0.9	-1.0
N. Sumatra	0.9	1.0	1.0	1.0	1.0	0.9	0.8	0.7	0.9	0.9	0.1	-0.2	0.0	0.0	0.0	-0.5	-0.5
W. Sumatra	0.9	0.8	0.9	0.9	1.0	1.0	0.6	0.6	0.6	0.7	-0.2	-0.2	0.0	0.0	-0.3	-1.6	-0.3
Riau	0.8	0.7	0.9	1.5	1.3	0.8	0.7	0.6	0.7	0.7	-0.1	0.0	-0.1	-0.1	-0.2	-1.1	-0.6
Jambi	0.6	0.6	0.6	0.6	0.6	1.0	0.8	1.1	0.7	0.7	-0.2	0.0	0.3	0.0	-0.3	-1.4	-0.4
S. Sumatra	0.8	0.8	0.7	0.8	0.8	1.1	0.9	1.0	1.2	1.1	-0.1	0.0	0.1	-0.1	0.0	-1.4	-0.7
Bengkulu	0.6	0.5	0.6	0.6	0.5	1.0	1.0	0.8	1.3	1.5	-0.1	0.1	-0.1	0.2	0.5	-1.2	-0.5
Lampung	0.6	0.5	0.6	0.6	0.5	0.9	1.5	1.2	1.3	1.4	-0.1	0.5	-0.2	0.1	0.5	-0.3	-0.6
Jakarta	4.6	4.5	4.2	4.7	5.0	0.4	0.1	0.2	0.2	0.3	-0.2	-0.1	0.0	0.1	-0.1	-1.1	0.0
W. Java	1.0	0.9	0.9	0.9	0.8	0.9	0.6	0.8	0.7	0.8	0.0	-0.2	0.2	0.1	-0.1	-0.7	-0.3
C. Java	0.5	0.6	0.6	0.6	0.6	1.2	1.2	1.2	1.3	1.3	0.1	0.0	0.0	0.0	0.1	-0.6	-0.6
Yogyakarta	0.8	0.8	0.8	0.7	0.7	0.9	1.1	1.1	1.1	1.3	0.1	0.1	0.1	0.2	0.5	-0.4	-0.4
E. Java	1.1	1.1	1.0	1.0	1.1	1.0	1.3	1.3	1.2	1.1	0.1	0.2	0.0	-0.1	0.1	-0.5	-0.8
Bali	1.0	1.0	1.2	1.0	1.0	0.7	0.4	0.4	0.4	0.3	-0.3	0.1	-0.1	-0.1	-0.3	-1.7	-0.3
W. Nusa Tenggara	0.5	0.5	0.5	0.5	0.5	1.4	1.8	1.4	1.5	1.6	0.1	0.3	-0.4	0.0	0.1	-0.6	-0.8
E. Nusa Tenggara	0.8	0.8	0.8	0.8	0.8	1.6	2.2	2.0	1.6	1.7	0.2	0.4	-0.2	0.1	0.1	-0.4	-0.8

Table 5.1 (continued)

District	GRP per capita without oil and gas (ratio)							Poverty ratio				Change in ratio					Change in poverty (ppt p.a.)	
	1993	1996	1999	2003	2010	1993*	1996*	1996	1999	2003	2012	1993-96*	1996*-96	1996-99	2003-12	1993-2012	1993-96	2003-12
W. Kalimantan	1.1	1.2	1.4	1.4	1.6	1.9	2.0	1.4	1.1	0.8	0.7	0.1	-0.6	-0.3	-0.2	-1.2	-1.1	-0.7
C. Kalimantan	1.3	1.2	1.1	1.1	1.0	1.5	1.0	0.8	0.6	0.7	0.5	-0.5	-0.2	-0.1	-0.1	-1.0	-3.2	-0.5
S. Kalimantan	0.5	0.4	0.5	0.5	0.5	1.4	1.3	0.5	0.6	0.5	0.4	-0.1	-0.8	0.1	0.0	-1.0	-1.4	-0.3
E. Kalimantan	2.0	1.8	2.0	2.0	2.0	1.0	0.8	0.6	0.9	0.7	0.6	-0.2	-0.3	0.3	-0.1	-0.5	-1.5	-0.5
N. Sulawesi	0.4	0.3	0.4	0.4	0.4	0.9	0.9	1.0	0.8	0.9	0.9	0.1	0.1	-0.2	0.1	0.1	-0.4	-0.4
C. Sulawesi	1.4	1.3	1.5	1.3	1.2	0.8	0.7	1.3	1.2	1.3	1.3	0.0	0.5	0.0	0.0	0.5	-0.8	-0.8
S. Sulawesi	0.2	0.2	0.2	0.3	0.3	0.7	0.7	1.0	0.8	0.9	0.9	0.1	0.2	-0.2	0.0	0.2	-0.3	-0.5
S.E. Sulawesi	0.8	0.7	0.8	0.8	0.6	0.8	0.8	1.7	1.3	1.3	1.1	0.0	0.9	-0.4	-0.2	0.3	-0.8	-0.9
Maluku	0.6	0.5	0.2	0.4	0.4	1.8	1.7	2.5	2.0	1.4	1.4	-0.1	0.8	-0.6	-0.1	-0.4	-1.6	-0.9
Papua	1.2	1.3	1.7	1.6	1.1	1.8	1.9	2.4	2.3	2.2	2.6	0.1	0.5	-0.1	0.3	0.8	-1.0	-0.9

a 1993 poverty rates are under the old poverty definition, and those for 1996 onward are under the new definition (although the change between 1993 and 1996 uses the old definition, for consistency). In the table, an asterisk denotes the use of the old definition.

Source: BPS; national accounts; authors' calculations.

*Figure 5.13   Ratio of provincial poverty to national average,
            1996 and 2012*

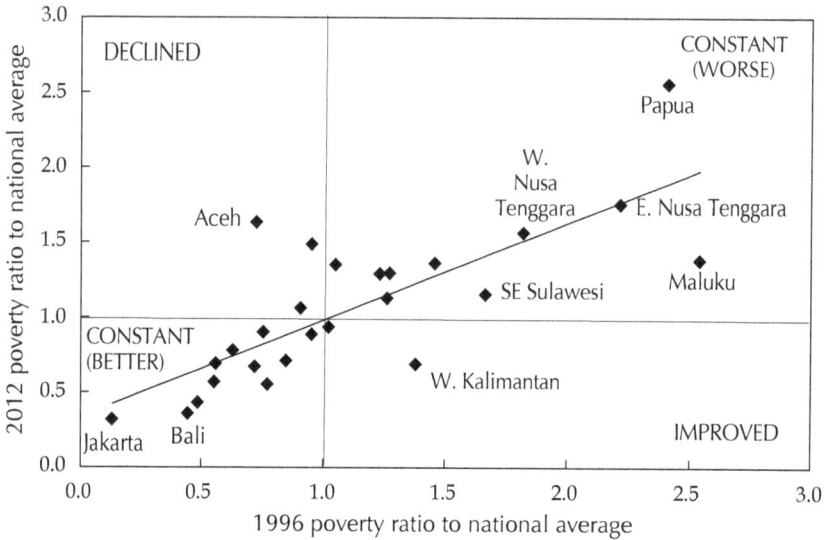

Source: Susenas; authors' calculations.

The consistently non-poor provinces are a more mixed story. Some have poverty rates not too far from the national average (North Sumatra, West Java and East Java), but some have considerably lower rates (West Sumatra, Central Kalimantan and especially Bali, which is second only to Jakarta in the poverty rankings). Aceh is the obvious outlier, with a poverty rate 1.6 times higher than the average. Most of the slipping-behind provinces have average or above-average poverty rates (South Sumatra, Bengkulu, Lampung, Central Java, Yogyakarta, North, Central and South Sulawesi, and Papua), as would be expected, but three (Jambi, and West and South Kalimantan) have considerably lower rates. So in general, the economic classification also holds for household poverty.

How has relative economic growth supported poverty reduction? We have already seen that provincial poverty reduction was negatively correlated with GRP per capita growth in 1993–96 and 2003–09. Nationally, while the growth elasticity of poverty is a respectable 0.7 (Balisacan, Pernia and Asra 2002), it is clear that the poor have not benefited as much from economic growth, either since the recovery from the crisis and the advent of decentralization (as popular media and academia alike remark), or in fact before it (contrary to current perceptions). Figure 5.14 presents the growth incidence curves for Indonesian household consumption between 1990 and 2010. Each curve shows the annualized

Figure 5.14   Growth incidence curves, 1990–2010

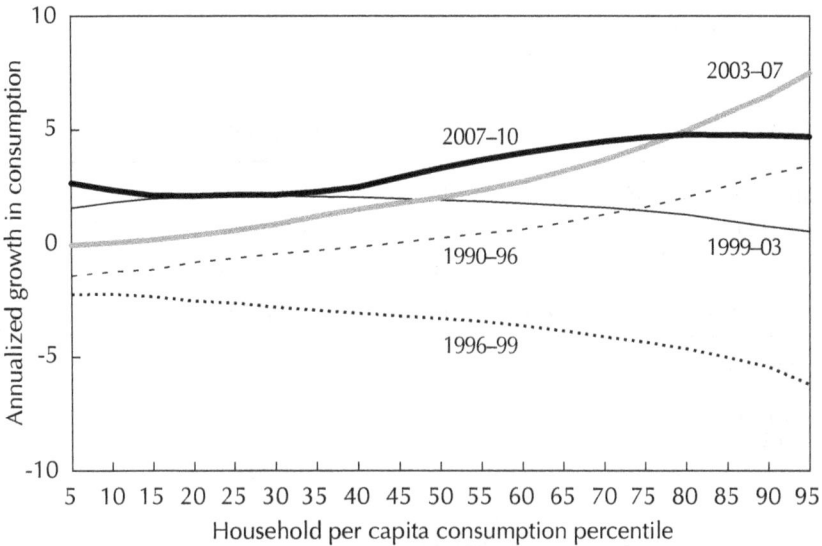

Source: Susenas; authors' calculations; World Bank (2011).

growth in household per capita consumption for each 1 per cent of the population, ordered from poorest to richest. For the periods 1990–96, 2003–07 and 2007–10, the curves are largely upward rising, with the richest part of the distribution enjoying greater growth than the middle and poorer parts.[21] The reverse is the case in 1996–99 and 1999–2003, representing the Asian financial crisis and the recovery respectively. As has been noted in this chapter and elsewhere in the literature, it was better-off urban households that were most affected by the crisis. Consequently, while all household percentiles experienced a decline in real per capita consumption, it was considerably greater for richer households, which also experienced the lowest growth rates during the recovery.[22] However, other than during the crisis and the recovery, economic growth in Indonesia has not been pro-poor.

The recent slowing in rates of national poverty reduction discussed in section 5.2 seems likely to continue without new policy action. No

---

21 The consumption data in the 1990 Susenas are not strictly comparable to those in 1996, so the negative growth for poor households may be an artifact of different questionnaires. However, the relative distributions and the pro-rich trend are likely to be accurate.

22 See World Bank (2011) for further discussion.

124   *Amri Ilmma and Matthew Wai-Poi*

Table 5.2   District characteristics in 2000[a]

District type	Number of districts	Poverty rate (%)	Mean household consumption per capita (Rp/month)	Median household consumption per capita (Rp/month)	Gini ratio	Net junior secondary enrolment
Early splits	88	22.0	185,507	160,506	25.4	53.2
Late splits	16	26.4	167,819	147,626	24.9	54.8
No splits	194	17.3	196,869	168,940	24.8	62.5
All districts	**298**	**18.9**	**192,504**	**165,714**	**25.0**	**59.4**

a   Mean and median household per capita consumption have been adjusted for spatial and temporal differences in the cost of living, using a relative poverty line approach. See Appendix A5.1 for more details. Data were available for only 298 of the 305 districts exising in 2000.

Source: Susenas; authors' calculations.

province with a poverty rate below 10 per cent in 2010 has seen poverty fall by more than 0.5 percentage points per year since then, with many rates flat. This suggests that while poorer provinces will continue to see poverty gains, less poor provinces (and more populous ones) are likely to have stagnant poverty rates, leading to lower national gains.

5.4   DISTRICT POVERTY PERFORMANCE UNDER DECENTRALIZATION

Finally, we briefly examine district-level outcomes under decentralization. The drivers of district poverty reduction, both before decentralization (Balisacan, Pernia and Asra 2002) and afterward (Chapter 12 by Sumarto, Vothknecht and Wijaya, this volume), have already been examined, using a panel regression approach. Instead, we look at another aspect of district development and decentralization: the fragmentation of districts (*pemekaran*).

Brodjonegoro and Asanuma (2000) predicted that decentralization would tempt districts to split into new ones, in order to generate and capture new rents. This has indeed come to pass; there are now 497 districts, compared with 298 in 1996 and 305 in 2000. We divide the districts that have split into two categories: early splits (those that broke away in or before 2005) and late splits (those that broke away after 2005), although there are relatively few of the latter. Table 5.2 compares district characteristics in 2000. In total, just over 100 of the 298 districts (based on

Table 5.3   Average change in district characteristics, 2000–10, using 2000 boundaries

District type	Poverty (percentage points)	Mean household per capita consumption (%)	Median household per capita consumption (%)	Gini ratio (percentage points)	Net junior secondary enrolment (percentage points)
Early splits	–7.3	30.1	20.0	4.4	10.8
Late splits	–9.7	28.5	19.9	2.5	9.5
No splits	–4.6	19.8	12.1	4.0	5.2
All districts	**–5.5**	**22.8**	**14.5**	**4.0**	**6.8**

Source: Susenas; authors' calculations.

pre-decentralization boundaries) had split into at least two districts. (Of the 497 districts in 2012, 62 had split more than once.) In 2000, districts that would later split were considerably poorer than those that would not, had lower mean and median per capita household consumption, and had lower net enrolment rates at the junior secondary school level.[23] Levels of income inequality were relatively similar in both splitting and non-splitting districts.

We now look at district outcomes between 2000 and 2010 (Table 5.3).[24] Whatever the reasons behind their decisions to break away, districts that have split have enjoyed better socio-economic outcomes than those that have not. Poverty fell by 7.3 percentage points on average in the districts that split early and 9.7 percentage points in those that split late, compared with 4.6 percentage points in districts that did not split. Mean and median household per capita consumption in the districts that split grew 50–65 per cent faster than in the districts that did not, and increases in net enrolment were twice as high. To some extent these outcomes may be due to convergence, but it is clear that on average splitting districts have performed better than non-splitting districts since decentralization.

---

23 We look at junior secondary (Sekolah Menengah Pertama, SMP) enrolment rates because primary (Sekolah Dasar, SD) enrolment is close to 100 per cent in all districts.

24 We use 2010 as the end year because the Susenas uses a new sampling methodology from 2011, as well as revised population weights based on the 2010 census. Although these changes are not likely to have a big effect on aggregate estimates at the provincial or national levels, district-level estimates may well be sensitive to the changes.

However, income inequality increased more in the districts that split early (that is, in the majority of splitting districts) than in those that did not split. Changing the period of comparison to 2003–10 does not qualitatively change the results.

We constructed a district mobility matrix for mean per capita household consumption by decile between 2003 and 2010.[25] It shows considerable mobility, both upward and downward. The matrix allows us to distinguish splitting from non-splitting districts. Given the better performance of splitting districts on average, it is unsurprising to find that they display more upward mobility. Of the districts that have split, 59 are in a higher decile in 2010 than in 2003, 24 in the same decile and 18 in a lower one. Conversely, of the districts that did not split, 48 are better off and 51 remain the same, but 90 are in a lower decile.

We also divide districts into those that are commodity intensive and those that are not, based on employment in mining and estate crops (oil palm, rubber, coffee and cocoa).[26] Of the 35 most commodity-intensive districts (counting under the boundaries before splitting), 19 are better off and only eight are worse off.

When we construct the corresponding district mobility matrix for poverty rates over the same period, we find a similar degree of mobility. Again, we break down the districts by type. Among the splitting districts, 41 are in a higher decile, 42 in the same decile and 18 in a lower one. That is, there is a skew towards improvement, as there was for the mean consumption breakdown, but to a lesser degree. The increase in income inequality observed in splitting districts, relative to non-splitting ones, suggests that some of the increased household consumption in the former group of districts is not going to the poor. In the commodity-intensive districts, 25 are better off, six remain the same and four are worse off, which is actually a more pro-poor result than was observed for the mean consumption table.

So far, descriptive analysis has suggested that splitting districts are enjoying greater poverty reduction. We conclude this section by exploring this idea more formally. Chart 3.3 in Bappenas and UNDP (2008) compares the poverty reduction records of 'control' districts (no splits) and 'divided' districts (splits) between 2001 and 2005.[27] It shows that the group of districts that will later split has a higher average poverty rate in 2001 than the control group, but that this gap narrows by 2005 (particularly over the first two years). However, much of this could be due to a convergence effect (which we have seen at the provincial level), and

---

25   The matrix is available from the authors upon request.
26   Classification details are available from the authors upon request.
27   It also compares 'parent' and 'new' districts, which we do not explore here.

not due to *pemekaran* alone. To deal with this and the related issue of confounding factors, we adopt a regression approach.

To do this, we look at the impact of *pemekaran* on the change in district poverty, controlling for a number of other potential drivers of poverty reduction. The other explanatory variables we include are change in per capita GRP (with and without oil and gas); change in mean per capita consumption; change in district revenue (total and just DAU transfers); capital expenditure and personnel expenditure as proportions of total district expenditure; initial enrolment rate for junior secondary school; whether the district is commodity intensive; and which regional grouping it belongs to. Crucially, we include the initial poverty rate, which will control for any convergence effect. We conduct this analysis for the period 2003–09. This period is chosen for reasons of both data and timing. First, detailed revenue and expenditure data are available only until 2009. Second, 2002–03 marks the beginning of the commodity price boom. But most importantly, beginning earlier than 2002 or 2003 risks including poverty reduction that was due to the recovery from the crisis, rather than decentralization. In addition, any potential poverty reduction effects from decentralization are likely to take a year or two to become measurable.

Table 5.4 presents the main results. A particularly interesting one to note is that districts that have split enjoy 9–12 per cent faster poverty reduction than those that have not, even after controlling for other factors. Other interesting results include clear evidence of convergence at the district level – around 1 per cent faster reduction for each additional point of initial poverty, counter to Seymour and Turner's (2002) expectation that the gap between rich and poor regions would increase;[28] strong evidence of a negative relationship between poverty and growth in household consumption, as anticipated by Hill, Resosudarmo and Vidyattama (2008) and Balisacan, Pernia and Asra (2002); and little evidence for such a relationship with growth in GRP per capita (with or without oil).[29] We also see that commodity-intensive districts enjoy stronger poverty reduction.

These are very preliminary results, and much more work is required to test their robustness. Further work will need not only to include further explanatory variables, but also to examine regional variation;

---

28 Note, however, that faster poverty reduction can still be consistent with slower mean consumption growth under certain distributional outcomes.

29 The coefficient for GRP per capita without oil is negative, but it is significant only at the 10 per cent level, and it is not robust to the period of analysis; this result becomes insignificant if the period is changed to 2002–09, whereas all other results remain effectively the same.

Table 5.4   District-level drivers of poverty reduction

Dependent variable: percentage change in poverty	1	2	3	4
2003 poverty rate	−0.89***	−0.88***	−0.90***	−0.89***
Growth in GRP per capita (with oil & gas)	−0.13		−0.12	
Growth in GRP per capita (without oil and gas)		−0.16*		−0.15*
Growth in mean per capita household consumption	−0.67***	−0.68***	−0.66***	−0.67***
Growth in total district revenue	0.00	−0.01		
Growth in district DAU revenue			0.00	0.00
Capital expenditure as share of total district expenditure	0.25	0.23	0.25	0.24
Personnel expenditure as share of total district expenditure	0.29	0.26	0.30	0.26
2003 net enrolment in junior secondary school	−0.08	−0.06	−0.08	−0.06
District splits before 2005	−9.05**	−8.78**	−9.58**	−9.41**
District splits after 2005	−11.76**	−11.82**	−12.06**	−12.22**
Commodity-intensive district	−14.00***	−13.80***	−13.71***	−13.50***
Regional dummies	Yes	Yes	Yes	Yes
No. of observations	281	281	281	281
R^2	0.39	0.39	0.39	0.39
Adjusted R^2	0.35	0.36	0.35	0.36

*** $p<0.01$; ** $p<0.05$; * $p<0.1$. Standard errors are in brackets.

pemekaran has led to considerable conflict and adverse effects in Papua, for example (see Chapter 17 by Nolan, Jones and Solahudin).[30] However, if it is the case that splitting districts experience faster poverty reduction than non-splitting ones, even after controlling for initial poverty rates (convergence) and for economic growth, revenues and expenditures, then the subsequent – and critical – question becomes, what are the underlying mechanisms behind this phenomenon? Is it, as Seymour and Turner (2002) have speculated, that decentralization has led to greater local participation in governance and development? Why would it be

---

30 Regional dummies are included in our analysis, but an interaction between the regional and *pemekaran* dummies would be useful.

that decentralization has the potential to 'improve the conduciveness of poverty reduction policy' (Sumarto, Suryahadi and Arifianto 2004: 31)? Could it simply be that districts whose leaders are motivated and competent enough to engineer a split subsequently enjoy the fruits of such leadership? Or does the faster increase in inequality in splitting districts suggest a more cynical capture of public funds, with some distribution to the poor to shore up incumbents' positions? Finally, future research could investigate whether there are differences in economic and social outcomes for two different types of splitting districts: those that split away (children) and those that are split from (parents).

5.5 CONCLUSIONS

In the last 20 years, Indonesia has gone from decades of unbroken growth and poverty reduction, to an all-consuming economic, political and social crisis, to *reformasi*, democratization and decentralization, to renewed, albeit far from inclusive, economic expansion. Despite it being such an eventful period, the rate of poverty reduction has remained relatively unchanged, and broad-based declines are seen at both the provincial and district levels (with notable exceptions). There is clear evidence of convergence among provincial and district poverty rates, with initially poorer districts enjoying nearly one percentage point faster poverty reduction to 2010 for each additional percentage point of poverty in 2003. At a provincial level, this convergence represents a continuation of pre-crisis and pre-decentralization patterns of provincial poverty reduction.

At the same time, relative poverty rankings between provinces have remained largely unchanged since 1996. Few provinces have seen significant improvements or declines relative to the national average, with the notable but not unexpected exception of Aceh. Eastern Indonesia, especially Papua, remains considerably poorer than the rest of the country. Jakarta and Bali have the lowest poverty – nearly eradicated according to the official (but low) national poverty line – and Jakarta in particular is enjoying the benefits of renewed growth.

The implementation of decentralization seems to have neither greatly accelerated poverty reduction (as its proponents claimed it would) nor led to a significant slowing (as its critics had feared). Nonetheless, there is some initial evidence that districts that have taken advantage of decentralization to split into new regions have experienced a boost in poverty reduction. Further research is needed, however, to understand if this is a robust result, and, if it is, what the underlying mechanisms are. If lessons can be learned from these districts, it may help policy makers address the increasingly difficult challenge of reaching Indonesia's remaining poor, who still number 30 million.

REFERENCES

Asra, A. (2000) 'Poverty and inequality in Indonesia: estimates, decomposition, and key issues', *Journal of the Asia Pacific Economy*, 5(1/2): 91–111.

Balisacan, A.M., E.M. Pernia and A. Asra (2002) 'Revisiting growth and poverty reduction in Indonesia: what do subnational data show?', ERD Working Paper Series No. 25, Economics and Research Department, Asian Development Bank, Manila, October.

Bappenas (Badan Perencanaan Pembangunan Nasional) and UNDP (United Nations Development Programme) (2008) 'Evaluation of the proliferation of administrative region in Indonesia 2001–2007', Building and Reinventing Decentralised Governance (BRIDGE), July.

Brodjonegoro, B. (2002) 'The impact of the Asian economic crisis on regional development patterns in Indonesia', EADN Regional Project on the Social Impact of the Asian Financial Crisis, East Asian Development Network (EADN), January.

Brodjonegoro, B. and S. Asanuma (2000) 'Regional autonomy and fiscal decentralization in democratic Indonesia', unpublished paper, University of Indonesia, Jakarta.

Friedman, J. and J. Levinsohn (2002) 'The distributional impact of Indonesia's financial crisis on household welfare: a "rapid response" methodology', *World Bank Economic Review*, 16(3): 397–423.

Hill, H. (ed.) (1989) *Unity and Diversity: Regional Economic Development in Indonesia since 1970*, Oxford University Press, Singapore.

Hill, H., B.P. Resosudarmo and Y. Vidyattama (2008) 'Indonesia's changing economic geography', *Bulletin of Indonesian Economic Studies*, 44(3): 407–35.

Ministry of Finance (2012) *Desentralisasi Fiskal di Indonesia Satu Dekade Setelah Ledakan Besar* [Fiscal Decentralization in Indonesia a Decade after the Big Bang], University of Indonesia Press, Jakarta.

Miranti, R. (2007) 'The determinants of regional poverty in Indonesia: 1984–2002', PhD dissertation, Australian National University, Canberra.

Miranti, R. (2011) 'Regional patterns of poverty: why do some provinces perform better than others?', in C. Manning and S. Sumarto (eds) *Employment, Living Standards and Poverty in Contemporary Indonesia*, Institute of Southeast Asian Studies, Singapore.

Ratnawati, T. (2006) 'Mengevaluasi kebijakan pemekaran wilayah di Indonesia' [Evaluating the district splitting policy in Indonesia], in M.Z. Mubarak, M.A. Susilo and A. Pribadi (eds) *Blue Print Otonomi Daerah Indonesia* [Blueprint for Indonesian Regional Autonomy], Kerjasama YHB Center with the European Union and partners, Jakarta.

Ravallion, M. (1992) 'Poverty comparisons: a guide to concepts and methods', Living Standards Measurement Study, Working Paper No. 88, World Bank, Washington DC.

Ravallion, M. and B. Bidani (1994) 'How robust is a poverty profile?', *World Bank Economic Review*, 8(1): 75–102.

Sachs, J. and A. Warner (2001) 'The curse of natural resources', *European Economic Review*, 45: 827–38.

Sadli, M. (2000) 'Establishing regional autonomy in Indonesia: the state of the debate', paper presented at the University of Leiden, Leiden, 15–16 May.

Seymour, R. and S. Turner (2002) '*Otonomi daerah*: Indonesia's decentralisation experiment', *New Zealand Journal of Asian Studies*, 4(2): 33–51.

Suharyo, W. (2003) 'Indonesia's transition to decentralized governance: an evolution at the local level', SMERU Working Paper, SMERU Research Institute, Jakarta.

Sumarto, S., A. Suryahadi and A. Arifianto (2004) 'Governance and poverty reduction: evidence from newly decentralized Indonesia', SMERU Working Paper, SMERU Research Institute, Jakarta.

Sumarto, S., A. Wetterberg and L. Pritchett (1999) 'The social impact of the crisis in Indonesia: results from a nationwide *kecamatan* survey', World Bank working paper, World Bank, Jakarta.

Suryahadi, A., G. Hadiwidjaja and S. Sumarto (2012) 'Economic growth and poverty reduction in Indonesia before and after the Asian financial crisis', SMERU Working Paper, SMERU Research Institute, Jakarta.

World Bank (2011) 'Indonesian economic quarterly: turbulent times', World Bank, Jakarta, March.

World Bank (2012) 'Indonesian economic quarterly: adjusting to pressures', World Bank, Jakarta, July.

APPENDIX A5.1   DATA AND METHODOLOGY

Provincial poverty statistics are official figures from BPS, based on the National Socio-Economic Survey (Survei Sosio-Ekonomi Nasional, Susenas). All household indicators, such as mean per capita consumption, are our calculations from the Susenas.

Household consumption has been adjusted for spatial cost-of-living differences. To do this, provincial urban–rural adjustment factors are calculated as:

$$rpcexp = pcexp * (PL_{nat,2012} / PL_{i,t})$$

where *rpcexp* is household real (spatially adjusted) per capita consumption; *pcexp* is nominal per capita consumption; $PL_{nat,2012}$ is the population-weighted national poverty line in 2012; and $PL_{i,t}$ is the provincial urban or rural poverty line in year *t* in the area that the household resides in.

GRP data are from the national accounts, and local government revenue and expenditure data are from the Ministry of Finance. All are real in temporal terms.

Commodity-intensive districts are determined on the basis of the percentage of employment in mining or estate crops. Employment data are taken from the National Labour Force Survey (Survei Angkatan Kerja Nasional, Sakernas).

PART 2

Decentralization and governance

6 Twelve years of fiscal decentralization: a balance sheet

*Blane D. Lewis**

6.1 INTRODUCTION

The prevailing view among many policy makers, policy advisers and other interested observers in Indonesia is that decentralization has been somewhat of a disappointment. This assessment derives from the observation that local public service delivery has improved little, if at all, since the government began implementing its regional autonomy program in 2001, despite an apparently significant transfer of funds to provinces and districts to discharge their newfound responsibilities. A number of theories have been put forth to explain the seemingly meagre results of decentralization, each with its own set of policy reform prescriptions.

The main intent of this chapter is to review the experience with decentralization since 2001, to critically assess various explanations for the failure of regional autonomy to significantly improve local services and to gauge the prospects for reform going forward. First, the chapter provides a brief review of the history of fiscal decentralization in Indonesia (section 6.2). Next, it examines some of the empirical evidence on decentralized service delivery outcomes (section 6.3). It then discusses and appraises the standard rationales for poor service outcomes (section

* The author has served as an adviser to the Indonesian government on matters related to fiscal decentralization for many years, under the auspices of the Harvard Institute of International Development, the United States Agency for International Development and the World Bank, among others. The views in this chapter are the author's own and should not be attributed to any of the organizations for which he has worked.

6.4). In section 6.5, the chapter offers an alternative explanation for inadequate decentralized service delivery, and in section 6.6 it evaluates the near-term policy reform agenda for decentralization. The chapter concludes with a consideration of the likelihood of successful reform.

6.2   A BRIEF HISTORY OF FISCAL DECENTRALIZATION

Indonesia is a unitary country comprising central, provincial and local levels of government. Until 2001, the regional administration of public affairs operated through a hierarchical, multi-tiered and parallel system of deconcentrated central government agencies and nominally autonomous subnational units.[1] Throughout most of its history, Indonesia's public sector was counted among the most centralized in the world (Smoke and Lewis 1996; Lewis and Smoke 1998).

Many observers would date Indonesia's modern administrative and fiscal decentralization program to Law 5/1974 on Basic Principles on Administration in the Regions. This legislation did indeed provide a basis for greater involvement of decentralized subnational governments in the provision of those public services that existed at the time. In the early 1990s some implementing regulations were written and a pilot program for regional autonomy was undertaken, but little real progress was made in operationalizing the general principles outlined in the early law over the succeeding 25 years (Brodjonegoro and Asanuma 2000; Lewis 2002b).

Decentralization became more of a political imperative in the late 1990s, after the Suharto regime fell, and under the successive stewardships of Presidents Bacharuddin Jusuf Habibie and Abdurrahman Wahid. At that time, in the wake of East Timor's secession, decentralization was seen as a way of holding the country together. The impetus to move forward in a more assertive fashion derived from an important decree issued during a special session of the People's Consultative Assembly (Majelis Permusyawaratan Rakyat, MPR) in 1998. Under the MPR mandate, Indonesia embarked on an ambitious program of fiscal decentralization, perhaps one of the largest such experiments in the world (World Bank 2007).

The decentralization effort had its genesis in two laws, both promulgated in May 1999, one on administrative matters (Law 22/1999 on

---

1   In this chapter the term 'subnational' refers (collectively) to provinces and districts/municipalities. Districts/municipalities (or *kabupaten/kota* in the Indonesian language), which comprise the lowest tier of subnational government in Indonesia, are called 'local governments'.

Regional Government) and the other on fiscal and finance issues (Law 25/1999 on the Fiscal Balance between the Central Government and the Regions). In December 2000, the national parliament (Dewan Perwakilan Rakyat, DPR) passed an additional and essential piece of decentralization legislation on subnational government taxation, Law 34/2000 on Regional Taxes and Levies. In late 2004, Indonesia initiated a redesign of its basic decentralization framework by issuing revisions to the two major pieces of legislation: Law 32/2004 on Regional Government and Law 33/2004 on the Fiscal Balance between the Central Government and the Regions. In 2009, the DPR finalized an amendment to Law 34/2000 on subnational taxes (that is, Law 28/2009), completing the second-generation design of the decentralization system. The government is currently revisiting the design of its legal and regulatory system for decentralization yet again with a view to making improvements in the near future, some time after the presidential and general elections in 2014.

Administrative and fiscal decentralization of the public sector has been complemented by active developments in national and local-level democracy. Representatives of subnational parliaments (Dewan Perwakilan Rakyat Daerah, DPRD) have been popularly elected since 2001; these parliaments, in turn, elected subnational government executives. Since 2004, however, executive heads have been chosen through direct elections.

Current laws and regulations decentralize significant responsibilities to subnational governments, especially in the social and infrastructure sectors. Subnational expenditure now makes up about half of consolidated government spending net of interest payments and subsidies. Local (as opposed to provincial) governments carry out most subnational spending; local government expenditure makes up three-quarters of the total subnational spending (World Bank 2012).[2]

As in many developing countries, however, tax revenues in Indonesia remain very centralized (Lewis 2003b, 2003c). As a result, inter-governmental transfers dominate as a source of revenue for subnational governments, although they have almost complete discretion over how these transfers are spent (Lewis 2001, 2002a). The decentralization legislation also allows subnational governments to borrow for infrastructure development from a variety of sources: government, private financial institutions and capital markets.[3] All things considered, Indonesia has gone

---

2 This chapter focuses on local governments because of their relative importance in subnational fiscal affairs and service delivery.

3 See, for example, Lewis (2003a, 2007a), Lewis and Woodward (2010) and Petersen and Tirtosuharto (2013).

138   Blane D. Lewis

Figure 6.1   Local government expenditure and revenue, 2001–09

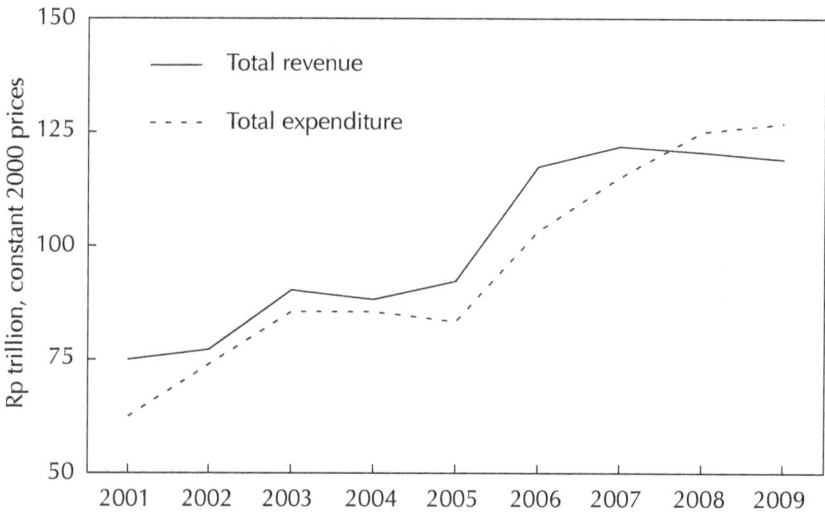

Source: Directorate General of Fiscal Balance, Ministry of Finance.

from one of the most fiscally centralized countries in the world to one of the most decentralized (Alm, Aten and Bahl 2001; World Bank 2007).

Figure 6.1 shows the changes to real aggregate local government spending and revenue between 2001 and 2009, the time period for which relevant subnational budget realization data are available.[4] Local government expenditure increased from 2001 to 2003 and then remained stable through 2005; spending then increased steadily until 2008 when it flattened out. Local government revenue followed a similar pattern until 2006, then remained fairly even until the end of the period.

The difference between total revenue and total expenditure in any given year indicates the annual local government surplus (or deficit). Figure 6.1 illustrates nicely the well-known build-up of fiscal reserves among local governments until 2007 (Lewis and Oosterman 2009). By 2008, however, total local government spending exceeded total own-source and transfer revenues, implying that local units had begun to draw down on their significant reserves.

Figure 6.2 shows local government bank deposits from 2001 until the end of 2012 and provides a different view of the accumulation of reserves at the local level. It illustrates two main points. First, it indicates that for

4 The lag in subnational fiscal data becoming available from the Ministry of Finance has increased considerably since 2001. The data for 2010, for example, are not expected to become available until late 2013 or early 2014.

Figure 6.2 Local government bank deposits, 2001–12

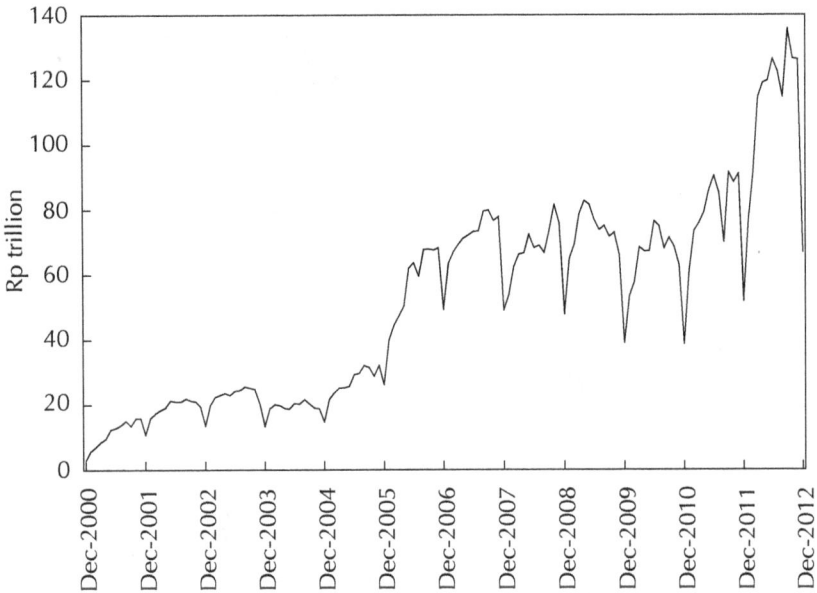

Source: Bank Indonesia.

any given fiscal year local governments tend to stockpile their revenue until the last quarter of the year, at which point they quickly deplete their available resources. This clearly shows the well-known tendency of local governments to delay a significant proportion of their spending until the last couple of months of the year.

Second, the figure shows the pattern of reserve accumulation across fiscal years. As can be seen, local governments saved considerably from 2001 through 2006, especially during the latter year. Local governments began to draw down on their reserves in 2008 (as indicated also in Figure 6.1), with the depletion lasting through 2010. The process of accumulation began again in 2011 and accelerated in 2012. The source of the rise in reserves in 2011 and 2012 seems to have been a significant increase in the general purpose block grant in those two years (Lewis and Smoke, forthcoming).

Total reserves are quite concentrated, especially in large urban centres and in districts rich in natural resources. Figure 6.3 shows the cumulative distribution of reserves across numbers of subnational governments;[5] it

---

5 The data, which come from Bank Indonesia, do not allow a breakdown between the provincial and district levels of governments.

Figure 6.3   *Cumulative distribution of bank deposits across subnational*
                governments, 2011

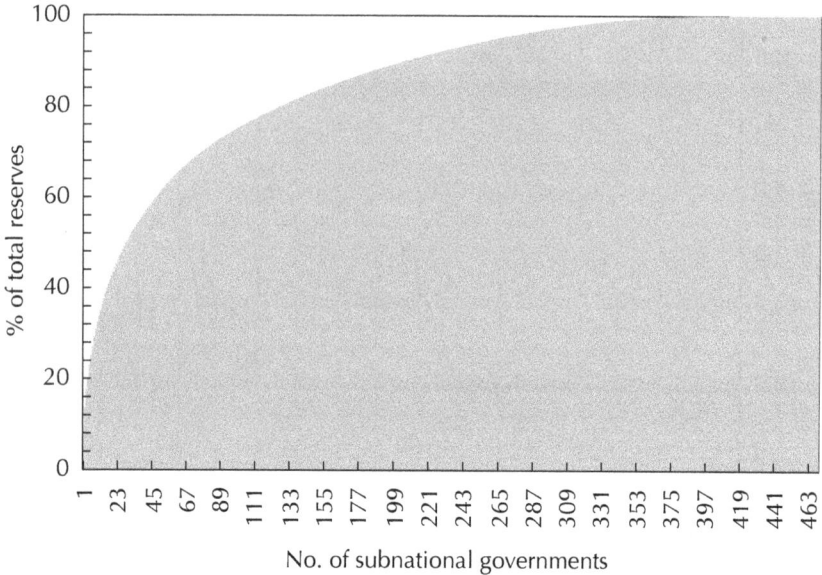

No. of subnational governments

Source: Bank Indonesia.

illustrates the concentration of reserves in a relatively small number of places. Table 6.1 provides a list of the top subnational government savers; the reserves of the 10 places listed in the table, all either large metropolitan cities or districts rich in natural resource revenues, comprise nearly one-third of total reserves.

In per capita terms, the reserves are clearly concentrated in natural resource-rich areas of the country. Figure 6.4 shows per capita reserves in 2010 and 2011 by island group and for the nation as a whole. Per capita reserves in Kalimantan are considerably larger than those found elsewhere and they increased significantly (by about 50 per cent in nominal terms) between 2010 and 2011.

Table 6.2 shows local government expenditure and revenue for 2001–09 by share of major budget category. In the most recent years for which data are available (2008–09), local governments spent just over a quarter of their expenditure budgets on general administration. Another 10 per cent was assigned to health, almost one-third to education and slightly less than a quarter to infrastructure. Local governments spent just under half of their budgets on personnel, about 15 per cent on goods and services (including maintenance) and around one-third on capital expenditures.

Table 6.1 Top subnational government savers, 2011 (Rp billion)

	Province	District/city	Reserves (Rp billion)	Cumulative reserves (Rp billion)	Cumulative (%)
1	DKI Jakarta	Central Jakarta	7,489.7	7,489.7	9.3
2	East Kalimantan	Samarinda city	3,509.5	10,999.3	13.7
3	West Java	Bandung city	3,096.4	14,095.7	17.6
4	Riau	Pekanbaru city	2,086.9	16,182.5	20.2
5	East Java	Surabaya city	2,085.6	18,268.1	22.8
6	East Kalimantan	Kutai Kartanegara district	1,813.5	20,081.6	25.0
7	Riau	Bengkalis district	1,652.9	21,734.5	27.1
8	Aceh	Banda Aceh city	1,606.8	23,341.3	29.1
9	Papua	Jayapura city	1,338.9	24,680.2	30.7
10	South Kalimantan	Banjarmasin city	1,174.5	25,854.8	32.2

Source: Bank Indonesia.

Figure 6.4 Subnational per capita reserves by island group, 2010 and 2011

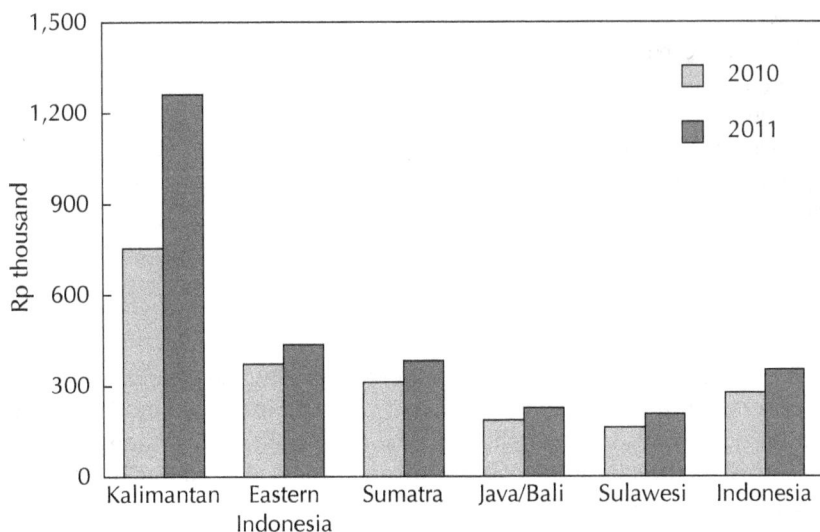

Source: Bank Indonesia.

Table 6.2   Local government expenditure and revenue by major budget category, 2001–09 (%)

	2001	2002	2003	2004	2005	2006	2007	2008	2009
Expenditure type									
By sector									
General administration	32.2	29.4	33.1	37.3	39.7	43.5	31.4	25.7	26.7
Health	6.1	6.4	6.6	6.9	7.0	6.6	8.7	9.7	9.7
Education	35.7	35.0	32.3	33.6	30.7	24.7	29.1	29.5	31.0
Infrastructure	12.0	13.1	15.0	12.1	12.8	15.1	19.2	24.7	22.0
Other	14.0	16.2	13.1	10.1	9.8	10.1	11.6	10.5	10.6
	100.0	100.0	100.0	100.0	100.0	100.0	100.0	100.0	100.0
By economic classification									
Staff	55.2	49.8	47.2	52.5	49.4	42.0	45.9	44.5	44.0
Goods & services	18.4	20.9	20.3	19.4	20.8	22.1	17.1	17.4	14.8
Capital	17.9	19.7	22.4	18.3	20.7	27.1	29.3	29.8	32.5
Other	8.5	9.7	10.1	9.9	9.1	8.8	7.7	8.3	8.6
	100.0	100.0	100.0	100.0	100.0	100.0	100.0	100.0	100.0
Revenue type									
Own-source revenue	6.7	8.0	7.6	8.3	7.8	6.8	7.7	7.3	7.3
Inter-governmental transfers									
Shared tax revenue	7.4	8.1	8.9	11.2	11.0	10.5	8.7	8.6	8.7
Shared natural resource revenue	10.9	10.2	9.6	7.2	12.6	10.1	8.2	9.9	8.6
General purpose grant	70.3	67.9	62.8	62.1	55.8	60.8	60.5	57.7	58.5
Special purpose grant	1.1	0.8	3.0	3.0	3.1	5.7	6.9	7.3	8.1
Other	3.6	5.1	8.1	8.2	9.6	6.2	8.0	9.2	8.7
	100.0	100.0	100.0	100.0	100.0	100.0	100.0	100.0	100.0

Source: Directorate General of Fiscal Balance, Ministry of Finance.

Expenditure shares fluctuated somewhat during the period. The share of general administration declined, that of health increased modestly and that of education dropped slightly. The most noteworthy changes were for infrastructure; its share of expenditure increased by about 10 percentage points between 2001 and 2009.[6] The share of personnel spending

6 Infrastructure spending comprises both capital and routine spending. Capital spending on infrastructure dominates routine spending in the sector. From

declined during the period, as did that of goods and services, while the importance of capital expenditures grew quite significantly.

As Table 6.2 indicates, inter-governmental transfers are by far the main source of revenue for local governments, comprising over 90 per cent of total local budgets. These transfers are of four main types: shared tax revenues, shared non-tax revenues (from natural resources), general purpose grants (Dana Alokasi Umum, DAU) and special purpose grants (Dana Alokasi Khusus, DAK). The DAU is quantitatively the most important transfer, making up almost 60 per cent of total local government revenue. Shared tax revenue and shared non-tax revenue each comprise about 9 per cent of total revenue, while the DAK makes up about 8 per cent of the total. Own-source revenue contributes only around 7 per cent of local government revenue.

Revenue shares have also changed somewhat over the period. The share of own-source revenue essentially remained flat during the period studied here, while that of shared tax revenue increased modestly and that of natural resource revenue decreased. The DAU has exhibited the most change; its share fell from 70 per cent in 2001 to less than 60 per cent in 2009. The share of the DAK, meanwhile, rose from just 1 per cent to about 8 per cent over the time frame.

6.3   DECENTRALIZED SERVICE DELIVERY OUTCOMES: A SYNOPSIS

When decentralization began in 2001, the general and strong expectation was that local public service delivery would much improve (Lewis 2005). This expectation was based on standard fiscal decentralization theory, which suggests that proximity of local governments to their constituents allows the former to better identify and respond to the service delivery needs of the latter (at least when compared to the central government). The effectiveness of decentralized service delivery has fallen short of expectations, however. Service delivery outcomes in major sectors such as health, education and infrastructure have proven decidedly mixed, at best.

Immunization rates have increased quite rapidly throughout much of the country but progress in reducing both child malnutrition and maternal mortality has stagnated in recent years (World Bank 2012). Net

---

2001 to 2009, for example, it made up just over 70 per cent of the total (not shown in Table 6.2). See Lewis and Oosterman (2010) and Lewis (2013a) for a discussion of capital spending and the impact of various transfers on such expenditure.

school enrolment rates have risen at all levels (except primary school, where rates were already near 100 per cent) but the quality of education remains problematic. While Indonesian students' reading scores on the Programme for International Student Assessment (PISA) examination improved steadily between 2000 and 2009, their maths scores did not advance and their science scores actually deteriorated (World Bank 2012).

Perhaps most problematic is the lack of improvement in infrastructure services. Some progress has been made on a few service delivery indicators; district road length, for example, has grown on average by 3.5 per cent per year since 2001. But road quality has deteriorated; about 40 per cent of district roads are currently classified as in poor condition, up from 35 per cent in 2001. Access to water services has also declined since decentralization; the percentage of households with access to safe water has actually dropped from 50 per cent to 48 per cent (World Bank 2013).

Indonesian businesses consistently identify the poor quality of infrastructure as a severe constraint on their operations. A recent survey by Regional Autonomy Watch (2011) found that nearly 40 per cent of enterprises throughout the country identified infrastructure as the single most important restriction on their business activities. (No other constraint was cited by more than 15 per cent of respondents.) Firms reported difficulties with most types of traditional infrastructure but singled out roads, and to a lesser extent power, as particularly problematic. Thus poor infrastructure is not only a 'consumer service' delivery problem in Indonesia but also one that constrains economic growth (Day and Lewis 2013; Lewis 2013b; Lewis and Niazi, forthcoming).

Indonesian public services also do not fare well from an international comparative perspective. The nation generally performs in the middle range of countries in the region on most health and education delivery indicators – typically better than Cambodia and India, for example, but worse than Thailand, Vietnam and the Philippines. But it ranks among the worst-performing countries in the world in terms of the quality of its infrastructure and, within the region, better only than the Philippines (World Bank 2013).

6.4   STANDARD RATIONALES FOR DEFICIENT SERVICE OUTCOMES: A CRITICAL REVIEW

A number of reasons have been offered to explain Indonesia's unsatisfactory local service delivery outcomes. Not surprisingly, perhaps, the explanations offered by the various institutions involved in the delivery of services differ considerably. Subnational governments and some central line agencies, such as the Ministry of Education and the Ministry of Public Works, argue that levels of provincial and district funding are inadequate. (The subnational governments want larger untied grants while the central agencies want more funds under their own control, of course.) Other central government departments, such as the Ministry of Finance and the Ministry of Home Affairs, claim that a lack of sub-national implementation capacity is the main constraining factor. Finally, many international agencies, including the World Bank, focus on various inadequacies in the inter-governmental fiscal system to explain the poor outcomes.

Levels of funding

The argument that regions, in general, lack sufficient funds to deliver improved public services seems implausible. Transfers to subnational governments now make up approximately one-half of the state budget, net of subsidies and interest payments, or about 6 per cent of GDP. It is hard to see how central–local transfers could be much larger than they are given the country's current fiscal circumstances. Qualitative evidence suggests that Indonesian local governments are better funded than their counterparts in most countries in the region (Lewis and Searle 2011). Although it is difficult to obtain hard data with which to compare a wide range of countries in the region, recent analysis shows that transfers to third-tier subnational governments make up only 0.4 per cent of GDP in India and 3 per cent in the Philippines, compared with approximately 5 per cent of GDP in Indonesia (Lewis 2013f). All things considered, it would appear that Indonesian local governments, in general, have suf-ficient funds to deliver services at a better standard than they currently do.[7]

A more credible proposition is that subnational governments spend their funds in an inefficient and ineffective manner. They spend too much on administration and personnel, for example, and not enough on actual service delivery. Recent analysis shows that administrative spending by districts in Indonesia, which amounts to more than one-quarter of total budgetary expenditure, far exceeds international best practice, which posits reasonable administrative spending of less than 5 per cent of budgets (Lewis 2006; Sjahrir, Kis-Katos and Schulze 2013). Other research implies that local government spending on personnel has a positive effect on education and health service outcomes only up to

---

7 Of course, given distributional problems related to transfers, it may be that some districts do not have enough funds to deliver services well. The argu-ment here, however, is that most local governments are sufficiently financed.

some point, beyond which the impact is negative (Lewis 2013d).[8] More broadly, the general level of spending appears to have little or no effect on a wide range of service outcomes (Lewis and Pattinasarany 2011; World Bank 2012).

There is one dimension of the funding inadequacy argument that appears more legitimate, however, and that concerns subnational loan finance. Subnational governments in Indonesia have borrowed exceedingly little both before and since decentralization. In real terms, total subnational borrowing – including that by water enterprises (*perusahaan daerah air minum*, PDAM) – over the past 35 years has amounted to less than 1 per cent of current GDP (Lewis 2007a). Contrast this with the situation in the Philippines, for example, where local governments have borrowed about 1 per cent of GDP per year in recent years (World Bank 2013). Of course, part of the explanation lies in the fact that the Philippines has dedicated financial institutions to lend to local governments for the construction of infrastructure whereas Indonesia does not. In any case, inadequate borrowing is not typically what proponents of the funding shortfall argument have in mind. In fact, subnational governments in Indonesia continue to show limited interest in borrowing for capital development – they typically (and unrealistically) prefer to have all their funds in grant form (Lewis and Woodward 2010).

Capacity

The issue of subnational implementation capacity is somewhat less straightforward to examine than the funding question. It is notoriously difficult to define and measure capacity well; there is no hard evidence in Indonesia that can be used to inform the debate. Indonesia is still a developing nation, so the capacity of subnational governments to deliver services tends not to be as high as it is in more modern countries. At the same time, experience shows that there is a great deal of variation across subnational governments in Indonesia, with the best among them being quite well run (Lewis 2010).

A specific illustration often used to bolster claims of a lack of capacity concerns the subnational build-up of fiscal reserves. The argument made is that subnational governments have insufficient capacity to spend even the funds they are allocated. However, as was shown in section 6.2 of this chapter, reserves tend to be concentrated in a relatively small number of places. This fact argues against the generality of the claim. Moreover, it is not clear that the fiscal reserves are in any way excessive, even

---

8 The point at which the effect of spending becomes negative was estimated to be around the 60th percentile of current district spending.

for those local governments that do maintain significant balances. It has been demonstrated, for example, that a not-implausible decrease in the price of oil could reduce revenue-sharing transfers to oil-rich local governments significantly; and that these reduced transfers could lead to the total elimination of fiscal reserves in a relatively short time, if local governments were to draw down on those reserves in order to maintain spending at a constant level (Lewis and Oosterman 2009). This calls into question the logic of even trying to spend all funds that are allocated.

Still, one may easily agree with the argument that a lack of capacity surely constrains local policy development and program execution to some extent, in some places. Deficiencies in local government planning and financial management (and, especially, the links between the two) merit some mention in this regard (Lewis 2010). The important question about potential capacity shortfalls, however, is to what extent they occur and where. The view here is that capacity constraints are not binding for a very large number of places. Otherwise put, the vast majority of subnational governments could deliver better quality services now with the capacity they already have.

Inter-governmental framework

A number of potential difficulties with the current inter-governmental fiscal arrangements have been raised over the years. Perhaps the most frequently discussed are the limited and improper role of provinces; unclear and unsuitable expenditure assignments; inadequate tax decentralization and own-source revenue mobilization; and the inappropriate structure and design of various inter-governmental transfers. Specific issues directly related to these areas of difficulty have been thoroughly reviewed elsewhere,[9] and recapitulation of the various arguments, conclusions and proposals for reform is beyond the scope of the current chapter. The discussion below focuses instead on two additional and broader issues that cut across each of the aforementioned problems: the 'one-size-fits-all' nature of the inter-governmental system, and the nearly complete dearth of fiscal incentives to encourage improved performance at the local level. These cross-cutting issues arguably subsume most other concerns.

9　The role of provinces is discussed in Ferrazzi, Dwiyanto and Effendi (2013); expenditure assignments in Lewis and Chakeri (2003) and Adrison, Martinez-Vazquez and Nurhalim (2013); tax assignments and own-source revenue mobilization in Lewis (2007b), Lewis and Sjahrir (2009) and Smoke and Sugana (2013); and inter-governmental transfer design and implementation in Lewis (2001, 2002a, 2002b), Shah, Qibthiyyah and Dita (2012), Agustina et al. (2013) and Lewis and Pattinasarany (2013).

It is unmistakably the case that the inter-governmental system treats local governments as if they were broadly similar entities. Expenditure and tax assignments are essentially the same for all districts, and the allocation of transfers (with the obvious exception of natural resource revenue sharing) tends not to differentiate sufficiently among types of local governments. Large municipalities, small and medium-sized cities, and rural districts are all treated more or less equivalently from a fiscal point of view. This aspect of the system clearly has some negative impact on the proper determination of subnational fiscal needs and capacities and therefore on the appropriate resourcing of provincial and local governments (that is, from an equalization standpoint). Its effect on actual service delivery is less clear, however, since level of funding appears to be weakly related to the quality of services.

The second issue of incentives in the inter-governmental system, or the lack thereof, has received significant attention in the past few years (Lewis and Smoke 2009, 2012). Two separate concerns may be identified in this regard. One relates to the so-called inadvertent or perverse incentives that exist in the framework, and the other to constructive incentives that might purposely be embedded in the system. The conventional wisdom is that the system needs to be redesigned to expunge perverse incentives, which negatively influence service delivery outcomes. In addition, many policy advisers have advocated that the government should incorporate more positive or constructive incentives into the system through the development and use of performance grants.

Recent studies cast doubt on at least some of the conventional wisdom, however. Lewis (2013e) and Lewis and Smoke (forthcoming), for example, argue that there is no empirical evidence to suggest that the magnitude of inter-governmental transfers, in general, provides a disincentive for local governments to increase their own-source revenues, as many observers have suggested. Neither does the evidence support the widely held assertion that the DAU, in particular, strongly discourages own-source revenue generation. On the other hand, the evidence is at least consistent with the assumption that the DAU provides an incentive for local governments to increase local personnel spending. However, since local governments probably want to spend funds on staff salaries and allowances anyway, any specific incentives in the DAU to promote such increased spending are likely to be redundant.

Research does seem to support the orthodox point of view on performance grants, at least tentatively. Indonesia is currently conducting two main experiments with inter-governmental performance grants: the DAK reimbursement scheme, and the water and sanitation grant (*hibah*). These programs have been in operation for a couple of years, and preliminary impact evaluations have now been carried out for both

(Lewis 2013c, 2013g). The initial evidence suggests mixed but promising results.

The DAK reimbursement scheme appears to have led to improved reporting on project implementation in a limited number of circumstances and to more stimulative local government capital spending. The water and sanitation initiative seems to have resulted in some increased local government equity investments in water enterprises (PDAM) and in more household water connections, especially for the poor. Beyond that, however, the Indonesian experience demonstrates that the design of successful performance grants is a challenging exercise and that positive effects are not easily achieved. Expectations about the impact of performance grants should therefore be measured carefully against the real prospects for success (Lewis and Smoke 2009, 2012).

Summary

The findings of this section do not support the argument that subnational governments are insufficiently funded, in general, although they should be given better access to finance for local infrastructure development. The claim that lack of subnational management capacity severely constrains service delivery also seems exaggerated, for all but a limited number of places. The uniform treatment of heterogeneous subnational units in policy design and implementation is clearly a problem for the proper resourcing of provinces and districts. The extent to which this approach affects the quality of local service delivery is unclear, however, since it appears that the level of funding has little to do with service outcomes. Perhaps it is best to think of this dimension of decentralization policy as more of a problem-in-waiting. The assertion that perverse incentives in inter-governmental transfers have major deleterious local fiscal effects seems mostly unfounded. Finally, the limited initial experience with inter-governmental performance grants appears positive in terms of encouraging better service delivery, although care must be taken not to overstate the likely positive impacts. In any case, while the legitimacy of some of the above obstacles is acknowledged, taken together they would seem insufficient to explain the meagre outcomes for local public service delivery under decentralization.

6.5 AN ALTERNATIVE EXPLANATION FOR WEAK SERVICE OUTCOMES

An alternative explanation for poor service delivery outcomes would focus on the lack of downward accountability of local governments towards their constituents (Lewis 2010; Wihardja 2013). It is well known from international experience that weak accountability and poor public services go hand in hand (Lewis 2010). Accountability in this context actually has two separate dimensions: an appeal from citizens for improvements to service quality, and a response by local governments to meet constituents' demands. Appeals from citizens implicitly presuppose in the first instance the existence of some reasonable measure of dissatisfaction with the status quo.

In Indonesia it turns out that citizens actually seem quite satisfied with the quality of local public service delivery. A fairly large survey found that 78 per cent, 90 per cent and 85 per cent of respondents were at least somewhat satisfied with the quality of local administrative, health and education services respectively. Less than 30 per cent of the randomly selected households in the study indicated that they wanted better administrative and social services and were willing to pay for them. In fact, only 7 per cent of households had ever formally complained about the quality of local government services. Of those that had not complained, more than 90 per cent said it was because they had no complaints about service quality (Lewis and Pattinasarany 2009). Other studies have reported similarly high levels of satisfaction with local public services in Indonesia (Research Triangle Institute 2006).[10]

So it would seem that the lack of downward accountability at the local level in Indonesia may in large measure be a function of insufficient citizen demand for higher service quality. This, in turn, provides a clear and robust explanation for the lack of observed improvements in local public service quality under decentralization. That is, if citizens are already reasonably satisfied with the quality of service delivery, there would seem to be little reason for local governments to strive to improve it. Of course, enhancing the quality of service delivery might reasonably be taken as a local government obligation, but most local officials in Indonesia apparently do not see it as such.

6.6   NEAR-TERM POLICY REFORM AGENDA

A reasonable policy agenda could be derived from the preceding discussion of constraints on improving local service delivery. Such an agenda

---

10 These high levels of satisfaction may be due in part to a courtesy bias among respondents. In the present context, Lewis and Pattinasarany (2009) conclude that while such a bias probably is present, it does not reverse the conclusion that Indonesians are quite satisfied with the quality of local public services. They argue that a more likely explanation for citizens' high levels of satisfaction relates to their low expectations of service quality.

might include the development of a special purpose vehicle for lending to subnational governments for infrastructure as well as specific, well-targeted capacity-building efforts. Policy makers might also focus on restructuring the system to account for the considerable heterogeneity that exists among local governments in Indonesia. This would entail reforming expenditure assignments, tax assignments and transfer allocation methods across local governments of different types: large municipalities, small and medium-sized cities, and predominately rural areas, for example. In addition, given the recent positive experience with inter-governmental incentive programs, the central government might expand its efforts to develop and implement performance grants. It is recognized, of course, that executing this agenda would be a major undertaking.

In any case, this does not seem to be what the Ministry of Finance has in mind, judging by current draft revisions of Law 33/2004 on the Fiscal Balance between the Central Government and the Regions. Instead, the ministry seems to be opting for a minimalist approach to reform of the inter-governmental system. Its line of attack implicitly assumes that for the most part the inter-governmental fiscal system is working quite well; in its view, tinkering at the margin may be called for but there is no need for a major overhaul. Many officials may recognize that there are problems with service delivery, of course, but they do not seem to believe that such difficulties are the fault of the central–provincial–local fiscal framework. The prevailing strategic view is that it is the ministry's job to deliver the funds to meet stated grant objectives, which focus largely on equalizing fiscal capacity across subnational governments of similar types (that is, provinces and districts), and to a lesser extent assuring neutrality in allocations, and that when this happens local public service delivery will take care of itself.

6.7   CONCLUSIONS: PROGNOSIS FOR SUCCESSFUL REFORM

There are two main problems with the Ministry of Finance's stance on the state of inter-governmental fiscal relations. First, the system does not perform particularly well even by its own standards – fiscal equalization and neutrality. It is well known that the current system of transfers results in wide disparities in resource allocation;[11] and the discussion above on perverse incentives suggests that the system is less neutral than it might be (at least with regard to staff expenditures). Second, principles of fiscal equalization and neutrality in grant design and allocation work

---

11   See, for example, Lewis (2002b), Arze (2005), Hofman et al. (2006), Fadliya and McLeod (2010) and World Bank (2012).

well in terms of assuring reasonable service delivery outcomes only in situations where there is strong local demand to guide (and insist on) the supply of public services. As noted above, this seems not to be the case in Indonesia. If the Ministry of Finance cannot be counted on to take a more proactive approach to inter-governmental fiscal policy design and implementation along the lines discussed above, then there is not much hope in the short term that service delivery outcomes will improve, even at the margin.

Of course, the other possibility is that the quality of local services in Indonesia is already good enough and that there is no real need for improvement. The objective evidence seems to indicate that this is not true, but on the other hand, it appears as if Indonesian citizens themselves are reasonably satisfied with the amount and quality of local service delivery. At least, they report that they are content and they declare that they are unwilling to pay for improvements to public services. If this is the situation, then Indonesians may already have the decentralized system of government that they want and deserve.

The view in this chapter is that the status quo is not acceptable, however. As such, it would seem that perhaps the most important initiative that could be undertaken to reform the fiscal decentralization system would be to convince the citizens of Indonesia that they deserve better and to encourage them to express their demands to their district leaders. Only then will local governments be forced to make good on the theoretical benefits of decentralization. This is clearly an objective that can only be realized in the long term.

REFERENCES

Adrison, V., J. Martinez-Vazquez and E. Nurhalim (2013) 'The reform of expenditure assignments at the local level in Indonesia', in *New Visions for Decentralization in Indonesia*, World Bank, Jakarta.

Agustina, C.D., A. Ehtihsam, D. Nugroho and H. Siagian (2013) 'Political economy of natural resource revenue sharing in Indonesia', in *New Visions for Decentralization in Indonesia*, World Bank, Jakarta.

Alm, J., R. Aten and R. Bahl (2001) 'Can Indonesia decentralise successfully? Plans, problems and prospects', *Bulletin of Indonesian Economic Studies*, 37(1): 83–102.

Arze, J. (2005) 'Fiscal equalization impact of changes to DAU allocation mechanism', unpublished paper, World Bank, Jakarta.

Brodjonegoro, B. and S. Asanuma (2000) 'Regional autonomy and fiscal decentralization in democratic Indonesia', *Hitotsubashi Journal of Economics*, 41(2): 111–22.

Day, J. and B.D. Lewis (2013) 'Beyond univariate measurement of spatial autocorrelation: disaggregated spillover effects for Indonesia', *Annals of GIS*, 19(3): 169–85.

Fadliya and R.H. McLeod (2010) 'Fiscal transfers to regional governments in Indonesia', Working Paper No. 2010/14, Crawford School of Economics and Government, Australian National University, Canberra.

Ferrazzi, G., A. Dwiyanto and C. Effendi (2013) 'The future role of the province in Indonesia in public service delivery and financing: understanding and assessing options', in *New Visions for Decentralization in Indonesia*, World Bank, Jakarta.

Hofman, B., Kadjatmiko, K. Kaiser and B.S. Sjahrir (2006) 'Evaluating fiscal equalization in Indonesia', unpublished paper, World Bank, Jakarta.

Lewis, B.D. (2001) 'The new Indonesian equalisation transfer', *Bulletin of Indonesian Economic Studies*, 37(3): 325–43.

Lewis, B.D. (2002a) 'The general purpose grant', in B. Resosudarmo, A. Alisjahbana and B. Brodjonegoro (eds) *Indonesia's Sustainable Development in a Decentralization Era*, Indonesian Regional Science Association, Bandung.

Lewis, B.D. (2002b) 'Indonesia', in P. Smoke and Y.-H. Kim (eds) *Intergovernmental Transfers in Asia: Current Practice and Challenges in the Future*, Asian Development Bank, Manila.

Lewis, B.D. (2003a) 'Local government borrowing and repayment in Indonesia: does fiscal capacity matter?', *World Development*, 31(6): 1,047–63.

Lewis, B.D. (2003b) 'Property tax in Indonesia: measuring and explaining administrative (under-) performance', *Public Administration and Development*, 23: 227–39.

Lewis, B.D. (2003c) 'Tax and charge creation by regional governments under fiscal decentralisation: estimates and explanations', *Bulletin of Indonesian Economic Studies*, 39(2): 177–92.

Lewis, B.D. (2005) 'Indonesian local government spending, taxing and saving: an explanation of pre- and post-decentralization fiscal outcomes', *Asian Economic Journal*, 19(3): 291–317.

Lewis, B.D. (2006) 'Local government taxation: an analysis of administrative cost inefficiency', *Bulletin of Indonesian Economic Studies*, 42(2): 213–33.

Lewis, B.D. (2007a) 'On-lending in Indonesia: past performance and future prospects', *Bulletin of Indonesian Economic Studies*, 43(1): 35–57.

Lewis, B.D. (2007b) 'Revisiting the price of residential land in Jakarta', *Urban Studies*, 44(11): 2,179–94.

Lewis, B.D. (2010) 'Indonesian fiscal decentralization: accountability deferred', *International Journal of Public Administration*, 33(12): 648–57.

Lewis, B.D. (2013a) 'Local government capital spending in Indonesia: impact of intergovernmental fiscal transfers', *Public Budgeting and Finance*, 33(1): 76–94.

Lewis, B.D. (2013b) 'Urbanization and economic growth in Indonesia: good news, bad news and (possible) local government mitigation', *Regional Studies*, available at http://rsa.tandfonline.com/doi/abs/10.1080/00343404.2012.748980?journalCode=cres20.

Lewis, B.D. (2013c) 'DAK reimbursement performance grant impact analysis: district counterpart funding, reporting, and capital spending', policy note prepared for World Bank, Jakarta.

Lewis, B.D. (2013d) 'Explaining district education and health outcomes in Indonesia', analytical note prepared for World Bank, Jakarta.

Lewis, B.D. (2013e) 'Intergovernmental transfers and perverse incentives in Indonesia: unmet assumptions, unsatisfactory recommendations', policy note prepared for World Bank, Jakarta.

Lewis, B.D. (2013f) 'Municipal revenues, expenditures, and access to infrastructure services in India', background paper prepared for South Asia Urbanization Flagship, World Bank, Washington DC.

Lewis, B.D. (2013g) 'Water *hibah* impact: local government investments in PDAM and the establishment of household water connections', report prepared for Indonesian Infrastructure Initiative (IndII), Jakarta.

Lewis, B.D. and J. Chakeri (2003) 'Central development spending in the regions post-decentralisation', *Bulletin of Indonesian Economic Studies*, 40(3): 379–94.

Lewis, B.D. and T. Niazi (forthcoming) 'Fiscal decentralization in Indonesia: local infrastructure impact and finance', in Asian Development Bank, *Subnational Public Sector Finance and Financial Management in Asia*, Asian Development Bank, Manila.

Lewis, B.D. and A. Oosterman (2009) 'The impact of decentralization on subnational government fiscal slack in Indonesia', *Public Budgeting and Finance*, 29(2): 27–47.

Lewis, B.D. and A. Oosterman (2010) 'Subnational government capital spending in Indonesia: level, structure and financing', *Public Administration and Development*, 31(3): 135–228.

Lewis, B.D. and D. Pattinasarany (2009) 'Determining citizen satisfaction with local public education in Indonesia', *Growth and Change*, 40(1): 85–115.

Lewis, B.D. and D. Pattinasarany (2011) 'The cost of primary education in Indonesia: do schools need more money?', *Education Economics*, 19(4): 397–410.

Lewis, B.D. and D. Pattinasarany (2013) 'A new intergovernmental capital grant for Indonesia: a polemic in support of economic growth', in *New Visions for Decentralization in Indonesia*, World Bank, Jakarta.

Lewis, B.D. and B. Searle (2011) 'Asia-Pacific', in United Cities and Local Governments (ed.) *Local Government Finance: The Challenges of the 21st Century*, Edward Elgar, Cheltenham.

Lewis, B.D. and B.S. Sjahrir (2009) 'Local tax effects on the business climate', in N. McCulloch (ed.) *Rural Investment Climate in Indonesia*, Institute for Southeast Asian Studies, Singapore.

Lewis, B.D. and P. Smoke (1998) 'Reply to Beier and Ferrazzi', *World Development*, 26(12): 2,213–17.

Lewis, B.D. and P. Smoke (2009) 'Incorporating subnational performance incentives in the Indonesian intergovernmental framework', in National Tax Association (ed.), *NTA Proceedings from the 101st Annual Conference in Philadelphia, PA*, National Tax Association, Washington DC.

Lewis, B.D. and P. Smoke (2012) 'Incentives for better local service delivery: international experience and relevance for Indonesia', in *Fiscal Decentralization in Indonesia a Decade after the Big Bang*, Ministry of Finance, Jakarta.

Lewis, B.D. and P. Smoke (forthcoming) 'Intergovernmental transfers in Indonesia: local incentives and responses', *Fiscal Studies*.

Lewis, B.D. and D. Woodward (2010) 'Restructuring Indonesia's sub-national public debt: reform or reversion?', *Bulletin of Indonesia Economic Studies*, 46(1): 65–78.

Petersen, J. and D. Tirtosuharto (2013) 'Capital financing by Indonesian local governments: will subnational bonds (finally) play a part?', in *New Visions for Decentralization in Indonesia*, World Bank, Jakarta.

Regional Autonomy Watch (2011) 'Local economic governance: a survey of business operators in 245 districts/municipalities in Indonesia, 2011', Regional Autonomy Watch and Asia Foundation, Jakarta.

Research Triangle Institute (2006) 'Government opinion polling summary report', unpublished paper, USAID Local Government Support Project, Research Triangle Institute, Research Triangle Park, North Carolina, November.

Shah, A., R. Qibthiyyah and A. Dita (2012) 'General purpose central–provincial-local transfers (DAU) in Indonesia: from gap filling to ensuring fair access to essential public services for all', Policy Research Working Paper No. 6075, World Bank, Jakarta, June.

Sjahrir, B.S., K. Kis-Katos and G.G. Schulze (2013) 'Administrative overspending in Indonesian districts: the role of local politics', Discussion Paper Series No. 24, Department of International Economic Policy, University of Freiburg, Freiburg, July.

Smoke, P. and B.D. Lewis (1996) 'Fiscal decentralization: a new approach to an old idea', *World Development*, 24(8): 1,281–99.

Smoke, P. and R. Sugana (2013) 'Subnational own-source revenues and shared taxes in Indonesia: taking stock and looking forward', in *New Visions for Decentralization in Indonesia*, World Bank, Jakarta.

Wihardja, M.M. (2013) 'Political and institutional obstacles to delivering public goods and services', draft report, World Bank, Jakarta.

World Bank (2007) *Decentralizing Indonesia*, World Bank, Jakarta.

World Bank (2012) 'Indonesia subnational public expenditure review: optimizing subnational performance for better services and faster growth', World Bank, Jakarta.

World Bank (2013) 'Subnational debt policy technical assistance', World Bank, Manila.

7 Local governance and development outcomes

*Arianto A. Patunru and Erman A. Rahman**

7.1 INTRODUCTION

Improved local governance has been the spirit of decentralization in Indonesia. Enacted not long after the start of the *reformasi* era in 1998, and effective since 2001, Law 22/1999 on Regional Government explicitly stated that democratic principles and public participation would be the basis of regional autonomy. The law also referred to various decrees issued by the People's Consultative Assembly (Majelis Permusyawaratan Rakyat, MPR) in 1998 to reform governance and counter corruption. The revised law on regional government (Law 32/2004) continues to emphasise the importance of community empowerment, grassroots participation and democratic principles to accelerate people's welfare and improve regional competitiveness.

Globally, good governance is believed to be the main path to sustainable economic growth and improvements in welfare.[1] In Indonesia, a number of studies have examined the relationship between the quality of governance and economic growth.[2] This chapter complements those studies by analysing the correlation between various local governance indicators – economic, budget allocation and public sector financial management – and development outcomes, with the latter defined with ref-

* We thank Achmad Taufik, Boedi Rheza, Yuna Farhan and Ronaldo Oktaviano for data assistance.

1 See, for example, the papers in Abed and Gupta (2002) and Rodrik (2003).
2 See, for example, Brodjonegoro (2009), McCulloch and Malesky (2011), Pepinsky and Wihardja (2011) and Pambudhi (2013), as well as McCulloch and Malesky in Chapter 9 of this volume.

erence to household-level expenditures and the Human Development Index (HDI).

Section 7.2 discusses recent developments in local governance, including key reforms to lift standards, and describes the current state of public sector financial management. Section 7.3 focuses on issues related to local budget policy and execution, and section 7.4 provides a brief overview of levels of development across the country. Section 7.5 dwells on the correlation between economic and social outcomes, good governance indicators, budget policy indicators and administrative characteristics. The chapter concludes by offering some policy implications.

7.2   RECENT DEVELOPMENTS IN LOCAL GOVERNANCE

More than a decade after decentralization, it is not clear that the quality of local economic governance has improved. This is the main conclusion from two datasets derived from surveys of businesses conducted by Regional Autonomy Watch (Komite Pemantauan Pelaksanaan Otonomi Daerah, KPPOD) and the Asia Foundation in four provinces: East Java, West Nusa Tenggara and East Nusa Tenggara (as part of nationwide surveys conducted in 2007 and 2010–11) and Aceh (which was surveyed separately in 2008 and 2010) (KPPOD and Asia Foundation 2008a, 2008b, 2010, 2011).[3] These were the only four provinces to be surveyed twice, allowing comparison of the progress of local economic governance over time.

As Table 7.1 shows, no single province performed markedly better or worse on the various indicators of local economic governance identified in the surveys. In general, the performance of districts (*kabupaten/kota*) in East Java improved over time, while that of the districts in Aceh deteriorated.[4] This was not the case for all indicators, however: the performance of the districts in East Java worsened in terms of anti-corruption measures by the district head, security issues and the provision of business development programs; while that of the districts in Aceh improved in terms of ease of getting access to land, time to repair roads and the provision of business development programs. Interestingly, in spite of their geographical proximity, the two Nusa Tenggara provinces moved in opposite directions on some indicators. For instance, the performance

---

3 During the course of the surveys, KPPOD and the Asia Foundation interviewed businesses in 444 of the then 491 districts and municipalities, in 32 of the then 33 provinces (all but Jakarta).

4 Unless indicated otherwise, 'districts' refers to both districts (*kabupaten*) and municipalities (*kota*).

Table 7.1 Comparison of performance of districts in four provinces on selected local economic governance variables

Variable	Aceh		East Java		West Nusa Tenggara		East Nusa Tenggara	
	2008	2010	2007	2010–11	2007	2010–11	2007	2010–11
Ease of gaining access to land (% difficult or very difficult)	48	29	39	15	28	21	36	46
Land access constraints as an obstacle to doing business (% big or very big)	8	18	4	3	16	9	6	3
Perception of the quality of roads (% bad or very bad)	38	33	28	24	35	42	41	66
Perception of the quality of electricity supply (% bad or very bad)	35	73	10	7	33	42	48	48
Perception of the quality of water supply (% bad or very bad)	33	71	27	20	40	12	44	47
Frequency of blackouts (no. of blackouts per week)	5	6	2	1	3	2	3	4
Time to repair roads (days)	167	66	65	73	23	32	52	46
Infrastructure issues as an obstacle to doing business (% big or very big)	38	68	12	10	42	51	36	45
Ease of getting company registration licence (*tanda daftar perusahaan*, TDP) (% difficult or very difficult)	5	20	8	3	9	6	8	11
Business licence constraints as an obstacle to doing business (% big or very big)	9	17	5	2	7	7	8	8
District head takes strong action against corruption (% disagree or strongly disagree)	41	30	27	22	31	20	22	23
Issues in the integrity of the district head as an obstacle to doing business (% big or very big)	9	19	1	2	3	12	2	0
Issues in the interaction between local government & business as an obstacle to doing business (% big or very big)	9	22	4	4	8	19	8	0
Security issues as an obstacle to doing business (% big or very big)	8	13	2	8	5	24	13	0
Business development program constraints as an obstacle to doing business (% big or very big)	72	17	7	10	10	26	6	12
Transaction cost constraints as an obstacle to doing business (% big or very big)	6	13	5	3	9	5	2	1

Source: KPPOD and Asia Foundation (2008a, 2008b, 2010, 2011).

of the districts in West Nusa Tenggara improved (but that of East Nusa Tenggara worsened) in terms of ease of getting access to land, frequency of blackouts and ease of getting business licences; and the performance of the districts in East Nusa Tenggara improved (but that of West Nusa Tenggara worsened) in terms of anti-corruption measures, government–business interaction and security issues.

Over the last few years, the central government has introduced a number of measures to improve the quality of local economic governance. Interestingly, some of these were initiated by local governments themselves during the early stage of decentralization, and were later scaled up by the central government for deployment across the country. These measures were designed to promote organizational reform, improve transparency and increase efficiency at the local level, while reducing opportunities for corruption. Below we discuss the progress so far with three of these initiatives.

Establishment of one-stop shops for business licensing. The purpose of one-stop shops is to make it easier, cheaper and quicker for the private sector to obtain business licences, by providing clearer, more streamlined and more transparent procedures. According to Rustiani, Rahman and Mustafa (2012), the concept was initially introduced by the national government before decentralization, and was then scaled up in 2001–05 with the support of various development partners. Since 2006, the central government has required all subnational governments to establish such offices, leading to an increase in the number of district-level outlets from 111 (25 per cent of districts) in 2006 to 404 (82 per cent) in 2011. However, only 31 per cent of these one-stop shops are authorized to issue most or all of the most common types of licences (that is, 20 or more types of licences).[5] Moreover, the offices are yet to meet the expectations held for them. In 2011, for example, around half of the one-stop shops in Java failed to meet national service standards for the time taken to issue a company registration licence (*tanda daftar perusahaan*, TDP) or trading permit (*surat izin usaha perdagangan*, SIUP), and four-fifths did not meet the national service standards for the cost of such licences (Ministry of Trade 2011).

Adoption of electronic procurement systems (sistem pengadaan secara elektronik) and establishment of procurement service units (unit layanan pengadaan). Presidential Regulation 54/2010 on Public Procurement of Goods and Services requires all government agencies to use electronic procurement systems and to establish procurement service units. Electronic procurement is expected to improve the transparency, competitiveness and

---

5 Most local governments have over 100 types of licence at their disposal, many of which would never be issued.

efficiency of public procurement of essential goods and services. The city of Surabaya pioneered the use of e-procurement in Indonesia, starting in 2004, without donor support. Procurement service units are expected to conduct procurement on behalf of local governments' technical departments. In theory, centralizing procurement within one agency should help to reduce the number of staff dealing with procurement, make it easier to introduce new procedures such as electronic procurement, and eliminate conflicts of interest by separating procurement from the budgetary process and from the users of the procured goods or services.

A study by the Asia Foundation and B-Trust (2012) found that, by 2011, 378 districts (76 per cent of districts) and 31 provinces (94 per cent of provinces) had adopted electronic procurement systems, although 274 districts and nine provinces used them only to announce tenders. The study also found that 130 districts (26 per cent) and nine provinces (27 per cent) had established procurement service units. Even among the governments that made full use of e-procurement, electronic procurement systems were used to make only 21 per cent of expenditures on capital investment and goods and services in the case of provincial governments, and 11 per cent in the case of district governments. Based on case studies in eight regions, the Asia Foundation and B-Trust concluded that, on average, local governments made savings of less than 10 per cent through the use of electronic procurement, with an average number of bidders per tender of just five.

Establishment of provincial information commissions and appointment of information and documentation officers. With the support of development partners, around 15 local governments in Indonesia issued bylaws on freedom of information in 2000–05. These local initiatives placed pressure on the central government to draft a new national law on the transparency of public information, which was eventually enacted in 2008 (Law 14/2008 on Freedom of Information). The law requires each provincial government to establish an information commission, and each subnational government to appoint an information and documentation officer. According to the National Information Commission, 23 provincial commissions had been established by December 2013;[6] by 2011, about one-fifth of districts had appointed information and documentation officers (Seknas Fitra and Asia Foundation 2011, 2012). Based on accessibility tests, however, Seknas Fitra and the Asia Foundation concluded that only one-fifth of budget documents – mostly summaries – were accessible as required by the law.

Although the measures introduced by the central government to lift standards of local governance have had mixed outcomes, the auditor

---

6 See http://www.komisiinformasi.go.id/category/view/ki-provinsi.

opinions issued by the State Audit Agency (Badan Pemeriksa Keuangan, BPK) suggest that there has been a significant improvement in public sector financial management over the last few years.[7] The proportion of provincial and district governments whose financial reports were passed by BPK without qualification rose between 2007 and 2010–11 (Figure 7.1). In general, provincial governments performed better than their local government counterparts. Districts in Java–Bali and Sumatra were more likely than those in other island groups to be given a clean auditor's report, and those in Eastern Indonesia the least likely.[8] In 2011, for example, only 1 per cent of districts in Java–Bali, and 6 per cent of those in Sumatra, received a 'bad' auditor opinion (adverse or disclaimer), compared with 55 per cent of the districts in Eastern Indonesia.

Corruption is still a problem in local government. The Minister of Home Affairs made several public statements about standards of local governance in 2013, the latest indicating that 309 regional heads (governors, district heads or mayors) had broken the law, usually by acting corruptly (*Tempo*, 7 November 2013). Data from the Corruption Eradication Commission (Komisi Pemberantasan Korupsi, KPK) show that around one-third of all corruption cases handled by the commission between 2004 and 2013 involved subnational government officials (Table 7.2), including 10 cases involving governors and 35 involving district heads or mayors (KPK 2013a). In terms of both the number of cases and the share of the total handled by KPK, those involving subnational governments were higher in 2012 and 2013 than in any of the years from 2009 to 2011.

7.3   LOCAL BUDGET POLICY AND EXECUTION

As a result of decentralization, subnational governments now have substantial budgetary responsibilities, making local budgets very important. The per capita revenues of provincial governments increased continuously between 2008 and 2013, while those of districts and municipalities have fluctuated (Figure 7.2). Although Law 28/2009 on Regional Taxes and Levies gives subnational governments authority over some taxes, improving their capacity to generate revenue, the contribution of locally

---

7   This 'good news' should be treated with caution. Based on a detailed analysis of auditor opinions in eight regions in 2007–11, the Asia Foundation and B-Trust (2012) concluded that there was a high degree of variation in the thoroughness of audits between regions.

8   In this chapter, 'Eastern Indonesia' refers to the provinces of West Nusa Tenggara, East Nusa Tenggara, Maluku, North Maluku, West Papua and Papua.

Figure 7.1   Quality of financial reports of district and provincial governments, 2006–11[a]

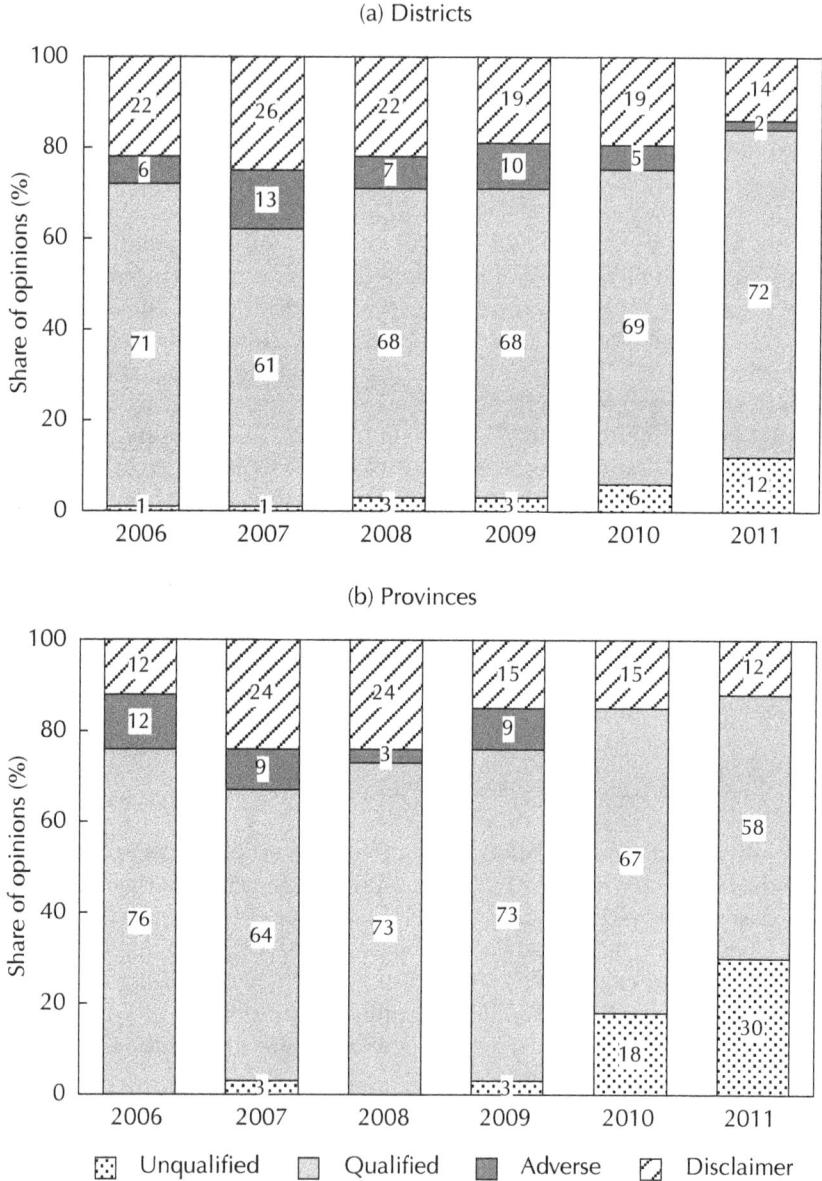

(a) Districts

(b) Provinces

a   Based on BPK auditor opinions for 419 districts and 33 provinces that are complete for the period 2006–11.

Source: BPK auditor reports, compiled by Seknas Fitra and processed by authors.

Table 7.2   Corruption cases handled by the Corruption Eradication Commission, 2004–13

Level of government	2004–07		2008		2009		2010		2011		2012		2013		Total	
	(no.)	(%)	(no.)	(%)	(no.)	(%)	(no.)	(%)	(no.)	(%)	(no.)	(%)	(no.)	(%)	(no.)	(%)
Central government	28	39	13	28	13	35	16	40	23	59	18	38	43	65	154	44
Subnational governments	25	35	23	49	9	24	8	20	10	26	23	48	21	32	119	34
Other	19	26	11	23	15	41	16	40	6	15	7	15	2	3	76	22
Total	**72**	**100**	**47**	**100**	**37**	**100**	**40**	**100**	**39**	**100**	**48**	**100**	**66**	**100**	**349**	**100**

Source: KPK (2013b).

Figure 7.2   Total budget revenue per capita by type of subnational government, 2008–13[a]

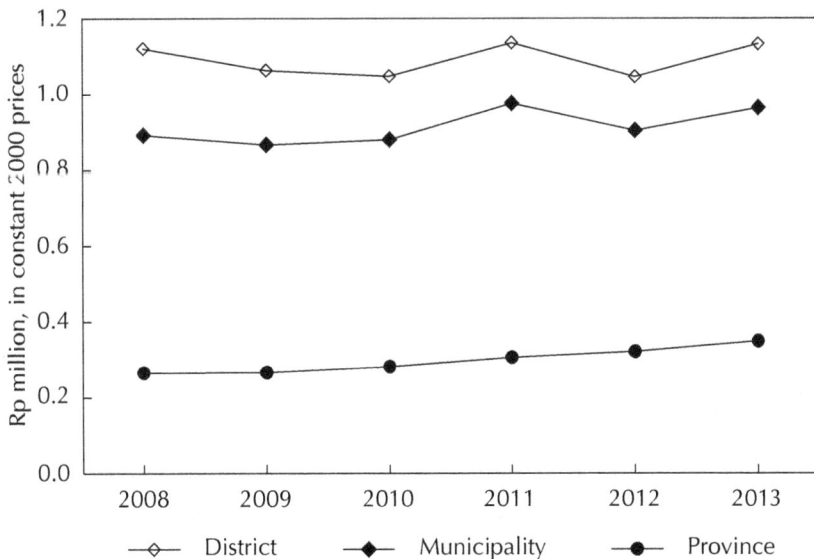

a   Based on valid data for 354 districts, 86 municipalities and 33 provinces that are complete for the period 2008–13. Figures for 2008–11 are based on realized budget reports, and those for 2012 and 2013 on budget plans.

Source: Regional Financial Information System (Sistem Informasi Keuangan Daerah, SIKD), Ministry of Finance, compiled by Seknas Fitra and processed by authors.

Figure 7.3   Distribution of budget revenue by revenue source and type of subnational government, 2008–13ᵃ

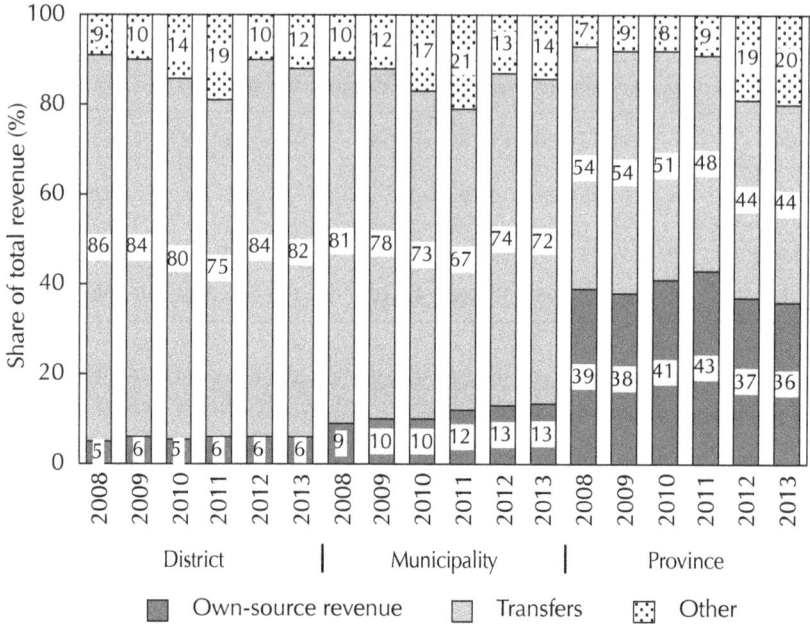

a   Based on valid data for 354 districts, 86 municipalities and 33 provinces that are complete for the period 2008–13. Figures for 2008–11 are based on realized budget reports, and those for 2012 and 2013 on budget plans.

Source: Regional Financial Information System (Sistem Informasi Keuangan Daerah, SIKD), Ministry of Finance, compiled by Seknas Fitra and processed by authors.

sourced revenue (*pendapatan asli daerah*, PAD) to total revenue has been stagnant in districts and provinces (Figure 7.3). It has increased, however, in municipalities, from 9 per cent in 2008 to 13 per cent in 2013. Despite declining in share since 2008, transfers from the central government continue to be the dominant source of revenue for all three types of subnational governments. The main types of transfers are grants from the General Purpose Fund (Dana Alokasi Umum, DAU) and the Special Purpose Fund (Dana Alokasi Khusus, DAK), and transfers from the Revenue Sharing Fund (Dana Bagi Hasil, DBH).

An interesting aspect of the data is the increasing contribution of 'other' sources of revenue to subnational government budgets. The main component of this revenue category is the Adjustment Fund (Dana Penyesuaian), for channelling infrastructure development funds to subnational governments. Rahman, Farhan and Taufik (2012) identify several problems with this new type of transfer. For example, it duplicates the grants for specific sectors provided through the DAK, but with less transparent and clear criteria. This is concerning given that the DAK itself has been described as 'quite complex' (Fadliya and McLeod 2010). With the increase in the number of sectors that can be funded by DAK grants (from 13 in 2009 to 22 in 2011) and by Adjustment Fund grants (from six in 2008 to 17 in 2011), the discretion of subnational governments over budget allocation is getting smaller. Moreover, the non-transparent procedures for Adjustment Fund allocations have led to allegations of a corrupt 'budget mafia' within the national parliament (*Tempo*, 16 October 2011). There are also administrative deficiencies in the way the grants are treated in local budgets; they are recorded only during the budget revision process, leaving limited time to implement the projects that are being funded (Seknas Fitra and Asia Foundation 2011, 2012).

On the expenditure side of subnational government budgets, the share of spending on personnel and administration has been increasing among districts and municipalities, and that of transfers at the provincial level of government (Figure 7.4).[9] The share of development expenditure (capital investment and spending on goods and services), on the other hand, has generally been declining; this is particularly evident in 2008–10 at the district level and in 2011–13 at the provincial level. For all three types of subnational governments, the share of development expenditure was lower in 2013 than it had been in 2008.

Across the five major island groups, there is very little variation in the revenue per capita received by municipalities, but much wider differences between districts and provinces. On average, in 2008–13 the municipalities in Kalimantan received Rp 1.1 million per capita (the highest among the five island groups), while those in Java–Bali received Rp 0.7 million (the lowest).[10] Over the same period, however, the districts in Eastern Indonesia received Rp 2.2 million per person, about six times the per capita income of districts in Java and Bali; and the provincial governments in Eastern Indonesia received Rp 0.5 million per capita, or around 2.6 times more than those in Sulawesi.

Given their large populations, it is not surprising to find that districts in Java–Bali spend less, per capita, on both personnel–administration and development than districts in other islands (Table 7.3). They spend more on personnel and administration than the other districts, however, as a share of total expenditures. The districts in Eastern Indonesia spend

---

9   Spending on personnel and administration covers salaries (civil servant, contractor and so on), interest, contingencies and other items. Transfers include financial assistance and transfers to other levels of government, social assistance and grants.

10   Unless stated otherwise, all values are based on 2000 constant prices.

Figure 7.4   Distribution of budget expenditure by expenditure category and type of subnational government[a]

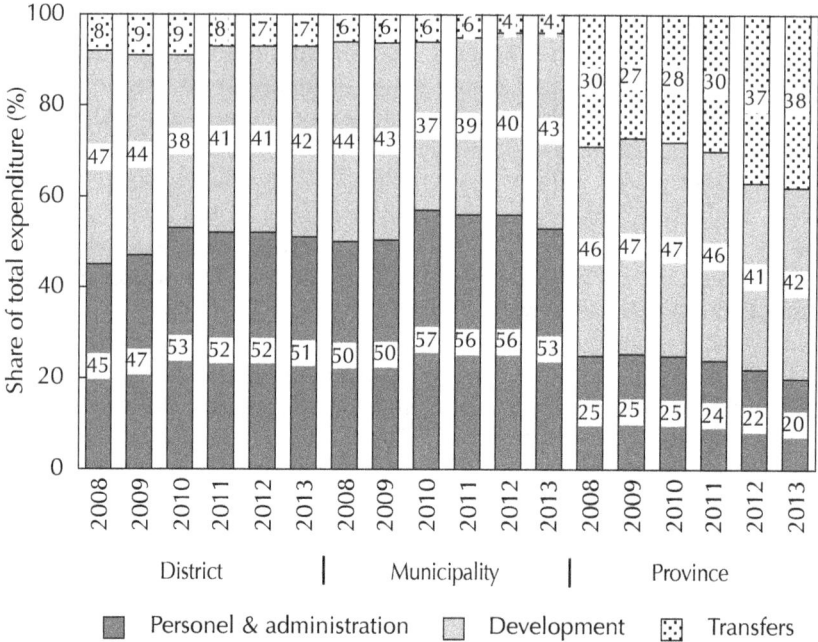

a Based on valid data for 354 districts, 86 municipalities and 33 provinces that are complete for the period 2008–13. Figures for 2008–11 are based on realized budget reports, and those for 2012 and 2013 on budget plans.

Source: Regional Financial Information System (Sistem Informasi Keuangan Daerah, SIKD), Ministry of Finance, compiled by Seknas Fitra and processed by authors.

significantly more per capita on both personnel–administration and development – but they are also the only districts where per capita spending on development actually fell between 2008 and 2013. Districts in Kalimantan have the lowest proportion of spending on personnel and administration, and the highest proportion on development expenditures.

Another interesting trend in local budget policy is for district governments to transfer increasing amounts to their village counterparts. On average, in 2008 grants to village governments comprised only 1.6 per cent of total district expenditures, or Rp 14,000 per head of district population (Table 7.4). In 2013 they reached 2.9 per cent of total district expenditures (Rp 33,000 per capita). In per capita terms, villages in Kalimantan and Eastern Indonesia receive the highest amounts; as a proportion of total expenditures, villages in Java and (again) Kalimantan receive the highest allocations.

Table 7.3   District expenditure on personnel–administration and development by island group, 2008 and 2013

Island group	Personnel & administration				Development			
	Rp million per capita (in 2000 constant prices)		% of total expenditure		Rp million per capita (in 2000 constant prices)		% of total expenditure	
	2008	2013	2008	2013	2008	2013	2008	2013
Sumatra	0.41	0.53	46	52	0.47	0.49	47	43
Java–Bali	0.23	0.29	55	57	0.15	0.19	35	35
Kalimantan	0.46	0.65	35	41	0.93	1.08	57	53
Sulawesi	0.38	0.53	46	54	0.42	0.44	48	41
E. Indonesia	0.59	0.79	37	47	1.40	1.15	55	47

a   Based on valid data for 354 districts and 86 municipalities that are complete for the period 2008–13. Figures for 2008 are based on realized budget reports, and those for 2013 on budget plans.

Source: Regional Financial Information System (Sistem Informasi Keuangan Daerah, SIKD), Ministry of Finance, compiled by Seknas Fitra and processed by authors.

Table 7.4   District expenditure on village grants by island group, 2008 and 2013

Island group	2008		2013	
	Rp thousand per capita	% of total expenditure	Rp thousand per capita	% of total expenditure
Sumatra	12.4	1.5	27.5	2.5
Java–Bali	7.9	2.2	17.0	3.6
Kalimantan	23.0	1.7	66.1	3.2
Sulawesi	7.3	0.9	25.8	2.6
E. Indonesia	26.3	1.4	50.0	2.8
Indonesia	**14.0**	**1.6**	**32.7**	**2.9**

a   Based on valid data for 354 districts and 86 municipalities that are complete for the period 2008–13. Figures for 2008 are based on realized budget reports, and those for 2013 on budget plans.

Source: Regional Financial Information System (Sistem Informasi Keuangan Daerah, SIKD), Ministry of Finance, compiled by Seknas Fitra and processed by authors.

*Figure 7.5   Share of unspent budget in total revenue by type of
subnational government, 2008–13*[a]

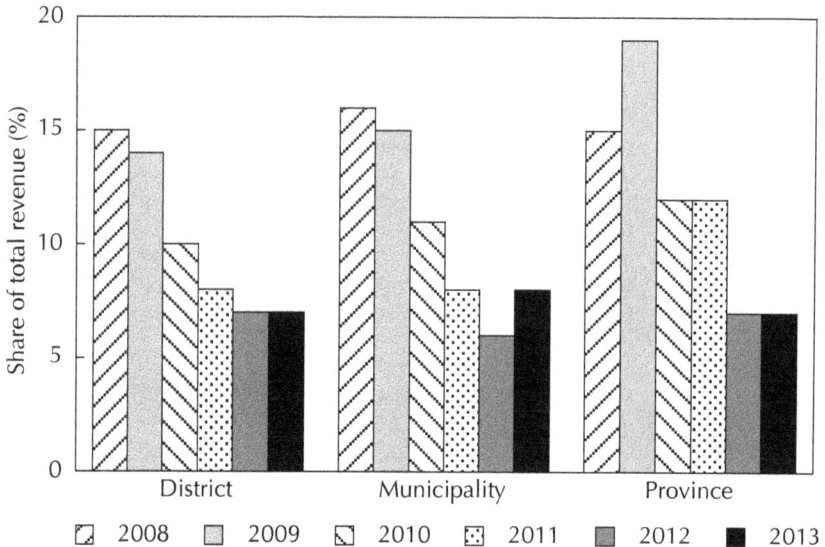

| ☒ 2008 | ▢ 2009 | ◸ 2010 | ⊡ 2011 | ▪ 2012 | ■ 2013 |

a   Based on valid data for 354 districts, 86 municipalities and 33 provinces that are complete
for the period 2008–13. Figures for 2008–11 are based on realized budget reports, and
those for 2012 and 2013 on budget plans.

Source: Regional Financial Information System (Sistem Informasi Keuangan Daerah, SIKD),
Ministry of Finance, compiled by Seknas Fitra and processed by authors.

One indicator of an improvement in budget execution may be a
decline in unspent funds (*sisa lebih pembayaran anggaran*, SILPA) as
a share of total revenue (Figure 7.5). Between 2008 and 2013, unspent
budget from the previous year fell from around 15 per cent of the total
revenues of district, municipal and provincial governments to just 7 per
cent. The narrowing of the gap between planned, revised and realized
budgets suggests an improvement in budget execution – although this
could also be interpreted as an inability to make savings on procurement
(Asia Foundation and B-Trust 2012).

The improvements in budget execution have not been evenly distributed across regions (Figure 7.6). In 2013, the share of unspent funds
in district budgets comprised around 7 per cent of total revenues in
Sumatra and Java–Bali, and around 3 per cent in Eastern Indonesia and
Sulawesi. In Kalimantan, however, the share was around 17 per cent,
most of it contributed by the districts in the rich province of East Kalimantan. Unspent funds comprised more than 50 per cent of total revenue
in five of East Kalimantan's 14 districts, 25–50 per cent in another five
and 20–25 per cent in two.

Figure 7.6   Share of unspent budget in total district revenue by island group, 2008–13[a]

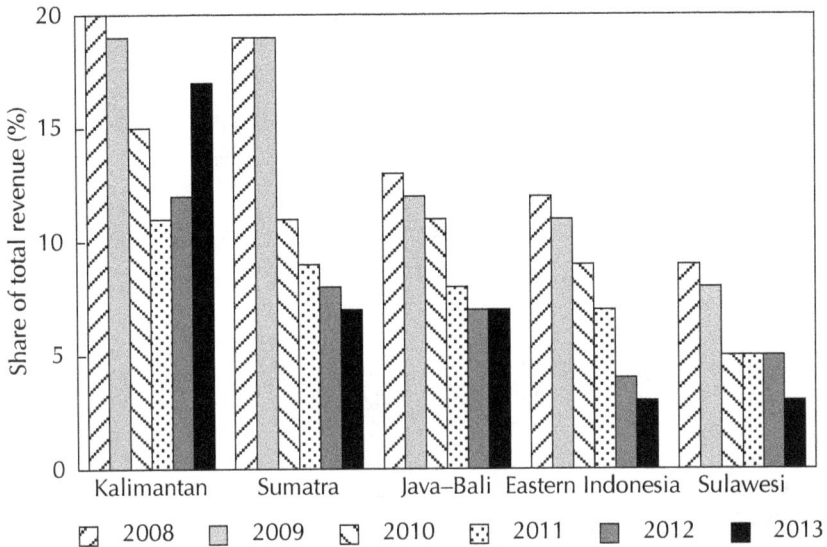

a   Based on valid data for 354 districts and 86 municipalities that are complete for the period 2008–13. Figures for 2008–11 are based on realized budget reports, and those for 2012 and 2013 on budget plans.

Source: Regional Financial Information System (Sistem Informasi Keuangan Daerah, SIKD), Ministry of Finance, compiled by Seknas Fitra and processed by authors.

7.4   DEVELOPMENT OUTCOMES

To give a broad idea of levels of development across Indonesia, Table 7.5 shows income per capita, the Gini ratio, the poverty rate and the Human Development Index (HDI) for each of the 33 provinces in 2010–11. Although national GDP per capita was almost $3,000 in 2010, the provincial figures vary widely, from around $600 to $10,000. The capital, Jakarta, and the resource-rich provinces of Riau and East Kalimantan stand out as the regions with the highest incomes per capita. Their levels of wealth are in stark contrast to those in Maluku and North Maluku, varying by a factor of more than 10.

Although most of the provinces with low incomes per capita are located in the eastern part of the country, poverty headcount ratios are more widely dispersed. The provinces with high poverty incidence include several in Java and other parts of 'wealthier' western Indonesia.

The above facts suggest a worrying level of inequality – as confirmed by provincial Gini ratios that hover between 0.30 and 0.40 (where 0 represents perfect equality of incomes, and 1 maximum inequality).

Table 7.5   Levels of development and inequality by province, 2010–11

Province	GDP per capita, 2010 ($)[a]	Gini ratio, 2011[b]	Headcount poverty ratio, 2010[c]	Human Development Index, 2010[d]
Aceh	1,898	0.34	19.6	71.7
North Sumatra	2,337	0.36	11.3	74.2
West Sumatra	1,980	0.39	9.0	73.8
Riau	6,809	0.36	8.5	76.1
Jambi	1,915	0.36	8.7	72.7
South Sumatra	2,330	0.37	14.2	73.0
Bengkulu	1,157	0.37	17.5	72.9
Lampung	1,552	0.39	16.9	71.4
Bangka Belitung	2,312	0.30	5.8	72.9
Riau Islands	4,693	0.33	7.4	75.1
Jakarta	9,875	0.47	3.8	77.6
West Java	1,970	0.43	10.7	72.3
Central Java	1,510	0.41	15.8	72.5
Yogyakarta	1,451	0.41	16.1	75.8
East Java	2,286	0.41	14.2	71.6
Banten	1,765	0.42	6.3	70.5
Bali	1,886	0.41	4.2	72.3
West Nusa Tenggara	1,207	0.42	19.7	65.2
East Nusa Tenggara	651	0.40	21.2	67.3
West Kalimantan	1,514	0.40	8.6	69.2
Central Kalimantan	2,118	0.34	6.6	74.6
South Kalimantan	1,776	0.39	5.3	69.9
East Kalimantan	9,945	0.38	6.8	75.6
North Sulawesi	1,785	0.39	8.5	76.1
Central Sulawesi	1,539	0.39	15.8	71.1
South Sulawesi	1,614	0.42	10.3	71.6
Southeast Sulawesi	1,640	0.42	14.6	70.0
Gorontalo	852	0.45	18.8	70.3
West Sulawesi	1,043	0.48	13.9	69.6
Maluku	580	0.38	23.0	71.4
North Maluku	571	0.34	9.2	69.0
West Papua	3,260	0.42	31.9	69.2
Papua	3,474	0.42	32.0	64.9
Indonesia	**2,981**	**0.41**	**12.5**	**72.3**

a   GDP per capita is provincial GDP in 2010 current US dollar prices (converted from Indonesian rupiah using the average exchange rate in 2010 from Bank Indonesia), divided by the provincial population, taken from BPS.
b   Gini ratios are calculated based on the National Socio-Economic Survey (Survei Sosio-Ekonomi Nasional, Susenas) for the first quarter of 2011.
c   Headcount poverty ratio is the proportion of the population under the poverty line, taken from BPS.
d   Human Development Index figures are taken from BPS.

7.5 LOCAL GOVERNANCE AND DEVELOPMENT OUTCOMES: IS THERE ANY CORRELATION?

We are interested in finding answers to the following questions. Is good governance associated with better development outcomes? Is good budget allocation associated with better development outcomes? What are the characteristics of districts that have good budget allocations? And what types of districts obtain good auditor opinions from BPK?

Model

To examine the relationship between governance and levels of development, we estimate the following model:

$$Out = f(GG, BA, Admin, control) \tag{7.1}$$

where *Out* is economic or social outcomes; *GG* is a good governance indicator; *BA* is budget policy or budget allocation; and *Admin* is administrative characteristics.

To assess the relationship between budget allocation and administrative characteristics, and between auditor opinions and administrative characteristics, we also examine:

$$BA = f(Admin) \tag{7.2}$$

and

$$GG = f(Admin) \tag{7.3}$$

We should emphasize that the purpose of these exercises is not to seek causality between the variables, but rather to assess the correlation between them.

Data

The main sources of data are the local economic governance surveys undertaken by Regional Autonomy Watch (KPPOD) and the Asia Foundation in districts and municipalities across the country. In each locality, around 50 firms were asked to rate various aspects of local economic governance, mainly the quality of the local government. We make use of four sets of surveys: the nationwide 2007 and 2010–11 local economic governance surveys, and the 2008 and 2010 Aceh surveys (KPPOD 2008a, 2008b, 2010, 2011).[11] These surveys use similarly structured questionnaires,

---

11 For analyses of the individual surveys, see McCulloch and Malesky (2011) on the 2007 survey and Pambudhi (2013) on the 2010–11 survey.

allowing for direct comparison. The 2007 survey covers 243 districts/ municipalities in 15 provinces, and the 2010–11 survey covers 245 districts/municipalities in 19 provinces.[12] In addition to Aceh, three provinces, East Java, East Nusa Tenggara and West Nusa Tenggara, were surveyed twice, allowing a panel examination (as in Table 7.1 above).

The Local Economic Governance Index constructed from the survey data has nine subindices: land access; local infrastructure; business licensing; local-level regulations; transaction costs; capacity and integrity of district head/mayor; local government and business interaction; provision of business development programs; and security and conflict resolution.

It is tempting to pool the indices from the 2007 and 2010–11 surveys. This is not possible, however, because each index is constructed from subindices, each of which is constructed in turn from all responses to the associated question. We therefore test our hypotheses separately on the 2007 survey and the 2010–11 survey, which together cover all provinces except Aceh and Jakarta (31 provinces).[13] We attempt, however, to carry out a combined regression using selected individual variables (as opposed to pooled indices or subindices). In this pooled regression, 32 provinces are represented (all but Jakarta). Table 7.6 provides a short description of all variables.

Some studies have pointed out that the quality of regional GDP data is rather unsatisfactory (see, for example, McCulloch and Malesky 2011). To address this problem, in model 7.1 we use growth in household consumption per capita in 2007–11 as our proxy for economic growth. Another dependent variable is the change in the HDI during 2007–11. We regress these two variables on the governance indices constructed from the 2007 survey and the 2010–11 survey separately (both the standalone indices and the breakdown subindices). We also include another proxy for governance (the 2008 auditor opinions issued by BPK) and a set of 2008 budget allocation variables (the ratio of development expenditure to total expenditure, the ratio of personnel expenditure to total expenditure, and the ratio of unspent funds to total revenue).[14]

For administrative characteristics, we use two dummies representing the subdivision of a region to create new administrative units (a process

---

12 A total of 260 districts were surveyed in 2010–11, but 15 were excluded from index construction for various reasons (KPPOD and Asia Foundation 2011: 5).

13 As noted earlier, Aceh is the subject of separate surveys, and Jakarta is not covered by the national surveys.

14 We also tried using per capita budget allocations. The results did not differ significantly.

known in Indonesia as *pemekaran*). The first dummy captures the year of establishment of a new district. There are four possible categories in this group: Generation 0 for districts established before 1999 (that is, before decentralization); Generation 1 for those established in 1999; Generation 2 for those established in 2001–03; and Generation 3 for those established in 2007–09.[15] The second dummy is for whether or not a particular district has split during the decentralization era. We also include regional dummies for whether a region is a district (Kabupaten) versus a municipality (Kota), and for island clusters (Sumatra, Java–Bali, Kalimantan, Sulawesi and Eastern Indonesia). Finally, we control for initial conditions, namely per capita consumption (in the case of the economic growth regression), the HDI (in the case of the HDI change regression), population size, and the level of access to clean drinking water, decent sanitation and education – all in 2007.

For the combined regression, instead of the Local Economic Governance Index and its subindices, we choose a few individual variables from the local economic governance surveys. After conducting some correlation tests, we end up with three individual variables each of which has a distribution (that is, mean and standard deviation) that is not significantly different across the 2007 and 2010–11 samples. These are the proportions of respondents saying their leaders (district head or mayor) are corrupt, that access to land is important, and that road infrastructure is important.

For the budget allocation model (7.2), we use administrative characteristics only as the independent variables, with the 2012 budget allocation as the dependent variable. For model (7.3), we regress BPK auditor opinions on the overall Local Economic Governance Index and all the administrative characteristics. Unlike the previous models, which use ordinary least squares, model 7.3 employs a simple logit estimation. To simplify interpretation, in this model we convert the Local Economic Governance Index into a binary variable, where 'high' and 'low' refer to better or worse local governance, using the median value as the cut-off point.

Results

Tables 7.7 and 7.8 show the results of regressing economic growth and change in the HDI, respectively, on good governance indicators, along with budget policy indicators and administrative characteristics. In both

---

15 More new districts have been established since 2009. We do not include them because our outcome variables are only until 2011 and our governance indicators are for 2007 and 2010–11.

Table 7.6 Summary of variables

Variable	Description	Source	Base: 2007 LEG survey data					Base: 2010–11 LEG survey data				
			Observations	Mean	SD	Min.	Max.	Observations	Mean	SD	Min.	Max.
Dependent												
gepc711	Growth of real exp. per capita, 2007–11	Susenas	243	5.9	3.4	–6.9	16.1	235.0	7.5	4.3	–6.4	27.6
HDI711	Change in Human Development Index, 2007–11	BPS	243	0.7	0.2	0.4	1.7	259.0	0.8	0.2	0.3	1.8
Independent: initial conditions												
DEV12	Development exp./total exp., 2012	MOF	242	38.3	10.0	17.8	72.7	259.0	43.5	10.7	22.5	80.3
SILPA12	Unspent funds/total revenue, 2012	MOF	242	0.1	0.1	0.0	0.7	259.0	0.1	0.1	0.0	0.5
Person12	Personnel exp./total exp., 2012	MOF	242	55.4	10.4	21.5	75.0	259.0	50.5	11.1	15.4	73.8
lrepc7	Log of real exp. per capita, 2007	Susenas	243	11.9	0.3	11.1	12.7	235.0	11.8	0.3	11.0	12.5
gwater7	% of population with access to decent water supply, 2007	Susenas	243	81.3	15.6	25.1	100.0	235.0	69.9	21.7	6.3	100.0
gsanit7	% of population with access to decent sanitation, 2007	Susenas	243	44.1	21.5	0.4	94.8	235.0	32.1	21.4	0.0	85.5
gedu7	% of population with at least junior secondary education, 2007	Susenas	243	58.4	8.2	39.6	80.0	235.0	59.0	8.1	43.9	88.0
lPop7	Log of population, 2007	BPS	243	13.0	0.9	10.6	15.3	259.0	12.3	1.0	8.7	14.8
Independent: governance indicator												
index	Local Economic Governance (LEG) Index	KPPOD/AF	243	61.7	6.4	41.4	76.0	245.0	62.3	7.2	39.4	79.0
land	LEG subindex: land access & security of tenure	KPPOD/AF	243	71.3	10.3	39.7	99.4	245.0	74.1	11.7	39.7	99.4
licence	LEG subindex: business licensing	KPPOD/AF	243	60.0	8.3	32.2	84.6	245.0	61.2	8.4	31.1	84.6
interact	LEG subindex: government–business interaction	KPPOD/AF	243	55.4	9.8	26.3	80.1	245.0	51.3	10.2	25.0	77.8

Code	Description	Source									
BDP	LEG subindex: business devt program	KPPOD/AF	243	43.0	12.1	15.0	86.5	245.0	38.5	14.9	0.0	76.3
integrity	LEG subindex: capacity/integrity of district head/mayor	KPPOD/AF	243	56.9	10.8	23.9	87.9	245.0	52.3	11.8	14.9	89.8
trcost	LEG subindex: transaction costs	KPPOD/TAF	243	69.6	12.2	27.3	96.1	245.0	79.8	11.3	27.3	100.0
infra	LEG subindex: infrastructure	KPPOD/F	243	65.6	12.1	26.3	89.0	245.0	67.6	12.6	29.5	89.0
secure	LEG subindex: security & conflict resolution	KPPOD/AF	243	60.0	11.5	27.4	96.7	245.0	66.4	12.2	2.4	96.7
bylaw	LEG subindex: local regulation	KPPOD/AF	243	84.2	13.9	1.1	100.0	239.0	82.1	13.7	1.1	100.0
pct_corr*	% of respondents saying leaders are corrupt (inverted)	KPPOD/AF	462	79.0	15.1	21.6	100.0	462.0	79.0	15.1	21.6	100.0
pct_landd*	% of respondents saying land access is difficult (inverted)	KPPOD/AF	462	65.8	19.7	5.7	100.0	462.0	65.8	19.7	5.7	100.0
pct_roadi*	% of respondents saying road infrastructure is bad (inverted)	KPPOD/AF	462	62.5	24.4	0.0	100.0	462.0	62.5	24.4	0.0	100.0
BPK8	Auditor opinion, 2008; 1 if good, 0 otherwise	BPK	243	0.8	0.4	0.0	1.0	259.0	0.5	0.5	0.0	1.0
SILPA8	Unspent funds/total revenue, 2008	MOF	242	0.2	0.1	0.0	0.9	236.0	0.2	0.1	0.0	0.6
DEV8	Development exp./total exp., 2008	MOF	242	42.5	11.2	23.8	76.7	236.0	49.3	12.6	21.0	80.9
Independent: administrative characteristics												
cNew	Dummy for *pemekaran*: Gen. 0 (pre-1999), Gen. 1 (1999), Gen. 2 (2001–03), Gen. 3 (2007–09); Gen. 0 is the base	MOHA	243	0.3	0.7	0.0	2.0	259.0	0.9	1.1	0.0	3.0
dsplit	Dummy: 1 if split, 0 otherwise	MOHA	243	0.2	0.4	0.0	1.0	259.0	0.3	0.5	0.0	1.0
Kabupaten	Dummy: 1 if district (*kabupaten*), 0 if municipality (*kota*)	MOHA	243	0.8	0.4	0.0	1.0	259.0	0.8	0.4	0.0	1.0
Java-Bali	Dummy: 1 if Java–Bali, 0 otherwise	MOHA	243	2.4	1.3	1.0	5.0	259.0	3.1	1.6	1.0	5.0

* = for all observations.

BPK = Badan Pemeriksa Keuangan (State Audit Agency); BPS = Badan Pusat Statistik (Statistics Indonesia); KPPOD/AF = Komite Pemantauan Pelaksanaan Otonomi Daerah (Regional Autonomy Watch) and Asia Foundation; LEG = local economic governance survey; MOF = Ministry of Finance; MOHA = Ministry of Home Affairs; Susenas = Survei Sosio Ekonomi Nasional (National Socio-Economic Survey).

Table 7.7 Economic growth and good governance

gepc711	Base: 2007 LEG survey data				Base: 2010–11 LEG survey data			
	(1)	(2)	(3)	(4)	(5)	(6)	(7)	(8)
index	0.0339 (0.0419)	0.0240 (0.0418)			0.0661 (0.0423)	0.0680 (0.0421)		
land			−0.0345 (0.0289)	−0.0323 (0.0288)			−0.0265 (0.0302)	−0.0267 (0.0300)
licence			−0.0208 (0.0343)	−0.0229 (0.0341)			−0.00849 (0.0357)	−0.00747 (0.0355)
interact			0.0810** (0.0400)	0.0755* (0.0395)			−0.0396 (0.0389)	−0.0489 (0.0391)
BDP			−0.0155 (0.0207)	−0.0140 (0.0206)			−0.0144 (0.0217)	−0.00977 (0.0217)
integrity			−0.0531 (0.0333)	−0.0549* (0.0331)			−0.0258 (0.0325)	−0.0224 (0.0321)
trcost			−0.0236 (0.0220)	−0.0242 (0.0218)			0.0165 (0.0293)	0.0169 (0.0291)
infra			0.0516* (0.0290)	0.0514* (0.0289)			0.0844*** (0.0273)	0.0842*** (0.0271)
secure			0.0235 (0.0262)	0.0214 (0.0261)			0.0325 (0.0271)	0.0348 (0.0270)
bylaw			0.0144 (0.0155)	0.0148 (0.0154)			−0.00202 (0.0186)	0.00273 (0.0187)
BPK8	0.000142 (0.552)	0.0812 (0.551)	−0.00844 (0.561)	0.0845 (0.561)	0.791 (0.584)	0.855 (0.581)	0.968* (0.573)	1.017* (0.570)
SILPA8	−0.117 (1.881)	−1.248 (1.929)	−0.0618 (1.898)	−1.203 (1.953)	1.142 (2.398)	0.833 (2.374)	0.291 (2.402)	0.00902 (2.380)
DEV8	0.0246 (0.0328)		0.0139 (0.0342)		0.0380 (0.0360)		0.0711* (0.0386)	

	(1)	(2)	(3)	(4)	(5)	(6)	(7)	(8)
Person8		-0.0610* (0.0334)		-0.0532 (0.0346)		-0.0717* (0.0391)		-0.100** (0.0421)
1. New99	-0.165 (1.002)	-0.482 (1.007)	0.00757 (1.002)	-0.296 (1.008)	-0.0150 (1.076)	-0.186 (1.052)	-0.638 (1.045)	-0.645 (1.018)
2.New01-03	0.470 (0.765)	0.277 (0.764)	0.502 (0.777)	0.317 (0.776)	1.237 (1.024)	0.963 (1.015)	1.485 (0.998)	1.309 (0.989)
3. New07-09					0.336 (1.941)	0.228 (1.932)	0.220 (1.904)	0.0747 (1.895)
dsplit	0.238 (0.648)	0.257 (0.644)	0.264 (0.657)	0.291 (0.653)	0.286 (0.770)	0.245 (0.766)	0.200 (0.755)	0.203 (0.751)
Kabupaten	0.102 (0.802)	-0.0155 (0.791)	0.501 (0.832)	0.420 (0.821)	-2.178* (1.265)	-2.599** (1.290)	-2.365* (1.265)	-2.833** (1.287)
Java-Bali	-1.955*** (0.739)	-1.780** (0.714)	-2.374*** (0.789)	-2.202*** (0.772)	-1.800* (0.938)	-2.007** (0.941)	-1.958** (0.959)	-2.175** (0.957)
lrepc7	-2.172* (1.219)	-2.597** (1.236)	-2.031* (1.229)	-2.432* (1.249)	-2.651** (1.336)	-3.175** (1.370)	-4.304*** (1.468)	-4.895*** (1.512)
gwater7	0.0194 (0.0207)	0.0192 (0.0204)	0.0223 (0.0209)	0.0223 (0.0206)	-0.0420** (0.0185)	-0.0435** (0.0184)	-0.0319* (0.0186)	-0.0342* (0.0185)
gsanit7	0.0232 (0.0164)	0.0261 (0.0164)	0.0199 (0.0165)	0.0230 (0.0165)	0.00592 (0.0232)	0.0102 (0.0233)	0.00569 (0.0227)	0.0101 (0.0228)
gedu7	8.94e-05 (0.0402)	0.00949 (0.0403)	0.00252 (0.0418)	0.0118 (0.0420)	-0.0155 (0.0500)	-0.0153 (0.0497)	0.0163 (0.0520)	0.0180 (0.0518)
lPop7	-0.458 (0.351)	-0.381 (0.346)	-0.537 (0.363)	-0.462 (0.359)	-0.194 (0.449)	-0.00783 (0.456)	-0.127 (0.471)	0.0355 (0.480)
Constant	32.62** (14.54)	40.80*** (15.07)	32.69** (14.59)	39.57*** (15.13)	39.92** (17.86)	49.13*** (18.52)	56.26*** (19.91)	69.02*** (20.83)
No. of obs.	242	242	242	242	230	230	224	224
R^2	0.160	0.170	0.199	0.207	0.191	0.199	0.270	0.278

*** = $p < 0.01$; ** = $p < 0.05$; * = $p < 0.1$. Standard errors are in parentheses. LEG = local economic governance survey.

Table 7.8 HDI change and good governance

HDI711	Base: 2007 LEG survey data				Base: 2010–11 LEG survey data			
	(1)	(2)	(3)	(4)	(5)	(6)	(7)	(8)
index	0.00223 (0.00150)	0.00192 (0.00150)			0.00579*** (0.00158)	0.00572*** (0.00158)		
land			-0.00138 (0.00103)	-0.00135 (0.00103)			-0.000800 (0.00109)	-0.000793 (0.00109)
licence			0.000743 (0.00121)	0.000636 (0.00120)			-0.00223* (0.00132)	-0.00225* (0.00132)
interact			0.00319** (0.00141)	0.00295** (0.00140)			0.00136 (0.00144)	0.00142 (0.00145)
BDP			-0.000668 (0.000728)	-0.000615 (0.000726)			-0.000349 (0.000806)	-0.000342 (0.000808)
integrity			-0.000377 (0.00117)	-0.000415 (0.00117)			0.00124 (0.00120)	0.00115 (0.00119)
trcost			0.00151* (0.000777)	0.00149* (0.000777)			0.00254** (0.00109)	0.00254** (0.00109)
infra			-0.000435 (0.00101)	-0.000389 (0.00101)			0.00224** (0.000990)	0.00228** (0.000990)
secure			-0.000620 (0.000924)	-0.000637 (0.000923)			-6.42e-05 (0.00102)	-7.81e-05 (0.00102)
bylaw			-0.000329 (0.000547)	-0.000328 (0.000546)			-0.000192 (0.000688)	-0.000239 (0.000697)
BPK8	-0.0408** (0.0196)	-0.0378* (0.0196)	-0.0487** (0.0197)	-0.0457** (0.0198)	-0.00777 (0.0218)	-0.00920 (0.0218)	-0.00464 (0.0212)	-0.00454 (0.0213)
SILPA8	0.157** (0.0665)	0.118* (0.0685)	0.156** (0.0664)	0.118* (0.0690)	0.0809 (0.0901)	0.0926 (0.0898)	0.0687 (0.0894)	0.0662 (0.0891)
DEV8	0.000800 (0.00115)		-0.000370 (0.00119)		-2.03e-05 (0.00129)		-0.00125 (0.00134)	

	(1)	(2)	(3)	(4)	(5)	(6)	(7)	(8)
Person8		-0.00195* (0.00116)		-0.000948 (0.00119)		0.000772 (0.00137)		0.00124 (0.00142)
1. New99	-0.0169 (0.0333)	-0.0308 (0.0340)	-0.0223 (0.0333)	-0.0342 (0.0340)	-0.0112 (0.0403)	-0.00486 (0.0396)	-0.0106 (0.0388)	-0.0136 (0.0380)
2. New01-03	-0.0575** (0.0271)	-0.0643** (0.0271)	-0.0673** (0.0273)	-0.0738*** (0.0274)	-0.0495 (0.0386)	-0.0423 (0.0382)	-0.0385 (0.0372)	-0.0397 (0.0370)
3. New07-09					-0.149** (0.0722)	-0.149** (0.0722)	-0.218*** (0.0706)	-0.217*** (0.0707)
dsplit	0.0242 (0.0230)	0.0241 (0.0228)	0.0172 (0.0231)	0.0177 (0.0231)	0.0209 (0.0288)	0.0222 (0.0288)	0.0285 (0.0280)	0.0280 (0.0280)
Kabupaten	-0.0102 (0.0286)	-0.0122 (0.0280)	-0.00541 (0.0291)	-0.00342 (0.0287)	0.0374 (0.0487)	0.0404 (0.0489)	-0.000749 (0.0497)	0.00334 (0.0501)
Java-Bali	-0.0168 (0.0262)	-0.0114 (0.0253)	-0.0116 (0.0276)	-0.00505 (0.0271)	0.0367 (0.0352)	0.0387 (0.0354)	0.0582 (0.0356)	0.0609* (0.0356)
HDI7	-0.0355*** (0.00286)	-0.0360*** (0.00286)	-0.0357*** (0.00288)	-0.0360*** (0.00289)	-0.0303*** (0.00300)	-0.0304*** (0.00299)	-0.0357*** (0.00361)	-0.0357*** (0.00361)
gwater7	0.000106 (0.000738)	8.95e-05 (0.000728)	0.000184 (0.000737)	0.000230 (0.000730)	0.000893 (0.000687)	0.000900 (0.000686)	0.000794 (0.000698)	0.000812 (0.000699)
gsanit7	0.000365 (0.000609)	0.000425 (0.000607)	0.000220 (0.000607)	0.000276 (0.000607)	-0.00190** (0.000869)	-0.00191** (0.000868)	-0.00142 (0.000861)	-0.00143* (0.000862)
gedu7	0.00295** (0.00143)	0.00315** (0.00142)	0.00294** (0.00147)	0.00310** (0.00147)	0.00805*** (0.00204)	0.00798*** (0.00204)	0.00755*** (0.00208)	0.00756*** (0.00208)
lPop7	0.0156 (0.0121)	0.0172 (0.0119)	0.0178 (0.0123)	0.0198 (0.0122)	0.0125 (0.0168)	0.00828 (0.0171)	-0.00481 (0.0175)	-0.00505 (0.0178)
Constant	2.664*** (0.332)	2.815*** (0.326)	2.751*** (0.349)	2.778*** (0.346)	1.795*** (0.426)	1.817*** (0.400)	2.592*** (0.495)	2.477*** (0.470)
No. of obs.	242	242	242	242	230	230	224	224
R^2	0.581	0.586	0.608	0.609	0.545	0.545	0.598	0.598

*** = $p < 0.01$; ** = $p < 0.05$; * = $p < 0.1$. Standard errors are in parentheses. LEG = local economic governance survey.

tables, columns 1–4 are based on the good governance indicators in the 2007 local economic governance survey, and columns 5–8 on those in the 2010–11 survey.

The results in Table 7.7 indicate that the quality of infrastructure appears to be a very significant factor affecting household expenditure growth. Government–business interaction also contributes positively in some models. Unexpectedly, however, the variable for leaders' integrity is negative. Obtaining a good auditor opinion from BPK, higher development expenditures and lower personnel expenditures are all associated with higher economic growth. Finally, districts outside Java–Bali enjoy higher growth in household expenditure than those in Java–Bali, and municipalities (Kota) exhibit higher growth than districts (Kabupaten).

Table 7.8 shows that government–business interaction, transaction costs and infrastructure are significant factors affecting change in the HDI. Surprisingly, the business licensing and BPK audit variables have negative signs, suggesting a negative association with change in the HDI. In the latter case, this may be due to the very strong correlation between a poor audit result, a district's 'youth' and a district's location outside Java–Bali (see Table 7.11 below). Table 7.8 also shows that newly established districts (and those located outside Java–Bali) experience less change in the HDI. Another interesting finding is that higher personnel expenditures are also associated with less change in the HDI.

As discussed earlier, we cannot pool the indices and subindices from the 2007 and 2010–11 surveys, but we can pool selected, non-indexed, individual variables. Table 7.9 provides the results of pooling survey data for individual variables. Among other things, it shows that better road infrastructure is significantly associated with higher economic growth (as proxied by per capita expenditure growth), while land access is more important in terms of change in the HDI. Development expenditures contribute positively to economic growth, but personnel expenditures have the opposite effect. Newly established districts experience less change in the HDI than 'old' districts. The impact of recent establishment on growth in household expenditure, however, is insignificant. Finally, districts outside Java–Bali have higher growth in per capita expenditure.

Table 7.10 addresses the question of what affects budget policy. It appears that newly established districts tend to have higher development expenditures and lower spending on personnel than those that have not split. Municipalities (Kota) have higher personnel expenditures than districts (Kabupaten), and districts outside Java–Bali have higher development spending than those in Java–Bali.

Finally, Table 7.11 indicates that newly established districts are less likely to obtain a good auditor opinion than those that have not split, that municipalities (Kota) are more likely to obtain a good auditor opinion

Table 7.9   Economic growth, HDI change and good governance: pooled data

Variable	gepc711 (1)	gepc711 (2)	HDI711 (3)	HDI711 (4)
pct_corr	−0.0108 (0.0122)	−0.00949 (0.0122)	0.000222 (0.000462)	0.000230 (0.000462)
pct_landd	0.0138 (0.00974)	0.0126 (0.00968)	0.000730* (0.000374)	0.000724* (0.000374)
pct_roadi	0.0159* (0.00850)	0.0155* (0.00844)	0.000351 (0.000320)	0.000348 (0.000320)
BPK8	0.248 (0.434)	0.332 (0.431)	−0.00262 (0.0163)	−0.00207 (0.0163)
SILPA8	−1.107 (1.380)	−1.763 (1.389)	0.0796 (0.0521)	0.0748 (0.0530)
DEV8	0.0409* (0.0232)		0.000138 (0.000871)	
Person8		−0.0703*** (0.0241)		−0.000333 (0.000897)
1. New99	−0.431 (0.704)	−0.620 (0.697)	−0.0573** (0.0263)	−0.0591** (0.0263)
2. New01-03	0.719 (0.625)	0.492 (0.622)	−0.0642*** (0.0236)	−0.0658*** (0.0236)
3. New07-09	−0.147 (1.563)	−0.330 (1.555)	−0.0205 (0.0590)	−0.0212 (0.0591)
dsplit	−0.381 (0.506)	−0.406 (0.502)	−0.00107 (0.0190)	−0.00134 (0.0190)
Kabupaten	−0.668 (0.718)	−0.929 (0.720)	0.00182 (0.0275)	0.00129 (0.0274)
Java–Bali	−1.520** (0.593)	−1.609*** (0.584)	−0.0355 (0.0226)	−0.0356 (0.0224)
lrepc7	−2.985*** (0.890)	−3.349*** (0.898)		
HDI7			−0.0295*** (0.00226)	−0.0295*** (0.00226)
gwater7	−0.0346** (0.0138)	−0.0351** (0.0137)	0.00102** (0.000518)	0.00102** (0.000518)
gsanit7	0.0185 (0.0141)	0.0220 (0.0141)	−0.000304 (0.000546)	−0.000300 (0.000546)
gedu7	0.0229 (0.0313)	0.0245 (0.0311)	0.00228* (0.00125)	0.00230* (0.00125)
lPop7	−0.203 (0.281)	−0.0952 (0.279)	0.00950 (0.0106)	0.0102 (0.0105)
Constant	43.13*** (11.29)	51.36*** (11.36)	2.368*** (0.273)	2.377*** (0.253)
No. of observations	436	436	436	436
R^2	0.189	0.199	0.453	0.453

*** = $p < 0.01$; ** = $p < 0.05$; * = $p < 0.1$. Standard errors are in parentheses.

Table 7.10   Budget allocation and administrative characteristics

Variable	DEV12 (1)	Person12 (2)	SILPA12 (3)
1. New99	9.870*** (1.587)	–11.35*** (1.668)	0.0224 (0.0141)
2. New01-03	10.35*** (1.270)	–11.22*** (1.335)	–0.00997 (0.0113)
3. New07-09	16.28*** (1.848)	–16.90*** (1.942)	0.00300 (0.0165)
dsplit	2.655** (1.214)	–2.973** (1.276)	–0.0140 (0.0108)
Kabupaten	–0.242 (1.116)	–2.182* (1.174)	0.0108 (0.00995)
Java–Bali	–3.895*** (1.165)	1.713 (1.225)	–0.00594 (0.0104)
Constant	37.60*** (1.157)	59.24*** (1.217)	0.0672*** (0.0103)
No. of observations	461	461	461
R^2	0.330	0.307	0.015

*** = $p < 0.01$; ** = $p < 0.05$; * = $p < 0.1$. Standard errors are in parentheses.

than districts (Kabupaten) and that districts in Java–Bali are more likely to obtain a good auditor opinion than those located outside Java–Bali.

7.6   CONCLUSIONS AND POLICY IMPLICATIONS

We conclude that infrastructure development, reductions in transaction costs, and improved financial management and budget allocation are the keys to optimizing the benefits from decentralization. *Pemekaran*, on the other hand, might hinder such an endeavour.

With regard to infrastructure development, relevant policies might include, first, reforming the system of budgetary transfers from the central government to subnational governments, by streamlining the DAK, improving the procedures for deciding and allocating DAK grants, and completely eliminating separate (Adjustment Fund) grants for infrastructure. The second priority is to increase the efficiency of local government procurement procedures, and reorient procurement towards the provision of better-quality infrastructure. Third, there need to be

Table 7.11   *Auditor opinions and administrative characteristics*

Variable	Base: 2007 LEG survey data		Base: 2010–11 LEG survey data	Base: 2007 & 2010–11 LEG survey data
	BPK8 (1)	BPK11 (2)	BPK11 (3)	BPK11 (4)
dindex	0.316 (0.361)	−0.135 (0.446)	0.114 (0.320)	
1. New99	0.596 (0.689)	0.725 (0.813)	−1.088* (0.630)	−0.164 (0.483)
2. New01–03	−0.115 (0.499)	−0.276 (0.546)	−1.715*** (0.541)	−1.164*** (0.375)
3. New07–09			−2.272*** (0.611)	−1.869*** (0.487)
dsplit	−0.220 (0.447)	−0.380 (0.500)	−0.850 (0.527)	−0.573 (0.373)
Kabupaten	−0.0967 (0.415)	−0.346 (0.571)	−1.180* (0.669)	−0.706 (0.430)
Java–Bali	0.635 (0.414)	3.413*** (1.067)	1.812* (1.081)	3.027*** (1.037)
Constant	1.096** (0.438)	1.691*** (0.559)	3.092*** (0.753)	2.443*** (0.441)
No. of observations	243	243	259	462

*** = $p<0.01$; ** = $p<0.05$; * = $p<0.1$. Standard errors are in parentheses.

stronger incentives for subnational governments to increase the share of spending on infrastructure.

Enforcing the implementation of Law 28/2009 on Regional Taxes and Levies so that local governments collect only the taxes and charges they are entitled to is important to reduce businesses' transaction costs. Improving budget allocation policies is also necesssary, but more for development outcomes than for other aspects of public sector financial management.

Finally, to discourage the subdivision of regions (*pemekaran*), and con-sistent with the new draft decentralization law, the rules governing the circumstances in which a new district can be created should be tightened.

REFERENCES

Abed, G.T. and S. Gupta (eds) (2002) *Governance, Corruption and Economic Performance*, International Monetary Fund, Washington DC.

Asia Foundation and B-Trust (2012) 'Enhancement of the subnational procurement monitoring', unpublished report, Asia Foundation and B-Trust, Jakarta.

Brodjonegoro, B. (2009) 'Fiscal decentralization and its impact on regional economic development and fiscal sustainability', in C.G.J. Holtzappel and M. Ramstedt (eds) *Decentralization and Regional Autonomy in Indonesia: Implementation and Challenges*, Institute of Southeast Asian Studies, Singapore.

Fadliya and R.H. McLeod (2010) 'Fiscal transfers to regional governments in Indonesia', Working Paper No. 2010/14, Crawford School of Economics and Government, Australian National University, Canberra.

KPK (Komisi Pemberantasan Korupsi) (2013a) 'Penanganan TPK berdasarkan profesi/jabatan' [Criminal corruption cases by profession/position], KPK, Jakarta, available at http://acch.kpk.go.id/statistik-penanganan-tindak-pidana-korupsi-berdasarkan-tingkat-jabatan.

KPK (Komisi Pemberantasan Korupsi) (2013b) 'Penanganan TPK berdasarkan instansi' [Criminal corruption cases by institution], KPK, Jakarta, available at http://acch.kpk.go.id/statistik-penanganan-tindak-pidana-korupsi-berdasarkan-instansi.

KPPOD (Komite Pemantauan Pelaksanaan Otonomi Daerah) and Asia Foundation (2008a) *Local Economic Governance in Indonesia: A Survey of Businesses in 243 Regencies/Cities in Indonesia, 2007*, KPPOD and Asia Foundation, Jakarta.

KPPOD (Komite Pemantauan Pelaksanaan Otonomi Daerah) and Asia Foundation (2008b) *Tata Kelola Ekonomi Daerah Aceh: Survei Pelaku Usaha di 23 Kabupaten/Kota di Aceh, 2008* [Local Economic Governance in Aceh: A Survey of Business Operators in 23 Districts/Municipalities in Aceh, 2008], KPPOD and Asia Foundation, Jakarta.

KPPOD (Komite Pemantauan Pelaksanaan Otonomi Daerah) and Asia Foundation (2010) *Tata Kelola Ekonomi Daerah Aceh dan Nias: Survei Pelaku Usaha di 25 Kabupaten/Kota di Aceh dan Nias, 2010* [Local Economic Governance in Aceh and Nias: A Survey of Business Operators in 25 Districts/Municipalities in Aceh and Nias, 2010], KPPOD and Asia Foundation, Jakarta.

KPPOD (Komite Pemantauan Pelaksanaan Otonomi Daerah) and Asia Foundation (2011) *Local Economic Governance: A Survey of Business Operators in 245 Districts/Municipalities in Indonesia, 2011*, KPPOD and Asia Foundation, Jakarta.

McCulloch, N. and E. Malesky (2011) 'Does better local governance improve district growth performance in Indonesia?', IDS Working Paper No. 369, Institute of Development Studies, University of Sussex, Brighton.

Ministry of Trade (2011) 'Laporan sintesis hasil review monitoring dan supervisi penerbitan SIUP dan TDP di 100 kabupaten/kota tahun anggaran 2010' [Synthesis report on the monitoring and supervision of trading permits and company registration certificates in 100 districts/municipalities in fiscal year 2010], Ministry of Trade, Jakarta.

Pambudhi, P.A. (2013) 'Local economic governance and growth: empirical evidence from decentralized Indonesia', paper presented at the Ash Center for Democratic Governance and Innovation, Harvard Kennedy School, Cambridge.

Pepinsky, T.B. and M.M. Wihardja (2011) 'Decentralization and economic performance in Indonesia', *Journal of East Asian Studies*, 11(3): 337–71.

Rahman, E.A., Y. Farhan and A. Taufik (2012) 'How local governments utilize their funds and how local elections influence local budget policies', paper presented at the Human Development and Capability Association conference, Jakarta, 3–7 September.

Rodrik, D. (ed.) (2003) *In Search of Prosperity: Analytic Narratives on Economic Growth*, Princeton University Press, Princeton.

Rustiani, F., E.A. Rahman and M. Mustafa (2012) 'Six years after "nationalization" of one stop shop for business licensing: what are the issues and challenges we are facing now?', paper presented at the Human Development and Capability Association conference, Jakarta, 3–7 September.

Seknas Fitra (Sekretariat Nasional Forum Indonesia untuk Transparansi Anggaran) and Asia Foundation (2011) *Analisis Anggaran Daerah: Studi terhadap Anggaran Tahun 2007–2010* [Local Budget Analysis: A Study of Local Budgets in 2007–2010], Seknas Fitra and Asia Foundation, Jakarta.

Seknas Fitra (Sekretariat Nasional Forum Indonesia untuk Transparansi Anggaran) and Asia Foundation (2012) *Analisis Anggaran Daerah 2011* [Local Budget Analysis 2011], Seknas Fitra and Asia Foundation, Jakarta.

8   Decentralization, governance and public service delivery

Günther G. Schulze and Bambang Suharnoko Sjahrir*

8.1   INTRODUCTION

Has Indonesia's decentralization in 2001 been successful at improving service delivery and governance quality at the local level? Has democratization in the districts helped foster the quality of public services? More than 10 years into decentralization, we are able to provide an assessment based on systematic empirical evidence from the districts. This chapter reports results from large panel data analyses studying the effects of decentralization and local democratization on government spending (Kis-Katos and Sjahrir 2014), on governance quality (Sjahrir, Kis-Katos and Schulze 2014) and on public service delivery (Schulze and Sjahrir 2014). A synopsis of these three perspectives allows a well-rounded, balanced picture of the impact of these two far-reaching structural reforms on the quality of local government behaviour. It allows us to portray and identify the effects of these reforms on the production process for public services, comprising inputs, technology (governance) and output.

The effect of decentralization and democratization on the quality of government behaviour has been a contentious issue in the academic

*   This chapter is based on joint research with Krisztina Kis-Katos. We are grateful to her for her contribution and for valuable comments on this paper. We are indebted to Antonio Farfán-Vallespín and Judith Müller for helpful comments. The research underlying this paper has been supported by the German Ministry of Education and Research (BMBF) under grant number 01UC0906. We are also grateful to the Indonesia Project at the Australian National University for generous support.

debate, both theoretically and empirically. The first generation of the fiscal federalism literature stressed that decentralization allowed easier generation of location-specific knowledge and better preference matching (Hayek 1948; Oates 1972 and others); moreover, mobile individuals could sort themselves into the jurisdictions that offered the best mix of public services and taxes for them (Tiebout 1956). The second generation has focused on the effects of decentralization on accountability and the political process in general. Inter-jurisdictional competition for mobile factors (firms and individuals) curbs the ability of local governments to exploit their citizens and forces them to provide better services to attract these mobile factors (Brennan and Buchanan 1980). As decentralization brings decisions closer to the people, the transparency of and participation in the political process should be enhanced. Incumbents seeking re-election will be disciplined, at least partially, by the requirement to secure a majority of the vote (Ferejohn 1986). Decentralization implies unbundling of public goods provision, both regionally and by government function, which allows citizens to hold decision makers more directly accountable (Seabright 1996; Farfán-Vallespín 2014). Whereas, under centralization, a local constituency can hold the (central) decision maker accountable only in cooperation with other constituencies representing at least half the population, under decentralized rule a local constituency can hold its (local) decision maker directly accountable. The central policy maker can thus make up for poor performance in some districts with good performance in other districts, while the local policy maker cannot (Seabright 1996).[1] Moreover, citizens who are unable to assess the performance of their incumbents can still compare the policy outcomes in their own districts with those in neighbouring districts in a yardstick competition (Besley and Case 1995).

This optimistic view of decentralization stands in contrast to the notion that the political process at the local level may be dysfunctional. Voters may be uninformed, local media may be monopolized or captured (Besley and Prat 2006) and powerful local elites may dominate the political process (Prud'homme 1995; Bardhan and Mookherjee 2000). As a consequence, electoral competition may no longer discipline incumbents. Capture is easier at the local than at the central level because there is less public scrutiny of the political process and less media presence

---

1 A similar argument can be made with respect to government functions. Decentralization implies that some government functions are transferred to the local level while others are retained by the centre. Since, under decentralization, each level of government is responsible for fewer government functions than the central government was responsible for under centralization, the scope for balancing poor performance in some areas with good performance in others is significantly smaller under decentralization (Farfán-Vallespín 2014).

at the local level,[2] and because fewer actors need to be brought in line.[3] Decentralization implies the devolution of power to the local level, thereby providing powerful local elites, where they exist, with more scope for local capture. Examples of local capture are frequent in developing countries.[4] The success or failure of the decentralization cum local democratization reform thus becomes an empirical issue. The existing evidence is mixed and context-specific (Bardhan and Mookherjee 2006b). For instance, Blanchard and Shleifer (2001) show that while decentralization has stimulated growth in China (see also Qian and Weingast 1997), the opposite is true for Russia. Faguet (2004) finds that Bolivia's decentralization has made spending patterns more responsive to needs; poorer regions spend more on education, health and sanitation. Galiani, Gertler and Schargrodsky (2008) show that school decentralization in Argentina has increased the quality of educational outcomes but failed to provide benefits for the poor. The evidence may also vary within countries – some local jurisdictions may provide better governance and service delivery than the previously centralized one, while others may fall behind.[5]

Systematic empirical evidence on Indonesia's decentralization is only just beginning to emerge; so far it has been scant, often preliminary or limited to selected aspects. Lewis (2005, 2007) and Lewis and Oosterman (2009) analyse the fiscal behaviour of local governments after decentralization, looking at the aggregate spending, local taxation, savings and borrowing of local governments. Kaiser, Pattinasarany and Schulze (2006) examine the effects of decentralization on public service delivery shortly after decentralization in selected districts using the Governance and Decentralization Survey of the World Bank. Based on a different round of the same survey, Hofman, Kaiser and Schulze (2009) show that

---

2   The presence of media that is not captured enhances electoral accountability (Ferraz and Finan 2008) and reduces corruption (Brunetti and Weder 2003).

3   This idea goes back at least to Alexander Hamilton, who argues in Federalist Paper No. 10 that capture of the political process is more likely in smaller jurisdictions:

> Men of factious tempers, of local prejudices, or of sinister designs, may, by intrigue, by corruption, or by other means, first obtain suffrages, and then betray the interests, of the people. The question resulting is, whether small or extensive republics are more favorable to the election of proper guardians of the public weal; and it is clearly decided in favor of the latter … (Hamilton, Jay and Madison 1787 [2001: 59]).

4   See, for example, Reinikka and Svensson (2004), Galasso and Ravallion (2005), Bardhan and Mookherjee (2006a) and Olken (2007). See also Bardhan and Mookherjee (2006b) for a survey of the literature on decentralization and local capture, and Kis-Katos and Schulze (2013) for a survey of corruption in Southeast Asia.

5   See Baiochhi (2006) for such evidence for Brazil, and Chaudhuri (2006) for India.

corruption became more decentralized, but no less intense, shortly after decentralization. Skoufias et al. (2014) study the effects of direct local elections on district spending patterns, as do Kis-Katos and Sjahrir (2014), but they do not analyse the effects of decentralization. For other recent assessments of regional dynamics and decentralization impacts, see Hill and Vidyattama (Chapter 4) and Lewis (Chapter 6) in this volume.

Indonesia is a particularly interesting case to study the effects of decentralization and local democratization on public service delivery and local governance, not only because of its sheer importance as the fourth most populous nation in the world and the second-largest democracy in the developing world, but also because of its vast heterogeneity in terms of economic development, ethnic composition, religion and (possibly) governance quality, and because of the 'big bang' nature of its decentralization reform. It is also particularly suited to a large econometric analysis because its data quality is high and its districts numerous, and because more than a decade has passed since decentralization, allowing for large-scale panel analyses. Moreover, since democratization reforms at the local level were introduced in two steps, each at different, exogenously given points in time for the districts, the effects of democratization are econometrically well identified, as shown in Sjahrir, Kis-Katos and Schulze (2013).

The chapter proceeds as follows. In section 8.2 we report on decentralization and democratization (D&D) at the local level in Indonesia. Section 8.3 discusses methodological issues for the measurement of D&D effects. Section 8.4 reports the effects of D&D on the spending patterns of local jurisdictions and considers whether they have become more needs-oriented (Kis-Katos and Sjahrir 2014). Section 8.5 shows the pattern of administrative overspending, that is, excessive spending of local governments on their own district administrations, and asks whether local democratization has improved the situation (Sjahrir, Kis-Katos and Schulze 2014). Section 8.6 reports the results of a large-scale panel analysis of the effects of D&D on the quality of local public services in the areas of health, education and infrastructure (Schulze and Sjahrir 2014). Section 8.7 summarizes the results and describes the broad picture as we see it emerging from these three studies.

8.2   DECENTRALIZATION AND DEMOCRATIZATION AT THE LOCAL LEVEL

In 1998, towards the end of the Asian financial crisis, President Soeharto stepped down, paving the way for major structural reforms. The caretaker government led by President Habibie organized free national elections in June 1999 and pushed for far-reaching decentralization in a move to calm growing dissatisfaction with the centralist government and resurfacing separatist tendencies in the outer regions, especially Papua and Aceh. The national parliament approved the decentralization laws in May 1999, and decentralization took effect in January 2001.[6] The legislation devolved major authorities to the district level and gave provinces mainly backstopping and coordinating functions. The centre retained authority for defence, security, justice, foreign affairs, fiscal affairs, religion, forestry and currency, and all other functions were transferred to the districts. Law 22/1999 gave districts (*kabupaten*) and cities (*kota*) responsibility for health, education, public works, environment, communications, agriculture, industry and trade, investment, land, cooperatives, labour and infrastructure.[7] Except for a few local taxes, the power to tax was retained by the centre, thereby limiting the decentralization reform largely to the expenditure side. Decentralization therefore led to a large increase in transfers from the centre to the regions.[8] By 2011, local governments were in charge of around 35 per cent of consolidated Indonesian government expenditures; in contrast, they collected less than 2.5 per cent of total revenues (World Bank 2012). Decentralization also implied the transfer of two-thirds of all civil servants to the regions (World Bank 2003).

Fiscal decentralization was accompanied by stepwise democratization at the local level. District parliaments were freely elected in 1999 (along with the national parliament), but incumbent district heads (*bupati* and *walikota*), effectively appointed by the New Order regime, were allowed to serve their full terms. These terms came to an end at different points in time, after which district parliaments elected the district heads. The revised decentralization laws passed in October 2004 gave the provinces, as the representatives of the central government, supervisory rather than just coordinating powers, and introduced direct elections of district heads (*pilkada*), beginning in 2005. Again incumbents were allowed to serve their full terms so that this reform took effect gradu-

---

6   The legal framework for decentralization is given by Law 22/1999 on Regional Government and Law 25/1999 on the Fiscal Balance between the Central Government and the Regions (revised in 2004 as Law 32/2004 and Law 33/2004).

7   In this chapter the terms 'districts' or 'local governments' are used interchangeably to refer to both districts and municipalities (*kabupaten* and *kota*).

8   These transfers comprise grants from the formula-based General Purpose Fund (Dana Alokasi Umum, DAU) aimed at equalizing fiscal capacity across districts, as well as grants from the earmarked Special Purpose Fund (Dana Alokasi Khusus, DAK), shared tax revenues and shared (non-tax) natural resource revenues (Fadliya and McLeod 2011; Agustina, Fengler and Schulze 2012). While before decentralization all transfers from the centre were earmarked, after 2001 districts had considerably more freedom to use the transfers, subject to the general requirements of local public service provision.

ally. The reform was intended to increase accountability of district heads and to curb 'money politics', in particular, the practice of candidates for the position of district head making payments to local parliamentarians in exchange for their support (Buehler 2010). In fact, however, it simply shifted money politics from local parliaments to political parties, which began to sell nominations to *bupati* and *walikota* hopefuls (Mietzner 2006; Lindsay 2009; Buehler 2010).

Decentralization triggered the creation of new districts, which increased in number from 292 in 1999 to 477 in 2010.[9] The splitting of administrative units to form new ones, a process known in Indonesia as the 'blossoming' (*pemekaran*) of districts, was a bottom-up process that, however, needed approval from the centre. It was motivated by fiscal incentives, natural resource endowments, geographic dispersion, and political and ethnic diversity (Fitrani, Hofman and Kaiser 2005). Some of the new districts lacked the human capital and infrastructure to deliver public services effectively (Decentralization Support Facility 2007).

While these reforms – democratization at the national and regional levels and decentralization involving the devolution of more than a third of total government expenditures – were fundamental in nature and marked a major change in the political constitution of the Republic of Indonesia, many members of the old elites remained in dominant positions in the new system (Aspinall 2010; Mietzner 2010). At the local level, hierarchical accountability to an autocratic centre was replaced by democratic accountability to the local constituency of the young democracy.

8.3 METHODOLOGICAL ISSUES: MEASURING THE EFFECTS OF DECENTRALIZATION AND DEMOCRATIZATION

Measuring the effects of decentralization and democratization at the local level poses two major challenges (beyond the normal challenges of empirical research). First, how do we identify the effects of decentralization and of democratization and separate them from each other, and second, what precisely should we measure? We will discuss each of these issues in turn.

Decentralization, democratization and the problem of identification

Decentralization by its very nature affects all local jurisdictions at the same time. This makes it hard to identify its effects if other important

---

9   These figures are based on Ministry of Finance data on the number of districts receiving DAU each year.

events take place or changes are implemented at the same time. Notably, decentralization is often accompanied by major democratization reforms at the local level, or may be made possible only by major events (such as political or economic crises) that have hit the country at (almost) the same time. Such a situation is not uncommon, as decentralization itself is endogenous (Arzaghi and Henderson 2005). This problem of identification is inherent in the analysis of decentralization, and an econometric analysis that is devoted to answering relevant questions on the effects of this reform needs to address the issues in the best way possible.[10]

In the case of Indonesia, the effects of decentralization and democratization are relatively easily measurable and identifiable. First, the Asian financial crisis and the rebound from that crisis (1997–99) sufficiently precede the decentralization reform (2001) to be distinguishable from the effects of decentralization. Second, the two steps of local democratization, the indirect, and then direct, elections of local government heads, are clearly identified, as they take place at very different times in the districts. That makes them distinguishable from the decentralization reform. Table 8.1 shows the increase in the number of districts and the gradual change from appointed to indirectly elected to directly elected district heads.

The second inherent problem in identifying and quantifying the effect of decentralization is the missing counterfactual. How would districts have performed if decentralization had not taken place? One obvious approach is to project the past trend into the future to create a synthetic counterfactual. Another approach is to use theory in order to predict which socio-economic characteristics make a local jurisdiction profit more from decentralization, that is, those factors that ensure high levels of accountability to the local constituency and good governance. Prime candidates are the competitiveness of the political system as proxied by the distribution of seats in the local parliament, media presence, the educational and income profile of the local population, and ethnic heterogeneity (see above). If these factors significantly influence post-decentralization performance, but not (or to a significantly lesser extent) pre-decentralization performance, decentralization has been shown to have an effect. We follow both approaches.

---

10 In economic analysis there is often a trade-off between the relevance of the question asked and the elegance of the econometric technique that can be used to answer the question. Although devoted to elegance, we think relevance should take precedence.

Table 8.1   *Increase in districts, and the transition from appointed to indirectly elected to directly elected district heads, 1999–2010*

Year	No. of districts	District heads			
		Indirectly elected		Directly elected	
		No.	%	No.	%
1999	292	42	14.4		
2000	299	111	37.0		
2001	336	178	53.0		
2002	348	208	59.8		
2003	370	316	85.4		
2004	410	392	95.6		
2005	434	248	57.1	186	42.9
2006	434	192	44.2	242	55.8
2007	434	164	37.8	270	62.2
2008	451	49	10.9	402	89.1
2009	477	74	15.5	403	84.5
2010	477	0	0.0	477	100.0

Source: Number of districts: based on Ministry of Finance data on the number of districts receiving block grants (DAU) each year; indirectly and directly elected district heads: Ministry of Home Affairs, General Elections Commission (Komisi Pemilihan Umum KPU), Asia Foundation and World Bank Indonesia, adapted from Sjahrir, Kis-Katos and Schulze (2013).

What to measure? An approach on three levels

Districts produce local public goods, especially in the areas of health, education and infrastructure. They use inputs, mainly financial resources, to purchase factors of production (labour, physical capital, human capital), which are combined to produce a public service, the output. The produced output leads to a final, observable outcome. For instance, districts decide on their health budgets, hire midwives, doctors and other medical personnel, and purchase equipment (input stage); these medical personnel produce health services such as assistance at births (production stage); this leads to the number of assisted births (output stage). This has an influence on the incidence of child and maternal mortality (the outcome). D&D potentially affects all three stages of the production process: input, production and output. This is shown in Figure 8.1.

At the *input stage*, governments need to decide on the expenditure composition. Since the budget is largely given by transfers from the

Figure 8.1   The process of public service production

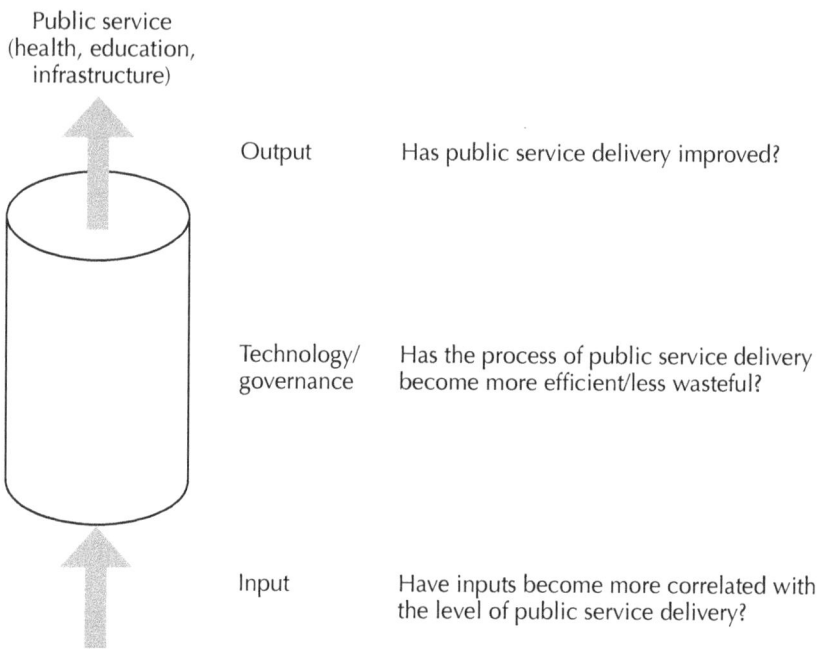

Public service
(health, education,
   infrastructure)

	Output	Has public service delivery improved?
	Technology/ governance	Has the process of public service delivery become more efficient/less wasteful?
	Input	Have inputs become more correlated with the level of public service delivery?

centre,[11] local governments can mainly decide on the sectoral allocation of a given budget. If the allocation becomes more needs-oriented
– that is, if resources are redirected to sectors in which the jurisdiction
is lagging – decentralization has made the government more responsive to the demands of the local population. This approach to evaluating decentralization is taken by Faguet (2004) and Kis-Katos and Sjahrir
(2014). It indicates the willingness of governments to improve services
in the aggregate, by analysing one of the most important decisions local
governments can make: to which use they want to channel their scarce
resources. Yet, it does not show the performance of the governments. A
local government may make the right input choices, but the process of
public service production may be so inefficient that this has little effect.[12]

---

11 On average local governments' own-source revenue is less than 10 per cent
    of their total revenue.
12 A government may change its sectoral input choices in order to make it easier
    for top bureaucrats to extract rents, as some sectors are more conducive to
    corruption than others (Shleifer and Vishny 1993; Mauro 1998). If this coin-
    cides with a stronger needs orientation, the results may be misleading.

The *production process* for public services may differ tremendously between sectors and across jurisdictions, in which case input data may be misleading. For instance, if teacher absenteeism is a big issue in one district but not in another, educational outcomes may differ significantly even if financial endowments do not. Corruption in particular may compromise the ability of local governments to deliver services effectively (Reinikka and Svensson 2004). Since reliable corruption data for Indonesia at the district level are unavailable in a panel format, we cannot trace the influence of D&D on the level of corruption. Similarly wasteful, however, is the excessive spending of districts on administration, which on average amounts to a third of the entire district budget. This is a clear sign of governance failure, for which we do have data throughout the period since decentralization. We use these data as a proxy for the efficiency of the production technology (Sjahrir, Kis-Katos and Schulze 2014). This shows to what extent a district government remains below its possible level of service delivery.

In the end it is the level of public services that matters. This is directly observable. The *output stage* thus links the selected output measures to the socio-economic characteristics of the district, its fiscal endowments, its political composition and the measures of the D&D reforms. In addition, interaction effects with the reform variables need to be included in order to investigate whether certain socio-economic or political characteristics make districts respond differently to D&D. It is important to select output variables that the district has direct control over, for instance, junior secondary school enrolment but not university enrolment, or the number of community health centres (*puskesmas*) per person but not the number of hospitals (*rumah sakit*). Output measures need to be reliable and representative of a sector's performance.[13] Direct output measures are the most obvious candidates for evaluating a local jurisdiction's performance and the effect of decentralization thereon. Even so they are not perfect, as they do not take into account the widely differing fiscal endowments and production technologies (levels of graft and other in-efficiencies) of districts, and the differing needs of local populations. For instance, if an area is relatively rich, many inhabitants would be able to afford private health care and so would not need to use community health centres. Thus, a lower provision of health centres by the district would not necessarily be a sign of insufficient provision of this service.

---

13 Selecting a representative indicator is a difficult task. For instance, if the pupil–teacher ratio is the measure of choice, one needs to be convinced that teacher absenteeism is not a big issue and that there is no quantity–quality trade-off in the choice of teachers.

In short, we can measure the effects of D&D at the input, the technology (governance) and the output stage. These analyses are very informative but still have deficiencies if looked at in isolation. A well-rounded picture emerges only through a synopsis of all these approaches. The aim of the research we are reporting on in this chapter is to provide such a comprehensive picture.

Data and empirical approach

We report the main results of three empirical contributions using panel data for 418 local governments in Indonesia from 1994 until 2010. Local governments in Aceh and Papua are excluded because of missing data, and districts in DKI Jakarta because they are not decentralized. For some of the analyses we use balanced panels, collapsing 'child' districts back into their 'parent' districts; for others, we use unbalanced panels.[14] The dataset consists of fiscal indicators from the Ministry of Finance's Regional Financial Information System (Sistem Informasi Keuangan Daerah, SIKD), socio-economic indicators generated from various surveys and censuses conducted by the central statistics agency (Badan Pusat Statistik, BPS), and socio-political indicators from various sources, such as the General Elections Commission (Komisi Pemilihan Umum, KPU), the Ministry of Home Affairs, the Asia Foundation and the World Bank.

8.4   DECENTRALIZATION AND BUDGET STRUCTURES

In 'The impact of fiscal and political decentralization on local public investments in Indonesia', Kis-Katos and Sjahrir (2014) analyse the determinants of local governments' capital expenditures in the three main decentralized sectors: education, health and infrastructure. They test the hypothesis that D&D has made local government investments in these sectors more needs-oriented. They proxy needs by the level of public infrastructure in each sector, hypothesizing that local governments with relatively lower levels of public infrastructure in a particular sector will invest more, thereby creating convergence across districts.

Fiscal and administrative decentralization was implemented once and applied to all local governments in 2001. This may make it difficult to disentangle the effects of decentralization from an average time effect. However, Kis-Katos and Sjahrir argue that decentralization is by far the

---

14   If we use political variables, we need to employ either an unbalanced panel or a restricted panel including only those districts that have not split. This is because we do not have data on the composition of new district parliaments.

biggest policy change affecting local government finances and administration in Indonesia in the last 20 years. Therefore, it is likely that the average decentralization effect will not pick up the effects of other macroeconomic shocks.[15] As noted above, the timing of indirect and direct elections of local government heads was determined in a quasi-random way, because the incumbents were allowed to finish their terms before the new elections took place. These different timings can be traced back to the colonial era. Therefore, the democratization effect is nicely identified.

The authors analyse the effects of D&D on capital expenditure by estimating the following equation:

$$EXP_{it}^s = \beta_0^s PI_{it-1}^s + \beta_1^s DEC_{it}^s + \beta_2^s REV_{it}^s + \gamma_1^s PI_{it-1}^s \times DEC_{it} + \gamma_2^s REV_{it}$$
$$\times DEC_{it} + \beta_3^s DEM_{it}^s + \beta_4^s DIR_{it}^s + \gamma_3^s PI_{it-1}^s \times DEM_{it} + \gamma_4^s PI_{it-1}^s$$
$$\times DIR_{it} + X_{it}^s{}'\delta^s + \mu_t^s + \lambda_i^s + \varepsilon_{it}^s. \tag{8.1}$$

The superscript s represents the sectors: education, health and infrastructure. The dependent variable EXP_{it}^s is the natural logarithm of per capita annual capital expenditures of local government i in year t in sector s.[16] PI_{it-1}^s is the lagged value of the public infrastructure level in sector s.[17] For education, Kis-Katos and Sjahrir use the number of junior secondary schools per 100 children of junior secondary school age (children aged 13–15 years), for health the number of community health centres (*puskesmas*) per 10,000 people, and for infrastructure the share of villages with paved roads. These indicators are selected to best represent the responsibilities of local governments after the decentralization reform. DEC_{it}^s is the decentralization indicator; it equals one for all local governments starting from 2001. REV_{it}^s is the natural logarithm of per capita total fiscal revenue to control for a local government's fiscal size. The vector X_{it}^s represents further controls: the natural logarithm of per capita regional GDP, the urbanization rate, the natural logarithm of per capita sectoral

---

15 The monetary crisis that took place in 1997–98 may have affected the fiscal size and budgetary allocations of local governments. The authors control for the effect of the crisis years in some specifications and find that the results are not sensitive to this.

16 The paper uses development expenditure, which captures fiscal resources spent on investments in public infrastructure (Kis-Katos and Sjahrir 2014). The number of districts is 271, that is, the number existing before decentralization, excluding districts in Papua and Aceh because of missing data and districts in DKI Jakarta because they are not autonomous regions. The new districts created after decentralization are collapsed back into their parent districts to create a consistent panel.

17 The lagged levels are used to avoid instantaneous feedback from investments to public service delivery levels.

capital expenditures of the province, and an indicator for districts that have split. Kis-Katos and Sjahrir's coefficient of interest is γ_1^s, which represents the additional responsiveness of investments to levels of public infrastructure in a given sector after decentralization. A negative γ_1^s indicates that, after decentralization, local governments increased capital expenditures by more in places with lower levels of local public service infrastructure. This interpretation of the coefficient is the same as Faguet's (2004) interpretation of the same coefficient in his estimation. The coefficient γ_2^s represents changes in the revenue elasticity of capital expenditures after decentralization. DEM_{it}^s and DIR_{it}^s are dummy variables for democratically elected and directly elected local government heads respectively. Using the same interpretation as for γ_1^s, γ_3^s and γ_4^s represent additional responsiveness of investments to the level of public infrastructure in a given sector after having a democratically elected head and after having a directly elected head respectively. λ_i^s is local government fixed effects and μ_t^s is time fixed effects. Equation (8.1) is estimated in a seemingly unrelated regression framework to control for the inter-relation of sectoral fiscal decisions.

Kis-Katos and Sjahrir's main result is that decentralization has increased local governments' responsiveness to lower levels of public infrastructure in all three sectors. In the estimation using only decentralization interactions (with lagged levels of public infrastructure and with total revenue), the coefficients for γ_1^s are negative and significant for all three sectors. This indicates that capital expenditures increased significantly in districts with lower levels of public infrastructure in all three sectors.

Kis-Katos and Sjahrir do not find similar effects for democratization. Compared with appointed heads, neither district heads elected by the local parliament nor directly elected heads show higher responsiveness of local capital expenditures to lower levels of public infrastructure. β_3^s and γ_3^s are not significant in all three sectors. γ_4^s is significant only for health, which indicates that having a directly elected head seems to increase health capital expenditure in districts that already have higher levels of health infrastructure. The authors argue that this evidence indicates that the democratization reform has not yet improved local governments' responsiveness.

8.5 DECENTRALIZATION, DEMOCRATIZATION AND GOVERNANCE

In 'Administrative overspending in Indonesian districts: the role of local politics', Sjahrir, Kis-Katos and Schulze (2014) analyse whether democratization at the local level has curtailed the excessive spending of districts on their own administration. On average, Indonesian districts spend 30 per cent of their total budgets on administration; this is second only to education (34 per cent) and it is double the average allocation for infrastructure. Administrative expenditures comprise the following subcategories: general government (which makes up 86 per cent of the administration budget), development planning, unity and local politics, personnel, people and village empowerment, statistics, archives, and communication and informatics. These spending levels are clearly excessive by any international standard; large amounts of resources are taken away from the production of public services such as health, education, transport and infrastructure, and directed towards less productive or completely unproductive uses such as large government buildings, overstaffing of the central administration and expensive cars.[18] The high spending levels are fairly stable over time: while the share of administrative spending has decreased slightly since 2005, the per capita levels have increased along with the overall district budget (Figure 8.2).

Sjahrir, Kis-Katos and Schulze (2014) create an unbalanced panel for 399 districts covering the years 2001–09 and regress the realized administrative expenditure per capita on four groups of control variables. The authors include, first, variables that determine an efficient level of administrative spending, such as population size (to capture economies of scale) and characteristics of the district's geography and settlement pattern (for example, the number of villages, the share of landlocked villages, distance to Jakarta, district area and urbanization rate). Real GDP per capita portrays the demand for administrative services. Second, they include fiscal revenues per capita to capture the financial endowment of the district, hypothesizing that richer districts spend more on administration. Third, they include variables that portray accountability channels, with literacy rates being the proxy for the educational profile of the constituency and thus the degree to which citizens are able to effectively monitor local government behaviour. Also in this group is a dummy variable for resource-rich districts, as resource endowment has been shown to increase corruption (van der Ploeg 2011). Lastly, the authors include a set of dummy variables portraying the years before and after a split for the parent district and for the first years after a split for the child district, as well as time dummies.

Sjahrir, Kis-Katos and Schulze find evidence for scale economies in administrative spending. Administrative spending increases with the urbanization rate and the income level of the district. Richer districts

---

18 Sjahrir, Kis-Katos and Schulze (2014) provide some anecdotal evidence on the forms of overspending. Obviously administrative spending is not unproductive as such, but it is unproductive at such levels.

Figure 8.2   Share of administrative expenditure relative to total expenditure, 2001–09

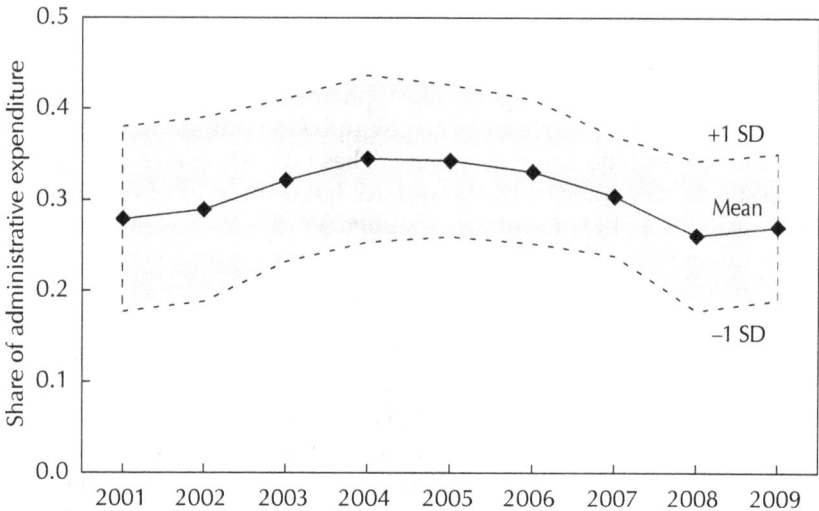

Source: Regional Financial Information System (Sistem Informasi Keuangan Daerah, SIKD), Ministry of Finance; Indonesia Database for Policy and Economic Research (DAPOER INDO), World Bank.

spend more on administration, with an elasticity close to one, whereas efficient spending levels should have a much smaller elasticity. The authors find no statistically significant evidence for literacy rates to reduce overspending. Moreover, the splitting of districts does not alter the aggregate level of administrative spending per capita (only its composition during a transition phase), indicating that *pemekaran* is not responsible for the high levels of administrative spending.

In a second set of regressions, the authors include dummies for direct and indirect elections of district heads and find no significant effect. In other words, they find no evidence that democratization has increased accountability and as a consequence reduced wasteful spending on district administration! Underlying this result is a heterogeneous reaction to direct elections: direct elections have reduced administrative spending for richer districts (those with already high levels of spending) and increased it for districts that are financially relatively poorly endowed. Overall, democratization has not improved governance. For the 197 districts that did not split, the authors include measures of parliament composition.[19]

---

19 Splitting districts elect new parliaments, the compositions of which are not reported centrally. Thus, these districts could not be included.

They find that districts with a higher political concentration (that is, less political competition) spend significantly more on administration.

Overall, the analysis shows a high level of wasteful government spending that benefits those who rule by increasing the perks of office, but not the citizens for whom the funds are intended. These levels are persistent and are little affected by the steps towards more democracy and more direct accountability of the elected leaders.

8.6   DECENTRALIZATION AND PUBLIC SERVICE DELIVERY

Finally, in 'Decentralization and public service delivery: the case of Indonesia', we analyse the effect of D&D on public service delivery levels for selected services (Schulze and Sjahrir 2014). This is arguably the most direct approach to measuring the effects of D&D, as delivering local public services for the benefit of citizens is the central task of local governments. Our dependent variables are the number of junior secondary schools per 100 children of junior secondary school age, the junior secondary net enrolment rate (NER), the number of *puskesmas* per 10,000 people, the share of births attended by medical personnel, the share of villages with paved roads and the share of households with access to clean water. We use these variables because they measure central services at the local level; the first five are under the direct control of district governments, and water provision is under their indirect control through district-owned water utility companies.

In a first set of regressions, we show that, after decentralization, districts with low levels of service provision have tended to increase their service levels faster than already relatively advanced districts. This result is in line with the result on the input side (Kis-Katos and Sjahrir 2014) and shows a general tendency for convergence in public service delivery. The trend is not uniform across sectors, however. Figure 8.3 shows that convergence is strongest in education, and the pattern is apparent both before and after decentralization. Health shows slight convergence before decentralization but no significant convergence after decentralization. Infrastructure shows stronger signs of convergence after decentralization than before it.

In a second set of regressions, we use the panel structure of our data and seek to explain service delivery levels using the seemingly unrelated regression approach for 418 districts. We control for revenues per capita, local GDP per capita, urbanization rates, literacy rates and population density; we also include time dummies and a dummy for a parent district. Our variables of interest are a decentralization dummy that equals one from 2001 onward, measuring the effect of decentralization on public

Figure 8.3   Service delivery patterns before and after decentralization[a]

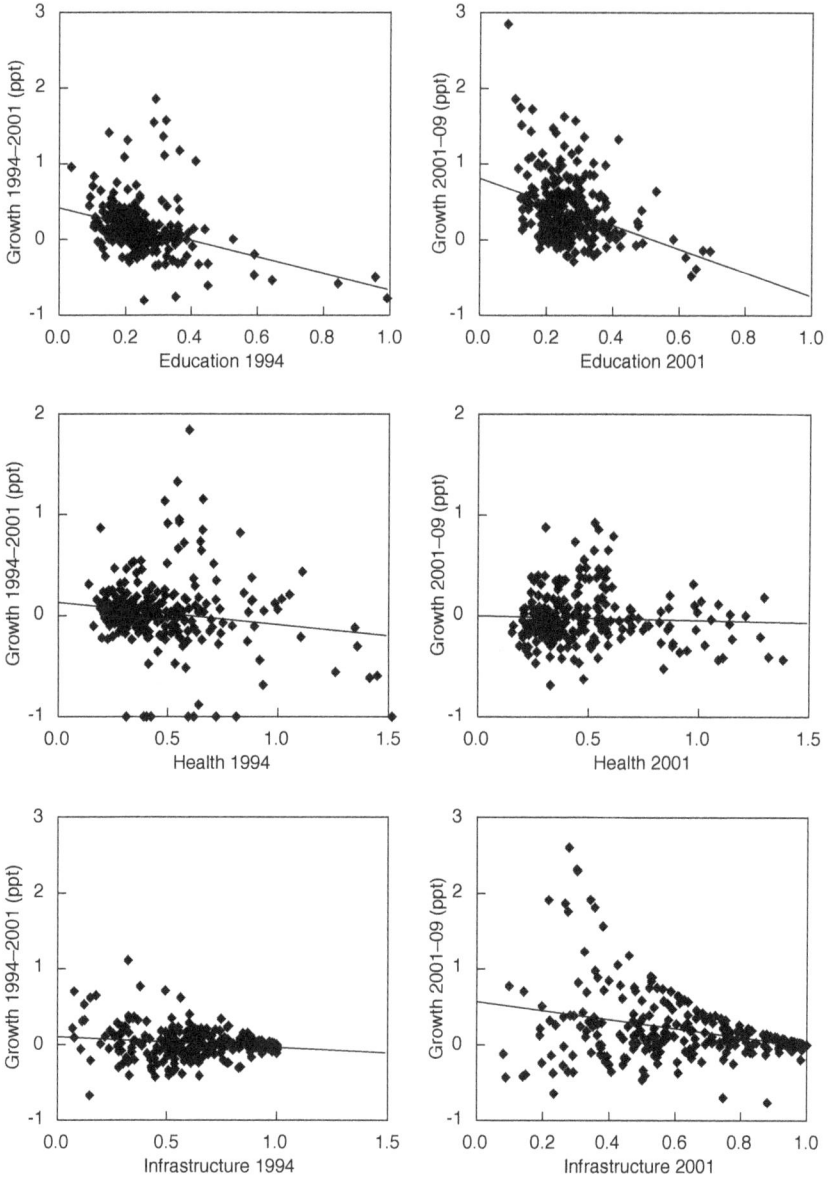

a   Service delivery indicators are the number of junior secondary schools per 100 children of junior secondary school age (education), the number of community health centres (*puskesmas*) per 10,000 people (health) and the share of villages with paved roads (infrastructure). The X axis indicates the service delivery indicators at the beginning of the period and the Y axis indicates growth of the service delivery indicator during the given period. The figures on the left are for the period before decentralization and the figures on the right for the period after decentralization.

service delivery; and two dummies indicating if the head is elected by the local parliament or elected directly by the constituency, measuring the effects of democratization at the local level. In addition, we include the interaction effects of these dummies with revenue per capita. In fixed effects (FE) and in pooled ordinary least square (OLS) regressions, decentralization tends to improve service delivery levels: for four of the six indicators performance improves after decentralization, while two indicators deteriorate in the pooled OLS model and one in the FE model. Again we have no clear effect of direct elections on service delivery levels. Direct elections reduce the number of junior secondary schools per 100 school-aged children and the ratio of *puskesmas* to population for the poor districts, but increase these indicators for the rich districts (FE regressions). For deliveries assisted by medical personnel and the share of villages with paved roads, the effects are the reverse. The effect of district revenues per capita is positive for the latter two indicators and for the number of secondary schools per 100 school-aged children. This shows the importance of fiscal endowment for service delivery levels.

In a third set of regressions, we restrict our sample to the districts that did not split, because data on ethno-linguistic fragmentation and the composition of the local parliament are available only for those districts. Ethno-linguistic fragmentation affects service delivery in a way that is contrary to expectations: more homogenous districts do not provide more public goods, and for some indicators the estimated coefficients are actually negative. The effect of political concentration in the local parliament is non-uniform: it has little effect on service delivery, except in the case of road and water infrastructure, which is better in districts with a higher concentration in the local parliament.[20] Direct elections do not have a differential effect for districts with higher political concentration, except in the case of road infrastructure, which improves even further in politically highly concentrated districts.

Overall, decentralization seems to have improved service delivery outcomes, even though the picture is not as clear-cut as might have been expected. Our results corroborate earlier findings for the input side that the structure of public budgets has become more needs-oriented (see section 8.4 and Kis-Katos and Sjahrir 2014). Democratization has less tangible effects that depend to a large extent on the fiscal endowments of the districts. This is again in line with earlier findings that direct elections have not (yet) improved accountability and thus governance quality in a significant way (see section 8.5 and Sjahrir, Kis-Katos and Schulze 2014). Higher literacy rates have mostly positive effects on public service

---

20 Political concentration is measured only for the reform period (beginning in 1999), when local parliaments could first be directly elected.

delivery outputs. A very clear result, however, is that financially better-endowed districts provide significantly better services than poorer ones.

8.7 CONCLUSION

This chapter has reported on three major studies examining the effects of decentralization and local democratization on public service delivery in Indonesia. The studies analysed the effects of these major institutional reforms on the input side by looking at the changes in budget structures, on the technology side by investigating to what extent democratization has reduced wasteful spending on district administration, and on the output side by analysing the effects on public service delivery levels. A coherent picture emerges from a synopsis of the results of these studies.

Decentralization seems to have improved service delivery and has made budgets more needs-oriented. The transfer of the authority to spend money on health, education and infrastructure to the local level seems to have resulted in better preference matching. In the aggregate decentralization has given districts the financial resources to deliver better services, although the distribution of revenues per capita is still quite uneven. Yet, this effect is not as uniform and as strong as proponents of this reform may have hoped. Democratization at the local level – as measured by the democratic election of district heads, first by democratically elected local parliaments and subsequently directly by local electorates – has not (yet) had a significant effect on budget composition or on the extent to which government resources are wasted through excessive spending on district administration. Consequently, there is no clear impact on service delivery levels. This mirrors observations that corruption has not receded since decentralization and local democratization, but rather has shifted to local actors and become more diffuse (Hill 2012; Hofman, Kaiser and Schulze 2009). Our findings clearly indicate, however, that money matters. Larger revenues per capita improve public service delivery significantly. Fiscal endowment also influences the way in which districts respond to democratization. Rich districts behave significantly differently to poorer districts (but not uniformly so across all sectors).

The results may be disappointing at first glance, as they contradict simple textbook notions of the positive effects of D&D reforms. Yet, a little more than a decade into decentralization and democratization at the local level, it may be too early to hand down the final verdict. Even though these reforms have been fundamental in the sense that they have empowered local actors and changed the way in which institutions interact and office holders are selected, they have not replaced the elites that established themselves under the New Order. The inclusion of potential veto players in the new system may have been a precondition for the success of these reforms (Aspinall 2010). It may thus be too naïve to assume that changing the formal rules of the game will have large, immediate effects. Instead we find evidence for some moderate and heterogeneous improvements only. We think that our results portray the reality quite well and that the situation has yet to change for the better in a more tangible way. However, these institutional reforms may have unleashed forces that will affect the quality of the political process over time. In particular, the emergence of a politically powerful civil society (including the business community), the increasing role of the Corruption Eradication Commission (Komisi Pemberantasan Korupsi, KPK) and the de-politicization of the military may lead to reforms that make the political system more open, more competitive and as a consequence more responsive and accountable. The future may hold more than we can currently see.

REFERENCES

Agustina, C.D., W. Fengler and G.G. Schulze (2012) 'The regional impact of Indonesia's fiscal policy on oil and gas: options for reform', *Bulletin of Indonesian Economic Studies*, 48(3): 369–97.

Arzaghi, M. and V. Henderson (2005) 'Why countries are fiscally decentralizing', *Journal of Public Economics*, 89: 1,157–89.

Aspinall, E. (2010) 'Indonesia: the irony of success', *Journal of Democracy*, 21(2): 20–34.

Baiochhi, G. (2006) 'Inequality and innovation: decentralization as an opportunity structure in Brazil', in P. Bardhan and D. Mookherjee (eds) *Decentralization and Local Governance in Developing Countries: A Comparative Perspective*, MIT Press, Cambridge.

Bardhan, P. and D. Mookherjee (2000) 'Capture and governance at local and national levels', *American Economic Review*, 90(2): 135–9.

Bardhan, P. and D. Mookherjee (2006a) 'Decentralisation and accountability in infrastructure delivery in developing countries', *Economic Journal*, 116(508): 101–27.

Bardhan, P. and D. Mookherjee (2006b) 'Decentralization, corruption and government accountability', in S. Rose-Ackerman (ed.) *International Handbook on the Economics of Corruption*, Edward Elgar, Cheltenham.

Besley, T. and A. Case (1995) 'Incumbent behavior: vote-seeking, tax-setting and yardstick competition', *American Economic Review*, 85(1): 25–45.

Besley, T. and A. Prat (2006) 'Handcuffs for the grabbing hand? Media capture and government accountability', *American Economic Review*, 96(3): 720–36.

Blanchard, O. and A. Shleifer (2001) 'Federalism with and without political centralization: China versus Russia', *IMF Staff Papers*, 48(4): 171–9.

Brennan, G. and J. Buchanan (1980) *The Power to Tax: Analytical Foundation of a Fiscal Constitution*, Cambridge University Press, Cambridge.

Brunetti, A. and B. Weder (2003) 'A free press is bad news for corruption', *Journal of Public Economics*, 87: 1,801–24.

Buehler, M. (2010) 'Decentralisation and local democracy in Indonesia: the marginalisation of the public sphere', in E. Aspinall and M. Mietzner (eds) *Problems of Democratisation in Indonesia: Elections, Institutions and Society*, Institute of Southeast Asian Studies, Singapore.

Chaudhuri, S. (2006) 'What difference does a constitutional amendment make? The 1994 Panchayati Raj Act and the attempt to revitalize rural local government in India', in P. Bardhan and D. Mookherjee (eds) *Decentralization and Local Governance in Developing Countries: A Comparative Perspective*, MIT Press, Cambridge.

Decentralization Support Facility (2007) *Costs and Benefits of New Region Creation in Indonesia: Final Report*, Decentralization Support Facility, Jakarta.

Fadliya and R.H. McLeod (2011) 'Fiscal transfers to regional governments in Indonesia', paper presented at the Decentralization and Democratization in Southeast Asia conference, University of Freiburg, Freiburg, 15–17 June.

Faguet, J.-P. (2004) 'Does decentralization increase government responsiveness to local needs? Evidence from Bolivia', *Journal of Public Economics*, 88: 867–93.

Farfán-Vallespín, A. (2014) 'Decentralization as unbundling of public goods provision', revised working paper, Department of International Economic Policy, University of Freiburg, Freiburg.

Ferejohn, J. (1986) 'Incumbent performance and electoral control', *Public Choice*, 50(1–3): 5–26.

Ferraz, C. and F. Finan (2008) 'Exposing corrupt politicians: the effects of Brazil's publicly released audits on electoral outcomes', *Quarterly Journal of Economics*, 123: 703–45.

Fitrani, F., B. Hofman and K. Kaiser (2005) 'Unity in diversity? The creation of new local governments in a decentralising Indonesia', *Bulletin of Indonesian Economic Studies*, 41(1): 57–79.

Galasso, E. and M. Ravallion (2005) 'Decentralized targeting of an antipoverty program', *Journal of Public Economics*, 89(4): 705–27.

Galiani, S., P. Gertler and E. Schargrodsky (2008) 'School decentralization: helping the good get better, but leaving the poor behind', *Journal of Public Economics*, 92(10–11): 2,106–20.

Hamilton, A., J. Jay and J. Madison (1787) *The Federalist: A Commentary on the Constitution of the United States*, ed. by R. Scigliano, Random House, New York, 2001.

Hayek, F.A. von (1948) *Individualism and Economic Order*, University of Chicago Press, Chicago.

Hill, H. (2012) 'Corruption and development: the Indonesian experience', in S. Khoman (ed.) *A Scholar for All: Essays in Honour of Medhi Krongkaew*, Thammasat University Press, Bangkok.

Hofman, B., K. Kaiser and G.G. Schulze (2009) 'Corruption and decentralization', in C.J.G. Holzappel and M. Ramstedt (eds) *Decentralization and Regional Autonomy in Indonesia*, Institute for Southeast Asian Studies, Singapore.

Kaiser, K., D. Pattinasarany and G.G. Schulze (2006) 'Decentralization, governance and public services in Indonesia', in P. Smoke, E.J. Gómez and G.E. Peterson (eds) *Decentralization in Latin America and Asia: Towards a Comparative Inter-disciplinary Perspective*, Edward Elgar, Cheltenham.

Kis-Katos, K. and B.S. Sjahrir (2014) 'The impact of fiscal and political decentralization on local public investments in Indonesia', Department of International Economic Policy Working Paper No. 25, University of Freiburg, Freiburg.

Kis-Katos, K. and G.G. Schulze (2013) 'Corruption in Southeast Asia: a survey of recent research', *Asian-Pacific Economic Literature*, 27(1): 79–109.

Lewis, B.D. (2005) 'Indonesian local government spending, taxing and saving: an explanation of pre- and post-decentralization fiscal outcomes', *Asian Economic Journal*, 19(3): 291–317.

Lewis, B.D. (2007) 'On-lending in Indonesia: past performance and future prospects', *Bulletin of Indonesian Economic Studies*, 43(1): 35–57.

Lewis, B.D. and A. Oosterman (2009) 'The impact of decentralization on subnational government fiscal slack in Indonesia', *Public Budgeting and Finance*, 29(2): 27–47.

Lindsay, J. (2009) 'Pomp, piety and performance: *pilkada* in Yogyakarta 2005', in M. Erb and P. Sulistiyanto (eds) *Deepening Democracy in Indonesia? Direct Elections for Local Leaders (Pilkada)*, Institute of Southeast Asian Studies, Singapore.

Mauro, P. (1998) 'Corruption and the composition of government expenditure', *Journal of Public Economics*, 69(2): 263–79.

Mietzner, M. (2006) 'Local democracy', *Inside Indonesia*, 85: 17–18.

Mietzner, M. (2010) 'Indonesia's direct elections: empowering the electorate or entrenching the new order oligarchy?', in E. Aspinall and G. Fealy (eds) *Soeharto's New Order and Its Legacy*, ANU Press, Canberra.

Oates, W. (1972) *Fiscal Federalism*, Harcourt Brace Jovanovich, New York.

Olken, B. (2007) 'Monitoring corruption: evidence from a field experiment in Indonesia', *Journal of Political Economy*, 115(2): 200–49.

Prud'homme, R. (1995) 'The dangers of decentralization', *World Bank Research Observer*, 10(2): 201–20.

Qian, Y. and B.R. Weingast (1997) 'Federalism as a commitment to preserving market incentives', *Journal of Economic Perspectives*, 11(4): 83–92.

Reinikka, R. and J. Svensson (2004) 'Local capture: evidence from a central government transfer program in Uganda', *Quarterly Journal of Economics*, 119(2): 679–705.

Schulze, G.G. and B.S. Sjahrir (2014) 'Decentralization and public service delivery: the case of Indonesia', University of Freiburg, Freiburg.

Seabright, P. (1996) 'Accountability and decentralisation in government: an incomplete contracts model', *European Economic Review*, 40(1): 61–89.

Shleifer, A. and R.W. Vishny (1993) 'Corruption', *Quarterly Journal of Economics*, 108(3): 599–617.

Sjahrir, B.S., K. Kis-Katos and G.G. Schulze (2013) 'Political budget cycles in Indonesia at the district level', *Economics Letters*, 120(2): 342–5.

Sjahrir, B.S., K. Kis-Katos and G.G. Schulze (2014) 'Administrative overspending in Indonesian districts: the role of local politics', *World Development*, 59: 166–83.

Skoufias, E., A. Narayan, B. Dasgupta and K. Kaiser (2014) 'Electoral accountability and local government spending in Indonesia', unpublished paper, World Bank, Washington DC.

Tiebout, C. (1956) 'A pure theory of local expenditures', *Journal of Political Economy*, 64(5): 416–24.

van der Ploeg, F. (2011) 'Natural resources: curse or blessing?', *Journal of Economic Literature*, 49(2): 366–420.

World Bank (2003) 'Decentralizing Indonesia: a regional public expenditure review overview report', World Bank, Jakarta.

World Bank (2012) 'Indonesia sub-national public expenditure review: optimizing subnational performance for better services and faster growth', World Bank, Jakarta.

9 What determines the quality of subnational economic governance? Comparing Indonesia and Vietnam

Neil McCulloch and Edmund Malesky[*]

9.1 INTRODUCTION

There is a large literature on the relationship between the quality of governance – broadly defined – and long-run economic performance (North
1990; Acemoglu, Johnson and Robinson 2002). The general conclusion
from this literature is that institutions, and the quality of their governance, matter for economic performance at the country level. There is also
evidence to suggest that subnational governance is related to economic
performance at the subnational level, although the evidence here is more
mixed (Eckardt 2002; McCulloch and Malesky 2011). This chapter asks
a different question: what are the drivers of the quality of subnational
economic governance? The general assumption in the literature, and by
policy makers, is that the quality of governance is a choice, that is, that

[*] We would like to thank Professor Hubert Schmitz for his leadership of the Economic and Social Research Council (ESRC) and Department for International
Development (DFID) research program from which this work derives. We
gratefully acknowledge comments by Nguyen Duc Nhat of VietSurvey, and
by participants of the 2013 Indonesia Update conference. The United States
Agency for International Development, the Vietnam Chamber of Commerce
and Industry and the General Statistics Office of Vietnam kindly provided
access to the Vietnamese data used; Regional Autonomy Watch (KPPOD),
the Asia Foundation and Statistics Indonesia (BPS) kindly provided the Indonesian data. We gratefully acknowledge funding from ESRC, DFID and the
Department of Foreign Affairs and Trade. Naturally all errors are our own.

'good' leaders choose to have good governance and 'bad' ones choose otherwise. Leadership is clearly critical (von Luebke 2009; Patunru, von Luebke and McCulloch 2012), but there may also be structural factors, such as the size of the local economy, its location and its natural resource endowments, that influence the quality of governance by shifting the incentives faced by local leaders. We explore the influence of such factors in both Indonesia and Vietnam using quantitative data on the quality of subnational governance and the characteristics of subnational regions.

To preview our results, we find some interesting similarities in the determinants of subnational governance between the two countries, but also some marked differences. In particular, we find support for the idea that the complexity and size of modern cities reduce the quality of local governance. But we also find that being located outside Java appears to have a negative impact on the quality of governance in Indonesia, as does the size of the local economy, whereas neither location nor GDP appears to influence the quality of governance in Vietnam. We suggest that the structure of the political institutions in the two countries has provided a different set of incentives for local leaders, and that it is this that may be responsible for the differences in the determinants of subnational economic performance in Vietnam and Indonesia.

The chapter is structured as follows. Section 9.2 describes the structural drivers of subnational economic governance in Indonesia. Section 9.3 examines the drivers of changes in the quality of governance at the provincial level in Vietnam, exploiting both quantitative and qualitative evidence. Section 9.4 outlines our hypothesis for what may be driving these different results, and Section 9.5 suggests some implications for policy.

9.2   STRUCTURAL DRIVERS OF SUBNATIONAL ECONOMIC GOVERNANCE IN INDONESIA

In 2008 the Asia Foundation, in conjunction with a national Indonesian non-government organization, Regional Autonomy Watch (Komite Pemantauan Pelaksanaan Otonomi Daerah, KPPOD), launched a new dataset measuring the quality of local economic governance in 243 districts across Indonesia (KPPOD 2008).[1] The dataset is based on a statistically representative, random sample of over 12,000 firms and 729 business

---

1 This dataset is one of a series measuring economic governance in Vietnam, Bangladesh, Sri Lanka, Cambodia and the Philippines, with support from the Asia Foundation. Further details can be found at www.asiafoundation.org.

associations throughout these districts.[2] Each sampled firm was asked a series of questions about nine different aspects of local governance:

1   access to land and security of tenure;
2   market entry and business licensing;
3   local government–business interaction;
4   business development programs;
5   the capacity and integrity of the district head or mayor;
6   local taxes, user charges and other transaction costs;
7   local infrastructure;
8   security and conflict resolution; and
9   access to information.

The responses of the 50 firms in each district to the questions in each of the nine areas were used to construct a set of subindices reflecting the quality of governance in each area.[3] The subindices were also aggregated into a single Economic Governance Index (EGI) for each district.[4]

One advantage of this measure of local economic governance is that it contains only things that are under the direct control of the local government. Often surveys of the subnational investment climate aim to rank the attractiveness of locations for investment and therefore include variables relating to the endowments of a district, such as its natural resources and its proximity to major markets. These are not characteristics that a district government can influence, however, and they are therefore not good measures of the quality of current local economic governance. The EGI focuses on attempting to measure the quality of governance rather than endowments.

The KPPOD survey shows that the quality of economic governance varies considerably across Indonesia's districts. For example, the city of

---

2   Within each district, the survey was stratified by firm size (firms with 10–19, 20–99 or 100+ employees) and by sector (production, trade or services). The survey is representative of all private sector firms with 10 or more employees in the non-primary sector. See KPPOD (2008) for full details.

3   For example, the land subindex was constructed from responses to questions about the time it took to obtain a land certificate, the ease of getting access to land, the frequency of land evictions and conflicts over land, and overall perceptions on whether there were significant land-related problems in the district. See KPPOD (2008) for a detailed description of the construction of the subindices.

4   In the analysis presented here, the EGI is a simple sum of the nine subindices. This differs from the calculation of the EGI by KPPOD (2008), which includes a measure of the quality of local legislation based on expert assessment, and uses weights of the relative importance of different subindices.

Blitar in East Java has an overall EGI score of 76, indicating a high quality of economic governance across the nine different areas measured by the index, whereas South Nias receives an EGI of only 41, primarily because of its very poor scores for infrastructure governance, the integrity and capacity of the mayor, and the quality of business–government interaction (KPPOD 2008).

What drives this wide variation in the quality of economic governance at the district level? One possibility is that the quality of local economic governance is determined by the district leadership. Indeed, the underlying rationale for the production of the index is that, by publicizing information about good or bad governance, it will bring pressure to bear on the local leadership to improve its performance. There can be little doubt that local leadership plays an important role in determining the quality of local governance (von Luebke 2009). However, the incentives faced by local leaders are often influenced by the structural economic context in which they operate, for example, whether the district is remote or close to a major city, whether it has major natural resources and so on. Hence it is valuable to ask whether there is a connection between the structural economic characteristics of a region and the quality of its economic governance.

What sort of structural characteristics might we expect, a priori, to influence these attributes of governance? Consider natural resources. There is a large literature on the natural resource 'curse' (for example, Ross 1999; Dunning 2008), the idea that the presence of natural resources gives rise to conflict over control of these resources and therefore, paradoxically, to slower growth. If this is true at a subnational level, we would expect that the quality of governance would be negatively correlated with measures of natural resource dependence.

Consider, also, the size of the local economy. One of the stylized facts from our data is that urban districts (*kota*) in Indonesia have worse overall governance scores than rural districts (*kabupaten*). One possible explanation for this is that urban areas have to deal with issues of congestion, overcrowding, crime and pollution to a greater extent than rural areas. Land management can also be more complex and contentious. However, urban areas also tend to have better infrastructure, including better internet access, enabling a greater degree of transparency.

Similarly, one might expect richer regions to have poorer governance than poorer ones if rent seeking is related to the size of the local economy. Larger local economies may be more prone to rent seeking simply because the incentives for such behaviour are greater in wealthier regions than in poorer ones. If this is the case, the size of the local economy should be an important predictor of the quality of governance. Conversely, one might argue that richer districts might have advantages, such as more competent local officials and, like urban areas, better communications infrastructure facilitating greater transparency.

Other structural variables include the size of the population. As with the size of the local economy, a larger population may create more opportunities for rent seeking. It may also make service delivery more complex, potentially reducing people's perceptions of the competence of the local government. Similarly, one might expect distance from the capital, Jakarta, to have a negative effect on the quality of governance. This is based on the idea that districts that are physically closer to the capital are more likely to come under the scrutiny of the centre, while those at the periphery of the country may find it easier to pursue rent-seeking policies. The same is true for ethno-linguistic fractionalization, which has been shown in other contexts to reduce economic performance through its influence on elite capture (Easterly and Levine 1997). Religious fragmentation might be expected to have a similar effect. In contrast, we might expect the general level of education in a district to have a positive influence both on the competence of the local administration and on the transparency and accountability of its government, leading to a positive correlation with measures of the quality of governance.

Our structural variables are based on data compiled from surveys conducted by Indonesia's central statistics agency, Badan Pusat Statistik (BPS). Data from the annual National Socio-Economic Survey (Survei Sosio-Ekonomi Nasional, Susenas) have been aggregated to provide comprehensive socio-economic indicators at the district level. Every three years BPS also conducts the Village Potential (Potensi Desa, Podes) census, collecting data on basic infrastructure and socio-economic conditions at the village level throughout the country. These data have also been aggregated to provide district-level indicators.

We estimate the following regression:

$$Gov = \beta_0 + \beta_1.\ln GDP + \beta_2.Miningshare + \beta_3.\ln Pop + \beta_4.City + \beta_5.Java$$
$$+ \beta_6.\ln Dist + \beta_7.Schooling + \beta_8.Ethnic + \beta_9.religious + \varepsilon$$

where *Gov* is a measure of the quality of district governance; $\ln GDP$ is the log of non-oil district GDP; *Miningshare* is the share of mining in district GDP; $\ln Pop$ is the log of the district population; *City* is a dummy for the district being an urban district (*kota*); *Java* is a dummy for the district being in Java; $\ln Dist$ is the log of the distance of the district from Jakarta; *Schooling* is the share of the adult population that has ever attended secondary school; *Ethnic* is a measure of ethno-linguistic fractionalization; *religious* is a measure of religious fragmentation; and ε is the usual error term. Table 9.1 shows the results of a series of regressions exploring the above hypotheses.

Table 9.1   *Structural determinants of local economic governance in Indonesia*

	Economic Governance Index (EGI)	Integrity of district head or mayor	Quality of licensing	Quality of local government–business interaction
Log non-oil gross regional product (GRP)	−1.972 (1.97)*	−4.559 (2.62)***	0.115 (0.11)	−0.500 (0.33)
Share of mining in GRP (2002)	1.562 (0.51)	6.573 (1.38)	0.392 (0.10)	2.888 (0.65)
Log population (2002)	−3.207 (5.46)***	−4.371 (3.65)***	−5.214 (6.20)***	−4.357 (3.85)***
City (*kota*)	−1.181 (0.67)	−2.565 (0.73)	−3.399 (1.48)	−0.675 (0.24)
In Java	9.365 (8.15)***	5.751 (2.16)**	7.907 (4.22)***	2.951 (1.30)
Log distance from Jakarta	1.980 (2.82)***	0.708 (0.48)	2.125 (2.23)**	0.807 (0.59)
Share ever attended secondary school (2002)	0.494 (0.05)	13.615 (0.65)	23.925 (1.68)*	−6.103 (0.35)
Ethno-linguistic fragmentation	4.998 (2.32)**	5.986 (1.29)	2.554 (0.88)	3.111 (0.74)
Religious fragmentation	−7.639 (2.43)**	−6.280 (0.86)	−20.314 (4.12)***	−5.593 (0.83)
Constant	112.291 (6.14)***	173.198 (5.30)***	108.741 (4.96)***	113.773 (3.69)***
R^2	0.30	0.13	0.27	0.14
N	195	197	197	197

* = $p < 0.1$; ** = $p < 0.05$; *** = $p < 0.01$. Standard deviations are in parentheses.

Column 1 shows the influence of the structural variables on the overall EGI.[5] The results confirm some of our prior expectations about the structural correlates of governance. For example, districts with large economies have worse governance than those with poorer economies. Similarly, districts with large populations have poorer governance. Both of these effects are statistically significant; but not large. For example, a

---

5   To minimize potential endogeneity, we have used 2001 values for all structural variables. The governance variables were measured in 2007.

10 per cent increase in the population of a district leads to a drop of about 0.3 in the EGI score, but the mean of the EGI score is 58, with a standard deviation of 6.1, so the impact is small. Interestingly, we find that there is no additional impact on governance of a district being a city (*kota*), as opposed to a rural district (*kabupaten*), once the size of the economy and population are taken into account.

We also find no statistically significant effect on governance associated with the share of mining in the local economy (and indeed the sign is the opposite of that expected).[6] Surprisingly, greater ethno-linguistic fragmentation appears to have a positive influence on the overall governance measure, but religious fragmentation has the expected negative effect. Districts outside Java are significantly and substantially worse governed than those in Java. Moreover, this effect is not due to the higher level of education in Javanese districts, which appears to have no statistically significant effect on the quality of governance. This provides tentative support for the idea that districts that are less 'visible' to Jakarta have poorer governance (Olken 2007). This effect is large, with districts outside Java more than one standard deviation worse governed than those in Java, even after controlling for the other determinants of governance.[7]

Columns 2, 3 and 4 of Table 9.1 explore the same relationship, using narrower definitions of governance, and employing some of the sub-indices that comprise the EGI. We look at three subindices: the integrity of the district head or mayor; the quality of licensing; and the quality of interaction between local government and business. We choose these three because they represent different dimensions of governance, and so we might expect that structural characteristics would have different effects on different dimensions. The results appear to bear this out. Integrity is closely associated with the measurement of rent seeking. As expected, we find that larger and more populous districts perform worse, consistent with the view that these characteristics encourage rent seeking. Surprisingly, however, we find that, after controlling for size and population, the share of mining in the local economy has no statistically significant effect on the quality of integrity at the local level. This runs counter to much qualitative evidence on the impact of natural resources on local governance (McCarthy 2002; RWI 2013), although it is consistent

---

6 This result also holds when we measure dependence on natural resources using a dummy for the presence of oil and gas in the district instead of the share of mining.

7 Including distance from Jakarta has a strong negative effect when no Java dummy is included. But this turns into a small positive effect when the Java dummy is included, suggesting that it is not distance per se but rather location outside Java that makes the difference.

with work suggesting that, historically, Indonesia has avoided the worst aspects of the resource curse (Haber and Menaldo 2011).

When the quality of licensing is used as the dependent variable, we find that the size of the economy no longer has a statistically significant impact. This is consistent with licensing quality reflecting the administrative competence of a district government. Districts with large populations continue to have poorer quality licensing, perhaps reflecting the administrative difficulties associated with serving such large numbers of customers. Interestingly, districts with high religious fragmentation also appear to have poorer licensing, suggesting that particular groups may be excluded from effective licensing services.

Finally, we look at the influence of structural variables on the quality of interaction between business and the local government. We choose this subindex because, other than the complexities associated with a large population, we would not expect structural variables to have an important influence on this aspect of governance; rather, the quality of interaction should depend on the quality of local leadership. The results in column 4 are consistent with this interpretation, with no structural variables other than population being associated with the quality of interaction.

9.3   STRUCTURAL DRIVERS OF SUBNATIONAL ECONOMIC GOVERNANCE IN VIETNAM

Unlike Indonesia, Vietnam has had an indicator of the quality of local economic governance at the provincial level for several years.[8] Its Provincial Competitiveness Index (PCI) measures different aspects of economic governance at the provincial level based on responses from a random sample of firms in each province, as well as hard data used to address perception bias among survey respondents. When combined with information on other provincial characteristics, these data allow us to test a range of hypotheses about the determinants of changes in the quality of provincial governance over time. We proceed by describing the data. We then set out a range of structural factors that might influence changes in governance and estimate their importance in driving reform.

---

8 In fact, Indonesia's EGI is based on Vietnam's Provincial Competitiveness Index. Several countries have undertaken similar exercises, but almost always for only one or two years. Vietnam is the only country with a long (six-year) time series of governance measures. See Asia Foundation (2011) for an overview of similar work in Bangladesh, Sri Lanka and Cambodia.

Data

To measure the quality of local economic governance we draw on the PCI, a composite index of provincial economic governance calculated each year since 2006 by the Vietnam Chamber of Commerce and Industry.[9] It is based on a mail-out survey to a random sample of firms in each of Vietnam's 63 provinces (five of which are major cities).[10] The survey asks a range of questions about firms' perceptions of local economic governance, as well as their concrete experiences of local governance. Like the Indonesian EGI, the PCI focuses on aspects of local governance that are under the control of the local – in this case provincial – administration. It therefore excludes factors such as the quality or availability of national roads, airports and ports that would bias the index in favour of larger cities or provinces. Firms' responses to the questions are combined into a set of nine subindices reflecting provincial performance on:

1 entry costs;
2 land access and security of tenure;
3 transparency;
4 time costs of regulatory compliance;
5 informal charges;
6 proactivity of the provincial government;
7 business support services;
8 labour policies; and
9 legal institutions.

Provincial scores on each subindex represent the province's performance on that topic relative to the performance of other provinces in Vietnam. The PCI is a combination of the subindices, yielding an overall score for the quality of economic governance in each province.[11] In

---

9   A pilot PCI survey was conducted in 2005 but this did not cover all provinces in the country.

10 The sampling frame for the survey is the list of firms provided by the provincial tax authority. For example, in 2007, 6,700 firms were chosen randomly from the list of 177,815 firms provided by the tax office. To ensure representativeness, the sample is stratified by legal type of enterprise, sector of business and firm age.

11 For full details of the construction of the PCI, see Malesky and Merchant-Vega (2011). The published PCI scores use a weighted sum of the subindices, with weights determined by the influence of each subindex in predicting different aspects of firm performance. Because our analysis requires a consistent index across time, we construct a mini-PCI using only those variables used in all years from 2006 to 2010, and combine the subindices using equal weights.

our analysis, we measure the speed of economic reform as the average annual growth rate of the PCI in each province between 2006 and 2010.

In addition to the PCI data, we rely on data from several other sources. In particular, we use data on the value of domestic investment drawn from the enterprise census conducted annually by the General Statistics Office (GSO) of Vietnam. This census attempts to cover all non-state enterprises with 10 or more employees (as well as a sample of smaller firms). We also draw on the GSO's national accounts data on GDP at the provincial level, as well as a range of provincial statistics from the GSO's *Statistical Yearbooks*.

Factors that might influence governance quality and reform

We anticipate that a range of structural characteristics may influence the quality of governance in Vietnam at any point in time. For example, the size of the local economy might induce rent seeking, reducing the quality of governance; and provinces that are close to Hanoi or Ho Chi Minh City may be more likely to be part of the discussion of economic reform nationally, and therefore to push through reforms, than those that are more remote. Similarly, major cities may be under more political pressure to pursue reforms because they are more visible on the national stage – but equally they have more complex economies that may make achieving good governance harder. The five national-level cities (Hanoi, Ho Chi Minh City, Hai Phong, Can Tho and Da Nang) also tend to generate much more revenue than other provinces. This makes them politically more powerful, since they are funders rather than supplicants of central government. Malesky (2008) has shown that this has given such provinces considerable autonomy to undertake policy reform. This may enable them to push forward faster with reforms than other, more dependent, provinces.

Column 1 of Table 9.2 shows the results of a regression of the PCI score on lagged structural variables. It shows that the size of provincial GDP, which had a statistically significant and detrimental effect on governance in Indonesia, does not appear to have any influence on the quality of local governance in Vietnam. The same is true for distance from Hanoi or Ho Chi Minh City, in contrast to the significant role played by location in Indonesia. However, being one of the five national-level cities has a large negative impact on the quality of governance (more than one standard deviation), although this is significant only at the 11 per cent level. Population size, interestingly, has a positive and statistically significant effect on governance. The level of education in the province appears to have no effect on the quality of governance. But whether a province is a net contributor of revenue to the centre has a strong and statistically significant positive influence on the quality of governance.

Table 9.2   Regression of governance change on structural and political variables in Vietnam[a]

	Provincial Competitiveness Index (PCI)	Average PCI growth rate (2006–10)
Log GDP per capita	0.390 (0.41)	0.002 (0.57)
Distance to Hanoi/ Ho Chi Minh City	0.232 (0.34)	0.001 (0.41)
National-level city dummy	−4.914 (1.67)	−0.015 (1.58)
Log population	2.526 (2.28)*	−0.001 (0.16)
Percentage of secondary school graduates	−0.011 (0.10)	−0.001 (3.79)**
Net revenue contributor	3.982 (2.16)*	0.013 (2.03)*
PCI (2006)		−0.002 (3.43)**
Constant	27.659 (1.33)	0.191 (2.72)**
R^2	0.23	0.43
N	128	64

* $= p < 0.1$; ** $= p < 0.05$; *** $= p < 0.01$. Standard deviations are in parentheses.
a   Column 1 is a pooled regression of the PCI in 2008 and 2007 on lagged explanatory variables. Column 2 is a regression of the average growth of the PCI from 2006 to 2010, with explanatory variables from 2006 unless otherwise indicated. All regressions include dummies for the provinces of Lang Son and Bac Kan, which were strong outliers.

We are fortunate to have a panel of governance measures over time for Vietnam. This allows us to explore the influence of our structural variables not only on the level of governance at one point in time, but also on the changes in the quality of governance over time. Column 2 of Table 9.2 shows the average annual growth rate of the PCI between 2006 and 2010 regressed against the same set of structural variables. We also include the base level of the PCI in 2006 to capture any potential conditional convergence effect.

We find that provinces that started with low PCI scores in 2006 were significantly more likely than provinces with high scores to have higher growth in their PCI scores over the period. This is consistent with qualitative evidence suggesting that a key motivation for trying to improve governance is to avoid the embarrassment of being publicly ranked near the bottom. A province with an average value of 48.4 on the PCI in 2006 (and average values for all the other variables above) typically experienced growth in its PCI score of 0.25 per cent per year from 2006 to 2010; a province with the same characteristics but an initial PCI score five points lower typically experienced much higher growth of 1.35 per cent per year.

Neither the size of the economy nor the distance from Hanoi or Ho Chi Minh City makes any difference to performance in reforming governance. However, the pace of reform appears to be slower in the five major cities, although this effect is significant only at the 12 per cent level. This may point to the difficulties of reform in the major cities, perhaps due to the higher political visibility of measures that contravene national regulations, even if they improve the investment climate. Better-educated provinces tend to have slower PCI growth; this is consistent with other work showing that education does not necessarily translate into better governance (McCulloch and Malesky 2011).

As expected, we find a large and statistically significant effect on PCI growth of being a province that is a net contributor of revenue to the centre, consistent with the literature suggesting that provinces with large fiscal resources have greater policy autonomy to pursue reform (Malesky 2008). This is also supported by evidence from qualitative work that provinces that have a degree of autonomy (outside the high-profile national cities), as well as those that are embarrassed by their initially poor scores, proactively pursue reform (Schmitz et al. 2012).

The results for Vietnam are rather different from those obtained for Indonesia, a puzzle to which we now turn.

Comparing the determinants of governance in Vietnam and Indonesia

It is instructive to compare the structural determinants of governance and of reform in Vietnam and Indonesia. First, the size of the economy is a strong correlate of poor local governance in Indonesia, but the same is not true in Vietnam. Why might this be the case? In Indonesia, there is ample qualitative evidence for rent seeking in locations with higher levels of economic activity – the results for the integrity subindex in Table 9.1 confirm as much. The fact that there is no such link in Vietnam suggests that the state plays a more proactive role in regulating the quality of governance, which is certainly plausible given the fact that the centre uses the PCI as a monitoring tool.

This would also help to explain why we find a strong connection between location and the quality of governance in Indonesia but not in Vietnam. Javanese districts are significantly and substantially better governed than those outside Java (even after taking into account their higher GDP per capita). This is probably a reflection of the strong central state that existed prior to 1998 under Suharto, when there was a marked Java bias. However, running counter to the 'out of sight, out of mind' theory, we find that, after accounting for Java's better governance performance, districts that are further from Jakarta have better, rather than worse, governance. Autonomy appears to trump neglect in influencing the quality of local governance. In Vietnam, in contrast, there is no connection between distance to the major centres of power and the quality of governance. Again, this probably reflects the enduring presence of a strong central state, ensuring robust information flow and monitoring between the centre and the provinces, regardless of location.

A further difference concerns the role of population. Large populations are associated with poorer governance in Indonesia, but with better governance in Vietnam. This may reflect the fact that the formula for the distribution of central resources to the districts in Indonesia does not fully reflect the size of the local population. As a result, locations with large populations receive substantially lower per capita resources than those with smaller populations (although this is also true to some extent in Vietnam).

The role of cities provides another area of contrast. Vietnam's five national cities have substantially poorer governance than other provinces with revenue autonomy. In Indonesia, however, being a city (*kota*) has no impact on governance, once one accounts for the size of the local economy. The difference is almost certainly due to the different meanings of these two variables. In Vietnam, the cities in question are national cities, facing problems of urbanization (less land to convert, more use of infrastructure and services, greater demand for licences). The manner in which these strategic cities operate is subject to substantial political interference by the centre. The *kota*, on the other hand, are much more numerous, being defined simply as locations that meet a specified set of criteria on population density and the availability of urban facilities. It is therefore not surprising that being a *kota* has no significant influence on the quality of governance, once the size of the economy has been taken into account.

Finally, we find evidence in Vietnam that revenue autonomy is strongly associated with improved governance. Such autonomy also appears to speed up the process of reform. Unfortunately there is no corresponding measure for Indonesia, because its districts have very little revenue autonomy, with almost all of their resources coming from the centre. The Vietnamese result is particularly interesting because, of the 15 provinces that have a degree of revenue autonomy, five are the national cities. It would appear that reform is fastest in non-national cities that have a degree of autonomy but not the political interference associated with being a national city.

In summary, the differential impact of structural variables in determining the quality of subnational governance in Vietnam and Indonesia appears to be driven largely by the different political institutions and incentives in the two countries. Vietnam, with its strong central state, appears to have ensured a distribution of resources and flows of information such that the size of the economy, location and population size do not have a significant influence on governance. These factors matter a great deal in Indonesia, where the centre's control has been significantly weakened since decentralization took effect in 2001. At the same time, we find evidence from Vietnam that political interference has a negative effect on the quality of local governance. But there is also evidence from both countries that autonomy matters. In Vietnam, provinces that get to keep some of the revenues they raise have substantially better governance (and faster improvements in governance) than those that do not; in Indonesia, distance from Jakarta has a positive effect on the quality of governance after controlling for the influence of Java.

We now consider how the structure of the political institutions in the two countries may give rise to the observed results.

9.4 COMPARING THE POLITICAL INSTITUTIONS AND INCENTIVES IN VIETNAM AND INDONESIA

Political institutions and incentives in Vietnam

Vietnam has a nominally centralized system of government controlled by the dominant Vietnamese Communist Party (VCP). The 1992 Constitution makes this clear, stating unambiguously that the national administration is a centralized and unified system from the centre to the local level, with the central government presiding over that system. Thus, while Vietnam has engaged in a great deal of decentralization over the years, residual central control of political promotions and the role of the VCP in cadre selection and evaluation have ensured elements of upward accountability that have encouraged economic reform.

Over the course of the past two decades, however, the centralization of economic reform policy has slowly eroded (Fritzen 2002; van Arkadie et al. 2010). A range of expenditure and regulatory decisions have been delegated to the provinces, and a specific set of provinces has been granted central permission to experiment with economic reform, in much the same way that China allowed its coastal regions to serve as laboratories. The economic reform program in Vietnam has therefore followed a unique pattern, with one province 'fence breaking' or pushing forward with an unsanctioned experiment, a few other provinces copying the success of the initial reform (as market-preserving federalism would expect) and the central government then either legislating that reform at the national level, allowing the experiment to continue in a few provinces, or squelching it entirely. Land reform, the early creation of property rights, privatization (or, as the Vietnamese call it, 'equitization') and the creation of industrial zones have all followed this pattern (Fforde and de Vylder 1996; Kerkvliet 2005; Malesky 2004, 2008). In general the central government appears to tolerate fence breaking, allowing such experimentation to continue for long periods while it gauges its success.

In China, the combination of increased decentralization of decision making in constrained policy settings together with continued party control of promotions has been theorized as 'regionally decentralized authoritarianism' (RDA) (Landry 2008; Xu 2011). The RDA model argues that central authorities in China have designed a system that links regional economic performance to promotion (Whiting 2006). This essentially creates a tournament for local officials that encourages market reform and innovation. A number of studies have demonstrated associations between economic performance and promotion in China (Yang 2004; Chen, Li and Zhou 2005; Landry 2008). The RDA model also argues that central authorities have integrated experimentation into the decision-making process, by comparing local initiatives and selecting those that could be useful in resolving major national policy issues.

The RDA hypothesis gained currency in political analyses of China because it improved on previous explanations of local experimentation – such as the notion of market-preserving federalism developed by Montinola, Qian and Weingast (1995) – by illustrating how regional experimentation was connected to cadre evaluation and management. It also helped explain anomalies in the classic decentralization explanations for Chinese and Vietnamese success, in particular the lack, in both countries, of the capital and labour mobility necessary to generate competition between subunits. Under the household registration system (*hukou* in China, *hộ khẩu* in Vietnam), households had to possess a certificate of residence before becoming eligible for public health and education. This limited labour mobility to experimenting provinces, although the policies were always imperfectly enforced and have been relaxed over time (Young 2000; Gordon and Li 2003; Naughton 2003).

The evidence seems to suggest that Vietnam has adopted 'RDA-lite'. As in China, top officials in Vietnam appear to encourage fence breaking, rather than being renegade local officials simply trying to steal a march on central planners. Gainsborough (2004), for instance, has shown how leaders in some of the leading fence-breaking provinces have had similar career histories and party roles to those of less innovative leaders, suggesting that all local leaders are tied together by the party hierarchy. He also describes how central leaders have used major corruption cases to rein in provincial leaders who were gaining too much power.

Nevertheless, Vietnam and China do differ in one important way. Cadre evaluation as a constraint on decentralized experimentation has had less bite in Vietnam, because it has made far less use of rotation policies to move leaders out of their home provinces and has been significantly less likely to promote officials outside their home provinces (Malesky 2008). Whereas only 18 per cent of Chinese provincial party and state leaders serve in their provinces of birth, 70 per cent of top Vietnamese provincial officials do so. In fact, if one includes Vietnamese officials who have spent the bulk of their careers in a province after arriving from somewhere else at a young age, 90 per cent of Vietnamese officials can be considered native (Pincus et al. 2012). As a result, the long-term horizons of Vietnamese officials are more likely to be associated with the economic success of their home provinces, as opposed to their careers in the central bureaucracy. Table 9.3 shows the key political institutions in Vietnam (and Indonesia).

Incentives facing local leaders in Vietnam

A typical career trajectory for a successful Vietnamese official is to start out as an official in a commune or district before being promoted to head the provincial department of a line ministry. Each central ministry is duplicated at the provincial level in the form of departments. After heading a department, a successful official will seek promotion either within the provincial People's Committee or, more rarely, to Hanoi through the line ministry. A successful chair of a provincial People's Committee (*Ủy ban nhân dân*) aims to become the provincial party secretary (*Bí thư tỉnh ủy*). Very successful provincial party secretaries will move on to high-ranking employment in the central government in Hanoi, but this is quite rare. More likely, the official will remain in the province but aspire to be appointed to the VCP Central Committee, the most powerful policy-making body in the country (Malesky, Abrami and Zheng 2011). It is in charge of devising the country's 10-year socio-economic plans, and is responsible for selecting the general secretary of the Central Committee and members of the Politburo.

From the perspective of local economic governance, the most important position is the chairmanship of the provincial People's Committee.

Table 9.3   Key political institutions in Vietnam and Indonesia

Vietnam	Indonesia
Central Committee • Top policy-making body in Vietnam • Most, but not all, provincial party secretaries will be members **Line ministries** • National line ministries are replicated at the local level • Dual subordination means that the heads of line ministries report both to the central line ministry and to the chair of the provincial People's Committee **Provincial party secretary** • Top leadership position at the provincial level • Represents the party at the local level • Responsible for interpreting the Constitution locally • Receives funding independently of the People's Committee • Other members of the local party committee may include local line ministry chiefs, members of the People's Committee and members of the People's Council **Chair of the People's Committee** • Executive head of the province • Controls the budget for the line ministries **People's Council** • Elected by the general public, from candidates approved by the party • Advises the People's Committee and elects its members, from candidates approved by the party • Has oversight of budget expenditures	**National parliament (DPR)** • Elected by the public every five years, based on multi-member constituencies • Candidates must be members of national parties • Only parties that receive over 3 per cent of the national vote can gain seats in parliament • Approves national legislation and the national budget **Provincial head (governor)** • Directly elected by the public on a single ticket with the deputy governor • Plays dual role of being the central government's representative and representing the interests of the province to the central government • Has limited powers over district heads in the province **District head or mayor (bupati or walikota)** • Directly elected by the public on a single ticket with the deputy district head or mayor • Chief executive of the district • Controls most of the budget for local line ministries **Line ministries** • Responsible for range and staffing of provincial and district line ministries as determined by central regulations • Funded from central, provincial and district budgets **Local parliaments (provincial and district DPRDs)** • Elected by the public every five years (at the same time as the national parliament), based on multi-member constituencies • Approve regional budgets

DPR = Dewan Perwakilan Rakyat (People's Representative Council); DPRD = Dewan Perwakilan Rakyat Daerah (Regional People's Representative Council).
Source: Authors.

A chairman has three sets of incentives: prestige and power; pecuniary benefits for him/herself and related family businesses; and community interests in providing employment and better living conditions for citizens. Increasing provincial revenue in whatever way possible is the primary means by which People's Committee officials achieve these goals. Nguyen Dinh Cung of the Central Institute for Economic Management put it this way in a 2001 interview with one of the authors: 'Provincial revenue is the most important indicator of success and power of all provinces. It is their primary target.'

The financial system provides a major impetus for provinces to maximize their revenues; Hanoi sets national taxes through the Ministry of Finance but returns to the provinces all revenue they generate above a biannually negotiated target (World Bank 1996). As Fritzen (2002: 11) puts it:

> The fiscal system is set up to reward, with greater administrative discretion and resources, those provinces which garner greater levels of FDI and tax revenue ... Since both are highly concentrated on a few provinces, the situation of provinces with respect to de facto administrative discretion can be quite divergent.

The chair of a provincial People's Committees balances this incentive against a few other goals, such as the desire for promotion (success in managing the province and generating revenue and employment may lead to promotion to the position of party secretary); the desire to advance personal interests (most own, or have relatives who own, businesses in the province that would benefit from economic growth and opportunity); and the desire to promote pecuniary interests (a growing province creates more opportunities for rent seeking and personal reward, including opportunities for sweetheart land deals and procurement kickbacks).

Political institutions and incentives in Indonesia

Indonesia's political institutions are somewhat different from those in Vietnam (Table 9.3). Since the fall of the highly centralized Suharto regime in 1998, Indonesia has undergone a profound political transformation. The country now has free and fair elections and, since the introduction of two key laws in 1999, a high degree of decentralization. The president and vice president are directly elected by the people every five years, with the president selecting the national executive. The national parliament is made up of representatives elected by the public from multi-member constituencies. Candidates must be members of national political parties, with only those parties that receive more than 3 per cent of the national vote allowed to take up seats in parliament.

A similar structure exists at the provincial level, with direct elections of provincial governors and deputy governors, and of provincial parliaments. However, the decentralization laws deliberately jumped over the provincial level to provide most authority to the districts,[12] which now number over 500. As a result, the most important position from the perspective of local economic governance is that of the district head or mayor (*bupati* or *walikota*). District heads and their deputies have been directly elected since 2005, giving them (and the parties they represent) a strong measure of downward accountability to the people. District heads are also accountable to their local parliaments (elected in more or less the same manner as the provincial and national parliaments), because they are the bodies responsible for approving the local budget and the district head's annual accountability report.

District heads, however, have another important form of accountability – horizontally to their funders. Since a change in the law in 2005, political parties have received virtually no state funding (Mietzner 2007). As a result, they have to rely heavily on funding from local business oligarchs or, in the case of incumbents, their privileged access to the local budget. The result has been an explosion of allegations of local corruption as both state resources and regulatory authority have become distorted to benefit the interests of major party funders.

Incentives facing local leaders in Indonesia

Given the structure of political institutions in Indonesia, the incentives facing local leaders are rather different from those in Vietnam. In principle, district heads and mayors should be more regarding of their citizens, considering that they are directly elected by the people. Indeed, there is growing evidence that political parties are increasingly taking into account the popularity and reputation of candidates, because unknown or unpopular candidates tend not to be successful. At the same time, running for office is prohibitively expensive. A district election will typically cost the candidate (or his or her backers) several million dollars, depending on location; provincial elections cost tens of millions of dollars. There is therefore a very strong incentive for ambitious local leaders to do all they can to accumulate cash or to commit to regulatory decisions that will win the backing of major funders. At the same time, there is little effective monitoring of district performance by either governors or the central government, and no sanctions in place for non-performance.

---

12 This was done to minimize the incentives for provinces to break away from the centre – a major concern at the time of the change (Fitrani, Hofman and Kaiser 2005).

Moreover, promotion, in the form of selection as a candidate for the position of governor, or election to an important party post that might make one a candidate for a ministerial position, is not related to economic success at the local level. Consequently, despite its more democratic selection mechanism, Indonesia's form of decentralization does not appear to be any more successful than Vietnam's in stimulating the policies and actions necessary for local economic development.

9.5 CONCLUSIONS

We have presented evidence that structural factors such as the size of the local economy, population size and geographical location play a significant role in determining the quality of local economic governance in Indonesia. These same factors do not appear to play the same role in Vietnam, although we find evidence in both countries that the extent of genuine autonomy is positively associated with better governance.

We suggest that the explanation for the differing influence of such structural factors on local governance can be found in the different nature of the two countries' political institutions and incentives for local leaders. In Vietnam, decentralized authority for the provinces coexists with a strong central state that exercises influence over local policy making through the VCP. Although movement of local leaders out of a province is rare, the ability of the party to monitor and reward local performance through promotion appears to have provided incentives for promoting economic growth.

In Indonesia, on the other hand, there seems to be little association between local performance and the career incentives of local leaders, despite strong downward accountability to local electorates. Without any meaningful upward accountability, leaders are often driven more by the need to raise funds than by the necessity to generate local-level growth. This may help to explain why governance is poorer in places with larger economies outside Java.

The policy conclusion from this work is not that local democracy should be abandoned. Rather, it is that Indonesia's decentralization could be enhanced by strengthening upward accountability for district-level leaders, while at the same time introducing and enforcing limits on campaign expenditure to weaken the pressure on candidates to respond to local oligarchs rather than to their own electorates.

REFERENCES

Acemoglu, D., S. Johnson and J.A. Robinson (2002) 'Reversal of fortune: geography and institutions in the making of the modern world income distribution', *Quarterly Journal of Economics*, 117(4): 1,231–94.

Asia Foundation (2011) *Innovations in Strengthening Local Economic Governance in Asia*, Asia Foundation, San Francisco.

Chen, Y., H. Li and L.-A. Zhou (2005) 'Relative performance evaluation and the turnover of provincial leaders in China', *Economics Letters*, 88(3): 421–5.

Dunning, T. (2008) *Crude Democracy: Natural Resource Wealth and Political Regimes*, Cambridge Studies in Comparative Politics, Cambridge University Press, Cambridge.

Easterly, W. and R. Levine (1997) 'Africa's growth tragedy: policies and ethnic divisions', *Quarterly Journal of Economics*, 112(4): 1,203–50.

Eckardt, S. (2002) 'Russia's market distorting federalism: decentralisation, governance and economic performance in Russia in the 90s', Free University, Berlin.

Fforde, A. and S. de Vylder (1996) *From Plan to Market: The Economic Transition in Vietnam*, Westview Press, Boulder.

Fitrani, F., B. Hofman and K. Kaiser (2005) 'Unity in diversity? The creation of new local governments in a decentralising Indonesia', *Bulletin of Indonesian Economic Studies*, 41(1): 57–79.

Fritzen, S. (2002) 'The "foundation of public administration"? Decentralization and its discontents in transitional Vietnam', paper presented at the Asia Conference on Governance in Asia, City University of Hong Kong, Hong Kong, 5–7 December.

Gainsborough, M. (2004) *Changing Political Economy of Vietnam: The Case of Ho Chi Minh City*, Routledge, London.

Gordon, R.H. and W. Li (2003) 'Government as a discriminating monopolist in the financial market: the case of China', *Journal of Public Economics*, 87(2): 283–312.

Haber, S. and V. Menaldo (2011) 'Do natural resources fuel authoritarianism? A reappraisal of the resource curse', *American Political Science Review*, 105(1): 1–26.

Kerkvliet, B.J. (2005) *The Power of Everyday Politics: How Vietnamese Peasants Transformed National Policy*, Cornell University Press, Ithaca.

KPPOD (Komite Pemantauan Pelaksanaan Otonomi Daerah) (2008) *Local Economic Governance in Indonesia: A Survey of Businesses in 243 Regencies/Cities in Indonesia, 2007*, KPPOD and Asia Foundation, Jakarta.

Landry, P.F. (2008) *Decentralized Authoritarianism in China*, Cambridge University Press, New York.

Malesky, E. (2004) 'Leveled mountains and broken fences: measuring and analysing de facto decentralisation in Vietnam', *European Journal of East Asian Studies*, 3(2): 307–36.

Malesky, E. (2008) 'Straight ahead on red: how foreign direct investment empowers subnational leaders', *Journal of Politics*, 70(1): 97–119.

Malesky, E. and N. Merchant-Vega (2011) 'A peek under the engine hood: the methodology of subnational economic governance indices', *Hague Journal on the Rule of Law*, 3(02): 186–219.

Malesky, E., R. Abrami and Y. Zheng (2011) 'Institutions and inequality in single-party regimes: a comparative analysis of Vietnam and China', *Comparative Politics*, 43(4): 409–27.

McCarthy, J.F. (2002) 'Turning in circles: district governance, illegal logging, and environmental decline in Sumatra, Indonesia', *Society and Natural Resources*, 15(10): 867–86.

McCulloch, N. and E. Malesky (2011) 'Does better local governance improve district growth performance in Indonesia?', IDS Working Paper No. 369, Institute of Development Studies, University of Sussex, Brighton.

Mietzner, M. (2007) 'Party financing in post-Soeharto Indonesia: between state subsidies and political corruption', *Contemporary Southeast Asia: A Journal of International and Strategic Affairs*, 29(2): 238–63.

Montinola, G., Y. Qian and B.R. Weingast (1995) 'Federalism, Chinese style: the political basis for economic success in China', *World Politics*, 48(1): 50–81.

Naughton, B. (2003) 'How much can regional integration do to unify China's markets?', in N.C. Hope, D.T. Yang and M.Y. Li (eds) *How Far across the River? Chinese Policy Reform at the Millennium*, Stanford University Press, Palo Alto.

North, D.C. (1990) *Institutions, Institutional Change and Economic Performance*, Cambridge University Press, Cambridge.

Olken, B. (2007) 'Monitoring corruption: evidence from a field experiment in Indonesia', *Journal of Political Economy*, 115(2): 200–49.

Patunru, A., C. von Luebke and N. McCulloch (2012) 'A tale of two cities: the political economy of local investment climate in Indonesia', *Journal of Development Studies*, 18(7): 799–816.

Pincus, J., V.T. Anh, P.D. Nghia, B. Wilkinson and N.X. Thanh (2012) 'Structural reform for growth, equity, and national sovereignty', policy discussion paper prepared for the Vietnam Executive Leadership Program (VELP), Harvard Kennedy School, Cambridge, 13–17 February.

Ross, M. (1999) 'The political economy of the resource curse', *World Politics*, 51(2): 297–322.

RWI (Revenue Watch Institute) (2013) 'Oil, gas and minerals for the public good: the Revenue Watch 2013 Resource Governance Index', RWI, New York.

Schmitz, H., D.A. Tuan, P.T.T. Hang and N. McCulloch (2012) 'Who drives economic reform in Vietnam's provinces?', IDS Research Report No. 76, Institute of Development Studies, University of Sussex, Brighton.

van Arkadie, B. et al. (2010) 'Joint country analysis: development challenges in a middle-income Viet Nam', United Nations, Hanoi.

von Luebke, C. (2009) 'The political economy of local governance: findings from an Indonesian field study', *Bulletin of Indonesia Economic Studies*, 45(2): 201–30.

Whiting, S.H. (2006) *Power and Wealth in Rural China: The Political Economy of Institutional Change*, Cambridge University Press, Cambridge and New York.

World Bank (1996) *Vietnam: Fiscal Decentralization and the Delivery of Rural Services*, World Bank, Hanoi.

Xu, C. (2011) 'The fundamental institutions of China's reforms and development', *Journal of Economic Literature*, 49(4): 1,076–51.

Yang, D.L. (2004) *Remaking the Chinese Leviathan: Market Transition and the Politics of Governance in China*, Stanford University Press, Stanford.

Young, A. (2000) 'The razor's edge: distortions and incremental reform in the People's Republic of China', *Quarterly Journal of Economics*, 115(4): 1,091–135.

PART 3

Local-level perspectives

10 Dilemmas of participation: the National Community Empowerment Program

John F. McCarthy, Dirk Steenbergen,
Greg Acciaioli, Geoff Baker, Anton Lucas,
*Vivianti Rambe and Carol Warren**

10.1 INTRODUCTION

In 2006, the Indonesian government committed to a community-driven development program on a nationwide scale. Project planners subsequently rolled out this program across nearly 70,000 villages in 6,681 subdistricts (*kecamatan*) from Aceh to Papua. A scaled-up version of a program pioneered by the World Bank, the initiative created one of the largest and most publicized international examples of a 'social capital' turn in development programming. Over the period 2007–12, $1,200 million (Rp 1.2 trillion) was allocated to the program.[1]

The National Community Empowerment Program (Program Nasional Pemberdayaan Masyarakat, PNPM) came out of years of research and policy work on the need for beneficiary participation in development (Hickey and Mohan 2005), and followed the mainstreaming of social

* This research was conducted as part of an Australian Research Council Discovery Project on 'Social capital, natural resources and local governance in Indonesia' (DP0880961). The authors wish to acknowledge the contributions to the data used in this study by two other members of the research group, Jodie Goodman and Johan Weintre, working in Lombok and West Kalimantan respectively.

1 See http://www.pnpm-mandiri.org and http://simpadu-pnpm.bappenas. go.id/Desinventar/home/view/644&lang=.

capital ideas in public policy (Bebbington et al. 2004; Fine 2010).[2] This approach derives from the original argument that social capital not only facilitates collective action and economic development, but also is ultimately the mechanism that connects the two (Woolcock 2010: 481). Social capital, embedded in participatory groups and encompassing shared understandings of fairness, leadership, rights and duties, has come to represent a resource that can be mobilized and built upon for developmental ends (Nakagawa and Shaw 2004).

Through its Social Capital Initiative, the World Bank took up this idea and applied it across the globe in community-driven development (CDD) and social fund approaches. These aimed to get communities involved in choosing how funds might be spent and monitoring the progress of the projects they chose, thereby developing interventions that more effectively supported community development and fostered local accountability mechanisms. In some respects this represented a logical extension of the decentralization of government taking place across Indonesia. However, rather than devolving authority through state actors who were to be held downwardly accountable, the new CDD initiatives aimed to avoid accountability deficits within the state by establishing parallel frameworks to engage local participation.[3] Accordingly, the PNPM program has two main components: facilitation of participation in the selection, design and implementation of local development projects, and accountability mechanisms to achieve this goal (King, Samii and Snilstveit 2010).

The PNPM program focuses on improving participation in the allocation and management of block grants to fund community development. By strengthening the role of local communities in this way, it seeks to harness the energies of civil society beyond formal government structures to improve transparency and accountability, and to stimulate community ownership of development goals, encompassing poverty alleviation and gender equity. In many respects PNPM is the village-level flagship

---

2 PNPM is actually a suite of programs. Beginning with PNPM Mandiri Perdesaan and PNPM Mandiri Perkotaan, covering rural and urban projects respectively, since 2007 it has developed a number of spin-off programs. These include PNPM Generasi, focusing on medical and educational initiatives for the upcoming generation, PNPM Lingkungan Mandiri Perdesaan, also known as PNPM Green (environmentally oriented projects), PNPM Pariwisata (tourism), PNPM Peduli (initiatives targeting the poorest households), PNPM Pisew (public infrastructure) and other similarly organized programs run by various ministries.

3 Hence the term *mandiri* in the title of many PNPM programs, as they are supposed to foster the 'self-reliance' or 'independence' of participating communities.

program for democratization and decentralization reform in the post-Suharto era.[4] Consequently, the program provides a litmus test for grass-roots reform. It deserves serious attention in any consideration of where democratic decentralization has taken a nation characterized by such a high degree of socio-economic, cultural, political and ecological diversity.

The social capital-inspired turn in public policy is not uncontested, however (Fox 2007; Fine 2010; Woolcock 2010). Among other concerns, critics point to the tendency of policy applications to instrumentalize social life (Fine and Green 2000; Mosse 2005). They also note the ambiguous implications of the concept, especially insofar as it supports existing interest groups (Fine 2001, 2010). Finally, critics argue that the social capital approach fits with a form of poverty analysis that tends to cast responsibility for poverty reduction on the poor themselves, setting aside deeper structural considerations and the case for large-scale public action to engage with the drivers of poverty and vulnerability (Li 2007).

Despite these criticisms, the questions raised by the social capital thesis – understood here as networks and social relationships that facilitate collective action (Fox 2007: 142) – converge with an analysis of poverty and development and are relevant to understanding the impact of PNPM.[5] The ability of individuals and communities to leverage resources depends on the character of their engagements through particular social arrangements (Mosse 2010: 1,158). Internal organizational capacities and differentiation of access to social resources are important to an analysis of how social advancement and disadvantage are (re)produced within vertical and horizontal networks that facilitate (or do not facilitate, as the case may be) access to opportunities and benefits. Engagements between communities, donors and the state can then be analysed in terms of how resources and information flow; what dynamics shape access to external resources; and how internal community resources are mobilized, and for whose benefit.

This chapter sets out to understand the key dynamics shaping PNPM, the complex range of local-level responses and the effects generated by the program. The ambiguous outcomes associated with the program are indicative of key dilemmas facing rural Indonesia, and at the same time highly suggestive of contradictions at the heart of the CDD agenda.

---

4   This is because PNPM provides a vehicle for the transfer of funds directly to villages, in the process avoiding mediating networks of contractors and officials (Perdana and Maxwell 2011).

5   We are interested in both the horizontal (associational) and collective dimensions of the social capital concept invoked by Robert Putnam and the vertical (status hierarchic) individual dimensions that are the focus of Pierre Bourdieu's work.

10.2   SOCIAL FUNDING: THE PNPM APPROACH

At the time of the collapse of the New Order government in 1998, a CDD program pioneered by the Social Capital Initiative unit of the World Bank found its calling. The Kecamatan Development Program – also known by its Indonesian title, Program Pengembangan Kecamatan (PPK) – focused on participation and capacity-building mechanisms at the community level to identify, finance and implement small-scale public investments. The objective was to improve access to economic and social infrastructure and services among the poor, while avoiding the weaknesses associated with the top-down investment planning that was typical of state agencies under the New Order (Bebbington et al. 2004).

Under the current president, Susilo Bambang Yudhoyono, the Kecamatan Development Program has been scaled up and framed as a key strategy to tackle poverty. Now called the National Community Empowerment Program (PNPM), it aims to address entrenched poverty and increase the participation in development planning of marginalized sectors of Indonesian society, including the poor, women, remote traditional (*adat*) communities and other groups previously excluded from local decision making and development planning.[6] As well as accelerating poverty reduction by 'empower[ing] rural and urban communities to proactively participate in development' (Voss 2008b: 3), PNPM's objectives include improving the accountability and representative capacity of local governance through better communication, engaging communities and securing the involvement of non-government organizations. The core PNPM Mandiri program is administered by the Ministry of Home Affairs.

Under the PNPM program, each subdistrict is given a block grant to fund small projects. Like the Kecamatan Development Program, PNPM includes a deliberative mechanism to allow villages themselves to identify priority projects and compete with other villages to have their proposals funded. After ranking project options according to program criteria, members of a subdistrict committee, composed of representatives of all villages in the subdistrict, collectively choose the projects to be funded each year. The successful villages receive the funds to carry out the selected projects under accountability procedures designed to avoid corruption. Because they are identified and carried out by local communities themselves, it is expected that the projects will contribute to social capital formation and enhance the local capacity for community-driven development (Baron, Harjoto and Jo 2009).

---

6   See http://www.pnpm-mandiri.org/index.php?option=com_content&view
    =article&id=54&Itemid=267.

PNPM has five formal stages – socialization, planning, implementation, evaluation and monitoring – requiring differing levels of community involvement (Figure 10.1). We assessed various aspects of the program through an in-depth study of 15 villages (*desa*) in nine provinces to date: two villages in each of the provinces of Aceh, Bengkulu, West Kalimantan, West Nusa Tenggara, Central Sulawesi and Southeast Sulawesi, and one village in each of the provinces of Bali, Maluku and Papua. Using the household as the unit of measurement, in each village we surveyed approximately 40 households, selected following stratified random sampling on the basis of proportional representation at the subvillage or hamlet level. We collected information on levels of public knowledge about the program, as well as degrees of participation, roles in decision making, patterns of leadership, and responses to PNPM projects as well as other community-driven social and environmental capital-building initiatives. We also collected qualitative data beyond the 15 villages based on interviews and participant observation.

Participation and capacity building

A number of assessments of the Kecamatan Development Program and PNPM find that they have provided a more effective and efficient way to allocate funds for building local infrastructure, including by providing temporary low-skilled employment opportunities (McLaughlin, Satu and Hoppe 2007; Voss 2008a, 2012). Most of the village leaders we interviewed agreed with this positive view of the PNPM program, saying it had provided an improved mechanism for decision making, delivering a system that allocated funds in response to village requests, in contrast to the previous state-driven process.

Our survey results on degrees of community involvement in PNPM are revealing. We found that knowledge of the program was high across the board, with 79 per cent of all villagers surveyed saying they had received information about the program (Table 10.1, Figure 10.2). Satisfaction with the program was more qualified, however, with only 51 per cent saying they were very or moderately satisfied with the local PNPM program (the remainder were dissatisfied, uncertain or unable to respond). In 11 of the 15 villages surveyed, a majority of respondents expressed satisfaction; in only one (Sst in Lombok, West Nusa Tenggara)[7] did the proportion of respondents who were dissatisfied (15.9 per cent) exceed the share of those who were satisfied (13 per cent), with an unusually high percentage giving no opinion.

---

7 We use abbreviations for village names in order to comply with the ethical requirement that respondents should not be identifiable.

*Figure 10.1   Project management system for PNPM Mandiri Perdesaan
(PNPM-Rural)*

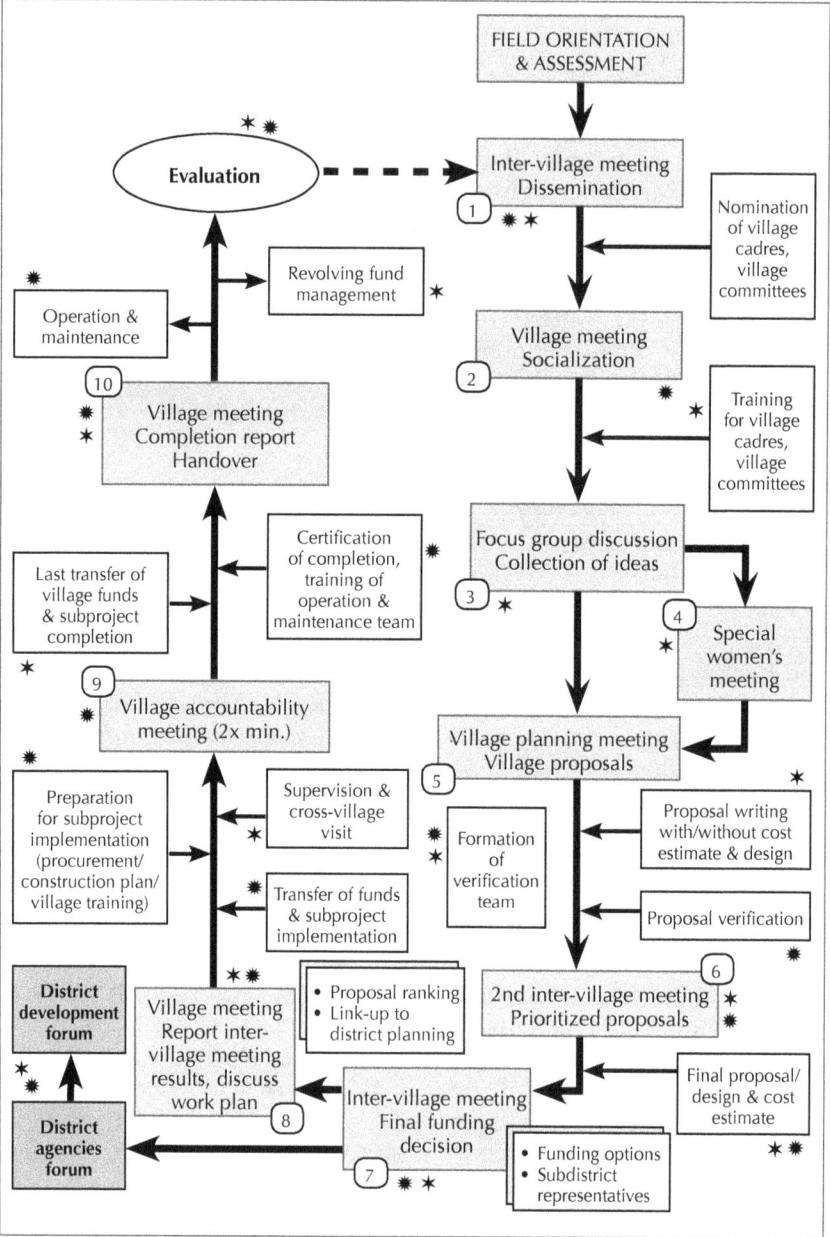

✶ = subdistrict community facilitator; ✹ = technical facilitator.
Source: Adapted from World Bank (2011: 22).

Table 10.1   *Share of survey households in each village that had received information about PNPM, were satisfied with the PNPM program and had participated in PNPM activities (%)[a]*

	Information		Satisfaction		Participation	
	Yes	No	Yes	No	Yes	No
Lms (Aceh)	80.0	17.5	70.0	23.3	35.0	35.0
TuK (Aceh)	90.2	4.9	68.3	12.2	43.9	56.1
BA (Bengkulu)	75.0	22.5	56.4	25.6	27.5	52.5
LP (Bengkulu)	57.5	30.0	38.9	36.1	22.5	62.5
KD (West Kalimantan)	97.5	0.0	82.5	15.0	50.0	50.0
Mlp (West Kalimantan)	90.0	2.5	57.5	22.5	57.5	32.5
Prk (Bali)	82.5	17.5	57.9	2.6	30.0	62.5
LS (Lombok)	68.6	31.4	21.6	5.9	23.5	74.5
Sst (Lombok)	60.0	40.0	13.0	15.9	10.0	90.0
Lgk (Central Sulawesi)	93.6	4.3	51.1	40.4	97.9	2.1
Pr (Central Sulawesi)	88.6	4.5	46.5	39.5	59.1	34.1
Wrt (Southeast Sulawesi)	62.5	25.0	56.8	37.8	32.5	52.5
HJ (Southeast Sulawesi)	77.5	7.5	55.0	45.0	35.0	45.0
TaK (Maluku)	76.2	21.4	69.2	28.2	52.4	38.1
MM (Papua)	100.0	0.0	61.9	38.1	69.0	28.6
Total	**79.1**	**16.4**	**51.1**	**25.3**	**42.0**	**49.5**

a   The discrepancy for each variable between the sum of the 'yes' and 'no' responses and the total response per village (100 per cent) is due to the portion of respondents who answered 'don't know'.

Participation, one of the primary objectives of the CDD model, was highly variable. In the disaffected Lombok village (Sst), only 10.0 per cent of respondents participated in any stage of the program. In contrast, 97.9 per cent of respondents in one of the Central Sulawesi villages (Lgk) participated, with virtually the entire village benefiting from waged employment in building an access road to carry crops to a local loading point. In six of the study villages, a majority of respondents (more than 50 per cent) participated in one or more stages of the local PNPM program. In only three did participation levels fall below 25 per cent.

Figures 10.3 and 10.4 show that most of the respondents who participated were involved in just one stage of the PNPM development process (20.7 per cent of respondents), mostly through employment in the implementation stage (57.5 per cent); the next highest level of participation was

Figure 10.2   Share of survey households in each village that had received information about PNPM, were satisfied with the PNPM program and had participated in PNPM activities

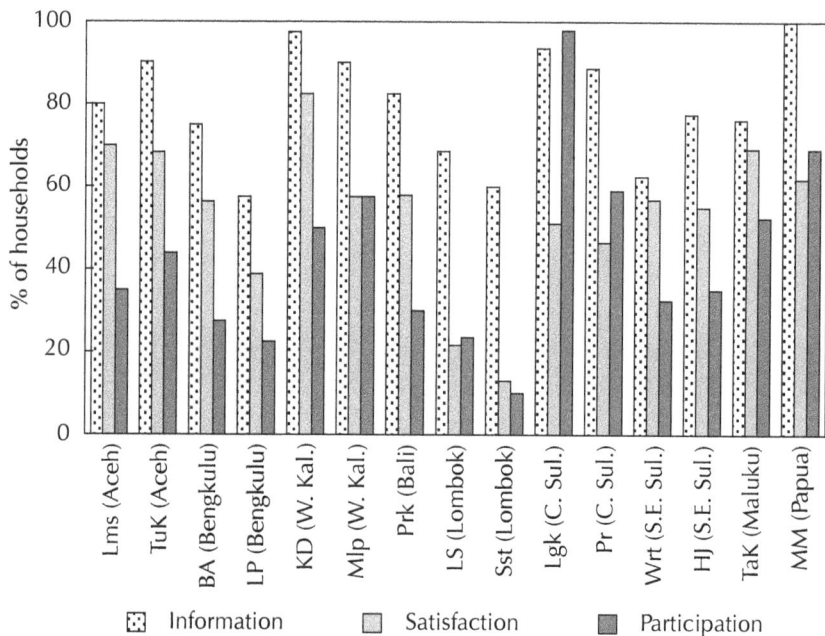

Figure 10.3   Distribution of survey households involved in one stage of the PNPM cycle[a]

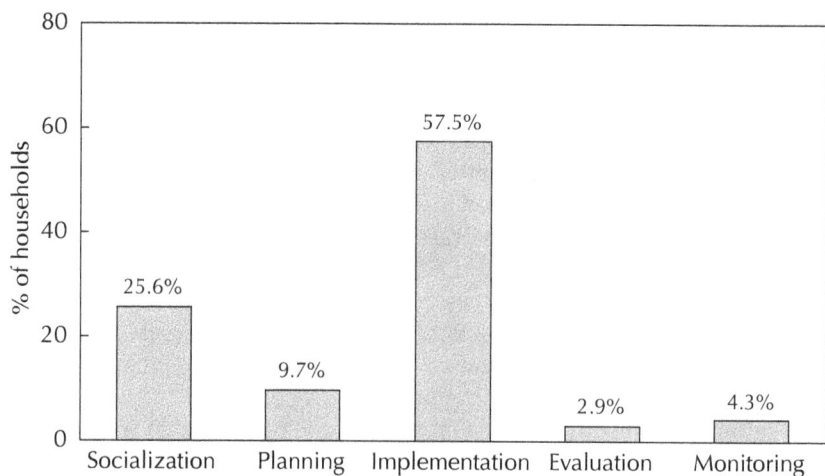

a   Note that the graph includes data only from the group of respondents who identified as having participated in *one* stage of the PNPM program cycle.

Figure 10.4   Distribution of survey households by involvement in stages of the PNPM cycle (bar chart)[a] and by economic status (scatter diagram)[b] (N = 647)

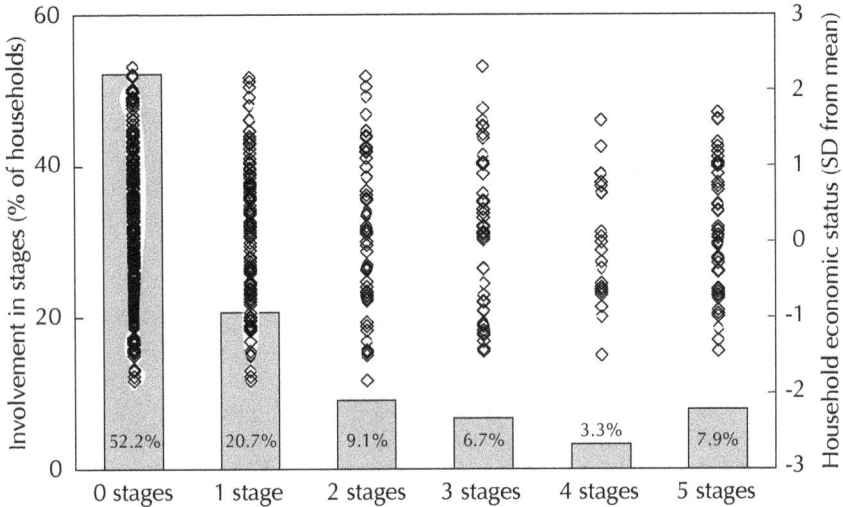

a   There is a 5.8 per cent difference between the number of respondents indicating participation in the PNPM program (42.0 per cent) in Table 10.1 and the number indicating involvement in the follow-up question (47.8 per cent) in Figure 10.4. This is due to a group of respondents who initally answered 'no' or 'don't know' to the question on participation but subsequently indicated involvement in some stage of the project.

b   A composite score for the economic status of each household is measured by a series of proxy indicators derived from the quantitative survey. These include income, ownership of land and other assets, and experience of financial hardship. The score is expressed as a z-score with zero as the mean and positive or negative scores reflecting standard deviations from the mean.

for the first stage of socialization, introducing the program (25.6 per cent). A substantial proportion of participants (16.6 per cent of those reporting participation, and 7.9 per cent of all respondents) were involved in all five stages of the PNPM process. Interestingly, no significant relationship was found between degree of involvement or non-involvement in the different stages of the program and economic status as measured by a composite of economic indicators comprising asset ownership, occupation and degree of difficulty in meeting basic needs. The scatter diagram in Figure 10.4, superimposed on the bar graph showing the percentages of households involved in the PNPM stages, indicates the distribution of households (each represented by a diamond) across the economic status scores derived from this composite calculation.

The results of the survey questions on knowledge, satisfaction and participation lead us to question views that the CDD approach has not had a significant effect on levels of participation among previously marginalized groups or on the monopoly of decision making by privileged socio-economic groups. There is at least some evidence that PNPM has created opportunities for a larger segment of the population to become involved than was the case previously, although the data do not allow us to say anything conclusive about the quality of that participation, or the extent to which the new processes associated with PNPM have been transferred to or otherwise affect wider patterns of local governance.[8]

Consistent with the social capital thesis, our field-level interviews revealed that project decision-making processes were strongly affected by pre-existing village networks and institutional arrangements. Where local decision making was dominated by elite interests, ordinary villagers regarded the program as unlikely to provide significant assistance; they believed that funding was likely to be used opportunistically by powerful actors and that work opportunities would be awarded to those close to the project facilitators. The extent to which communities were able to hold local elites accountable depended heavily upon prevailing local structures. In Aceh, for instance, where land ownership was highly concentrated, the survival of the poorest in rural communities often depended upon maintaining good relations with those mediating access to livelihood opportunities (McCarthy 2013). Here, we found that villagers were unable to hold the powerful village actors dominating PNPM processes accountable. In Bali, on the other hand, where the smallest percentage of respondents expressed dissatisfaction with the PNPM program (2.6 per cent), the importance of strong hamlet-level organization, where discussions on PNPM activities took place, may have ensured greater accountability. Other assessments of CDD programs have also found that intervention processes tend to be shaped by existing social relations, and that they are not readily able to circumvent domination by strategically placed actors (Mosse 2008; Vajja and White 2008).[9]

In an earlier assessment of the Kecamatan Development Program, Voss (2008a: vi) found that 'despite an inclusive approach to community organizing that seeks to bring all community members into the decision-making process, the results indicated that disadvantaged groups are not benefiting'. In his 2012 evaluation of PNPM, he found that the poorest groups were positively affected by the program, but that this did not extend to particular disadvantaged groups, such as female-headed households or households whose head lacked a primary education (Voss

---

8   However, an evaluation of the PNPM program by Voss (2012: 20) found that while there was strong evidence of achievement of project goals with regard to information dissemination, inclusion and satisfaction of beneficiaries, these outcomes did not extend to village governance beyond this program.

9   This is a key point in Mosse's (2008) work on participatory development, largely using South Asian examples.

2012: 16). Our interviews revealed that the exclusion or passivity of disadvantaged groups could be attributed to a combination of reticence, risk aversion and lack of time to commit to the participatory demands of projects. The transaction costs of participating in CDD activities were found to be high.[10] A number of informants in the villages we studied alleged that discussions to generate proposals for new PNPM projects tended to occur outside formally constituted forums, during informal meetings involving key villagers. These villagers would then bring a set of priorities to the general meeting at which proposals were to be discussed, at times making their acceptance a foregone conclusion.

In several of the villages, the people who assumed formal roles in the PNPM program were closely associated with the dominant social institutions in the village and often maintained several other leadership positions simultaneously. In the Maluku village, the social standing of the PNPM village representative within the traditional kinship structure – he was the son of a highly respected traditional clan leader – made him by default the primary candidate for leadership within PNPM. For the same reason he assumed a leading role on village government boards and was closely associated with other NGO development projects. As one villager remarked, 'He [the PNPM village representative] is familiar with how the system works because he has done a lot of these projects, so it is best that he is in this position'. In one of the Central Sulawesi villages, the leaders of the project implementation team were largely drawn from church elders.

In Aceh, where PNPM projects were provided with outside facilitators (in addition to the village representatives, who were chosen internally) and subjected to an externally directed process of guidance, monitoring and supervision, projects worked much more effectively than in many other Acehnese villages where post-tsunami interventions had been implemented (McCarthy 2013). Nonetheless, the process was still clearly embedded in village networks. The subdistrict PNPM facilitator in Aceh noted that, with so many villages to handle, it was beyond the capacity of the program's facilitators to overcome many types of problems: 'If there are problems [in PNPM decision making and implementation], it's the responsibility of all sides, not just us; if the village is good, PNPM will go well; if the village is weak, it will be weak'. Given the dependence of projects on functioning village networks, the facilitator admitted that staff found it difficult to circumvent dominant actors: 'If the facilitators openly take the side of the poorer people in the village, then the project does not succeed'. Paradoxically, however, in the two Southeast Sulawesi

10 See the essays that pursue this theme in Cooke and Kothari (2001) and Hickey and Mohan (2004).

cases – one a traditional village where the *adat* leaders were supported by strong customary institutions, and the other a more recent, migrant village with a respected village head – a high level of trust in leadership was associated with relatively low levels of participation. In these two villages, 45.0 per cent and 52.5 per cent of respondents respectively indicated no involvement in any stage of the PNPM process.

Despite the tendency to fall back on previous leadership roles and development patterns, PNPM's CDD model did lead to debates, controversy and even demonstrations by villagers about the most appropriate ways of spending the block grants. A key problem in many villages was that local needs and priorities did not sufficiently match the types of activities that could be implemented under PNPM guidelines. In several study sites, villagers were disappointed to discover that funds could not be allocated, for example, to the construction or repair of religious buildings (King, Samii and Snilstveit 2010).

Governance

Assessments of PNPM have noted that many problems emerged when the Kecamatan Development Program was scaled up to the national level (Akatiga 2010). Our study showed heavy reliance on facilitators, PNPM village representatives and village heads as the main sources of information about the program; they also often influenced the type and success of proposals. In one of the Southeast Sulawesi villages in our study, for example, inadequate information given by a facilitator resulted in the dismissal of a proposal at the subdistrict selection stage, whereas in the other case study village, the facilitator managed to steer its proposal to a successful outcome. One subdistrict facilitator argued that although facilitators could offer subtle suggestions to guide villagers towards appropriate projects, they should not impose their own ideas on them or try to determine the outcome of a bid. However, it is clear that the more skilled facilitators were in a position to influence the success of a proposal, at least insofar as it could be tailored to fit PNPM criteria.

By most accounts, overt misappropriation of project funding by village heads was rare. Yet, in one Bengkulu village (BA), the village head systematically creamed off 10–20 per cent of PNPM project funds, circumventing accountability processes at the village level through nepotism and bribery. By paying off the district and subdistrict bureaucracies, he was able to rely on them to ignore complaints that surfaced repeatedly in survey and interview responses.[11]

---

11 Similar practices occurred in other villages in the same district, and were widely reported on by local journalists. As a result, several village heads

Ironically, in one of the Aceh villages, the control of the program by powerful actors – descendants of a traditional aristocratic family who owned most of the land – allowed PNPM project funds to be bundled with other funds to support an irrigation system extension that improved the livelihoods of the villagers. In this case, the same powerful village actors whom villagers had criticized for arbitrary and self-serving behaviour, also advocated successfully on behalf of the village in PNPM subdistrict meetings. One village elder lamented the control over project monies exercised by the village elite. But given that the interests of landlords and poor sharecroppers were in alignment on this issue, he was happy that Rp 2 billion would now be put into improving the village's irrigation channels, in the hope of increasing production for both the poor and the elite. He reserved judgement on the outcome, however: 'We need to see how this works out … If people are serious, it will work, but if it's manipulated, then something else will occur'.

In contrast, in the other Acehnese village, where power relations were much more symmetrical and processes more participatory, village leaders did not succeed in harnessing CDD opportunities to fix the village's irrigation system or to construct a road to facilitate access to cash crop gardens for the benefit of the poor. This was because the villagers were unable to come to a clear consensus: some felt that irrigation should be the priority for funding, but one vocal villager opposed the project because most of the benefits would flow to outsiders who owned land in the village. The way that villages compete for funds works against cooperation between villages on common projects and undercuts the possibility of villages collectively supporting larger-scale investments that would be to their mutual benefit.

Ambiguity of funding criteria, poor facilitation, inability to evaluate the technical requirements of some (especially hydro-electric) projects and discontent with the competitive ranking process determining how subdistrict block grants would be spent were among the complaints registered by village leaders and ordinary villagers in our study. While recognizing that PNPM provided important public goods and a stimulus for planning and cooperation at the village level, many respondents felt that its framework was too rigid, leading to a mechanical approach to the project phases and to apathy (Voss 2012: xii). Villagers did not always

---

were investigated by the police and detained. According to one NGO activist: 'PNPM Pisew [for infrastructure projects] is the PNPM with the most problems in [this district]. Not only have malfeasance and corruption occurred, but management at the district level has also posed serious problems. [As a result] since 2011 PNPM Pisew has been discontinued in [this district]' (Anton Lucas, personal communication, 18 October 2013).

accept established PNPM criteria or the need to compete for funds.[12] Some saw the funds as an entitlement, and resented the bureaucratic burden imposed by the program.

Poverty alleviation, cash for work and infrastructure development

The capacity of CDD activities to alleviate poverty remains an open question, with some studies suggesting that this approach plays only a minor role in assisting the chronically poor and other marginalized groups (Rao and Ibanez 2003). In places where the poor are invisible minorities, democratic 'participation' may actually work against giving priority to poverty alleviation. In some communities a focus on infrastructure, for example, is rationalized as being of benefit to everyone, whereas projects specifically targeting people classified as poor are open to contestation.

As PNPM funds had to be spent on public goods, funds awarded to the villages in most of our case study sites were spent predominantly on small-scale village infrastructure.[13] In Aceh, this was the case even though extensive infrastructure had been built during the immediate post-tsunami period, and the more urgent need was for livelihood programs. One village leader in Aceh argued that PNPM funds should focus explicitly on livelihood problems, instead of the established preference for infrastructure by actors who benefited from contracting. This had led to the installation of drains and gutters that the village simply did not need. The case for drainage projects to receive priority in the relatively dry west Balinese village in our study was also questionable, although two other projects – to construct a pre-school building and to provide basic housing for the elderly – were widely regarded as satisfying important needs, as was a project to supply domestic piped water to about half the population in LP village in Bengkulu.

In some cases, greater levels of participation did not ensure practical outcomes. In the early stages of the Kecamatan Development Program in the Maluku village, for instance, several public health facilities were built, including fresh ground-water wells, a maternity ward and public

---

12 Balinese facilitators reported that the competitive aspects of the program were modulated in various ways. During the subdistrict selection process, village representatives typically came to an informal accommodation of competing interests, adopting a rotational principle or subdividing grant allocations to ensure that, over time, all villages would be awarded some funds for projects proposed.

13 In 2009, across the whole of Indonesia, 66 per cent of PNPM's block grant funding was devoted to public infrastructure, 13 per cent to education, 4 per cent to health and 17 per cent to micro-credit (Voss 2012: 6).

toilets. Within a matter of months, however, these structures were either abandoned or converted to other uses: older wells were preferred to the newly dug ones, which yielded brackish water; the maternity ward became a locally run pre-school classroom because women preferred to give birth at home; and the public toilets were deemed unsanitary because of the associated foul smell.[14] In cases where developmental outcomes were minimal, project benefits were limited to cash-for-work opportunities for those villagers who had gained employment from infrastructure construction.

Relatively high levels of satisfaction with the new access roads for producers in the Central Sulawesi villages show the continuing importance of investment in rural infrastructure and of the unskilled wage-labour opportunities they provide. Central Sulawesi villagers earned daily wages of Rp 35,000 ($3.50) working on these roads, whereas previous development projects had required unpaid contributions of labour as an expression of mutual cooperation (*gotong royong*).[15] Our surveys revealed that the necessity for, and satisfaction with, the types of infrastructure proposed and selected depended very much on the degree of isolation and infrastructure deficit, as well as perceptions of fairness in the distribution of benefits, especially work opportunities.

In response to the question, 'What type of PNPM community development activity would you wish to propose for the future?', physical infrastructure was by far the most commonly proposed option (49.4 per cent), with the combined share of the other most popular options – livelihood projects (19.2 per cent), education (10.9 per cent) and health care (8.1 per cent) – barely approaching this preference. This may partially be accounted for by the channelling effect of precedence, with decades of village development funds committed to physical infrastructure; but it is also due to the real need in remote regions for roads, drainage ditches, bridges and irrigation canals, which enhance access to markets and are therefore vital for rural economies.

Respondents in the village in Papua noted also that physical infrastructure had the advantage of highly visible outcomes, allowing villagers to

---

14 Similar facilities were provided during the New Order under the state-driven development model, with varying degrees of success. In the Central Sulawesi study area, the public toilets funded by a local women's organization fell into disuse for much the same reasons described here. In the PNPM context, the choice of such projects even today betrays the influence of local leaders still inculcated with New Order ideals of 'proper' development – old wine in new bottles, one might say.

15 Unpaid contributions of labour are in fact also expected for some PNPM projects.

assess who had, and had not, benefited.[16] Visibility also deterred corrupt syphoning-off of project funds. As one villager observed:

> If the house is not finished we know the project is not finished, very easy to see. We know also who is being paid ... and so we can see very easily where the problem is. ... The way money is managed in those other proposals [micro-credit] is difficult to follow and gets lost in the books ... Some people get very rich without us [villagers] knowing. This way we can see clearly who has gotten their share by looking at the completed houses (interview by Dirk Steenbergen, MM (Papua), 12 February 2010).

Notably, respondents in the two Aceh villages (24.4 per cent and 33.3 per cent) and in the Balinese village (25.8 per cent) showed the lowest level of interest in infrastructure development. In Aceh, the large investments in infrastructure development that occurred after the tsunami accounted for this disinterest, while in Bali, the location of the village near the district capital and just off a major inter-island road corridor meant that it already had sufficient access to markets and government services to warrant consideration of other priorities.

The SPP micro-credit program and women's empowerment

PNPM mandates that a proportion of the projects it funds (up to 25 per cent) be oriented towards the needs of women.[17] The major vehicle for accomplishing this is the micro-finance facility known as Savings and Credit for Women (Simpan Pinjam Perempuan, SPP), which provides revolving funds to develop small-scale income-generating activities. Since 2008, the rural arm of PNPM, PNPM Mandiri Perdesaan (PNPM-Rural), has facilitated the granting of loans under this program in addition to its main development scheme.

SPP provided one of the few sources of capital in many of our study villages, and it specifically targeted women. To receive a loan, women were required to form a group and develop a credible business plan that would enable repayment within a 12-month period. Under a system of peer control, there were clear sanctions for default. The group as a whole had responsibility for meeting repayments. The measure of success was that loans flowed and repayments were on schedule. If repayments did

---

16 While Scott (1998) has argued that a primary aim of development projects in the Global South has been to render communities visible to the state, the experience with PNPM demonstrates that the reverse may also be the case – that villages prefer development spending on infrastructure because it is visible.

17 See http://simpadu-pnpm.bappenas.go.id/Desinventar/home/view/644& lang=.

not meet the required 95 per cent threshold, the village would not receive SPP loans or PNPM funding during the next round.[18]

Across our case study areas, we found that the poorest women were not participating in the SPP program. Poor women without secure livelihoods were hesitant to take out loans because they were not confident they could manage the repayment schedule. In this case, collective responsibility for default proved to be a disincentive to creative efforts to include women from the poorest households. Indeed, in the Balinese village, ownership of a motorbike or equivalent item was listed as collateral for each of the applicants, even though the program was not intended to require such surety.

Women complained of a lack of guidance on where their business activities might best be channelled, and which markets they might develop.[19] Other assessments have drawn similar conclusions, noting that, in the absence of practical information, networks and training, women's income-generating activities were often not viable. In addition, supporting activities to help with marketing or the bulk purchase of goods were generally absent. Consequently, the micro-credit funds for women were able to improve livelihoods in only a few cases (Akatiga 2010).

Most women reported using the loans for productive purposes such as petty trade, livestock development, cake production or other household industries, or to purchase agricultural inputs. However, given the lack of other sources of credit in many communities, some respondents had used the funds for non-productive purposes such as buying refrigerators or floor tiling. In general, there appeared to be little oversight concerning whether SPP funds were being used in accordance with program criteria. The clear priority of the women involved in the program was to meet the procedural requirements of the organizers for loans to be repaid. It remains unclear if PNPM has in any way succeeded in overcoming the vulnerability of marginalized households by providing SPP funds. Also, despite the focus on bookkeeping and auditing, we found at least one case of embezzlement: in one of the Central Sulawesi villages, a

---

18 The 95 per cent threshold is mandated in official guidelines, but some discretion is applied in the enforcement of those guidelines. In one subdistrict in Central Sulawesi, the implementing officials agreed to maintain the 95 per cent threshold in determining whether SPP funds could be dispersed in a subsequent cycle, but lowered the threshold to 80 per cent in determining whether villages would be eligible to compete for the next round of PNPM-Rural grants.

19 In one of the Central Sulawesi villages, a suggestion to expand the production of mats using a unique type of reed found only on the banks of the nearby lake was abandoned because it would have required too much expertise and hard work to be of wide benefit.

PNPM-SPP team member faced a possible jail term for misappropriation of SPP funds.

Key weaknesses in the PNPM–SPP program were the lack of training for recipients in such aspects as practical business planning to ensure market outlets, and the tendency to replicate the same micro-credit development options among participants in the same village. In Aceh, for example, several women were given funding each to set up a food stall (*warung*) at the local waterfall, while another group received a bridal make-up course and equipment so that they could work as make-up artists for village weddings. Given that a number of *warung* were already operating at the waterfall and that only three marriages had taken place in the village during the previous year, it seemed unlikely that these activities would generate a secure stream of income.

The tendency for all women in a group to choose the same type of small business project points to shortcomings in how SPP is implemented; women face a poverty of options, and significant risks. The literature on micro-credit schemes globally has pointed to unrealistic expectations that credit alone can provide the conditions to establish the poor in secure income-generating occupations. Insufficient training and a lack of access to stable markets on reasonable terms of trade, not to mention a lack of support for other basic prerequisites to 'participation', are widely found to undermine the rosy picture painted by micro-credit promoters.[20]

Although efforts are being made to integrate PNPM with broader subdistrict planning and development programming, this disjunction remains a problem for SPP. In this regard, the fact that PNPM is designed to bypass normal village governance channels may cause serious waste and aggravate the vulnerabilities that poor women face. An extraordinary example of poor facilitation and liaison with important local institutions occurred in one of the Central Sulawesi villages. There, the women's project chosen for 2010 was to use SPP credit for the preparation and marketing of dried salted fish from the nearby lake. However, within two months of the disbursal of funds, the village *adat* council declared the lake closed to commercial fishing and imposed traditional conservation restrictions (*ombo*) due to dwindling stocks. As a result, the women were no longer able to access any fish for drying and salting and thus had no opportunity to use the credit extended to them for the purpose for which it had been allocated. This example demonstrates how perilous the credit program for women can be when not explicitly articulated with other conservation and development initiatives.

---

20 See http://www.forachangingworld.com/2009/09/microfinance-in-indonesia/. For a critique of micro-credit programs, see Isserles (2003).

While women's participation in project planning, and in employment on construction projects, is a hallmark of PNPM-Rural, there is little evidence that women have achieved a significant role in decision making beyond the SPP program. One of our case study villages (LP in Bengkulu) provides an instructive example of the largely token empowerment of women through PNPM capacity building to date. In the 2009 PNPM round, the village's women put forward a proposal for residential street drainage to prevent flooding of homes,[21] while the men proposed the construction of concrete laneways to provide access to their cash crop gardens. According to one woman who attended the meeting called to discuss these proposals:

> Many women came to the meeting. In the end things got rather tense (*agak keras*). The women were defeated in debates with the men (*kalah omong-omong*), who wanted concrete laneways to get [their motorbikes] up to their gardens. The women wanted concrete street culverts so their houses would not be flooded. The women's voice was defeated (*kalah suara*), although there was no actual voting (interview by Anton Lucas, LP (Sumatra), 22 March 2010).

The women were promised that the proposal for street drains would be submitted in the next round.

Even more distressing for the women was what happened on the third day of laneway construction: 40 women employed on the project were told there was no longer any work for them. This happened after the village headman forced the project leader, who was committed to prioritizing women, to resign, claiming to the PNPM subdistrict office that he was no longer able to work with him.[22] His replacement, a crony of the headman, then declared that carrying buckets of sand and cement up the steep hillside was too onerous for women, and that strict project deadlines could not be met with women's casual labour because they worked too slowly. Instead, he rented a mechanical concrete mixer and hired motorbikes and male drivers for Rp 50,000 per day to cart the materials up the hill. This was a particularly heavy blow for the poorer

---

21 The houses in two of the hamlets in the village were built beside a road around a steep hillside, and water was constantly flooding across the road and into the houses located on the downhill side of the road.

22 This was because the project leader had refused to pay the headman (his brother-in-law) the 2 per cent commission on the total PNPM project budget that he had demanded. The headman had married into the dominant local family, but could not rely on them for support because they opposed his corrupt activities. There was no such counter-elite opposition to the headman's power in the other Sumatran study village (BA).

women whose husbands were away working in local goldmines for long periods, only intermittently sending money back to their families.[23]

Other streams within PNPM, such as PNPM Peduli (targeting the very poor) and PNPM Pariwisata (tourism), do not always deploy the community-driven, participatory procedures of the main program. In the PNPM Peduli program recently introduced in Bali, for example, non-government organizations were asked to decide the locations and types of schemes, with after-the-fact assessments to determine whether the funds had actually supported the 'concern' (*peduli*) to redress exclusion of the most marginalized villagers. In the case of the Balinese fishing village in our study as well, PNPM Pariwisata funds were not allocated through the complex bottom-up process that is supposed to characterize PNPM. In this case, the funds were used to purchase several flat-bottomed boats (*sampan*) for the transport of tourists. The boats were bought from the village head, whose need for them had declined with the collapse of the local fishery. The broadly based community development objectives of the program would have been better suited by a scheme using the traditional *jukung* outrigger boats belonging to local fishers, who could have supplemented their marginal livelihoods by offering tourist excursions. In neither case were public deliberations involved in the allocation of these PNPM special purpose funds.

10.3   CONCLUSIONS

For all its lofty rhetoric, the PNPM suite of programs has attracted mixed reviews. The ambiguous outcomes associated with the program are indicative of many of the key dilemmas facing rural Indonesia and the CDD agenda itself.

While decentralization can be considered an important step towards developing downward accountability, the full promise of democratized governance has yet to eventuate in post-reform Indonesia (Warren and McCarthy 2009). As Buehler (2010: 281) has noted: 'administrative performance as measured by the quality of public service delivery has not improved significantly at the local level since 1999, despite decentralisation initiatives'. Our studies indicate that, compared with state-level planning processes, PNPM offers a more effective means of channelling central government funds to the village level and an improved approach to planning and delivering local infrastructure, by providing mecha-

---

23 Voss (2012) similarly found that poorer women, especially those heading households without resident husbands or fathers, were excluded from many of the potential benefits of PNPM projects.

nisms for increased participation. The program also offers opportunities for adaptive learning at the village level through an iterative process of deliberation over successive years of planning. An indicator of PNPM's popularity is that state planners have begun to use its processes to substitute for the dysfunctional *musrenbang* district planning process.[24] Various other ministries have harnessed PNPM's participatory aspect for their own development programs, including the Department of Public Works' Rural Infrastructure Development Program (Program Pembangunan Infrastruktur Perdesaan).

The potential for PNPM to address poverty remains a vexed question. One widely quoted assessment found that consumption among poor households in PNPM villages increased by 9.1 per cent between 2007 and 2010 (Voss 2012: xi). The economic benefits were both a direct result of what amounted to a cash-for-work program, and an indirect result of the associated increases in economic activity within the villages. Yet, the continued emphasis on infrastructure limits the capacity of the program to deliver sustainable, long-term community development. The choice of infrastructure is shaped by a menu that allows only for specific forms of public goods and by the limitation on funds available for any particular project. The competition between villages embedded in the program's design works against whole-of-subdistrict planning and expenditure to address wider, supra-village infrastructure problems. Also, in some cases village decision makers felt they did not have the experience, capacity or expertise required to implement projects, yet the program did not provide the resources necessary to remedy this situation. It is questionable whether the PNPM system of multiple small grants can achieve sustainable, long-term outcomes. The program has been unable to deal in any systematic fashion with production problems, unequal pricing arrangements, limited access to land, water and agricultural inputs, lack of financial services and paucity of seasonal employment opportunities, or with other structural drivers of poverty.

These limitations are evident in the revolving credit schemes (SPP) for women. While in some cases the micro-credit schemes have provided an adaptation strategy for women and their families, in others many poor women have opted out because of the risk of being unable to repay the debt. Micro-credit may have enabled some villagers to develop enterprises, but many were simply not in a position to choose viable economic

---

24 *Musrenbang*, an abbreviation of *musyawarah perencanaan pembangunan* (development planning meeting), refers to the deliberative meetings of village representatives. For more details on the use of PNPM processes in district-level planning, see http://arali2008.wordpress.com/2011/03/07/ catatanku-musrembang-kecamatan-integrasi-pnpm-mandiri-pedesaan/.

options for a small business. The lesson here is that more support is needed to improve livelihoods through micro-credit schemes (Akatiga 2010: 7). This points to a wider problem: that PNPM has been confronted with the challenges of up-scaling to the national level, despite having limited capacity to oversee such an ambitious program (Mosse 2008). A crucial consideration is the quality of facilitators and village cadres, because of their key role in driving CDD processes (Akatiga 2010). Where the choice of PNPM village cadres has had more to do with existing networks of power than aptitude and qualifications for the position, outcomes have been poor.

PNPM's problems derive from a contradiction at the heart of the CDD approach. PNPM offers an opening – an opportunity – for village demand-driven infrastructure planning. It does so by providing processes to increase participation, transparency and accountability. However, this involves lengthy and complicated planning and implementation procedures with considerable transaction and opportunity costs. These drawbacks constitute a disincentive for involvement of the poor. The scope of deliberation processes, which shape whose voices are heard, is much narrower than the participatory framework would suggest. The capacity of the resource-poor and marginalized, especially women and other disadvantaged groups, to access benefits and opportunities remains circumscribed. Although they are the ones who are supposed to be the primary beneficiaries of empowerment under the PNPM program, often they cannot afford the opportunity costs of involvement.

Other research has shown that external interventions tend to have a catalytic effect in promoting collective action and cooperation, where dynamic leaders emerge as prime movers (Krishna 2007; Upton 2008). The achievement of CDD outcomes tends to be tied to community capacity and the enabling political context (Voss 2012). It is difficult to develop project-level collective action if such conditions are absent.

PNPM faces a fundamental problem in dealing with established hierarchies, one that lies at the heart of the social capital debate.[25] On the one hand, the CDD approach aims to build on constructive vertical as well as horizontal networks and the capacities associated with good leadership. On the other hand, CDD processes need to avoid elite capture of decision making. It remains difficult to transcend this inherent tension. While our

---

25 The different concepts of social capital derived from Pierre Bourdieu's work on social capital as a resource deployed by individuals and Robert Putnam's on social capital as a resource for collective action focus on different elite/leadership roles. Leadership is a critical, but double-edged, dimension of this debate.

study did find examples of village patrons who had taken advantage of the PNPM opportunity to pursue activities of wide benefit to their communities, we also encountered cases of elite capture of project benefits by established interests. Efforts to democratize access to benefits, particularly in areas where the poor are embedded in patronage networks that work against governance approaches attempting to build in vertical accountability, have proved intractable to date.

PNPM's empowerment agenda opens up space for village self-organization, setting up processes to minimize the problem of elite capture. Yet the question remains: to what extent can a template of intervention processes offer empowerment to marginalized communities? The literature on participation suggests that empowerment requires a much more transformative process (Hickey and Mohan 2004; Li 2007). In the absence of this, CDD processes are mapped onto existing power relations. To a large degree, pre-existing vertical and horizontal networks work to structure interventions. PNPM projects provide new opportunities for some, but fail to overcome the marginalization of others where structures of disempowerment and vulnerability persist.

Somewhat against the grain, our survey does nevertheless show a roughly proportionate degree of involvement in PNPM processes of all socio-economic groups within the study villages (Figure 10.4). Although this says little about the quality of participation of lower socio-economic groups, it does indicate that the program is an important stepping-stone towards increasing their role in decision making. Along with significant levels of satisfaction expressed by survey respondents, the responses on participation suggest that PNPM's defects should be addressed by building upon, rather than wholesale jettison of, the program.

The hybrid articulation of state and non-state institutional arrangements in the PNPM model offers the benefits of opening up decision-making structures. However, in bypassing existing structures, it inadequately addresses the weakness of representative arrangements in formal village governance. The hoped-for transfer of democratization, transparency and accountability from PNPM to village governance has generally so far failed to materialize. In the words of Voss (2012: xii):

> Key findings from the qualitative study indicate that while the program was effective in creating participation, transparency and accountability for processes within the PNPM program, these impacts did not spill over into general local/village governance as the capacity of communities to impact elite control of decision-making was limited.

The 2004 revisions of the 1999 national laws on regional autonomy were clearly aimed at restoring executive over legislative authority at the village level. The revived constraints on the authority of village councils (Badan Permusyawaratan Desa, BPD) in this legislation,[26] and the fact that PNPM processes ignore them, has to be considered one of the serious structural problems that must be addressed in order to overcome deficiencies in achieving the program's objectives. Antlöv and Eko (2012: 1) explicitly make this point and recommend restoration of the provisions in the 1999 regional autonomy law relating to the separation of powers at the village level and the accountability of the village head to the public through the BPDs:

> At a time of increased transfers of funds and authority to villages, it would be desirable to further strengthen the independence and oversight function of the Village Council (BPD). ... Making the village government accountable to the community and the BPD would improve responsiveness and capacity to manage funds and provide services. This could be done by returning to formulations in Law 22/1999 on BPD.

Ultimately, the PNPM goals of community-driven development and poverty alleviation are inextricable from broader processes of democratization of village governance as a whole, which in turn cannot be separated from reform at other levels of decentralized governance.

The Kecamatan Development Program and PNPM were intended to bypass provincial and district governments in order to avoid the decentralization of corruption that has characterized regional autonomy to date. In focusing on the subdistrict as the administrative meeting point of PNPM village representatives and central government funding, the program runs counter to the official focus on structural decentralization to the district level. Many villages have benefited from the PNPM program in ways they may not have done from the regional autonomy reforms of formal government, except in the few districts where political strategies have come to depend on mass mobilization and populist health and education policies (Buehler 2010; Rosser and Wilson 2012).

In sum, PNPM provides a more effective approach to village-level planning and funding allocation, and its participatory, decentralized approaches to decision making and spending have generated considerable social learning. Yet, we find that in partially bypassing formal government structures – for all the advantages this may have in circumventing the longstanding, executive-driven, top-down development model and established rent-seeking arrangements – the program does not adequately contribute to the reform of decentralized local govern-

---

26 Notably, the Village Representative Council (Badan Perwakilan Desa) was relabelled the Village Deliberative Council (Badan Permusyawaratan Desa) in the new legislation, which also does not specify a process of election for this body (Law 32/2004 on Regional Government, articles 199–209).

ance more generally.[27] Given that it cannot substitute for more systematic approaches to addressing the underlying drivers of vulnerability, on its own it provides only a limited mechanism for poverty alleviation.

There are clear lessons from PNPM that provide indications of ways forward that build on local experiences with this and other CDD approaches. These include the importance of long timeframes for effective 'adaptive' institutional development and for fostering 'institutional bricolage' (Cleaver 2012), as well as the need to reform social structures by encouraging more thorough-going democratization of the legal framework of local government, by improving the articulation between formal government and the PNPM program, by institutionalizing more effective checks and balances and by providing enabling conditions for inclusive governance.

REFERENCES

Akatiga (2010) 'Marginalized groups in PNPM-Rural', Akatiga, Bandung.

Antlöv, H. and S. Eko (2012) 'Village and sub-district functions in decentralized Indonesia', paper prepared for a Decentralization Support Facility (DSF) Workshop on Alternative Visions for Decentralization in Indonesia, Jakarta, 12–13 March.

Baron, D.P., M.A. Harjoto and H. Jo (2009) 'The economics and politics of corporate social performance', Research Paper No. 1993R, Stanford Graduate School of Business, Stanford, April.

Bebbington, A., S. Guggenheim, E. Olson and M. Woolcock (2004) 'Exploring social capital debates at the World Bank', *Journal of Development Studies*, 40(5): 33–64.

Buehler, M. (2010) 'Decentralisation and local democracy in Indonesia: the marginalisation of the public sphere', in E. Aspinall and M. Mietzner (eds) *Problems of Democratisation in Indonesia: Elections, Institutions and Society*, Institute of Southeast Asian Studies, Singapore.

Cleaver, F. (2012) *Development through Bricolage: Rethinking Institutions for Natural Resource Management*, Routledge, New York.

Cooke, B. and U. Kothari (2001) *Participation: The New Tyranny?* Zed Books, London and New York.

Fine, B. (2001) *Social Capital versus Social Theory: Political Economy and Social Science at the Turn of the Millennium*, Routledge, London and New York.

Fine, B. (2010) *Theories of Social Capital: Researchers Behaving Badly*, Pluto Press, New York.

Fine, B. and F. Green (2000) 'Economics, social capital, and the colonization of the social sciences', in S. Baron, J. Field and T. Schuller (eds) *Social Capital: Critical Perspectives*, Oxford University Press, Oxford and New York.

---

27 Insofar as PNPM is being taken up by other central government ministries, it is in the context of a central–local dynamic that is at least partly outside the mainstream processes of provincial and district bureaucracies, with diverse benefits and shortcomings that arise from complex, context-specific factors.

Fox, J.A. (2007) *Accountability Politics: Power and Voice in Rural Mexico*, Oxford University Press, Oxford and New York.

Hickey, S. and G. Mohan (2004) *Participation: From Tyranny to Transformation? Exploring New Approaches to Participation in Development*, ZED Books, London and New York.

Hickey, S. and G. Mohan (2005) 'Relocating participation within a radical politics of development', *Development and Change*, 36(2): 237–62.

Isserles, R. (2003) 'Microcredit: the rhetoric of empowerment, the reality of "development as usual"', *Women's Studies Quarterly*, 31(3/4): 38–57.

King, E., C. Samii and B. Snilstveit (2010) 'Interventions to promote social cohesion in sub-Saharan Africa', *Journal of Development Effectiveness*, 2(3): 336–70.

Krishna, A. (2007) 'How does social capital grow? A seven-year study of villages in India', *Journal of Politics*, 69(4): 941–56.

Li, T.M. (2007) *The Will to Improve: Governmentality, Development, and the Practice of Politics*, Duke University Press, Durham and London.

McCarthy, J.F. (2013) 'Community led development and vulnerability in a post-disaster context: caught in a sad romance', AAS Working Papers in Social Anthropology, Volume 26, Austrian Academy of Sciences, Vienna.

McLaughlin, K., A. Satu and M. Hoppe (2007) 'Kecamatan Development Program qualitative impact evaluation', World Bank, Jakarta.

Mosse, D. (2005) *Cultivating Development: An Ethnography of Aid Policy and Practice*, Pluto Press, London and Ann Arbor.

Mosse, D. (2008) 'PNPM and social development work in Indonesia: a visit report', unpublished draft report.

Mosse, D. (2010) 'A relational approach to durable poverty, inequality and power', *Journal of Development Studies*, 46: 1,156–78.

Nakagawa, Y. and R. Shaw (2004) 'Social capital: a missing link to disaster recovery', *Journal of Mass Emergencies and Disasters*, 22: 5–34.

Perdana, A. and J. Maxwell (2011) 'The evolution of poverty alleviation policies: ideas, issues and actors', Arndt-Corden Department of Economics, Australian National University, Canberra.

Rao, V. and A.M. Ibanez (2003) 'The social impact of social funds in Jamaica: a mixed-methods analysis of participation, targeting, and collective action in community-driven development', Policy Research Working Paper No. 2970, World Bank, Washington DC, February.

Rosser, A. and I. Wilson (2012) 'Democratic decentralisation and pro-poor policy reform in Indonesia: the politics of health insurance for the poor in Jembrana and Tabanan', *Asian Journal of Social Sciences*, 40: 608–34.

Scott, J.C. (1998) *Seeing Like a State: How Certain Schemes to Improve the Human Condition Have Failed*, Yale University Press, New Haven and London.

Upton, C. (2008) 'Social capital, collective action and group formation: developmental trajectories in post-socialist Mongolia', *Human Ecology*, 36(2): 175–88.

Vajja, A. and H. White (2008) 'Can the World Bank build social capital? The experience of social funds in Malawi and Zambia', *Journal of Development Studies*, 44(8): 1,145–68.

Voss, J. (2008a) 'Impact evaluation of the second phase of the Kecamatan Development Program in Indonesia', World Bank, Jakarta.

Voss, J. (2008b) 'PNPM-Rural baseline report', World Bank, Washington DC.

Voss, J. (2012) 'PNPM Rural impact evaluation', PNPM Support Facility, Jakarta, April.

Warren, C. and J.F. McCarthy (eds) (2009) *Community, Environment and Local Governance in Indonesia: Locating the Commonweal*, Routledge, London and New York.

Woolcock, M. (2010) 'The rise and routinization of social capital, 1988–2008', *Annual Review of Political Science*, 13: 469–87.

World Bank (2011) 'Project appraisal document on a proposed loan in the amount of US$531.19 million to the Republic of Indonesia for the fourth National Program for Community Empowerment in Rural Areas', World Bank, Jakarta.

11 Governing fragile ecologies: a perspective on forest and land-based development in the regions

Ida Aju Pradnja Resosudarmo, Ngakan Putu Oka, Sofi Mardiah and Nugroho Adi Utomo

11.1 INTRODUCTION

It is now over a decade since Indonesia embarked on massive administrative and political decentralization, including in the land-based natural resource sector. The arguments for the decentralization of natural resources hinge on the assumptions that 'locals know best' and that reducing the distance between decision makers and ordinary citizens will result in policies that better address local needs and circumstances. The dynamics of decentralization in the natural resource sector, especially the forest sector, during the early post-reform years have been widely documented.[1] Despite a lack of capacity, local governments scrambled to take the new opportunities to exploit the forests in their regions, resulting in distinct and undesirable patterns of governance – in particular, the indiscriminate allocation of timber licences, the benefits of which accrued disproportionately to local elites, and a failure to reinvest the proceeds in the forests. Inconsistencies in the legal framework led to incoherency in the workings of government institutions, and to a struggle between the different tiers of government for authority over natural resources. The critical elements of a national system of checks and balances, and downward and upward accountability of local governments, were missing or weak.

---

1 See, for example, McCarthy (2004), Resosudarmo (2004), Oka et al. (2005), Barr et al. (2006) and Moeliono, Wollenberg and Limberg (2009).

What has happened since those early years of decentralization? Has there been a change in direction over the past decade? What have been the effects of decentralization in the forest and land-based sectors? Can recent initiatives in these sectors improve the management of Indonesia's forest estate (*kawasan hutan*)? Focusing on the governance of forest lands, this chapter examines whether decentralization has fundamentally changed the ways in which the fragile ecologies of Indonesia's Outer Islands are managed.

We focus on forests and forest lands for at least three reasons. First, from a conservation perspective, Indonesia's forests house an invaluable wealth of biodiversity, much of it found nowhere else and some of it yet to be fully explored.

Second, the country's forest lands remain an important economic resource. It is true that, with the exception of the pulp and paper industry, the readily measurable economic returns from timber and wood products have declined, particularly when compared with the rising shares in national GDP of other natural resource-based sectors. Large-scale logging continues in pockets of Kalimantan and Papua, but the sector is no longer the major engine of development – through timber-derived foreign exchange – that it was in the 1970s through 1990s (Resosudarmo 2002). The significance of Indonesia's forests and forest lands today lies, rather, in their vast area and in how their official status either promotes or constrains other economic activities. Indonesia has a land mass of 187 million hectares, of which nearly 130 million hectares (70 per cent) has been officially recognized as *kawasan hutan* and placed under the purview of the Ministry of Forestry. This means that any type of forest or non-forest activity taking place within 70 per cent of the country's land area must comply with laws and regulations governing forest lands. This has significant implications, because most of Indonesia's mineral and geothermal resources are found within forest lands.

Third, Indonesia's forests and peatlands have the potential to play an important role in climate change mitigation. Peatlands have an extremely high carbon content, and are a major source of carbon emissions when cleared and drained. Indonesia's forests contain some 20 million hectares of peatlands, bringing them to international attention as a target of conservation efforts.

In section 11.2 of this chapter, we discuss land-use dynamics in the Outer Islands, focusing on forest lands, spatial planning processes, the licensing regime and the post-decentralization expansion of agriculture and mining. In section 11.3 we describe climate change mitigation initiatives associated with the United Nations' Reducing Emissions from Deforestation and Degradation (REDD+) scheme. This is followed by a brief conclusion.

To simplify discussion, in this chapter we use the terms 'forests' and 'forest lands' interchangeably when referring to the Indonesian forest estate. Because of their high concentrations of forests, we focus on the Outer Islands of Sumatra, Kalimantan, Sulawesi and Papua – forest lands make up 59 per cent, 72 per cent and 61 per cent of the land mass of Sumatra, Kalimantan and Sulawesi respectively, and a massive 94 per cent of the land mass of Papua (Ministry of Forestry 2013a). It should be noted, however, that not all of Indonesia's forest lands are actually forested; some of this land may have very little forest cover.

11.2   LAND-USE DYNAMICS

Forest lands (*kawasan hutan*) and spatial planning

Table 11.1 shows the main regulatory and policy instruments governing the management of forest lands in Indonesia. At the broadest level, the administration of land is governed by two laws: Law 41/1999 on Forestry (the Forestry Law) and Law 5/1960 on Basic Regulation of Agrarian Principles (the Basic Agrarian Law). The former regulates areas within the *kawasan hutan*, and the latter areas outside the *kawasan hutan*.[2] Although the Decentralization Law (Law 22/1999 on Regional Government and its revised version, Law 32/2004) grants authority over natural resource sectors to the regions, the Forestry Law gives the central government, through the Ministry of Forestry, the authority to manage the Indonesian forest estate. The ministry has responsibilities in four major domains: stipulating which areas are to be formally recognized as forest lands; delineating the specific categories of forest areas (protection, conservation or production); managing and conserving forests; and issuing licences authorizing commercial activities within the forests. The Ministry of Forestry therefore has the authority to determine whether and where forestry and non-forestry activities within forest lands can take place, and the location and area of forest lands to be released for non-forest uses such as agriculture.[3] Central to its decisions is the status of the area, that is, whether it has been categorized as a protection forest (for watershed management or erosion control), a conservation forest (for the

---

2 In theory the Basic Agrarian Law governs the entire land base of the nation, but in practice the National Land Agency (Badan Pertanahan Nasional, BPN) administers only the areas outside the *kawasan hutan*.

3 Note that the release of protected areas and areas that have strategic importance for the country requires, in addition, the approval of the national parliament.

Table 11.1   *Main regulatory and policy framework for the management of forest lands*

Regulation/policy	Content
Law 5/1960 on Basic Regulation of Agrarian Principles (Basic Agrarian Law)	Governs land administration
Law 41/1999 on Forestry (Forestry Law)	Defines forest area & places forest lands under the purview of the Ministry of Forestry
Law 22/1999 & Law 32/2004 on Regional Government (Decentralization Law)	Sets out the responsibilities devolved to the regions & those retained by the central government
Law 25/1999 & Law 33/2004 on the Fiscal Balance between the Central Government & the Regions	Regulates the sharing of natural resource revenues between the central, provincial & district levels of government
Law 18/2004 on Agricultural Plantations	Gives local governments authority over agricultural licensing
Law 26/2007 on Spatial Planning	Requires provinces to complete their spatial plans within two years, & districts within three years
Law 4/2009 on Minerals & Coal Mining	Gives local governments authority over mineral & coal licensing
Law 32/2009 on Environmental Protection & Management	Requires assessment & evaluation of the environmental impact of land-based activities, with sanctions for non-compliance
Greenhouse gas reduction target, 2009	Sets the goal of a 26 per cent reduction in greenhouse gases by 2020, mostly from the land-use, land-use change & forestry sectors
Presidential Instruction (Inpres) 10/2011 on the Suspension of New Concession Permits & the Improvement of Governance for Primary Natural Forests & Peatlands, extended by Inpres 6/2013	Places a moratorium on the conversion of primary forests & peatland until May 2015

protection of biodiversity, wildlife and ecosystems) or a production forest (for forest or non-forest commercial uses).

The authority of local governments is confined to areas outside forest lands, technically about 30 per cent of the country's land mass. Given that most natural resource and land-based development opportunities are found within or concern forest lands, local governments have only limited formal powers to make decisions on the allocation and commercial use of land within their jurisdictions (although they do have responsibility for the day-to-day management and monitoring of protection forests).

The allocation of forest and land-based activities in the Outer Islands is guided by two sets of instruments: maps of forest land use based on consensus (*tata guna hutan kesepakatan*, TGHK) and maps based on the regional spatial plans (*rencana tata ruang wilayah*, RTRW) of provinces and districts. The TGHK were initially drawn up in 1982. They classified approximately 141 million hectares of Indonesia's land mass of 187 million hectares (about 74 per cent of the total) as forest lands. Prepared to provide a legal reference to secure and manage forests, the TGHK had drawbacks. These included the complexity associated with the extensive coverage of the maps, the use of (then) limited spatial mapping technology and the coarse scale of the maps (1:500,000). The TGHK were thus largely indicative and often did not reflect actual conditions on the ground. In some cases, for example, the 'forest lands' in the maps included settlements and towns, or ignored the customary land-use rights claimed by traditional (*adat*) communities. Although inherently conflict-laden, the TGHK nevertheless became the main legal reference for land-use planning and activities in forested regions, and locally initiated activities were officially confined to areas not covered by the maps.

A decade later, Law 24/1992 on Spatial Planning required provinces and districts to prepare regional spatial plans (RTRW Propinsi and RTRW Kabupaten), to be used as the basis for local development strategies. The plan of each government had to conform to that of the jurisdiction above it, making it essential to align the maps accompanying the regional spatial plans with the TGHK. As this process of reconciliation (*paduserasi*) was completed, the Ministry of Forestry produced new forest-land designation maps (*peta penunjukan kawasan hutan*) to replace the TGHK. In provinces where agreement was not reached, the original TGHK continued to be used as the basis for decision making.

The process of *paduserasi* was not easy, and in some provinces was drawn out for many years. By 2001, the Ministry of Forestry had issued designation maps for 23 provinces, with three provinces, North Sumatra, Riau and Central Kalimantan, yet to complete the process (Santoso 2003: 8). In 2005, the province of North Sumatra finally managed to complete its spatial plan to the satisfaction of the ministry, but the provinces of Riau and Central Kalimantan had yet to do so. This meant that there was no Ministry of Forestry decree delineating the forest lands in these important forest-rich provinces. Thus, in these areas, the 1982 TGHK continued to be the official reference for land-use allocation and land-based development decisions.

In 2007, the government passed a new spatial planning law, Law 26/2007, requiring all provincial and district governments to revise their spatial plans to conform to current circumstances and needs. The provincial plans were to be completed and formalized with a provincial regulation within two years of the issuance of the law, and the district plans were to be completed and formalized with a district regulation within three years. The implementing regulation for this law, however, was not issued until 2010.

Because their authority to manage lands is restricted to areas outside forest lands, subnational governments clearly have an interest in maximizing the area of non-forest lands within their jurisdictions. For its part, the Ministry of Forestry is equally keen to retain its control over land use, and thus to maximize the area of forest lands. The ministry's reluctance to release forest lands to the regions has made the process of completing regional spatial plans very protracted. By the end of 2013, half of Indonesia's provinces had not had their spatial plans endorsed in the form of a provincial regulation.[4] These delays have caused legal uncertainty over land use and significantly undermined development activities and investment in the regions, including the implementation of the priority projects for 2011–25 listed in the national government's Masterplan for the Acceleration and Expansion of Indonesia's Economic Development (MP3EI).

Not surprisingly, the provinces that had not had their spatial plans endorsed by the end of 2013 were those with significant areas of forest, among them Papua, West, Central and East Kalimantan, Aceh and Riau. Riau, for example, prepared draft spatial plans twice, the first for the period 1994–2005 and the second for the period 2001–15, but neither was ever finalized and approved. At the time of writing, the province's current draft plan had not been finalized either.

A similar situation holds in Central Kalimantan. The absence of a single map that both local and central governments can agree on has led to a complex and conflicting array of forest-use and land allocation procedures. In 1982, 15.3 million of the province's 15.4 million hectares were defined as forest lands: 11 million hectares as permanent forests and 4.3 million hectares as forests for conversion and other uses.[5] This left only 80,000 hectares of land for non-forest uses. As mandated by Law 24/1992 on Spatial Planning, the provincial government issued a spatial plan in

---

4 By November 2013, 17 provinces (52 per cent of provinces), 249 districts (63 per cent of districts) and 67 municipalities (72 per cent of municipalities) had formalized their spatial plans by issuing local regulations.

5 Minister for Agriculture Decree 759/Kpts/Um/10/1982 on the Designation of Forest Lands in the Territory of Central Kalimantan.

1993 in the form of a provincial regulation, but the process of reconciling the content of the plan with the 1982 TGHK was never completed or finalized. In 2003, the provincial government issued a new spatial planning regulation reducing the area of designated forest lands to 10.3 million hectares and increasing the area of non-forest land to 5.1 million hectares. The legality of this regulation was uncertain because, until 2011, the Ministry of Forestry continued to base its decisions on the TGHK. The differences between the TGHK and the 2003 spatial plan meant that some of the non-forest areas in the provincial plan overlapped with areas of forest lands in the TGHK. Relying on the provincial regulation as the basis of their authority, since 2003 district governments in Central Kalimantan have issued agricultural and mining licences, and endorsed other non-forestry activities, within such areas.

The divergence between the national maps (TGHK and designation maps) and conditions on the ground, compounded by pressure for non-forestry development, has fostered disagreement between governments and other actors over what constitutes, and should be retained as, forest lands. This is exacerbated by inconsistencies within the Forestry Law itself. In particular, one article of the law stipulates that an area needs to be gazetted in order to fall within the legal definition of forest lands, while another article suggests that state (Ministry of Forestry) designation alone is sufficient to give it the requisite legal status. To date, only 16 per cent of Indonesia's 130 million hectares of forest lands has been gazetted (Directorate General of Forestry Planology 2012a). Thus, the legitimacy of forest lands continues to be tested, both in practice and in the law courts. In practice, local governments often issue licences over areas that overlap with areas of centrally issued concessions or extend into protected areas. They also tolerate small-scale mining and agricultural activities that encroach on forest lands. The tussle over the status of forest lands culminated in a Constitutional Court review of the definition of forest lands in the Forestry Law, in response to a request by five district heads (*bupati*) in Central Kalimantan who potentially faced litigation over the issuance of 'illegal' licences. In 2011 the Constitutional Court ruled that, in future, land would need to be formally gazetted in order to meet the definition of forest lands (Constitutional Court Decision 45/2011, issued on 21 February 2012).

To resolve some of the uncertainty, in May 2011 the Ministry of Forestry issued a decree defining 12.7 million hectares of land in Central Kalimantan as *kawasan hutan*, and issued a new designation map replacing the three-decade-old TGHK.[6] The provincial government is prepar-

---

6 Ministry of Forestry Decree 292/2011, updated by Ministry of Forestry Decree 269/2012.

ing a revised spatial plan in consultation with the central government (although, at the time of writing, it had still not been formally endorsed). The government has also moved to resolve the deadlock over the designation of forest lands by setting aside disputed areas ('holding zones') for consideration at a later date. This allows the preparation of spatial plans to move forward, although the legal uncertainty over these areas persists and no institution is accountable for their oversight. Some of the holding zones are very large; in Central Kalimantan, for instance, they cover an area of over 200,000 hectares.

It is not only the various levels of governments that have produced conflicting reference maps; national and local government departments also have their own maps focusing on sectoral responsibilities, often without reference to the maps of other sectors. In addition to the Ministry of Forestry, for example, the Ministry of Home Affairs, the Ministry of Energy and Mineral Resources and the National Land Agency (Badan Pertanahan Nasional, BPN) each produces its own maps. This gets in the way of consistent planning, management and development of land-based activities. These inconsistencies at the policy level are exacerbated by the reality on the ground of coexisting systems of land tenure: the nationwide, de jure system of formal land rights put in place by successive national governments, and the de facto system based on the claims of traditional communities that exists throughout much of the Outer Islands (Resosudarmo et al. 2014). This has long been a source of conflict.

Spatial plans provide a starting point for consistent and guided development of regions. In the absence of agreement on such plans, the central government continues to refer to the TGHK or the forest land designation maps when allocating land-based activities, while local governments tend to refer to their proposed spatial plans. The uncertainty stemming from the lack of a set of spatial plans and maps recognized as legitimate by all parties concerned complicates planning and implementation, encourages overlaps, contributes to the inappropriate allocation of activities and leads to conflict and high transaction costs. It is within this muddle that national and regional policies on land and natural resources are currently being implemented. Eventually, however, the formalization of spatial planning should provide the clarity required for land-based development in the regions, including the projects identified in the MP3EI, and improve the management of forest lands.

Local government finances and the licensing regime

Decentralization has altered the balance of power between the central government and local governments. The devolution of responsibilities to the regions has boosted local governments' interest in allocating land uses according to their own priorities, and in developing the natural resources in their jurisdictions.

Broadly speaking, local government revenues consist of central government transfers and locally generated revenue (*pendapatan asli daerah*, PAD). The routine expenditures of local governments are met through the block grants provided by the central government. Development activities associated with local government decisions, however, are mostly financed through natural resource transfers and PAD. For resource-rich regions, natural resource transfers are a significant source of revenue (Ministry of Finance 2013). Because the size of these transfers is dependent on the amount of natural resource taxes and royalty payments collected in the respective jurisdictions, local governments have an incentive to maximize natural resource extraction. Locally generated revenue creates an even bigger incentive, as it goes directly into local government coffers to be used in any way the government wishes.

Natural resource taxes, royalty payments and PAD are secured by issuing natural resource and land-based activity licences. Regions' licensing powers are acquired through regulatory provisions in the forestry sector as well as other land-based sectors, all of which have implications for forests and forest lands. During the early years of decentralization, ministerial regulations granted local governments the power to issue timber licences. This prompted widespread and indiscriminate licensing, leading to accelerated deforestation, massive forest degradation and intensified conflict among local stakeholders (Resosudarmo 2004; Barr et al. 2006; Moeliono, Wollenberg and Limberg 2009). The central government quickly withdrew this authority. However, the subsequent promulgation of laws in related sectors, such as Law 18/2004 on Agricultural Plantations and Law 4/2009 on Minerals and Coal Mining (Table 11.1), gave the regions a new source of leverage: licensing authority over agricultural establishments and mining (with the exception of oil and gas). These two legal instruments essentially shifted control over important land-based activities and resource extraction to the regions, by giving districts authority over the resources located in their jurisdictions, and provinces authority over resources spanning more than one district.

Although the authority of local governments is limited to areas outside forest lands, their ability to issue agricultural and mining licences still has implications for the country's forests. First, a significant portion (16 per cent) of the land outside designated forest areas still has good forest cover (Ministry of Forestry 2012), and some of these forests shelter deep peatland with a high carbon content (Murdiyarso and Kauffmann 2011). Second, local governments continue to issue licences over areas that transgress the boundaries of forest lands. Third, in practice, even activities authorized in areas outside forest lands can impinge on adjacent forest lands owing to weak regulatory enforcement. Finally, the licensing regime puts the Ministry of Forestry under pressure from district governments and commercial interests to release forest lands, including protection and conservation forests, for other uses.

Agriculture and its 'prima donna', oil palm

Lacking good infrastructure and strong manufacturing bases, the regions of Sumatra, Kalimantan, Sulawesi and, more recently, Papua, rely mainly on the employment and income generated by agricultural expansion to lift local living standards. The most popular commodities are coffee (in, for example, South Sumatra and Lampung), rubber (Riau, Jambi, West and Central Kalimantan), oil palm (North Sumatra, Riau, Jambi, most of Kalimantan, some parts of Sulawesi and Papua) and cocoa (Central Sulawesi). Of these, oil palm is the most economically attractive and the most widespread. Despite cyclical variations in prices, and pressure from environmental groups, Indonesia continues to be the world's largest palm oil producer (Sheil et al. 2009). In 2013, the area under oil palm far outweighed the area under other commodities (Handoyo and Ayudi 2013). Generally favourable world prices, strong demand and national policies encouraging exports have steadily increased the production and export of this 'green gold'. Domestically, demand for palm oil is supported by the country's large population and a cooking culture that makes heavy use of vegetable oil; Indonesia's consumption of palm oil rose from 3.3 million tons in 2000 to 6.1 million tons in 2010.[7] Official figures suggest that the area of land planted with oil palm has more than doubled since decentralization, from 4.1 million hectares in 2000 to 9 million hectares in 2011 (Figure 11.1). This trend is likely to continue, not only to cater to household demand for vegetable oil, but also to provide sufficient palm oil for non-food uses such as biofuel.[8]

Oil palm attracts both large-scale plantation companies and smallholders. The profitability of palm oil compared with other agricultural commodities is reflected in the rapid increase in the area under oil palm plantations, and in the support provided by financial institutions to this sector (Figure 11.1). Oil palm plantations are seen as a profitable business, and both state and private banks are eager to fund its expansion.[9]

---

7 See   http://www.indexmundi.com/agriculture/?country=id&commodity=palm-oil&graph=domestic-consumption.

8 Caroko et al. (2011: 4) estimated that 10.25 million hectares of land would be required by 2015 to supply the amount of biofuel needed to meet the national biofuel target.

9 Personal communication with Commissioner of Bank Danamon, 21 September 2013.

Figure 11.1   Trends in area, production and exports of palm oil, and bank credit for agriculture, 2005–11

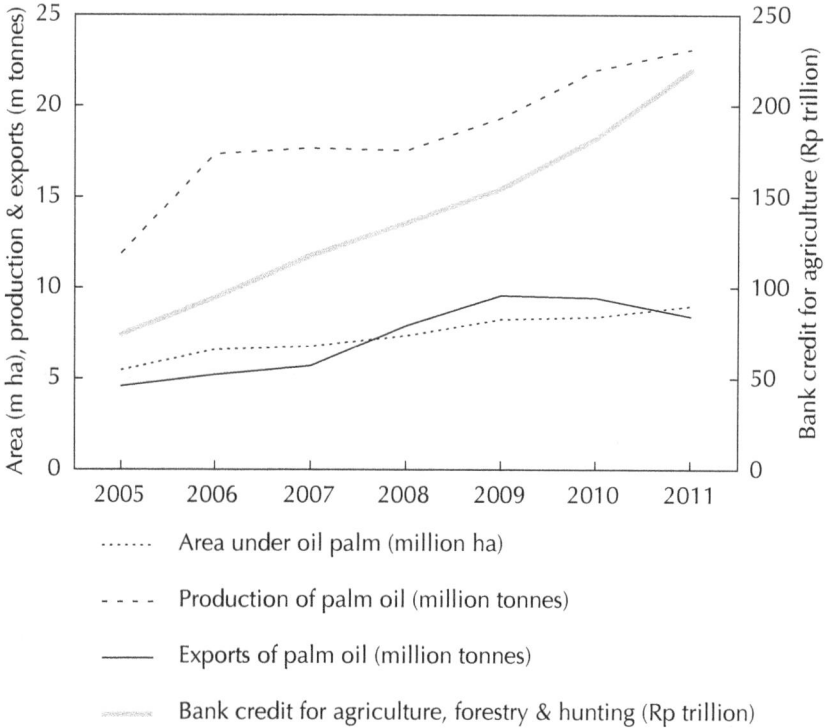

.... Area under oil palm (million ha)

- - - - Production of palm oil (million tonnes)

———— Exports of palm oil (million tonnes)

▬▬▬ Bank credit for agriculture, forestry & hunting (Rp trillion)

Source: Area and production: Agricultural Statistics Database, Ministry of Agriculture, http://aplikasi.deptan.go.id/bdsp/newkom.asp; exports: United Nations Commodity Trade Statistics Database, http://comtrade.un.org/db/; credit: Bank Indonesia, http://www.bi.go.id/web/id/Statistik/Statistik+Perbankan/Statistik+Perbankan+Indonesia/.

For smallholders, oil palm is attractive because it provides a significant, steady, long-term source of income (Feintrenie, Chong and Levang 2010). For example, a Riau farmer with a two-hectare plot of oil palm can expect to make Rp 2–3 million a month (Resosudarmo 2010), a sum comparable to the minimum labour wage in Jakarta. When well maintained, an oil palm tree can be harvested for 20–25 years. Oil palm is an appealing livelihood option for poor villagers living in the country's rural forested regions; over 38,000 Indonesian villages are located within or close to forest lands (Ministry of Forestry and BPS 2009). It is also attractive to people who have been forced out of illegal logging and thus need to find other means of livelihood.

The pressure to convert forests to agriculture is reflected in the area of forest lands released, or projected to be released, for agriculture. Between

2007 and 2011, official data show that 5.7 million hectares of forest lands were released for agricultural use (Ministry of Forestry 2012). During the first half of 2013, another 120,000 hectares were released for agriculture and a further 150,000 hectares set aside for future oil palm concessions (Ministry of Forestry 2013b). This will go only some way to meeting demand: between January and June 2013, 23 companies were seeking approval for the release of over 360,000 hectares of forest lands for oil palm development (Ministry of Forestry 2013b).

While official figures provide a general portrait of the extent of oil palm development, they do not include forest lands that have been illicitly converted to oil palm and other agricultural commodities (Dabu 2011; Suharman 2011). District governments continue to issue licences based on maps suggesting that the areas in question are outside forest lands, despite Ministry of Forestry maps showing them lying within forest lands. A joint investigation by the Ministry of Forestry and the Judicial Mafia Eradication Task Force found that, in Central Kalimantan alone, some 350 plantations covering an area of 4.6 million hectares lay within forest lands in 2011.[10]

Aggravating this situation is the lack of coordination between local governments and the regional offices of the central government. Law 18/2004 on Agricultural Plantations and Law 4/2009 on Minerals and Coal Mining, and their implementing regulations, do not explicitly require coordination with the Ministry of Forestry and its regional offices as part of the licensing process, even if the area proposed for agriculture or mining is located within forest lands. Clearly this increases the likelihood of local licences being issued over areas within forest lands, including areas with good forest cover that would otherwise be protected or conserved. In fact, the income from the sale of timber felled to clear land for other uses is an additional incentive for local governments to issue licences that stray into areas with good forest cover. Thus, it is not unusual to find that licences have been issued over areas that intrude into protected and conservation areas, that overlap with areas under active (and legal) timber concessions or that overlap with areas covered by other licences, such as mining or even other oil palm plantation licences.

Outside the designated forest lands, ecological and social safeguards over land use are minimal. There are no effective control mechanisms to ensure that district governments' allocations of land for agricultural development are environmentally or socially appropriate. Environmental impact assessments for the licensing process are often 'made to order', a desk exercise carried out by external consultants who do not

10 Press release on violations of forest lands in Central Kalimantan, 1 February 2011.

understand the situation on the ground and are interested only in satisfying administrative requirements. Law 32/2009 on Environmental Protection and Management is quite strong and comprehensive, but has yet to show its teeth because of the absence of implementing regulations and a lack of resources on the part of the Ministry of Environment as the executing agency. Consequently, even deep, ecologically fragile peatland forests risk being cleared for other activities. While providing some guidelines, Regulation 14/2009 of the Ministry of Agriculture limiting the allowable clearing of peatland forests to places where the peat is less than three metres in depth has proved difficult to enforce in practice. Plantations often cover large areas, and it is likely that at least some parts of the land cleared to make way for them extend into areas where the peat is more than three metres deep. It should also be remembered that even peatlands that are *less* than three metres deep store substantial quantities of carbon.

Local governments, as the issuing authorities, virtually absolve themselves of the responsibilities associated with the granting of these licences. Despite requests by the Ministry of Forestry that they not grant licences over areas within forest lands, and revoke those already granted,[11] some district governments continue to do so. In issuing licences, local governments place the burden on the applicant to ensure that the land in question meets the Ministry of Forestry's administrative requirements. Thus, if the area impinges on or is situated within forest lands, it becomes the responsibility of the applicant to apply to the ministry for its release. Many companies ignore this requirement, and begin operations on the ground immediately after obtaining a licence from the district government, without waiting for the Ministry of Forestry to release the land in question. In the absence of effective oversight, control or sanctions, local governments have little incentive to abide by the regulations of the ministry, or to pay attention to ecological considerations.

The responsibility for settling matters with communities whose lands will be affected by the decision to grant a licence is also placed on the applicant. This was affirmed by a recent ministerial regulation, Ministry of Agriculture Regulation 98/2013 on the Guidelines for the Licensing of Agricultural Establishments (article 24). A legal instrument delinking decisions from responsibilities creates a further disincentive for local governments to incorporate social considerations into their decision-making processes.

Under conditions such as these, social controls can be the last gatekeeper for land-related allocation decisions. But in some areas, the tight-

---

11 See, for example, Ministry of Forestry Letters 1712 of 2001, S.51 of 2005 and
    S.31 of 2008.

knit and environmentally aware communities of the past are slowly breaking down, to become more individualistic and more concerned with economic than environmental outcomes (Resosudarmo et al. 2014). It is not surprising that some communities have turned to oil palm and support the clearing of forests, considering that non-timber forest products such as rattan provide far less income. In addition, communities' attachment to and stewardship of the forests are constantly being tested by oil palm companies, which are aggressive in pursuing negotiations for the conversion of local forests with community leaders, and quick to make promises to win community support.

To complicate matters further, land rights are a contentious issue in the Outer Islands, where almost all land is *de jure* state land, but *adat* communities nevertheless claim large swathes of forest as their own (Resosudarmo et al. 2014). This dual system of land tenure promotes uncertainty, and sows the seeds of conflict between *adat* communities and the external actors interested in establishing oil palm plantations. It is also not uncommon to find divisions among communities themselves, with some supporting the conversion of forests and others supporting the developers. Legal uncertainty over community land rights, and the reality that local governments are able to issue licences over community lands, can propel communities to minimize their losses by converting forests to oil palm themselves, or by acceding to their conversion in return for compensation. Under such circumstances, social controls are losing their force and in some places have become ineffective.

What about vertical accountability? The Ministry of Agriculture has no control or monitoring authority over how much or where locally initiated agricultural expansion takes place. Neither the ministry nor its regional offices are involved in the process of issuing licences, and there is no obligation for local governments to report their licensing activities to the ministry or to any other institution. This constrains the development of a holistic, nationwide, ecologically and economically sound agricultural strategy. The lack of formal avenues of vertical accountability between district governments and the ministry perpetuates the indiscriminate issuance of licences.

With both large companies and rural farmers attracted to oil palm, land has become an increasingly expensive traded commodity in, for example, Central, West and South Sulawesi. And while the process of oil palm expansion may vary by region, the ultimate impact on forests is the same: deforestation. In Kalimantan, licences are issued to companies within forest lands. In Sulawesi, oil palm plantations are being developed on community-controlled lands. In parts of Sulawesi and Riau, indigenous land owners have sold their land to migrants for oil palm and other agricultural commodities, only to clear other areas of forest later on to meet their own needs. While the individual impact of such activities may appear trivial in comparison to large-scale clearing by companies, the cumulative impact is large.

Forests are also being cleared in response to the national policy of improving the country's capacity to grow its own food and supply its own energy. This policy has resulted, for example, in parts of the districts of Bulungan in East Kalimantan and Ketapang in West Kalimantan being earmarked for the development of estates growing food products for domestic consumption. As land becomes increasingly scarce in Kalimantan and Sumatra, pressure on land for agricultural development has moved eastward into Papua and Maluku, the last frontiers of Indonesia's natural forests. The district of Merauke in Papua has been identified as a site for the development of food and energy estates. In 2013, the Ministry of Forestry designated an area of 300,000 hectares for future sugarcane developments in Maluku.

Mining

Mining is another activity with important repercussions for forest cover and the environment. The geological features of Indonesia are such that most mineral deposits, including gold, bauxite, zircon, nickel and coal, are found in forest areas. As with agriculture, decentralization, favourable economic conditions and export-oriented policies have encouraged local governments to issue scores of licences. As a result, production has increased significantly. Coal production, for example, doubled between 2004 and 2011, making Indonesia the world's fifth-largest producer.[12] Much of this coal is exported, but domestic consumption is also rising steadily to meet the needs of industry and to feed Indonesia's power plants (Resosudarmo, B.P. et al. 2009).

One could argue that, in contrast to agricultural expansion, which involves the permanent clearing of large tracts of forest, mining involves smaller areas and does not have a significant or long-term effect on forest cover. In fact, however, mining operations in the Outer Islands do have severe long-term impacts on forests. First, although deforestation caused by direct mining activities may seem insignificant compared with deforestation from agriculture, the indirect activities associated with mining, including the construction of extensive transport networks and new settlements, substantially affect forest cover.[13] Second, although reclama-

---

12 'Mengapa China mengimpor batu bara dari Indonesia?' [Why does China import coal from Indonesia?], *Tambangnews*, 7 September 2010.
13 Personal communication with senior official in the Directorate General of Forestry Planology, Ministry of Forestry, 24 June 2011.

tion is supposedly mandatory, many mining operations abandon their sites without fulfilling this obligation upon closure. Third, the activities of illegal miners and companies that have secured licences through improper procedures contribute significantly to production but are not captured by the official statistics, masking the true impact of mining on forest lands.

As stated above, the Ministry of Forestry is responsible for authorizing the release of forest lands for other uses. However, mining companies do not need to obtain such a release; rather, they need to obtain a lease-use permit (*ijin pinjam pakai kawasan hutan*) for the period of the intended operations.[14] By December 2012, the ministry had issued active lease-use permits over 359,000 hectares for production and 2.35 million hectares for exploration, for all types of mining, and had granted in-principle approvals over another 498,000 hectares (Directorate General of Forestry Planology 2012b). It also continues to honour the permits for open pit mining issued over nearly 850,000 hectares of protected land before the passage of the Forestry Law.[15] These figures understate the extent of mining in forest areas, however, because illegal mining activities and those of companies operating under local government licences without securing lease-use permits from the Ministry of Forestry would go unrecorded.

As in the case of oil palm licences, the responsibility for ensuring that licence holders meet other obligations, in this instance securing lease-use permits, is placed on the applicants themselves. Also, the fact that the licensing process occurs at the district level, with minimal involvement of the district forestry service or the Ministry of Forestry's regional offices, and with no vertical, sanctioned obligation to report the licences to the ministry, means that licences can be issued over forest lands without the ministry being aware of it. Lacking on-the-ground monitoring capacity, the Ministry of Forestry has not been able to rigorously enforce the requirement for mining companies to obtain lease-use permits. Of the 299 mining concessions in the Meratus Protection Forest in East Kalimantan, for example, reportedly only one has a lease-use permit from the ministry.[16]

---

14 Government Regulation 24/2010 on the Use of Forest Areas; Ministry of Forestry Regulation 18/2011 on Guidelines for Lease-use Permits in Forest Lands.

15 Although the Forestry Law permits open pit mining only in production forests – not in conservation or protection forests – the 13 or so companies that had secured permits before the passage of the law have been allowed to continue to operate within protection forests.

16 'Penambangan memprihatinkan' [Mining activities cause concern], *Kompas*, 25 January 2010.

The provision of lease-use permits is intended to secure government revenues and at the same time to control the expansion of mining operations within forest lands. For areas in production forests that are already the subject of a forest-use licence (such as a timber concession), Ministry of Forestry Regulation 18/2011 on Guidelines for Lease-use Permits in Forest Lands sets a maximum limit on mining operations of 10 per cent of the area in question; for areas that are not the subject of another licence, or that are located in protection forests, the limit is 10 per cent of the total forest area (although these restrictions do not apply to exploration activities). Although this may seem adequate to ensure sustainable forest management, in practice it is difficult to curb illicit mining activities within these same forest areas. Thus, in reality, the maximum limit can easily be exceeded.[17]

Small-scale illegal mining operations are persistent (Resosudarmo, B.P. et al. 2009; Spiegel 2012). They are also difficult to track, as the miners are quick to move on to other areas once a deposit has been depleted. In areas where the opportunities for mining attract large numbers of immigrants, they are a cause of conflict between the original inhabitants and the new arrivals. Local governments often turn a blind eye to artisanal mining, recognizing the limited availability of alternative livelihoods and for fear of arousing community discontent.[18]

The issuance of scores of mining licences without due regard for central government regulations and procedures, and often overlapping with other permits, has led to uncontrolled extraction of mineral resources, serious environmental problems, economic losses to the government, social conflict and business uncertainty. At one point, the Ministry of Forestry reported that in Kalimantan alone, over 900 mining units were operating illegally on an area of over 5.3 million hectares without undergoing the proper procedures to obtain permits, resulting in estimated state losses of no less than Rp 110 trillion.[19]

The number of mining licences issued by local governments has increased sharply since the regional autonomy laws were passed, from 597 in 2000 to over 10,000 in 2011. Of these, no less than 8,000 were reportedly problematic (Rakhmanto 2011). They included licences that had been obtained without going through the proper (national) procedures, licences issued over overlapping areas or activities, and licences

---

17 Interview with senior official in the Ministry of Forestry, June 2011.
18 Personal communication with senior officials of Kapuas and Berau districts (Kalimantan), 15 May 2013.
19 '5,3 juta hektar hutan Kalimantan ditambang tidak prosedural' [5.3 million hectares of Kalimantan forests mined without appropriate procedures], *Majalah Tambang*, 23 March 2011.

that remained in force despite a company's failure to meet its rent and royalty obligations. Although the Ministry of Energy and Mineral Resources has a supervisory role in the management of the country's mineral resources, weak vertical linkages between local governments and the ministry mean that it is often oblivious of the mining licences issued by local governments.

Clearly, the tangible benefits flowing from agricultural and mining activities have amplified local governments' interest in exploiting local resources. Notably, local governments generate revenue from the various levies and charges (*retribusi*) associated with the licensing process, from taxes and from 'negotiated' contributions imposed on businesses.[20] The latter include direct contributions to the local government concerned, as well as payments in kind such as improvements to roads and other public facilities.

In addition to official income, informal incentives not reflected in the accounting books are another important driver of resource extraction. These are more difficult to assess. Burgess et al. (2011) find that rates of deforestation are linked to increases in the number of political jurisdictions, and rise sharply in the years leading up to local elections. Tans (2012) describes the powerful 'timber mafia' that grew up in South Tapanuli district, North Sumatra, during the early years of decentralization, involving the district head, law enforcement agencies, forestry officials and logging interests. The role of informal incentives in the granting of rights to expand agricultural plantations is exemplified by the graft case involving Amran Batalipu, the district head of Buol (Central Sulawesi), and Siti Hartati Murdaya, one of Indonesia's most successful business tycoons.[21] Similar cases have occurred in the mining sector (see, for example, Bakhori 2012; Yozami 2012).

In an effort to rein in the proliferation of licences, the Ministry of Energy and Mineral Resources now requires local governments to report all their licences to the ministry, and licence holders to undergo an assessment to ensure their licences are clean and clear. A licence is classified as clean and clear if it has been obtained through the correct administrative procedures, the area covered by the licence does not overlap with the area of another licence, the company has obtained a lease-use permit for areas located within forest lands, and the company has fulfilled its land rent and royalty obligations. Mining companies have a strong

---

20 For example, the district of Bulungan in East Kalimantan extracts a proportion of company profits in return for licensing agricultural establishments.

21 Amran Batalipu was found guilty and given a gaol term. See, for example, 'Bekas bupati Buol Amran divonis 7,5 tahun penjara' [Amran, the former district head of Buol, is sentenced to 7.5 years in gaol], *Tempo*, 11 February 2013.

incentive to obtain clean and clear status because this is now officially linked to exporting requirements. Nevertheless, in July 2013, only 5,957 of a total of 10,884 mining business licences had been classified as clean and clear.[22] The main bottlenecks have been overlapping licences and licences without lease-use permits. This once again highlights the difficulty of coordinating procedures between the various levels of government, and the lack of effective vertical accountability mechanisms.

In a bid to improve coordination between levels of government and better manage forest lands, the Ministry of Forestry is decentralizing forest management to locally based forest management units (*kesatuan pengelolaan hutan*). Responsible for specific areas of forest, these forest management units operate on four principles: transparency, active participation of all stakeholders, accountability, and ecosystem-based management. They are responsible for the management of forests (planning, organization, implementation, monitoring and evaluation), for the interpretation and implementation of national, provincial and district policies, and for attracting investment opportunities to support the objectives held for the particular category of forest (conservation, protection or production). Over 170 forest management units had been established, on paper, by January 2013. But details of how they will actually work, particularly with regard to the relationship and sharing of tasks with the provincial and district offices of national institutions, and with the existing provincial and district forestry institutions, are yet to be sorted out.

11.3   REDD+ IN INDONESIA

It is clear that both the national and local governments are under great pressure to clear forests to make way for much needed local livelihood and development activities. Can forests be relied on to supply these needs with minimal disruption to their ecological and biological diversity? One possible option to reconcile these competing needs is the Reducing Emissions from Deforestation and Forest Degradation (REDD+) scheme, an international initiative to reduce greenhouse gas emissions from forests, while also offering livelihood opportunities (Angelsen et al. 2012).

REDD+ is a climate change mitigation initiative to give forested developing countries an incentive to reduce greenhouse gas emissions from deforestation and forest degradation, and to support the conservation and sustainable management of forests. Essentially the REDD con-

---

22 'Sebanyak 5.957 perusahaan tambang pemegang IUP berstatus CnC' [5,957 holders of mining licences have clean and clear status], *EnergiToday*, 19 July 2013.

cept involves payments to countries to prevent deforestation and forest degradation, with the '+' signalling active measures to improve forest management and to conserve and restore forests. Indonesia's forests and forest lands are very important in a global context, not only because they have been disappearing at an alarming rate, but also because they contain over 20 million hectares of peatlands with a very high carbon content (Murdiyarso and Kauffman 2011). Deforestation and forest and peatland degradation are the largest sources of greenhouse gas emissions in Indonesia: land-use change and forestry, together with peat fire-related emissions, contributed 59.6 per cent of the country's total emissions in 2000, and 62.9 per cent in 2005 (Ministry of Environment 2010). The climate change dimension of forests has put Indonesia's tropical forests in the spotlight, presenting an opportunity to save them amidst strong pressure to convert them to other uses.

Indonesia aims to reduce its greenhouse gas emissions by 26 per cent on its own, or by 41 per cent with international support, by 2020. Most of these reductions will be achieved through the forestry and peatland sectors.[23] REDD+ initiatives will be an important element in achieving these targets.

The actual implementation of REDD+, when envisioned in terms of compensation for reduced emissions, has taken some time to get off the ground. So far, most effort has been focused on the preparatory phase of establishing a national policy framework for REDD+, and the accompanying institutional architecture. Progress has been slow, in part due to the uncertainty caused by the lack of commitment to REDD+ financing by developed nations during a series of United Nations Framework Convention on Climate Change (UNFCCC) negotiations. Domestic political and bureaucratic inertia and pressure from influential domestic interests have also played a part, despite the strong political commitment of the president to REDD+ (Luttrell et al. 2014). This is not surprising given that the scheme is operating in a domain where there is strong competition to secure land for activities such as agriculture, mining and logging. The progress of REDD+ has also been hampered by the inherent complexity of forest governance, including, as we have seen, a lack of coordination and cooperation between agencies and between different levels of government (Resosudarmo 2007). The technical aspects of REDD+, including the determination of deforestation rates, emissions and reference emission levels, are also challenging and can be politically sensitive.

Despite the difficulties, significant progress has been made in laying the foundations for REDD+. The government has passed various

---

23 Presidential Decree 61/2011 on the National Action Plan to Reduce Greenhouse Gas Emissions.

REDD+-related regulations, published a National Action Plan to Reduce Greenhouse Gas Emissions, prepared a National REDD+ Strategy, placed a moratorium on the conversion of primary forests and peatlands, and developed conceptual frameworks for REDD+ financing and benefit sharing, and for the measurement, reporting and verification of greenhouse gas emissions from forests in relation to REDD+. In 2013, the president established a national REDD+ agency tasked with coordinating REDD+ policies and activities, and reporting directly to the president, through Presidential Decree 62/2013. Particularly important and relevant to the issues discussed in this chapter is the now widely acknowledged need to have a single set of maps that can be used as a reference by all levels of government, all sectors and the public, and a policy commitment to work towards this goal.

At the provincial and local levels, REDD+ initiatives take various forms.[24] Mostly still in the early stages of development, they include demonstration activities implemented by bilateral aid agencies or international conservation NGOs (such as the Kalimantan Forest Climate Partnership in Central Kalimantan and the Berau Forest Carbon Program in East Kalimantan), ecosystem restoration projects led by the private sector (for example, the Rimba Raya Conservation Project in Central Kalimantan), community projects (such as the Ketapang Community Carbon Pool initiative to preserve peat forest in West Kalimantan) and large-scale local government projects (as in Aceh, where the provincial government initially endorsed the use of carbon finance mechanisms to avoid deforestation in the Ulu Masen area).

At this stage it is too early to determine whether REDD+ will work as a sustainable conservation vehicle for Indonesia's forests. The nuts and bolts of the regulatory framework and other required mechanisms are not yet in place for the scheme to be fully implemented. Whether REDD+ can achieve the goals held for it will depend on its attractiveness compared with other conservation activities, and the reception of relevant stakeholders at both the national and local levels. One might anticipate, for example, that the long-term nature of REDD+ initiatives may not fit with the short-term horizons of local government politicians, coinciding with their terms in office (Resosudarmo and Oka 2013). Also, for the most part, local communities are interested in REDD+ only if it improves their incomes and livelihoods (Resosudarmo et al. 2012). The

---

24 A comprehensive list of REDD projects to March 2012, providing both information and maps, has been compiled by the Forest Climate Center (Sekala); see http://forestclimatecenter.org/files/2012-03-26%20Indonesia%20-%20 REDD%20Demonstration%20Activities.pdf. See also http://www.redd-indonesia.org/proyek-percontohan.

scheme has, however, helped highlight the crucial role of forests and the importance of improved forest governance, putting this issue firmly on the political map, and on the agenda of decision makers.

11.4   CONCLUSION

Decentralization has shifted responsibility for land and natural resources from the central government to subnational governments, but it has not led to any fundamental improvement in the ways in which the fragile ecologies of Indonesia's Outer Islands are managed. The extraction of natural resources to satisfy development and livelihood needs has been prioritized over longer-term environmental considerations. The main change that has taken place since 2001 has been a shift in emphasis from logging to agriculture and mining, propelled by local governments' increased authority, changes in national policy, tighter controls on timber harvesting and weak enforcement of national regulations in other sectors.

Development is necessary, and impingement on or the conversion of forested areas is clearly unavoidable. But it is also essential to ensure the optimal use of land through integrated and careful planning, and to implement and enforce appropriate policies. The reconciliation of regional and national forest maps, the production of a single, overarching set of reference maps containing basic geospatial information, the harmonization of central and local government laws and regulations, better coordination of central and local government procedures and the implementation of effective accountability mechanisms would all help to optimize the use of forests and forest lands, and to embed ecological considerations in land-use decisions.

The United Nations' flagship climate change mitigation program, REDD+, is being presented as an option ultimately to curb the suboptimal use of forest lands and forest resources. Still in its infancy, situated within a complex maze of forest and natural resource regulations and obliged to compete with other attractive economic and livelihood activities, REDD+ faces a range of obstacles. Whether it can reshape the current development agendas in the regions and put the management of forests on a more sustainable path remains to be seen.

REFERENCES

Angelsen, A., M. Brockhaus, W.D. Sunderlin and L. Verchot (eds) (2012) *Analyzing REDD+: Challenges and Choices*, Center for International Forestry Research (CIFOR), Bogor.

Bakhori, S. (2012) 'Satgas: ada bupati terlibat kasus ijin tambang' [Task force: district heads involved in mining licence cases], *Tempo*, 9 May.

Barr, C., I.A.P. Resosudarmo, A. Dermawan, J.F. McCarthy, M. Moeliono and B. Setiono (eds) (2006) *Decentralization of Forest Administration in Indonesia: Implications for Forest Sustainability, Economic Development and Community Livelihoods*, Center for International Forestry Research (CIFOR), Bogor.

Burgess, R., M. Hansen, B. Olken, P. Potapov and S. Sieber (2012) 'The political economy of deforestation in the tropics', Discussion Paper No. 9020, Center for Economic Policy Research, London.

Caroko, W., H. Komarudin, K. Obidzinski and P. Gunarso (2011) 'Policy and institutional frameworks for the development of palm oil-based biodiesel in Indonesia', Working Paper No. 62, Center for International Forestry Research (CIFOR), Bogor.

Dabu, P. (2011) 'Negara merugi 311,4 triliun dari bisnis ilegal di hutan' [State losses from illegal business in forests reach Rp 311.4 trillion], *Kontan*, 28 April.

Directorate General of Forestry Planology (2012a) 'Kebijakan percepatan pemantapan kawasan hutan' [Policies to accelerate gazettal of forest lands], paper presented at the workshop Menuju Kawasan Hutan yang Berkepastian Hukum dan Berkeadilan [Towards Equitable Forest Lands with Legal Certainty], Ministry of Forestry, Jakarta, 13 December.

Directorate General of Forestry Planology (2012b) 'Data dan informasi planologi kehutanan tahun 2012' [Forestry planology data and information 2012], Ministry of Forestry, Jakarta, December, available at http://www.dephut.go.id/uploads/files/23e5b973df2453cb1c0192af2387e8a5.pdf.

Feintrenie, L., W.K. Chong and P. Levang (2010) 'Why do farmers prefer oil palm? Lessons learnt from Bungo district, Indonesia', *Small-scale Forestry*, 9(3): 379–96.

Handoyo and M.E.R Ayudi (2013) 'Industri perkebunan diperketat' [Commodity plantation industry tightened], *Kontan*, 17 October.

Luttrell, C., I.A.P Resosudarmo, E. Muharrom, M. Brockhaus and F. Seymour (2014) 'The political context of REDD+ in Indonesia: constituencies for change', *Environmental Science and Policy*, 35: 67–75.

McCarthy, J.F. (2004) 'Changing to gray: decentralization and the emergence of volatile socio-legal configurations in Central Kalimantan, Indonesia', *World Development*, 32(7): 1,199–223.

Ministry of Environment (2010) *Indonesia Second National Communication under the United Nations Framework Convention on Climate Change (UNFCCC)*, Ministry of Environment, Jakarta, November.

Ministry of Finance (2013) 'Laporan keuangan transfer ke daerah TA 2012' [Financial report on fiscal transfers to the regions, budget year 2012], Ministry of Finance, Jakarta.

Ministry of Forestry (2012) *Statistik Kehutanan Indonesia 2011* [Forestry Statistics of Indonesia 2011], Ministry of Forestry, Jakarta, July.

Ministry of Forestry (2013a) 'Buku basis data spasial kehutanan tahun 2013' [Book of forestry spatial data 2013], Ministry of Forestry, Jakarta, available at www.webgis.dephut.go.id.

Ministry of Forestry (2013b) 'Laporan perkembangan pelepasan kawasan hutan untuk budidaya perkebunan' [Report on the release of forest lands for commodity plantations], Ministry of Forestry, Jakarta, available at http://www.dephut.go.id/index.php/news/details/9341.

Ministry of Forestry and BPS (Badan Pusat Statistik) (2009) 'Identifikasi desa di dalam dan di sekitar kawasan hutan 2009' [Identification of villages in and around forest lands, 2009], Ministry of Forestry and BPS, Jakarta.

Moeliono, M., E. Wollenberg and G. Limberg (eds) (2009) *Decentralization of Forest Governance: Politics, Economics and the Fight for Control of Forests in Indonesian Borneo*, Earthscan, London and Sterling VA.

Murdiyarso, D. and B. Kauffman (2011) 'Addressing climate change adaptation and mitigation in the tropical wetland ecosystems of Indonesia', Infobrief No. 41, Center for International Forestry Research (CIFOR), Bogor.

Oka, N.P., P.O. Ngakan, A. Achmad, D. Wiliam, K. Lahae and A. Tako (2005) 'Dinamika proses desentralisasi sektor kehutanan di Sulawesi Selatan' [The dynamics of decentralization in the forestry sector in South Sulawesi], Case Study 11, Center for International Forestry Research (CIFOR), Bogor.

Rakhmanto (2011) 'Pemerintah menyetop sementara izin tambang' [Government temporarily halts mining permits], *Kontan*, 24 May.

Resosudarmo, B.P., I.A.P. Resosudarmo, W. Sarosa and N.L. Subiman (2009) 'Socioeconomic conflicts in Indonesia's mining industry', in R. Cronin and A. Pandya (eds) *Exploiting Natural Resources: Growth, Instability, and Conflict in the Middle East and Asia*, Henry L. Stimson Center, Washington DC.

Resosudarmo, I.A.P. (2002) 'Timber management and related policies: a review', in C.P. Colfer and I.A.P. Resosudarmo (eds) *Which Way Forward: People, Forests, and Policymaking in Indonesia*, Resources for the Future, Washington DC.

Resosudarmo, I.A.P. (2004) 'Closer to people and trees: will decentralization work for the people and the forests of Indonesia?', *European Journal of Development Research*, 16(1): 110–32.

Resosudarmo, I.A.P. (2007) 'Has Indonesia's decentralization led to improved forestry governance? A case study of Kutai Barat and Bulungan districts, East Kalimantan', PhD thesis, Australian National University, Canberra.

Resosudarmo, I.A.P. (2010) 'Drivers of deforestation and land use change in Riau, Indonesia, and their implications for REDD+', unpublished draft report commissioned by the Australian National University, Canberra.

Resosudarmo, I.A.P. and N.P. Oka (2013) 'What does REDD+ mean for local authorities? The case of Sulawesi, Indonesia', unpublished paper, Center for International Forestry Research (CIFOR), Bogor.

Resosudarmo, I.A.P., A.E. Duchelle, A.D. Ekaputri and W.D. Sunderlin (2012) 'Local hopes and worries about REDD+ projects', in A. Angelsen, M. Brockhaus, W.D. Sunderlin and L.V. Verchot (eds) *Analyzing REDD+: Challenges and Choices*, Center for International Forestry Research (CIFOR), Bogor.

Resosudarmo, I.A.P., S. Atmadja, A.D. Ekaputri, D.Y. Intarini, Y. Indriatmoko and P. Astri (2014) 'Does tenure security lead to REDD+ project effectiveness? Reflections from five emerging sites in Indonesia', *World Development*, 55: 68–83.

Santoso, H. (2003) 'Forest area rationalization in Indonesia: a study on the forest resource condition and policy reform', World Agroforestry Centre (ICRAF), Bogor.

Sheil, D., A. Casson, E. Meijaard, M. van Nordwijk, J. Gaskell, J. Sunderland-Groves, K. Wertz and M. Kanninen (2009) 'The impacts and opportunities of oil palm in Southeast Asia: what do we know and what do we need to know?', Occasional Paper No. 51, Center for International Forestry Research (CIFOR), Bogor.

Spiegel, S.J. (2012) 'Governance institutions, resource rights regimes, and the informal mining sector: regulatory complexities in Indonesia', *World Development*, 40(1): 189–205.

Suharman, T. (2011) '891 perkebunan dan pertambangan di Kalimantan Tengah ilegal' [891 commodity plantations and mining operations in Central Kalimantan are illegal], *Tempo Interaktif*, 1 February.

Tans, R. (2012) 'Mobilizing resources, building coalitions: local power in Indonesia', Policy Studies 64, East-West Centre, Honolulu.

Yozami, M.A. (2012) 'Banyak kepala daerah keluarkan IUP palsu' [Many local authorities issue fake licences], *hukumonline*, 16 February.

12 Explaining regional heterogeneity of poverty: evidence from a decentralized Indonesia

*Sudarno Sumarto, Marc Vothknecht and Laura Wijaya**

12.1 INTRODUCTION

Over the past decade Indonesia has made significant progress in reducing poverty. According to official statistics produced by the national statistics agency (Badan Pusat Statistik, BPS), the poverty rate fell from 23.4 per cent in 1999 to 11.4 per cent in 2013. Viewed from any angle, this is a tremendous achievement. However, as demonstrated also by Amri Ilmma and Matthew Wai-Poi in Chapter 5 of this volume, Indonesia's success at the national level masks the existence of substantial regional differences. This chapter focuses on this regional heterogeneity in poverty indicators. It relates district performance in reducing poverty to characteristics of the decentralization program implemented in Indonesia since 2001.

We argue that the system of governance for managing Indonesia's 'big bang' decentralization lacks key institutional requirements, notably adequate performance measures and an effective framework of constraints,

* The views expressed in this chapter are those of the authors and do not necessarily represent the views of the organizations for which they work. We are grateful to Asep Suryahadi, Adama Bah, Daniel Suryadarma, Indunil De Silva and Hector Salazar, who provided useful comments on an earlier draft. Any remaining errors and weaknesses are ours.

as reflected in the shortcomings in the system of controls for central government oversight of local governments (World Bank 2006). Moreover, the division of responsibilities between the different levels of government is unclear, clouding the lines of accountability required to improve service delivery. An additional challenge stems from the uniform implementation of decentralization regardless of regional differences. This is a problem in a country as diverse as Indonesia, where each region differs in local government capacity and available resources. All these factors have undoubtedly had an effect not only on the implementation of the national poverty reduction strategy, but also on the development of local poverty reduction initiatives.

A review of experiences in 19 countries conducted by the OECD Development Centre finds that decentralization has led to improvements in poverty reduction in only one-third of cases (Jütting, Corsi and Stockmayer 2005). The authors argue that lower middle-income countries that have literacy rates above 80 per cent, and whose political processes are relatively open, are more likely to experience decreases in poverty following the adoption of decentralization measures. Overall, they conclude that decentralization is more likely to have a positive impact on poverty if there is an adequate commitment by the central government to the decentralization process, if the actors involved have the requisite (financial and technical) capacity, and if checks and balances are established at the local level to prevent rent seeking and corruption.

In this chapter we aim to uncover the factors associated with the differing performances of district governments in reducing poverty. Through an analysis of a district-level panel dataset containing annual observations for the period 2005–10, we find support for the argument that heterogeneity in poverty levels across districts is associated with heterogeneity in local governments' resources and capacity. Specifically, we find that poverty appears to have decreased more in districts that have: (1) an established local office for the coordination of poverty reduction initiatives (TKPKD); (2) a higher share of total fiscal revenues (including both locally generated revenue and transfers from the central government); (3) a higher average level of educational attainment; (4) a larger share of local leaders with secondary education; and (5) a higher share of urban population.

The remainder of the chapter is organized as follows. Section 12.2 describes the observed heterogeneity in poverty across Indonesian regions between 2005 and 2010. Section 12.3 discusses the factors that are likely to be associated with different levels of poverty reduction at the local level. Section 12.4 presents the data and estimation strategy, and section 12.5 summarizes the results. Section 12.6 offers some concluding remarks.

12.2   OBSERVED HETEROGENEITY IN REGIONAL POVERTY

Indonesia has made significant strides in reducing poverty since the Asian financial crisis in 1997–98. This has been achieved through a combination of high economic growth and the implementation of poverty reduction programs. However, a different picture emerges when one looks at growth and poverty at the provincial and district levels.

Large disparities in the headcount poverty ratio can be observed at both the provincial and district levels. At the provincial level, in 2012 densely populated provinces such as Jakarta (with a headcount poverty ratio of 3.7 per cent) and Bali (4.0 per cent) had lower levels of poverty than provinces in the eastern part of Indonesia, such as Papua (30.7 per cent) and West Papua (27.0 per cent). At the district level as well, we find that in 2005 – the starting year for this chapter's empirical analysis – the highest incidence of poverty is observed in Eastern Indonesia, in particular districts in Papua (especially the highlands), West Papua, Maluku and East Nusa Tenggara (Figure 12.1). But there are large regional variations, with pockets of poverty also observed in richer Java and Sumatra. In fact, the absolute number of poor people is highest in Java, given its high population density.

A similar picture emerges when we consider the severity or depth of poverty, as measured by the poverty gap, with the areas of greatest poverty once again in the eastern part of the country. This geographic concentration of poverty suggests the existence of geographic poverty traps, whereby households in poor areas remain isolated from the general improvements in living standards enjoyed by identical households living in better-endowed areas in other parts of the country (Jalan and Ravallion 2002; Bloom, Canning and Sevilla 2003).

Figure 12.2 maps the absolute changes in the headcount poverty ratio between 2005 and 2010. Reflecting the trend towards convergence in poverty rates, regions with higher initial levels of poverty tend to experience larger decreases in poverty. However, substantial heterogeneity remains in poverty rates and trends both across and within regions.

12.3   REVIEW OF THE DETERMINANTS OF REGIONAL PERFORMANCE IN REDUCING POVERTY

A country's poverty reduction efforts depend on both the availability of public income and the adequate use of that income to fund public services, as well as participation by citizens in social, economic and political decision making at the local, regional and national levels (Sumarto, Suryahadi and Arifianto 2004). A priori, decentralization can either

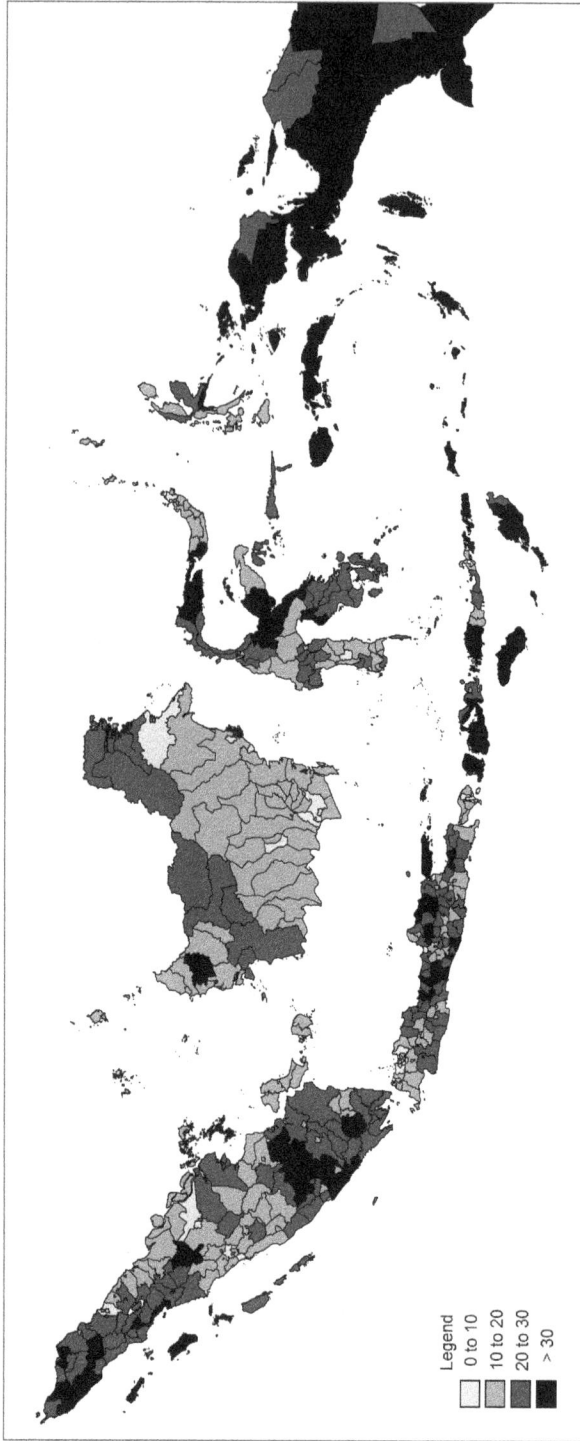

Figure 12.1   Headcount poverty at the district level, 2005 (%)

Legend
0 to 10
10 to 20
20 to 30
> 30

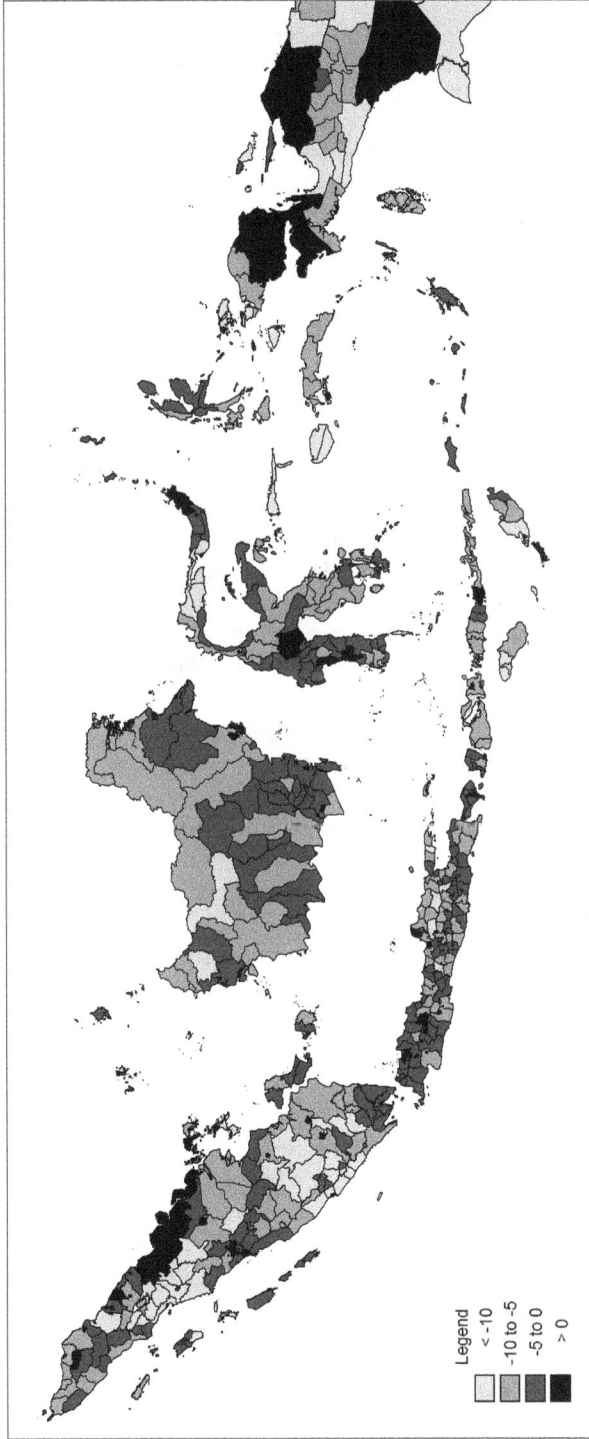

Figure 12.2   Change in headcount poverty at the district level, 2005–10 (percentage points)[a]

Legend
☐ < -10
▨ -10 to -5
▩ -5 to 0
■ > 0

a   Positive values (black) indicate an increase in poverty.

support or undermine a country's poverty reduction efforts. In this section, we examine the factors associated with the observed heterogeneity in poverty levels across Indonesia, in the context of the decentralization program implemented since 2001. First, we consider district governments' capacity to generate income, their fiscal capability and their ability to deliver services. Next, we discuss some of the implications of the decentralization process for governance, and a recent institutional innovation introduced to enhance the capacity of local governments to implement poverty reduction policies.

Income generation capacity at the local level

Under the decentralization laws introduced in 1999 and revised in 2004,[1] local governments (that is, districts and municipalities) have the legal authority to generate their own revenue by imposing taxes and levies (ADB 2010). Own-source revenue (*pendapatan asli daerah*, PAD) refers to the income produced directly by local governments through taxes and levies. The amount of PAD collected varies according to the ability of each district to generate income, giving some more scope than others to provide services and to introduce poverty reduction initiatives. On average, PAD represents 7 per cent of district income; the districts' main source of income is transfers from the central government, as discussed in more detail in the next subsection.

Not all taxes collected by the district governments are productive, with several authors concluding that some local governments have actually harmed the investment climate by introducing complex and problematic regulations that overlap with national regulations (Aten 2011; Butt and Parsons 2012). Between 2002 and 2009, the Ministry of Home Affairs cancelled 1,887 local regulations. In 2010, it reviewed over 3,000 local regulations and found 407 of them to be problematic. This figure was even larger in 2011, when the ministry revised 9,000 local regulations and found 351 to be problematic (Aten 2011). Law 28/2009 on Regional Taxes and Levies was supposed to prevent regional governments from introducing counterproductive taxes designed to collect revenue rather than achieve policy objectives (Aten 2011). Its failure to do so has discouraged investors at a time when Indonesia is in need of funding for its long-term development goals. There is therefore an urgent need for the central government to introduce rigorous and efficient monitoring and control mechanisms, to prevent local taxation from creating distortions that discourage investment and economic activity.

---

1   Law 22/1999 on Regional Government and Law 25/1999 on the Fiscal Balance between the Central Government and the Regions, now Laws 32/2004 and 33/2004 respectively.

Another feature of the new fiscal framework is that it allows regions to keep a given share of the revenue generated by their natural resources (World Bank 2003a). District income is therefore affected by the presence of natural resources, with areas that are rich in resources able to generate more income. This is likely to increase inequality between areas.

Local government fiscal capability

Local government budgets (*anggaran pendapatan dan belanja daerah*, APBD) depend on revenue from two sources: the part generated by each district (PAD, as discussed above) and the part provided by the central government (see below). Despite the large-scale decentralization of authorities to local governments, they remain heavily dependent on the central government to fund their expenditures. In 2011, for example, the Ministry of Finance estimated that the central government accounted for 91 per cent of all revenue collected and 64 per cent of direct spending by districts.

The General Purpose Fund (Dana Alokasi Umum, DAU) is the main mechanism by which the central government provides the funds to finance provincial and district government expenditures (Shah, Qibthiyyah and Dita 2012). The formula for distributing these unconditional block grants takes account of both the needs and economic potential of each region (Hofman and Kaiser 2002).

In addition, poorer provinces and districts are eligible to receive additional grants from the central government through the Special Purpose Fund (Dana Alokasi Khusus, DAK), the Adjustment Fund (Dana Penyesuaian, DP), the Regional Incentive Fund (Dana Insentif Daerah, DID), other types of grants (*hibah*) and, in the case of Aceh, Papua and West Papua, the Special Autonomy Fund (Dana Otonomi Khusus, DOK) (Shah, Qibthiyyah and Dita 2012). DAK transfers are intended to be spent on areas of national priority; they account for around 6 per cent of central government transfers and fund 5 per cent of subnational expenditures. The purpose of Adjustment Fund transfers is to provide special ad hoc assistance. According to Ministry of Finance estimates for 2012, on average DAU funding comprised 42 per cent of a district's total revenue, DAK funding 7 per cent and own-source revenue (PAD) only 7 per cent (Ministry of Finance 2012).

According to the World Bank (2011), the current system of transfers has not had a major impact on reducing inter-regional inequality because it fails to sufficiently take account of the particular challenges facing some areas. An additional problem with the DAU is that the current allocation mechanism gives districts an incentive to subdivide into smaller administrative units (Harjowiryono 2011) – because 'two new districts get effectively twice as much as the larger old district' from which they were formed (Fitrani, Hofman and Kaiser 2005: 66). In South

Table 12.1   Subdivision of districts and central government transfers in South Kalimantan and Yogyakarta, 2001and 2011

Province/city	Number of districts		Districts' total DAU (Rp billion)		Change in DAU, 2001–11 (%)
	2001	2011	2001	2011	
South Kalimantan	6	14	0.9	5.5	528
Yogyakarta	5	5	0.9	2.7	216

Source: Harjowiryono (2011); Shah, Qibthiyyah and Dita (2012).

Kalimantan, for example, the number of new districts more than doubled between 2001 and 2011, while the amount of DAU each district received more than quintupled (Table 12.1). Considering the financial incentive, and the 'vertical coalitions' of self-interested politicians moving between the provincial and local levels of government (Kimura 2007), it is unsurprising to find that four new provinces were created between 2001 and 2013, and that the number of districts grew from 336 to 511.

This 'blossoming' (*pemekaran*) of districts has led to a notable increase in their wage bills for civil servant salaries, which are largely funded by the central government. The proliferation of districts has also complicated governance, because it is more difficult for the central government to monitor a larger number of districts. The level of financial accountability appears to have decreased with *pemekaran*; there is no consolidated record of the total amount spent in all provinces and districts (Isdijoso 2012).

Local government performance in delivering public services

Service delivery improves in decentralized settings if citizen participation and public sector accountability go hand in hand with the decentralization of decision making on public services (Huther and Shah 1998). However, decentralization is often undertaken without paying enough attention to the need for improvements in service delivery (Robinson 2007). Ahmad et al. (2005) argue that one of the main problems affecting public service delivery is the lack of capacity of local governments to exercise responsibility over the services they are expected to provide. This lack of capacity is evident in two main areas: fiscal capacity (the ability of local governments to raise revenue) and technical capacity (the ability of local governments to manage and allocate their resources).

The main way in which a lack of fiscal capacity affects the provision of local public services is by eroding the ability of local governments to build on programs funded by the central government. In the health sector, for instance, local governments are supposed to complement the national health insurance program for poor households (Jaminan Kesehatan Masyarakat, Jamkesmas) with locally funded health insurance (Jaminan Kesehatan Daerah, Jamkesda) for those not covered by the national scheme. But although central government spending on health doubled between 2007 and 2013, many poor households remain without such cover. The coverage of Jamkesda varies from region to region according to budget constraints, with some areas, such as Jakarta and Bali, approaching universal coverage of the poor and others still failing to cover a large part of this population. There are also big differences in regional spending on education: in 2008, the district of Bandung spent nearly Rp 250 million in addition to the funds provided by the central government, while the district of North Mamuju in West Sulawesi allocated less than Rp 40 million to education in the same year. The differing levels of district spending on health, education and other public services are likely to lead to different outcomes in different areas – although the World Bank (2011) points out that there can be a mismatch between local government spending and service delivery outcomes.

Like a lack of fiscal capacity, a lack of technical capacity also has consequences for public service delivery, for instance, by creating misalignments between sectoral allocation decisions and service delivery needs. In the infrastructure sector – the key to developing access to markets, off-farm employment and social services (Balisacan, Pernia and Asra 2002) – a lack of technical capacity by local governments in carrying out large-scale projects has held back progress in improving access to roads, telecommunications and even electricity. About two-thirds of villages in the more remote parts of Indonesia do not have access to a telecommunications network, and more than 70 million Indonesians do not have access to an electricity supply (Aswicahyono and Friawan 2008). Local governments that suffer from a lack of technical capacity therefore find themselves dependent on the central government not only for funding, but also for the implementation of much needed local infrastructure projects.

Local government performance in delivering public services to constituents is further hindered by the absence of transparent lines of authority and clear accountability for policy implementation. According to Heywood and Harahap (2009), district governments have little discretion over the use of public funds to improve local health outcomes. The authors argue that this is likely to be an important reason for the lack of improvement in publicly funded health services. Key decisions on the amount and use of funds in health as well as other sectors are still made by the central government. As a result, no one is held accountable for the performance of those sectors – the district government blames the central

government for any failings, and vice versa, leaving no actor accountable to the public. The World Bank (2003b) has expressed concern that
the maintenance of infrastructure is also being underfunded due to the
unclear assignment of government responsibilities and shortcomings in
the inter-governmental fiscal transfer system.

Finally, spending on services is increasingly crowded out by the significant sums spent on the local government apparatus. According to
estimates by the Indonesian Forum for Budget Transparency, 298 of 491
districts in 2011, and 302 of those districts in 2012, spent over 50 per cent
of their total budgets on wages (Farhan 2012). This is an inefficient use
of funds, as less is allocated to improving public services and reducing
poverty, both of which have positive, sustainable multiplier effects.

Governance aspects of decentralization

Good governance is crucial for achieving better public service management, improved public service delivery, faster economic growth and
more economic, political and social opportunities for the poor (Blaxall
2000; Eid 2000; Gupta, Davoodi and Tiongson 2000; Sumarto, Suryahadi
and Arifianto 2004). It is also essential for an effectively managed decentralization process. Crook and Sverrisson (2001) show that decentralization has positive effects only in countries with well-established public
participation schemes, where local governments apply the principles of
good governance and where there are functioning checks and balances
involving both the central government and the general public. According to the World Bank (2006), however, Indonesia's decentralization
took place in the absence of a comprehensive policy framework, and the
Indonesian system therefore lacks some of the key governance requirements for an effectively managed decentralization scheme. This can have
unintended consequences, among the most harmful for poverty reduction being violence and conflict.

Political decentralization is regarded as a way of diffusing social
and political tensions and ensuring local cultural and political autonomy (Bardhan 2002). McLaughlin and Perdana (2010) find low levels
of reported electoral conflict and conflict stemming from the abuse of
local power in Indonesia. They conclude that political decentralization
has not brought about a notable increase in violence, with few localities
suffering from high levels of ethnic or religious conflict. There may be
a link between administrative decentralization and conflict, however.[2]

---

2 Murshed and Tadjoeddin (2008) have also found a link between levels of
   expenditure and violence. They find that the probability of routine violence is
   higher in districts where local public spending is lower.

The International Crisis Group argues that in some areas conflict is a by-product of the *pemekaran* process, especially where decisions are made without public consultation (ICG 2005). In West Sulawesi, for example, conflict erupted over the formation of the new district of Mamasa, with some members of the community supporting the administrative changes and others bitterly opposing them. The report argues that the Mamasa incident is an example of what can happen when there is no clear procedure to resolve disputes in the *pemekaran* process. An open democratic procedure is therefore needed to reduce the probability of conflict occurring.

Despite the uniform implementation of fiscal decentralization, experiences at the subnational level vary. Overall, it appears that decentralization has led to an increase in inequality, with 80 per cent of shared taxes and natural resource revenue accruing to the richest 20 per cent of districts.

District institutional capacity for poverty reduction

Under a presidential regulation issued in 2005, district governments have been encouraged to establish teams to oversee and coordinate the design and implementation of local poverty reduction strategies (Tim Koordinasi Penanggulangan Kemiskinan Daerah, TKPKD). The main responsibilities of the TKPKDs are to develop and manage local poverty indicators and poverty information systems, and to establish early warning systems on various aspects of poverty. Members include district heads and mayors (*bupati* and *walikota*), local government officials from departments such as health, education and community empowerment, and representatives from district BPS offices. The distribution of TKPKD offices across districts is shown in Figure 12.3.

Several challenges exist in using TKPKDs as a poverty reduction tool. First, in 2010 about 20 per cent of districts – nearly half of them located in the eastern part of the country – had not established a TKPKD. In addition, the length of time for which the existing TKPKDs have been established varies widely across districts. Our data reveal that districts with longer-established TKPKDs have been more successful in reducing poverty, as indicated by Figure 12.4.

The success of the TKPKDs in contributing to local poverty reduction efforts depends on a number of intertwined factors. First, the support of local elites, especially district heads and members of parliament, is crucial in fostering the role of the TKPKDs. Second, the operations of the TKPKDs need to be adequately funded, regardless of the fiscal capacity of the local government. Third, local governments, and therefore TKPKDs, need to have a well-developed capacity to undertake program planning and budgeting.

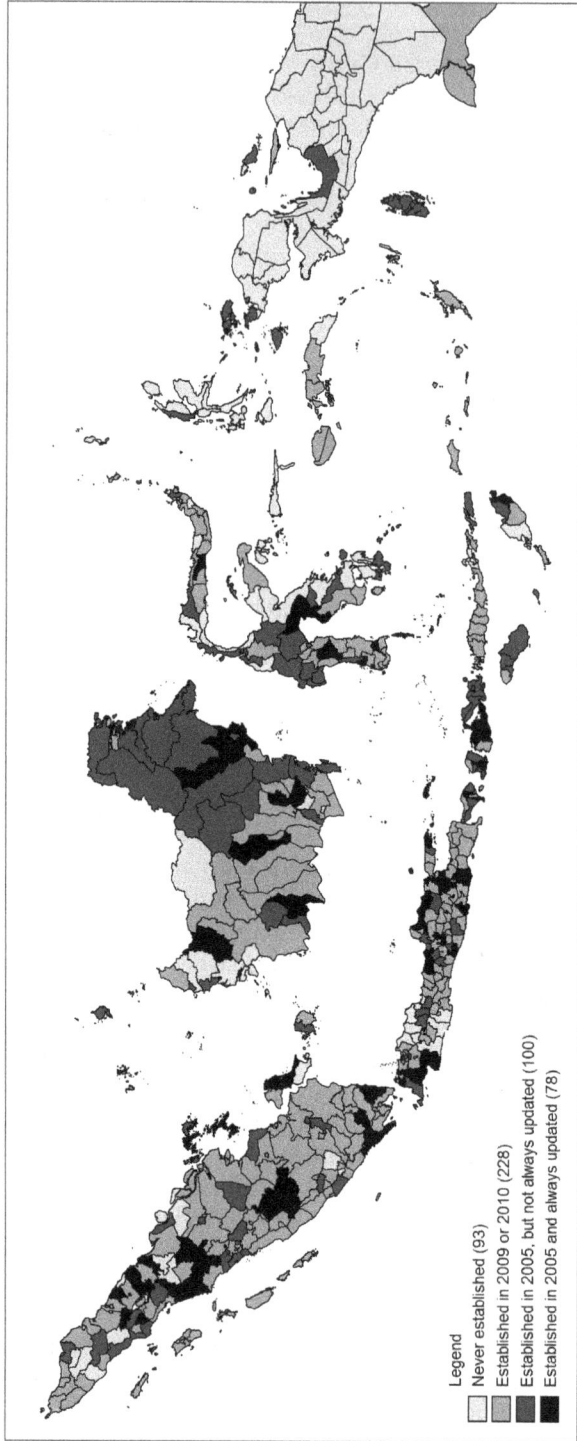

Figure 12.3   Distribution of TKPKD offices across districts

Legend
Never established (93)
Established in 2009 or 2010 (228)
Established in 2005, but not always updated (100)
Established in 2005 and always updated (78)

Figure 12.4   Correlation between existence of TKPKD offices and reductions in poverty

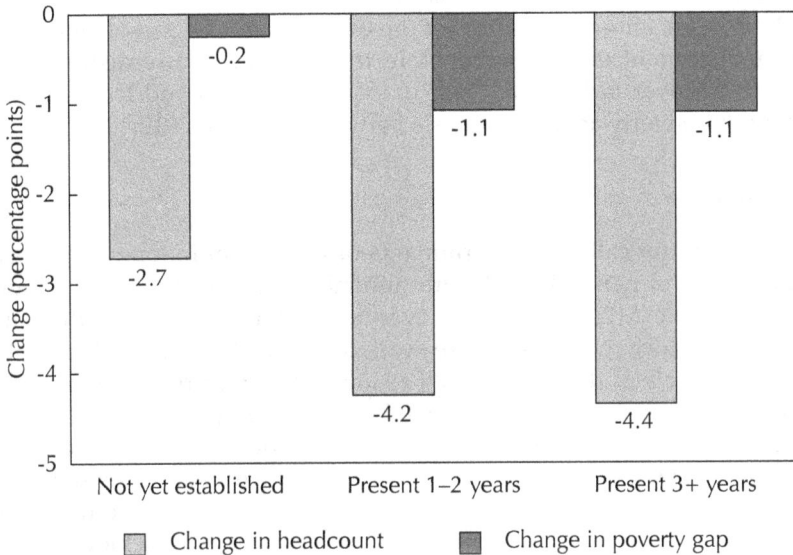

To address some of these issues, between 2005 and 2010 the presidential office issued several further regulations reforming the composition and role of the TKPKDs. In 2010, it established the National Team for the Acceleration of Poverty Reduction (Tim Nasional Percepatan Penanggulangan Kemiskinan, TNP2K) to coordinate and oversee the national poverty reduction strategy, and to support and develop the capacity of the TKPKDs to plan and implement local poverty reduction programs and policies. However, the local government bodies suffer from high staff turnover, making it difficult to maintain a focal point for mainstreaming poverty reduction initiatives. To address this issue, some local governments, such as the governments of Central Java province and Indramayu district, have issued regulations to minimize the rotation of civil servants across local government departments.

12.4   DATA AND ESTIMATION STRATEGY

In their study of differences in poverty reduction at the subnational level in the 1990s, Balisacan, Pernia and Asra (2002) highlight several advantages of using Indonesia as a case study. First, the country is highly diverse geographically, and with respect to institutional attributes and economic performance. This diversity allows for a critical assessment of the influence on poverty of economy-wide policies and initial conditions, including institutions and geographic attributes. Second, cross-sectional and time-series data are available for the subnational units (provinces and districts), allowing analysis of the determinants of growth and poverty reduction at the district level. In this section, we use district-level data to uncover factors that help to explain regional and local heterogeneity in poverty across Indonesia between 2005 and 2010.

Data sources

To assess empirically the determinants of poverty in Indonesia, we use a district-level panel dataset with annual observations for the period 2005–10. Table A12.1 provides an overview of the data sources, the time period for which the variables are available and, where applicable, problematic aspects of the data as well as adjustments made in response to those problems. A general challenge in constructing the database arises from the post-Suharto decentralization legislation and the related formation of new districts. The *pemekaran* process led to an increase in the number of districts from 440 in 2005 to 497 in 2010. We have therefore realigned the data to match the 2005 district borders, to achieve a uniform dataset of 440 districts throughout.

Descriptive statistics

Table 12.2 presents descriptive statistics. In addition to the mean, maximum and minimum values, we show standard deviations decomposed into their 'between' and 'within' components, that is, the variation across districts in a given year (*between*) and the variation within districts over time (*within*). Some of the structural characteristics we are interested in do not vary substantially over the sample period (education, demographics, infrastructure, institutional quality), which restricts our econometric options.

Before turning to the regression analysis, we take a closer look at regional and local heterogeneity in poverty levels and trends. Table 12.3 provides a provincial-level overview of headcount poverty and the poverty gap in both 2005 and 2010. On average, the incidence of poverty fell by 4.2 percentage points, from 21.1 per cent in 2005 to 16.9 per cent in 2010; over the same period, the poverty gap narrowed from 4.0 per cent to 2.8 per cent. There are substantial variations between provinces, however. With the exception of West Papua, we see that all provinces with poverty rates above 30 per cent in 2005 were able to reduce poverty by at least five percentage points, with the highest reduction observed for the province of Gorontalo. The absolute reductions in poverty tend to be lowest for provinces with lower levels of poverty in 2005.

Table 12.2   Descriptive statistics for the district-level panel dataset, 2005–10

Variable	No.	Mean	Mini-mum	Maxi-mum	Standard deviation		
					Overall	Between	Within
Social factors							
Poverty head count	2,640	18.44	2.10	63.50	10.520	10.070	3.080
Poverty gap	2,640	3.38	0.00	22.30	2.740	2.470	1.200
Gini coefficient (based on household consumption)	2,640	27.07	13.10	62.00	4.450	3.290	2.990
Average years of education	2,640	7.64	4.50	12.90	1.080	1.030	0.340
Share of population with primary education	2,640	0.82	0.18	0.93	0.076	0.074	0.017
Share of population with junior secondary education	2,640	0.39	0.04	0.72	0.117	0.114	0.027
Economic factors							
Real GDP per capita	2,640	0.86	0.06	20.91	1.380	1.371	0.163
Share of agriculture in GDP	2,640	0.32	0.00	0.85	0.188	0.187	0.023
Share of mining in GDP	2,640	0.07	0.00	0.95	0.160	0.159	0.017
Share of workers in agriculture	2,640	0.48	0.00	1.00	0.251	0.250	0.025
Share of workers in mining	2,640	0.02	0.00	0.37	0.036	0.036	0.007
Unemployment rate, total	1,760	0.07	0.00	0.22	0.039	0.036	0.014
Underemployment rate, total	1,760	0.36	0.07	0.91	0.130	0.122	0.046
Annual growth rate of GDP per capita	2,640	0.06	–0.40	0.87	0.043	0.022	0.037
Total fiscal revenues per capita	2,604	0.24	0.01	3.20	0.315	0.300	0.098
Total fiscal revenues as a share of GDP	2,604	0.44	0.01	5.45	0.560	0.543	0.136
Demographic factors							
Total population	2,640	5.05	0.10	41.10	5.740	5.740	0.010
Population density	2,640	10.65	0.00	205.00	24.970	25.000	0.020
Share of urban population	2,640	0.35	0.00	1.00	0.319	0.319	0.000
Ethnic diversity (more than one ethnicity, based on Podes village surveys)	2,640	0.73	0.07	1.00	0.232	0.222	0.067
Other factors							
Share of villages with asphalt main road	2,640	0.64	0.00	1.00	0.284	0.279	0.055
Primary health care facility easy to reach	2,640	0.94	0.00	1.00	0.107	0.095	0.051
Police station easy to reach	2,640	0.85	0.00	1.00	0.188	0.178	0.061
Share of village heads with no secondary education	2,640	0.10	0.00	1.00	0.157	0.150	0.049
Recent history of large-scale extended violence	2,640	0.23	0.00	1.00	0.422	0.422	0.000

Table 12.3   *Provincial overview of headcount poverty and the poverty gap, 2005 and 2010*

Province	Headcount poverty			Poverty gap		
	2005	2010	Change	2005	2010	Change
Aceh	28.2	23.4	−4.8	5.3	4.2	−1.1
North Sumatra	17.6	14.4	−3.2	3.1	2.3	−0.7
West Sumatra	13.7	11.6	−2.1	2.2	1.8	−0.4
Riau	15.7	13.1	−2.6	3.1	2.4	−0.7
Jambi	14.7	10.6	−4.1	2.2	1.5	−0.7
South Sumatra	25.0	18.2	−6.8	4.5	3.0	−1.5
Bengkulu	26.1	20.0	−6.1	4.7	3.5	−1.2
Lampung	24.3	21.3	−3.0	4.8	3.8	−1.0
Bangka Belitung	13.4	9.8	−3.5	2.7	1.4	−1.3
Riau Islands	13.4	11.3	−2.1	2.9	1.9	−1.0
Jakarta	4.8	5.4	0.6	0.8	0.9	0.1
West Java	16.1	14.3	−1.8	3.1	2.2	−0.9
Central Java	24.4	19.4	−4.9	4.5	3.3	−1.2
Yogyakarta	21.6	18.3	−3.3	4.4	2.6	−1.7
East Java	23.6	17.7	−5.9	4.5	2.9	−1.6
Banten	11.7	10.5	−1.2	2.0	1.7	−0.3
Bali	8.4	7.3	−1.2	1.2	1.1	−0.1
West Nusa Tenggara	30.0	25.1	−5.0	5.9	4.5	−1.5
East Nusa Tenggara	32.3	25.7	−6.7	7.0	4.9	−2.0
West Kalimantan	17.3	11.5	−5.9	3.0	1.8	−1.2
Central Kalimantan	14.1	10.0	−4.1	2.1	1.6	−0.6
South Kalimantan	9.0	7.6	−1.4	1.5	1.1	−0.4
East Kalimantan	13.3	11.1	−2.2	2.8	2.1	−0.7
North Sulawesi	11.8	12.7	0.9	2.1	2.1	0.0
Central Sulawesi	25.8	21.1	−4.7	5.1	4.0	−1.1
South Sulawesi	16.3	14.0	−2.3	2.8	2.3	−0.4
Southeast Sulawesi	24.7	20.0	−4.7	4.7	3.4	−1.3
Gorontalo	34.9	19.9	−15.0	7.8	3.4	−4.4
West Sulawesi	20.7	17.8	−2.9	0.0	2.8	2.8
Maluku	37.6	31.8	−5.8	8.4	7.0	−1.4
North Maluku	17.3	12.8	−4.6	2.7	2.2	−0.5
West Papua	41.3	40.8	−0.4	8.1	11.9	3.8
Papua	46.6	38.3	−8.3	12.9	9.2	−3.6
Indonesia	**21.1**	**16.9**	**−4.2**	**4.0**	**2.8**	**−1.2**

Figure 12.5 Convergence in poverty rates: headcount poverty

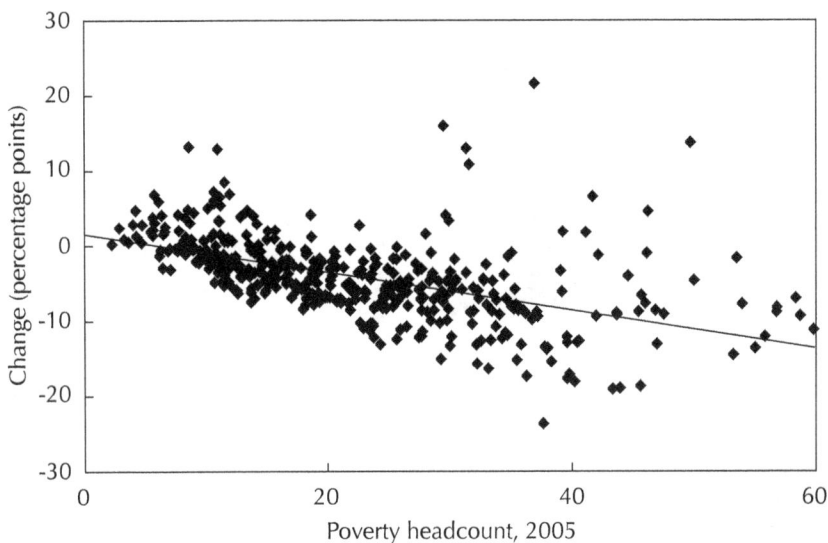

The underlying trend of convergence in poverty levels is confirmed when we plot changes in headcount poverty and the poverty gap against the 2005 levels of these indicators for the 440 districts in the sample (Figures 12.5 and 12.6). While the graphs show an overall negative correlation between the initial levels of poverty and the changes over time, they also illustrate substantial deviations from this general trend and hence point to diverging local experiences across the archipelago.

Table A12.2 shows that there are close correlations between some of our socio-economic control variables. This implies a choice to be made about the inclusion of the most relevant correlates of poverty to avoid potential issues of multi-collinearity. We have chosen not to include measures of labour market participation and local infrastructure, which are highly correlated with per capita GDP and with the share of urban population.

Econometric approach

To exploit the longitudinal dimension of the dataset, we run panel regression models on both poverty incidence and poverty severity. As a number of our control variables show relatively low variation over the 2005–10 period,[3] we first apply a random effects (RE) model. The

---

3 See the within-district standard deviations reported in Table 12.2.

Figure 12.6   Convergence in poverty rates: poverty gap

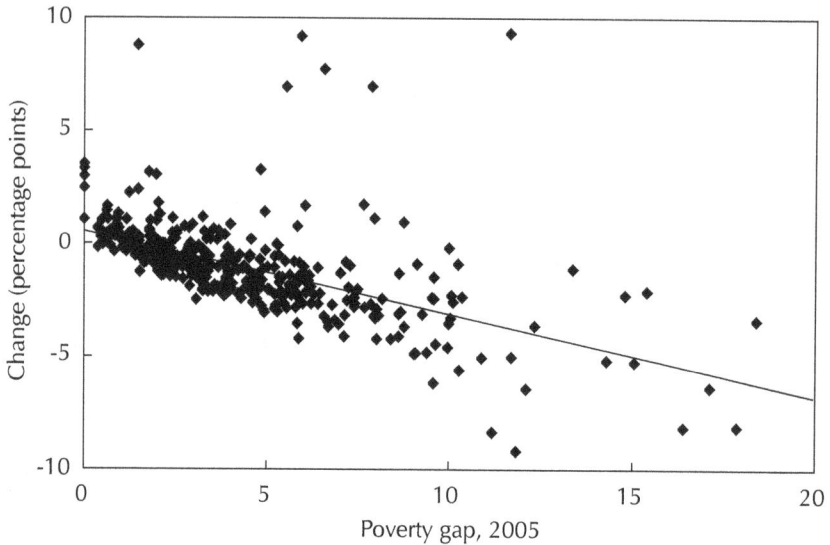

RE model allows us to account for unobserved district heterogeneity that might affect poverty levels beyond the observable explanatory factors, and at the same time to include the control variables that either exhibit low variation over time or are time-invariant. The flexibility of the RE model relies on the rather strong assumption of orthogonality between the district-specific random effect and the explanatory variables. For comparison and robustness, we therefore also run fixed effects (FE) models using a reduced set of time-varying control variables. The introduction of fixed effects allows us to capture district-specific underlying cultural values, as well as other time-invariant or long-term, slowly changing determinants of poverty. Note that we forego the inclusion of time (year) dummies for this analysis. By capturing the overall improvement in poverty levels in Indonesia in recent years, time dummies would absorb substantial parts of the variation in poverty in our sample. We are mainly interested in identifying general correlations between poverty and socio-economic conditions, which would be at least partly eliminated by the introduction of time dummies.

Finally, we estimate standard ordinary least squares (OLS) regressions on the absolute changes in headcount poverty and the poverty gap between 2005 and 2010, controlling for initial conditions in 2005 as well as changes in explanatory factors over this period. As the observations within districts are likely to be interdependent over time, we cluster the standard errors at the district level to allow for such intra-group correlation.

Given the complex and often reciprocal links between poverty and other socio-economic conditions, it is important to note that we do not claim to provide causal explanations, but rather to describe the relationship between the local environment and the prevalence of poverty. The analysis aims to further understanding of the factors related to local poverty (reduction) in a decentralized Indonesia.

12.5   RESULTS

Table 12.4 presents the main regression results at the district level for both the RE and FE models. We use a balanced panel of 434 districts over the six-year period from 2005 to 2010.[4] In regression (1) on headcount poverty, we include only a core set of control variables. The incidence of poverty is found to be lower in districts with: (1) higher GDP per capita; (2) a higher share of total fiscal revenues; (3) a higher average level of educational attainment; (4) a larger share of local leaders with secondary education (as a proxy for the quality of local governance); and (5) a higher share of urban population.

While the role of education in reducing poverty is uncontroversial, views on the poverty consequences of urbanization differ. The newer, more optimistic view is summarized by Whiting and Unwin (2009: 1,737), who note that 'greater urbanization in low income countries is an essential component of economic development and from this perspective is both inevitable and desirable', and is also clearly evident in the World Bank's (2009) *World Development Report*.

Districts with relatively larger public budgets (compared to the size of their local economies) appear to have slightly lower levels of poverty, and this effect seems to be independent of the quality of the local government (proxied by the educational attainment of local leaders). All else being equal, an increase of one year in the average number of years of schooling is estimated to be correlated with a 2.1 percentage point reduction in the poverty rate. On average, poverty levels are found to be about nine percentage points higher in rural districts, reflecting a substantial rural–urban divide.

To assess the correlation between the presence of a TKPKD office and the level of poverty, we include two dummy variables indicating the presence of a TKPKD office for one to two years, and for at least three years. Compared to districts where no office has been established, poverty is found to be more than one percentage point lower in districts that

---

4   We exclude the six districts in Jakarta from the panel, given the distinct characteristics of the capital region and the lack of data on their fiscal revenues.

Table 12.4 Determinants of poverty at the district level: regression results

	Poverty headcount				Poverty gap		Change in headcount	Change in gap
	RE (1)	RE (2)	RE (3)	FE (4)	RE (5)	FE (6)	OLS (7)	OLS (8)
Real GDP per capita (without mining)	-0.80 (0.307)	-0.72 (0.331)	-0.77 (0.150)	-0.37 (0.696)	-0.06 (0.590)	-0.10 (0.758)	-0.05 (0.753)	0.03 (0.677)
Fiscal revenue as share of GDP	-1.99*** (0.004)	-2.63*** (0.000)	-3.54*** (0.000)	-4.99*** (0.000)	-0.97*** (0.000)	-2.01*** (0.000)	1.97*** (0.002)	0.90*** (0.000)
Education: average years of schooling	-2.10*** (0.000)	-2.05*** (0.000)	-2.03*** (0.000)	-1.99*** (0.000)	-0.34*** (0.000)	-0.33*** (0.003)	-0.06 (0.868)	-0.10 (0.482)
Village heads without secondary education	11.81*** (0.000)	10.13*** (0.000)	7.77*** (0.004)	6.56** (0.027)	1.15 (0.306)	-0.49 (0.719)	5.30** (0.012)	0.62 (0.452)
Share of urban population	-8.90*** (0.000)	-4.02 (0.227)	-4.30 (0.128)		-1.29* (0.099)		3.29*** (0.010)	-0.22 (0.643)
TKPKD active for 1–2 years[a]	-1.35*** (0.000)	-1.30*** (0.000)	-1.13*** (0.000)	-1.35*** (0.000)	-0.16** (0.026)	-0.32*** (0.001)	-0.91 (0.169)	-0.18 (0.494)
TKPKD active for 3+ years	-3.89*** (0.000)	-3.70*** (0.000)	-3.43*** (0.000)	-3.79*** (0.000)	-0.66*** (0.000)	-0.92*** (0.000)	-1.61** (0.017)	-0.41 (0.121)
Agriculture as share of GDP		8.61 (0.156)	9.09* (0.085)	11.27 (0.205)	1.27 (0.339)	1.36 (0.745)		
Mining as share of GDP		1.97 (0.642)	4.52 (0.229)	10.91* (0.091)	0.77 (0.385)	2.95 (0.293)		
Gini coefficient		0.05* (0.069)	0.04 (0.132)	0.03 (0.234)	0.07*** (0.000)	0.06*** (0.000)	0.05 (0.442)	0.06** (0.022)

	(1)	(2)	(3)	(4)	(5)	(6)	(7)	(8)
Recent history of large-scale violence		6.24***	4.44***		1.05***		0.52	0.27
		(0.000)	(0.000)		(0.000)		(0.470)	(0.333)
Region[b]								
Sumatra			-2.51***		-0.35*		-0.30	-0.09
			(0.002)		(0.055)		(0.609)	(0.689)
Kalimantan			-10.87***		-2.06***		-2.87***	-1.12***
			(0.000)		(0.000)		(0.001)	(0.001)
East & West Nusa Tenggara			2.08		0.74**		1.15	0.39
			(0.187)		(0.027)		(0.168)	(0.227)
Sulawesi			-2.38**		-0.39*		0.51	-0.04
			(0.023)		(0.091)		(0.494)	(0.878)
Maluku & North Maluku			1.89		1.50*		-0.10	0.78
			(0.569)		(0.072)		(0.944)	(0.163)
Papua			14.81***		5.80***		3.64**	2.99***
			(0.000)		(0.000)		(0.011)	(0.000)
Headcount poverty or poverty gap in 2005							-0.36***	-0.62***
							(0.000)	(0.000)
Change in share of fiscal revenues, 2005–10							0.50	-0.50
							(0.589)	(0.161)
Change in Gini coefficient, 2005–10							0.07	0.11***
							(0.208)	(0.000)
Constant	39.26***	31.95***	33.90***	31.70***	4.41***	5.12***	1.51	0.73
	(0.000)	(0.000)	(0.000)	(0.000)	(0.000)	(0.007)	(0.593)	(0.485)
Year dummies	No	No	No	No	No	No	No	No
No. of observations	2,598	2,598	2,598	2,598	2,598	2,598	434	434
Pseudo-R^2 (7) or adjusted R^2 (8)	0.286	0.300	0.309	0.314	0.128	0.145	0.468	0.516

* = significant at 10 per cent; ** = significant at 5 per cent; *** = significant at 1 per cent. P-values are in parentheses. Standard errors are clustered at the district level.
a   Reference category is districts with no active TKPKD in the past.   b   Reference category is Java/Bali.

have had a TKPKD office for at least one year, and nearly four percentage points lower in those that have had a TKPKD office for at least three
years.

We then extend the list of control variables, introducing additional
economic factors (regression 2). Again, the incidence of poverty is found
to be lower in districts with higher GDP per capita, although the result is
not statistically significant. The share of mining in district GDP is not correlated with poverty incidence. Similarly, the share of agriculture in district GDP is not significantly correlated with poverty, probably because
the share of the urban population accounts for the predominance of the
agricultural sector in the district economy.

All else being equal, poverty incidence appears to be slightly higher
in districts that have higher rates of inequality, as measured by the Gini
coefficient. This finding is consistent with the general observation that
the poverty reduction effect of growth increases with regional output, but
at a decreasing rate due to the non-linear tail effects of the distribution of
income. Several studies have emphasized the importance of inequality
in determining the responsiveness of poverty to output growth (Ravallion 1997; Easterly 2000; Adams 2004). Based on the specification that the
growth elasticity of poverty decreases with inequality, Ravallion (1997)
econometrically tested the 'growth elasticity argument' that while low
inequality helps the poor share in the benefits of growth, it also exposes
them to the costs of a contraction in growth. In essence, our results suggest that the poverty reduction effect of output growth may occur in part
through inequality reduction effects.

Finally, a recent history of large-scale violence appears to be highly
and positively correlated with poverty incidence. Controlling for a wide
range of socio-economic control variables, we find that headcount poverty is about six percentage points higher in provinces that were affected
by large-scale violence in the early years of the country's political and
economic transition. The direction of causality is unclear, however, as we
cannot rule out the possibility that areas with (persistently) high levels of
poverty may be particularly prone to violence, or that areas that experience high levels of violence have performed less well in reducing poverty.
One set of theories stresses the role that political repression, or what are
sometimes called 'grievance' factors, may play in driving regional conflict. In this view, ethnic groups that experience discrimination should
be the most likely to organize armed insurrections against the state, and
conflict should be most likely to erupt in undemocratic states and those
with pronounced social divisions. A second set of theories focuses on
economic rather than political factors. In this view, rising poverty and
falling incomes are the factors most likely to spark civil conflicts. This
may be either because poverty breeds armed violence aimed at looting

assets and natural resources, or because poor areas simply have limited institutional capacity to repress armed uprisings.

To ensure that our results are not driven by structural differences between major regions, we introduce regional dummies, with the islands of Java and Bali as the reference category (regression 3). This also allows us to account for region-specific characteristics that are constant over time, such as socio-cultural norms or habits. The results for the other control variables are mostly unchanged, suggesting that different degrees of poverty within regions are mainly related to the same factors that explain the overall heterogeneity in poverty at the national level. The regional dummies also provide evidence on the overall spatial trends in poverty. While the interpretation of the coefficients is not straightforward, as the factors driving the differences between regions are unknown, the strong coefficients observed in particular for Kalimantan (where, *ceteris paribus*, poverty levels are 11 percentage points lower than in Java/Bali) and Papua (where, *ceteris paribus*, they are 15 percentage points higher than in Java/Bali) suggest that factors other than the socio-economic conditions we control for considerably shape poverty outcomes in these regions.

The appropriateness of the RE model relative to the more restrictive FE model can be assessed using the Hausman specification test. The null hypothesis of consistent estimates from the RE model is rejected, implying that the use of the FE model is more appropriate.[5] We therefore assess the robustness of the findings on the determinants of headcount poverty by estimating an FE model (regression 4). The time-invariant control variables (share of urban population, history of conflict, regional dummies) are excluded from the FE model, which focuses solely on the within-district evolution of poverty over time. The results largely confirm, and provide a valuable complement to, those from the RE estimations. In particular, we find that the incidence of poverty remains about four percentage points lower in districts that have had a TKPKD office for at least three years. The negative correlation between fiscal revenues and poverty incidence also appears to be strongly supported. The main difference between the two sets of results is that the share of mining in GDP becomes significant in the FE model; the result suggests that poverty incidence is nearly 11 percentage points higher in districts where the mining sector makes a significant contribution to district GDP.

Regressions (5) and (6) report the RE and FE results on the determinants of the poverty gap. Although the same set of control variables is included, we obtain a somewhat different picture of the determinants of the intensity of poverty. In line with expectations, greater inequality in

---

5 The same holds for the regressions on the poverty gap; the Hausman test confirms the use of the FE model.

consumption contributes to a higher poverty gap. The estimated effect is rather marginal, though, with a one standard deviation (4.45) increase in the Gini coefficient leading to an increase in the poverty gap of 0.11 standard deviations.

As for poverty incidence, we find that rural areas and provinces with a recent history of conflict are generally more affected by severe poverty. Moreover, a relatively high level of fiscal revenues relative to the size of the economy is linked to reduced levels of poverty severity, with a one standard deviation (0.55) increase in the share of fiscal revenues leading to a decrease in the poverty gap of 0.20 standard deviations. The existence of a TKPKD office also reduces poverty severity, although the difference between the offices established for one to two years and those established for at least three years is smaller than was the case for poverty incidence. Although poverty severity is found to be uncorrelated with the educational achievements of local leaders, it is negatively and significantly correlated with average years of schooling, suggesting reduced severity of poverty in districts with higher average educational attainment.

Finally, we consider the absolute changes in district-level poverty (for both the headcount and gap measures of poverty) between 2005 and 2010 (regressions 7 and 8) and assess the factors that explain the *changes* in poverty indicators. We estimate standard OLS regressions and include the core control variables used in the previous regressions, in the form of both levels (2005 values) and changes over the period, where appropriate. Some general trends appear to hold for both headcount poverty and the poverty gap. The phenomenon of converging poverty levels is strongly confirmed by the significantly negative coefficients associated with the 2005 baseline levels of poverty. The higher headcount poverty and the poverty gap in 2005, the larger the reduction in these measures observed between 2005 and 2010. Beyond the socio-economic factors controlled for, districts in Kalimantan appear particularly successful in reducing poverty, while the opposite is observed for districts in Papua. Urbanization is associated with greater reductions in headcount poverty, but not the poverty gap. Similarly, the existence of TKPKD offices is linked to larger decreases in headcount poverty (1.6 percentage points in districts with offices operating for at least three years), but not in the poverty gap. Reductions in the poverty gap seem more contingent on the income distribution and low levels of consumption inequality.

Surprisingly, a higher initial share of fiscal revenues appears to be linked to less success in poverty reduction. Further investigation into the role of fiscal revenues in poverty reduction reveals this correlation to be non-linear in nature. Up to a moderate level of fiscal revenues, a relatively larger public budget contributes to a reduction in poverty; however, districts in which such revenues represent 50 per cent or more of the size of the local economy seem to have been less successful in mitigating poverty over the 2005–10 period (results not reported).

12.6   CONCLUSION

In this chapter we have considered heterogeneity in the evolution of poverty over time across Indonesian districts, in the context of the rapid implementation of decentralization since 2001. Our econometric results suggest that the differing experiences of districts in reducing poverty between 2005 and 2010 are related to differences in their local GDP per capita, availability of resources to fund public expenditures, service delivery outcomes, quality of governance and institutional capacity to implement poverty reduction policies. Regional heterogeneity in poverty across Indonesia also appears to be related to the level of education, the existence of conflict and the degree of urbanization.

Poverty incidence is found to be lower in districts with higher GDP per capita, higher average educational attainment, a larger share of local leaders with secondary education and a higher degree of urbanization. Regional output per capita is a major factor behind falling poverty rates; but inequality also has a statistically significant effect on poverty across all districts in Indonesia. Moreover, there appears to be a positive link between inequality and poverty, suggesting that a successful poverty reduction strategy requires both economic growth *and* a sound redistribution policy.

Our finding is consistent with previous studies, which have generally revealed that growth in GDP per capita is an important means of reducing poverty. This result is especially true when income distributions are relatively stable over time, as output per capita has the general effect of raising incomes for all members of society, including the poor. On average, poverty levels are found to be around 14 percentage points higher in rural districts, reflecting a substantial rural–urban divide. The share of fiscal revenues in district GDP has a significant negative correlation with both poverty incidence and poverty severity. A district's institutional capacity to carry out poverty reduction initiatives appears to be a strong and consistent predictor of the evolution of poverty over time. Compared to districts where no TKPKD office has been established, poverty is found to be significantly lower in districts with active TKPKD offices. As one would expect, the correlation increases over time, with districts where a TKPKD office has been active for at least three years having four percentage points lower headcount poverty than those where no office has been established. In addition, substantially higher poverty incidence and poverty severity is found in districts with a recent history of large-scale violence, although the direction of causality is yet to be established.

Poverty reduction in Indonesia therefore appears to be confronted by several challenges related to the decentralization process. The main challenge is to address the limited capacity and resources of local governments to develop and implement poverty reduction strategies, and to provide good public services. Second, decentralization has occurred too quickly and therefore lacks a comprehensive policy framework. The correlation between the establishment of TKPKD offices and reductions in poverty suggests, however, that there are opportunities to address the institutional barriers to an effective decentralization framework. Based on the TKPKD model, the government could, for instance, develop a more comprehensive policy framework that helped to clarify the lines of responsibility and accountability in the delivery of public services, to support the reduction of poverty at a similar pace across the country.

In summary, the principal message that emerges from this study is that regional output, income distribution and poverty reduction are strongly inter-related, so a successful development strategy requires effective, region-specific combinations of growth and distribution policies. Rapid and sustainable growth in regional economic output is viewed as the primary vehicle for poverty reduction. The basic proposition is that if poor, lagging districts in Indonesia can increase their economic output rapidly enough, and their income distributions are not unusually skewed against the poor, poverty reductions should occur.

REFERENCES

Adams, R.H. (2004) 'Economic growth, inequality and poverty: estimating the growth elasticity of poverty', *World Development*, 32(12): 1,989–2,014.

ADB (Asian Development Bank) (2010) 'Asian Development Bank support for decentralization in Indonesia', ADB, Manila.

Ahmad, J., S. Devarajan, S. Khemani and S. Shah (2005) 'Decentralization and service delivery', Policy Research Working Paper No. 3603, World Bank, Washington DC, May.

Aswicahyono, H. and D. Friawan (2008) 'Infrastructure development in Indonesia', in N. Kumar (ed.) *International Infrastructure Development in East Asia: Towards Balanced Regional Development and Integration*, ERIA Research Project Report 2007-2, IDE-JETRO, Chiba.

Aten, R. (2011) 'Decentralization in Indonesia as a partial solution to Indonesian conflicts', International Network for Economics and Conflict, United States Institute of Peace, 7 November.

Balisacan, A.M., E.M. Pernia and A. Asra (2002) 'Revisiting growth and poverty reduction in Indonesia: what do subnational data show?', ERD Working Paper Series No. 25, Economics and Research Department, Asian Development Bank, Manila, October.

Bardhan, P. (2002) 'Decentralization of governance and development', *Journal of Economic Perspectives*, 16(4): 185–205.

Blaxall, J. (2000) 'Governance and poverty', paper presented at the Joint Workshop on Poverty Reduction Strategies in Mongolia, World Bank, Ulaanbaatar, 4–6 October.

Bloom, D.E., D. Canning and J. Sevilla (2003) 'Geography and poverty traps', *Journal of Economic Growth*, 8: 355–78.

Butt, S. and N. Parsons (2012) 'Reining in regional governments? Local taxes and investment in decentralised Indonesia', *Sydney Law Review*, 34(1): 91–106.

Crook, R.C. and A.S. Sverrisson (2001) 'Decentralisation and poverty-alleviation in developing countries: a comparative analysis *or*, is West Bengal unique?', IDS Working Paper No. 130, Institute of Development Studies, University of Sussex, Brighton.

Easterly, W. (2000) 'The effect of IMF and World Bank programs on poverty', unpublished paper, World Bank, Washington DC.

Eid, U. (2000) 'Good governance for poverty reduction', paper presented at the Asian Development Bank Seminar on the New Social and Poverty Agenda for Asia and the Pacific, Chiang Mai, 5 May.

Farhan, Y. (2012) 'Naikan gaji kepala daerah: presiden bangkrutkan daerah' [By increasing the salary of regional heads: the president will make regions bankrupt], press release, Forum Indonesia untuk Transparansi Anggaran, Jakarta, available at http://seknasfitra.org/wp-content/uploads/2013/02/Siaran-Pers-Tolak-Kenaikan-Gaji-Kepala-Daerah1.pdf.

Fitrani, F., B. Hofman and K. Kaiser (2005) 'Unity in diversity? The creation of new local governments in a decentralising Indonesia', *Bulletin of Indonesian Economic Studies*, 41(1): 57–79.

Gupta, S., H. Davoodi and E. Tiongson (2000) 'Corruption and the provision of health care and education services', IMF Working Paper No. 00/116, International Monetary Fund, Washington DC, June.

Harjowiryono, M. (2011) 'Lessons learned from Indonesia's fiscal decentralization', paper presented at the International Conference on Fiscal Decentralization in Indonesia a Decade after the Big Bang, Ministry of Finance, Jakarta.

Heywood, P. and N.P. Harahap (2009) 'Public funding of health at the district level in Indonesia after decentralization: sources, flows and contradictions', Health Research Policy and Systems, 7(5), available at http://www.health-policy-systems.com/content/7/1/5.

Hofman, B. and K. Kaiser (2002) 'The making of the big bang and its aftermath: a political economy perspective', paper presented at a conference called Can Decentralization Help Rebuild Indonesia? George State University, Atlanta, 1–3 May.

Huther, J. and A. Shah (1998) 'Applying a simple measure of good governance to the debate on fiscal decentralization', Policy Research Working Paper No. 1894, World Bank, Washington DC, March.

ICG (International Crisis Group) (2005) 'Decentralisation and conflict in Indonesia: the Mamasa case', Asia Briefing No. 37, ICG, Singapore/Brussels, May.

Isdijoso, W. (2012) 'Assessing the performance of Indonesian decentralization (and democratization): what is to be assessed and how?' paper presented on behalf of the SMERU Institute at a conference on The Performance of Indonesian Decentralization during Its First Decade: Policy and Priorities for the Second, Bappenas, PGSP-UNDP and Strategic Asia Indonesia, Jakarta, 25 June.

Jalan, J. and M. Ravallion (2002) 'Geographic poverty traps? A micro model of consumption growth in rural China', *Journal of Applied Econometrics*, 14(4): 329–46.

Jütting, J., F. Corsi and A. Stockmayer (2005) 'Decentralisation and poverty reduction', Policy Insights No. 5, OECD Development Centre, OECD, Paris, January.

Kimura, E. (2007) 'Provincial proliferation: territorial politics in post-authoritarian Indonesia', PhD dissertation, University of Wisconsin-Madison, Madison.

McLaughlin, K. and A. Perdana (2010) 'Conflict and dispute resolution in Indonesia: information from the 2006 Governance and Decentralization Survey', Indonesian Social Development Paper No. 16, World Bank, Jakarta, January.

Ministry of Finance (2012) 'Profil APBD TA 2012' [Local government budget (APBD) profile for 2012], Ministry of Finance, Jakarta, available at http://www.djpk.depkeu.go.id/attachments/article/163/Profil_APBD_TA2012.pdf.

Murshed, S.M. and M.Z. Tadjoeddin (2008) 'Is fiscal decentralisation conflict abating? Routine violence and district level government in Java, Indonesia', MICROCON Research Working Paper No. 7, MICROCON, Brighton, July.

Ravallion, M. (1997) 'Can high-inequality developing countries escape absolute poverty?', *Economics Letters*, 56: 51–7.

Robinson, M. (2007) 'Introduction: decentralising service delivery? Evidence and policy implications', *IDS Bulletin*, 38(1): 1–6.

Shah, A., R. Qibthiyyah and A. Dita (2012) 'General purpose central–provincial-local transfers (DAU) in Indonesia: from gap filling to ensuring fair access to essential public services for all', Policy Research Working Paper No. 6075, World Bank, Jakarta, June.

Sumarto, S., A. Suryahadi and A. Arifianto (2004) 'Governance and poverty reduction: evidence from newly decentralized Indonesia', SMERU Working Paper, SMERU Research Institute, Jakarta, March.

Whiting, D. and N. Unwin (2009) 'Cities, urbanization and health', *International Journal of Epidemiology*, 38(6): 1,737–42.

World Bank (2003a) 'Decentralizing Indonesia: a regional public expenditure review', Report No. 26191-IND, East Asia Poverty Reduction and Economic Management Unit, World Bank, Washington DC, June.

World Bank (2003b) 'Indonesia: selected fiscal issues in a new era', Report No. 25437-IND, East Asia Poverty Reduction and Economic Management Unit, World Bank, Washington DC, February.

World Bank (2006) *East Asia Decentralizes: Making Local Government Work*, World Bank, Washington DC.

World Bank (2009) *World Development Report 2009: Shaping Economic Geography*, World Bank, Washington DC.

World Bank (2011) 'Indonesia economic quarterly: turbulent times', World Bank, Jakarta, October.

Table A12.1   Data sources, data availability and potential problems

Variable	Source	Years	Comments or problematic aspects
Regional GDP (district-level GDP data)	BPS	2005–2010	
Unemployment/ underemployment (workers per sector)	Sakernas (July)	2007–2010	Representative at the district level from 2007 onward; disaggregation by sex and/or age is not possible.
Workers per sector	Sakernas (July)	2005–2010	Disaggregation by sector may not be representative for small districts.
Total fiscal revenues (including own-source revenues & central government transfers)	SIKD, Ministry of Finance	2005–2010	Data for Jakarta are entirely missing, as there is only one budget for the capital (the six Jakarta districts do not have separate budgets)
Household expenditure, poverty rates, inequality, average years of education, enrolment rates	Susenas	2005–2010	2005 data for Papua and Aceh are missing (2004–06 average is used). 2008 data are not suitable for panel analysis (2007–09 average is used).
Population figures	Susenas	2005–2010	There is a structural break in 2008 (2006 baseline figures are used). Disaggregation by age (for example, share of young population) is problematic.
TKPKD	TNP2K	2005–2011	
Local infrastructure (roads, public services) and institutions (education of village head, presence of police stations and security posts), ethnic diversity	Podes village surveys	2005, 2008	

BPS = Badan Pusat Statistik (Statistics Indonesia); Podes = Potensi Desa (Village Potential); Sakernas = Survei Angkatan Kerja Nasional (National Labour Force Survey); SIKD = Sistem Informasi Keuangan Daerah (Regional Financial Information System); Susenas = Survei Sosio-Ekonomi Nasional (National Socio-Economic Survey); TKPKD = Tim Koordinasi Penanggulangan Kemiskinan Daerah (Local Coordinating Team for Poverty Reduction); TNP2K = Tim Nasional Percepatan Penanggulangan Kemiskinan (National Team for the Acceleration of Poverty Reduction).

Table A12.2 Correlations between selected variables

	Head-count poverty	Poverty gap	GDP per capita	TKPKD	% of agriculture in GDP	% of mining in GDP	Fiscal rev. per capita	Fiscal rev. as % of GDP	Unemployment rate	Underemployment rate	Gini coefficient	Average years of education	% of urban population	Ethnic diversity	Asphalt main road
Poverty gap	0.89	1.00													
GDP per capita	-0.17	-0.08	1.00												
TKPKD	-0.20	-0.19	0.07	1.00											
% of agriculture in GDP	0.47	0.33	-0.38	-0.08	1.00										
% of mining in GDP	-0.02	0.02	0.39	0.00	-0.22	1.00									
Fiscal revenues per capita	0.28	0.34	0.22	0.01	0.07	0.22	1.00								
Fiscal revenues as % of GDP	0.51	0.48	-0.16	-0.12	0.36	-0.11	0.63	1.00							
Unemployment rate	-0.31	-0.24	0.24	-0.02	-0.59	0.01	-0.10	-0.24	1.00						
Underemployment rate	0.37	0.28	-0.29	-0.06	0.65	0.08	0.08	0.27	-0.54	1.00					
Gini coefficient	-0.10	0.05	0.19	0.03	-0.32	-0.05	0.04	-0.02	0.20	-0.24	1.00				
Average years of education	-0.47	-0.33	0.24	0.13	-0.65	-0.12	-0.06	-0.26	0.52	-0.59	0.31	1.00			
% of urban population	-0.50	-0.37	0.27	0.09	-0.79	-0.13	-0.17	-0.32	0.62	-0.74	0.35	0.78	1.00		
Ethnic diversity	-0.48	-0.40	0.21	0.11	-0.31	0.09	-0.04	-0.22	0.29	-0.32	0.16	0.34	0.38	1.00	
Asphalt main road	-0.47	-0.42	0.06	0.12	-0.56	-0.22	-0.36	-0.42	0.39	-0.47	0.15	0.56	0.67	0.22	1.00
Heads with no secondary education	0.50	0.54	0.03	-0.14	0.27	0.17	0.55	0.59	-0.19	0.17	0.01	-0.33	-0.33	-0.26	-0.56

PART 4

Migration, cities and connectivity

13 Migration patterns: people on the move

Salut Muhidin

13.1 INTRODUCTION

In the last few decades, Indonesia has witnessed many changes in its demographic and socio-economic characteristics. Today, Indonesians have smaller families, longer life expectancy and more education. The average number of children per woman, as measured by the total fertility rate, declined from 4.6 in 1980 to 2.6 in 2010 (BPS 2012). Over the same period, life expectancy increased from 57.6 to 69.4 years. The implementation of compulsory education started with six years of schooling in 1984, increasing to nine years in 1994 and 12 years in 2012. This has significantly increased school enrolment rates; the net enrolment rate for senior secondary school, for example, increased from 17 per cent in 1975 to 51 per cent in 2012 (BPS 2013). In response to such significant changes, and the concomitant developments in local and global economic conditions, population mobility and migration patterns have also changed considerably.

At the same time, there have been significant improvements in transport, especially road and air transport, and in communications technology, which have also facilitated population mobility. The growing Indonesian diaspora, estimated to number 3–6 million (Muhidin and Utomo 2013), is further evidence of Indonesians' willingness to migrate. Mobility is a complex process involving the interaction of a wide range of factors, both personal and to do with the regions of destination and origin. Using the concept of a 'mobility continuum', Pooley, Turnbull and Adams (2005: 3) have observed that population mobility may include simple mobility (travel for work, shopping or leisure), circular mobility (involving regular longer travel) and longer-distance residential migration. The latter concept of mobility is the focus of this chapter.

According to the 2010 population census, Indonesia is home to 238 million people, about 27 million (12 per cent) of whom live outside their provinces of birth (BPS 2011). The proportion of such migrants varies widely across regions, however, from less than 3 per cent in the provinces of East Java, West Nusa Tenggara and Central Java, to as much as 42 per cent in Jakarta and 48 per cent in Riau Islands. These regional variations can be attributed to differences in socio-economic development, culture, geographic settings and patterns of human settlement, among other factors. Allied to this are marked variations in fertility and mortality, which not only shape the growth and composition of populations, but also provide an incentive for mobility in general, and drive urbanization (Ananta and Muhidin 2005; Hugo 2005).

In a large and regionally diverse country such as Indonesia, population mobility is an important issue. It is closely linked to the development process, both as a result and as a cause of changes in regional socio-economic and demographic characteristics. The decentralization reforms implemented in Indonesia since 2001 are highly relevant in this context. District (*kabupaten/kota*) governments now have greater autonomy, resulting in a growing interest in population distribution issues, including migration and urbanization.

Although much is known about demographic indicators such as fertility and mortality, surprisingly little attention has been paid to Indonesian migration patterns over time and space. In part, this may be because their sheer scale and complexity presents a formidable challenge to scholarship. In addition, understanding of the dynamics of mobility has been hampered by a lack of suitable time-series data and statistical measures that capture the multiple dimensions of population movement (Bell and Muhidin 2009). Studies typically concentrate on a single period of observation; where temporal comparisons have been made, they generally involve simple comparisons of gross or net inter-regional flows.

This chapter aims to contribute to a better understanding of the dynamics of migration patterns in Indonesia over the last three decades, and during the most recent decade of regional autonomy in particular. I begin by describing the data sources (section 13.2) and current patterns of regional population distribution (section 13.3). Next, using a fairly comparable set of migration data derived from four national censuses (1980, 1990, 2000 and 2010), I explore regional variations in lifetime and recent migration levels, and patterns of spatial redistribution (section 13.4). In section 13.5, I review the links between migration and development before describing some of the determinants of migration, including differences in levels of socio-economic development across regions.

I conclude by identifying commonalities and differences, and by exploring the idea of a distinctive regional mobility transition (section 13.6).

This chapter uses the concept of mobility transition developed by Zelinsky (1971, 1979, 1983) and later modified by Skeldon (1990). Zelinsky argued that there were 'definite, patterned regularities' in the growth of mobility, linked to the modernization process. He identified five stages in a mobility transition, paralleling those in a demographic transition, in which the levels and forms of mobility changed over time. He described these five stages as 'a kind of outward spatial diffusion of successively more advanced forms of human activity' during the progression from a 'pre-modern traditional society' to an 'early transitional society', a 'late transitional society', an 'advanced society' and a 'future super-advanced society' (Zelinsky 1971: 230–31). Critics argued, however, that Zelinsky's thesis was time-bound and Euro-centric, incorrectly characterized traditional societies as immobile, overlooked the importance of colonial invasion and government regulation, and failed to recognize the diversity of cross-national contexts within which migration occurs. This led Skeldon (1990) to suggest that, as societies develop, patterns of population mobility change from being dominated by short-distance migration to being dominated by long-distance, rural–urban temporary migration, then by long-distance, rural–urban permanent migration, and finally by commuting. Because rural–urban migration is still applicable in the context of Indonesia, in the following analysis I also take into consideration Harris and Todaro's (1970) concept of migration decisions and expected income differentials.

13.2   DATA SOURCES

In the analysis that follows, the main sources of data for estimating the levels and composition of internal migration are the 1980, 1990, 2000 and 2010 Indonesian population censuses. In addition, for descriptive purposes, the chapter uses published BPS data from other sources, such as the Inter-censal Population Survey (Survei Penduduk antar Sensus, Supas) and the National Socio-Economic Survey (Survei Sosio-Ekonomi Nasional, Susenas).

The analysis focuses on lifetime migration and recent migration. Information on lifetime migration is obtained by comparing the place of current residence with the place of birth, and information on recent migration by comparing the place of residence at the time of a census with the place of residence five years earlier. Lifetime migration is used to capture the past history of a migrant, and indicates the impact of chain migration rather than that of recent migration flows. Using the definition of recent migration and applying it to the data sources, we are able to obtain four periods of data on recent migrants: 1975–80, 1985–90, 1995–2000 and 2005–10.

The geographical units of analysis are the major island groups, provinces and districts. This classification captures longer-distance, more or less permanent migration across island, provincial and district boundaries. Census data are available for a longer period for the provinces (1980–2010) than for the districts (2000–10), so this study focuses mainly on the provinces. Indonesia has seven main groups of islands: Sumatra, Java, Bali and Nusa Tenggara, Kalimantan, Sulawesi, Maluku and Papua. The number of provinces fell from 27 to 26 when East Timor became an independent country in August 1999. The introduction of the regional autonomy laws in late 1999 encouraged the establishment of new provinces, bringing the total to 33 by the time of the 2010 census. The seven new provinces established since the laws were implemented in 2001 are Bangka Belitung (formerly part of South Sumatra), Riau Islands (Riau), Banten (West Java), Gorontalo (North Sulawesi), West Sulawesi (South Sulawesi), Northern Maluku (Maluku Islands) and West Papua (Papua). Although information on district-level migration is provided only in the 2000 and 2010 censuses, it provides valuable preliminary insights into changes in migration patterns associated with the implementation of the regional autonomy policy since 2001.

13.3   REGIONAL POPULATION DISTRIBUTION

Table 13.1 provides data on the size of the Indonesian population from 1980 to 2010, at the national, island and provincial levels. It also provides some information on regional demographic indicators, namely population growth rate, population density, share of urban population, total fertility rate and life expectancy at birth.

Discussions of Indonesian population distribution usually highlight the contrast between the country's most developed regions, Java and Bali, and the rest of Indonesia. Java remained the most populous island in 2010, with 136.6 million people (58 per cent of the total population) living on 7 per cent of the nation's land area. The three most populous provinces in Indonesia were all in Java – West Java (43 million), Central Java (32 million) and East Java (37 million) – despite the latter two having the country's lowest population growth rates in 2000–10. Unsurprisingly, population densities were also higher in Java, ranging from 784 persons per square kilometre in East Java to 14,469 persons per square kilometre in Jakarta. The only other province with a comparable figure was Bali, with 673 persons per square kilometre. The range of population densities in Java is actually not as extreme as it is in other islands, however, if one excludes Jakarta. Although Jakarta has been spreading into the neighbouring province of West Java since the beginning of the 1990s, its population density continues to be far higher than that of any other province.

In 2010, the rest of the country (Sumatra, Bali and Nusa Tenggara, Kalimantan, Sulawesi, Maluku and Papua) was home to 97 million people (42 per cent of the total population), scattered across huge areas comprising 93 per cent of Indonesia's land area. The population densities of these islands ranged from eight or nine persons per square kilometre in the sparsely populated Papuan provinces, to 115–220 persons per square kilometre in the four most densely populated Sumatran provinces: North Sumatra, West Sumatra, Riau Islands and Lampung. Lampung's high population density is explained by the high levels of in-migration under the government's transmigration program, which reached a peak in the 1970s and 1980s (Tirtosudarmo 2009). The high population densities of North Sumatra, West Sumatra and Riau Islands (especially Batam Island) can be explained by location; these provinces are situated close to Malaysia and Singapore, with direct access to the trade routes of the Malacca Straits. Trade with these dynamic economies has provided an incentive for job creation and helped to create links with both international and domestic markets.

The population of Indonesia grew at an average rate of 1.5 per cent per annum between 2000 and 2010, down from 2.0 per cent in 1980–90. The provinces with higher growth rates than the national average in 2000–10 tended to be the newly established ones: Riau Islands (5.0 per cent), Bangka Belitung (3.1 per cent), Banten (2.8 per cent), Gorontalo (2.3 per cent) and West Papua (3.7 per cent). Other provinces with higher than average growth rates were Riau (3.6 per cent) and East Kalimantan (3.8 per cent). Most of the provinces with the lowest population growth rates were located in Java, such as Central Java (0.4 per cent), East Java (0.8 per cent) and Yogyakarta (1.0 per cent). Other provinces with lower than average growth rates were West Kalimantan (0.9 per cent) and North Sumatra (1.1 per cent).

The other indicators shown in Table 13.1 may help to explain these trends. High rates of urbanization, for example, may explain the relatively high population growth rates in Riau Islands (where the share of the urban population in the total population was 82.8 per cent), Banten (67.0 per cent), Bali (60.2 per cent) and East Kalimantan (62.1 per cent). Jakarta's high population growth rate is explained by the pull of the city as a fast-growing metropolitan region, and that of West Java by its location next to the capital, as well as its high fertility rate (although it also has lower than average life expectancy). As Jakarta has grown, much of its excess population has spilled over into the neighbouring province

Table 13.1 Population indicators by island and province, 1980–2010

Region/province	Total population (million)				Growth, 2000–10 (% p.a.)	Density, 2010 (persons per km²)	Urban pop./ total pop., 2010 (%)	Total fertility rate, 2010	Life expec- tancy, 2010 (years)
	1980	1990	2000	2010					
Indonesia	**147.5**	**179.4**	**206.3**	**237.6**	**1.5**	**124**	**49.8**	**2.6**	**69.4**
Sumatra	**28.0**	**36.5**	**43.3**	**50.6**	**1.6**	**105**	**39.1**		
Aceh	2.6	3.4	3.9	4.5	1.4	78	28.1	2.8	68.7
North Sumatra	8.4	10.3	11.7	13.0	1.1	178	49.2	3.0	69.5
West Sumatra	3.4	4.0	4.2	4.8	1.3	115	38.7	2.8	69.5
Riau	2.2	3.3	5.0	5.5	3.6	64	39.2	2.9	71.4
Riau Islands				1.7	5.0	205	82.8	2.6	69.8
Jambi	1.4	2.0	2.4	3.1	2.6	62	30.7	2.3	69.1
South Sumatra	4.6	6.3	6.9	7.5	1.9	81	35.8	2.8	69.6
Bangka Belitung			0.9	1.2	3.1	74	49.2	2.6	68.9
Bengkulu	0.8	1.2	1.6	1.7	1.7	86	31.0	2.2	69.9
Lampung	4.6	6.0	6.7	7.6	1.2	220	25.7	2.7	69.5
Java	**91.3**	**107.6**	**121.4**	**136.6**	**1.2**	**1,055**	**58.5**		
Jakarta	6.5	8.3	8.4	9.6	1.4	14,469	100.0	2.3	73.2
West Java	27.5	35.4	35.7	43.1	1.9	1,217	65.7	2.5	68.2
Banten			8.1	10.6	2.8	1,100	67.0	2.5	64.9
Central Java	25.4	28.5	31.2	32.4	0.4	987	45.7	2.5	71.4
Yogyakarta	2.8	2.9	3.1	3.5	1.0	1,104	66.4	2.1	73.2
East Java	29.2	32.5	34.8	37.5	0.8	784	47.6	2.3	69.6

Table 13.1 *(continued)*

Bali & Nusa Tenggara	**7.9**	**9.4**	**11.1**	**13.1**	**1.7**	**179**	**39.2**	**2.3**	**70.7**
Bali	2.5	2.8	3.2	3.9	2.2	673	60.2	2.3	70.7
W. Nusa Tenggara	2.7	3.4	4.0	4.5	1.2	242	41.7	2.8	62.1
E. Nusa Tenggara	2.7	3.3	4.0	4.7	2.1	96	19.3	3.3	67.5
Kalimantan	**6.7**	**9.1**	**11.3**	**13.8**	**2.0**	**25**	**42.1**	**3.1**	**66.6**
West Kalimantan	2.5	3.2	4.0	4.4	0.9	30	30.2	3.1	66.6
Central Kalimantan	1.0	1.4	1.9	2.2	1.8	14	33.5	2.8	71.2
South Kalimantan	2.1	2.6	3.0	3.6	2.0	94	42.1	2.5	63.8
East Kalimantan	1.2	1.9	2.5	3.6	3.8	17	62.1	2.8	71.2
Sulawesi	**10.4**	**12.5**	**14.9**	**17.4**	**1.5**	**92**	**33.6**	**2.6**	**72.2**
North Sulawesi	2.1	2.5	2.0	2.3	1.3	164	45.2	2.6	72.2
Gorontalo			0.8	1.0	2.3	92	34.0	2.6	66.8
Central Sulawesi	1.3	1.7	2.2	2.6	2.0	43	24.3	3.2	66.6
South Sulawesi	6.1	7.0	8.1	8.0	1.2	172	36.7	2.6	70.0
West Sulawesi				1.2	2.7	69	22.9	3.6	67.8
Southeast Sulawesi	0.9	1.4	1.8	2.2	2.1	59	27.4	3.0	67.8
Maluku & Papua	**2.6**	**3.5**	**4.2**	**6.2**	**3.9**	**12.0**	**29.4**		
Maluku	1.4	1.9	1.2	1.5	2.8	33	37.1	3.2	67.4
North Maluku			0.8	1.0	2.5	32	27.1	3.1	66.0
Papua	1.2	1.6	2.2	2.8	5.4	9	26.0	3.5	68.6
West Papua				0.8	3.7	8	30.0	3.7	68.5

Source: 1980, 1990, 2000 and 2010 population censuses; BPS (2012).

of West Java. This has resulted in the emergence of an extended metro-politan region, which continues to grow rapidly. Indeed, since the early 1990s, Jakarta's periphery (the outer ring in West Java) has been growing more rapidly than the city's core (see Firman, Chapter 15). In the provinces outside Java and Bali, higher than average growth rates may be explained by factors such as government resettlement programs (Jambi, Bengkulu and Lampung) and industrial development (mining in East Kalimantan, Central Kalimantan and Papua, manufacturing and other industries in Riau and Riau Islands, and trading and agro-business in Sulawesi).

Together with Indonesia's remarkable array of ethnicities, cultures, languages and geographic settings, these uneven regional population distributions provide a unique context for population mobility on a range of temporal and spatial scales.

13.4   MIGRATION PATTERNS

This section describes internal migration patterns in Indonesia at the island and provincial levels in 1980–2010, and at the district level in 1995–2000 and 2005–10 (the periods of recent migration covered by the 2000 and 2010 censuses). It examines trends in lifetime and recent migration by gender and age, and relates these trends to levels of regional development. Migration patterns are also examined for evidence of spatial clustering, to ascertain whether there are clear longitudinal trends.

Overall levels of migration

Table 13.2 summarizes the trends in inter-regional migration among both recent migrants (those that have migrated within the last five years) and lifetime migrants (those that were born in a different place from the current place of residence). Despite an increase in the absolute volume of migration over time, the intensity of recent migration at the higher spatial levels – that is, at the inter-island and inter-provincial levels – has fluctuated only slightly: it declined in 1980–2000, but then increased again in 2000–10. At the lower spatial (district) level, however, the intensity of recent migration has increased over time. Lifetime migration, in contrast, has increased at all geographical levels over time – from 6.8 per cent in 1980 to 11.5 per cent in 2010 at the inter-provincial level, for example.

Among both recent and lifetime migrants, mobility appears to be highest at the lowest geographical level. In 2010, for example, there were about 12.4 million recent migrants and 45.1 million lifetime migrants at the inter-district level. Recent migrants made up 5.8 per cent of the

Table 13.2 Patterns of recent and lifetime migration by spatial level and gender, 1980–2010

	Share of migrants in total population (%)				Share of migrants in urban areas to share in rural areas, 2010 (%)	No. of migrants, 2010 (million)
	1980	1990	2000	2010		
All migrants (% of total population)						
Recent migration						
Inter-island	1.2	1.1	0.8	0.9	2.1	1.9
Inter-province	2.4	2.9	2.1	2.4	3.1	5.1
Inter-district[a]			4.0	5.8	1.7	12.4
Lifetime migration						
Inter-island	3.6	4.2	4.1	4.8	1.5	11.3
Inter-province	6.8	8.2	8.4	11.5	2.7	27.2
Inter-district[a]				19.1	2.8	45.1
Male migrants (% of male population)						
Recent migration						
Inter-island	1.3	1.3	0.9	1.0		1.0
Inter-province	2.6	3.1	2.2	2.5		2.7
Inter-district[a]			4.0	5.9		6.3
Lifetime migration						
Inter-island	4.0	4.6	4.3	5.1		6.1
Inter-province	7.3	8.7	8.7	12.0		14.3
Inter-district[a]				19.5		23.1
Female migrants (% of female population)						
Recent migration						
Inter-island	1.1	1.0	0.8	0.8		0.9
Inter-province	2.3	2.7	2.0	2.3		2.4
Inter-district[a]			4.0	5.7		6.0
Lifetime migration						
Inter-island	3.3	3.8	3.8	4.5		5.2
Inter-province	6.4	7.7	8.1	11.0		12.9
Inter-district[a]				18.7		21.9

a Data on inter-district migration are available only in the 2000 and 2010 censuses.
Source: 1980, 1990, 2000 and 2010 population censuses; IPUMS-International (University of Minnesota).

population at the inter-district level, compared with 0.9 per cent at the inter-island level and 2.4 per cent at the inter-provincial level. For life-time migrants, the figures were 19.1 per cent, 4.8 per cent and 11.5 per cent respectively.

The dominance of inter-district migration is also apparent in Figure 13.1, which shows the age profiles for inter-island, inter-provincial and inter-district migration in 1995–2000 and 2005–10 (the periods of recent migration covered by the 2000 and 2010 censuses). For all age groups, it is evident that migration levels are higher at the inter-district level than at the inter-island and inter-provincial levels. Although the numbers of migrants have increased over time, evidence from the 2000 and 2010 censuses indicates that migration age profiles have not changed much in shape at any geographical level. That is, levels of migration are low during early childhood and fall until ages 10–14; they then increase to reach a peak at ages 20–24, before dropping away to low levels by the age of retirement. These patterns are similar to the migrant schedules studied by Rogers and Castro (1981), and can be explained mainly by patterns of employment and urbanization. Young people mainly migrate in search of jobs and other economic opportunities. The most attractive employment opportunities are found in urban areas, where formal sector jobs offering pension and other benefits are concentrated. Because levels of urbanization in Indonesia are still relatively low (although increasing over time), migration at older ages is accordingly relatively low. The pro-portion of Indonesians living in urban areas climbed from 23.4 per cent in 1980 to 30.9 per cent in 1990, 41.9 per cent in 2000 and 49.7 per cent in 2010 (Firman 2013).

The ratio of the proportion of migrants in urban areas to the propor-tion in rural areas shows that the migration intensity in urban areas is two to three times higher than in rural areas (Table 13.2). For example, in 2010 the proportion of migrants was 1.2 per cent in urban areas and 0.6 per cent in rural areas (2.1) in the case of inter-island migration, and 3.7 per cent and 1.2 per cent respectively (3.1) in the case of inter-provincial migration. Clearly, more Indonesian migrants are settling in urban areas than in rural areas.

Analysis by gender shows that males are more mobile than females in the Indonesian context (Table 13.2). At the inter-district level, for exam-ple, Indonesia's 6.3 million recent male migrants made up 5.9 per cent of the total male population in 2010, while the country's 6.0 million recent female migrants accounted for 5.7 per cent of the total female population. In line with the overall trend for migration to become more common over time, the proportions of lifetime migrants, both male and female, gen-erally recorded an increase during 1980–2010. The increased levels for females in particular can be explained by a number of factors, including

Figure 13.1   *Age profile of recent migrants by spatial level, 1995–2000 and 2005–10*

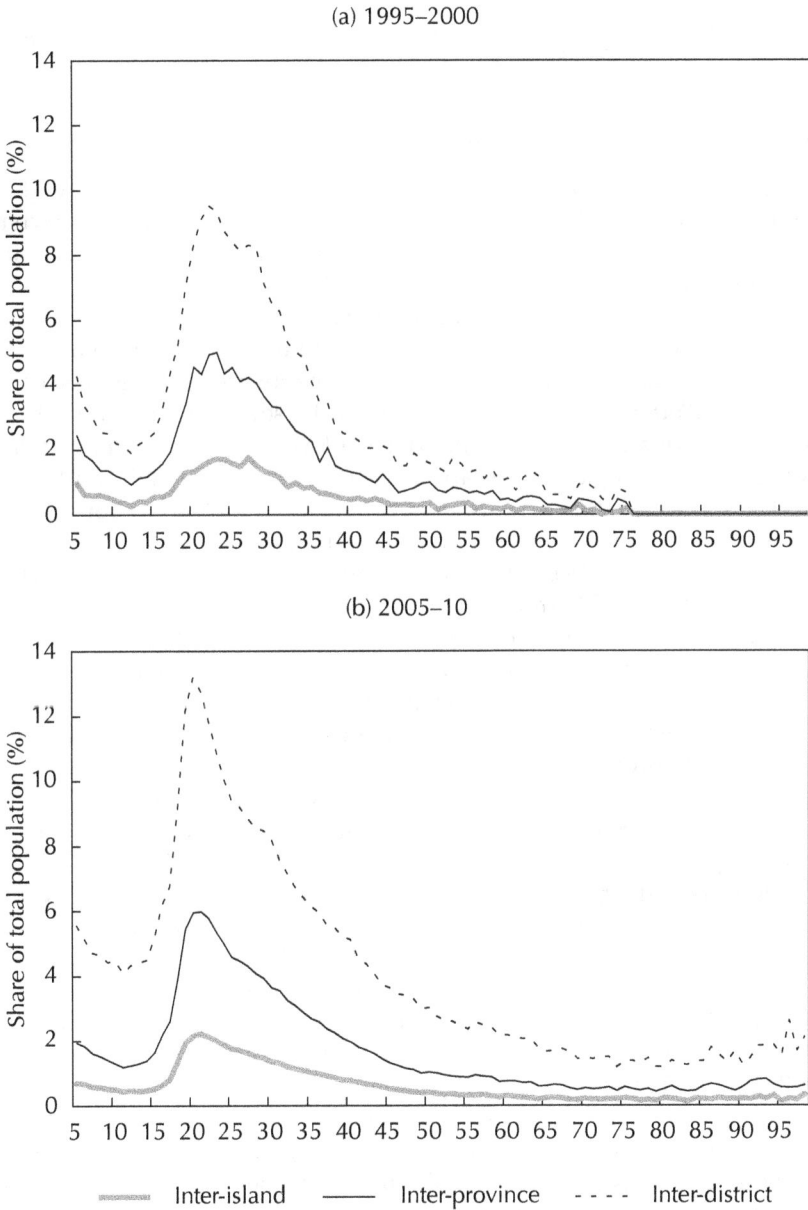

(a) 1995–2000

(b) 2005–10

Inter-island   Inter-province   - - - - Inter-district

Source: 2000 and 2010 population censuses; IPUMS-International (University of Minnesota).

a decline in fertility rates and an increase in women's educational levels and labour participation rates. By 2010, about 22 per cent of Indonesian females had a secondary or tertiary education, and a significant proportion of these better-educated women (27 per cent) were participating in the labour force (BPS 2013).

Regional patterns of migration

Table 13.3 focuses on changes in recent migration (migration within the five years preceding each census). It shows that the share of recent migrants in the total population has declined in most provinces, despite some fluctuations, particularly in 1995–2000. The late 1990s were a period of great political and economic uncertainty for Indonesia, encompassing the Asian financial crisis and the ensuing political crisis, which affected almost every aspect of society (Beegle, Frankenberg and Thomas 1999; Sumarto, Wetterberg and Pritchett 1999). In some provinces, such as Aceh, Maluku and the former province of East Timor, many inhabitants fled into nearby regions to escape a rise in violence and civil conflict. In Aceh and Maluku, this led to high negative rates of net migration, of –9.5 per cent and –7.4 per cent respectively. In the case of East Timor, most of those who fled to West Timor in late 1999 reportedly returned in 2000, although about 50,000 Indonesian nationals are thought to have settled permanently in West Timor or other regions (Muhidin 2002).

In 1980, recent migrants constituted more than 10 per cent of the population in four provinces: Jakarta (13.6 per cent), Lampung (12.9 per cent), East Kalimantan (10.6 per cent) and Bengkulu (10.2 per cent). By 2010, however, the proportion was below 10 per cent in all provinces except recently established Riau Islands (14.3 per cent). It is not surprising to see that provinces with higher levels of industrialization have received more migrants, including East Kalimantan (with its mining industry) and Riau Islands (the closest province to Singapore). This indicates that investments in extractive industries and manufacturing have attracted incoming migrants, with employment also being a significant pull factor. Migration levels in the four provinces that had attracted the most migrants in 1980 fell over the next three decades, to 7.4 per cent in Jakarta, 1.3 per cent in Lampung, 6.8 per cent in East Kalimantan and 3.1 per cent in Bengkulu. Lampung and Bengkulu were the main destination regions for the government's transmigration program in the 1970s and 1980s. As the numbers of migrants reached saturation point, however, migration to these regions began to slow. Jakarta also attracted many migrants in the 1970s and 1980s because of its higher levels of socio-economic development and relatively good infrastructure. But in the last decade or so, industrial development has encroached on many residential areas, with

Table 13.3   *Share and net share of recent migrants by island and province, 1980–2010*

Region/province	Share in population (%)				Net share (%)			
	1980	1990	2000	2010	1980	1990	2000	2010
Indonesia	**2.8**	**3.3**	**3.0**	**2.5**				
(million)	(3.6)	(5.1)	(5.3)	(5.4)				
Sumatra	**5.1**	**3.7**	**3.7**	**2.8**				
Aceh	2.3	1.9	1.0	1.6	1.0	0.2	−9.5	0.6
North Sumatra	1.2	1.2	1.4	1.1	−1.2	−1.9	−2.2	−2.2
West Sumatra	3.1	3.6	2.8	3.0	−2.1	−1.3	−3.3	−0.5
Riau	5.2	8.6	12.5	6.1	2.5	5.4	6.4	3.5
Riau Islands				14.3				10.7
Jambi	8.8	7.7	5.1	4.0	5.9	4.1	1.2	−0.7
South Sumatra	5.6	3.9	2.5	1.8	2.3	0.3	0.5	1.4
Bangka Belitung			4.5	5.6			0.3	−8.6
Bengkulu	10.2	8.1	5.0	3.1	8.1	5.3	2.4	2.0
Lampung	13.0	4.0	2.5	1.4	12.1	1.5	0.0	0.6
Java	**2.2**	**3.1**	**2.8**	**2.4**				
Jakarta	13.6	11.1	9.1	7.4	7.0	−2.2	−1.9	−2.8
West Java	2.2	4.3	3.4	2.7	0.4	2.8	1.5	1.2
Banten			8.6	4.9			5.7	−5.4
Central Java	0.8	1.5	1.2	1.0	−3.3	−3.1	−2.4	0.7
Yogyakarta	3.8	6.0	6.7	7.1	1.1	1.5	2.3	−9.4
East Java	0.8	1.1	0.5	0.7	−1.4	−1.1	−1.1	0.2
Bali & Nusa Tenggara	**1.2**	**1.5**	**1.3**	**1.7**				
Bali	1.7	2.6	1.5	2.9	−0.7	0.4	1.9	1.7
W. Nusa Tenggara	1.0	1.2	1.7	1.2	−0.6	0.0	0.3	0.2
E. Nusa Tenggara	1.0	0.9	0.8	1.2	−0.4	−0.7	0.5	−0.4
Kalimantan	**4.5**	**5.1**	**4.3**	**3.9**				
West Kalimantan	1.8	1.6	1.5	1.1	0.5	0.0	0.1	0.0
Central Kalimantan	6.1	6.5	7.8	6.2	4.3	3.5	6.2	4.5
South Kalimantan	3.4	4.2	3.3	3.2	0.9	1.0	1.0	1.5
East Kalimantan	10.7	11.6	7.1	6.8	9.1	7.7	5.2	4.5
Sulawesi	**2.6**	**2.6**	**2.5**	**2.3**				
North Sulawesi	2.4	1.5	3.0	2.3	0.4	−0.7	0.9	0.1
Gorontalo			1.3	2.9			−3.3	−1.3
Central Sulawesi	7.6	4.6	4.2	2.7	6.2	2.8	2.5	−6.3
South Sulawesi	1.1	1.8	1.1	1.7	−1.6	−0.7	−1.5	1.1
West Sulawesi				3.7				2.0
Southeast Sulawesi	6.4	6.2	7.0	3.3	2.8	3.0	5.7	2.3
Maluku & Papua	**3.8**	**4.8**	**3.6**	**3.2**				
Maluku	3.8	4.3	1.8	2.2	1.7	1.9	−7.4	−0.1
North Maluku			2.5	2.7			−2.4	1.1
Papua	3.4	5.1	4.3	2.7	1.9	3.1	1.7	1.1
West Papua				8.2				5.6

Source: 1980, 1990, 2000 and 2010 population censuses; IPUMS-International (University of Minnesota).

the former residents generally moving to the municipalities surrounding Jakarta (Bogor, Tanggerang and Bekasi). Evidence from the 1990, 2000 and 2010 censuses shows that one-third of the in-migrants to West Java came from Jakarta.

Turning to the net migration figures, in the last three decades the provinces of Riau, South Sumatra, Bengkulu, Lampung, West Java, Central, South and East Kalimantan, Southeast Sulawesi and Papua have consistently had positive net migration (more in-migrants than out-migrants) (Table 13.3). The provinces of Bali and West Nusa Tenggara can also be included in this group, although they had more out-migration than in-migration in the 1970s (as recorded in the 1980 census). The provinces of North Sumatra, West Sumatra and (since 1990) Jakarta, on the other hand, have continuously had more out-migration than in-migration (negative net migration). Trends in the other provinces have fluctuated. Some provinces that were less attractive to migrants (with negative net migration) in 2000 had become more attractive by 2010 (Central Java, East Java and South Sulawesi), while others that were more attractive to migrants (with positive net migration) in 2000 had become less attractive by 2010 (Jambi, Yogyakarta and Central Sulawesi).

At least three different explanations can be offered to explain these patterns. First, migration can be historically bound, that is, due to officially sanctioned transmigration, as in the provinces of Lampung, Bengkulu, South Sumatra and North Sumatra. Second, migration can be ingrained in a society or culture (Muhidin 2002). For instance, a culture of out-migration (*merantau*) is well established among the Minangkabau in West Sumatra, the Batak in North Sumatra, the Sundanese in West Java, the Rotinese in East Nusa Tenggara, the Banjarese in South Kalimantan and the Bugis in South Sulawesi. These ethnic communities have a reputation as traders and seafarers, within a cultural framework of temporary out-migration. Third, migration can be economically motivated. This is the main reason for migration, as shown by the high levels of in-migration to Jakarta, and to other provinces in Java–Bali where regional development is more advanced. The various economic reforms implemented since the mid-1980s to boost foreign investment have resulted in the creation of job opportunities in other places as well, such as Batam Island in Riau Islands, and the provinces of East Kalimantan and Papua.

We now consider patterns of recent migration at the district level, focusing on the most recent period, 2005–10 (the five-year period derived from the 2010 census). Table 13.4 shows the districts where the proportion of recent migrants in the total population was above 10 per cent. Most of the districts in this group in Java and Sumatra also had higher levels of urbanization, but the pattern was much more mixed elsewhere. In the district of North Mamuju in West Sulawesi, for example, the proportion

Table 13.4   Patterns of recent migration by district, 2010

Province	District	Share in district pop. (%)	Net share (%)	Urban pop./ total pop. (%)
Sumatra				
Aceh	Kota Sabang	12.4	4.0	62.4
Aceh	Aceh Besar	12.3	9.1	27.9
Aceh	Banda Aceh city	25.4	9.1	100.0
West Sumatra	Bukittinggi city	14.6	−6.5	100.0
West Sumatra	Solok city	13.3	1.4	98.5
West Sumatra	Padang Panjang city	12.5	−4.6	94.8
Riau	Kampar	12.4	8.1	23.0
Riau	Pelalawan	16.2	12.1	21.0
Riau	Pekanbaru	14.0	1.5	98.2
Riau Islands	Batam	25.9	19.4	97.2
Riau Islands	Riau Islands	13.8	9.7	61.5
Java				
West Java	Depok	13.6	9.7	100.0
West Java	Bekasi	13.9	11.0	100.0
Banten	South Tangerang	19.1	18.0	100.0
Yogyakarta	Yogyakarta	16.2	−5.5	100.0
Yogyakarta	Sleman	15.8	12.4	91.1
Bali & Nusa Tenggara				
Bali	Denpasar	12.6	6.4	100.0
E. Nusa Tenggara	Kupang	14.9	10.7	93.9
Kalimantan				
Central Kalimantan	Seruyan	21.5	19.8	19.0
Central Kalimantan	Sukamara	17.8	14.4	28.5
Central Kalimantan	Lamandau	15.3	10.6	18.8
Central Kalimantan	West Kotawaringin	14.5	10.5	45.2
Central Kalimantan	Palangka Raya	13.6	6.7	90.3
South Kalimantan	Banjarbaru	22.8	17.8	96.1
East Kalimantan	East Kutai	16.6	12.6	40.7
Sulawesi				
West Sulawesi	North Mamuju	14.7	11.6	8.3
Southeast Sulawesi	Kendari	14.0	4.9	91.4
Papua				
Papua	Jayapura city	14.0	8.5	91.1
Papua	Sarmi	16.4	12.9	19.2
Papua	Boven Digoel	12.4	11.5	22.5
West Papua	Teluk Wondama	30.3	29.0	0.0
West Papua	Teluk Bintuni	25.8	23.4	27.3
West Papua	Kaimana	13.1	9.4	41.7
West Papua	Raja Ampat	13.6	12.3	0.0

Source: 2010 population census; IPUMS-International (University of Minnesota).

of recent migrants was 14.7 per cent, with positive net migration (more in-migrants than out-migrants), but the urbanization level was only 8.3 per cent. Four districts in West Papua (Teluk Wondama, Teluk Bintuni, Kaimana and Raja Ampat) and two districts in Papua (Sarmi and Boven Digoel) also had low levels of urbanization but relatively high proportions of migrants. It is worth noting that the district of North Mamuju and the four West Papuan districts are all located in provinces established since the regional autonomy laws took effect in 2001. In other words, it is possible that the regional autonomy policy is creating the conditions for people to look beyond the usual migration destinations, and consider migrating to less urbanized regions in search of fresh economic and other opportunities.

Spatial directions of inter-regional migration

Figure 13.2 shows patterns of recent migration by province of origin and island of destination in the two five-year periods preceding the 1990 and 2010 censuses, 1985–90 and 2005–10. It indicates that the preferences for destination regions have changed slightly during that time. In the earlier period, Java attracted high proportions of migrants from other parts of Indonesia (Figure 13.2(a)). By 2005–10, however, migrants from the provinces in Sumatra, Kalimantan, Sulawesi and Eastern Indonesia had become more likely to move to another province within the same island group (Figure 13.2(b)). There are many possible explanations for these changing preferences, including an individual's desire to stay close to family and friends, and improvements in socio-economic conditions that have eroded the incentive to move away.

To take some specific examples, Figure 13.2 indicates that out-migration by recent migrants from the province of Riau to another province within Sumatra increased from 50 per cent in 1985–90 to 69 per cent in 2005–10, while migration from the same province to Java fell from 44 per cent to 25 per cent. Out-migration from the province of North Sulawesi also significantly changed direction, with 31 per cent of recent migrants going to Java and 34 per cent to another province within Sulawesi in 1985–90, but 49 per cent moving to a neighbouring province, and only 16 per cent going to Java, in 2005–10.

This has not been the pattern for all provinces, however. For example, most recent migrants from the provinces of Aceh, North Sumatra, West Sumatra and West Kalimantan continue to prefer to migrate to Java and Sumatra than elsewhere, and migrants from the provinces of East Java, South Sulawesi, and West and East Nusa Tenggara still favour Kalimantan as a destination region. But for many migrants, neighbouring or adjacent provinces are the more immediate destination. A high proportion of out-migration from the province of Jakarta, for example, is to West Java.

Figure 13.2   *Distribution of recent migrants by province of origin and island of destination, 1985–90 and 2005–10*

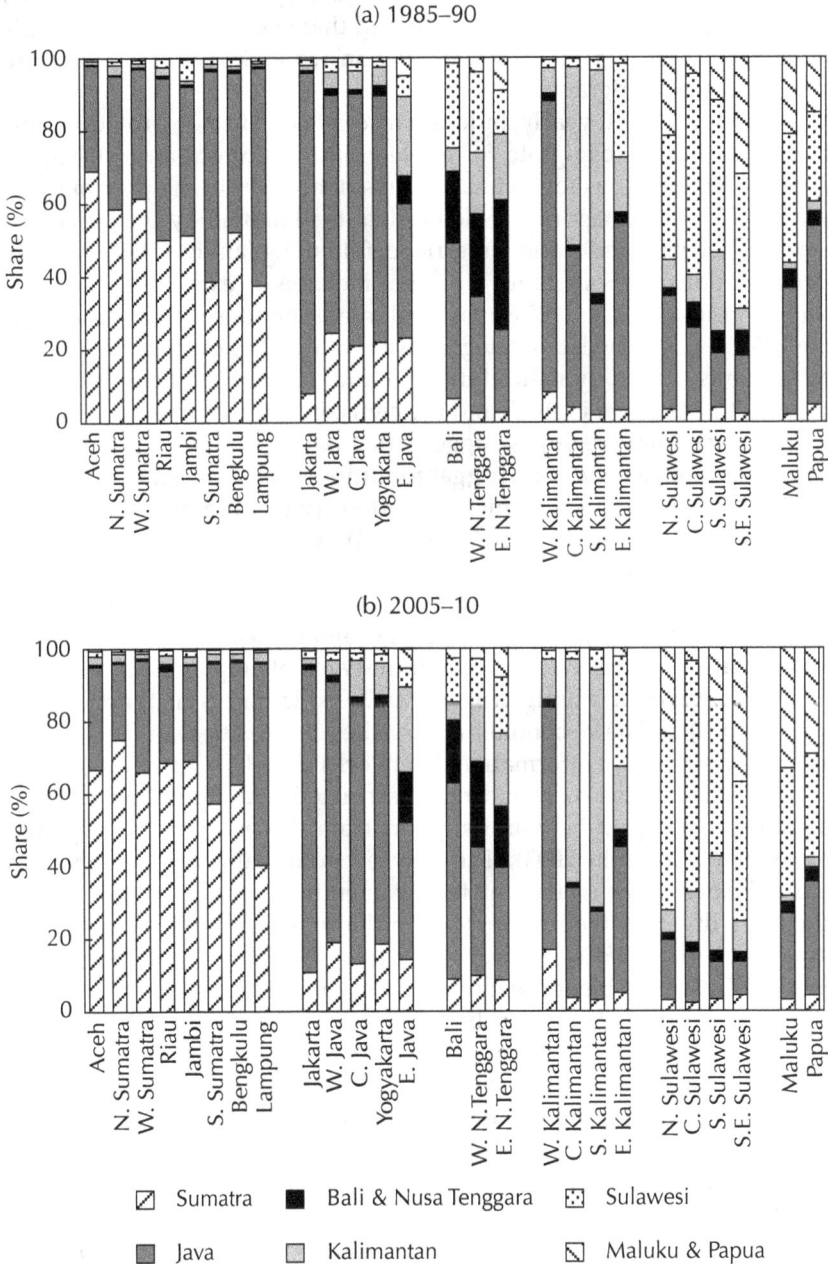

(a) 1985–90

(b) 2005–10

| ⊠ Sumatra | ■ Bali & Nusa Tenggara | ⊡ Sulawesi |
| ▨ Java | ▢ Kalimantan | ◺ Maluku & Papua |

Source: 1990 and 2010 population censuses.

13.5   REASONS TO MIGRATE

It is clear from the preceding discussion that regional migration patterns in Indonesia have changed over time, and that many factors affect trends in and levels of migration. In this section we look more closely at the determinants of migration.

Although the 10-yearly Indonesian censuses do not provide information on reasons to migrate, fortunately, the inter-censal surveys (Supas) do record the reasons for a change of residence within the previous five years. The main categories of determinants identified by the Supas are work, job seeking, education, marriage, following family, following relatives and housing. Sometimes the Supas includes an extra reason, such as transmigration (in the 1985 Supas) and migration for security reasons (in the 2005 Supas). The latter category was included to capture population movements caused by natural disaster and internal conflict (in particular, the 2004 tsunami in Aceh and the civil conflict in Maluku).

Evidence from the Supas suggests that family reasons (marriage and family reunion) are the main trigger for Indonesians to migrate within the country, followed by economic motivations (work and job seeking) (see Manning and Purnagunawan, Chapter 14). According to the 2005 Supas, for example, about 47 per cent of people migrated for family reasons (38 per cent to join immediate family, 5 per cent to join other relatives and 4 per cent to marry), and 36 per cent for economic reasons (21 per cent for work-related reasons and 15 per cent in search of employment).

The dominance of family reasons can be explained using the structural (or network) and new economic approaches to migration. In the network approach, social and informational networks (family, relatives and social networks) lower the costs and risks associated with migration, because migrants can expect help and support from those who have migrated previously (Muhidin 2003). The new economic approach emphasises the risk-sharing behaviour of family members, in which individuals choose to diversify their resources in order to minimize the risks to family income (Stark 1991). Hence, rather than the entire family migrating, it may be more viable for just one or a few family members to migrate, allowing those left behind to benefit from remittances, and to join the migrant members later on, once they have settled in the new destination. In other words, migration occurs in order to improve the income of the household rather than the economic situation of the individual. The network and new economic approaches are mutually reinforcing, making migration a self-perpetuating process (known as chain migration).

In Indonesia, it is still common practice for family members to be economically dependent on a household head or parent. This makes it important to strive to reunite the family if the wage earner in the family (the parent or head of household) migrates. Thus, chain migration (migration in the track of former migrants, who may or may not be related) is a very real phenomenon among Indonesian migrants. In the Javanese context, decisions related to marriage, work and education are still usually taken in consultation with parents or other family members, through a process of consensus (*musyawarah*). The role of the family in the migration decision is likely to weaken, however, as changes in family relationships, levels of education and the structure of governance (policy) strengthen the influence of other factors.

At the same time, the migration decision is related to the economic contexts of migration (for example, the urban–rural differences in expected earnings described by Harris and Todaro 1970) and to the personal traits of migrants (for instance, the behavioural aspects of the decision to migrate described by Wolpert 1965). That is, the process of migration decision making can be interpreted as an individual choice in response to stresses posed by the home environment and to perceptions of the differential between current wage earnings and expected wage earnings in the future. This is similar to the push–pull theory proposed by Lee (1966).

To provide a practical illustration of the influence of environmental factors, Table 13.5 shows the relationship between migration and levels of development and employment. Regions are classified according to whether they have low, medium or high rates of migration. The development indicator is the ratio of the Human Development Index (HDI) in the destination region to that in the region of origin, where a ratio of more than 1 indicates that the level of development in the destination region is higher than that in the region of origin. The employment indicator is the ratio of unemployment in the region of origin to that in the region of destination, where a ratio of more than 1 indicates that the level of unemployment in the destination region is lower than that in the region of origin.

The analysis indicates that most people migrate in the expectation of being better-off: 86.1 per cent of migrants moved to a region where the HDI level was higher than in the region of origin, and 75.3 per cent to one where the unemployment rate was lower than in the region of origin. Among those who moved to a region where development and employment conditions were less advantageous than in the region of origin (that is, the 13.9 per cent who moved to a region with a lower HDI and the 24.7 per cent who moved to a region with a higher unemployment rate), family reasons are likely to have been an important factor. In other words, the existence of a trigger or motive for migration is a necessary antecedent for a move to take place, regardless of whether it is to a more or less advantageous region.

Table 13.5   Distribution of recent migrants by level of development and employment in the regions of origin and destination, 2010

Indicator	Migration rate (%)			Total (%)
	Low (< 5%)	Medium (5–10%)	High (>10%)	
Ratio of HDI (destination/origin)				
<1 = lower HDI in destination region	12.6	1.0	0.3	13.9
>1 = higher HDI in destination region	78.1	6.0	2.0	86.1
Total	**90.7**	**7.0**	**2.3**	**100.0**
Ratio of unemployment rate (origin/destination)				
<1 = higher unemployment in destination region	22.0	2.0	0.7	24.7
>1 = lower unemployment in destination region	68.7	5.0	1.6	75.3
Total	**90.7**	**7.0**	**2.3**	**100.0**

Source: Author's calculation.

Figure 13.3 shows the proportions of recent migrants who gave educational or work-related reasons for migrating in the five years preceding the 2005 inter-censal survey, by province of residence at the time of the survey. Migrants to the provinces of Yogyakarta, West Sumatra, Bengkulu and South Sumatra were the most likely to have migrated to obtain an education (Figure 13.3(a)). Outside Java, educational facilities and the availability of transport are generally poor, and the best schools, from primary through to senior secondary, tend to be located in the provincial or district capitals. This explains the high levels of inter-district migration for educational reasons in provinces such as West Nusa Tenggara and West Kalimantan. To get a good tertiary education, however, Indonesians living outside Java need to travel further afield. This is reflected in the generally higher figures for inter-island and inter-provincial migration among the provinces outside Java.

Figure 13.3(b) shows that many people have moved to developing regions that are experiencing strong economic growth. The efforts to boost foreign investment since the mid-1980s have apparently been successful in creating job opportunities in places such as Batam Island in Riau Islands, with its dynamic industrial sector, and East Kalimantan and Papua, with their vigorous mining sectors. Provinces with higher

Figure 13.3   Share of recent migrants migrating for educational or work-related reasons, by province of current residence, 2000–05

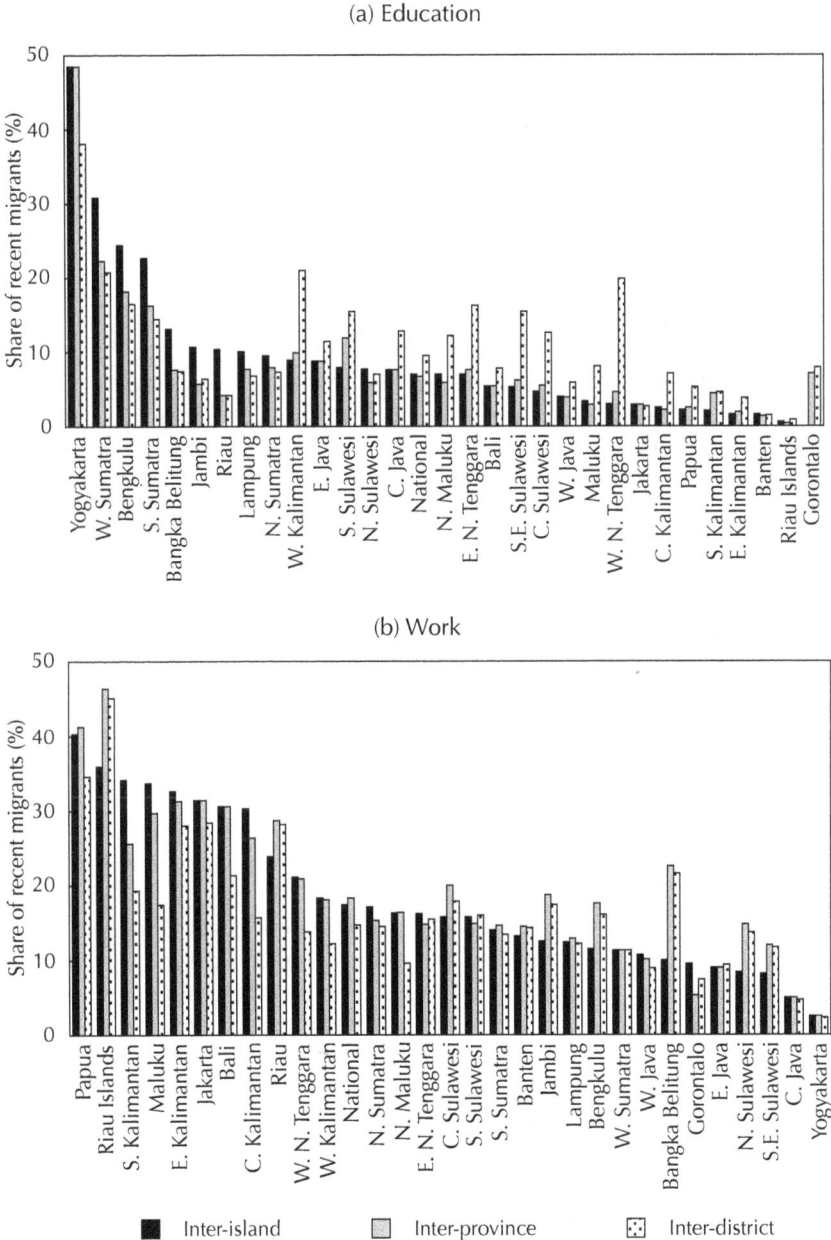

(a) Education

(b) Work

■ Inter-island   ▢ Inter-province   ⠿ Inter-district

Source: 2005 Inter-censal Population Survey (Supas).

levels of economic development, notably Jakarta and Bali, also continue to be attractive to job seekers from other islands and provinces. The province of Bangka Belitung has relatively high proportions of migrants who have moved from other provinces and districts for work-related reasons. It is one of the new provinces established since the introduction of the regional autonomy policy, so one could speculate that some of the inter-provincial and inter-district migration to Bangka Belitung was related to expectations of higher levels of development, and therefore new economic opportunities.

13.6   CONCLUSION

This chapter has described migration dynamics in Indonesia over the last three decades, emphasizing in particular patterns of regional migration during the decade since the implementation of the regional autonomy policy in 2001. Indonesia is a geographically fragmented country, with widely varying socio-economic and demographic conditions. Some regions have better socio-economic indicators than others; some are more urbanized; and some are richer in natural resources. Indonesia's remarkable regional diversity provides a unique context for the study of population migration dynamics.

Using information on lifetime and recent migrants obtained from the national censuses, the analysis has demonstrated that the composition of migration in Indonesia has changed over time. At the inter-provincial level, the proportion of lifetime migrants in the total population increased from 7 per cent in 1980 to 12 per cent in 2010. At the inter-district level, the figure was much higher, with 19 per cent of the total population living outside the district of birth in 2010. The share of recent migrants, on the other hand, has remained fairly stable at the inter-provincial level, despite a slight decline from 2.9 per cent in 1980 to 2.4 per cent in 2010. Analysis by age group showed that the age profile of Indonesian migration has not changed much at any geographical level. That is, levels of migration are low during early childhood and old age, and highest among young adults aged 20–24 years. This is a typical age–migration profile for developing countries such as Indonesia (Rogers et al. 2007). Analysis by gender indicated that males have been more mobile than females, although the gap between the shares of male/female migrants in the total male/female population has remained stable over time. The proportion of females living outside the province of birth has nevertheless increased, from 6 per cent of the total female population in 1980 to 11 per cent in 2010. Most migration is to urban areas, as indicated by the higher proportions of migrants in urban than in rural areas.

Patterns of regional migration have also changed significantly in response to changes in demographic conditions, levels of socio-economic development and the structure of governance (policy) across the country. Some provinces and districts are already in the later stages of a demographic and mobility transition, while others are still in the early stages. For example, Jakarta has emerged as a mega-city, with a population of 9.6 million in 2010 and slowing rates of in-migration, while many of the provinces in the more remote islands are just beginning to experience the demographic and socio-economic changes that lead to higher levels of development and migration. Government policies, on regional development and population-related matters in particular, certainly affect migration dynamics. Since the implementation of the regional autonomy policy, for example, some newly established districts and provinces have attracted more migrants, despite being less urbanized. Expectations that these places will offer new economic opportunities are one of the common explanations for this phenomenon.

Returning to the five phases of a mobility transition hypothesized by Zelinsky (1971), the analysis in this chapter suggests that most of the provinces in Java, Bali and Sumatra would be in the third stage ('late transitional society') or the fourth stage ('advanced society'), while the provinces in the rest of Indonesia would be in the third stage. A late transitional society is characterized by an increase in circular migration, but a decline in population movement from rural areas to cities. In an advanced society, residential mobility has levelled off and oscillates at a high level; movement from rural areas to cities continues but has fallen in both absolute and relative terms; there is vigorous movement of migrants from city to city and within urban agglomerations; and there is significant circular migration motivated by economic conditions and recreational factors. A province like Jakarta could even be considered to be in the final stage of a mobility transition ('future super-advanced society'), where there is a decline in the level of residential migration and some forms of circulation as transport and communication technologies improve.

Overall, the levels of both lifetime and recent migration indicate that mobility is most prevalent at the short-distance, inter-district level. This could be related to the longstanding phenomenon of circular migration in Indonesia. A large number of studies by Hugo (2005), Deshingkar (2006) and others have documented a steady increase in circular labour migration, where workers leave their families behind to work in other regions for periods from one week to two years. In fact, circular labour migration is so commonplace in Indonesia that workers often use shorthand expressions to describe it. 'PJKA', for example, stands for *'pulang Jumat kembali Ahad'*, which literally means 'back home on Friday and going away again on Sunday'. Construction workers are among those who have long had to commute to earn a living. This type of work is available in both urban and rural areas, and has traditionally attracted male labourers from the agricultural sector since the early 1980s.

REFERENCES

Ananta, A. and S. Muhidin (2005) 'Completion of vital transition and changing migration in Indonesia: empirical results and projection scenarios', *Population Review*, 44(1): 36–55.
Beegle, K., E. Frankenberg and D. Thomas (1999) 'Measuring change in Indonesia', Labor and Population Program Working Paper Series 99-07, Rand Corporation, Los Angeles
Bell, M. and S. Muhidin (2009) 'Cross-national comparisons of internal migration', Human Development Research Paper 2009/30, United Nations Development Programme, New York, July.
BPS (Badan Pusat Statistik) (2011) 'Population of Indonesia: results of the 2010 population census', BPS, Jakarta.
BPS (Badan Pusat Statistik) (2012) 'Indonesia demographic and health survey 2012', BPS, Jakarta.
BPS (Badan Pusat Statistik) (2013) *Statistical Yearbook of Indonesia*, BPS, Jakarta.
Deshingkar, P. (2006) 'Internal migration, poverty and development in Asia: including the excluded', *IDS Bulletin*, 37(3): 88–100.
Firman, T. (2013) 'Demographic patterns of Indonesia's urbanization, 2000–2010: continuity and change at the macro level', paper presented at the International Union for the Scientific Study of Population (IUSSP) International Population Conference, Busan, 26–31 August.
Harris, J.R. and M.P. Todaro (1970) 'Migration, unemployment and development: a two-sector analysis', *American Economic Review*, 60(1): 126–42.
Hugo, G. (2005) 'Migration in the Asia-Pacific region', paper prepared for the Policy Analysis and Research Programme of the Global Commission on International Migration (GCIM), September.
Lee, E.S. (1966) 'A theory of migration', *Demography*, 3(1): 467–57.
Muhidin, S. (2002) *The Population of Indonesia: Regional Demographic Scenarios using a Multiregional Method and Multiple Data Sources*, Rozenberg Publishers, Amsterdam.
Muhidin, S. (2003) 'Migrated household in Indonesia: an exploration of the intercensal survey data', in Chotib, S.-E. Khoo, S. Muhidin, Z. Hao and S.K. Singh, *Asians on the Move: Spouses, Dependants and Households*, Asian MetaCentre Research Paper Series No. 8, National University of Singapore, Singapore.
Muhidin, S. and A. Utomo (2013) 'How many overseas Indonesians are there?', Discussion Paper Series No. 1/2013, Indonesia Diaspora Network, Sydney, December.
Pooley, C., J. Turnbull and M. Adams (2005) *A Mobile Century? Changes in Everyday Mobility in Britain in the Twentieth Century*, Ashgate, Aldershot.
Rogers, A. and L.J. Castro (1981) 'Model migration schedules', IIASA Research Report RR-81-030, International Institute for Applied Systems Analysis (IIASA), Laxenburg.
Rogers, A., B. Jones, V. Partida and S. Muhidin (2007) 'Inferring migration flows from the migration propensities of infants: Mexico and Indonesia', *Annals of Regional Science*, 41(2): 443–65.

Skeldon, R. (1990) *Population Mobility in Developing Countries: A Reinterpretation,* Belhaven Press, London.

Stark, O. (1991) *The Migration of Labor,* Basil Blackwell, Cambridge MA and Oxford.

Sumarto, S., A. Wetterberg and L. Pritchett (1999) 'The social impact of the crisis in Indonesia: results from a nationwide *kecamatan* survey', World Bank working paper, World Bank, Jakarta.

Tirtosudarmo, R. (2009) 'Mobility and human development in Indonesia', Human Development Research Paper 2009/19, United Nations Development Programme, New York.

Wolpert, J. (1965) 'Behavioral aspects of the decision to migrate', *Papers of the Regional Science Association,* 15(1): 159–69.

Zelinsky, W. (1971) 'The hypothesis of the mobility transition', *Geographical Review,* 61(2): 219–49.

Zelinsky, W. (1979) 'The demographic transition: changing patterns of migration', in International Union for the Scientific Study of Population (IUSSP) (ed.) *Population Science in the Service of Mankind,* IUSSP, Liège.

Zelinsky, W. (1983) 'The impasse in migration theory: a sketch map for potential escapees', in P. Morrison (ed.) *Population Movements: Their Forms and Functions in Urbanization and Development,* Ordina Editions, Liège.

14 Regional labour markets in 2002–12: limited convergence but integration nonetheless

Chris Manning and Raden Muhamad Purnagunawan

14.1 OVERVIEW

Like many large countries, Indonesia has a geographically fragmented labour market. Physical and economic contrasts between and within the major islands govern patterns of employment, wages and unemployment. The labour market still bears the signs of a dualistic division, dating from colonial or even pre-colonial times, between densely populated, poorer Java–Bali and most of the more land-abundant Outer Islands. Rapid national economic growth based on both export-oriented development and resource booms altered that historical pattern during the Soeharto years. The process became more complicated in the post-Soeharto democratic reform era after Indonesia's radical decentralization. Manufacturing stagnated in Java, while in the Outer Islands better governance and the return of revenue to resource-rich provinces provided more opportunities in some regions than in others for human resource development and economic diversification.

The widely varying rates of poverty discussed by Ilmma and Wai-Poi (Chapter 5) and Sumarto, Vothknecht and Wijaya (Chapter 12) are reflected to a large extent in differences in labour productivity across island groups and provinces. Labour productivity in Jakarta and East Kalimantan is more than twice the national average, whereas in Gorontalo and East Nusa Tenggara it is less than half. Most people in the former two provinces work in the formal sector in services, mining and manufacturing. In contrast, high levels of poverty and low labour productivity in the latter two provinces are closely associated with a concentration of employment in agriculture and the informal sector.

At the same time some indicators, such as inter-regional migration, suggest quite high levels of integration for a country of Indonesia's size and spread. There are also signs of convergence in labour productivity among some provinces and regions, as poorer provinces shed agricultural workers.[1] Remarkable similarities across the country in trends towards greater formalization and improvements in unemployment rates and wages also suggest a degree of integration in the national economy. This has meant that some of the worse-off provinces have not been left behind. Nevertheless, in other provinces, high rates of population growth, low levels of schooling and associated low levels of out-migration have kept much of the workforce trapped in low-productivity agriculture.

Forces outside the labour market, such as different rates of investment, have contributed most to inter-provincial differences in employment and wages. However, government regulation of wages appears to have slowed manufacturing employment growth across the country, especially in Java in the early and latter part of the 2000s. This was due partly to national legislation (the labour law of 2003), but also to regional wage variation and the union and political party alliances formed to push up wages in manufacturing around the capital city in 2011–13.

This chapter explores some of these issues through a focus on regional labour market structures and change in the period 2002–12. We try to capture both general patterns and the range of experience among regions. The chapter clusters provinces into five island groups, then uses two provinces from each group to illustrate contrasts within island groups and nationally. The approach is descriptive and the coverage broad, seeking to understand rather than account for patterns, although we do offer some thoughts on possible explanations for difference and change.

Section 14.2 of the chapter briefly describes the approach used in the analysis, and the main characteristics of the island groups and case-study provinces. In section 14.3 we present a few key features of the national labour market, setting the scene for our discussion of regional patterns and trends. Section 14.4 examines regional dimensions of labour supply trends, focusing especially on workforce growth rates and the supply of educated labour. Section 14.5 deals with labour demand patterns, proxied by patterns of employment in agriculture, manufacturing and

---

1 Indicators of integration include high levels of inter-regional migration and low levels of dispersion in wages and unemployment. 'Convergence' refers to the reduction in dispersion of these indicators over time.

services and in the formal and informal sectors. The sixth section looks at two indicators of labour market outcomes: unemployment and wages.

14.2   APPROACH AND SUMMARY DATA

Our approach acknowledges that regional contrasts in labour markets tend to be assocated with socio-demographic characteristics of the workforce as well as with economic structure and change by occupation and industry.[2] Variations by region per se are typically associated with barriers to labour mobility, especially imperfect information flows and transport costs. They can also be due to institutional factors such as social barriers to entry into occupations or industries. Macroeconomic instability and short-term shocks like the 1997–98 Asian financial crisis tend to affect different regions differently – workers in Jakarta and more urbanized regions suffered more than those in many rural areas away from the main economic and financial centres. Longer-term causes of regional variation in labour markets relate mainly to the cumulative effects of policies that influence physical investment and human capital. Key indicators of longer-term regional imbalance are differences in the profile of the workforce, in labour productivity and wages across industries and occupations, and in unemployment or underemployment.[3] These variables are the focus of this chapter.

The analysis is based on data from the August round of the National Labour Force Survey (Survei Angkatan Kerja Nasional, Sakernas) conducted annually (and in recent years biannually) over the past three decades by the central statistics agency (Badan Pusat Statistik, BPS). Statements in the text are based on data from this source unless otherwise indicated.

In this analysis we have broken the archipelago into five main island groups, Sumatra, Java–Bali, Kalimantan, Sulawesi and (other) Eastern Indonesia. Many of the main contrasts are still between Java–Bali and the other regions. But there are some interesting differences among the Outer Island groups, especially between Kalimantan and Eastern Indonesia at two extremes, with Sumatra and Sulawesi somewhere in between.

To capture some of the diversity within and between island groups we have taken two provinces, one high and one low in labour productiv-

---

2 For examples of analysis of regional labour markets, see various editions of the OECD's *Employment Outlook* (for example, OECD 2000: Ch. 2).

3 As is well known, underemployment is as important as unemployment – if not more so – as an indicator of labour market imbalance in developing countries, including Indonesia.

ity, as case studies for each group.[4] The 10 case-study provinces are North Sumatra and Lampung in Sumatra; Banten and Central Java (Java); East Kalimantan and West Kalimantan (Kalimantan); North Sulawesi and Gorontalo (Sulawesi); and Papua and East Nusa Tenggara (Eastern Indonesia). We have also added Jakarta to the Java case studies, to capture the unique features of the national capital. Some of the disparities between these case-study provinces and between the island groups, in population size, per capita output, output per worker and poverty, are shown in Table 14.1. The data indicate that output per worker was generally positively associated with GDP per capita and negatively associated with the poverty rate. GDP per capita and output per worker were slightly higher in Kalimantan and much lower in Eastern Indonesia than in the other island groups. This mirrored poverty rates, which were lower than the national rate in the former and higher in the latter.

At the provincial level, output per worker was well above the national average in Jakarta and East Kalimantan, and lowest by a considerable margin in Gorontalo and East Nusa Tenggara. Within island groups (and excluding Jakarta), the differences were most marked in Kalimantan and Sulawesi. Although poverty rates seem to be negatively correlated with output per worker, this was not always the case: Papua with its abundant natural resources is one exception; West Kalimantan, where poverty rates were only slightly below those of much richer East Kalimantan (and also well below the national level), is another.

14.3   THE INDONESIAN LABOUR MARKET, 2002–12

To set the scene for the discussion of regional labour market developments, Table 14.2 provides some basic data on the Indonesian labour market in 2012 and on changes over the preceding decade. The labour force is expanding at a moderate rate (1.6 per cent per annum over the decade), with much faster increases occurring among more educated Indonesians, especially those with a tertiary education. There is still some controversy about future population growth rates (McDonald 2014), but it seems likely that an expanding labour force will continue to contribute significantly to economic growth for another 10–15 years.

Two points are important to an understanding of the human capital base across the country. First, even in 2012, two-thirds of the workforce

---

4 In almost all cases we have selected the province with the highest and the lowest labour productivity in each island group. The exception is Sumatra, where no 2002 data were available for the province of Riau Islands, formed by separation from Riau province in 2004.

Table 14.1   Some characteristics of the island groups and case-study provinces, 2012

Island group/ province	Population (million)	Ratio, Indonesia = 1.0[a]		
		GDP per capita	Value added per worker	Poverty rate
Sumatra	**50.6**	**0.9**	**0.9**	
North Sumatra	13.0	1.0	1.1	0.9
Lampung	7.6	0.6	0.6	1.4
Java–Bali	**140.5**	**1.1**	**1.1**	
DKI Jakarta	9.6	4.7	4.3	0.3
Banten	10.6	0.9	1.0	0.5
Central Java	32.4	0.6	0.6	1.3
Kalimantan	**13.8**	**1.3**	**1.2**	
East Kalimantan	3.6	2.3	2.4	0.6
West Kalimantan	4.4	0.8	0.8	0.7
Sulawesi	**17.4**	**0.7**	**0.8**	
North Sulawesi	2.3	0.9	1.0	0.7
Gorontalo	1.0	0.3	0.4	1.4
Eastern Indonesia	**15.3**	**0.5**	**0.5**	
Papua	2.8	0.8	0.7	2.6
East Nusa Tenggara	4.7	0.3	0.3	1.7
Indonesia	**237.6**	**1.0**	**1.0**	**1.0**

a   In 2012, Indonesia's GDP per capita was Rp 32.4 million and output per worker Rp 21.4 million (both non-oil and gas); the national poverty rate was 12 per cent.
Source: BPS (2013); Sakernas, 2012.

was educated only to primary or junior secondary level. It will take some 20 years before the educational profile of the Indonesian workforce approaches that of middle-income countries like Malaysia, as older, less-educated workers retire.

But at the same time, the composition of the workforce has been changing quickly. Well over 50 per cent of the total increase in the workforce during the period 2002–12 consisted of senior secondary and tertiary graduates. Meanwhile the absolute number of primary school graduates in the workforce began to decline. Very few Indonesians are now leaving school before they have completed primary school, and very few urban Indonesians leave before completing junior secondary school. As we shall see, these patterns are remarkably uniform across island groups.

Table 14.2 Working age population, labour force, employment and unemployment, Indonesia, 2002–12

	2012	Growth (% p.a.)		
		2002–07	2007–12	2002–12
Working age population (million)	174	2.0	1.2	1.6
Labour force (million)	118	1.7	1.4	1.6
≤ Primary	55.9	0.0	–1.1	–0.5
Junior high	21.9	3.7	0.8	2.3
Senior high – general	19.1	4.5	4.5	4.5
Senior high – vocational	10.5	0.6	7.3	3.9
Diploma I/II	1.0	8.5	–7.1	0.7
Tertiary	9.5	7.3	10.4	8.9
Employment (million)	110.8	1.7	2.1	1.9
Agriculture	38.9	0.1	–0.6	–0.4
Non-agriculture				
Formal	39.6	2.5	7.1	4.8
Informal	32.3	3.1	0.8	2.0
Unemployment (million)	7.2	1.8	–6.5	–2.3
Real wages (Rp million/month, in 2012 prices)				
Agriculture	0.8	0.2	6.4	3.3
Non-agriculture	1.6	0.6	2.8	1.7

Source: Sakernas, 2002, 2007 and 2012.

On the demand side, employment is very roughly partitioned into three main groups: the agricultural sector and the formal and informal sectors outside agriculture. The former two groups each account for a little over one-third and the latter a little under one-third of all employment (Table 14.2). From the perspective of labour productivity this presents a huge challenge. It means that well over half of the employed population is engaged in low-productivity activities. Approximately 60 per cent of the workforce is in agriculture and low-productivity services, where output per worker is around half or less of the national average.[5]

---

5 Even when the data are adjusted for differences in hours worked, output per worker in agriculture was less than one-third of that in all non-agricultural sectors in 2012. The difference was smaller in the cases of personal and social

Many low-productivity informal jobs are in petty trade, including the omnipresent small stalls (*warung*). These low-productivity activities are also skewed in their distribution across regions – they are much more prominent in parts of Eastern Indonesia and in rural Central and East Java than in and around Jakarta and in parts of Sumatra and Kalimantan.

Output growth and job creation have been slower in manufacturing than in most service sectors, a pattern that we shall see is very clear for most provinces across Indonesia. Three sectors (mining, utilities and financial services) had high output per worker but accounted for a very small share of total employment (around 5 per cent overall). In two of them (mining and financial services), growth of jobs was very fast, helping to explain improved labour market conditions in several booming regions in and around Jakarta, and also in Kalimantan.

Overall employment has been growing faster than the labour force, helping to explain the decline in unemployment rates shown in Table 14.2. Nationally, wage growth has been modest, especially in non-agricultural activities (see the last two rows of Table 14.2). Recently, however, trends in minimum wages have differed across regions, with important implications for the distribution of investment (see below).

In sum, the national labour market appears to have responded reasonably well to moderate rates of economic growth in the first decade of the twentieth century, as shown by declining rates of unemployment, by the movement of more workers into high-productivity sectors and by rising real wages. Table 14.2 suggests, moreover, that growth in formal sector jobs and a decline in agricultural jobs have been particularly marked since around the mid-2000s, after the oil price rises of 2005 and the macroeconomic adjustments that these entailed. Economic growth rates in 2007–12 were faster in almost all sectors (not shown in the table) than in the early to mid-2000s, despite the global financial crisis of 2008–09. While they had suffered greatly from the Asian financial crisis in 1997–98, most Indonesian provinces and regions were spared the worst effects of the global crisis a decade later.

14.4   LABOUR SUPPLY AND UNEMPLOYMENT

Labour force growth historically has been slower in Java–Bali than in most of the Outer Island regions. In the latter it has been driven by higher rates of population growth and, to a lesser extent, by inter-regional migration out of more densely populated Java, and from South Sulawesi

---

services, and trade, restaurants and hotels (in both of which output per worker was around 30–40 per cent above that in agriculture).

Figure 14.1   Annual growth of working-age population and labour force by island group, 2002–12

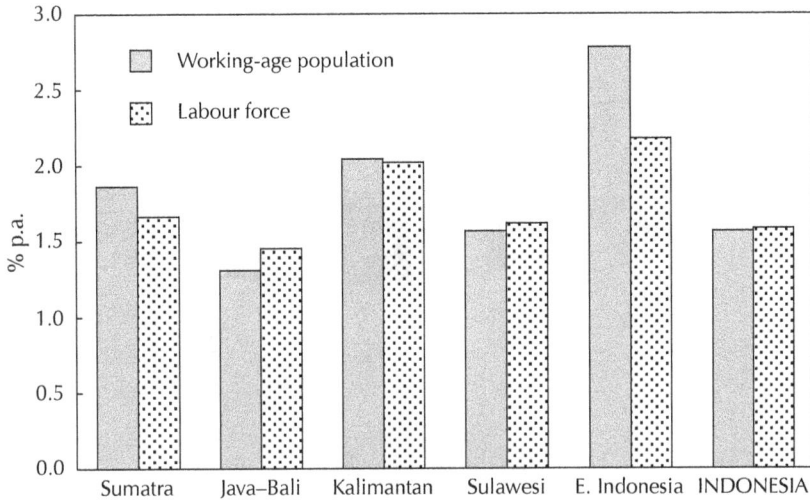

Source: Sakernas, 2002 and 2012.

and the poorer regions of Eastern Indonesia. The contrast in labour supply growth between Java and the main Outer Island regions was still marked in the 2000s. There now appears to be greater differentiation within the Outer Islands than in the past, however. While the working-age population and labour force were growing at less than 1.5 per cent in Java–Bali and approaching replacement rate, they were expanding at closer to 2.5 per cent per annum in Eastern Indonesia and 2 per cent in Kalimantan (Figure 14.1). On the other hand, growth rates were closer to 1.5 per cent in Sulawesi, and were especially low in relatively densely populated South Sulawesi, which is renowned for having high rates of out-migration.[6]

The pattern of rapid expansion of senior secondary and especially tertiary schooling was remarkably consistent across island groups and provinces. This is reflected for all island groups in sharp increases in the representation of workers educated to these levels among new entrants to the workforce during the decade 2002–12 (Figure 14.2). Even though tertiary graduates still make up less than 8 per cent of the workforce,

---

6 Both the working-age population and the labour force hardly increased at all over the decade to 2012 in South Sulawesi, the most populous of the Sulawesi provinces.

Figure 14.2   *Educational composition of labour force, 2012, and share of increase in workforce by educational category, 2002–12, by island group*

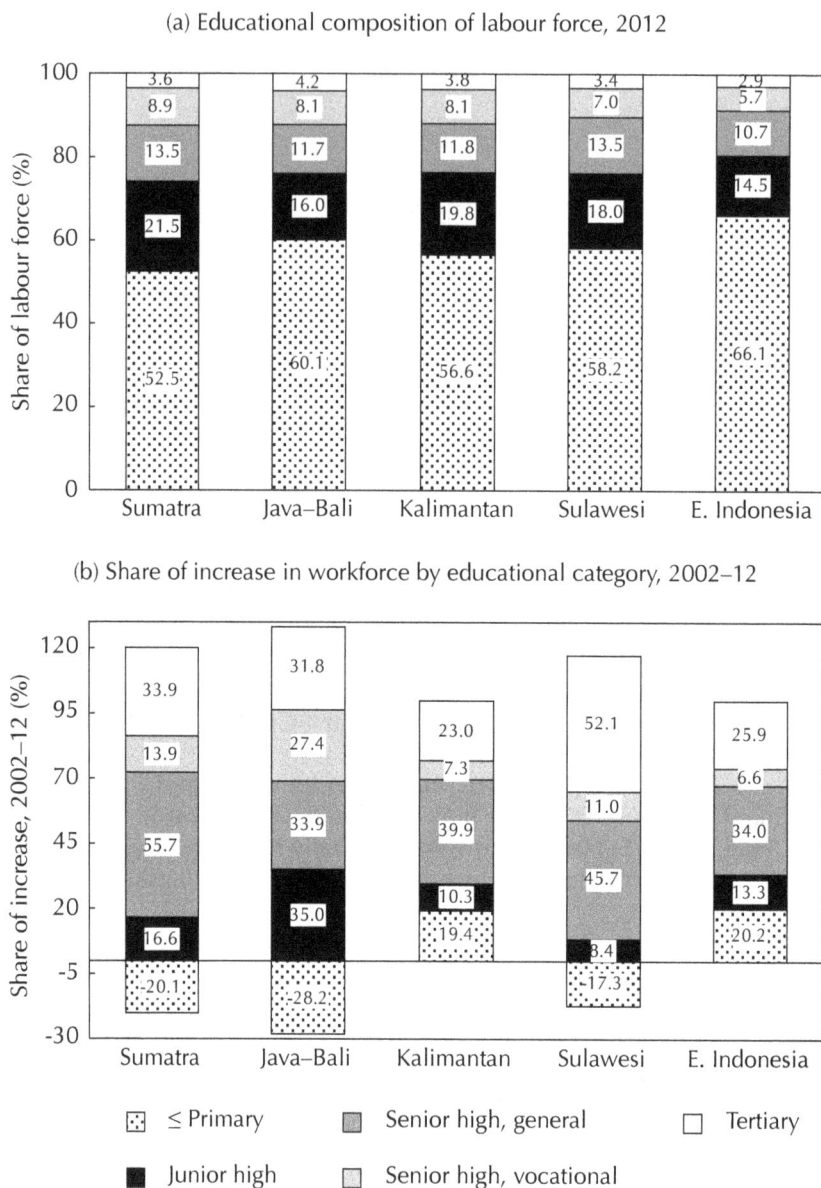

(a) Educational composition of labour force, 2012

(b) Share of increase in workforce by educational category, 2002–12

☐ ≤ Primary   ▨ Senior high, general   ☐ Tertiary

■ Junior high   ▨ Senior high, vocational

Source: Sakernas, 2002 and 2012.

in 2012 they accounted for over 20 per cent of new entrants nationally. Although rates of tertiary education remain fairly low across all island groups, the increases in tertiary enrolments were quite dramatic in some regions such as Sulawesi, where tertiary graduates made up over 40 per cent of all new additions to the workforce in the period 2002–12.

Despite the supply-driven expansion of secondary and tertiary education and the low and seemingly declining quality of tertiary schooling in particular (Hill and Thee 2012), Sakernas data suggest that demand has been able to keep up with the increasing supply of secondary and tertiary graduates. Such huge increases in supply could not have occurred without some impact on the quality of schooling, especially at the tertiary level, where the cost of education is typically much higher per student than at lower levels. But it is interesting that unemployment has actually declined across all provinces in recent years, even though it has been somewhat more 'sticky' for tertiary graduates, whose unemployment rates tend to be well above those of less well-educated Indonesians. Nationally, for all levels of schooling, we show below that the decline was a huge 33 per cent, from 9.1 per cent in 2007 to just over 6 per cent in 2012. All the island groups registered falls in unemployment, ranging from nearly 50 per cent in Sulawesi to 26 per cent in Eastern Indonesia. For tertiary graduates, national unemployment rates fell at a slower rate, but in this case there was more variation among island groups and provinces. One explanation may be that tertiary graduates are beginning to 'bump' secondary graduates out of many modern sector jobs as supply increases, although this is not yet reflected in higher unemployment rates among senior secondary graduates.

14.5   LABOUR DEMAND AND EMPLOYMENT

Agriculture is still the main sector for employment in all major island groups and in most provinces. Between 2002 and 2012, the decline in the workforce in low-productivity agriculture was marked in some cases. These included the poorer regions of Java and Lampung, where a quite sharp reduction in the agricultural workforce contributed to above-average growth in labour productivity. Expansion of work in some social sectors such as education and health care appears to have contributed especially to a rising share of formal sector work across the archipelago. This is likely to have led to some regional convergence in labour market indicators. However, the continuing heavy concentration of work in low-productivity agriculture in several regions outside Java, such as Papua and West Kalimantan, has had the opposite effect.

Table 14.3   Agriculture: employment, productivity and output by island group and case-study province, 2002–12

Island group/ province	Share of agriculture in total employment 2012 (%)	Value added per worker in agriculture 2012 (Rp thousand)	Growth 2002–12 (% p.a.) Agricultural output	Growth 2002–12 (% p.a.) Agricultural employment
Island group				
Sumatra	46	10,854	3.4	–0.4
Java–Bali	27	8,255	2.9	–1.0
Kalimantan	46	9,946	3.7	1.6
Sulawesi	44	10,655	4.5	–0.9
Eastern Indonesia	57	4,602	3.2	1.3
Indonesia	35	8,909	3.3	–0.4
Case-study province				
North Sumatra	43	12,331	4.2	–0.4
Lampung	48	9,748	4.0	–1.7
Banten	13	12,003	4.3	–4.3
Central Java	31	7,249	2.8	–1.5
East Kalimantan	28	17,692	3.2	6.6[a]
West Kalimantan	59	6,592	4.2	0.5
North Sulawesi	33	12,110	4.4	–2.4
Gorontalo	38	5,555	5.6	0.6
Papua	73	3,600	3.6	3.2[a]
East Nusa Tenggara	62	3,804	2.7	–0.5

a   The rate of increase in the agricultural workforce is unusually high in both Papua and East Kalimantan (especially in 2007–12). This may be partly the result of sampling error in relatively dispersed rural environments in both provinces.

Source: National accounts and Sakernas, 2002 and 2012.

Agriculture

A key feature of regional labour markets that underpins rates of poverty and disadvantage across island groups and provinces is the share of the population concentrated in low-productivity agriculture. Table 14.3 summarizes the distribution of the workforce and labour productivity in agriculture in 2012, as well as growth rates in agricultural output and employment in 2002–12, for the main island groups and for our high- and low-productivity case-study provinces. Among the island groups, Eastern Indonesia stands apart, with by far the highest share of the workforce employed in agriculture (just under 60 per cent) and the lowest average level of labour productivity in agriculture. Moreover, like Kalimantan, Eastern Indonesia was still absorbing more people into agriculture in 2002–12, whereas in Sumatra, Java–Bali and Sulawesi the agricultural workforce had begun to decline.[7]

Labour productivity in agriculture was generally lower in the case-study provinces with low than with high overall labour productivity in each island group – in Lampung, Central Java, West Kalimantan and Gorontalo. It was also very low in East Nusa Tenggara, but in this case it was only slightly below that in Papua, whose average labour productivity in all other sectors was much higher (Table 14.1). The good news is that workers were beginning to move out of the sector in several of these poorer provinces and that output growth was robust – in several provinces exceeding 4 per cent per annum in real terms, a quite impressive growth rate for agriculture.

Papua stands out as the only case-study province where average labour productivity is quite high – owing to the presence of enclave mining projects – but agricultural labour productivity is nevertheless very low. A high share of the population continues to depend on agriculture for a living. This underlines the great challenge for Papua: raising agricultural productivity in isolated regions, especially in the densely populated central highland areas, where transport and marketing costs are very high, and in isolated villages scattered elsewhere across the main island (Resosudarmo et al. 2009). The data suggest, moreover, that the agricultural labour force is still increasing in Papua, one factor that helps explain the enduring high levels of poverty.[8]

Sumatra, Sulawesi and Kalimantan contrast with Java–Bali and Eastern Indonesia in terms of agricultural labour productivity and agricultural output. Kalimantan was home to the case-study province with the highest level of agricultural labour productivity in 2012 – East Kalimantan. The island's agricultural labour force was still growing, partly because of the relative abundance of land and partly because of the recent expansion of its oil palm plantations. Growth in agricultural employment, too, was particularly marked in East Kalimantan, which

---

7 In Kalimantan, however, where agricultural labour productivity in 2012 was more than twice as high as it was in Eastern Indonesia, many people appear to have been drawn into agriculture to achieve a higher standard of living, rather than pushed into it by a shortage of other employment opportunities.

8 The official data on the increase in employment in Papuan agriculture seem implausibly high; see Table 14.3, note a.

actually experienced de-industrialization of the workforce owing to a decline in its wood-based industries. This occurred despite an economy that was booming in most sectors. Workers, many of them from outside the region, were drawn into both oil palm plantations and coal mining ventures during this period.

Manufacturing and services

Turning to the non-agricultural sectors, we find that the services sector dominates non-agricultural employment in all major island groups and in all provinces. In this respect Indonesia is not unique in Southeast Asia (Aswicahyono, Hill and Narjoko 2011). But it does mean that the country faces a major challenge in absorbing a large backlog of workers currently employed in low-productivity sectors.

Manufacturing

The share of jobs in Indonesia's manufacturing sector is very low by the standards of East Asian countries that have grown rapidly in the past several decades. Before the Asian financial crisis in 1997–98, it appeared that new jobs created in export industries might become the driving factor lowering poverty in many regions of Indonesia. Workers in Java–Bali and nearby provinces were absorbed into the rapidly growing, mostly labour-intensive and export-oriented industries (Manning 1998). After 1998 this process was interrupted, although there was a noticeable recovery in manufacturing employment growth in 2010–12.

Around 80 per cent of all jobs in manufacturing are concentrated in Java–Bali. For the entire period 2002–12, the growth of manufacturing jobs in Java–Bali was a little above the average for all employment growth in that region and in Indonesia as a whole (Table 14.4). Employment grew more quickly in Banten to the west of Jakarta, and in Central Java, where much of the small-scale industry is concentrated (Figure 14.3). It grew less quickly not only in increasingly service-sector-dominated Jakarta but also in West Java and East Java. Certain regions in the latter two provinces, such as Sidoardjo and Bandung, had previously been the centres of major export-oriented industries such as textiles, garments and footwear, which take advantage of economies of scale and agglomeration in relatively low-wage, labour-surplus environments.[9] Poor infrastruc-

---

9   Thus, employment in West Java, which encompasses the modern manufacturing hubs of Bekasi, Bogor and Bandung, grew at only 2 per cent during the period, well below the 5–6 per cent per annum achieved in the late 1980s and the first half of the 1990s.

Table 14.4 *Manufacturing and services: employment, productivity and output by island group, 2002–12*

	Share of sector in total employment 2012 (%)	Value added per worker 2012 (Rp thousand)	Growth 2002–12 (% p.a.)	
			Output	Employment
Manufacturing				
Sumatra	7.3	57,634	3.1	3.8
Java–Bali	18.6	34,833	5.0	2.5
Kalimantan	5.0	113,242	–1.4	–4.3
Sulawesi	6.4	27,001	6.5	4.7
Eastern Indonesia	5.9	21,115	14.6	0.1
Indonesia	**13.9**	**38,380**	**4.2**	**2.4**
Services				
Sumatra	45.1	23,716	6.9	4.7
Java–Bali	53.5	27,043	6.8	3.1
Kalimantan	42.6	28,269	7.3	3.6
Sulawesi	48.1	19,440	8.5	5.5
Eastern Indonesia	35.2	15,512	6.5	4.7
Indonesia	**49.6**	**25,477**	**7.0**	**3.6**

Source: National accounts and Sakernas, 2002 and 2012.

ture and connectivity and, to a lesser extent, tight and uncertain labour regulations have been suggested as the main explanations for the decline in these industries in West and East Java.

As real wages began to rise in China's major cities and the investment climate became more uncertain in Vietnam around the time of the global financial crisis in 2008–09, some of the investment in these labour-intensive industries refocused on Java. But a haphazard process of regional minimum wage adjustments in 2011–13, fanned by a more united union movement, seems to have put some of the new investment in and around the capital city on hold, particularly in 2013.[10] Populist statements by

---

10 See below for further discussion of minimum wage trends. The impact seems to have been particularly strong in the footwear industry, where an estimated 30,000 jobs were lost following large increases in minimum wages in and around Jakarta in the first half of 2013. See Prasetyantoko et al. (2013) for a further discussion of these impacts.

Figure 14.3   *Share of manufacturing in total employment, 2012, and*
                 growth in manufacturing output and employment, 2002–12,
                 by case-study province

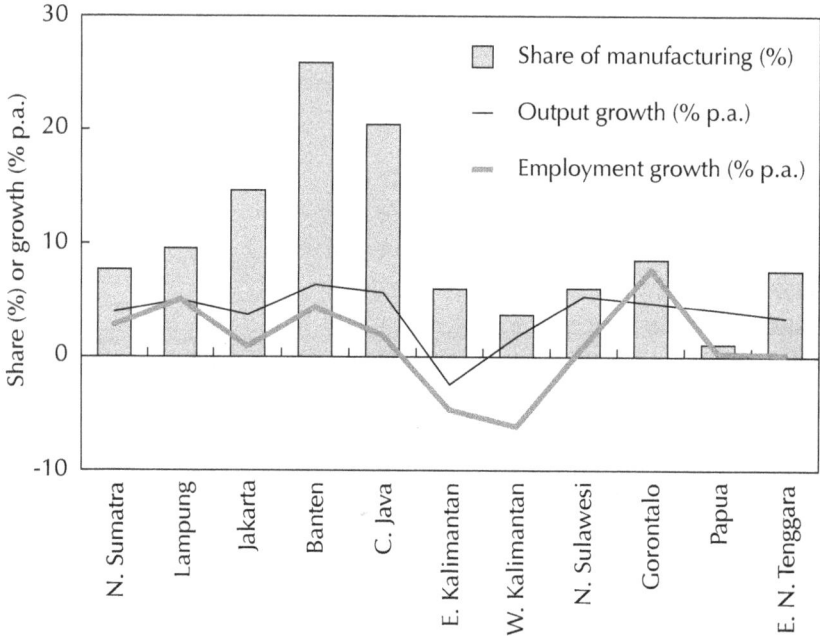

Source: National accounts and Sakernas, 2002 and 2012.

the central government in 2012, proudly announcing its determination
to end the 'low-wage era', added to investor uncertainty.

Manufacturing employment grew more quickly in Sulawesi and
Sumatra than in Java–Bali in 2002–12, though from a small base (Table
14.4). In these regions, both resource and agriculture-based processing
and consumer goods industries have flourished to meet the demands of
a growing middle class. But jobs in industry hardly grew at all in Eastern
Indonesia, despite quite significant increases in output in manufacturing
(from an even smaller base). And employment actually declined in Kalimantan, where a key factor has been the demise of timber-based industries such as plywood as sources of new logs have dried up.

Table 14.4 does not show data for the mining industry, which accounts
for a small share (just under 1.5 per cent) of all employment. Jobs grew
quite rapidly in this industry outside Java in the period after the Asian
financial crisis, especially in East and Central Kalimantan, where small-
scale coal miners took advantage of the high international prices of coal
to increase supply. Mining accounted for 10 per cent of all jobs in East

Kalimantan in 2012, and made up a significant share of employment growth in the region from the early to mid-2000s.

Services

The story of employment in services has generally been very different from that in manufacturing. Service industries have been boosted by high rates of domestic consumption growth, and this has been reflected in job creation across the board in services in most regions. In all island groups except Eastern Indonesia, employment has grown strongly in the small financial and business services industry (especially modern and smaller-scale banking and financial services) and less rapidly in the much larger trade sector.[11] Output per worker is very high in financial services across all island groups, as it is in mining.

In contrast, jobs growth has been much slower in trade, restaurants and hotels, a subsector that has typically been dominated by small retail stalls and peddlers. Perhaps increasing urban density and the spread of franchised mini-markets and supermarkets in the main cities has contributed to the slow growth of jobs in trade. However, it is worth noting that employment in trade, restaurants and hotels has still been growing in all island groups, and slightly faster than manufacturing jobs in most.

Perhaps surprisingly, jobs growth has also been slow in transport and communications in most regions. This is despite the remarkable growth of this sector (around 10 per cent per annum since 2000), driven mainly by the communications revolution. Again, as with trade, backwash effects may have been important, with larger-scale, more capital-intensive subsectors in transport in particular dominating growth in output. For example, employment growth was close to 10 per cent per annum in airline services in the first decade of the 2000s, but it was very slow in land and sea transport (Aswicahyono and Manning 2011).

Expansion of employment opportunities in services has been on the high side in Sulawesi and, to a lesser extent, Eastern Indonesia.[12] Increased government investments in education and health, including poverty alleviation programs, are likely to have played a major role in employment growth in public and social services in Eastern Indonesia. In contrast to these two regions, services sector employment growth has been slower in Java and intermediate in Sumatra and Kalimantan.

---

11 See Manning and Aswicahyono (2012) for a breakdown of service sector job creation nationally between 2000 and 2010.

12 This has been especially so in construction in Sulawesi and in public, social and private services in both regions.

Figure 14.4   Growth in services output and employment by case-study province, 2002–12

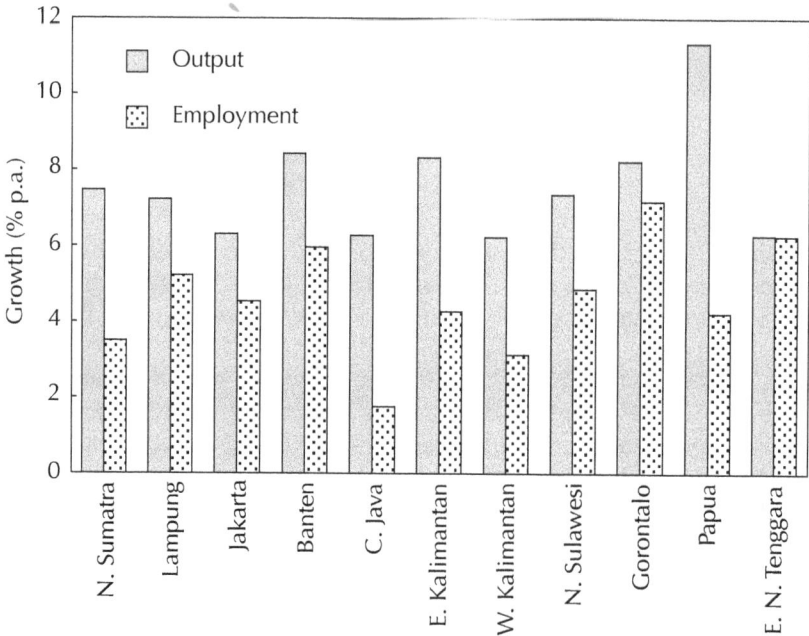

Source: National accounts and Sakernas, 2002 and 2012.

Figure 14.4 shows that service sector output growth was strong in all case-study provinces, both the high and the low labour productivity ones, in the period 2002–12. The resource-rich regions of Papua and East Kalimantan and the strong manufacturing centre of Banten, west of Jakarta, stand out, as does Gorontalo. One might expect linkages from strong resource-based growth and manufacturing to have contributed directly and indirectly to growth in service industries. The employment impacts were more muted, however, except in the case of Banten, Gorontalo and East Nusa Tenggara.[13] In the case of Banten it seems likely there were strong links with manufacturing growth, whereas in East Nusa Tenggara a considerable share of jobs expansion may be related to public spending in social sectors and to growth of the informal sector (which we discuss below).

Labour productivity in service sectors varied considerably across island groups and provinces (Figure 14.5). As might be expected, labour

---

13 See Aswicahyono and Manning (2011) on linkages between manufacturing and service sector employment at the national level.

Figure 14.5   *Index of labour productivity in manufacturing and services by case-study province, 2012 (Indonesia = 1.0)*[a]

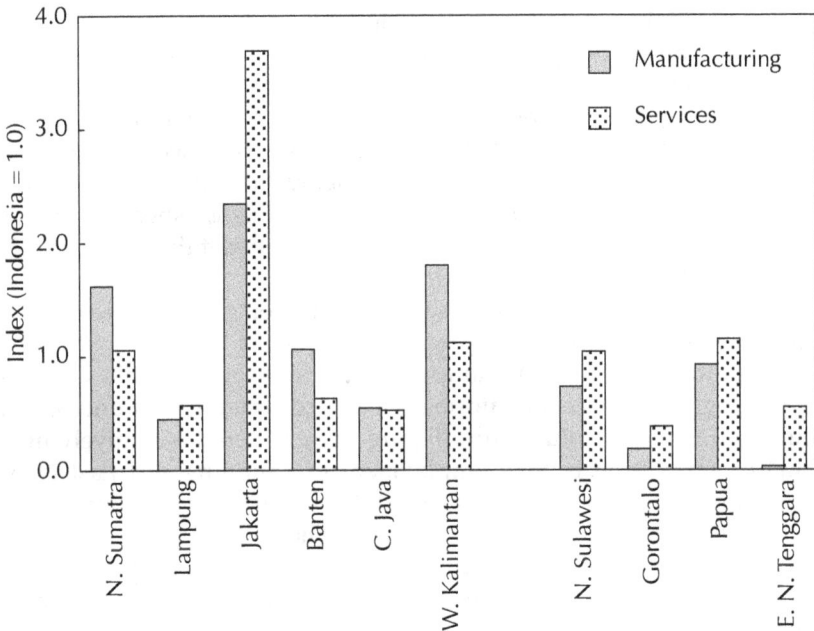

a   Data are not shown for East Kalimantan, which records values well above all other regions in manufacturing, as a result of oil and gas and related industry processing and refining.

Source: National accounts and Sakernas, 2012.

productivity was higher in both services and manufacturing in the higher-income or resource-rich regions such as Jakarta, Papua and North Sumatra, and lower in the poorer ones (East Nusa Tenggara, Gorontalo, Central Java and Lampung). The former have been drawing in some of the more educated workers, whereas the latter depend more on older workers with less formal schooling.

In general, however, one would not expect jobs growth to bear a close relationship to output growth across provinces, given huge differences in labour productivity among subsectors (airline industries versus trishaw drivers in transport; home industries versus oil refining in manufacturing). For example, one could expect to find large within-sector differences in labour productivity when comparing Central Java and Lampung on one hand with East Kalimantan and Papua on the other. These relationships are likely to be linked in part to different concentrations of workers in the formal and informal sectors. We return to this subject in the next section.

Formal and informal jobs

The informal sector still provides many jobs in Indonesia. This is reflected in the quite high share of jobs outside agriculture that can be classified as informal in all island groups and across most provinces.[14] While informal work is more visible outside the central business districts of cities, it is also a major feature of non-agricultural employment in rural areas. Indeed, one of the important shifts in rural household welfare has been a diversification of rural work to non-agricultural and mainly informal jobs in many parts of Indonesia (Booth 2012). This is especially true in the land-scarce regions of Java and Bali and in some of the more densely populated Outer Island regions.

Figures 14.6 and 14.7 provide some information on this subject. Informal work is especially widespread in the poorer provinces with low labour productivity, such as Lampung, Central Java, Gorontalo and East Nusa Tenggara, where the informal sector accounted for around 50 per cent of all non-agricultural jobs (Figure 14.6). Given the relatively high share of agriculture in total employment in Lampung and East Nusa Tenggara (around 50 per cent or more), the availability of formal sector work was quite limited in these provinces. The sector provided employment opportunities for only around one-quarter or less of the labour force, mainly in the public sector. It is therefore not surprising that both provinces are areas of out-migration (especially from East Nusa Tenggara to jobs in East Malaysia).

Informal sector work appears less prevalent in Jakarta. The data do not tell the whole story, however. Many informal businesses operate in Jakarta, but most of their owners and workers reside on its outskirts in districts that are part of West Java and Banten, and commute to the city to work. The informal sector workforce is also relatively small in the resource-rich provinces of East Kalimantan and Papua. However, this seems to be due more to the isolated and enclave nature of many of the mining and related industries in both provinces.

Over time, the informal sector has shrunk considerably, having expanded after the Asian financial crisis, when many people lost formal sector jobs. Among the five island groups, formal sector jobs contributed close to, or more than, 75 per cent of all new jobs in 2002–12. This was

---

14 The crude definition of 'informal sector' work is used here: all workers who are 'self-employed' or 'employed in a small family business', and those people classified as family workers. The formal sector consists of all wage employees (casual and permanent) and employers. (A more refined definition would also take account of occupation, classifying self-employed professionals, for example, as formal rather than informal sector workers. The numbers of such workers are, however, quite small overall.)

Figure 14.6   *Non-agricultural employment in the formal and informal sectors by case-study province, 2012*

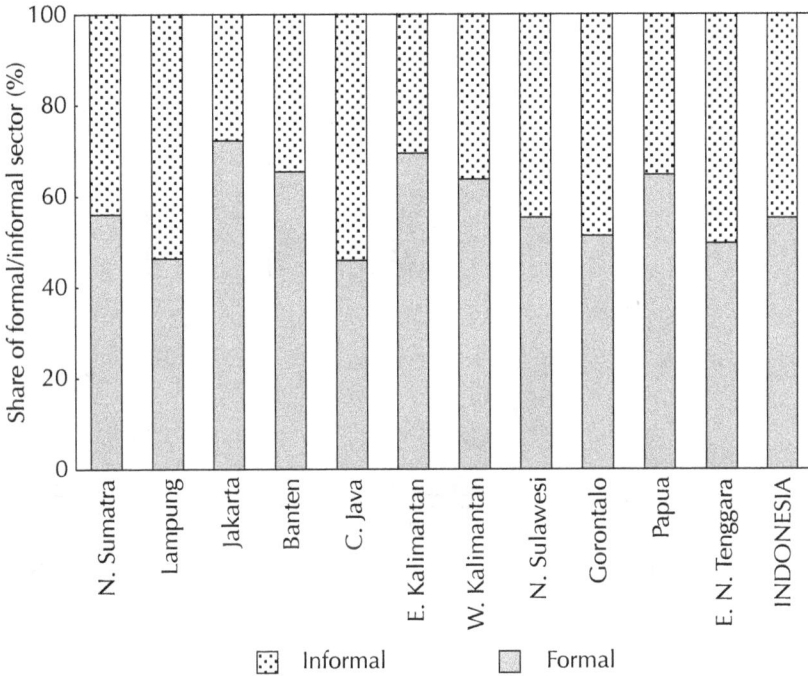

Source: National accounts and Sakernas, 2002 and 2012.

also true of most of the provinces covered in this study, although the experience of provinces was more varied than that of island groups. The poorer regions such as Lampung, Central Java, Gorontalo and East Nusa Tenggara continued to depend for employment on a relatively high share of new informal jobs outside agriculture (Figure 14.7).

A higher proportion of both formal and informal sector jobs were in services than in manufacturing in 2012 (Table 14.4), even in regions where manufacturing employment was more heavily concentrated, such as Banten and Jakarta. Services also accounted for well over half of the growth in both formal and informal sector employment outside agriculture in all regions in the 2000s. Although the manufacturing employment record has not been good, the service sector has been able to take up the slack. While many service sector jobs have relatively low levels of productivity, a significant share are in modern services with fairly high levels of productivity, such as banking, business services, real estate, and hotels and restaurants.

Figure 14.7 *Distribution of the increase in non-agricultural employment in the formal and informal sectors by case-study province, 2002–12*

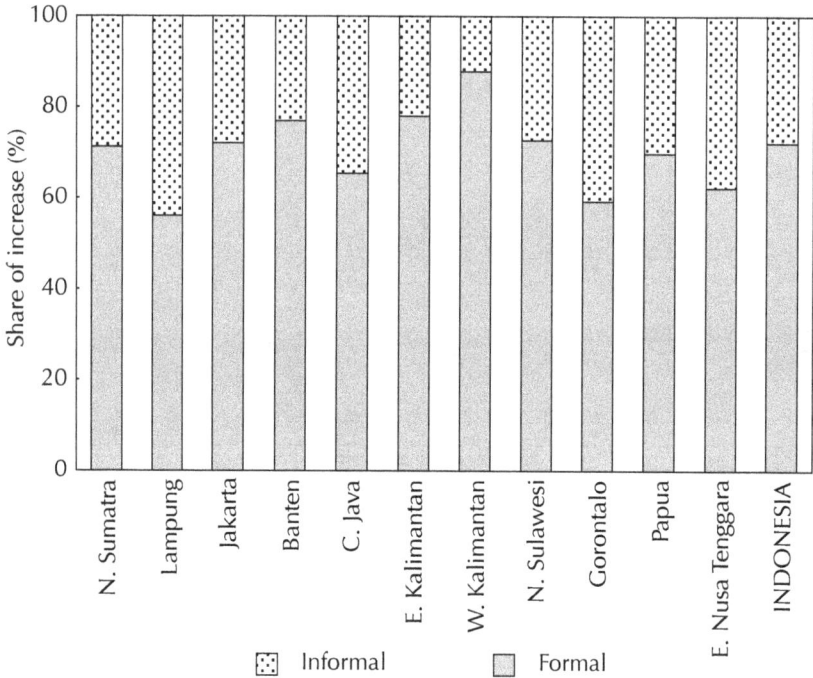

Source: Sakernas, 2002 and 2012.

14.6 UNEMPLOYMENT AND WAGES

Both unemployment and wage trends registered significant improvements across Indonesia in 2002–12, despite slower rates of economic growth than in most of the previous decade. Unemployment rates rose in the first half of the decade and then fell quite steeply from 2006 onward in almost all island groups and provinces. In regard to inter-provincial differences, three patterns stand out. First, unemployment tended to be highest in the more urbanized and faster-growing regions – Jakarta, Banten and East Kalimantan – and lowest in those regions where the informal sector and agricultural employment were more widespread, such as West Kalimantan, Gorontalo and East Nusa Tenggara. Thus, in 2012 the highest unemployment rate was recorded in Banten (10.1 per cent), followed by Jakarta (9.9 per cent) and East Kalimantan (8.9 per cent), and the lowest rates were close to one-third of these levels, with East Nusa

Table 14.5 *Unemployment rates and wages of regular non-agricultural workers by island group and case-study province, 2002–12*

Island group/ province	Index of unemployment rate (Indonesia = 1.0)			Wages of non-agricultural workers	
	2002	2007	2012	Rp million/ month 2012	Real wage growth 2002–12 (% p.a.)[a]
Sumatra	**1.0**	**1.0**	**0.9**	**1.7**	**1.3**
N. Sumatra	1.1	1.1	1.0	1.6	1.3
Lampung	0.9	0.8	0.8	1.4	0.5
Java–Bali	**1.0**	**1.0**	**1.1**	**1.6**	**1.9**
DKI Jakarta	1.6	1.4	1.6	2.2	2.2
Banten	1.6	1.7	1.7	1.9	1.8
C. Java	0.7	0.8	0.9	1.3	1.7
Kalimantan	**1.0**	**0.8**	**0.9**	**2.0**	**1.5**
E. Kalimantan	1.3	1.3	1.5	2.4	1.6
W. Kalimantan	0.9	0.7	0.6	1.6	1.2
Sulawesi	**1.2**	**1.1**	**0.9**	**1.7**	**0.9**
N. Sulawesi	1.3	1.4	1.3	1.9	0.6
Gorontalo	1.5	0.8	0.7	1.5	1.7
Eastern Indonesia	**0.7**	**0.7**	**0.7**	**1.9**	**1.6**
Papua	0.7	0.6	0.6	2.6	1.1
E. Nusa Tenggara	0.5	0.4	0.5	1.6	1.6
Indonesia	**1.0**	**1.0**	**1.0**	**1.7**	**1.7**
National rate (%)	*9.1*	*9.1*	*6.1*		

a Adjusted by increases in the national CPI, 2002–12.
Source: Sakernas, 2002, 2007 and 2012.

Tenggara at 2.9 per cent, West Kalimantan and Papua at 3.5 per cent and Gorontalo at 4.4 per cent. Some of the contrasts are shown for 2002, 2007 and 2012 in Table 14.5, presented as an index of the all-Indonesia rates (1.0). Clearly unemployment was not positively related to poverty, or negatively to per capita incomes and productivity. Indeed, quite the opposite: more rapid growth encouraged potential job seekers to look for employment and created longer job queues in regions such as Banten and East Kalimantan.

Second, variations were greatest within rather than across island groups. Average unemployment rates ranged within quite a narrow band across the main island groups, from 6.7 per cent in Java–Bali to 5.2 per cent in Sulawesi, although the rate in Eastern Indonesia was a lower 4.4 per cent. Geography per se does not seem to have a close relationship to unemployment.

Finally, relative unemployment rates were reasonably stable across island groups and provinces over the 10-year period. They remained highest and even increased slightly in the more industrialized and faster-growing regions, but remained low in comparative terms in the less advanced and more agricultural regions.

High unemployment rates tended to be associated with higher wages in urbanized, industrialized and faster-growing regions of Indonesia. Hence the wages of regular non-agricultural workers were highest in Jakarta, Banten, East Kalimantan, North Sulawesi and Papua (close to Rp 2 million or more per month in 2012), and lowest in Lampung, Central Java and Gorontalo, where they were Rp 1.5 million or less. To a considerable extent these differences reflect variations in the cost of living across provinces and regions. For example, after adjustment for the Workers Decent Basic Needs Index (Kebutuhan Hidup Layak, KHL), which is used as a basis for determining minimum wages, wage rates in the former group of provinces were on a par with or even lower than those elsewhere in Indonesia in 2012.[15]

Real wage growth between 2002 and 2012 was positive but quite slow across all regions (Table 14.5). The rate of increase does not appear to be associated with obvious indicators such as the rate of manufacturing and service sector growth, or of minerals development.[16] High rates of inter-regional migration to resource-rich areas such as East Kalimantan and Papua suggest that wage growth there has been tempered by an abundant supply of unskilled workers. Civil service rates, which are uniform

---

15 For example, after adjustment for the KHL, wage levels in Jakarta and North Sumatra were found to be on a par with those in Central Java, at Rp 1.3 million a month; they were actually lower in East Kalimantan and Papua, where the KHL was close to twice its level in Central Java. The narrower gap in 'real' wages may be overstated somewhat, however, if one uses the KHL as a basis for adjustment. The estimated KHL is probably higher than is justified by the real cost of living in some of the high-wage provinces. Strong trade union involvement in estimating the index tends to push the official KHL above that justified by actual changes in the provincial cost of living as measured by BPS.

16 In a number of provinces real wage growth was negative in the early 2000s (2002–07). Wages then began to rise quite steeply, with real wage growth averaging around 3 per cent per annum in the five years to 2012.

across provinces (with cost-of-living adjustments in some regions), probably also contributed to bunching of rates of growth in wages.

Although compliance tends to be low away from the main cities and in smaller establishments, minimum wage adjustments have influenced wage levels and wage growth. This is especially true in regions where labour unions are stronger, particularly across the greater Jakarta region (Jabodetabek, covering Jakarta and the nearby municipalities and districts of Bogor, Depok, Tangerang and Bekasi), and to a lesser extent in and around Surabaya, in Batam and in Medan. In Java, minimum wages are adjusted annually at the district level, and the range in these adjustments can be substantial depending on union activism and local political factors.[17] In 2012, for example, a concerted union campaign to raise wages in greater Jakarta resulted in annual increases for 2013 of 30–70 per cent (with the median around 40 per cent) across its districts and municipalities. In contrast, average increases across some 25 districts in Central Java in the same year were closer to 10 per cent, with the highest increase being 22 per cent in the capital of Semarang. In Jakarta, labour-intensive manufacturers in and around the city were understandably disturbed by these developments. A strong social media campaign mounted by the Indonesian Employers Association (Asosiasi Pengusaha Indonesia, Apindo) managed to persuade the governor of Jakarta, Joko Widodo, to award a much more modest increase of 10 per cent in his city, a decision followed by most of the surrounding districts for 2014.

One cannot but be impressed by the extent of labour market integration that these data imply for such a large and diverse country. Not only has the range in unemployment rates and real wages been relatively modest (after taking into account cost-of-living differences) but the rates have also almost universally moved in the same direction over the medium term (2007–12). There have been fears from time to time that decentralization would tend to reduce the chances for households in poorer regions to move to areas where there are more opportunities. The data for 2002–12 suggest that these fears are unfounded.

14.7   CONCLUSION

In this chapter we have sought to identify regional patterns of integration and shifts towards greater convergence across Indonesia's island groups and selected provinces in the period 2002–12. The chapter has focused on both differences and similarities in the experience of the island groups,

---

17 Many regional minimum wage rates in the Outer Islands are still set at the provincial level.

and of the provinces selected to represent high and low labour productivity. The island groups show some important differences that reflect their contrasting resource and population endowments. But the main differences tend to be within island groups, between the low-productivity, mainly agriculture-based provinces in Kalimantan, Sulawesi and Eastern Indonesia and those where either natural resource wealth or industrial concentration has contributed to high levels of labour productivity and formal sector employment.

We have stressed a number of factors contributing to a more integrated national labour market, especially the rapid improvement in the educational qualifications of the workforce, service sector job growth and falling unemployment in almost all of the case-study provinces. While it would be too hasty to suggest there has been convergence in labour market indicators, there is no doubt that the provinces and regions of Indonesia are closely bound together in regard to labour market developments.[18] This degree of integration has probably intensified over the past decade or so. In particular, the communications revolution, typified by the spread of mobile phones and access to the internet at all levels of society, has surely contributed to greater mobility of people, capital and ideas within the archipelago.

No attempt has been made to cover all provinces, and there has been no coverage of data at the district level, where dynamic changes are occurring in response to innovative programs introduced by local leaders. Rather, we have sought to identify some of the main patterns of labour force growth, employment and wages, and to suggest possible explanations. More careful econometric work is needed to validate some of the tentative conclusions advanced in this chapter.

REFERENCES

Aswicahyono, H. and C. Manning (2011) 'Exports and job creation in Indonesia before and after the Asian financial crisis', Working Paper in Trade and Development, Arndt-Corden Department of Economics, Crawford School, Australian National University, Canberra.

Aswicahyono, H., H. Hill and D. Narjoko (2011) 'Indonesian industrialization: jobless growth?', in C. Manning and S. Sumarto (eds) *Employment, Living Standards and Poverty in Contemporary Indonesia*, Institute of Southeast Asian Studies, Singapore.

18 It has been suggested, for example, that regional contrasts in labour market outcomes are probably greater in the Philippines than in Indonesia, partly because economic power is less concentrated in Jakarta than in Manila, and partly because Indonesia has higher rates of inter-regional mobility than the Philippines (Esguerra and Manning 2007).

Booth, A. (2012) 'Indonesian agriculture', in A. Booth, C. Manning and Thee K.W. (eds) *Land, Livelihood, the Economy and the Environment in Indonesia: Essays in Honour of Joan Hardjono*, Obor Foundation, Jakarta.

BPS (Badan Pusat Statistik) (2013) *Statistical Yearbook of Indonesia 2013*, BPS, Jakarta.

Esguerra, E. and C. Manning (2007) 'Regional labour markets and economic development in the Philippines', in A. Balisacan and H. Hill (eds) *The Dynamics of Regional Development: The Philippines in East Asia*, Edward Elgar, Cheltenham.

Hill, H. and Thee K.W. (2012) 'Indonesian universities in transition: catching up and opening up', *Bulletin of Indonesian Economic Studies*, 48(2): 229–52.

Manning, C. (1998) *Indonesian Labour in Transition: An East Asian Success Story?* Trade and Development Series, Cambridge University Press, Cambridge.

Manning, C. and H. Aswicahyono (2012) 'Trade and employment in services: a report for the ILO', draft, International Labour Organization, Jakarta, 8 February.

McDonald, P. (2014) 'The demography of Indonesia in comparative perspective', *Bulletin of Indonesian Economic Studies*, 50(1), forthcoming.

OECD (Organisation for Economic Co-operation and Development) (2000) *OECD Employment Outlook 2000: June*, OECD Publishing, Paris.

Prasetyantoko, A., H. Aswicahyono, N. Poerwana and T. Hervino (2013) 'Dampak dan respon dunia usaha terhadap kebijakan upah minimum provinsi (UMP) 2013: industri alas kaki dan garmen' [The impact and response of the business sector to the 2013 provincial minimum wage policy: the footwear and garment industries], unpublished report, Atmadjaja University, Jakarta.

Resosudarmo, B.P., C. Manning, L. Napitupulu and V. Wanggai (2009) 'Papua I: challenges of economic development in an era of political and economic change', in B. Resosudarmo and F. Jotzo (eds) *Working with Nature against Poverty: Development, Resources and the Environment in Eastern Indonesia*, Institute of Southeast Asian Studies, Singapore.

15 The dynamics of Jabodetabek development: the challenge of urban governance

Tommy Firman

15.1 INTRODUCTION

Recent urban development in many Asian countries has been marked by the physical growth of cities, radiating from the centre in all directions and spilling over beyond their formal administrative boundaries. This development has been characterized by a mixture of many different kinds of land uses and economic activities, including the appearance of new towns and large housing and industrial estates alongside existing agricultural activities. This phenomenon, often referred to as 'mega-urbanization',[1] has occurred in many Asian countries, including Indonesia, China, India, Malaysia and Vietnam.[2]

In earlier research (Firman 2009), I have identified seven characteristics of mega-urbanization in Indonesia:

1 development of economic activities on a global scale;
2 division of functions between the core and the outskirts of large cities;
3 change from single-core to multi-core urban areas;
4 land-use change in the city centre and conversion of farmland to urban uses on the outskirts;

---

1 See McGee (1995, 2005), Douglass (2000) and Douglass and Jones (2008).
2 See Hugo (2006), Firman, Kombaitan and Pradono (2007) and McGee (2011) on Indonesia; Webster (2001), Sit (2005) and Xu and Yeh (2011b) on China; Dupont (2006) and World Bank (2013) on India; Wong (2006) on Malaysia; Anh (2008) on Vietnam; and, on Asian mega-cities more generally, Jones (2008).

5   large-scale urban infrastructure development;
6   greatly intensified use of space; and
7   considerable increases in commuter numbers and commuting times.

Over the past decade, the development of Indonesia's mega-urban regions has also reflected the urban fragmentation resulting from the new decentralization policy implemented since 2001 (Firman 2008, 2009).

One of the biggest challenges in mega-urban development is how to build an appropriate mechanism of governance that can optimize the potential of an urban region to improve its competitiveness and the quality of life of its residents.[3] Governance includes the power exercised not only by formal government institutions, but also by civil society and the private sector. Against this backdrop, this chapter examines mega-urbanization in the greater Jakarta metropolitan area, which has the country's largest concentration of economic activities and urban population, and the governance systems that could be used to manage urban development in the region. In addition, the chapter will update my earlier research on the development of the greater Jakarta area (Firman 2004, 2008, 2009, 2010).

The greater Jakarta area consists of the city of Jakarta and the surrounding metropolitan area, including Bogor, Depok, Tangerang and Bekasi – hence its acronym Jabodetabek, consisting of the first two or three letters of each region. It is made up of nine administrative areas occupying different tiers of government: the Special Capital Region of Jakarta (DKI Jakarta), which has the status of a provincial government; the municipalities (*kota*) of Bogor, Depok, Tangerang, South Tangerang and Bekasi; and the districts (*kabupaten*) of Bogor, Tangerang and Bekasi. The municipalities and districts of Bogor, Bekasi and Depok are within the province of West Java, while the municipalities of Tangerang and South Tangerang, and the district of Tangerang, are within the province of Banten. Thus, two provincial governments (West Java and Banten) are in a position to influence development in the capital, in addition to the provincial government of Jakarta.

Jabodetabek plays an important role in the national economy, generating about one-quarter of Indonesia's non-oil and gas GDP (Firman 2012). By comparison, Surabaya, Medan, Semarang and Makassar, constituting the next tier of major metropolitan areas, together contribute about 15 per cent, with other urban areas collectively contributing about the same amount.

---

3   See Laquian (2005a, 2005b, 2008), Bird and Slack (2007), Freire (2007) and Xu and Yeh (2011a).

This chapter consists of two main sections. Section 15.2 discusses recent socio-economic and physical development in Jabodetabek, including urban population, land conversion, new towns, industrial estates, infrastructure development and the potential impact of climate change. Section 15.3 examines the need for better governance institutions in Jabodetabek in the decentralization era. The final section offers some concluding comments.

15.2   SOCIO-ECONOMIC AND PHYSICAL DEVELOPMENT

Urban population

The population of Jabodetabek grew at an average rate of 3.6 per cent per annum between 2000 and 2010, reaching 27.9 million in the latter year. In 2010 Indonesia had 11 cities with a population of at least 1 million, five of them in Jabodetabek: Jakarta, Bekasi, Tangerang, South Tangerang and Depok. In this sense, Jabodetabek is a 'primate city'. The city (province) of Jakarta had a population of almost 9.6 million in 2010. In addition, approximately 2 million people commuted daily from the surrounding cities to work in Jakarta, resulting in a daytime population of about 11.6 million.

The population density of Jabodetabek has increased significantly, from 25.5 persons per square hectare in 1990 to 37.6 in 2000 and 44.6 in 2010. The population density of Jakarta city itself has increased more slowly, from 126.1 persons per square hectare in 1990 to 128.0 in 2000 and 145.9 in 2010 (Salim 2013). Jakarta's share of the population of Jabodetabek has declined significantly, from 54.6 per cent in 1990 to 43.2 per cent in 2000, then further to 35.5 per cent in 2010, reflecting the process of suburbanization of Jabodetabek's peripheral areas.

Population growth is slowing in Jakarta, as it is as in most of Indonesia's large cities; the rate of growth slowed from 3.1 per cent per annum in 1980–90 to just 0.4 per cent in 1990–2000, although it then rose to 1.5 per cent in 2000–10. In contrast, Jabodetabek's peripheral areas are experiencing much more rapid population growth. For instance, the populations of Bekasi city and Tangerang city grew by 3.4 per cent and 3.2 per cent per annum respectively in 2000–10, while that of Depok city grew even faster, at 4.2 per cent. The districts within Jabodetabek have also experienced faster population growth than Jakarta, with Bogor's population growing by 2.4 per cent and Bekasi's by 4.7 per cent. It should be noted, however, that the high population growth rates in these peripheral areas were not wholly due to in-migration, but also to the reclassification of rural villages (*desa*) to incorporate them into larger urban municipalities (*kota*) in the 2010 census.

Urban land-use conversion

Over the last four decades, industrial, commercial and residential development in Jabodetabek has resulted in land conversion in both the city of Jakarta and its fringe areas. Within Jakarta city, many previously residential areas are now commercial districts dotted with high-rise apartments and condominiums, while sizeable areas of prime agricultural land in the fringe areas have been converted into large-scale residential areas and new towns, industrial estates, golf courses and tourist resorts.

By the early 2000s, about 8,000 hectares of primary forest and 4,000 hectares of paddy fields had been converted into residential and industrial areas in south Jabodetabek. Situated upstream from Jakarta, this land was previously designated a conservation zone because of its importance as a water recharge area. Over the past decade, the pace of urban land conversion in Jabodetabek has been much faster in the periphery than in the city centre: whereas the built-up areas of Jakarta increased from 560 to 594 square kilometres between 2000 and 2010 (that is, by 0.6 per cent per annum), those in the periphery, including Bogor, Tangerang, Depok and Bekasi, expanded significantly from 544 to 850 square kilometres (4.6 per cent per annum) (Salim 2013; see also Figure 15.1).

The rapid pace of land conversion in Jabodetabek has been driven in part by developers attracted by the lucrative opportunities to extract high rents. Another factor has been the weak enforcement of government planning regulations, which has allowed private developers and local governments to violate land use regulations in regional spatial plans (*rencana tata ruang*). Many of the development proposals have been submitted by developers who have close formal or informal connections with the authorities. This is concerning, bearing in mind that the implementation of land-use plans is negotiable, and that the capacity of local governments to monitor and control land-use conversion is weak.

Shopping mall and apartment development in Jakarta city

As many as 40 large shopping malls had been built in Jakarta by 2010, including the city's first mall, Ratu Plaza, which was constructed in the early 1980s. The land area covered by the city's shopping malls has increased greatly, from 1.7 million square metres in 2000 to 4.8 million square metres in 2009 (Suryadjaja 2012). One of the largest commercial areas is the Sudirman Superblock, consisting of about 2 million square metres of residential, hotel, entertainment and business space. At present there are about 20 large malls in the Jakarta central business district, including Taman Rasuna and Grand Kuningan, Central Park Jakarta, Mall Taman Anggrek, Senayan City, Cilandak Town Square (Citos) and Pluit Junction. Another seven are to be built between 2013 and 2016: Cipinang

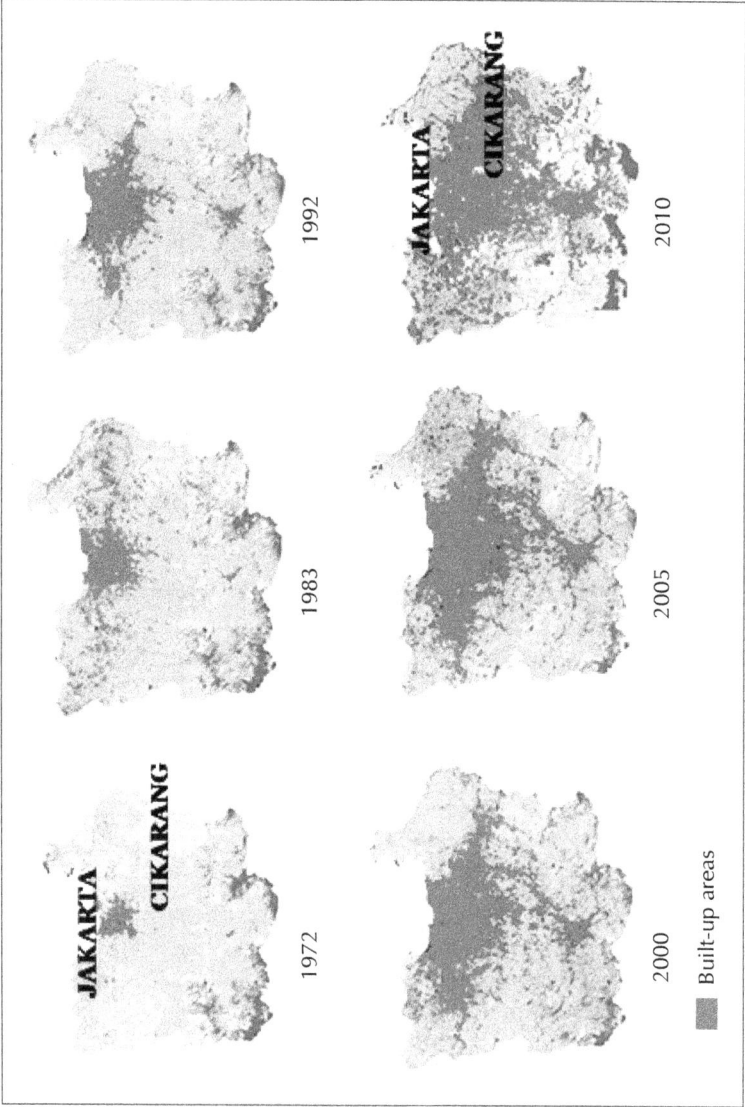

Figure 15.1   Macro land-use development in Jabodetabek, 1972–2010

JAKARTA
CIKARANG
1972

1983

JAKARTA
CIKARANG
1992

2000

2005

JAKARTA
CIKARANG
2010

■ Built-up areas

Source: Ministry of Public Works.

Indah Mall, The Baywalk@Green Bay Pluit and St Moritz (2013); Mall at the City Centre, the Gateway and Pantai Indah Kapuk Mall (2014); and Pondok Indah Mall 3 (2016). In addition, the city has around 40 medium-sized shopping malls. As well as the Sudirman Superblock, a number of other mixed-use 'superblocks' consisting of high-rise apartments, shopping malls, leisure facilities and commercial outlets have been built in Jakarta, covering an area of about 33,200 square metres (Herlambang 2010, cited in Padawangi 2012: 4).

The physical development of Jakarta over the past decade or so has also been shaped by the construction of luxury high-rise apartments in many areas. In many cases these are purchased for speculative purposes rather than owner occupation, in anticipation of rapidly rising prices. As many as eight high-rise apartment blocks, containing nearly 6,200 apartments, were completed in Jakarta in 2012 alone. These included Menteng Square in central Jakarta, consisting of three towers with 1,600 apartments, and Green Palace in South Jakarta with 1,260 apartments (Colliers International 2012a). In addition, another seven high-rise apartment projects offering a total of almost 4,200 apartments have just been launched, the two biggest being Madison Park (1,400 apartments) and Metro Park 2 (1,200 apartments), both in West Jakarta. Another 10 large apartment buildings are currently under construction. According to Jones Lang LaSalle, 14,900 condominiums from 40 completed projects were expected to come onto the market in 2012 (*Jakarta Post*, 20 February 2012). Shopping malls and high-rise apartment buildings are also now being built in Jakarta's fringe areas, including Bekasi and Tangerang.

It is worth noting that the 1997–98 financial crisis was triggered in part by a bubble in the property sector. Nevertheless, many of today's major residential developers seem to be convinced that the property sector, especially the residential segment for both houses and apartments, will not experience a repeat of those events (Grazela 2013).

Large-scale residential areas, new towns and industrial estate development in fringe areas

A number of new towns and large residential developments have been built on the fringes of Jakarta since the early 1980s, in response to demand for modern, secure, quiet living environments (Leisch 2002). This has been motivated in part by developers' expectations of large and quick financial returns, but it also reflects changes in the global economic environment to allow capital to move freely across borders and sectors, including in the property sector (Douglass 2000). Among middle and upper-income Indonesians, the main reasons for living in these new towns are to enjoy a more secure living environment with higher-quality infrastructure, and to avoid the air pollution and congestion of the city centre while still retaining access to it for work and shopping.

Many individual private developers have been involved in new town developments in Jabodetabek, with the result that the towns are poorly linked to the existing large infrastructure system or even violate the spatial plans of the region's districts and cities (Firman 2009). Often, the towns are designed as 'gated communities', surrounded by walls separating them from existing local communities, since most of the new residents do not want to live in culturally and socially mixed areas for security reasons. The new towns are frequently equipped with golf courses, in turn intensifying the pressure for land conversion in the Jabodetabek region. But many of the houses in those towns stand vacant because the residents purchased them for speculative reasons rather than to meet their own accommodation needs.

By 2010, 33 large new town projects had been developed in Jabodetabek (Figure 15.2), most with areas ranging from 500 hectares (Paramount Land Development) to 8,000 hectares (Kapuk Naga, Salim Group), but some up to 30,000 hectares (Bukit Jonggol). In addition, a number of smaller towns have been developed in the hilly and temperate region straddling Bogor, Puncak and Cianjur. This is believed to have contributed to severe flooding in Jakarta during most rainy seasons, as the new towns have been built in a designated conservation area that serves as a water catchment.

Driven by both domestic and foreign direct investment, demand for industrial land in Jabodetabek has increased sharply (Hudalah and Firman 2012). Cumulative foreign investment in Indonesia, excluding oil and gas, reached $64.8 billion over the period 2000–04 alone, almost 60 per cent of it invested in Jabodetabek. By mid-decade, industrial estates in the region covered some 11,000 hectares. About 40 per cent of this was in the district of Bekasi, the site of the largest agglomeration of manufacturing activities in Indonesia (Colliers International 2005). Some of these estates were very large, including Cikarang Industrial Estate, Lippo City Industrial Park, Bekasi International Industrial Estate and MM 2100 Industrial Estate. By 2010, industrial estates in Jabodetabek had expanded further to cover about 18,000 hectares (Hudalah 2013).

Another 400 hectares of industrial estates were added in Jabodetabek in 2012. Almost 60 per cent of this land was turned over for use by automotive industries, underscoring the rapid growth of this industry in the capital city region. In 2012, land prices for industrial estates ranged from about $105.7 per square metre in the district of Bogor to $175.1 per square metre in the district of Bekasi (Colliers International 2012b).

With the demand for industrial land in the capital greatly exceeding supply, industrial estates have sprung up in the districts bordering

Figure 15.2   New residential developments in Jabodetabek, 2010

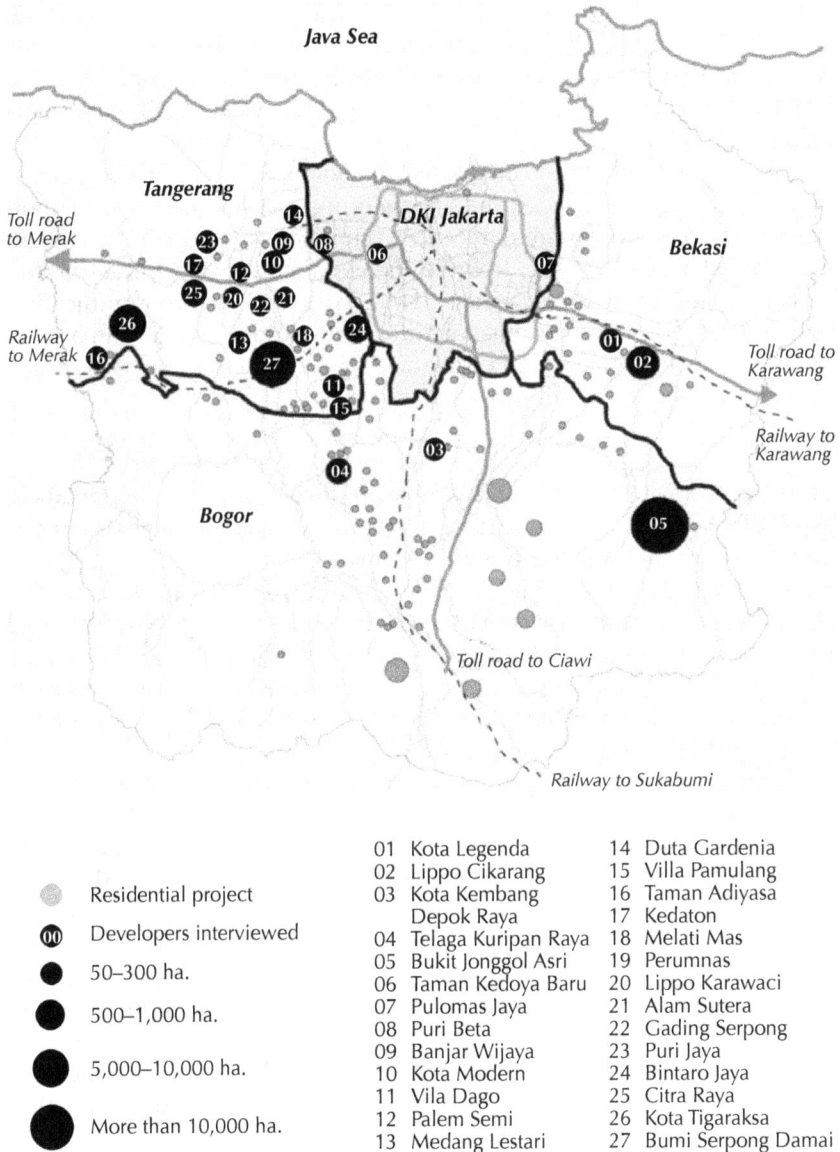

	01 Kota Legenda	14 Duta Gardenia
Residential project	02 Lippo Cikarang	15 Villa Pamulang
Developers interviewed	03 Kota Kembang Depok Raya	16 Taman Adiyasa
50–300 ha.	04 Telaga Kuripan Raya	17 Kedaton
500–1,000 ha.	05 Bukit Jonggol Asri	18 Melati Mas
5,000–10,000 ha.	06 Taman Kedoya Baru	19 Perumnas
More than 10,000 ha.	07 Pulomas Jaya	20 Lippo Karawaci
	08 Puri Beta	21 Alam Sutera
	09 Banjar Wijaya	22 Gading Serpong
	10 Kota Modern	23 Puri Jaya
	11 Vila Dago	24 Bintaro Jaya
	12 Palem Semi	25 Citra Raya
	13 Medang Lestari	26 Kota Tigaraksa
		27 Bumi Serpong Damai

Source: Based on Herlambang (2011).

Jabodetabek, notably Karawang in the east and Serang in the west, both officially outside Jabodetabek. In fact, Karawang now has the largest concentration of industrial estates in the wider capital region. In 2013, about 36 per cent of all industrial estates in Jabodetabek and surrounds were located in this district, with the next highest concentrations in the districts of Bekasi (26 per cent) and Serang (21 per cent) (Colliers International 2012b).

The various industrial centres in Jabodetabek are becoming increasingly diversified and specialized, intensifying the trend for the metropolitan region to become more polycentric (Hudalah et. al. 2013). At present, each industrial estate tends to build its own facilities and infrastructure – roads, water and waste-water treatment plants, telecommunication networks and so on – without overall coordination, resulting in a fragmented industrial complex (Hudalah 2013).

Transport development

The most pressing issue in infrastructure development in Jabodetabek, especially Jakarta city, is how to reduce traffic congestion. The provincial government of Jakarta has announced mass rapid transport (MRT) and monorail projects to respond to the transport problems in the city. The MRT is expected to improve Jakarta's public transport capacity, cut travel times, reduce the city's total transport-related carbon dioxide emissions and create job opportunities. It is to be integrated with other modes of transport that already exist in the city, to encourage a shift away from the use of private means of transportation.

Planning for the MRT project began in the early 1980s, based on the build–operate–transfer (BOT) model, but stopped in the late 1990s due to the severe economic crisis gripping Indonesia at the time. Work resumed in the mid-2000s, funded by a ¥120 billion loan package from the Japanese government through the Japan International Cooperation Agency (JICA). When finished, the MRT will have two parts, a north–south corridor and an east–west corridor. The north–south corridor will be constructed in two stages, with phase I connecting Lebak Bulus to Hotel Indonesia Circle (Bundaran H.I.), a distance of about 15 kilometres, and phase II extending the line from Hotel Indonesia Circle to Kampung Bandan. The east–west corridor, which is expected to become operational in 2027, is still in the feasibility study stage.

After a short review, the newly elected governor of Jakarta, Joko Widodo, agreed to list the MRT as a high-priority project in the 2013 provincial government budget. Construction was expected to start in 2013, with operations to begin in 2017. The project will be managed by PT Mass Rapid Transit Jakarta, a company owned by the Jakarta city government.

The planned monorail system for Jakarta city will have two lines: a Green line of about 14 kilometres operating in South Jakarta, and a Blue Line of about 10 kilometres connecting Kampung Melayu in East Jakarta to Tanah Abang in West Jakarta. Construction actually began in 2004, but stopped in 2008 due to financial constraints. The new Jakarta governor agreed to allow construction to recommence in 2013, with services scheduled to begin in 2016. When finished, the monorail is expected to carry about 275,000 passengers per day, each paying a fare of Rp 10,000 per trip. The project is being managed by a private consortium, PT Jakarta Monorail, with support from several foreign and other Indonesian companies. In addition, a consortium of five state-owned companies is planning a third and much longer monorail line connecting the suburb of Cibubur in East Jakarta to the Jakarta central business district, to serve about 192,000 passengers daily.

The monorail development in Jakarta has been contentious, with some non-government organizations arguing that it could cost as much as $808 million, whereas improvements to the Bus Rapid Transit and Bus Way systems could be made at a much lower capital cost and would require fewer subsidies. They are also sceptical about the long-run sustainability of the MRT project because of the high maintenance costs involved and the substantial potential burden on the Jakarta provincial government budget.

In a broader context, the Indonesian and Japanese governments have agreed to invest $24 billion in fast-tracking a number of high-priority infrastructure projects for Jabodetabek to improve the region's competitiveness in the Asian economy (Umezaki, n.d.). The projects for the capital listed in the national government's Masterplan for the Acceleration and Expansion of Indonesia's Economic Development 2011–2025 (MP3EI) include improving and expanding the port of Tanjung Priok; constructing a new international airport; building the Jakarta MRT; expanding Sukarno-Hatta Airport; upgrading the city's road network; improving the commuter railway system; developing new sources of clean water supply; constructing a solid waste treatment and disposal plant in West Java; and rebuilding a pumping station at Pluit in North Jakarta.

Floods and the potential impact of climate change

Jakarta is a low-lying coastal city, with some areas actually below sea level. The Jakarta delta is traversed by 13 streams flowing from the higher areas outside the city into Jakarta Bay. The city is vulnerable both to natural disasters such as floods and rising seawater, and to man-made problems caused by air and water pollution and the excessive extraction of groundwater (Firman et al. 2010). Jakarta is considered to be very vulnerable to climate change – one of the most vulnerable coastal cities in Southeast Asia (Yusuf and Francisco 2009).

Jakarta has always been prone to flooding, with the first major flood recorded in 1670 (Caljouw, Nas and Pratiwo 2005). Now, however, the city floods during almost every rainy season, and the intensity of floods has increased. Major flooding occurred in 2002, 2007 and 2013. The 2002 flood inundated more than 16,000 hectares, or about one-fifth of the city (Firman et al. 2010). The far worse 2007 flood submerged about two-fifths of Jakarta after four days of rain from 29 January to 2 February, interrupting regular activity, causing considerable damage to infrastructure and facilities (Padawangi 2012) and displacing about 430,000 people (Steinberg 2007). Such floods are particularly hard on vulnerable poor communities, especially those living along Jakarta's riverbanks.

The primary cause of the floods in Jakarta has been identified as the environmental degradation of the upstream water catchment areas of the Ciliwung and Cisadane rivers (Salim and Firman 2011). Other factors include the failure of land-use regulations to prevent development in conservation areas – especially water recharge areas – and land subsidence in many parts of the city due to excessive groundwater extraction. The rate of groundwater extraction in Jakarta reportedly increased from 17 million cubic metres per year in 1998 to 22.5 million cubic metres in 2007 (Firman et. al. 2010). In fact, the extraction of groundwater in Jakarta now exceeds aquifer recharge capabilities.

To help prevent flooding, the Dutch colonial government built canals in the east and west of the city (Banjir Kanal Timur and Banjir Kanal Barat). The central government and the Jakarta provincial government have continued to build canals in the independence era, especially under Jakarta governors Ali Sadikin (1966–77), Sutiyoso (1997–2007), Fauzi Bowo (2007–12) and Joko Widodo (2012–). It is obvious, however, that the city's problem with floods cannot be solved with canals alone. It should not be left to the Jakarta city government to implement the measures necessary to prevent major flooding in the city centre; other local governments in the Jabodetabek region, and also the central government, have a responsibility to implement an integrated water resource management plan for the region, because all have contributed to the unsustainable conversion and development of land in the important upstream areas, most notably in the Puncak area between Bogor and Cianjur.

According to Soehodho (2012), Jakarta city needs an integrated flood control strategy that would include optimizing the function of rivers and main channels; controlling flows from upstream areas through the recovery and development of ponds and reservoirs and the normalization of riverside environments; improving drainage systems; constructing dikes to anticipate rising sea levels; and increasing the supply of 'blue space' around the city's rivers. These engineering solutions are certainly very important for solving the flood problem in Jakarta, but there should also be a larger conceptual solution that includes governance and planning for urban and regional development in Jabodetabek as a whole.

Although it is not possible to say that climate change is the cause of sea-level rise and heavy rain in Jabodetabek, it is clear that Jakarta can expect to continue to experience climate-related disasters, especially flooding caused by rain and tides. It is projected that some areas of the city could be permanently inundated by 2050 if global warming continues on its current trajectory (Susandi 2009). Despite its importance, however, the issue of climate change is still largely misunderstood and neglected by the public at large, which is given very little information on such matters. At present the Jakarta city government does not have any concrete program to tackle the problems resulting from climate change, and there is no clear roadmap for mitigation and adaptation strategies to cope with the effects of climate change in Jakarta (Firman et. al. 2010).

The central and Jakarta provincial governments have in fact taken some measures to cope with flooding in Jakarta, including developing a mitigation program and an early warning system. However, these must be considered reactive rather than proactive attempts to respond to the problems resulting from climate change. Future efforts to deal with the effects of climate change on urban development should be framed in a long-term perspective, not just on an after-the fact basis. Also, the urban spatial plan for Jakarta needs to take greater account of the hazards facing the capital, including flooding due to high tides.

15.3 TOWARDS AN URBAN GOVERNANCE INSTITUTION FOR JABODETABEK

Both the central government and the Jakarta city government have done a great deal to respond to the problems of urban development in Jabodetabek, but without much success. One of the difficulties has been that no governance institution exists to handle urban problems in the region as a whole, in a comprehensive manner. Jabodetabek should be considered an integrated, compact urban region, rather than being managed in a fragmented way by the various local governments in the region. Laquian (2008: 19) has argued that inclusive development in Asia's mega-urban regions, including Jabodetabek, can be achieved by closely integrating urban and rural areas within the region; by including all levels of local government in planned development and governance schemes; and by integrating all urban infrastructure and services in area-wide networks.

Under the decentralization policy (Law 32/2004 on Regional Government), each local government in Indonesia, including in Jabodetabek, has the discretion to plan and implement development affecting its own region, without consulting neighbouring local governments. This situation has resulted in problems in supplying services that require cross-border partnerships, such as water supply and solid waste management.

Wielding their greatly increased powers under decentralization, local governments have been exploiting land, water and other natural resources in their areas ever more intensively in order to generate more own-source revenues (*pendapatan asli daerah*, PAD). Bogor and Cianjur districts, for example, continue to permit developers to build large housing estates and tourist resorts in the beautiful, scenic, temperate area of Puncak to the south of Jabodetabek (Firman 2009), even though this is suspected of causing intensified flooding in Jakarta. In a broader context, this situation reflects the fragmented and ineffective – even conflicting – approaches to development in the region, and the urgent need for an effective metropolitan governance institution to plan, manage and ensure the sustainability of such development (Firman 2008). Although not a new issue for Jabodetabek, or for other metropolitan areas in Indonesia, the need for an effective governance institution has become even more pressing under the new decentralization policy.

There is in fact already an institution in Jabodetabek whose main task is to coordinate and monitor development in the region: the Jabodetabek Development Cooperation Agency (Badan Kerjasama Pembangunan, BKSP). It was jointly established by the provincial governments of Jakarta and West Java in 1975, and later reinforced by Decree 29/1980 of the Minister of Home Affairs and Decree 125/1984 of the National Planning Minister. BKSP Jabodetabek is jointly headed by the governors of Jakarta, West Java and Banten, with an executive secretary appointed for five years in rotation by the home affairs minister on the recommendation of the respective provincial governments. As well as the three provincial governors, all heads of district and municipal governments (*bupati* and *walikota*) in the region are members. However, BKSP Jabodetabek has no authority to override the decisions made by the various member local governments. It is an ineffective and powerless body.

There are three main options to improve mega-urban governance in Jabodetabek (Firman 2008). The first is to establish a single authority that would include all provincial and local governments in the region, as in the greater Tokyo area (Vogel 2005). The second is to set up a two-tier regional municipality with legislative and executive functions, as in the greater Vancouver area in Canada. There, the metropolitan region is administered by a mayor who works in cooperation with a regional municipal council consisting of representatives of each municipality's council as well as directly elected councillors (Laquian 2005b). A third option would be to empower BKSP Jabodetabek, given its political acceptance as a coordinating forum by all provincial and local governments in the region.

The first option seems to be out of the question because it would create strong political tensions, particularly among the three provincial governments. In fact, when former Jakarta governor Sutiyoso proposed the formation of 'Megapolitan Jabodetabek', essentially in line with this option, many local leaders and officials in West Java and Banten opposed the idea, and even accused Sutiyoso of intending to bring parts of Bogor, Tangerang and Bekasi under the jurisdiction of Jakarta, with himself as governor or minister in charge of Jabodetabek development (Firman 2009). The second option also would not work in the Indonesian context because the country's amended Constitution does not recognize multi-tier regional municipalities. Therefore, the most viable option is to enhance the role and functions of BKSP Jabodetabek in order to make this institution work more effectively.

Law 29/2007 on the Government of the Special Capital Region of Jakarta stipulates that the Jakarta provincial government can establish a partnership with the provincial governments of Banten and West Java, together with all local governments neighbouring Jakarta city, to plan, use, monitor and control spatial development (*tata ruang*) in Jakarta city and the surrounding areas. In addition to spatial development, there are three other areas of concern for urban governance in the region: watershed planning and implementation; solid waste management; and transport (Salim and Firman 2011). It should also be kept in mind that the involvement of the central government is very important for Jabodetabek urban governance, not only because the management of mega-cities, particularly the capital, 'requires a voice at the highest level of government' (von Einsiedel 1999: 135-6, cited in Talukder 2006: 101), but also because infrastructure development in the region will require huge financial outlays that are beyond the capacity of the provincial and local governments in the region to supply.

The most suitable model for urban governance in Jabodetabek may be a mixed model in which all levels of government - central, provincial and local - play an important role (Firman 2009). In this model, BKSP Jabodetabek would be given the authority to plan and develop major infrastructure for the whole region, including spatial development, watershed management, solid waste management and transport, and the provincial governments would consequently relinquish their authorities over those functions. This would not mean establishing a new level of government. Rather, it would mean enhancing the authority of the existing but powerless BKSP, within the areas permitted by Law 32/2004 (which is currently being revised) and Law 29/2007, to enable implementation of a development plan that is relevant to the challenges of Jabodetabek development, while allowing the provincial and local governments to retain their other authorities over socio-economic development and public services. The central government would be expected to contribute financial and technical expertise. However, the main necessity is for all heads of governments in the region to display leadership and a willingness to cooperate to secure the best long-term outcomes for the greater Jakarta area. In short, Jabodetabek needs to be developed as a compact urban region, rather than being considered a collection of individual entities where development decisions can be made for the benefit of each district or municipality.

15.4   CONCLUDING REMARKS

The mega-urbanization of Jabodatebek has proceeded at a faster pace over the last decade than in the 1980–2000 period, but the process seems largely uncontrolled. Recent development in the region has been characterized by high urban population growth, intensified land-use conversion, the growth of apartment, condominium and other infrastructure projects in Jakarta city, and the spread of new towns, large-scale residential areas and industrial estates in the fringe areas. The region is vulnerable to natural disasters such as floods and rising sea levels, and to man-made disasters such as land subsidence caused by the excessive extraction of groundwater and illness caused by air and water pollution. More generally, the patterns of recent development in Jabodetabek reflect how liberalization of the economy has affected patterns of mega-urban development, and how Indonesia's new decentralization policy has resulted in urban fragmentation in the region (Bunnell and Miller 2011).

One of the biggest challenges in Jabodetabek mega-urban development is to build an appropriate mechanism of governance that can optimize the potential of the region to improve its competitiveness and the quality of life of its citizens, responding to the trend of fragmentation of the Jabodetabek urban region. The most obvious option is to enhance the role and functions of BKSP Jabodetabek to make it more effective in coordinating and supervising development, as all provincial and local governments in the region are members and recognize its existence as a coordinating forum.

The first step is to give BKSP Jabodetabek stronger powers to plan and develop major infrastructure for the whole region. Although the three provincial governments in the region would need to cede authority over those functions, this would not mean establishing a new level of government, which would be against the Constitution. The involvement of the central government in Jabodetabek urban governance is also critical, not only because Jakarta is the national capital, but also because the provincial and local governments in the region have only a limited capacity to finance infrastructure.

REFERENCES

Anh, D.N. (2008) 'The mega-urban transformations of Ho Chi Minh City in the era of Doi Moi renovation', in G.W. Jones and M. Douglass (eds) *Mega-urban Regions in Pacific Asia: Urban Dynamics in a Global Era*, National University of Singapore, Singapore.

Bird, R. and E. Slack (2007) 'An approach to metropolitan governance and finance', *Environment and Planning C: Government and Policy*, 25: 729–55.

Bunnell, T. and M.A. Miller (2011) 'Jakarta in post-Suharto Indonesia: decentralisation, neo-liberalism and global city aspiration', *Space and Polity*, 15(1): 35–48.

Caljouw, M., P.J.M. Nas and Pratiwo (2005) 'Flooding in Jakarta: towards a blue city with improved water management', *Bijdragen tot de Taal-, Land- en Volkenkunde*, 161(4): 454–84.

Colliers International (2005) 'Jakarta property market', Colliers International, Jakarta, September.

Colliers International (2012a) 'Research and forecast report: Jakarta apartment market, 2nd quarter 2012', Colliers International, Jakarta.

Colliers International (2012b) 'Research and forecast report: Jakarta industrial market, 2nd quarter, 2012', Colliers International, Jakarta.

Douglass, M. (2000) 'Mega-urban regions and world city formation: globalization, the economic crisis, and urban policy issues in Asia Pacific', *Urban Studies*, 37: 2,315–36.

Douglass, M. and G.W. Jones (2008) 'The morphology of mega-urban regions expansion', in G.W. Jones and M. Douglass (eds) *Mega-urban Regions in Pacific Asia: Urban Dynamics in a Global Era*, National University of Singapore, Singapore.

Dupont, V. (2006) 'Conflicting stakes and governance in the peripheries of large Indian metropolises: an introduction', *Cities*, 24(2): 89–94.

Firman, T. (2004) 'New town development in Jakarta metropolitan region: a perspective of spatial segregation', *Habitat International*, 28: 344–68.

Firman, T. (2008) 'In search of a governance institution model for Jakarta metropolitan area (JMA) under Indonesia's new decentralization policy: old problems, new challenges', *Public Administration and Development*, 28(4): 280–90.

Firman, T. (2009) 'The continuity and change in mega-urbanization in Indonesia: a survey of Jakarta–Bandung region (JBR) development', *Habitat International*, 33: 327–39.

Firman, T. (2010) 'Impact of climate change on Jakarta', *Jakarta Post*, 9 October.

Firman, T. (2012) 'Demographic patterns of Indonesia's urbanization, 2000–2010: continuity and change at the macro level', paper presented at the Plano-Cosmo International Conference, Bandung Institute of Technology, Bandung, 8–9 November.

Firman, T., B. Kombaitan and P. Pradono (2007) 'The dynamics of Indonesia's urbanization, 1980–2006', *Urban Policy and Research*, 25(4): 413–34.

Firman, T., I.M. Surbakti, I.C. Idroes and H.A. Simarmata (2010) 'Potential climate-change related vulnerabilities in Jakarta: challenges and current status', *Habitat International*, 30: 400–405.

Freire, M. (2007) 'Sustainable cities: the role of local governance in managing change', paper presented at the conference, A Global Look at Urban and Regional Governance: The State–Market–Civic Nexus, Emory University, Atlanta, 18–19 January.

Grazela, M. (2013) 'House, apartment prices continue to rise but bubble unlikely', *Jakarta Post*, 22 July.

Herlambang, S. (2010) 'On city commercialization: a preliminary research', paper presented at International Colloquium 2010: The Strategy and the Concept for Sustainable Future of Jakarta, Tarumanagara University, Jakarta.

Herlambang, S. (2011) 'Profil pengembangan kota baru di Jabodetabek, 1985–2010' [Profile of new town development in Jabodetabek, 1985–2010], Power-point presentation to a discussion organized by *Kompas Daily*, Jakarta, 2 July.

Hudalah, D. (2013) 'Industrial boom in greater Jakarta and inclusive development', *Jakarta Post*, 9 March.

Hudalah, D. and T. Firman (2012) 'Beyond property: industrial estates and post-suburban transformation in Jakarta metropolitan region', *Cities*, 29: 40–48.

Hudalah, D., D. Viantari, T. Firman and J. Woltjer (2013) 'Industrial land development and manufacturing deconcentration in greater Jakarta', *Urban Geography*, 34(7): 950–71.

Hugo, G. (2006) 'Population development and the urban outlook for Southeast Asia', in T. Wong, B.J. Shaw and K. Goh (eds) *Challenging Sustainability: Urban Development and Change in Southeast Asia*, Marshal Cavendish Academic, Singapore.

Jones, G.W. (2008) 'Comparative dynamics of the six mega-urban regions', in G.W. Jones and M. Douglass (eds) *Mega-urban Regions in Pacific Asia: Urban Dynamics in a Global Era*, National University of Singapore, Singapore.

Laquian, A.A. (2005a) 'Metropolitan governance reform in Asia', *Public Administration and Development*, 25: 307–15.

Laquian, A.A. (2005b) *Beyond Metropolis: The Planning and Governance of Asia's Mega-urban Regions*, Woodrow Wilson Center Press, Washington DC, and Johns Hopkins University Press, Baltimore.

Laquian, A.A. (2008) 'The planning and governance of Asian mega-urban regions', paper presented at the United Nations Expert Group Meeting on Population Distribution, Urbanization, International Migration and Development, New York, 21–23 January.

Leisch, H. (2002) 'Structures and functions of private new towns in Jabotabek', in P.J.M. Nas (ed.) *The Indonesian Town Revisited*, LIT Verlag, Münster.

McGee, T. (1995) 'Retrofitting the emerging mega-urban regions of ASEAN: an overview', in T.G. McGee and I. Robinson (eds) *The Mega-urban Regions of Southeast Asia*, University of British Columbia Press, Vancouver.

McGee, T. (2005) 'Distinctive urbanization in the peri-urban regions of East and Southeast Asia: renewing the debates', *Jurnal Perencanaan Wilayah dan Kota*, 16(1): 39–55.

McGee, T. (2011) 'Deconstructing the mega-city: a case study of the Jakarta mega-urban region (Jabodetabek) in the first decade of the 21st century', unpublished paper, Kyoto.

Padawangi, R. (2012) 'The right to flood-free homes: urban floods, spatial justice and social movements in Jakarta, Indonesia', in J. Widodo, J. Rosemann, B.L. Low and A. Gonzales-Brun (eds) *Global Visions: Risks and Opportunities for the Urban Planet*, National University of Singapore, Singapore.

Salim, W. (2013) 'Urban development and spatial planning of greater Jakarta', Powerpoint presentation to Forum Komunikasi Pembangunan Indonesia, Jakarta, 18 March.

Salim, W. and T. Firman (2011) 'Governing the Jakarta city–region: history, challenges, risks and strategies', in S. Hamnett and D. Forbes (eds) *Planning Asian Cities: Risks and Resilience*, Routledge, London.

Sit, V.F.-S. (2005) 'China's extended metropolitan regions', *International Development Planning Review*, 27(3): 297–331.

Soehodho, S. (2012) 'Balancing economic growth and environmental sustainability', Powerpoint presentation by the Deputy Governor for Industry, Trade and Transportation, Jakarta Capital City Government, to the 11th Plenary Meeting of the Asian Network of Major Cities 21 (ANMC21), 30 June.

Steinberg, F. (2007) 'Jakarta: environmental problems and sustainability', *Habitat International*, 31: 354–65.

Suryadjaja, R. (2012) 'Jakarta's tourism evolution: shopping center as urban tourism', Powerpoint presentation to the 5th International Forum on Urbanism, Barcelona, 25–27 February.

Susandi, A. (2009) 'Integration of adaptive planning across economic sectors', paper presented at the NWP Technical Workshop on Integration of Approaches to Adaptation Planning, Bangkok, 12–14 October.

Talukder, S.H. (2006) 'Managing megacities: a case study of metropolitan governance for Dhaka', PhD dissertation, Murdoch University, Perth.

Umezaki, S. (n.d.) 'Infrastructure development in Indonesia and the way forward', Economic Research Institute for ASEAN and East Asia, Jakarta.

Vogel, R.K. (2005) 'Decentralization and urban governance: reforming Tokyo metropolitan government', in B.A. Ruble, R.E. Stren, J.S. Tulchin and D.H. Varat (eds) *Urban Governance around the World*, Woodrow Wilson International Center for Scholars, Washington DC.

von Einsiedel, I.N. (1999) 'Managing mega-cities of Asia Pacific: governance and institutional challenges', *Asia-Pacific Development Monitor*, 1(1), Asia-Pacific Development Centre, Kuala Lumpur.

Webster, D. (2001) 'Inside out: peri-urbanization in China', unpublished paper, Asia-Pacific Research Center, Stanford University, Palo Alto.

Wong, T. (2006) 'Achieving a sustainable urban form? An investigation of the Kuala Lumpur mega-urban region', in T. Wong, B.J. Shaw and K. Goh (eds) *Challenging Sustainability: Urban Development and Change in Southeast Asia*, Marshal Cavendish Academic, Singapore.

World Bank (2013) 'Urbanization beyond municipal boundaries: nurturing economics and connecting peri-urban areas in India', World Bank, Washington DC.

Xu, J. and A.G.O. Yeh (2011a) 'Governance and planning of mega-city regions: diverse processes and reconstituted state spaces', in J. Xu and A.G.O. Yeh (eds) *Governance and Planning of Mega-city Regions: An International Comparative Perspective*, Routledge, New York.

Xu, J. and A.G.O. Yeh (2011b) 'Coordinating the fragmented mega-city regions in China: state reconstruction and regional strategic planning', in J. Xu and A.G.O. Yeh (eds) *Governance and Planning of Mega-city Regions: An International Comparative Perspective*, Routledge, New York.

Yusuf, A.A. and H. Francisco (2009) 'Climate change vulnerability mapping for Southeast Asia', Economy and Environment Program for Southeast Asia (EEPSEA), Singapore.

16 Challenges of implementing logistics reform in Indonesia

Henry Sandee, Nanda Nurridzki and
Mohamad Adhi Prakoso Dipo

16.1 INTRODUCTION

The rural hinterlands of Medan in North Sumatra and Pontianak in West Kalimantan are known for growing lots of oranges. You can find oranges from those areas in supermarkets in Jakarta and Surabaya, although their market share is limited because of strong competition from countries such as China. The main reason for this is that trade logistics costs in Indonesia are high – so high that it is cheaper to ship oranges to Jakarta from China (and even the United States) than from Medan and Pontianak. The cost of shipping a container from China to Jakarta is about $400, but as much as $600 from Pontianak. A study by the World Bank (2010) found that 70 per cent of the difference in the prices of staple agricultural commodities across the Indonesian archipelago was explained by a region's degree of remoteness. Essentially this reflects the poor state of logistics, especially the low quality of transport infrastructure. The distance from the large industrial estates in Cikarang in West Java to the port of Tanjung Priok in Jakarta, and from the industrial estates in Pasir Gudang to the port of Tanjung Pelepas in Malaysia, is more or less the same: about 55 kilometres. However, there is a substantial difference in the cost of transporting containers from these areas to the ports. In Indonesia, it costs about $750 to transport a container from Cikarang to Tanjung Priok, but in Malaysia it costs only $450 to transport a container from Pasir Gudang to Tanjung Pelepas.

The Indonesian government recognizes the importance of efficient transport networks to promote inclusive economic development. As a huge archipelago, the country depends on efficient, affordable and reliable shipping services to glue the nation together. Seeing itself more and more as a 'maritime economy', Indonesia has prepared both a Shipping Law and a Port Master Plan in recent years. The importance of toll roads and highways to bring down land transport costs has also been recognized. For example, when the toll road between Surabaya and Jakarta is finished, it is estimated that travel time between the two cities will fall from 18 to eight hours.

In recent years, the issue of logistics has attracted increased attention. Ministries have opened logistics directorates, universities are offering bachelor and master degrees in logistics, and the number of round tables, conferences and seminars on this topic has tripled. The most important development may well be the government's National Logistics Blueprint, set out in Presidential Decree 26/2012. Its motto is for the country's logistics system to be 'domestically integrated and globally connected for economic development and social welfare'. The blueprint presents a long-term strategy and action plan to strengthen the country's transport network. It recognizes the importance of both regulatory reform and better infrastructure to achieve its goal of lower logistics costs and more reliable transport services throughout the archipelago. Implementing the blueprint is a huge undertaking, involving both the public and private sectors, and central as well as local government agencies.

This chapter analyses the challenges Indonesia faces as its attempts to reduce logistics costs. We first provide a snapshot of Indonesia's current logistics performance and draw some comparisons with neighbouring countries (sections 16.2 and 16.3). Next, we describe the main features of the National Logistics Blueprint (section 16.4). We then draw on two case studies in particular – the port of Tanjung Priok in Jakarta (section 16.5) and the cattle industry in Sumbawa (section 16.6) – to highlight the enormous challenges in achieving logistics reform. These include the need to synchronize the involvement of various line ministries and agencies, to harness the participation of the private sector, to select priorities given limited resources and to coordinate the activities of central and regional authorities.

16.2   INDONESIA'S LOGISTICS PERFORMANCE IN REGIONAL PERSPECTIVE

Good trade logistics are a vital prerequisite for a nation to compete internationally and to supply domestic markets efficiently. Trade logistics involve a wide range of elements, including transport infrastructure, cargo consolidation and warehousing, border clearance and in-country distribution and payment systems. The performance and quality of customs, trade-related infrastructure, inland transit services, logistics services, information systems and port efficiency are all critical factors determining a country's ability to trade goods and services on time and at a low cost. Logistics is not only about cost, but also about the reliability and timeliness of delivery (Arvis et al. 2012).

The current focus on trade logistics is clearly related to the growing importance of global production networks. The steps to advance economic integration within ASEAN add a regional dimension to the importance of this debate. Firms are repositioning themselves to find the best locations to serve regional markets now that trade barriers within ASEAN are being reduced (Findlay 2011). A recent survey found that, when considering whether to stay in or locate to Indonesia, Japanese entrepreneurs were bothered not so much by Indonesia's high logistics costs as by the unreliability of delivery (JTPA 2012). Just-in-time production systems are increasingly important in production networks that frequently include up to 10 countries. A production system is only as strong as its weakest link, and for many businesspeople, the weakest link is the growing uncertainty about when goods imported into Indonesia will reach the factory floor.

There are various indicators comparing Indonesia's trade logistics performance with that of its neighbours. Infrastructure is one of the most important, because good infrastructure is the basis of a solid logistics system. A paper by Seneviratne and Sun (2013) compares infrastructure in five ASEAN economies: Indonesia, Malaysia, the Philippines, Thailand and Vietnam. The authors observe that although economic activity in these countries has rebounded to the levels observed before the Asian financial crisis, in most, investment in infrastructure has never fully recovered. This is certainly true for Indonesia, where infrastructure investment as a share of GDP has remained around 3 per cent, compared with pre-crisis levels of around 7 per cent (World Bank 2013). In practice, this means that the port of Tanjung Priok in Jakarta is using the same port infrastructure and access roads as five years ago, despite a doubling of the number of containers.

Seneviratne and Sun (2013) construct quantitative and qualitative indexes to compare infrastructure in the five ASEAN countries. They concentrate on three key basic infrastructure sectors: communications, power and roads. The indexes suggest that Malaysia and Thailand have better infrastructure, both in quantity and quality, than the other countries. Indonesia performs worst on the infrastructure quantity index and the Philippines worst on the infrastructure quality index. Both countries are archipelagos, where the main challenge is to improve connectivity between islands. In both, one can find many impediments to competitive manufacturing, including production and processing facilities located on different islands with poor sea transport infrastructure, and a restrictive regulatory regime.

The Logistics Performance Index (LPI) published by the World Bank measures a wider set of indicators of logistics performance across 155 countries. It is based on primary data collected from express carrier companies and freight forwarders involved in importing and exporting. In the case of Indonesia, the majority of respondents are international service providers that do business at the ports and airports of Jakarta and Surabaya. So far the results have been published in 2007, 2010 and 2012 (Arvis et al. 2007, 2010, 2012), with the next edition slated to appear in 2014.

Although the 2010 and 2012 reports focus solely on international performance, the 2007 report also included a number of quantitative and qualitative indicators of the domestic logistics environment (Arvis et al. 2007: 1). In 2007, Indonesia's ranking on the overall LPI was 43 out of 155 countries. However, its ranking on domestic logistics costs was much worse (92), reflecting the poor state of intra-island and inter-island connectivity.

The quality of domestic logistics – a very important indicator for an archipelagic country such as Indonesia – was dropped from subsequent editions of the LPI. Since 2010, the index has been calculated from six indicators: logistics competence of service providers; tracking and tracing; timeliness of delivery; availability of international shipments when required; functioning of border agencies; and quality of infrastructure. The LPI provides information on the import–export trade logistics performance of both the public and private sectors. Typical indicators of public sector performance would be the efficiency of border control agencies and the quality of infrastructure. The other indicators are in the private sector domain, but performance would of course be partly subject to the regulatory regime.

Figure 16.1 suggests that Indonesia's logistics performance has been catching up with that of its neighbours. The country's ranking improved by 16 places, from 75 in 2010 to 59 in 2012, while those of several neighbouring countries worsened or remained stagnant. Nevertheless, Indonesia's absolute score remains lower than those of countries such as Thailand, Malaysia and Vietnam.

Figure 16.2 shows that the quality of infrastructure remains a weak link in the performance of Indonesia's logistics sector. High costs and time losses are incurred due to congested and poorly maintained roads, ports, airports and so on. The rankings of several neighbouring countries also dropped between 2010 and 2012, suggesting that they have not been able to maintain appropriate levels of infrastructure either. But

Figure 16.1   Change in ranking on Logistics Performance Index, selected Asian countries, 2010–12

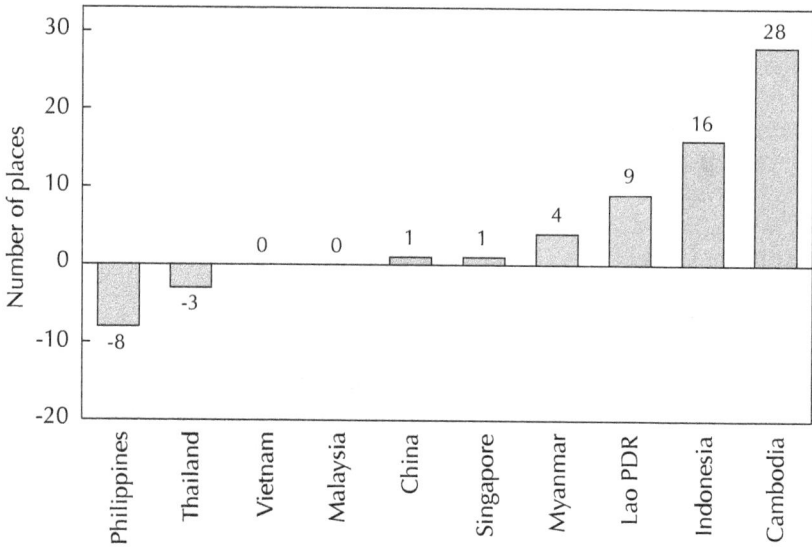

Source: Arvis et al. (2010, 2012).

Figure 16.2   Change in ranking on infrastructure component of the Logistics Performance Index, selected Asian countries, 2010–12

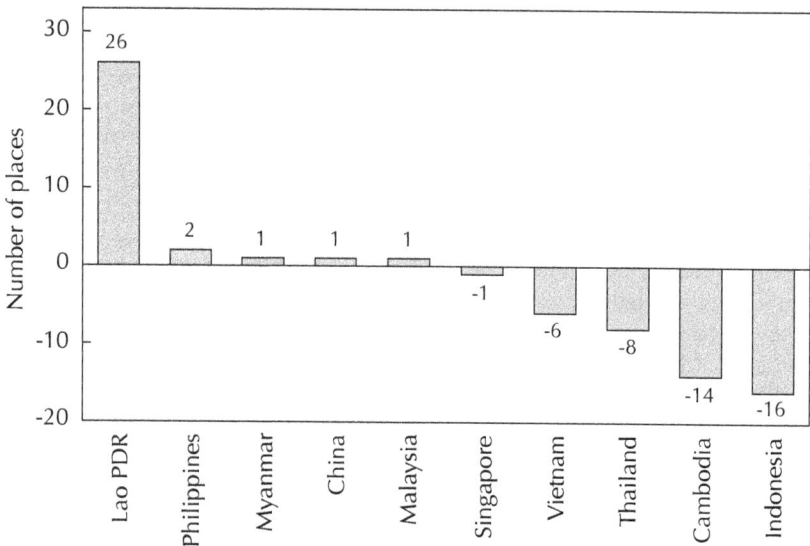

Source: Arvis et al. (2010, 2012).

Indonesia's ranking dropped the most, from 69th place in 2010 to 85th in 2012. Clearly, to improve its trade logistics and competitiveness, Indonesia needs to do much more to improve its infrastructure.

16.3 A CLOSER LOOK AT INDONESIA'S LOGISTICS PERFORMANCE

Because of the importance of trade logistics for competitiveness and a more efficient domestic distribution of goods, many countries have started to design logistics strategies and prepare annual overviews that make it possible to measure progress. Indonesia launched its first annual 'State of logistics' report in September 2013 (ITB 2013). The report includes a first attempt to estimate logistics costs as a percentage of GDP. Owing to the limited availability of data, the estimate is based chiefly on companies that are listed on the Jakarta Stock Exchange and that publish information annually on transport, inventory and administration costs. The estimates suggest that logistics costs declined slightly between 2004 and 2011, from 27.6 per cent to 24.6 per cent of GDP (ITB 2013: 16). Transport costs, the most important component, comprise almost 50 per cent of overall logistics costs. Land transport costs make up over 72 per cent of total transport costs, pointing to the current dominance of trucking to move goods in Indonesia. Inventory costs are another major component of logistics costs. They make up more than 30 per cent of total logistics costs, which is high in comparison with many neighbouring countries. This is most likely explained by the unreliability of delivery in Indonesia, which forces firms to hold larger stocks.

In addition to the published studies, there is a body of unpublished evidence on the state of trade logistics in Indonesia. Much of it derives from the bi-monthly logistics roundtables organized by the World Bank in collaboration with the Chamber of Commerce and Industry (Kamar Dagang dan Industri, Kadin) and the Ministry of Trade in Jakarta. Based on the World Bank's Trade Logistics Roundtables 2009–2010 (World Bank 2010), Wihardja (2013: 6–7) summarizes some of this evidence as follows.

- The price of a bag of cement in certain parts of Papua is 20 times that in Java. The price of a gallon of water in Medan is double that in Jakarta. Oranges from China are cheaper than oranges from Pontianak (Kalimantan). High domestic transport costs are the main reason for these price differences.
- About 70 per cent of the difference in rice prices across provinces can be explained by the degree of remoteness, which in turn is a reflection of poor logistics and inadequate transport infrastructure.

- The availability and prices of basic commodities fluctuate widely in remote areas. For instance, gasoline prices in Kisar island (Maluku) are three times higher in the rainy season than in the dry season.
- High-quality products with good commercial potential, such as prawns from Eastern Indonesia, cannot be processed commercially in Java, while commodities such as pineapples are canned abroad because it is cheaper to transport them to Malaysia than to ship them to Java.
- Indonesia's manufacturing sector is poorly integrated with international production networks because of the country's unreliable transport network and high logistics costs.
- The costs of transporting containers from Jakarta's main industrial sites are double those in Malaysia and Thailand.
- Some 10 per cent of Indonesian exports are delayed in Indonesian ports and so do not reach regional transhipment ports on time. Ships bound for local destinations are frequently delayed.
- In some export sectors, such as cocoa, rubber and coffee, more than 40 per cent of total logistics and transport costs are incurred before shipment, in inland transport and other expenses.
- Approximately 70 per cent of freight in Indonesia is transported by truck. A majority of the trucks on the road in Indonesia are old and poorly maintained.
- A truck making a round trip from Bandung to Jakarta is likely to spend up to 75 per cent of its time parked, due to customs processes, warehouse delays and lift-on/lift-off queues.
- Trade and transport logistics still mainly use paper-based systems; this increases logistics costs and provides scope for illegal fees.
- National and regional authorities continue to issue laws and regulations without any clear assessment of their impact on trade flows and logistics costs.

The poor state of inter-island logistics is evident from the above list. This is also apparent when one compares the cost of transporting a 20-foot container by sea to a number of different domestic destinations and to Singapore. According to the World Bank (2011: 36), it costs 2.7 times as much to transport such a container to Padang than to transport it to Singapore, 1.7 times as much to transport it to Makassar, 1.4 times as much to transport it to Jayapura and 1.3 times as much to transport it to Balikpapan. The cost for passengers to fly between the same destinations shows the opposite pattern: it is relatively much cheaper for a passenger to fly from Jakarta to a domestic destination than to fly to Singapore. Air transport costs have declined in Indonesia following liberalization of the sector and the increase in competition between airlines (World Bank

2011: 36). The maritime sector in Indonesia is characterized by free entry and freely determined fees. Nevertheless, there is a lack of competition on most routes to Eastern Indonesia, contributing to high costs. In general, the costs of domestic shipping are significantly higher than international shipping costs.

16.4   THE NATIONAL LOGISTICS BLUEPRINT

Over the last few years, Indonesia has released a number of mutually supporting, and sometimes overlapping, policy documents that are all aimed at improving intra-island, inter-island and international connectivity. They are intended to fit into the overall umbrella of the ambitious Masterplan for the Acceleration and Expansion of Indonesia's Economic Development 2011–2025 (MP3EI).

The National Logistics Blueprint issued in 2012 is one of these supporting documents. The main areas of action advocated by the blueprint are regulatory reform to facilitate the upgrading of infrastructure and to make the business environment more conducive to lower logistics costs; upgrading the quality of human resources in logistics; strengthening the competitiveness of domestic service providers; and promoting the use of information and communications technology throughout the logistics sector.

The blueprint includes a detailed matrix of actions to be taken by coordinating and line ministries, agencies and institutions. These are also being integrated into the country's mid-term development plans to ensure that the proposed measures are implemented and monitored, and that they are adequately funded.

The National Logistics Blueprint is a product of public–private consultation, with many Indonesian thinktanks and universities involved in its drafting, and many private sector leaders and academic experts currently participating in its implementation. To gain the cooperation and involvement of regional governments, the government's national logistics team has also signed memorandums of understanding with some district governments. There is awareness across the board that implementing logistics reform is a multi-faceted task that requires substantial horizontal and vertical coordination among government bodies, and between government and the private sector. Below, we discuss some recent examples showing the enormous challenges of bringing about lasting logistics reform, focusing in particular on intra-island and inter-island connectivity.

16.5   CONNECTING TANJUNG PRIOK PORT WITH JAKARTA'S INDUSTRIAL AREAS

Proposals to improve operational efficiency

The port of Tanjung Priok in Jakarta handles the majority of Indonesia's container imports and exports. The throughput of the port grew from the equivalent of 3.7 million containers in 2007 to close to 7 million containers in 2013. The port is congested, mainly because no substantial investments to improve productivity and to start planning for an extension were made for many years. The port is operated and regulated by a state-owned monopoly that, until recently, was more interested in seeking rents from existing operations than in investing in new ones. The port provides a good example of why investment in infrastructure has remained so low for so many years in Indonesia.

Law 17/2008 on Shipping attempted to change this situation by increasing competition at the port and separating the port regulator from the port operator. One of the key tasks of the regulator was to prepare tenders for investments in the upgrading and expansion of the port and its terminals. This process was delayed by the lack of institutional capacity of the regulator, which had no experience in tenders and literally had to start from scratch. Although new terminals are now being constructed, it will take another three to five years before they become operational. Also, the capacity of the new container-handling facilities to reduce logistics costs will depend on improvements to access roads linking the port with industrial areas.

Tanjung Priok handles freight to and from the industrial estates situated to the east, west and south of Jakarta, as well as the city itself.[1] The industrial conglomeration to the east of the city is Indonesia's largest manufacturing zone; it alone was responsible for over 60 per cent of the port's total throughput in 2011 (ITB 2013: 40). Clearly, to reduce delays and congestion at Tanjung Priok, it is important to improve the operational efficiency of the port. However, given the growing importance of the eastern spoke, the government has also been trying to increase the freight-handling capacity of Cikarang Dry Port, situated in the industrial heartland to the east of the capital. Cikarang is intended to serve as an extension to Tanjung Priok, with the two ports offering integrated logistics facilities and services. This means that freight can be transported directly from Tanjung Priok to the dry port, where it would be subject to the usual requirements for clearance by border agencies, and payments.

---

1   See Figure 6.1 in ITB (2013: 40) for a schematic representation of the 'hub and spoke' concept for connecting Tanjung Priok and Cikarang ports with Jakarta's industrial areas.

Eventually this should allow importers to obtain their goods in just a few days, and escape the congestion at Tanjung Priok. This model has proved successful for Lam Chae Bang port near Bangkok, which uses a nearby dry port to handle more than 25 per cent of imported containers.

The major short-term challenges for the national logistics team are to improve the operational efficiency of the Jakarta port and to optimize the use of Cikarang Dry Port. Both measures are of great importance to reduce dwell time – that is, the time between a container being unloaded at, and released from, a port. The length and also variability of dwell time is of great concern to the business community. Both make it necessary for firms to invest more in inventory, which drives up costs. Reducing dwell time is a priority for many Indonesian ministries and agencies, and has even become a key performance indicator for specific departments. In December 2012, the Coordinating Minister for Economic Affairs said that the government aimed to reduce dwell time to three days by early 2014, from around six days at the time. The need to reduce dwell time in order to boost Indonesia's competitiveness and reduce logistics costs was reinforced by the president himself in a speech marking a new phase of construction at Tanjung Priok in March 2013 (Osman 2013).

Working with the national logistics team, the various government committees set up to improve Indonesia's logistics performance have agreed on a number of proposals, including the need to:

- establish an integrated clearance system encompassing customs, food and drug, and quarantine inspections;
- facilitate electronic payments and full use of a paperless, one-stop national single window to make payments and meet import clearance requirements;
- increase the number of importers with priority-lane status, allowing them to submit clearances after their containers have left port;
- introduce round-the-clock services to make use of ports' unused capacity at night and on weekends; and
- promote Cikarang Dry Port as an alternative to Tanjung Priok for the clearance of imported containers.

Performance in improving operational efficiency

Figure 16.3 depicts dwell time for the Jakarta International Container Terminal in 2012 and 2013.[2] It shows that, despite all the effort directed to

---

2 The Jakarta International Container Terminal is the largest and most advanced container terminal at Tanjung Priok, handling more than 70 per cent of its container traffic. It is safe to assume that dwell time at other terminals is worse.

Figure 16.3   Dwell time at Jakarta International Container Terminal, 2012–13

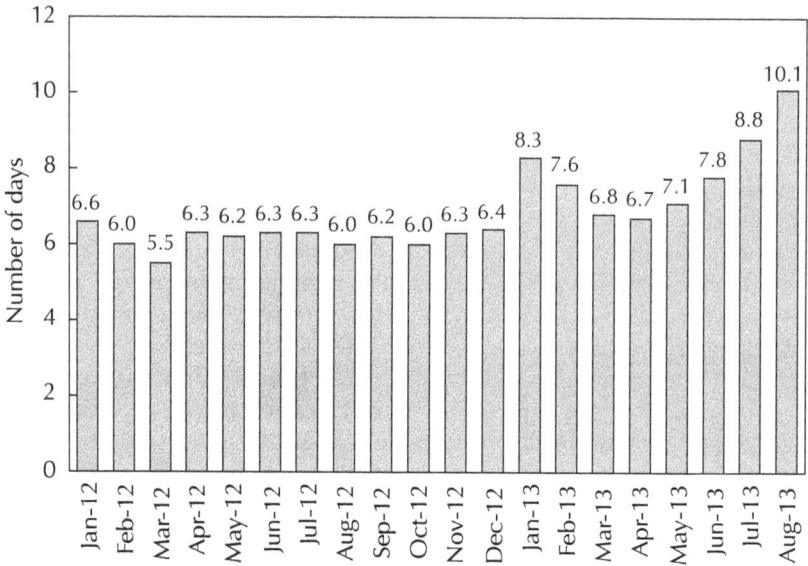

Source: Jakarta International Container Terminal.

reducing dwell time, it has actually increased since mid-2013. By August it was more than 10 days, or twice the number of days needed to release containers from Lam Chae Bang port near Bangkok.

Why has dwell time increased despite the priority given to logistics reform? Of course, part of the increase may be considered a 'good sign'; it signals that the economy is expanding, putting Indonesia's current port facilities under strain. However, there is also evidence that agencies are finding it hard to hand over their powers, making it difficult to integrate clearance facilities. This is holding up the roll-out of the national single window to facilitate online clearance and payments, which is currently behind schedule.

Pre-clearance procedures – the requirement to complete all paper-work and make all payments before obtaining customs clearance – are a major factor in the longer dwell time. Customs clearance itself is quite fast; this is also generally true for the post-clearance process, covering the time needed to pick up a container from the port once customs clearance has been obtained.

Tanjung Priok is probably the only port in the ASEAN region that has not yet increased the number of importers with priority-lane status. Many countries consider this to be an important strategy to improve the operational efficiency of ports. However, in Indonesia customs authorities argue that fewer than 100 of 10,000 importers fulfil the requirements to be placed in this category. Companies, in turn, complain that the procedure for requesting priority-lane status is so cumbersome that many do not want to apply.

Another explanation for the longer dwell time at Tanjung Priok is the increase in the number of time-consuming physical inspections of goods. The proportion of red-lane inspections actually increased in the latter part of 2013, due to new regulations issued by the Ministry of Trade. These require firms that import semi-finished goods to set up and register new companies if a portion of those goods will be sold to other companies in Indonesia. These 'new' importing firms are automatically classified as red-lane importers. The increase in the number of random red-lane inspections causes delays and uncertainty about when imported goods will be delivered. This has been duly noted by the business community, which is likely to reconsider investments in Indonesia to serve regional markets.

The government has attempted to reduce dwell time for imports by making it obligatory for all government entities at the port to remain open 24 hours a day, seven days a week. This was supposed to shorten the time needed to complete paperwork and make payments, and to reduce congestion on weekends in particular, when traffic was most dense. However, this measure was taken without providing any additional budget for the relevant agencies, and without coordination with the private sector. Freight forwarders, shipping line companies and banks kept to their regular business hours, with the result that the number of containers arriving on Saturday and Sunday continued to be higher than on other days, while the number of containers cleared on weekends remained low (Figure 16.4).

The national logistics team has also done much to promote the use of the dry port at Cikarang in West Java. Perhaps because the concept of a dry port was new to Indonesia, it took the private owners of the port some 10 years to collect all the permits they needed to start operating their business. Some licences had to be issued by local governments, such as project approvals, building permits, licences to employ staff and so on. However, the port also required national permits, such as a licence to operate as an international port of destination with the same status as a seaport. In addition, it needed a licence to be allowed to carry out customs clearances.

The dry port at Cikarang currently handles less than 1 per cent of all containers passing through Jakarta. It is only an option at present for companies that have already listed the dry port as the final destination for their containers in their shipping manifests. In the case of freight

Figure 16.4   Container arrivals and clearances at Tanjung Priok Port, March 2012

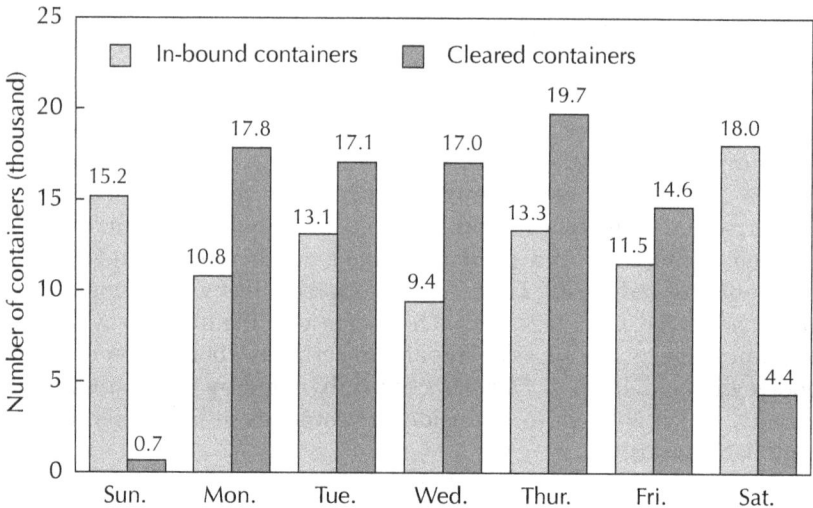

Source: ITB (2013: 36), based on Customs and Jakarta International Container Terminal data.

bound for Bangkok, in contrast, importers can easily change the final destination of their cargo from seaport to dry port whenever there is congestion at Lam Chae Bang, within 24 hours. This is not possible in Indonesia. Moreover, the accessibility of Cikarang remains poor because the government has not yet finished the new access road to the port.

Challenges for the national logistics team

The lack of progress in tackling trade logistics costs between the port of Tanjung Priok and the capital's industrial hinterland does not bode well for the further integration of Indonesia into global markets. Logistics costs remain high despite being high on the agenda of the team responsible for implementing the National Logistics Blueprint. One of the main reasons for these persistently high costs is the poor infrastructure at the port. The last two or three years have seen serious attempts to upgrade productivity, but for at least a decade before that there was virtually no attempt to expand or upgrade the port or its terminals. Indonesia is now clearly suffering the consequences of the failure to upgrade its main gateway to global networks. Moreover, so far the measures proposed to improve operational efficiency at the port have not been very effective. The major constraints to improved performance remain the lack of coordination among relevant government agencies, and the lack of collaboration between these agencies and the private sector. There is a port authority, but its powers and mandate are limited. The state-owned enterprise that operates most of the port's terminals remains in full control and makes key decisions on fees, investments and the possible role that the private sector can play in the port.

The same is true for Cikarang Dry Port. After several rounds of consultation, the national logistics team has come up with a list of recommendations to improve the functioning of the port. However, it does not have the power to overrule other agencies and departments. Therefore, the promised new access road connecting the dry port to the Jakarta–Cikampek toll road remains unfinished. The dry port can still only handle imported containers that list Cikarang as the destination on the ship's manifest, and there is no flexibility to change that on arrival in Tanjung Priok even if congestion renders clearance in the dry port a better option.

16.6   CONNECTING JAVA WITH THE OUTER ISLANDS

The cost of domestic shipping as an impediment to inter-island trade

Magiera (2003) observed that, in the 1990s, pineapples grown in Lampung were being shipped to Malaysia, rather than Java, for processing and canning. The reason was very simple: it was cheaper to transport the fruit to Malaysia, with the cost savings making it possible for Indonesian canned pineapples to compete with those produced in Thailand. The high cost of domestic sea transport between islands remains a major bottleneck for Indonesia. Oranges from Medan and Pontianak have difficulty competing with those from China in supermarkets in Jakarta and Surabaya, not only because Indonesian shipping costs are higher, but also because domestic shipping companies use much smaller vessels than the liners plying between Guangzhou and Jakarta. In addition, the domestic shipping companies confront the problem of 'backhaul', where vessels returning to Jakarta from Medan, Pontianak and other ports are, on average, only 30 per cent filled. Also, port productivity in places like Medan and Pontianak is low, and ships may have to wait several days or more before they can dock and unload. All these factors drive up the costs of domestic shipping.

Another much discussed factor contributing to Indonesia's high domestic shipping costs is the introduction of the cabotage principle through Law 17/2008 on Shipping. It limits the movement of cargo between Indonesian ports to Indonesia-flag vessels. Thus, it is not possible for an international shipper to unload cargo in Jakarta, pick up local cargo and unload it in Makasssar, and pick up cargo there for the international return trip.

Cabotage affects trade of perishable goods between the Outer Islands and Java. Previously, well-equipped foreign ships with reefer (cold storage) facilities could dock in ports outside Java, discharge their cargoes and load goods requiring cold storage for transport to the ports of Jakarta and Surabaya. This is no longer possible, because all cargo between the Outer Islands and Java must be carried exclusively by Indonesian vessels. This is the case even though most Indonesian vessels are not equipped with cold storage facilities, seriously hampering trade in fresh produce.

The introduction of cabotage also seems to have encouraged illegal trade between Eastern Indonesia and neighbouring countries. For example, fresh fish and prawns from Maluku cannot be profitably shipped to Jakarta in the absence of proper cold storage facilities in this and most other Eastern Indonesian islands. However, there is plenty of evidence to suggest that these products are being collected illegally by foreign vessels with reefer facilities, and taken to Bangkok and Manila for processing.

Trade between Eastern Indonesia and the main ports in Jakarta and Surabaya is especially problematic. Shipping a container to places like Maumere in East Nusa Tenggara and Jayapura in Papua can cost as much as $1,000, or 40 per cent more than shipping such a container from Jakarta to western Europe. Backhaul is a serious problem on these routes, with container ships returning from Eastern Indonesia to Java often less than 10 per cent filled. Port productivity in Eastern Indonesia is low, and shippers say that it sometimes makes more sense to unload and return empty rather than wait until enough containers have arrived from a port's hinterland to fill the ship. In the absence of a good planning system, shippers often do not know when those containers will arrive, a problem frequently made worse by the bad roads linking Eastern Indonesian ports to production centres. The virtual absence of cold storage facilities in most Eastern Indonesian ports means it is not possible to collect and store goods in advance, ready for loading before ships need to depart. It is difficult to understand why Indonesian shipping lines, traders and freight forwarders have not joined forces to invest in cold storage facilities that would render east–west trade in perishable and time-sensitive products more profitable. It would be interesting to assess to what extent this disinterest of the private sector is a consequence of the regulatory framework, including cabotage.

Transporting cattle from West Nusa Tenggara to Java

Modified ferries are used to ship cattle to Java from the islands of Lombok and Sumbawa (both in West Nusa Tenggara). These ferries are frequently government owned and subsidized. In 2012–13, the government ordered additional vessels to accommodate growth in domestic demand and to further its policy of becoming more self-sufficient in beef production. The government also has plans to rent cattle ranches in Australia to serve the Indonesian market exclusively. Cattle from Eastern Indonesia and Australia serve different market segments in Indonesia. However, the large-scale and well-organized trade from Australia makes it cheaper to transport livestock from Australia to Jakarta than from Sumbawa to the capital. This is partly to do with scale economies. Cattle from Australia are professionally imported, with large vessels sailing directly to the ports of Surabaya and Jakarta, whereas the local cattle trade is small in scale and suffers from irregular shipping services.

Rather than being taken by ship all the way from Sumbawa to Jakarta, domestic cattle are shipped in relatively small ferries only as far as the port of Surabaya. There, they are transferred to trucks that take them to abattoirs in Jakarta and surrounding areas (an 18-hour journey). The reasons for shipping cattle only as far as Surabaya are mainly economic: it is cheaper to truck cattle from Surabaya because the costs of domestic shipping are so high; and there is also a serious backhaul problem, with ferries usually returning empty to Eastern Indonesia. It should also be noted, however, that the trucking sector in Java is highly competitive, and that it benefits from access to cheap fuel, whereas the ferry sector does not.

The costs of shipping cattle from Sumbawa to Jakarta can be divided into three components. First, there is the cost of collecting information on cattle that are ready to be transported, taking them to the port of Bima, checking their health and readiness for shipping, obtaining licences and permits, and loading the cattle onto the ferries. Second, there is the cost of transporting the cattle from Bima to Jakarta. Third, there is the cost of slaughtering the cattle in abattoirs in Jakarta. We estimate local costs, transport costs and costs in Jakarta at Rp 680,000, Rp 650,000 and Rp 178,000 respectively, per head of cattle. It is striking that the costs associated with the first leg of the supply chain, from rural Sumbawa to the port of Bima, are almost as high as the transport costs from Bima to Jakarta, including transhipment in Surabaya.

Further analysis reveals that the high costs in Sumbawa are partly due to the absence of good information systems on the availability of cattle. The poor road infrastructure in rural Sumbawa is another factor driving up costs in this leg of the supply chain. Finally, an often overlooked factor is the wide variety of fees, taxes and quarantine duties that have to be paid to local governments. Our estimates show that the latter may add up to more than 60 per cent of total local costs in Sumbawa. The main bottleneck in the second leg of the supply chain is the unreliability and high cost of shipping. Cattle are transported from Sumbawa to

Surabaya on old ferries, with limited competition on these routes. There are also restrictions on licences for ferries that want to dock in the port of Bima. The situation is very different after cattle are transferred to trucks in Surabaya. On that leg of the journey, cut-throat competition between trucking companies drives down costs.

Challenges for the national logistics team

Reducing logistics and transport costs is high on the agenda of the national logistics team. Members are well aware that some of the factors contributing to high costs in Eastern Indonesia will not be easy to address. Congestion and delays in the port of Bima cannot be avoided, in the absence of better terminals and a full overhaul of port management. The high costs of ferry transport are also unlikely to change in the short run. The Ministry of Transport has ordered additional ferries, but it is not clear when they will be deployed or whether they will lead to more competition in the cattle transport industry. There is also little that can be done to improve cattle trucking without a total overhaul of the trucking industry, although finalization of the Trans-Java Expressway should reduce transport times between Surabaya and Jakarta from 18 to eight hours.

Nevertheless, the national logistics team has identified some areas where it may be able to score quick wins to reduce costs. In particular, it is looking at the complex licensing and tax system in Sumbawa itself. At present, traders pay when cattle enter the port and make a further payment when they leave it. There are also many licences to be obtained and payments, both legal and illegal, to be made when cattle move from farms in rural Sumbawa to Bima port. The national logistics team believes that it should be possible to reduce the amount of red tape quite quickly, directly feeding into lower supply chain costs. It is also worth noting, however, that the costs of red tape are firmly embedded in the local political economy. They provide an important source of income for local officials, who are not bothered that it leads to higher prices for consumers in Java. We found that it was not easy to convince such officials that reducing the amount of red tape might not lead to lower incomes, but rather result in higher incomes because trade would start to flourish.

The above discussion illustrates another dilemma facing Indonesia as it attempts to promote logistics reform: the lack of coordination between government agencies. We have noted already that this has impinged on attempts to reduce congestion in the port of Tanjung Priok. In the case of cattle transport as well, it is clear that the interests of local and national government agencies and officers do not always run parallel.

16.7   CONCLUDING REMARKS

In this chapter we have highlighted the importance and challenges of logistics reform in Indonesia. In response, the government has issued a National Logistics Blueprint, and various action plans have been approved. Evidence from the World Bank's Logistics Performance Index suggests that Indonesia has made some progress, although it is too early to tell whether or not these improvements are structural. The LPI indicates that logistics improvements have primarily taken place in the private sector; the improved expertise of Indonesian logistics service providers is a good example. The record is much less impressive, however, when it comes to logistics activities in international and domestic supply chains, which are primarily the responsibility of the national government. There also appears to have been little improvement in the performance of the border agencies that monitor and facilitate imports and exports at ports and airports.

We have presented two case studies amply illustrating the main logistics challenges facing Indonesia. First, the problems at Tanjung Priok Port suggest that a lack of international connectivity is constraining Indonesia's competitiveness and limiting the country's participation in global and regional production networks. Not only is it more expensive to export containers from Indonesia than from most neighbouring ASEAN countries, but the reliability and timeliness of Indonesian exports (and imports) are less predictable than elsewhere. Second, the supply chain for transporting cattle from Sumbawa to Jakarta nicely illustrates the transport and logistics bottlenecks holding back inter-island trade. Our analysis suggests that it is not only high transport and port costs that are a bottleneck to more trade between Java and the Outer Islands, but also local regulations, taxes and levies.

Despite the focus on clearing bottlenecks and reducing costs, so far the implementation of logistics policies has had limited success. There appear to be three main reasons for this. First, the basis of a solid logistics system is well-functioning infrastructure. Without good roads, railways and ports, it is very difficult to make much progress in improving logistics. Decentralization has made it more difficult to coordinate the implementation of many infrastructure projects, and gaining access to land remains problematic. For example, investors are ready to build a new port in West Java, and feasibility studies have been carried out. However, the road or railway line connecting the port with the industrial zones in West Java will need to pass through fertile land that is currently being used for rice production. The problem of gaining access to that land has not yet been solved.

Second, implementing logistics reform requires a high level of coordination among central government ministries, and between these ministries and regional authorities. There are plenty of examples of action plans that have been jointly formulated – to reduce dwell time in the port of Jakarta, for instance – but the parties often fail to carry out the actions assigned to them. Because it is so difficult to gain cooperation from other parties, there is a tendency for highly motivated departments to take their own initiatives and to avoid collaboration with other line ministries and regional authorities. In the case of cattle transport from Eastern Indonesia to Jakarta, the attempts by the central government to reduce local taxes and levies to make domestic trade more competitive have not been welcomed by the local authorities.

Third, a very important but sometimes overlooked factor is that many of the policies and regulations issued by the national government actually impede efforts to promote logistics reform. Two recent policy measures taken by the Ministry of Trade are illustrative. The ministry has expanded its pre-shipment verification policy, with the result that more goods now need to be inspected at the port of origin, and many imported goods that were previously exempt from pre-shipment verification have lost their priority-lane status. This new policy has especially affected intra-ASEAN trade, particularly from ports such as Bangkok and Manila. In many cases, shippers complain that the verification process takes longer than it does to sail the ships to Jakarta. In the absence of a pre-shipment verification letter from the port of origin, clearance in Jakarta cannot start, resulting in delays and higher logistics costs. This has become a bottleneck for successful participation of Indonesian firms in regional production networks.

The second regulation that has frustrated attempts to reduce logistics costs relates to companies that import semi-finished goods and spare parts and (occasionally) sell some of those goods to other companies in Indonesia. The new regulation requires these companies to set up new business entities to conduct such sales. These new entities are automatically subject to red-lane customs inspections that can increase dwell time by up to 16 days.

To conclude, logistics reform in Indonesia faces many challenges. These include not only the difficulties of promoting and enforcing coordination across ministries and with local authorities, but also the issuance of new laws and regulations that actually stymie Indonesia's attempts to reduce logistics costs, to improve the country's competitiveness and to promote a more efficient domestic distribution of goods.

REFERENCES

Arvis, J.-F., M.A. Mustra, J. Panzer, L. Ojala and T. Naula (2007) *Connecting to Compete 2007: Trade Logistics in the Global Economy*, World Bank, Washington DC.

Arvis, J.-F., M.A. Mustra, L. Ojala, B. Shepherd, D. Saslavsky (2010) *Connecting to Compete 2010: Trade Logistics in the Global Economy*, World Bank, Washington DC.

Arvis, J.-F., M.A. Mustra, L. Ojala, B. Shepherd and D. Saslavsky (2012) *Connecting to Compete 2012: Trade Logistics in the Global Economy*, World Bank, Washington DC.

Findlay, C. (ed.) 'ASEAN+1 FTAs and global value chains in East Asia', ERIA Research Project Report 2010-29, Economic Research Institute for ASEAN and East Asia (ERIA), Jakarta.

ITB (Institut Teknologi Bandung) (2013) *State of Logistics Indonesia 2013*, Center of Logistics and Supply Chain Studies (Institut Teknologi Bandung), Asosiasi Logistik Indonesia, Panteia/NEA, STC-Group and World Bank, Jakarta.

JTPA (Japan Transportation Planning Association) (2012) 'Study on new urban transportation system project in Cikarang, Republic of Indonesia', paper prepared for the Ministry of Economy, Trade and Industry, Tokyo.

Magiera, S.L. (ed.) (2003) 'Readings in Indonesian trade policy, 1991–2002', collection of policy papers, Jakarta, March.

Osman, N. (2013) 'Yudhoyono kicks off RI's largest port project', *Jakarta Post*, 23 March.

Seneviratne, D. and Y. Sun (2013) 'Infrastructure and income distribution in ASEAN-5: what are the links?', IMF Working Paper No. 13/41, Asia and Pacific Department, International Monetary Fund (IMF), February.

Wihardja, M.M. (2013) 'Looking at the G20 initiatives on infrastructure investment from a developing country's perspectives: Indonesia', draft paper for Regional Think20 Meeting, 28 June.

World Bank (2010) 'Connecting Indonesia: a framework for action', World Bank, Jakarta, June.

World Bank (2011) 'Indonesia economic quarterly: current challenges, future potential', World Bank, Jakarta, June.

World Bank (2013) 'Indonesia economic quarterly: continuing adjustment', World Bank, Jakarta, October.

PART 5

Challenges for
Indonesia's periphery

17 The political impact of carving up Papua

Cillian Nolan, Sidney Jones and Solahudin

17.1 INTRODUCTION

Administrative fragmentation, through the process known as *pemekaran*, is transforming political dynamics in Papua, strengthening clan identities, generating a new assertiveness among elected Papuan officials and nurturing new conflicts.[1] Papua has undergone greater administrative division than any other area of Indonesia. What in 1999 was a single province with 10 subprovincial districts or municipalities (*kabupaten/kota*) has become two provinces, Papua and West Papua, with 42 districts and municipalities, and further new units in process – all of this taking place in one of the poorest and most violence-wracked regions of Indonesia.

Papua is historically and culturally different from the rest of Indonesia. Whereas the rest of the former Dutch East Indies secured independence in 1949, the western half of the island of New Guinea was incorporated into Indonesia only in 1969 following a controversial United Nations-supervised referendum. It has been home to an active independence movement ever since. It is culturally Melanesian, not Malay, and it has over 200 indigenous ethnic groups. In addition, a large migrant population from the rest of Indonesia has grown up over the last several decades, including migrants from both Java and elsewhere as part of an official resettlement program during the 1970s and 1980s, as well as many others who came on their own to trade or to take jobs in the

---

1 In this chapter we use 'Papua' to refer to the two provinces together, and 'Papua province' when referring specifically to the province known as Papua.

civil service. In 2001, the Indonesian government granted Papua 'special autonomy' in the hope that this would weaken the independence movement, but whatever good will might have emerged from this initiative was destroyed two years later when, without consultation, the government divided the province first into three, then back into two, provinces. In the decade since special autonomy came into force, there has been limited progress on devolving political powers that would be significantly greater than those enjoyed by other Indonesian provinces; the main impact has been to flood Papua and West Papua with cash, much of which has disappeared through corruption. Both provinces remain at or near the bottom of the country's Human Development Index (HDI), despite huge wealth from various extractive industries and, increasingly, palm oil.

It is in this context that the 'blossoming' *(pemekaran)* of administrative units is taking place today, without any clear strategy or development logic, other than the tired refrain of 'bringing government closer to the people'. In the early 2000s, in the immediate aftermath of East Timor's independence, government security advisers in Jakarta were the major drivers of division in Papua as an antidote to separatism.[2] Now it is overwhelmingly local elites pushing the process, motivated by a search for status and spoils. Ambitious local officials have an interest in creating more villages *(kampung)* to access block grants for village development programs, and more subdistricts *(distrik, called kecamatan elsewhere in Indonesia)* to reach the requisite number for a new district, where political and fiscal power is concentrated. A greater number of districts raises the possibility of more provinces, and today at least three are under serious consideration.

Along the way, there is a strong incentive to inflate population statistics: more people can mean more central government subsidies, higher allocations of civil servants and more seats in local legislatures. Unreliable population data also lead to the drawing up of poor voter lists for direct elections. When these lists are combined with reliance on a supposedly 'traditional' practice of voting by community consensus, the results can be massive fraud, unverifiable results and violent conflict. Particularly in the central highlands, where the proliferation of new districts and subdistricts has been most pronounced, local candidates have even drawn relatives associated with the armed Free Papua Movement (Organisasi Papua Merdeka, OPM) into their electoral disputes.

---

2 A small armed group known as the Free Papua Movement (OPM) has been waging a low-intensity rebellion against Indonesian security forces since 1964; a broader political movement has campaigned for independence. For more on the separatist movement, see ICG (2010).

All this has meant that *pemekaran* in Papua, once viewed as a useful divide-and-rule tactic, is now a gigantic headache for Jakarta. The Ministry of Home Affairs has been urging a moratorium on any further division of Papua, even as Commission II, the national parliamentary body responsible for overseeing regional autonomy, approves dozens of new units that almost certainly are not economically viable. The ministry would like to go backwards, rejoining some of the non-performing districts with their 'parent' units and ending direct local elections in favour of the old system in which district legislatures chose the executive. Instead of piecemeal dissection, it would prefer to see a 'grand design' – not just for Papua but for the whole of Indonesia – reflected in amendments, now under discussion, to Law 32/2004 on Regional Government.

But it is going to be very hard to stop, let alone reverse, *pemekaran* in Papua. In the meantime, it will continue to affect efforts to redirect policy on Papua, whether this is in terms of expanded autonomy (*otsus plus*), accelerated development or greater dialogue with Jakarta. *Pemekaran* is shifting the locus of political strength from the coast to the central highlands. It is producing a growing number of elected officials – currently numbering over 1,000 across Papua and West Papua – who want more power and are becoming more effective at lobbying in Jakarta, where many of them spend far too much of their time. But it is also producing heightened clan identities and competition among local elites that may hinder their efforts to join forces in search of resolution to Papua's enormous political, social and economic problems.

17.2   A SHORT HISTORY OF *PEMEKARAN*

Administrative fragmentation since 1999

If the Ministry of Home Affairs is now talking about the need for a 'grand design', it reflects the lack of any overriding strategy in the carving up of Papua over the last 15 years. There have been several key steps along the way.

In October 1999, citing the need to improve government services and support further economic development, the national parliament passed Law 45/1999 on the Creation of West Irian Jaya and Central Irian Jaya, which divided the then province of Irian Jaya along straight-line borders that made no sense geographically, culturally or politically. The bitter loss of East Timor in a referendum the previous August was a factor in the division.[3] Four new districts (Puncak Jaya, Mimika, Paniai and

---

3 One analysis says that then president Habibie and the parliament pushed the law through 'in anticipation' of problems similar to those in East Timor arising

Sorong city) were created at the same time, but the provincial division was never implemented due to opposition from Papuan leaders.[4]

In 2001, the national parliament passed Law 21/2001 granting Papua special autonomy. It explicitly stated that the creation of any new province could take place only with the approval of a new body called the Papuan People's Council (Majelis Rakyat Papua, MRP), charged with upholding Papuan values.[5]

In 2002, 14 new districts were created: Asmat, Boven Digoel and Mappi (carved out of Merauke); Keerom and Sarmi (Jayapura); Yahukimo, Tolikara and Pegunungan Bintang (Jayawijaya); Waropen (Yapen Waropen); Kaimana (Fak-Fak); Teluk Bintuni and Teluk Wondama (Manokwari); and Raja Ampat and South Sorong (Sorong).

In 2003, under pressure from Indonesian intelligence to block expansion of the separatist movement after a rise in pro-independence activity, President Megawati Sukarnoputri divided Papua into two by fiat in what was perhaps the single act by any post-Suharto government that most convinced Papuans of Jakarta's continued bad faith. There was no consultation with the MRP, which indeed did not yet exist because Jakarta had delayed its establishment. The decree was supposed to implement the 1999 law dividing the province into three, but in the end only West Irian Jaya, later named West Papua, was created. The damage the division did to Jakarta–Papua relations, let alone to the idea within the Papuan elite that autonomy was an acceptable alternative to independence, is incalculable.

In the same year, the island of Biak was divided in two to create the district of Supiori out of Biak Numfor. Then, after a four-year lull, the divisions began to come thick and fast:

- In 2007, part of the district of Sarmi on the north coast was hived off to create Mamberamo Raya.
- In 2008, special autonomy was extended to West Papua and the district of Tambrauw was hived off from Sorong. In the same year, seven more districts were created in Papua province. Four were carved out

---

in Papua; see 'Inpres itu mengundang emosi' [Inpres invites an emotional reaction], available at http://www.unisosdem.org/article_detail.php?aid=1311&coid=3&caid=22&gid=2.

4 The four districts had initially been established as administrative districts (*kabupaten administratif*) in 1996, meaning that they were able to develop local executive structures but had no local legislatures.

5 Article 76 of Law 21/2001 on Special Autonomy for Papua states that any division of Papua into new provinces can be done only with the approval of the MRP and the Papua provincial assembly after considering socio-cultural unity as well as the existing human and economic resources available.

of Jayawijaya (Nduga, Lanny Jaya, Yalimo and Central Mamberamo), two out of Paniai (Deiyai and Intan Jaya) and one out of Nabire (Dogiyai).

- In 2009, Maybrat became the fifth district to be carved out of Sorong.
- In 2012, two new districts were created in the West Papuan district of Manokwari: South Manokwari and Pegunungan Arfak.
- In October 2013, the national parliament proposed draft legislation that would create a further 30 new districts and three new provinces across Papua and West Papua, subject to approval by the president after consulting the government. The president has not publicly addressed the issue but the Ministry of Home Affairs has said it has no intention of signing off on these proposals. It is unlikely they will come into being before the 2014 elections.[6]

The drivers of administrative fragmentation

Various interests are driving the push for the division of Papua into smaller administrative units, particularly at the district level. *Pemekaran* appears largely to be about gaining access to resources – especially central government revenue streams – but it is also about promoting the interests of clans (*suku*) and subclans.

Fiscal transfers

One factor driving the proliferation of new districts in Papua is that the fiscal transfers local governments receive from Jakarta – already higher in per capita terms than elsewhere in Indonesia – increase significantly as a consequence of such splits. Local governments across the country have only limited authority to raise funds locally; they are dependent on fiscal transfers from the central government.[7] Those transfers include a confusing range of different allocations, but the largest are grants from the General Purpose Fund (Dana Alokasi Umum, DAU), which is the source of over 70 per cent of local government revenues across Papua province. The DAU is calculated annually and is a function of a locality's

---

6 Institute for Policy Analysis of Conflict (IPAC) telephone interview with Director General of Regional Autonomy, Jakarta, 16 September 2013.

7 Dependence on fiscal transfers from Jakarta seems particularly high in Papua, where collection rates for ancillary taxes are low and other opportunities to generate local revenues are limited. The exceptions are a few areas with strong mining revenues (Nabire, Mimika) or natural gas revenues (Teluk Bintuni). Some of the newer districts have negligible local revenues. This is the case, for example, in Puncak, where in 2012 locally generated revenue (*pendapatan asli daerah*, PAD) accounted for just 0.13 per cent of local government spending.

population, area, HDI, construction price level and per capita economic output.[8] Confusingly, the allocation rewards areas with smaller populations, creating a strong incentive for division.[9]

Local governments in both Papua and West Papua do exceedingly well out of the DAU because they have low population densities and low scores on the HDI. Since 2003, the share of the national DAU allocated to Papua and West Papua has grown from 4.6 per cent to 7.4 per cent, although the combined population remains just over 1 per cent of the national total.[10] In individual areas, the growth in DAU allocations has been even higher: in the two years following the 2008 division of Jayawijaya into five districts, their combined DAU allocations increased fourfold (compared to growth of 7 per cent in the total national allocation).[11]

Papua and West Papua also benefit from significant separate allocations, known as *dana otsus*, under Papua's 2001 special autonomy framework. This funding does not vary with population – instead, it is a flat 2 per cent of the national DAU (1.4 per cent for Papua and 0.6 per cent for West Papua). The district governments currently receive 60 per cent of this amount, although the governor of Papua province, Lukas Enembe, has announced plans to increase this share to 80 per cent. New districts thus receive a direct share of these additional funds, which totalled Rp 5.5 trillion (roughly $550 million) for Papua and West Papua together in the 2012 national budget (Ministry of Finance 2013).

Jobs provide another incentive to create new administrative units. Often the public campaigns for *pemekaran* come with the promise of new civil service positions. The rise in the number of new districts in Papua has seen the size of the local civil service triple, from 37,000 in 2000 to 114,419 just over a decade later (BKN 2013a, 2013b). Each district in Papua employs an average of 2,744 staff, providing an important source of stable employment in an area where there are very limited private sec-

---

8 Law 33/2004 on the Fiscal Balance between the Central Government and the Regions sets the total DAU at just over a quarter of net domestic revenues, with 90 per cent of this amount going to district-level governments and the remainder to the provinces.

9 The per capita value of a local government's DAU allocation has been shown to decrease with increases in population, for no obvious policy reason (Fadliya and McLeod 2010).

10 The allocation in 2003 for the two Papuan provinces and all of their districts was Rp 3.6 trillion. In 2012 it was nearly six times that amount, at Rp 20 trillion.

11 See the annual presidential regulations for 2008, 2009 and 2010 on the division of the DAU among provinces, districts and municipalities (PP 110/2007, PP 78/2008 and PP 53/2009).

tor opportunities – indeed, very limited opportunities for employment at all.

The incentive to merge groups of isolated households to form new villages is also clear, especially following the creation of the Strategic Village Development Plan (Rencana Strategis Pembangunan Kampung, Respek), which delivers annual block grants of Rp 100 million (about $10,000) to every village in Papua province.[12] Initiated by former governor Barnabas Suebu in 2007, the program was introduced in part as a way of ensuring that the economic benefits of special autonomy were not hoarded in the provincial or district capitals but reached local communities. But as the grants have become a significant source of funds, the number of new villages has skyrocketed. Between January 2011 and December 2012 alone, 860 new villages were created – an increase of 21 per cent. With rumours that the village grants may rise to Rp 300 million under the Enembe government, the push for new villages is likely to continue.

Clan divisions

As Papua continues to be divided into ever smaller units, it is increasingly fracturing along clan lines.[13] The case of Jayawijaya is instructive. In 1999 it covered most of the central highlands, an area of 67,448 square kilometres (half the size of Java), but it has since been carved into 10 different districts. Four of them were created in one wave in 2008: Lanny Jaya (home primarily to ethnic Lani), Yalimo (Yali), Nduga (Nduga) and Central Mamberamo (home to five smaller clans). Yahukimo, one of the largest new districts to be carved out of Jayawijaya, was created in 2002. Its name is an acronym for the district's four major clans: Yali, Hubla, Kimyal and Momuna. Now smaller clans are pushing for further divisions so that they can wield greater influence and control over jobs.[14]

In West Papua, Pegunungan Arfak was carved out of Manokwari after an ethnic Arfak, Dominggus Mandacan, was defeated in the 2012 gubernatorial election. In an area where many people, including the governor, are ethnic Biak or Serui, the Arfak saw themselves as being shut

---

12 The Respek program operates only in Papua province. Since 2008 technical administration of the program has been carried out through the national PNPM program (Sari, Rahman and Manaf 2011).

13 For details on some of the elite divisions at play in *pemekaran* in Papua between 1999 and 2004, see Timmer (2005).

14 The national parliament's October 2013 draft legislation includes a proposal to carve five new districts out of Yahukimo: Yalimek, North Yahukimo, West Yahukimo-Ser Highlands, Southwest Yahukimo and East Yahukimo.

out of economic opportunities in Manokwari, and demanded their own district.

Similar motives drove the creation in 2009 of the district of Maybrat, home to both the Aifat clan and the traditionally more dominant Aymaru clan. A dispute then arose over where to locate the capital. This was a key decision because, for the town chosen, a change in status could be an important source of economic stimulus and lead to a sharp rise in land values, largely through a surge in demand for construction and services. In 2013, the district head (*bupati*) of Maybrat successfully petitioned the Constitutional Court to move the capital from the small and isolated town of Kumurke to Aymaru.[15] The Aifat community refused to accept the court's ruling; after it was announced a crowd gathered to burn down the home of the district head, and blocked the roads in front of the nearest police station, in Sorong.[16] The police, the army and a handful of local leaders then worked out a deal in which they agreed to ignore the court's decision. A few days later, a Ministry of Home Affairs official suggested that the best solution might be to speed up the establishment of Maybrat Sau, a proposed new district whose capital would be Aymaru.[17]

Similar demands for new districts based on perceptions of neglect or marginalization of one clan by a more dominant one are being made across both provinces. They include a proposal to carve two districts out of Yahukimo that is causing discord between the Yali and Mek clans, and proposals for the further division of the districts of Boven Digoel and Mappi along clan lines.[18]

Elections are often a trigger for *pemekaran*, as support for the creation of new districts becomes a form of patronage. Proposals for new districts require both the support of the district that is being divided and approval from the national parliament. Parliamentary support for the

---

15 See the Constitutional Court's decision in case 66/PUU-XI/2013, delivered on 19 September 2013. The question of where to establish the capital of Maybrat had been before the court before, in 2009, when a group of residents argued that making Kumurke the capital ignored the true aspirations of the community. Much of their argument centred on the assertion that the Aymaru and Aifat clans together formed one *suku*. The court threw out the case after determining that the complainants had no legal standing. See case 18/PUU-VII/2009, decided on 24 November 2009.

16 'Rumah bupati Maybrat dibakar massa' [Maybrat district chief's house burned down by crowds], *Cenderawasih Pos*, 21 September 2013.

17 'Minimalisir konflik, percepat pemekaran Maybrat Sau' [To reduce conflict, speed up the division of Maybrat Sau], *Cenderawasih Pos*, 27 September 2013.

18 On the discord between the Yali and Mek clans, see 'Masyarakat Yali dan Mek diminta tetap tenang' [Yali and Mek communities asked to maintain calm], *Cenderawasih Pos*, 14 September 2013. For more on Boven Digoel, see ICG (2007).

2008 wave of *pemekaran* in Papua was driven in part by national political parties hungry to shore up their electoral support in advance of the 2009 general elections; parties that pledged support for *pemekaran* did well in the central highlands whereas others foundered.[19] In Jayawijaya district in 2011 and 2012, the district head, Jhon Wetipo, had repeatedly made clear his opposition to any further division. But that changed in the lead-up to the September 2013 local election, when Wetipo, running for a second term, announced he would support the proposals for new districts.[20]

The outcomes of administrative fragmentation

Three outcomes of *pemekaran* in Papua have been poor governance, corruption and conflict. If the idea was to bring government closer to the people, then it may have done so in a physical sense, with palatial new government buildings in areas where there was no such impressive government presence before. Many of these buildings are half empty, however, and absenteeism of local officials is a chronic problem.[21] But there is also undoubtedly pride in having officials of one's own ethnicity.

In terms of the delivery of social services, many of the new districts are at the very bottom of the central government's rankings for effective governance. In 2011, the Ministry of Home Affairs published a performance review of 205 new local government units. West Papua was the worst-performing province, and seven of the 10 worst-performing districts were in either Papua or West Papua. In September 2013 the home affairs minister, Gamawan Fauzi, threatened four new districts with cancellation (or 'return' to their former status); three of these (Nduga, Deiyai and Maybrat) were in Papua or West Papua.[22]

The two Papuan provinces also have the highest poverty rates in Indonesia, with the worst rates generally found in some of the newest districts. Papua province has a poverty rate of 36.8 per cent and West Papua a rate of 34.9 per cent, compared to a national average of 13.3 per cent. Four districts in West Papua – Maybrat, Tambrauw, Teluk Wondama and Teluk Bintuni – have poverty rates that exceed 40 per cent; all are new districts formed through *pemekaran* (TNP2K 2011a, 2011b). Papua and West Papua also perform very poorly on the HDI. Papua

---

19 IPAC interview with Papuan member of the national parliament, Jakarta, 6 September 2013.
20 'Masyarakat sampaikan aspirasi ke bupati' [Community conveys its vision to the district chief], *tabloidjubi.com*, 4 June 2013.
21 For a description of civil servant absenteeism in Puncak Jaya in 2011, see ICG (2011).
22 'Pemekaran 4 daerah terancam dibatalkan' [Division of four administrative regions may be cancelled], *Tempo*, 13 September 2013.

province has the lowest HDI by province in Indonesia, while West Papua fares somewhat better with the fifth-lowest HDI, primarily because of its higher literacy rate and higher average number of years in school. Within Papua province, HDI levels are worst in the highlands, where literacy rates and years in school are far lower than elsewhere in Papua.[23]

The new governments have faced repeated allegations of corruption. Auditing standards remain poor in both the provincial and district administrations; the State Audit Agency (Badan Pemeriksa Keuangan, BPK) has given the Papua provincial administration a 'disclaimer' rating for the last three years, noting unsound financial accounting standards.[24] All 44 members of the provincial assembly of West Papua recently faced trial for their role in the alleged misuse of Rp 22 billion in unspent funds that were 'loaned' to members to help them build or renovate their homes.[25]

17.3   *PEMEKARAN* AND ELECTION VIOLENCE

Many of the problems thrown up by *pemekaran* – weak institutions, poor leadership, poor security, corruption – have become manifest during local elections, especially at the district level.

On a technical level, some of the problems arise from the difficulty of finding neutral members in the regional election commissions (Komisi Pemilihan Umum Daerah, KPUD) and in having them accepted as such by candidates and their supporters. Lack of coordination between district, provincial and national party offices, logistical difficulties in delivering ballots and inflated voter rolls have all been problems. Such problems are not unique to Papua, but they are particularly pronounced in some of the new districts where electoral disputes fall along clan or subclan lines. One consequence has been to place significant pressure on local budgets, because district governments often feel obliged to pay compensation for deaths in clan conflicts as a form of reconciliation. This practice may in turn be fuelling further violence.

---

23 In Intan Jaya, which has the lowest HDI score in Papua, the average number of years in school was just 2.07 in 2010 (TNP2K 2011a).

24 'Tiga tahun, laporan keuangan Papua buruk' [Three years of dismal financial reporting in Papua], *Bintang Papua*, 29 August 2013.

25 'Seluruh anggota DPR Papua Barat jadi tersangka korupsi' [Entire West Papua provincial assembly named as corruption suspects], *JPNN.com*, 20 July 2013.

Violence in Puncak

One of the most serious outbreaks of electoral violence to date in Papua took place in the district of Puncak in July 2011. Carved out of Puncak Jaya in 2008, this district now has a population of about 93,363. Its first election was scheduled for November 2011. On 29 July, a local notable, Elvis Tabuni, registered at the KPUD as the Gerindra party's candidate for district head. The next day another candidate, Simon Alom, tried to register, also claiming backing from Gerindra, and three other parties. The commission rejected his application, saying that two candidates could not be backed by the same party.

Simon Alom's supporters attacked Elvis Tabuni's followers in the town of Ilaga with stones and arrows. Four people were killed when police fired live ammunition to try and break up the fighting. Then Alom's supporters attacked the local Gerindra head, who was a member of Tabuni's clan, leading to 13 deaths on the party chief's side and four on Alom's. More deaths followed, bringing the total to 23 by the end of the first week, and the election was postponed.

The KPUD and Gerindra traded barbs about who was responsible for the mix-up. The provincial Gerindra office said that from the beginning it had supported Simon Alom alone, and accused the commission of bias in allowing Elvis Tabuni to register based only on the recommendation of his clansman (the local Gerindra head), rather than the party's provincial office (Arios 2012).

At this point, allegations of OPM involvement began to emerge. Goliat Tabuni, an OPM commander based in Puncak Jaya, reportedly sent a group of his men, led by a commander named Militer Murib, to help out the Tabuni faction. On the other side, Alom drew on the support of members of his own Damal clan in the village of Kwamki Lama in Timika.[26] Some were reportedly former members of Satgas Rajawali, a secret militia established by Indonesian Special Forces (Kopassus) to fight the OPM in the mid-1990s. Goliat Tabuni was one of those who had fought against this group in the past.

Simon Alom's men began looking for weapons to buy in Timika after learning that Militer Murib was helping Elvis Tabuni. In October 2011 they contacted John Lokbere, an ethnic Nduga from Mapenduma, who dealt in arms on the side. Lokbere in turn got his weapons from a gun dealer from Maluku with access to homemade *rakitan* weapons left over from the Ambon conflict. On 3 December 2011 fighting erupted again,

---

26 Timika is home to a large number of Damal people, many originally from the areas around Beoga and Ilaga, who came to the area in the 1970s looking to make a living following the start of Freeport operations. Some of them settled in the Kwamki Lama area.

and on 24 December, Lokbere and the Maluku dealer were arrested in Timika with the weapons Simon Alom had ordered.[27]

More fighting took place on 4 January 2012, resulting in six more fatalities, including that of the head of the district health care clinic (*puskesmas*), who was killed by gunfire. Police suggested that the gun used had been stolen by the OPM in an earlier raid on a police post.[28]

In early January 2013, in an effort at reconciliation, the Puncak government paid out compensation totalling an astounding Rp 17 billion (roughly $1.87 million) to the victims: Rp 300 million for each person killed and Rp 1 million for each person wounded.[29] If ever there was an incentive to engage in deadly conflict, these blood payments were it.

The election finally went ahead on 14 February 2012. Five candidates entered the election along with their deputies: Elvis Tabuni and Hery Dosinaen; Petrus Tabuni and Yansen Ferdinan Tinal; Ruben Wakerwa and Septinus Poahabol; Yopi Murib and Marten Uamang; Simon Alom and Yosia Tembak; and Willem Wandik and Repinus Telenggen. The actual voting proceeded without incident, but tensions began to rise about a week later.

On 20 February, it became clear that the victor was Willem Wandik, a leader of the push for the creation of Puncak whose candidacy had been backed by a coalition of 11 parties led by the Democrat Party (Partai Demokrat, PD). Elvis Tabuni claimed he had been cheated of victory and that 8,000 votes for him had gone missing from the subdistrict of Sinak.

There are three versions of what happened next. According to the police, Elvis Tabuni contacted Goliat Tabuni to ask for help in blocking the KPUD from holding a meeting, scheduled for 23 February, at which the victors would be officially announced. On 21 February, Goliat Tabuni's troops attacked Indonesian military troops in Sinak (Puncak) and in Tingginambut (Puncak Jaya). Eight soldiers and four civilians were killed.

---

27 Arms trading is a very profitable business in Papua. A *rakitan* weapon bought in Ambon for a few million rupiah can be sold in Timika for 10 times that amount. The dealer had earlier sold three *rakitan* weapons to Lokbere for a price of Rp 100 million ($10,280). He agreed to look for more weapons, and at the end of December 2011 brought two long-barrelled *rakitan* and one home-made pistol with two magazines and 61 bullets from Maluku to Timika.

28 'Senjata di Puncak Jaya diduga hasil rampasan' [Weapons in Puncak Jaya allegedly acquired in raid], *Tempo.com*, 8 January 2012. Like much of the reporting in the national press, this article confuses the districts of Puncak and Puncak Jaya.

29 '17 milyar untuk santunan korban konflik pilkada Kab. Puncak' [17 billion in compensation for victims of Puncak election conflict], *Bintang Papua*, 3 January 2013.

Elvis Tabuni maintained in a petition to the Constitutional Court that OPM leader Lakagak Telenggan, linked to Goliat Tabuni, had become angry because Willem Wandik had failed to deliver on a promise to pay him Rp 150 billion if his men helped intimidate voters in Sinak. They had therefore attacked to try and prevent the election results from being announced. The court dismissed Tabuni's petition.[30]

For its part, the OPM claimed responsibility for the attack but explicitly denied any link to the election results.[31]

Willem Wandik was eventually announced the winner and installed as district head in April 2013.

The Puncak story shows how weak local election processes can play into existing clan rivalries with disastrous results – in this case for two candidates who both lost anyway.

Violence in Nduga

Another case of election violence involved the district of Nduga, one of five new units carved out of Jayawijaya province in 2008. On its formation, it had eight subdistricts. The first election for district head in February 2011 was bitterly contested, and while the winner, Yairus Gwijangge, easily outstripped his rivals, one of the losing candidates submitted a petition to the Constitutional Court, alleging fraud.

The challenger, Yakoba Lokbere, a member of the Nduga district assembly (Dewan Perwakilan Rakyat Daerah, DPRD) who was also the wife of the district head of Jayawijaya, argued that the number of registered voters had increased suspiciously from 35,134 at the time of the presidential election in 2009 to 53,701 when the district election took place two years later. The actual number of votes cast as announced by the KPUD was 53,689, meaning that only 12 eligible voters did not vote.

Yakoba Lokbere claimed that only 36,000 ballots had been distributed and that no counting had taken place at the polling places, so it was not clear where the other votes had come from. The court ruled that she had

---

30 'MK tolak seluruh gugatan pemilukada Puncak' [Constitutional Court rejects Puncak election challenge], *Radar Sorong*, 27 March 2013.

31 See the statement entitled 'TPNPB-OPM bertanggung jawab atas semua aksi penembakan terhadap TNI & Polri: Indonesia hentikan penggunaan stigma sipil bersenjata, GPK & OTK' [TPNPB-OPM responsible for all TNI and Polri shooting attacks: Indonesia should stop stigmatizing armed civilians as security disturbance groups (GPK) and unidentified persons (OTK)], 23 February 2013, signed by the chief of general staff of the West Papua National Liberation Army (Tentara Pembebasan Nasional Papua Barat, TPNPB), Terianus Sato.

not produced enough evidence to justify overturning the results.[32] From then on, she reportedly used her power and wealth to persuade other DPRD members to oppose the Nduga district head. Other members held their own grudges; one, Paulus Ubruangge, wanted revenge on Yairus Gwijangge because he believed he had put a spell on his older sister, causing her death. Relations between the DPRD and the district head were thus already poor, but they worsened dramatically in early 2013.

On 23 March 2013, in anticipation of the coming general elections in April 2014, the district government held a coordination meeting at a hotel in Wamena, attended by Yairus Gwijangge and other senior officials, the heads of political party factions in the DPRD and members of the KPUD. Based on new population data from the Ministry of Home Affairs showing that the population of Nduga was 194,142 in December 2012, the KPUD, with the district head's support, decided to increase the number of subdistricts from eight to 32 and the number of villages from 32 to 211. In the process they added one electoral district, arbitrarily raised the number of eligible voters from 53,701 to 119,964, and increased the number of seats in the Nduga DPRD from 20 to 25, based on the alleged increase in population.[33]

The DPRD members present opposed the creation of the new subdistricts, saying they had not been consulted, that the changes had no basis in law and that the data on which the increases were based were completely fictitious. A fight then broke out between the district head's men and the DPRD members, during the course of which one of the former, the head of administration for the district of Nduga, Yustinus Gwijangge, was stabbed to death. The victim's relatives combed the streets of Wamena looking for the attacker, and fighting also broke out between the two sides in the village of Elekma, in the subdistrict of Napua, Jayawijaya.

On 29 May a member of the Nduga DPRD, Eke Bujangge, was hacked to death with machetes in Sentani, Jayapura, by three males – one of them a high school student in Wamena – who later said they were acting on orders from a senior official in the district government. According to the police, the attackers believed that Eke Bujangge had been one of those involved in the death of Yustinus Gwijangge. The next morning, fighting again broke out in Elekma, with the district head's supporters massed in Elekma Bawah and the DPRD's followers gathered in Elekma Atas. They

---

32 Constitutional Court case 74/PHPU.D-IX/2011, 5 July 2011.
33 Ministry of Home Affairs (2011) data for January 2011 show a population of only 15,763 for Nduga in 2011, although a zero may accidentally have been dropped from the total.

fought for two days, leaving two people dead and 22 wounded.[34] The police and military then carried out a search for arms in the two hamlets, a joint operation that temporarily stopped the fighting.

During the four months in total that the conflict continued, eight people were killed and hundreds wounded. The fighting only truly stopped after a meeting between the Nduga district head and the DPRD in Jayapura on 7 June 2013, facilitated by Governor Lukas Enembe. The parties agreed that the creation of the subdistricts would be halted, that the agreed-on population of the district would be 79,000, not 194,000, and therefore that the original number of eligible voters – 53,701 – would apply. It was as though population statistics had become a negotiable commodity rather than an established fact.

The parties also agreed on compensation for the victims, with the Nduga government handing over a total of Rp 18.5 billion (about $1.6 million) to the victims on both sides.[35] The family of each person killed received Rp 1 billion; the rest went to compensate families who had sustained injury or loss of property. The district head noted at the peace ceremony that spending large amounts of money on blood payments for victims of clan fighting was not an appropriate use of the district budget.[36]

The after-effects of the violence are still continuing. As of late August 2013, not a single candidate had registered for the DPRD, raising the prospect that Nduga will not have a legislative body after the 2014 elections.[37]

The Puncak and Nduga cases highlight how local elections in relatively new districts can exacerbate existing social fault lines, cause deadly conflict and strain local budgets. Many of the new units cover huge swathes of difficult terrain but have only a single police post with just seven to ten personnel and no capacity to enforce the law, let alone prevent violence.

---

34 'Dua suku Nduga bentrok, dua tewas, 22 luka' [Two clans clash in Nduga: two killed, 22 injured], *Sindonews.com*, 30 May 2013.

35 'Pemkab Nduga alokasikan Rp 18,5 miliar' [Nduga district government allocates Rp 18.5 billion], *Harianpagipapua*.com, 16 July 2013.

36 'APBD bukan untuk bayar kepala: Rp. 18 milliar untuk kompensasi perang suku' [District budget is not for blood money: Rp 18 billion for compensation in tribal war], *Kompasiana*, 15 July 2013.

37 'Belum ada caleg DPRD Kabupaten Nduga Papua yang mendaftar' [As yet no candidates have registered for Nduga district assembly], *Tribunnews.com*, 20 August 2013.

17.4   *NOKEN* AND THE GUBERNATORIAL ELECTION

The election for the governorship of Papua province in 2013 shows how the proliferation of districts in the central highlands may have helped Lukas Enembe, the province's first highland governor, get elected – through a system of voting that is susceptible to massive fraud.

Throughout the New Order and until the advent of direct elections, most of the top members of the Papuan elite, including all indigenous Papua governors, were from coastal areas, perhaps reflecting the greater accessibility to education and opportunities, and underscoring many highlanders' sense of neglect and discrimination. The creation of so many highland districts after the fall of Suharto strengthened the lobbying capacity of their local elites, leading to the formation of the 10-member Association of Central Highland District Heads in 2008.[38] It took off as an advocacy group after Enembe, then serving as district head of Puncak Jaya, was chosen by acclamation as its head for the 2010–12 period.

The association initially focused on how to divert more resources to infrastructure development in the highlands, where, it claimed, only 5 per cent of provincial infrastructure funds were being spent. Members also talked about pressing for the creation of a central highlands province, especially since there were now enough districts to make this feasible.[39]

It soon became clear to Enembe, however, that being governor of an undissected Papua would give him more influence than running a much smaller and poorer new province, and in retrospect, his advocacy on behalf of the highlands seems to have been a stepping-stone on his way to building support for another run at Papua's top job. He had narrowly lost the previous election in 2006 to Barnabas Suebu. Shortly thereafter, President Yudhoyono met with him to commiserate, offering to make him provincial chair of PD and pledging the party's support for next time.[40] Enembe went on to be elected district head of his native Puncak Jaya in 2007 and became active in supporting the campaigns of a number of other highlander district heads and legislators. In the 2009 general elections, Papuan voters gave highlanders a plurality in the provincial parliament.

---

38   It consists of the district heads of Jayawijaya, Puncak Jaya, Pegunungan Bintang, Tolikara, Yahukimo, Nduga, Yalimo, Lanny Jaya, Central Mamberamo and Puncak.
39   'Pembentukan provinsi pegunungan tengah dideklarasikan' [Creation of a central highlands province is declared], *Cenderawasih Pos*, 23 February 2013.
40   IPAC interview with Lukas Enembe, Jayapura, 23 March 2012.

By early 2012 Enembe was confident of victory – he explained that he had used the intervening years to build up control over 'all the infrastructure', including the KPUD, the provincial parliament and the MRP.[41]

The election should have taken place in mid-2011, timed to coincide roughly with the end of Suebu's term in July, but it became mired in a series of legal battles centring largely on efforts by Enembe's allies to prevent Suebu from running again.[42] In September 2012, when the Constitutional Court finally ordered the election to proceed, there was pressure to organize it as soon as possible. The KPUD, however, had done very little to prepare the voter rolls or to organize logistical support.[43] It announced in early December that its cleaned-up list of voters contained just over 2.7 million names (KPU Papua 2013). That figure was nearly equal to the entire population of the province according to the 2010 census, and it was over 30 per cent higher than the total used in the 2009 parliamentary polls.[44] The greatest increases were recorded in highland areas; the largest discrepancy was in Yahukimo, where the number of registered voters exceeded the total 2010 census population by 57 per cent.

But pressure from nearly all sides to get the poll under way meant that there was little space for objection. One Papuan member of the national parliament explained that he had raised concerns over the apparently inflated figures with the Jayapura representatives of several political parties, only to find that they were reluctant to intervene because they all believed that the padding in the rolls would work in their favour.[45] For the highlanders, an ostensibly traditional practice called the *noken* system was an added advantage.

Evolution of the *noken* system

The *noken* system is named for the traditional bag woven from bark that highlanders use as a carry-all. In an electoral context, people vote by placing their ballot paper in a *noken* bearing the picture or name of their preferred candidate. But the term is also associated with a diverse range of largely unregulated voting practices, all of which appear to share two features: voting by consensus, in which communities (or community leaders) come to an agreement before the poll on how everyone will

---

41 IPAC interview with Lukas Enembe, Jayapura, 23 March 2012.
42 For more on this dispute, see ICG (2012: 17).
43 IPAC interview with Benny Sweny, Chair of KPU Papua, Jayapura, 26 September 2012.
44 'Pemilih di Papua bertambah 100 ribu orang lebih' [Number of voters in Papua rises by more than 100,000], *detiknews*, 31 May 2009.
45 IPAC interview, Jakarta, 6 March 2013.

vote, and an absence of any marking of ballots. Some Papuans, including Enembe, have argued that the practice has a rich history, that it preserves a fragile harmony at village level and that it is the most practical way of facilitating voting in areas where literacy rates are still low. The Constitutional Court has upheld the practice in three separate cases since 2009, in decisions that were probably well-meaning efforts to defend local customs but in fact reinforced the notion of Papuans as backward and needing fewer constitutional guarantees than other Indonesian voters.

Supporters of the system claim that it has been used since the 1991 general elections,[46] but its use seems to have expanded dramatically in the 2009 elections, prompting a challenge in the Constitutional Court. The specific case concerned voting for the Regional Representative Council (Dewan Perwakilan Daerah, DPD), in the highland district of Yahukimo. In its decision, the court defended the practice of collective voting, which it termed voting by community consensus (*kesepakatan warga*), on the grounds that it formed part of a local tradition that, if disrupted, might lead to conflict. The effect was to say that open electoral competition was alien to highland culture and posed so great a risk of sparking violence that it trumped the individual's right to a secret ballot.

The court refined its reasoning in a February 2012 decision on a dispute over results in the election for district head in Dogiyai.[47] A challenge filed by one of the losing candidates argued that under national electoral law, ballots that had not been punched were inadmissible. The court ignored the technical question and returned to its 2009 ruling, adding that recognition of votes cast using the *noken* system was important as a means of upholding customary rights, even though those rights had never been written into formal law.[48] The problem was that it was very difficult to find any highland community that in fact used the *noken* system as a method of choosing leaders. It was not customary practice at all, but rather someone's idea of 'local wisdom' that had found its way into law.

There were some calls from the KPUD for the practice to be addressed in a 2011–12 revision of the parliamentary elections law – one member of the commission estimated that 47 per cent of polling stations in Papua

---

46 This was the argument put forth by the head of the Jayawijaya KPU, Alexander Mauri, at the hearings on the validity of the January 2013 gubernatorial election results in Constitutional Court case 17/PHPU.D-XI/2013. A detailed account of the use of the noken system in the gubernatorial poll is available in a summary of the court proceedings, 'Risalah sidang: perkara nomor 14/PHPU.D-XI/2013, 15/PHPU.D-XI/2013, 16/PHPU.D-XI/2013, 17/PHPU.D-XI/2013', 5 March 2013.

47 For more details, see ICG (2012).

48 See Constitutional Court decision 3/PHPU.D-X/2012, paragraph 3.25.

were violating national law by not using standard polling systems.[49] But the provincial legislature, busy preparing a separate regulation on the arrangements for the gubernatorial election, left the issue alone.

The January 2013 election

The election for the governorship of Papua was finally held on 29 January 2013. Two weeks before voting day, the KPU agreed on technical guidelines (*petunjuk teknis*) for the *noken* system.[50] These created a basic legal framework for the acceptance of unpunched ballots but provided no guidance on minimum standards.[51] Instead they stressed that electoral officials would *not* be involved in supplying *noken* as a replacement for ballot boxes (*kotak suara*), but that 'if there exist groups of voters that use *noken*', they would be permitted to do so 'in keeping with existing and evolving local custom'.[52] Polling officials would then punch all the ballots in each *noken* in accordance with the voters' wishes and subject to supervision by community representatives.

The results offer the best illustration of the irregularities that resulted. Even with clearly bloated voter rolls, turnout exceeded 99 per cent in 13 highland districts.[53] Lukas Enembe performed best in many of these districts, winning more than two-thirds of the vote in eight of them and as much as 99.5 per cent in Puncak Jaya. Turnout was far lower in other areas where the *noken* system was not applied, such as Jayapura city (62.3 per cent), Merauke (59.5 per cent) and Biak Numfor (58.4 per cent), although the provincial turnout rate remained high at 86.6 per cent (KPU Papua 2013).

Reports by a handful of NGO observers and reporters noted the lack of any uniform standards in how voting was conducted in the highlands and the paucity of controls on who was allowed to vote or how many times people were allowed to vote.[54] In some areas community mem-

---

49 'KPU Papua minta RUU pemilu bahas noken' [KPU Papua asks for draft electoral law to address *noken*], *Tribunnews*, 20 October 2011.

50 KPU Papua, decision 01/Kpts/KPU Prov. 030/2013, 12 January 2013.

51 An adviser to the KPU later explained that the apparent diversity of practice in the highlands was an obstacle to creating clear guidelines: each area insisted on its own way of conducting polling. Interview with Budi Setianto, Jakarta, 20 June 2013.

52 KPU Papua, decision 01/Kpts/KPU Prov. 030/2013, article 2(3), 12 January 2013.

53 In nine of these (Tolikara, Puncak Jaya, Nduga, Central Mamberamo, Lanny Jaya, Puncak, Paniai, Dogiyai and Deiyai), turnout was exactly 100 per cent. The other four were Jayawijaya, Yahukimo, Pegunungan Bintang and Yalimo (KPU Papua 2013).

54 Interviews with poll observers, Jayapura, 15 March 2013; Anfrel (2013).

428   *Cillian Nolan, Sidney Jones and Solahudin*

bers wore *noken* bags around their necks, while in others the bags were hung on stakes – bags were not always available for every candidate.[55] In some polling stations, unused votes were later punched by polling station officials in what they called the 'representative system' (*sistem perwakilan*), whereby those who had not voted let local leaders choose for them (ALDP 2013a, 2013b).

The result was a landslide victory for Lukas Enembe and running mate Klemen Tinal, who secured 52 per cent of the vote, compared to 18 per cent for their closest challengers, Habel Suwae and Yop Kogoya. Voting was sharply divided along regional lines: Enembe swept the highland districts, with the exception of Pegunungan Bintang (home to candidates Wellington Wenda and Weynand Watory), Deiyai and Paniai (home to Noakh Nawipa) and Nduga (won by Golkar candidate Suwae). When the vote counts were assembled at provincial level in Jayapura on 13 February, only Enembe's team signed the record of votes; all the other teams walked out.

Six different challenges to Enembe's victory were filed with the Constitutional Court, alleging widespread irregularities and abuse of the *noken* system. The evidence presented in the different cases included some compelling examples, but it failed to meet the required threshold of 'structured, systematic and massive' violations that would have led the court to throw out the results.[56]

Despite the legal challenges, there was little evidence of disquiet leading up to Enembe's inauguration on 9 April 2013. If the losers and their supporters were unhappy with the results, there was also serious fatigue surrounding an election dispute that had dragged on for nearly two years.

Following the election

Highlanders now control the two major party bases in Papua, with Enembe having led PD to 19.6 per cent of the 2009 legislative vote from nearly nothing in 2004, and his running mate, Klemen Tinal, taking over the regional chairmanship of Golkar, which narrowly outperformed PD in the 2009 polls.[57]

Enembe also has strong allies in the provincial legislature, where Yunus Wonda, a fellow PD member from Puncak, has played the role

---

55 Interviews with poll observers, Jayapura, 15 March 2013.

56 The relevant Constitutional Court cases are 14/PHPU.D-XI/2013, 15/PHPU.D-XI/2013, 16/PHPU.D-XI/2013 and 17/PHPU.D-XI/2013, all issued on 11 March 2013.

57 Tinal took over the post from Habel Suwae, the Sentani-born former district head of Jayapura, who had performed disappointingly in the gubernatorial election.

of de facto head since the forced departure of John Ibo in a corruption case. Another close ally is Timotius Murib, the Puncak Jaya-born head of the MRP. While neither of these institutions is a homogenous bloc, these alliances give Enembe and his allies considerable influence over both the legislative and executive branches of government.

The legitimization of *noken* voting has strengthened the political power of highlander politicians in a way that appears irreversible. Because the system offers the potential to ensure huge turnout in an area with ever-expanding voter rolls, highlanders are likely to play an increasingly dominant role in the provincial legislature. The turnout rates will also make competition for Papua province's 10 seats in the national parliament more intense.[58] As the 2014 elections approach, *pemekaran* and in particular the increased population figures in the highlands have led to the addition of a seventh voting district (*daerah pemilihan, dapil*) in the highlands. It is difficult to know precisely what impact this change will have on the election, because at the same time the KPU redrew the borders of all the *dapil*, but the new configuration closely concentrates the population of highland areas where the *noken* system is used into four constituencies that together comprise 34 of the 55 seats in the provincial legislature.

17.5   NO END IN SIGHT

In October 2013, the national parliament approved the creation of draft legislation that would establish 30 new districts (21 in Papua and nine in West Papua)[59] and three new provinces (Central Papua, South Papua and Southwest Papua). The draft legislation now requires approval from the executive in the form of a presidential order (*amanat presiden*) and further, final approval from the parliament.[60]

Approval may not be forthcoming any time soon for two reasons. The Ministry of Home Affairs has said that it will seek to block any further divisions until after the 2014 elections. It also hopes to first secure passage of a new draft law on local government. The proposals for new provinces also face opposition from Lukas Enembe and Bram Atururi

---

58 Papua province and West Papua province are separate national-level constituencies; West Papua elects just three representatives to the national parliament.

59 These 30 were filtered down from proposals circulating earlier in the year for as many as 70 new districts.

60 'DPR usulkan 65 pemekaran daerah, Mendagri: ampres belum terbit' [Parliament proposes 65 new regions, Minister of Home Affairs: still no order from the President'], *Kompas*, 25 October 2013.

(the governor of West Papua), neither of whom wants to see any diminution of his power base.

Proposals for further provinces are nonetheless likely to continue to resurface, and without clearer parameters and controls on how the process should work, the issue may become increasingly fraught. The question of Central Papua poses the greatest potential for conflict. The proposed area is home to some of the most lucrative mining areas in Papua, including the Freeport mine but also other emerging mining areas in Mimika and Nabire. Importantly, the proposed province would be home to a significant non-Papuan population; both Mimika and Nabire are over 50 per cent non-Papuan. Conflict is likely between Timika, Nabire and Biak over which of the three should be the capital, although Timika would probably have the edge.

17.6   THE IMPACT OF *PEMEKARAN*

On the positive side, *pemekaran* has furthered the 'Papuanization' of local government, at least at the senior executive and legislative levels. It has permitted previously unrepresented clans to have a share and a stake in the political process. The proliferation of new districts in the central highlands has also helped focus attention on the lack of development there, although not all elected leaders from these areas have always had the best interests of their constituencies at heart.

But serious problems of conflict and corruption that are not helpful to either development or peace have also arisen in many of the new districts. When Nduga, one of the poorest districts in Indonesia, spends Rp 18 billion of its annual budget on blood payments for deaths in election-linked clan conflicts, something is seriously wrong.

Stopping direct elections in Papua will not solve the problem; indeed, having an electoral system for Papua that is less democratic than that for the rest of Indonesia will only reinforce perceptions of discrimination and inequity. There are things that the Ministry of Home Affairs could do other than roll back political rights. It could enforce the criteria for *pemekaran* more rigorously; put more resources into trying to gather accurate census data; make a major effort to clean up voter rolls; eliminate the *noken* system; provide more oversight over both the provincial and district-level election commissions; and change the incentive structure that makes the creation of new administrative units so financially rewarding.

On the broader issue of what *pemekaran* means for the long-term political process in Papua, it is difficult to know for sure. The increase in elected officials could mean that more Papuans have a stake in the political system; at the same time some, particularly in the highlands, are sympathetic to the independence movement. If divide-and-rule policies in the early 2000s were based on the premise that smaller units would help defeat separatism, we have seen in Puncak how feuds over local elections can lead the disgruntled loser to side with the OPM. At the very least, however, as a process of dialogue – or 'constructive communication' to use Jakarta's preferred term – evolves between Papuans and the central government, then the officials who owe their jobs to *pemekaran* represent an increasingly important constituency whose views need to be heard.

REFERENCES

ALDP (Aliansi Demokrasi untuk Papua) (2013a) 'Aneka model TPS, aneka aturan main pilgub di Wamena' [Different models of polling stations, different rules of play in the gubernatorial election in Wamena], Abepura, 30 January.

ALDP (Aliansi Demokrasi untuk Papua) (2013b) 'Kemana surat suara sisa pilgub Papua?' [Where did the leftover ballots go in the Papua gubernatorial election?], Abepura, 7 February.

Anfrel (Asian Network for Free Elections) (2013) 'Papua gubernatorial election 2013', mission report, Anfrel, Bangkok, 3 June, available at http://anfrel.org/papua-gubernatorial-elections-2013/.

Arios, R.L. (2012) 'Tindak kekerasan pada konflik pilkada: sebuah analisis teori konstruksi sosial' [Violence during local election disputes: a social constructionist analysis], *Kompasiana*, 18 March.

BKN (Badan Kepegawaian Negara) (2013a) 'Daftar nominatif PNS Prop. Papua Barat per golongan per 30 Agustus 2013' [List of civil servants by grade for West Papua as of 30 August 2013], BKN, Jayapura, available at http://www.bkn.go.id/kanreg09/en/wilayah-kerja/wilayah-kerja-1.html.

BKN (Badan Kepegawaian Negara) (2013b) 'Daftar nominatif PNS per golongan per 30 Agustus 2013' [List of civil servants by grade as of 30 August 2013], BKN, Jayapura, available at http://www.bkn.go.id/kanreg09/en/wilayah-kerja/wilayah-kerja-2.html.

Fadliya and R.H. McLeod (2010) 'Fiscal transfers to regional governments in Indonesia', Working Paper No. 2010/14, Crawford School of Economics and Government, Australian National University, Canberra.

ICG (International Crisis Group) (2007) 'Indonesian Papua: a local perspective on the conflict', Asia Briefing No. 66, ICG, Jakarta/Brussels, 19 July.

ICG (International Crisis Group) (2010) 'Radicalisation and dialogue in Papua', Asia Report No. 188, ICG, Jakarta/Brussels, 11 March.

ICG (International Crisis Group) (2011) 'Indonesia: hope and hard reality in Papua', Asia Briefing No. 126, ICG, Jakarta/Brussels, 22 August.

ICG (International Crisis Group) (2012) 'Indonesia: dynamics of violence in Papua', Asia Report No. 232, ICG, Jakarta/Brussels, 9 August.

KPU Papua (Komisi Pemilihan Umum Papua) (2013) 'Catatan pelaksanaan rekapitulasi hasil penghitungan suara pemilihan umum gubernur dan wakil gubernur Provinsi Papua' [Record of summary of results of vote counting in the election for governor and vice governor of Papua province], 13 February.

Ministry of Finance (2013), 'Laporan keuangan transfer ke daerah (audited), tahun anggaran 2012' [Financial report of transfers to the regions (audited) for fiscal year 2012], Ministry of Finance, Jakarta, 15 May, available at www.djpk.depkeu.go.id/attachments/article/342/LKTD%202012.pdf.

Ministry of Home Affairs (2011) 'Buku induk kode dan data wilayah administrasi pemerintahan per provinsi, kabupaten/kota dan kecamatan seluruh Indonesia' [Book of codes and government administrative area data, by province, district/municipality and subdistrict for all of Indonesia], attachment to Ministerial Regulation 66/2011, Ministry of Home Affairs, Jakarta, 28 December.

Sari, Y.I., H. Rahman and D.R.S. Manaf (2011) 'Final report. Evaluation of PNPM Respek: village infrastructure and institutional capacity', Akatiga Centre for Social Analysis, Bandung, October.

Timmer, J. (2005) 'Decentralisation and elite politics in Papua', SSGM Discussion Paper 2005/6, State, Society and Governance in Melanesia (SSGM) Program, College of Asia and the Pacific, Australian National University, Canberra.

TNP2K (Tim Nasional Percepatan Penanggulangan Kemiskinan) (2011a) 'Indikator kesejahteraan daerah Provinsi Papua' [Welfare indicators for Papua province], TNP2K, Jakarta, November, available at http://data.tnp2k.go.id/?q=category/data/data/ikr-daerah.

TNP2K (Tim Nasional Percepatan Penanggulangan Kemiskinan) (2011b) 'Indikator kesejahteraan daerah Provinsi Papua Barat' [Welfare indicators for West Papua province], TNP2K, Jakarta, November, available at http://data.tnp2k.go.id/?q=category/data/data/ikr-daerah.

18 Development in Papua after special autonomy

Budy P. Resosudarmo, Julius A. Mollet,
Umbu R. Raya and Hans Kaiwai

18.1 INTRODUCTION

The western part of the New Guinea islands is a unique part of Indonesia. Situated furthest from the nation's capital, Jakarta, it is Indonesia's most sparsely populated and geographically challenging region, and has some of the country's lowest socio-economic indicators. The combination of these difficult geographical and demographic conditions has meant that development in the region has always been challenging (Garnaut and Manning 1972, 1973; Manning and Rumbiak 1989).

Papua formally became part of Indonesia through a long and bitter process that took place between 1963 and 1969. At the time of annexation in 1969, the region was renamed West Irian (Irian Barat) and became a province of Indonesia, with Jayapura as its capital. In 1973, the name was again changed, to Irian Jaya. This controversial history led to the formation of movements among the local elites calling for Papua to become an independent state. Though relatively low level, sporadic and only intermittently violent, these independence movements have consistently challenged the legitimacy of Indonesian rule ever since (McGibbon 2006).

Over the ensuing decades, the Indonesian government attempted to weaken Papuan independence movements and accelerate development by allocating a higher level of funding per capita to Irian Jaya than to the other Indonesian provinces. Critics argued, however, that it was far less than the revenue generated by the region's natural resources. In particular, much of the revenue from the hugely profitable Freeport mine in Mimika district went straight to the central government, fuelling tensions between Jayapura and Jakarta (Resosudarmo et al. 2009a, 2009b).

The most critical time in the relationship between Jakarta and Jayapura was the period 1998–2001. The resignation of President Soeharto in mid-1998 and East Timor's successful demand for a referendum on independence intensified separatist hopes in Irian Jaya. When Abdurrahman Wahid became president at the end of 1999, he introduced a more accommodative and culturally sensitive approach to the question of ethnic conflict and separatist demands by changing the name of the province to Papua – the name by which parts of the main island were known before contact with the West (Sumule 2003; McGibbon 2004, 2006). To maintain good relations with the provincial elites, the president also endorsed the development of a draft bill on special autonomy for Papua. After a long series of debates, in late 2001 the national parliament finally enacted Law 21/2001 on Special Autonomy for Papua (Resosudarmo et al. 2009a; Widjojo 2010).

The special autonomy legislation gave the provincial government authority over decision making in all sectors except international affairs, defence, monetary and fiscal policy, religion and justice, as well as a far higher share of the revenue originating in Papua than applied to other provinces. It specified that the province would receive 80 per cent of the revenues from its forestry, fishery and mining sectors, and 70 per cent of the revenues from its oil and gas sector until 2026, and 50 per cent thereafter. In addition to the financial transfers from the central government that all provinces receive, until 2021 Papua will receive additional special autonomy funds (*dana otsus*) amounting to 2 per cent of the total national General Purpose Fund (Dana Alokasi Umum, DAU).

The Indonesian government was slow to implement Law 21/2001. In 2003, before the transition to special autonomy was complete, the central government split Papua into two provinces: Papua with Jayapura as its capital, and West Papua (initially called West Irian Jaya) with Manokwari as its capital.[1]

Despite the efforts of the central government to calm separatist tensions by providing special autonomy and increased funding, there is a widespread perception that development in Papua is a failed process. Critics argue that the benefits of development have been concentrated in resource-rich enclaves and urban areas, bypassing most indigenous Papuans (Widjojo 2010). This chapter investigates Papua's macro-economic and micro-economic performance to establish whether such a perception is warranted. It attempts to understand the factors behind some of the development failures in Papua over the past 10 years, while also drawing attention to the successes.

---

1   In the rest of the chapter, we refer to the entire region as 'Papua', and to the two provinces separately as 'Papua province' and 'West Papua province'.

We first review the general development performance of Papua over the past two decades, as represented by trends in economic growth and poverty reduction (section 18.2). In section 18.3, we look more closely at the drivers of growth in each province, especially mining (in the case of Papua province) and liquefied natural gas (LNG) (in the case of West Papua province). Section 18.4 focuses on social and demographic indicators in the two provinces, including poverty, equality, health, rural and urban population growth, and migration. We then discuss inter-provincial trends, particularly local government income and expenditure (section 18.5), before providing a few concluding remarks.

18.2   GENERAL DEVELOPMENT PERFORMANCE

The two measures adopted in this chapter to assess the general development performance of Papua province and West Papua province since the implementation of special autonomy are the growth of the economy and the progress with poverty alleviation. It is often asserted that the record of the two provinces in these respects has been inferior to that of the rest of the country, so we use the national situation as our benchmark for performance. If Papua province and West Papua province have performed at a similar level to the national average over the past decade or so, it could be argued that they have been doing rather well, in spite of the frequent assertions to the contrary (Widjojo 2010).

Figure 18.1 shows GDP, including and excluding mining, oil and gas, for Papua and for the whole of Indonesia over the two decades from 1993 to 2012, indexed at 100 in 1993. It shows that the region's growth rates have at least matched those of the national economy. Papua's total GDP increased somewhat faster than the national rate before the enactment of the special autonomy law, and at a similar rate thereafter. Excluding mining, oil and gas, there was a sharp decline in GDP in Papua during the early phase of implementation of the special autonomy law, followed by a recovery from the time of the division into two provinces in 2003.

GDP per capita in Papua grew by approximately 1.9 per cent per annum on average during the period 1993–2012. This was lower than the national rate of 2.9 per cent per annum. Nevertheless, in 2012 the average level of GDP per capita in Papua and in Indonesia as a whole was approximately the same, at Rp 31 million for Papua and Rp 32 million for Indonesia.

Economic growth has been relatively effective in reducing poverty in Papua. Figure 18.2 indicates that the proportion of the population living below the poverty line, as defined by the central statistics agency, Badan Pusat Statistik (BPS), declined in both provinces from about 55 per cent

Figure 18.1   GDP including and excluding mining, oil and gas, Papua
and Indonesia, 1993–2012

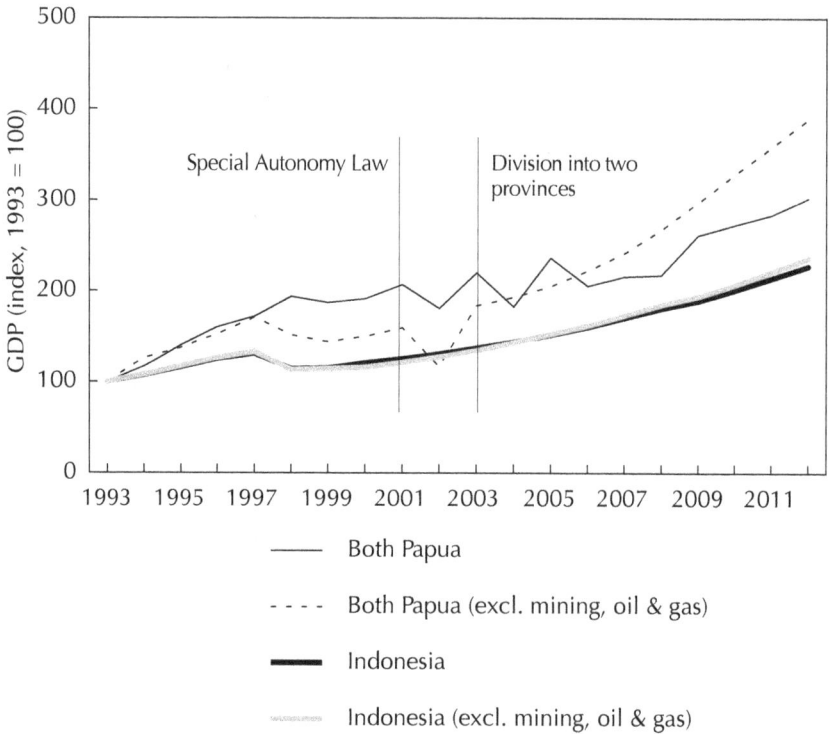

a   The figures for 1993–2002 are for the former province of Papua; those for 2003–12 are the
combined totals for Papua province and West Papua province.
Source: Provincial GDP data from BPS.

in 1999 to about 30 per cent in 2012. This was still much higher than the
national average, of around 12 per cent in 2012, even though poverty has
been declining faster than the national average in the two provinces for
several years. One could argue that the continuing high levels of poverty in Papua are mainly due to 'initial conditions', that is, to the high
proportion of poor people at the start of the special autonomy era (see
Ilmma and Wai-Poi, Chapter 5, and Sumarto, Vothknecht and Wijaya,
Chapter 12).

Given that the economy has been growing, and poverty declining,
at rates at least comparable to the national level since the implementation of special autonomy, it could hardly be argued that development in
Papua has been stagnant or has failed. On the contrary, it seems to have
been progressing at a relatively good rate. However, we need to look

Figure 18.2 Share of population below poverty line, Papua province, West Papua province and Indonesia, 1999–2012

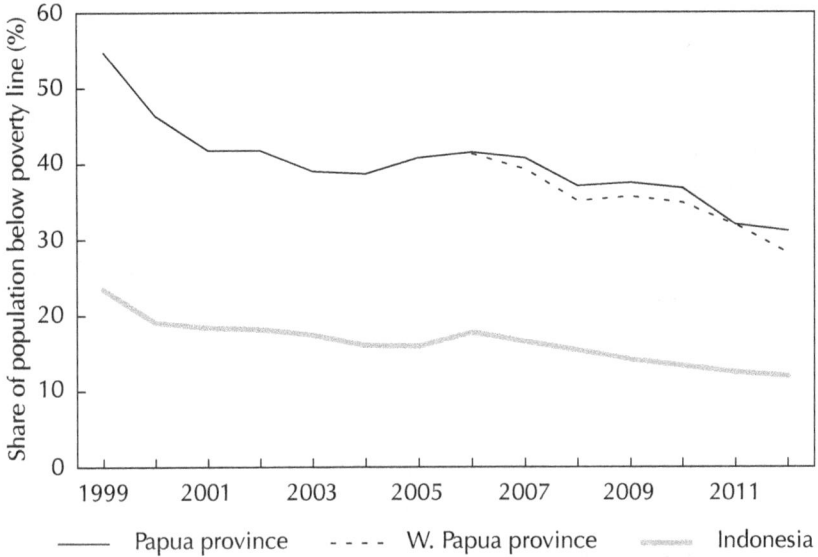

Source: BPS (various years).

more closely at the situation in each province before we can make this assertion with any confidence.

18.3 ECONOMIC PERFORMANCE

Economic growth and structural change

Although the legislation splitting Papua into two provinces was passed in 1999 (Law 45/1999), the process was completed only in 2003, when Abraham Atururi was elected the first governor of the province. Table 18.1 shows economic growth in the original province before it was split into two (1993–2001) and in each province since then (2003–12). On average, West Papua province has recorded yearly growth in GDP of 12.9 per cent since 2003, whereas Papua province has experienced almost no growth. The contrast between the two provinces is starker still when one examines the per capita figures: in 2003–12, GDP per capita grew at an average rate of 9.3 per cent per year in West Papua province, but declined by 5.2 per cent per year in Papua province. Clearly economic development in the region as a whole has been dominated by West Papua province.

Table 18.1   Components of GDP growth, Papua province and West Papua province, 1993–2012 (% p.a.)

Category/sector	Papua province		West Papua province 2003–12
	1993–2001	2003–12	
By expenditure category			
Private consumption	8.7	9.4	7.7
Government consumption	11.6	14.5	11.6
Fixed capital formation	9.1	12.7	6.1
Change in stocks	13.0	35.7	18.8
Exports	12.8	–9.7	15.2
Imports	12.1	5.9	7.5
By sector			
Agriculture	5.4	3.5	3.8
Mining & quarrying	12.1	-8.8	2.0
Manufacturing	5.8	4.0	30.8
Electricity, gas & water supply	2.0	6.4	9.0
Construction	–1.7	15.0	12.0
Trade, hotels and restaurants	6.4	9.8	8.6
Transport & communications	7.2	13.2	11.8
Finance & business	–2.0	19.0	14.5
Services	42.1	10.6	13.1
Total			
GDP	9.5	0.2	12.9
GDP per capita	6.8	–5.2	9.3

Source: Provincial GDP data from BPS.

The high economic growth rates in West Papua province are mainly due to the stellar performance of the LNG sector, which grew at an average annual rate of 31 per cent as production from PT BP Indonesia's Tangguh LNG project expanded. Most of this gas has been exported, making exports the main driver of growth on the expenditure side of GDP (Table 18.1). Government consumption is another important source of growth. As a new province and the recipient of generous special autonomy funding, West Papua province has been able to increase government expenditures quite rapidly. Together, the growth of Tangguh LNG and the expansion of government spending have induced growth in other sectors, such as finance, services, construction, transport and communications, and utilities.

Although Papua province has experienced almost no growth in GDP, the situation is not as serious as one might think. It is true that the mining sector, dominated by PT Freeport Indonesia, has been declining over the last decade or so, leading to a fall in the value of exports. On the other hand, government spending and fixed capital investment have both grown, by well over 10 per cent per year, contributing to growth in sectors such as finance, construction, transport and communications, and trade, hotels and restaurants. With so many sectors still experiencing respectable levels of growth, the impact of the stagnant economy on the welfare of the population will probably be limited. It should also be remembered that mining is typically an enclave activity; its impact on the general public is fairly limited, regardless of whether it is booming or contracting (Weisskoff and Wolf 1977).

Papua has depended heavily on natural resources, especially the mining, oil and gas sectors, since the mid-1970s (Manning and Rumbiak 1989; Resosudarmo et al. 2009a). Although this is still the case, there have been some structural changes in the two provincial economies since the split in 2003 (Table 18.2). The contribution of mining to the economy of Papua province declined from 62 per cent in 2003 to 47 per cent in 2012. The shares of agriculture and manufacturing also fell, but that of utilities remained the same. A few other sectors, notably construction and services, increased their shares during the period. Despite these structural changes, the economy of Papua province continues to be dominated by the mining sector, and in particular by a single company, Freeport Indonesia.

The structure of the West Papuan economy has also changed since the province was established in 2003. The manufacturing sector, dominated by the processing of natural gas from the Tangguh LNG project, sharply increased its share from 16 per cent in 2003 to 54 per cent in 2012, thereby reducing the relative contributions of all other sectors. One could therefore argue that the economy of West Papua province is also dominated by a single company, BP Indonesia, replacing the previous dependence on agriculture and on mining activities in the Salawati Basin.

On the expenditure side, private consumption and international trade have been the most prominent sectors in both provinces (Table 18.2). Import and export performance is determined mainly by the activities of Freeport Indonesia in Papua province, and those of BP Indonesia in West Papua province. In the former province, the growth in both private and government consumption suggests that higher public and private expenditures have compensated for some of the decline in Freeport Indonesia's exports.

Table 18.2   Structure of the economy, Papua province and West Papua province, 1993–2012 (%)

Category/sector	Papua province			West Papua province	
	1993	2003	2012	2003	2012
By expenditure category					
Private consumption	53.3	45.3	62.3	66.5	35.7
Government consumption	10.6	8.9	28.3	14.9	14.6
Fixed capital formation	37.5	21.2	39.8	42.7	23.5
Change in stocks	3.6	3.7	-3.6	3.4	12.1
Exports	42.3	71.8	36.7	50.4	47.5
Imports	47.3	50.9	63.6	78.0	33.3
By sector					
Agriculture	22.3	15.4	12.6	31.9	12.2
Mining & quarrying	50.9	61.5	46.5	18.4	6.5
Manufacturing	4.8	2.3	1.9	15.9	54.0
Electricity, gas & water supply	0.3	0.2	0.2	0.4	0.3
Construction	9.3	4.1	13.0	7.0	7.3
Trade, hotels & restaurants	5.7	5.1	6.8	10.0	6.6
Transport & communications	3.6	3.9	6.5	6.3	4.7
Finance & business	2.4	1.0	3.0	1.5	1.9
Services	0.7	6.5	9.5	8.5	6.6

Source: Provincial GDP data from BPS.

Observing the dynamics of economic growth and structural change in the two provinces, one can conclude that each is heavily reliant on a single industry – indeed, a single company – extracting natural resources. When the exports of either of those companies decline, due to a fall in world prices or to a reduction in output, inevitably the economy of the province concerned will contract or stagnate. To reduce the high dependency in both provinces on extractive industries, policies should be developed to encourage the development of other sectors. One option would be to expand the agricultural and agricultural processing sectors, because the contribution of agriculture to both provincial economies is second only to mining, and because these sectors could potentially absorb large numbers of workers. However, this does not mean that the development of other sectors, such as construction, and trade, hotels and restaurants, is not important.

Figure 18.3   Annual revenue of Freeport-Indonesia, 2005–12

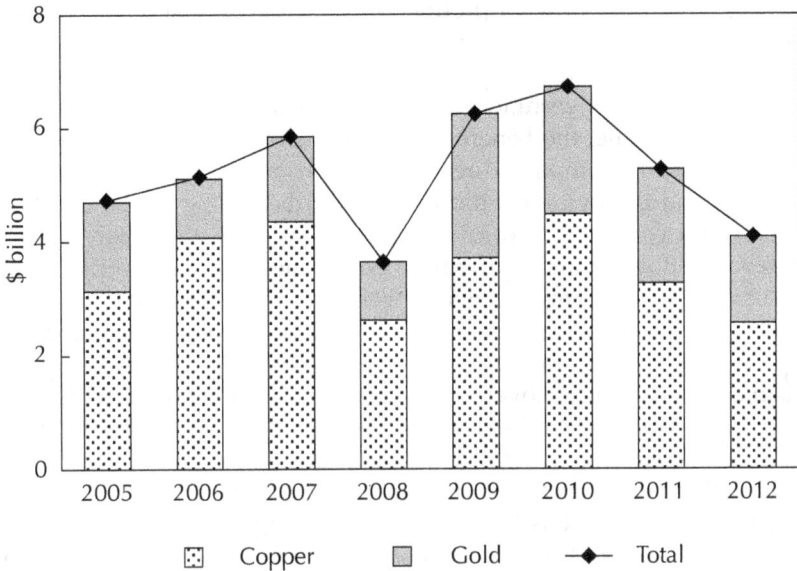

Source: Annual reports of Freeport-McMoRan Copper & Gold, Inc.

Mining and gas

PT Freeport Indonesia has long been the most significant mining operation in Papua province. It is part of Freeport-McMoRan Copper & Gold Inc., which has its headquarters in Phoenix, Arizona. The company initially mined copper and gold in the remote and rugged Ertsberg area, but since 1988 has concentrated on the Grasberg area, which is about 70 kilometres from the city of Timika (Ballard and Banks 2009). Since commencing operations in 1967, Freeport has grown into a hugely profitable company, mostly due to its exceptionally low production costs and its correspondingly high profit margins. In 2010 its annual revenue reached $6.7 billion, and in 2011 it paid about $1.9 billion to the Indonesian government in tax. The company directly employed over 24,000 staff in 2011, making Freeport one of the largest private sector employers in the whole of Indonesia (Freeport-McMoRan Copper & Gold Inc. 2013).

Freeport has dominated the economy of Papua for many years. For much of that time it constituted 50 per cent or more of the provincial economy and contributed 90 per cent of Papua's total exports. Since 2005, however, Freeport Indonesia's revenues have been fairly stagnant, or declining (Figure 18.3). The main reason for this is the relatively stable world copper prices during the period 2005–10, followed by a decline since then, without any corresponding significant increase in production. The fall in the value of production since 2005 is responsible for the decline observed earlier in the value of Papua province's exports.

The size of the mining industry is such that there is little incentive for the provincial government to make serious efforts to develop other sectors. Meanwhile, the benefits of this industry for local communities are debatable: the company directly employs only 4,000 or so indigenous Papuans, and the living conditions of the tribes living in the Grasberg area are still very basic. Critics also argue that the higher share of mining revenue flowing to the provincial government since the implementation of special autonomy has mainly benefited the residents of Jayapura, where most of the money has been spent. That is, the combination of a limited number of indigenous Papuans absorbed by this industry, the urban concentration of government spending and the failure to develop other sectors has greatly limited the benefits of the mining industry for Papuans in general, and for rural communities in particular.

West Papua province hosts two main types of mining activities. The longer-established one is the oil and gas mining in the seas off Sorong district and Salawati Island, which began in 1964 (Anggraeni 2007). This was important in the development of Sorong city and the surrounding areas, although its contribution paled beside that of Freeport. In 2001, for example, before Papua was divided into two provinces, oil and gas mining in the Salawati and Sorong areas contributed approximately 4.5 per cent of Papua's GDP and 3 per cent of its exports – far less than Freeport.

The more recent and much more significant activity is LNG extraction by BP Indonesia in the Bintuni Bay area. The company launched its Tangguh LNG project in 2005, with production commencing in 2009. Since then, this single company has dominated the economy of West Papua province. By 2012, the Tangguh LNG project accounted for about 42 per cent of the province's GDP and employed around 3,400 people, 54 per cent of them Papuan. The company is planning a major expansion of operations, so it is expected to remain the main driver of the provincial economy for some years to come (TIAP 2012).

Although BP Indonesia seems to have been able to recruit a higher proportion of Papuan employees than Freeport, the benefits of its extraction activities again appear to be concentrated in urban areas. As in Papua province, the large revenues flowing from this single sector can be expected to detract from efforts to develop other economic sectors. The impact of gas extraction on rural development could be limited unless there are concerted efforts to spread the benefits to other sectors, and to rural areas.

Figure 18.4   *Share of population below poverty line by urban/rural area,*
Papua province and West Papua province, 2006–12

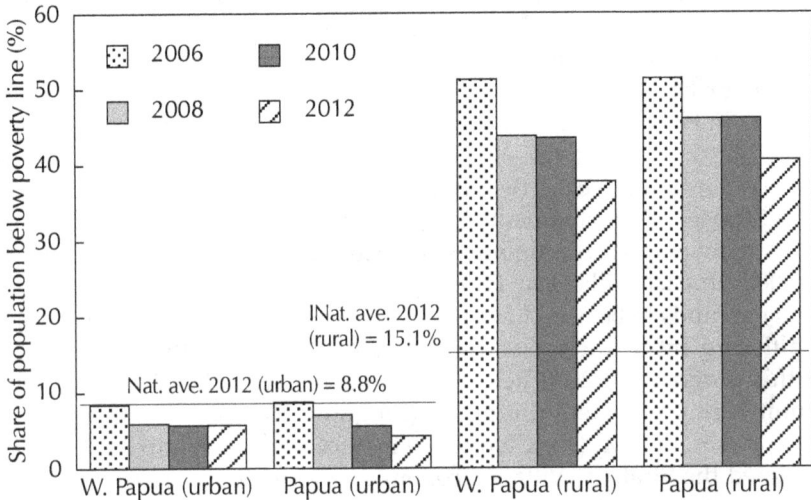

Source: BPS (various years).

18.4   SOCIAL AND DEMOGRAPHIC INDICATORS

Poverty

Although poverty in aggregate has declined in both Papuan provinces (see section 18.2), there may still be important differences in poverty levels within each region. In this section we investigate levels of poverty in rural and urban areas. This is a very relevant distinction in the case of Papua, where the rural and urban economies are very different. In particular, government and services are very important in urban areas, whereas agriculture dominates the rural economy. The composition of the urban and rural populations is also different, with relatively few migrants from other parts of Indonesia living in rural areas, and relatively few Papuans living in urban areas.

Figure 18.4 shows the proportion of the rural and urban populations living below the poverty line, as defined by BPS, in Papua and West Papua provinces. It can be seen that the level of both rural and urban poverty declined continuously in the two provinces between 2006 and 2012. Poverty fell faster in rural than in urban areas, but with no prospect of closing the gap. In 2012, urban poverty in both provinces was lower than the average for Indonesia's urban areas of approximately 9 per cent. This was far from the case for rural poverty, however, which was much higher than the national average for rural areas of around 15 per cent. Around 41 per cent of rural dwellers in Papua province, and 38 per cent in West Papua province, were classified as poor in 2012. In short, poverty in both provinces is very much a rural phenomenon.

Programs to develop rural areas and improve the productivity of the rural poor have arguably contributed to the observed decline in rural poverty in Papua. Yet, the fact that rural poverty remains very high does raise questions about the effectiveness of such programs. One of the more recent initiatives is the Strategic Village Development Plan (Rencana Strategis Pembangunan Kampung, Respek) introduced in 2007. It aims to develop local economies by distributing Rp 100 million (about $10,000) to each village in Papua province and West Papua province, with the funds to be used to improve nutrition, basic education, primary health care, infrastructure and livelihoods. To improve the effectiveness of this program, in 2008 Respek was merged with the National Community Empowerment Program (Program Nasional Pemberdayaan Masyarakat, PNPM) (see Chapter 10 by McCarthy et al.). In 2013, it was renamed the Strategic Village Economic and Institutional Development Program (Program Strategis Pembangunan Ekonomi dan Kelembagaan Kampung, Prospek), indicating an additional emphasis on village institutional development.

The success of this program is debatable, with both good and bad reports. In some villages, it has reportedly induced the development of some small-scale, post-harvest agricultural industries. In others, however, it appears to have discouraged indigenous farmers from growing staple foods and vegetables, thereby possibly reducing the availability of some foods in those villages. Apart from any conclusions that may be drawn about the program, combating poverty in rural areas is still the main development challenge facing the provinces of Papua and West Papua.

Income equality

The Gini coefficient is a measure of income distribution among a population, with a rise in the ratio representing an increase in inequality. The Gini increased from 0.37 in Papua province and 0.31 in West Papua province in 2007 to about 0.42 in both provinces in 2012. This was not very different from the ratios for Indonesia as a whole, of 0.33 in 2007 and 0.41 in 2012. The rise in income inequality in the two provinces, and in Indonesia, was not because the incomes of the poor were not growing – they have in fact grown – but rather because the incomes of the rich have been growing much faster than those of the poor.

Figure 18.5 shows average annual growth in household expenditure per capita in 2008–12, in real terms, from the poorest percentile of the

*Figure 18.5   Distribution of average annual growth in household
expenditure per capita, Papua and Indonesia, 2008–12*

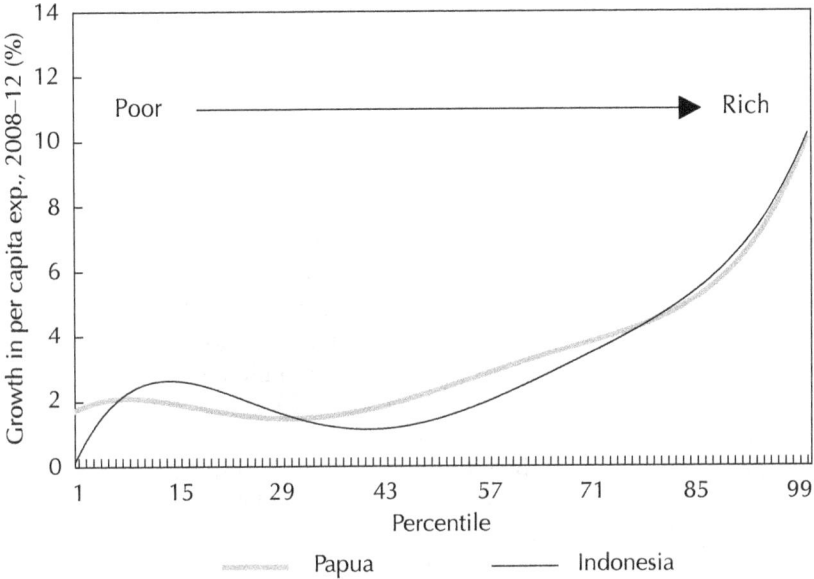

Source: Authors' calculation based on 2008 and 2012 Susenas.

population (on the left) through to the richest percentile (on the right), for both Papua and Indonesia. Expenditure per capita is used as a proxy of income, since it is typically difficult to obtain accurate information on income in developing countries such as Indonesia.

It can be seen that, on average, the income of the poorest 1 per cent of the population grew by less than 0.5 per cent per year in Papua (and less than 2 per cent in Indonesia as a whole), rising to roughly 10 per cent annually for the richest 1 per cent of the population, both in Papua and nationally. This suggests that the very rich have benefited more from development than other segments of the population. Since most rich people in Papua live in urban areas, and most of the poor in rural areas, it follows that urban dwellers have been the main beneficiaries of development. In Papua, a Gini coefficient of 0.42 in 2012 implies average household expenditure per capita for the poorest percentile of the population of about Rp 120,000 per month, rising to around Rp 5.5 million per month for the richest percentile.[2] That is, regardless of whether one

---

2 Based on data from the first quarter of the 2012 National Socio-Economic Survey (Survei Sosio-Ekonomi Nasional, Susenas).

considers the distribution of income growth or absolute levels of income, there is clearly a case for redistributing the benefits of development from the richer, mainly urban communities, to poorer rural populations. Among the solutions would be a more progressive tax system and social programs targeting the poor.

Health

Health outcomes are another commonly used welfare indicator. Here, we focus on the incidence of certain diseases. It is important to note, however, that in Indonesia the incidence of common diseases is generally based on reported cases in hospitals and health centres. These numbers may not be reliable, since many people who are in need of treatment do not attend health clinics or hospitals (Sedyaningsih and Gunawan 2009). In regions with poor services, low socio-economic indicators and difficult terrain, such as the provinces of Papua and West Papua, the numbers are almost certainly underestimates.

Figure 18.6 shows the incidence of three of the most serious diseases in Papua province and West Papua province – tuberculosis, malaria and AIDS – in comparison with other island groups. In 2010, the two provinces recorded the highest incidence of tuberculosis in the country, of 227 cases per 100,000 people in Papua province, and 195 in West Papua province. Maluku recorded the next highest incidence, with 170 cases per 100,000 people. The incidence of malaria is also higher in the two Papuan provinces than in any other island group – at least three times higher in 2010 than any other region except Nusa Tenggara.

Tuberculosis and malaria are among the biggest killers in Papua. Rates are persistently high in coastal areas, including urban coastal areas (Sedyaningsih and Gunawan 2009). This suggests that the efforts of the two provincial governments to target the diseases through various health programs have so far not been successful, even in urban areas where poverty is not widespread.

AIDS has also become a serious health problem, in Papua province in particular. In 2011, the cumulative number of recorded cases was approximately 180 per 100,000 people. Not only is this higher than in other regions in Indonesia, but it is also a significant increase on the 20 cases per 100,000 people recorded in 2002. The disease has now spread beyond sex workers and drug users into the general community, and beyond the mining towns into both urban and rural areas. The causes of the disproportionately high number of cases in Papua province can be traced to patterns of migration, poor literacy, inadequate education campaigns and a shortage of prevention and treatment programs (Freund 2007; National AIDS Commission 2009; Sedyaningsih and Gunawan

Figure 18.6   Incidence of tuberculosis, malaria and AIDS by major island group, 2010–11

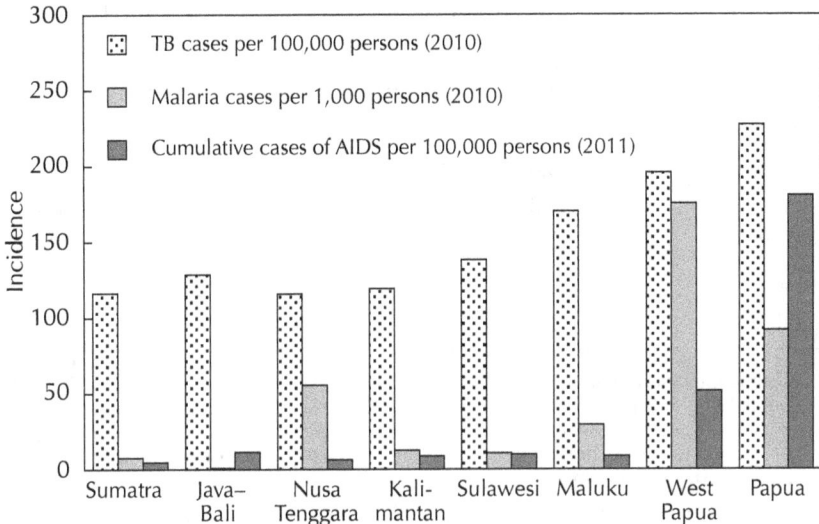

Source: Ministry of Health, Database Kesehatan, http://www.bankdata.depkes.go.id.

2009). More worrying still is the fact that the rates presented in Figure 18.6 are most likely substantial underestimates. Especially if they are living in rural areas, many Papuans are simply not aware that they may be infected and so do not show up at a hospital or health centre.

Population change and human development

According to the 2010 population census, the combined population of the two Papuan provinces is 3.6 million (Table 18.3). The population increased by 4.9 per cent annually between 2000 and 2010. This was three times the national rate, and higher than during the previous two decades, when the population grew by just over 3 per cent annually. Nevertheless, population density remains low, at around eight or nine people per square kilometre. This is half the density in other resource-rich provinces such as East Kalimantan (17 persons per square kilometre), and certainly much lower than in Sumatra and Java.

An influx of non-Papua-born citizens over the past decade or so has contributed significantly to Papua's high and rising population growth rates. During 2000–10, the annual growth rate of the non-Papua-born population was approximately 4.8 per cent for recent migrants and 6.7 per cent for lifetime migrants (Table 18.3). These migrants have tended

Table 18.3   Population dynamics in Papua, 1980–2010[a]

	Growth rate (% p.a.)			Share of total, 2010 (%)	Population (thousand)
	1980–90	1990–2000	2000–10		
Total	**3.5**	**3.0**	**4.9**	**100.0**	**3,594**
Lifetime migrant	10.6	3.1	6.7	19.1	686
Recent migrant	8.2	0.2	4.8	3.4	120
Non-migrant	2.3	3.1	4.5	77.6	2,787
Urban	5.1	5.5	4.6	26.1	937
Rural	3.5	2.3	5.0	73.9	2,657

a   Lifetime migrants are those who currently live in a province that is different from the province of birth. Recent migrants are migrants aged five years or over who reside in a different province from their province of residence five years previously. For purposes of comparison, people who were born in West Papua but now live in Papua province, and vice versa, are categorized as non-migrants.

Source: Authors' calaculation based on 1980, 1990, 2000 and 2010 population censuses.

to settle in urban areas, where they probably account for at least half the population (Resosudarmo et al. 2009a).

   One main cause of the high growth in the migrant population over the past few years has been the sudden increase in demand for skilled labour. For example, the activities of BP Indonesia in the Bintuni Bay area since 2009 have led to a sharp increase in demand for managerial and mining skills. Because of the limited availability of such skills among native Papuans, the company has had to recruit from other parts of the country, increasing the in-migration rate. BP Indonesia has set a quota for its Tangguh LNG project of 85 per cent of jobs to be filled by indigenous Papuans by 2029, but in 2012, 46 per cent of its 3,400 workers were still non-Papuan (TIAP 2012; BP 2013). Given the slow response from the Papuan side to the need for skilled labour, the likely expansion of the Tangguh LNG project and the prospect of new oil and gas tenements being developed in the future,[3] the demand for skilled labour from outside Papua is unlikely to abate soon.

   As well as being a recipient of skilled migrants, Papua has long been viewed as a suitable site for the central government's transmigration

---

3   In December 2009, the Indonesian government offered a new tender for 24 oil and gas blocks, including one in West Berau (near BP Indonesia's current site of operation) and five in Cenderawasih Bay; see 'Indonesia opens 24 new oil and gas blocks for tender and direct offer', *energy-pedia news*, 1 December 2009.

program because of its low population density. The Ministry of Trans-migration says it has identified 5.87 million hectares of land in Papua suitable for transmigration settlements. It aims to move around 10,000 people from West Java and East Java annually to other places in Indonesia, including Papua, where some previous sites have developed into thriving horticultural supply centres. In 2010, the governors of West Java and West Papua signed an agreement that would see 700 West Javanese farming households migrate annually to West Papua.[4]

Migrants entering Papua under government transmigration schemes and to meet the demand for skilled workers do not provide the entire explanation for the increase in the overall number of migrants in Papua over the last 10 years or so. Of course, in addition to skilled workers and transmigrants, many people come to Papua to work in service sectors such as transport and trade, hotels and restaurants, or to set up small businesses. Data from the 2010 population census suggest that, like skilled migrants and transmigrants, most of them have settled in urban areas.

Although the Papua-born population grew more slowly than the migrant population – by 4.5 per cent in 2000–10, compared with 6.7 per cent for lifetime migrants and 4.8 per cent for recent migrants (Table 18.3) – non-migrants still form the majority of the population (78 per cent in 2010). The rural population has been growing faster than the urban population: by 5.0 per cent per annum over the period 2000–10, compared with 4.6 per cent for the urban population. This could reflect improvements in health care in rural areas, but it is still a surprisingly high growth rate for Papua's slower-growing rural economy.

Overall, migrants are better educated than the average Papua-born citizen (Figure 18.7). The educational attainment of recent migrants is similar to that of lifetime migrants, with the majority having at least a junior secondary education. Most non-migrants, on the other hand, have gone no further than primary or junior secondary school. Among the non-migrants, West Papuans are better educated than Papuans: more than 50 per cent of Papuans, but only 20 per cent of West Papuans, have just a primary education.

Given the persistent shortage of specific skills in the mining and oil and gas sectors, and the expectation that more projects will come on stream in the future, the need for well-educated workers will only grow in the short to medium terms. For Papua-born citizens to play a bigger part in fulfilling this demand, local governments will need to invest more in education, especially tertiary education. This should be accompanied by strategies to ensure that knowledge and skills are transferred

---

4 '5 juta ha lahan transmigrasi di Papua Barat' [5 million hectares of trans-migration areas in West Papua], *Viva News*, 10 February 2010.

Figure 18.7   *Educational attainment among migrants and non-migrants,*
                 Papua province and West Papua province, 2010

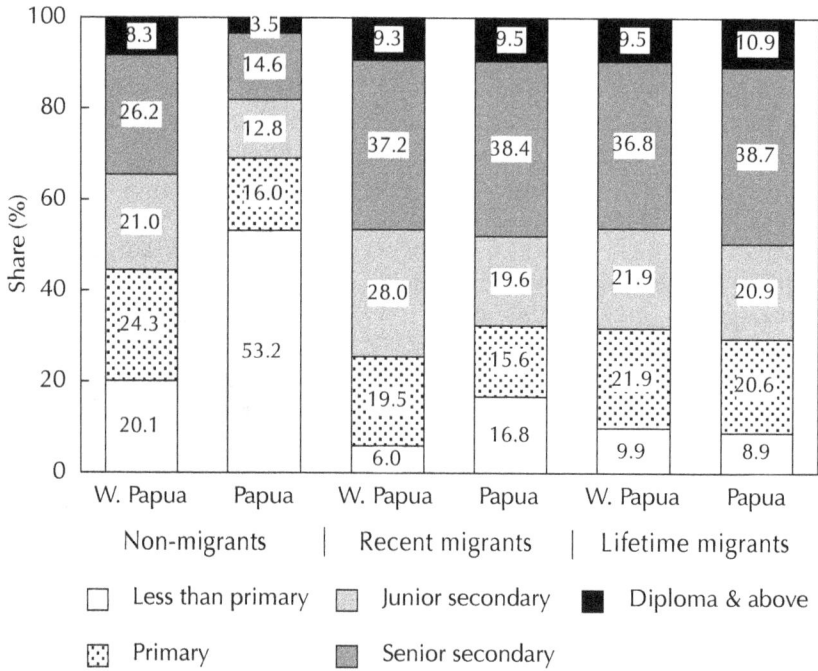

a   Lifetime migrants are those who currently live in a province that is different from the prov-
     ince of birth. Recent migrants are migrants aged five years or over who reside in a different
     province from their province of residence five years previously. For purposes of compari-
     son, people who were born in West Papua but now live in Papua province, and vice versa,
     are categorized as non-migrants.

Source: Authors' calculation based on 2010 population census.

from migrants to non-migrants, in order to improve the social returns to
education.

   Because most migrants are better educated than non-migrants, they
tend to have higher incomes than the average Papuan. They and the
richer Papuans generally live in urban areas. It is therefore not surprising
that the urban population has so far benefited disproportionately from
development in the two provinces.

18.5   REGIONAL DEVELOPMENT

In this section, we try to identify the areas within the provinces of Papua
and West Papua that have benefited most from development since the

Table 18.4 GDP and private expenditure by district, Papua province and West Papua province, 2003–11

District/group of districts	Growth of GDP, 2003–11 (% p.a.)	Growth of GDP per capita, 2003–11 (% p.a.)	GDP per capita, 2011 (Rp thousand)	Private expenditure per capita, 2011 (Rp thousand)
West Papua province				
Greater Sorong area[a]	4.6	2.0	36,209	8,450
Manokwari district	8.7	5.3	18,049	8,128
Teluk Bintuni district	39.5	33.6	298,731	11,555
Other districts	8.7	5.2	22,880	6,634
Papua province				
Greater Jayapura area[a]	12.0	8.3	31,050	9,960
Mimika district	−7.1	−12.0	239,083	10,354
Merauke district	6.9	4.8	21,234	7,135
Other districts	5.8	-4.5	7,035	5,315

a The greater Sorong area consists of Sorong district and Sorong municipality; the greater Jayapura area consists of Jayapura district and Jayapura municipality.

Source: Authors' calculation based on regional GDP data from BPS.

split in 2003. Table 18.4 shows regional GDP in the greater Sorong area (consisting of Sorong district and Sorong city), Manokwari district, Teluk Bintuni district and 'other' districts (within West Papua province); and in the greater Jayapura area (consisting of Jayapura district and Jayapura city), Mimika district, Merauke district and 'other' districts (within Papua province).

In West Papua province, the greater Sorong area and Teluk Bintuni district are both resource-based, development-driven regions. Oil and gas activities have driven development in Sorong, and the activities of Tangguh LNG in Teluk Bintuni. Growth in Manokwari district, on the other hand, has been heavily reliant on government spending. The capital cities of the districts of Sorong and Manokwari – Sorong city and Manokwari city – are relatively large municipalities that act as growth centres for the surrounding regions.

From Table 18.4 it can be seen that Teluk Bintuni's GDP has grown so rapidly that its income per capita was around 10 times that of the other regions in 2011. The greater Sorong area registered the slowest growth of both GDP and GDP per capita in 2003–11, due to the slower rate of expansion of oil and gas projects. Income per capita in Manokwari and the 'other' districts grew at about the same rate (just over 5 per cent) and their levels of per capita income in 2011 were broadly similar. Hence, if one excludes Teluk Bintuni, it appears that development has been relatively equally distributed across the province.

In Papua province, growth in the greater Jayapura area, including the capital city of Jayapura, has been driven by government spending, and that of Mimika by its resources. In Merauke, the relatively large capital city of Merauke once again acts as a growth centre for the surrounding district.

Both GDP and GDP per capita in Mimika district have contracted over the last few years as Freeport Indonesia's revenue and exports have slowed. Nevertheless, it remains a relatively rich region in terms of income per capita. The region with the fastest growth has been the greater Jayapura area, where GDP grew by 12 per cent per annum in 2003–11, and GDP per capita by 8 per cent, making it the second-richest region in Papua province after Mimika. GDP in Merauke and the 'other' districts grew at around half the rate of the greater Jayapura area. GDP per capita in the 'other' districts actually contracted between 2003 and 2011, with the result that they recorded the lowest income per capita in 2011. One can conclude that the greater Jayapura area has so far captured most of the benefits of development in Papua province.

Government expenditure

Government expenditure, by both the central government and local governments, is an important sector in the two Papuan provinces. As revealed in the regional accounts, it has been growing quite quickly – by over 10 per cent annually during the past decade or so. Government expenditure makes an important contribution to the economies of the two provinces, and creates significant multiplier effects in other sectors. For example, government spending on roads and transport not only directly expands the construction and transport sectors, but also induces expansion in other sectors such as trade, agriculture and manufacturing. This section discusses the size and types of local government expenditure, for both the provincial and district governments. It does not examine central government expenditures in the two Papuan provinces, which are more difficult to dissect.

Local governments in Papua derive most of their income from the DAU, from the special autonomy funds (*dana otsus*) available only to Papua and Aceh, and from their own natural resources (the latter through revenue sharing with the central government; see section 18.1 above). In 2011, these three sources of income accounted for about 46 per cent, 25

Figure 18.8   *Local government expenditure per capita by major island group, 2007 and 2011*

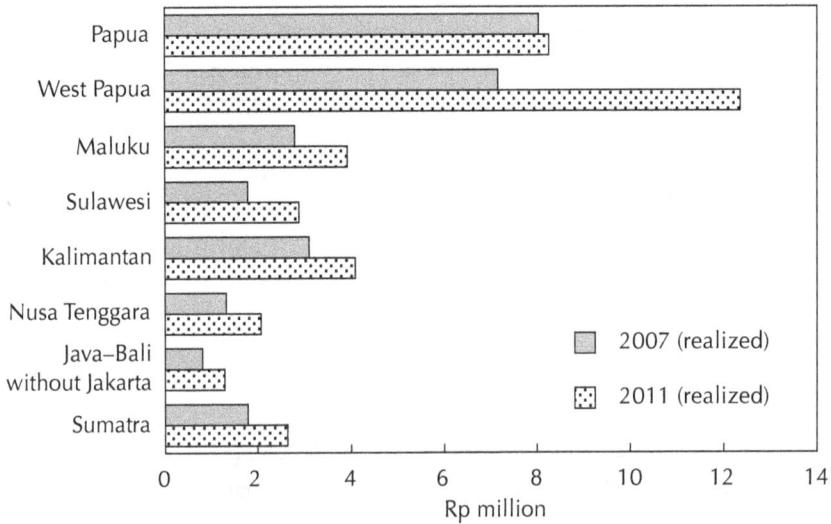

Source: Authors' calculation based on data from Directorate General for Fiscal Balance (2013).

per cent and 9 per cent respectively of total income in Papua province, and 34 per cent, 29 per cent and 21 per cent in West Papua province. By comparison, the shares of total income for all Indonesian provinces were 44 per cent (DAU) and 17 per cent (revenue sharing). Transfers from the Special Purpose Fund (Dana Alokasi Khusus, DAK) were more important for Papua province (7 per cent of total local government income) than for West Papua province (5 per cent). Own-source revenue (*pendapatan asli daerah*, PAD) has been relatively unimportant in both provinces, constituting just 3 per cent of total local government income in both provinces in 2011. Both provinces have put most of their income to use: Papua province was able to spend approximately 88 per cent of its income in 2011, and West Papua province 93 per cent.

Although small compared with those of middle-income and developed countries,[5] the per capita expenditures of the Papua and West Papua provincial governments are relatively large compared with those of other Indonesian provinces and some other developing countries. Figure 18.8 shows that, in both 2007 and 2011, realized per capita government expenditures in the two provinces were at least twice those in the other major island groups. In 2011, government expenditure was just

---

5 See http://www.principalglobalindicators.org/default.aspx.

Table 18.5   Structure of government expenditures in Papua province and West Papua province, 2010 (%)

Category	West Papua province	Papua province	National average
General services	53.5	49.1	32.5
Order & security	1.2	0.7	0.9
Economic	9.5	10.6	8.9
Environment	0.5	0.5	1.7
Housing & public facilities	17.4	16.1	14.5
Health	5.0	8.4	9.8
Tourism & culture	0.6	0.6	0.6
Education	10.1	12.5	29.7
Social protection	2.2	1.6	1.3

Source: Authors' calculation based on data from Directorate General for Fiscal Balance (2013).

over Rp 8 million per capita in Papua province, and more than Rp 12 million in West Papua province.

The main problem in Papua is not so much the amount of government expenditures but how the money is allocated. The largest expenditure item in the provincial budgets is general administration (employees' salaries, building maintenance and other items related to local government facilities), most of which is spent in urban areas (Table 18.5). In 2010, the national average for local government expenditure on general administration as a share of total expenditure was a rather high 33 per cent (see Lewis, Chapter 6), but in Papua province and West Papua province the shares were far higher, at 54 per cent and 49 per cent respectively. The consequence of this high spending on general administration is that not much is left over to fund other priorities. For example, although required by Law 20/2003 on the National Education System to spend at least 20 per cent of their budgets on education (Suryadarma and Jones 2013), in 2010 Papua province and West Papua province spent only 10 per cent and 13 per cent respectively on this sector. Spending on much needed social protection measures was lower still, at around 2 per cent of total expenditures in both provinces.

Clearly the structure of local government expenditures in both provinces needs to change so that far less is spent on general administration and far more on the economic, health, tourism, education and social protection sectors.

Figure 18.9   *Electricity consumption per capita by major island group*
                  (kWh per capita)

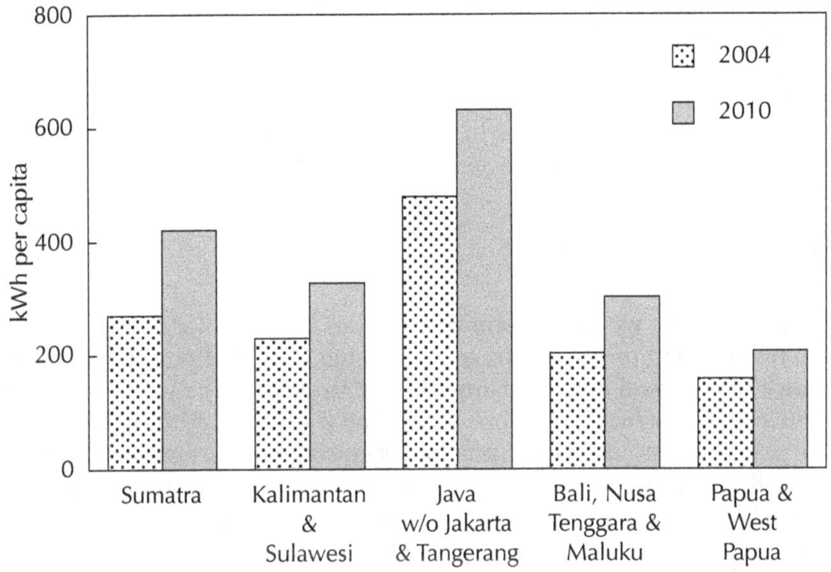

Source: BPS (various years).

Infrastructure

Although development in Papua has mainly benefited urban areas, most Papuans – including the vast majority of indigenous Papuans – are still dependent on the rural economy. Close to 74 per cent of the population lives in rural areas, with limited access to education and health services, electricity and other economic infrastructure. Improving conditions in rural areas is therefore essential to provide greater equality in education and welfare to Papua-born citizens – surely the main purpose of Papuan development.

One of the chief requirements is to improve rural infrastructure and facilities, with education, energy, trade and transport infrastructure all requiring attention. For example, the poor quality of educational facilities is certainly a factor in the current low levels of educational attainment among Papuans; and deficiencies in energy supply have been a major bottleneck for the development of various sectors, including trade, education and industry.

To provide an indication of the severity of the situation, Figure 18.9 shows electricity consumption per capita in Papua compared with that in the other major island groups. Electricity consumption by Papuan households in both 2004 and 2010 was lower than anywhere else in Indonesia; in fact, the per capita consumption of Papua in 2010 was similar to that of Bali and Nusa Tenggara six years earlier, in 2004. The shortage of electricity is especially acute in Papua's rural areas.

Although Papua's low population density and difficult terrain constrain the ability of governments to finance electrification and provide other essential infrastructure in rural areas, solving this problem needs to be a high priority in policy debate and practice.

18.6   FINAL REMARKS

In this chapter, we have examined various aspects of development in the two Papuan provinces. In general, using GDP and poverty levels as indicators of development, it appears that the region as a whole has been developing at a faster rate than the national average. Although GDP in the post-2003 province of Papua has been stagnant, economic activities other than mining have grown significantly. We therefore reject the argument that development has been stagnant. On the contrary, we argue that Papua has been one of the most dynamic regions in the country. Nevertheless, both Papuan provinces face serious development challenges.

The main one is to reduce rural poverty, which is still very high – about 41 per cent in 2012, or more than double the national average. Urban poverty, on the other hand, is roughly the same as in the country as a whole. Moreover, annual growth in household income has been much lower in rural than in urban areas, resulting in slower than expected poverty reduction in rural areas.

We have offered several explanations for the failure of rural poverty to decline as quickly as it should have. First, the economies of both provinces are heavily reliant on extractive industries, with the result that fewer government resources are directed to other sectors that could generate broader benefits, such as agriculture. Second, rural areas lack education, health and other infrastructure, resulting in low levels of educational attainment and employment generation. Third, most government spending has been on government administration, at the expense of programs to alleviate rural poverty. The existing poverty alleviation programs are neither adequately funded nor effective. Fourth, there has been a strong urban bias to development. Most of the government budget (including the salaries of government employees) has been spent either in urban areas or in the mining enclaves; these areas are also the beneficiaries of spending by private sector workers employed by extractive and other industries. This has made these areas attractive to migrants, many of whom have set up businesses servicing the surrounding communities.

This in turn has led to further increases in government budgetary spending in urban areas. Finally, rural population growth has been relatively high, so the benefits of economic growth in rural areas have had to be distributed among a larger population.

In addition to the factors mentioned above, governance and political issues are widely believed to exacerbate rural poverty in Papua. For example, a lack of transparency in the management of public finance has given bureaucrats opportunities to act corruptly. Traditional customary law on land and forest rights is another factor, as it commonly creates conflict between local communities and the government or investors, slowing down development. The process of subdivision of districts into ever-smaller administrative units (*pemekaran*) has also created conflict between competing elites over the spoils of government, thus inducing uncertainty and delaying the implementation of various poverty alleviation programs (see Nolan, Jones and Solahudin, Chapter 17).

There is also much to be done to improve other welfare indicators, such as public health outcomes. The incidence of tuberculosis, malaria and AIDS, for instance, is much higher in Papua than in other regions. One of the most convincing explanations for the poor health outcomes in Papua is the inadequate government health budgets and the failure to spend funds wisely.

Finally, we have argued that the dependence of both provinces' economies on just a few extractive sectors creates problems. First, the benefits of mining, oil and gas activities have not spread to the general population, particularly in rural areas. Second, the dominance of extractive industries means that there is less incentive to develop other sectors. But as a consequence, when there is a contraction in the extractive industries, the whole economy contracts as well.

Future policies in Papua province and West Papua province should focus on encouraging the development of sectors that would benefit the rural population, such as agriculture and agricultural processing. Larger and better-targeted programs to promote the development of rural infrastructure, education, and trade in goods and services between rural and urban areas should also be established. Finally, to the extent that the rapid growth of the rural population is due to high fertility rates, it may be advisable to re-establish a strong family planning program.

REFERENCES

Anggraeni, D. (2007) 'Pattern of commercial and industrial resource use in Papua', in A.J. Marshall and B.M. Beehler (eds) *The Ecology of Papua: Part Two*, Periplus, Singapore.

Ballard, C. and G. Banks (2009) 'Between a rock and a hard place: corporate strategy at the Freeport mine in Papua, 2001–2006', in B.P. Resosudarmo and F. Jotzo (eds) *Working with Nature against Poverty: Development, Resources and the Environment in Eastern Indonesia*, Institute of Southeast Asian Studies, Singapore.

BP (2013) 'Tangguh LNG and expansion', available at http://www.bp.com/en/global/corporate/careers/working-at-bp/our-projects/tangguh.html.

BPS (Badan Pusat Statistik) (various years) *Statistik Indonesia* [Indonesian Statistics], BPS, Jakarta.

Directorate General for Fiscal Balance (2013) 'Data keuangan daerah setelah TA 2006' [Regional financial data after financial year 2006], Ministry of Finance, Jakarta, available at http://www.djpk.depkeu.go.id/data-series/data-keuangan-daerah/setelah-ta-2006.

Freeport-McMoRan Copper & Gold Inc. (2013) *Expanding Resources: 2012 Annual Report*, Freeport-McMoRan Copper & Gold Inc., Phoenix.

Freund, A. (2007) 'The HIV/AIDS pandemic in West Papua', Australia West Papua Association, Newcastle.

Garnaut, R. and C. Manning (1972) 'An economic survey of West Irian: Part I', *Bulletin of Indonesian Economic Studies*, 8(3); 33–65.

Garnaut, R. and C. Manning (1973) 'An economic survey of West Irian: Part II', *Bulletin of Indonesian Economic Studies*, 9(1); 30–64.

Manning, C. and M. Rumbiak (1989) 'Irian Jaya: economic change, migrants, and indigenous welfare', in H. Hill (ed.) *Unity and Diversity: Regional Economic Development in Indonesia since 1970*, Oxford University Press, Singapore.

McGibbon, R. (2004) 'Secessionist challenges in Aceh and Papua: is special autonomy the solution?', Policy Studies 10, East-West Center, Washington DC.

McGibbon, R. (2006) *Pitfalls of Papua*, Lowy Institute for International Policy, Sydney.

National AIDS Commission (2009) 'Republic of Indonesia country report on the follow up to the declaration of commitment on HIV/AIDS (UNGASS): reporting period 2008–2009', National AIDS Commission Republic of Indonesia, Jakarta.

Resosudarmo, B.P., L. Napitupulu, C. Manning and V. Wanggai (2009a) 'Papua I: challenges of economic development in an era of political and economic change', in B.P. Resosudarmo and F. Jotzo (eds) *Working with Nature against Poverty: Development, Resources and the Environment in Eastern Indonesia*, Institute of Southeast Asian Studies, Singapore.

Resosudarmo, B.P., C. Manning and L. Napitupulu (2009b) 'Papua II: challenges for public administration and economic policy under special autonomy', in B.P. Resosudarmo and F. Jotzo (eds) *Working with Nature against Poverty: Development, Resources and the Environment in Eastern Indonesia*, Institute of Southeast Asian Studies, Singapore.

Sedyaningsih, E.R. and S. Gunawan (2009) 'How far is Papua from achieving the goals of Healthy Indonesia 2010?', in B.P. Resosudarmo and F. Jotzo (eds) *Working with Nature against Poverty: Development, Resources and the Environment in Eastern Indonesia*, Institute of Southeast Asian Studies, Singapore.

Sumule, A. (ed.) (2003) *Mencari Jalan Tengah Otonomi Khusus Provinsi Papua* [Finding the Middle Ground on Special Autonomy for Papua], PT Gramedia Pustaka Utama, Jakarta.

Suryadarma, D. and G.W. Jones (2013) *Education in Indonesia*, Institute of Southeast Asian Studies, Singapore.

TIAP (Tangguh Independent Advisory Panel) (2012) 'Report on operations of the Tanggug LNG project', TIAP, October, available at http://www.bp.com/content/dam/bp/pdf/sustainability/group-reports/TIAP_Report_2012_Final1.pdf.

Weisskoff, R. and E. Wolf (1977) 'Linkages and leakages: industrial tracking in an enclave economy', *Economic Development and Cultural Change*, 25: 607–28.

Widjojo, M.S. (ed.) (2010) *Papua Road Map: Negotiating the Past, Improving the Present and Securing the Future*, Institute of Southeast Asian Studies, Singapore.

19 Special autonomy, predatory peace and the resolution of the Aceh conflict

Edward Aspinall

19.1 INTRODUCTION

Since 2005, one of the most remarkable achievements in global peace making has occurred in the province of Aceh. The former rebel movement, the Free Aceh Movement (Gerakan Aceh Merdeka, GAM), has transformed itself into a largely civilian political movement that competes for power through elections. Political violence has declined dramatically, and most of the violence that does occur is not between Indonesian security forces and GAM supporters as it was during the conflict years. Most observers have ascribed the success of the peace process in part to the autonomy arrangements promised to GAM during the peace talks in Helsinki in 2005. GAM supporters describe these arrangements as 'self-government', while representatives of the Indonesian government typically use the term 'special autonomy'. These arrangements were embodied in Law 11/2006 on the Governing of Aceh a little over a year after the Helsinki peace agreement was signed. It has provided the framework for organizing Aceh's governmental affairs ever since.

While observers are right in attributing the success of the peace process to the compromise reached in Helsinki, and subsequently formalized in Law 11/2006, it would be a mistake to think that the autonomy package represents a set of ingredients that could successfully be transplanted to other conflict zones with similar results, regardless of circumstances. In fact, most of the ingredients had been tried before in Aceh but had failed. Following the fall of the Suharto presidency in 1998, the Indonesian government made several efforts to resolve the Aceh conflict by way of special autonomy, including two laws passed in 1999 and 2001. Many of the elements in the 2006 law had in fact already been included in the 2001 law, but were rejected at the time by GAM leaders as being a poor substitute for independence. Moreover, as we shall see, in several ways the autonomy arrangements put into effect in Aceh have fallen short of GAM supporters' expectations, and Jakarta retains decisive authority in various areas of Aceh's affairs.

What, then, has made the post-2005 special autonomy deal so successful? I argue that it boils down to a combination of two elements. First are the core political provisions in the Helsinki memorandum of understanding (MOU) and the 2006 law that have allowed GAM to transform itself into a political force and compete for power through elections. These provisions were missing from the 2001 law, and they were the deal breaker in the 2005 Helsinki peace talks. As a result of these provisions, candidates with GAM backgrounds won the gubernatorial elections in 2006 and 2011, occupy executive power in about half of Aceh's districts and dominate the provincial legislature as well as several district legislatures. Second are the economic arrangements that have meant that Aceh has been awash with government funds, providing many rent-seeking and illicit fund-raising opportunities for the former rebels who now dominate local politics. It is by observing the interaction between these political and economic elements that we may see the core dynamic at play in Aceh's local politics in the post-MOU era, a dynamic that might be characterized as 'predatory peace'.

The chapter advances this argument in three steps. First, it presents a brief historical survey of the efforts to achieve peace by way of autonomy arrangements in Aceh province in the post-Suharto period (section 19.2). Second, it describes some of the limits of the autonomy deal put in place since 2006, and the ways in which these arrangements fall short of the goal of 'self-government' set by supporters of GAM (section 19.3). Not only does Law 11/2006 contain many provisions that limit Aceh's authority to govern itself, but several key implementing regulations have not yet been passed. Finally, the chapter addresses the puzzle of why such a limited form of special autonomy has been so effective in consolidating peace (section 19.4). It explains that the situation has been made bearable for most leaders of the movement because of the two core components of special autonomy mentioned above: the mechanisms that have allowed former GAM supporters to dominate Aceh politically, and the economic arrangements that have enabled them to benefit materially from that dominance.

19.2   THE HISTORY OF SPECIAL AUTONOMY

For much of the decade following the resignation of President Suharto in 1998, attempts to resolve the conflict in Aceh focused on two processes that at first ran parallel, or even at cross purposes, but eventually combined successfully after the catastrophic December 2004 tsunami. First, various policy makers in Aceh and Jakarta tried to design a special autonomy package that would respond to Acehnese grievances and thus reduce political tensions in the province. They were motivated both by the spread of generalized unrest there (notably a series of large protests in 1999 and 2000 calling for a referendum on independence) and, more specifically, by the re-emergence of the GAM insurgency. Second, through talks first initiated in 1999, the central government attempted to deal directly with the insurgency by negotiating with GAM leaders. Initially, however, the GAM leaders saw these talks as an opportunity to internationalize the Aceh conflict and so achieve their goal of independence, and were dismissive of any compromise solution involving autonomy.

The first move to provide Aceh with extended autonomy outside the context of negotiations with GAM came during the dying weeks of the Habibie presidency in 1999. It was initiated by a group of legislators from the Islamic United Development Party (Partai Persatuan Pembangunan, PPP) who had just helped pass the nationwide decentralization laws and believed something more had to be done to placate Aceh. Together with many other policy makers in Jakarta, they recognized that the central government had never really acted in good faith to realize the promises to grant Aceh the status of a Special Territory (Daerah Istimewa) after an earlier armed conflict in the 1950s, and that the resulting disillusionment was still a cause of unrest in the province. Accordingly, in September 1999 all groups in the remaining Suharto-era national parliament (Dewan Perwakilan Rakyat, DPR) agreed to Law 44/1999 on Special Status for Aceh (Keistimewaan Aceh) before being replaced by legislators chosen in the June 1999 national elections.

A brief document consisting of 13 articles, the law acknowledged Acehnese forms of 'special status' in the fields of religious life, custom, education and the role of Islamic clerics (ulama) in the determination of regional policy. The law was designed as a salve to Acehnese aspirations, but it lacked detail. As in the Special Territory arrangements dating back to the 1950s, there was no clear delineation of authority between the national and provincial governments. The provincial government was required to produce regulations to bring the provisions of the law into effect. However, the initiators of the bill made it clear during the drafting process that all of the existing national law would continue to apply in Aceh.[1] As a result, the law had limited practical effect.

---

1 See, for example, 'Semua fraksi DPR RI setuju berlakunya syariat Islam di Aceh' [All parliamentary factions agree to the enforcement of Islamic shariah in Aceh], *Waspada*, 2 September 1999.

A more ambitious attempt came when Law 18/2001 on Special Autonomy for Nanggroe Aceh Darussalam was passed two years later. It significantly increased the range of concessions granted to Aceh. Responding to a longstanding grievance, it gave Aceh a much larger share of its oil and gas and other natural resource revenues than was provided to other provinces. It strengthened the ability of the province to enact Islamic law (*shariah*) regulations and to enforce them through a newly established Shariah Court. The law also contained several provisions on political arrangements, including one allowing direct elections of the governor and district heads, anticipating a similar provision that would come into force nationwide in 2005.

Several of the Acehnese legislators involved in drafting this law had participated in informal consultations with GAM leaders on its substance, and they hoped that certain provisions would help to accommodate GAM in a future peace deal. Notably, Law 18/2001 provided for the establishment of the office of Wali Nanggroe (Guardian of the State), the title GAM used to refer to the movement's founder and leader, Hasan di Tiro. However, most analyses of the law and its implementation concluded that special autonomy was a failure (McGibbon 2004; Miller 2006). Continuing conditions of conflict in the province meant that many of the law's provisions simply could not be implemented. Moreover, the fact that the 'concessions were offered unilaterally' (McGibbon 2004: 16) rather than as a product of a bargain struck with GAM meant that the law had no appreciable effect in lessening the conflict. On the contrary, GAM leaders condemned the law as falling far short of Acehnese aspirations for full independence.

Meanwhile, running parallel to these legislative initiatives were various efforts to resolve the Aceh conflict by way of negotiations between representatives of GAM and the government (Aspinall and Crouch 2003). These began under President Abdurrahman Wahid, not long after he came to power in 1999 and shortly after the passage of Law 44/1999 on Special Status for Aceh. Over the following three years the negotiations at times produced ceasefires, but they always foundered on the question of the final status of Aceh. GAM leaders did not budge from their goal of complete independence, and were dismissive of the special autonomy formulation. The continuing distance between the two sides on this fundamental issue meant that the ceasefires always broke down (Aspinall and Crouch 2003: 45). Eventually, the government declared a state of 'military emergency' in the province in 2003 and declared it would eliminate GAM once and for all.

This situation changed dramatically after new negotiations began in Helsinki in early 2005, immediately after the massive Indian Ocean tsunami of 26 December 2004. This is not the place to review the Helsinki process.[2] Two factors, however, made the negotiations different from preceding talks. First was the fact that the mediator, former Finnish president Martti Ahtisaari, insisted on a formula for the talks that 'nothing is agreed until everything is agreed', effectively making an autonomy deal of some sort a prerequisite for their successful conclusion. Second was the GAM leadership's acceptance of this logic and their announcement, on the eve of the second round of the talks, that they were prepared to accept a solution involving self-government for Aceh within Indonesia.

Once they had made this concession, the way was open for a final deal. The GAM negotiators (and adherents of the movement ever since) found solace in continuing to reject the term 'special autonomy'. They preferred 'self-government', a status they saw as conferring much greater powers, perhaps akin to those enjoyed by the Åland Islands in Finland or Hong Kong in China. The Helsinki MOU signed in August 2005 does not use either term (it does not even mention 'autonomy') but instead sets out a number of points delineating Aceh's authority and requiring central government action in areas such as local government, political participation, management of the economy, rule of law and human rights. It also details procedures for reintegration of and assistance for former GAM combatants and conflict victims, and for establishing mechanisms for organizing the peace process itself. Critically, the MOU stated that 'A new Law on the Governing of Aceh will be promulgated and will enter into force' (clause 1.1.1) to put into effect the key political provisions of the agreement.

19.3   THE LIMITS OF SPECIAL AUTONOMY[3]

In exchange for giving up their goal of independence, the GAM negotiators aimed to wring the maximum concessions possible from the Indonesian government in terms of the powers that would be granted to Aceh. For them, one of the key provisions in the Helsinki MOU was item 1.1.2(a):

> Aceh will exercise authority within all sectors of public affairs, which will be administered in conjunction with its civil and judicial administration, except in the fields of foreign affairs, external defence, national security, monetary and fiscal matters, justice and freedom of religion, the policies of which

---

2 Various works trace the negotiations from differing perspectives; see, for example, Aspinall (2005), Kingsbury (2006), Husain (2007) and Awaludin (2008).

3 Some of the material in this section is adapted from Chapter 4 (written by me) in Aspinall, Hillman and McCawley (2012).

belong to the Government of the Republic of Indonesia in conformity with the Constitution.

GAM leaders and some other political actors in Aceh argued that this provision meant that all areas of government except the six explicitly mentioned would be exclusively reserved to Aceh, making for the widest possible version of 'self-government'. This interpretation is still held by many Acehnese leaders, despite the fact that the wording of the provision is almost identical to that in Law 22/1999 on Regional Government (Indonesia's first major decentralization law), which obviously did not result in such an outcome elsewhere in Indonesia. As May (2008) has explained:

> The wording of the MOU does not justify this interpretation, and such an arrangement would also be unrealistic as there are numerous functions outside the six sectors mentioned in the MOU that need to be regulated and/ or implemented by central government. This is particularly true for those government functions that constitute the constitutional obligations of the central government, are related to international conventions that have been translated into national law, or to government functions, the implementation of which by the government of Aceh would affect other regions of Indonesia or even other countries.

Despite being committed to the peace agreement, central government leaders were also reluctant to concede too much to 'separatists'. After the Helsinki MOU was agreed to, several party leaders in the national parliament, as well as senior government and security officials, expressed concern about aspects of the agreement and its implications for Indonesia's unitary state system.

These differences in perception set the scene for protracted negotiations throughout late 2005 and much of the following year, leading to the formulation and passage of Law 11/2006 on the Governing of Aceh. Participating in these negotiations were representatives of GAM, Acehnese civil society and the Aceh government, as well as government officials and non-government actors at the national level, although of course it was the national parliament and government that finally approved the law.[4] There were major differences between the versions of the bill prepared in Aceh and those prepared by the central government, though compromises were reached on most matters. The preparation of the bill was thus in some ways a successful exercise in participatory democracy,

---

4 For one useful account of these negotiations, written before they concluded, see ICG (2006: 1-6). For an insider's account written by an Acehnese member of the national parliament who was integrally involved in the negotiations, see Hamid (2006).

with a significant range of Acehnese and national interests represented in the discussions.

However, this approach also had its costs. As May (2008) puts it:

> ... the direct involvement of an unusually large number of stakeholders with a vast scope of varying interests in all stages of the drafting process has led to many compromises, which often come at the cost of clarity and consistency of the law.

In some areas, the text of the law differed from that of the Helsinki MOU, leading to accusations by some in GAM and other groups that Law 11/2006 'deviated' from the peace agreement, or even 'betrayed' its core spirit. For example, there was a significant change on the key issue of central government powers. Whereas the Helsinki MOU listed six powers exclusively reserved to the central government (described above), Law 11/2006 (article 7.2) also reserved to the centre 'government functions (*urusan*) of national character', a broadly formulated phrase the elucidation of which was left to a further central government regulation (*peraturan pemerintah*). This government regulation had not been produced at the time of writing, even though central and Aceh government representatives have been negotiating its content for several years. Its eventual form will determine to what extent Aceh will be subject to standard national laws and regulations in a host of critical areas.

Another crucial point concerned the protection of the province's autonomy. In the Helsinki talks, GAM negotiators wanted to ensure that Aceh's envisaged new powers would not be whittled away by subsequent legislative or executive actions by Jakarta. They succeeded in having inserted into the agreement a provision that meant that new laws and administrative measures affecting Aceh and produced by either the national legislature or the national executive would need to be 'taken in consultation with and with the consent of the legislature of Aceh' (article 11.2(c)) or 'implemented in consultation with and with the consent of the head of the Aceh administration' (article 11.2(d)). These measures would have handed Aceh veto power over national laws and regulations affecting the province, and were therefore constitutionally dubious (May 2006: 14). Accordingly, they were translated into Law 11/2006 (article 8) in watered-down form, requiring not the consent but the 'consultation and advice' of the Aceh legislature (for laws) and the governor (for administrative measures), with the details of such consultations to be established by presidential regulation.

Crucially, the law adopted holus-bolus large parts of the 2004 decentralizations laws that applied throughout Indonesia (Law 32/2004 on Regional Government and Law 33/2004 on the Fiscal Balance between the Central Government and the Regions). Law 11/2006 also dealt with the substance of many sectoral laws (that is, laws governing this or that sector of economic, social or national life), adopting their provisions but

> ... modifying or adjusting [them] slightly to the Aceh situation, while at the same time all stipulations of these laws apply to Aceh as well, as long as they do not contradict the LOGA [Law on the Governing of Aceh] (May 2006: 52, quoting section 269.1 of Law 11/2006).

At many points, Law 11/2006 grants a power to Aceh that is then immediately modified by the phrase 'in accordance with regulations and laws' (this phrase occurs 49 times in the law, and there are various cognates), making the grant identical to one enjoyed by other provinces. To add to the complexity, it is not always clear in the law whether special autonomy in particular sectors accrues only to the province of Aceh, or also to its districts and municipalities (May 2006: 56–8). As a result of such compromises, the scope of Aceh's special autonomy or self-government (depending on which term one wants to use) is subject to significant limits. These limitations can be seen mostly in two areas.

Constraints on autonomy

First are the limits on Aceh's autonomy that flow from the various compromises summarized above. The fact that the majority of the legislative framework for government administration in the province is still essentially drawn from Laws 32/2004 and 33/2004 means that, in most matters, Aceh is governed by the same provisions that establish the framework for all other provinces, despite having been granted special powers. Only in a few additional key areas do the powers granted to Aceh significantly exceed those enjoyed by other provinces.

Moreover, there are many safeguards built into Law 11/2006 to ensure that those special powers are circumscribed. The strongest such provision, though one that is yet to be invoked, holds that the central government can cancel any regulation passed by the provincial parliament (*qanun*) simply if it contravenes the 'public interest' (article 235.2(b)). Some of the more specific and consequential safeguards concern symbolically charged political matters. For instance, article 82 on local political parties includes a provision prohibiting local parties from endangering the 'wholeness' of the Unitary State of the Republic of Indonesia, while the subsequent government regulation on local parties in Aceh (20/2007) gives the provincial office of the national Ministry of Law and Human Rights, rather than any organ of the provincial government, the authority to approve registration of local parties. Thus, when GAM members tried to register Partai Gerakan Aceh Merdeka (Partai GAM), they confronted a storm of protest from senior ministers, including the Minister of Law and Human Rights, who made it clear that it was within his rights to instruct the provincial office of the ministry to prevent any local party from adopting a name or symbol that would 'tend towards or promote the disintegration of the unitary state'.[5] Following negotiations with the central government, GAM leaders backed down and eventually chose 'Partai Aceh' as the name of their party.

Similar tensions were on display in 2013 when the Aceh parliament passed a *qanun* (3/2013) adopting, as the new flag for the province, a barely modified version of the Aceh flag GAM had used when struggling for independence. In this case the *qanun* did not fall foul of an article in Law 11/2006 but collided, rather, with a government regulation that had been passed after the law was formulated. Government Regulation 77/2007 on Regional Symbols prohibits any flag 'that bears similarity to the logo or flag of banned organizations or separatist movements, associations, institutions or organizations' (article 6(4)). This was an obvious example of a government regulation affecting Aceh that had been issued without consultation with the Aceh government, despite article 8 of Law 11/2006 mentioned above. This time, the Minister of Home Affairs issued a directive to the Aceh government requiring amendments to the *qanun* on 13 points, mostly relating to the design of the flag.[6]

A little different was the very serious conflict between Aceh's parliament and the Partai Aceh leadership on the one hand, and, on the other, the Jakarta government and Governor Irwandi Yusuf (a former GAM member who had been elected as an independent in 2006), over whether independent candidates should be allowed to run in local executive elections in the province. Law 11/2006 included a provision allowing independent candidates to contest such elections, but only in the first elections after the passage of the law (elections that were held in 2006). Subsequently the Constitutional Court held that this provision was unconstitutional, opening the way for independent candidates to continue to contest elections. Partai Aceh leaders argued that the court's decision violated article 8 of Law 11/2006 requiring consultation with Aceh's parliament if any national body wanted to change the rules governing Aceh. Their underlying goal was to prevent, or at least delay, Governor Irwandi's renomination (Aspinall 2011).

It is perhaps not surprising that there would be conflict between the Aceh government and the central government over such symbolically

---

5 'Soal Partai GAM Mattalata belum bisa perintah kanwil NAD' [Mattalata cannot yet give an order to the Aceh regional office on Partai GAM], *Serambi Indonesia*, 11 July 2007.

6 See ICG (2013) for a useful overview of this dispute, which had not been resolved at the time of writing.

loaded and politically important issues. But centralization persists also in more prosaic matters. Thus, there was a long-running dispute between the Aceh parliament and the national government during 2010 over whether the third deputy speaker of the Aceh parliament would represent the party with the fourth-largest vote (in accordance with national legislation), or Partai Aceh, which was what the majority in the parliament believed was possible under Law 11/2006.[7] More critically, as with regional regulations passed by any province, *qanun* passed by Aceh's parliament must be sent to the Ministry of Home Affairs in Jakarta, which has the right to annul them if it determines that they violate national regulations.[8] The minister also vets the provincial budget each year, striking out items that are not considered to be in keeping with national rules and regulations on expenditure.[9] In other areas the centre retains authority, but in ways that afford Aceh greater symbolic clout than other provinces. For example, whereas governors of other provinces must consult with the Minister of Home Affairs before appointing a regional secretary (the highest-ranking public servant in the provincial bureaucracy), in Aceh the governor must consult with the president.

It should also be noted at this point that in many of the areas where Aceh's authority *does* exceed that of other provinces, Law 11/2006 basically reproduces or extends provisions that were already in the 2001 special autonomy law (Law 18/2001). One obvious example concerns the implementation of *shariah*. The provisions in Law 11/2006 do not dramatically extend the scope of Aceh's authority to enforce *shariah* beyond what was already granted in the 2001 law, though they are more elaborate. Moreover, it should be remembered that Islamic law implementation was not a demand of GAM; rather, it was included in the special

---

7   'Penetapan Wakil Ketua III DPRA, Mendagri ultimatum Gubernur Aceh' [Minister of Home Affairs sends ultimatum to the Governor of Aceh on the appointment of the Third Deputy Speaker of the Aceh People's Representative Council], *Serambi Indonesia*, 25 October 2010.

8   According to one report, between 2002 and 2012 the central government annulled 45 *qanun* from Aceh, though all but one were produced by district or city governments, not the provincial government. See 'Agar dana tak terbuang sia-sia' [So that funds are not thrown out pointlessly], *Serambi Indonesia*, 21 May 2013.

9   See, for example, 'Mendagri koreksi APBA 2007 '[Home affairs minister corrects the 2007 Aceh budget], *Serambi Indonesia*, 27 June 2007; 'Mendagri koreksi APBA 2009' [Minister of Home Affairs corrects the 2009 Aceh budget], *Serambi Indonesia*, 25 February 2009. This is a source of conflict with the provincial government and parliament; see 'Koreksi Mendagri bagai tak dihirau: APBA 2009 disahkan tanpa diperbaiki' [Minister of Home Affairs' corrections apparently ignored: 2009 Aceh budget passed without improvements], *Serambi Indonesia*, 2 March 2009.

autonomy package offered to Aceh in 2001 as a means of undercutting popular support for the rebellion (Aspinall 2007a, 2009b: 209–13), even if several GAM-supported district heads and mayors have since become enthusiasts for *shariah* implementation.

Delays and limits in implementing regulations

The second limitation on Aceh's autonomy involves the requirement, in many crucial areas of governmental authority (99 by my count), for the power granted to Aceh in a particular article of Law 11/2006 to be 'regulated' (*diatur*) by further legal instruments. Specifically, the law requires the issuance of 12 national-level regulations (nine government regulations and three presidential regulations) and, according to the government of Aceh's own count, 59 *qanun* (Pemerintah Aceh 2010). As one senior official in the Aceh government put it, Law 11/2006 is only 'the skin' of special autonomy; the various implementing regulations will produce 'the contents'.[10] In other words, the passage of the law in 2006 marked only the beginning of the new era of extended autonomy for Aceh, rather than its culmination. Until the various regulations are issued it is hard to be definitive about just how far-reaching the grant of autonomy will be.

Legislative and regulatory productivity in Indonesia is notoriously glacial in pace, but the implementing regulations for Law 11/2006 have been especially slow in appearing. In the seven years that have elapsed since the law was passed (a period that exceeds the period of heightened conflict between 1999 and 2005 that prompted the peace deal in the first place), only four of the required 12 national regulations have been produced.[11] The missing regulations cover some of the most critical areas covered by the law, including delineation of national government authority in Aceh, transfer of the offices and powers of the National Land Agency (Badan Pertanahan Nasional, BPN) to Aceh, operation of the Sabang Free Port and powers over oil and gas. In the absence of these regulations, Aceh continues to be subject to standard national laws and regulations in a host of areas, including sensitive ones such as forestry and mining.

---

10 Interview with Burhan, Head of the Regional Autonomy Section, 6 December 2010.

11 Note that as this article was being finalized there were reports that this situation might be about to change and that at least some of the long-awaited regulations would soon appear. See, for example, 'Prof. Djohermansyah 95 persen RPP Aceh telah selesai' [Prof. Djohermansyah: 95 per cent of the draft government regulation on Aceh is complete], *Globe Journal*, 12 October 2013.

To give the national government due credit, part of the reason is that drafts of most (but not all) of the required regulations have been produced through a complex process of negotiation involving the Aceh government and various agencies in Jakarta. However, Aceh government officials express frustration with the drawn-out nature of these negotiations, blaming in part rapid staff turnover in the central government negotiating teams, and participation in them of relatively junior staff who are cautious in their approach to sensitive issues, with the result that discussions on simple provisions are often repeated multiple times. Another reported problem is the default tendency on the part of officials in the key ministries to rely on – indeed, often to duplicate – standard national sectoral regulations in designing the special autonomy regulations. One of the most dramatic examples of this came when the Minister of Finance approved a draft government regulation on the special port of Sabang in mid-2010 that ignored a text agreed earlier in the year after a protracted series of about 30 meetings between various levels of government. The new draft prompted Aceh's regional secretary to take the unusual step of publicly condemning the new proposal for 'being based only on national laws and regulations, without referring whatsoever to the Law for the Governing of Aceh'.[12] The regulation was withdrawn.

It is perhaps not surprising that the issues that have proven most difficult to resolve concern natural resources (oil and gas, forestry, land), given the central place that revenue from such resources plays for all governments, but also because of the important patronage streams they provide. The issue of land has been particularly problematic. Article 253 of Law 11/2006 mandated the transfer of the offices and powers of the National Land Agency (BPN) in Aceh to the provincial government by the beginning of 2008, with provincial officials arguing that this implied the transfer of the agency's important licensing functions. In late 2013, the transfer had still not occurred. This issue is significant for local development planning and in the implementation of the peace agreement. Numerous conflicts between development or agricultural companies and local communities have occurred at the grassroots level, putting strain on the peace process. Aceh government officials report that BPN officials in Jakarta have been reluctant to discuss the transfer of their authorities, and they offer a simple explanation: 'Now, to get the authority to open up a big palm oil plantation, for example, people need to go to Jakarta to get permission. That will shift to Aceh.'[13] Similar issues are involved in negotiating the draft national regulation on Aceh's oil and gas reserves,

---

12 'Menkeu anulir RPP Sabang' [Finance minister annuls draft government regulation on Sabang], *Serambi Indonesia*, 13 August 2010.

13 Confidential interview, 6 December 2010.

and the draft on national authorities in Aceh, which touches on issues such as forestry and mining.

It should also be noted that where national regulations *have* been issued, they usually contain articles that further circumscribe Aceh's autonomy. The regulation on local political parties has already been mentioned. Another regulation, one of the first to be produced, was intended to give effect to article 8 of Law 11/2006, on the procedures for consultation when the national government intends to issue a new law or regulation affecting Aceh. Presidential Regulation 75/2008 was promulgated on 24 December 2008 after lengthy negotiations between the Aceh and central governments. For this regulation, the Aceh government had proposed an elaborate dispute resolution mechanism in the event that consultations between Aceh and Jakarta produced disagreement. At one point it seemed that the national government was willing to approve elements of this procedure, but in the end it reverted to an earlier draft that reserved the final say to itself. Some Acehnese view the procedures set down in this presidential regulation as contravening the Helsinki MOU because, according to one adviser to the Aceh government, 'they basically leave all the power in the hands of the president to determine in the event of a failure or breakdown of the consultation process'.[14] In fact, the national government has been diligent in consulting with the Aceh government on most matters affecting the province (including the various outstanding regulations). Even so, the reservation of a final say to the national government has confirmed an outcome that the GAM negotiators in Helsinki had been concerned to avoid: a legal context in which Aceh's autonomy could be eroded piecemeal as a result of legislation and regulations issued in Jakarta.

My purpose in summarizing the chequered history of the new autonomy arrangements in Aceh is not to mount a critique of those arrangements. After all, tensions between national and subnational governments are a feature of all arrangements involving some degree of decentralization. In the Aceh case, many of the reservations of authority to the national government have doubtless been made with sound administrative principles in mind. My purpose, rather, has been to highlight how the outcome has been to place more limits on autonomy than was initially anticipated by many Acehnese. The autonomy currently in force in Aceh certainly falls far short of the goal of all-but-unfettered 'self-government' that GAM leaders aimed for in Helsinki, but nor does it make Aceh a 'state within a state', a fear sometimes articulated by officials in Jakarta.

Partai Aceh politicians and other former GAM leaders have frequently reiterated their disappointment with the outcome, sometimes in very bit-

---

14 Confidential interview with Aceh government adviser, 13 November 2009.

ter terms. As one Partai Aceh member of the Aceh legislature put it when speaking about the flag controversy: 'We have the impression that it's only Aceh that has to obey the wishes of the central government, while they can ignore provisions mandated by law'.[15] Such sentiments are typical of the views held by former GAM combatants; indeed, they often express them far more vividly, in terms of 'betrayal', 'broken promises' and 'deceit' by Jakarta – language that has resonance in Aceh given the territory's history and a powerful local narrative that holds that past conflicts in Aceh were caused by Jakarta's repeated acts of bad faith towards the territory (Aspinall 2009b: 136–7).

19.4   THE CRUX OF THE COMPROMISE

If autonomy has fallen so short of initial GAM expectations, how has it been so successful in cementing peace? Why have former GAM fighters stuck with a deal that has disappointed them in so many ways? There are two elements of the post-2006 autonomy arrangements that go much further than the 2001 special autonomy law, and help to answer these questions. First, the new dispensation produced by the Helsinki MOU and Law 11/2006 provides a series of mechanisms that have allowed former GAM leaders to engage in the political process locally, and in fact to dominate it. Second, new economic arrangements have swelled the coffers of Aceh's provincial and district governments. It is not simply these elements acting independently, however, that has shaped the peace; it is the combination that counts.

Political integration

The 2001 special autonomy law effectively *excluded* former GAM combatants and leaders from the political process, by requiring candidates for direct election to prove they had never been guilty of criminal acts (including subversion), or citizens of other countries (McGibbon 2004: 17–18). Key provisions of the Helsinki MOU and, subsequently, Law 11/2006 were designed specifically to *include* adherents of the movement. First, article 1.2.1 of the MOU allowed the establishment of local political parties in Aceh. (In other parts of the country parties have to show they have a broad national organizational presence before they can contest elections.) Second, article 1.2.2 gave the people of Aceh the 'right to

---

15 'Politisi Partai Aceh: ada kesan pemerintah pusat paksa Aceh ubah bendera' [Partai Aceh politician: there's an impression that the central government is forcing Aceh to change the flag], *Modus Aceh*, 23 May 2013.

nominate candidates for the positions of all elected officials', which was interpreted in Law 11/2006 as allowing independent candidates to stand in direct elections for local government heads. (In other parts of Indonesia at that time candidates had to be nominated by parties that had attained a certain share of the vote or the seats in legislative elections.)

Following these changes, members and supporters of GAM won a succession of election victories.[16] In the first round of direct elections of local government heads (*pilkada*) in 2006 and 2007, independent candidates supported by the movement (some ex-combatants, others supporters) won the governorship and 10 of the 23 district head posts in the province.[17] In the legislative elections in 2009, Partai Aceh became the dominant force in the local legislatures. It won 47 per cent of the vote and took 33 of 69 seats in the provincial parliament and, with the addition of three members of small parties, formed a faction (*fraksi*) that controls an absolute majority there. It also won 237 of the 645 district-level seats available in Aceh, including a majority of seats in seven district legislatures and a plurality in nine (Palmer 2010: 291). In the second round of post-MOU elections of local government heads, held from 2012, Partai Aceh candidates slightly increased their tally. They took the governorship after a bitter contest between the incumbent, Irwandi Yusuf, and the Partai Aceh nominee, Zaini Abdullah, both of whom had GAM backgrounds, following deep conflict caused by Partai Aceh's unsuccessful attempt to prevent Irwandi from standing as an independent. They also picked up three new districts (Aceh Besar, Southwest Aceh and Langsa), but lost two that GAM-supported candidates had won in 2006–07 (West Aceh and South Aceh). These victories had multiple sources. Intimidation was a factor in some places, but there was also a great deal of support for the movement, especially in parts of Aceh where the GAM insurgency had been strong, as well as an element of 'voting for peace' among citizens who felt that supporting the movement was the best way to avoid a return to violence (Clark and Palmer 2008).

This string of election wins propelled a layer of former combatants and other Acehnese nationalists into positions of political power, causing them to face serious challenges of adaptation in the process (Aspinall 2007b; Stange and Patock 2010), but also breathing life into autonomy provisions that had become moribund. For instance, both the 2001 and 2006 laws had included provisions allowing for an Acehnese flag and for the appointment of a Wali Nanggroe. But it was only after Partai Aceh

---

16 See, for example, ICG (2007), Clark and Palmer (2008), Barter (2011) and Palmer (2010).

17 These 10 districts were Sabang, Pidie, Pidie Jaya, Bireuen, North Aceh, Lhokseumawe, East Aceh, Aceh Jaya, West Aceh and South Aceh.

dominated the provincial parliament that *qanun* were passed to put these provisions into effect in ways that played to Acehnese nationalist sentiment, in the first instance by adopting a version of GAM's old flag, and in the second by investing the Wali Nanggroe (Malik Mahmud, the 'prime minister' of GAM) with new powers – prompting friction with Jakarta in the process.[18]

Economic integration

When interviewed in late 2010, the mayor of Aceh's capital, Banda Aceh, gave short shrift to the notion that Law 11/2006 had brought significant change to the way that the daily business of government was conducted in the province's districts: 'The only real change we've experienced since [the law was enacted] is an increase in money. There has been no other significant change ...'.[19] Mayor Mawardy Nurdin was speaking as the head of a city government where former GAM supporters had not fared well in elections, so the political earthquake that had occurred in other parts of Aceh had not much affected his government. But he was right to highlight the economic impact of the law.

In the 2001 special autonomy law, Aceh received additional funds as a result of the greater share of natural resource revenue (especially oil and gas revenue) granted to the province. However, by mid-decade Aceh's oil and gas reserves, and therefore revenues, had begun to decline. To compensate for this – and despite the lack of any such provision in the Helsinki MOU – Acehnese officials succeeded in having a new provision inserted in Law 11/2006 providing Aceh with an additional sum amounting to 2 per cent of the national General Purpose Fund (Dana Alokasi Umum, DAU) for 15 years, declining to 1 per cent for the following five years, with these funds thus lasting until 2027.[20] Although the share of natural resource revenue (*dana migas*) allocated to Aceh has been declining as a result of falling production in the province, the injection of the new special autonomy funds (*dana otsus*) has more than made up for the shortfall. The World Bank has estimated that over the 20 years they are to be provided, approximately Rp 78.6 trillion ($7.9 billion) will be transferred to Aceh, an amount that *exceeds* the total losses caused by the years of conflict in the province. In 2008 alone, the extra funds boosted

---

18 It should be noted that Partai Aceh legislators have been much less enthusiastic about implementing some other provisions of Law 11/2006, such as those mandating the establishment of a truth and reconciliation commission.

19 Interview with Mawardy Nurdin, 6 December 2010.

20 Apparently, the initial Acehnese proposal was for 5 per cent of the DAU, although the negotiators knew from the start that they would probably have to accept less than this (interview with Rusjdi Ali Muhammad, 9 March 2011).

provincial revenues by Rp 3.6 trillion (about $360 million) (MSR 2010: 150–51), leading to local media reports of a 'flood' of special autonomy money washing through Aceh.[21]

Predatory peace

There has been much interest in the effects of this revenue boost on local development (see **Chapter 20** by McCawley). For present purposes, however, we need only note that the increase constitutes a huge injection of resources for predatory capture and patronage purposes. Former GAM members and supporters who have moved into government, as well as their business and political allies, have been major beneficiaries. To some extent, this patronage has taken the form of direct budgetary transfers; in 2013, for example, the provincial budget included grants of Rp 127.5 billion (about $12.5 million) to the Aceh Transitional Committee (Komite Peralihan Aceh, KPA), the organization representing former GAM combatants,[22] with district governments where Partai Aceh is strong making similar, though smaller, transfers. For the first few years after the Helsinki peace deal, there was also a host of national and local government programs (cooperatives, land grants and the like) designed to assist the 'reintegration' of former GAM fighters. Such targeted support for ex-combatants has been in decline but KPA members are still well positioned to benefit from the general assistance programs run by local governments in GAM heartland areas.

Far more important, however, have been the opportunities for informal profiteering and patronage politics the new dispensation has fostered. One good example is a program of so-called 'aspiration funds' (*dana aspirasi*). These are a version of the constituency development funds available in many countries, whereby legislators are allocated a set budget to fund projects in their home electorates. The funds were originally designed as a payoff to the provincial parliament after it objected to the grant of 'working funds' (*dana kerja*) – a slush fund for all kinds of irregular payments – to the governor and deputy governor in 2009.[23] Initially grants were capped at Rp 2 billion (about $200,000) per legisla-

---

21 See, for example, 'Tahun 2008, Aceh Timur kebanjiran dana' [In 2008, East Aceh is flooded with funds], *Serambi Indonesia*, 22 January 2008.

22 'LSM kritisi dana hibah Rp 4,5 T' [NGO criticizes grant funds of Rp 4.5 trillion], *Serambi Indonesia*, 1 March 2013.

23 See, for example, 'Gurihnya perjalanan dinas, ranumnya dana aspirasi' [The tastiness of official travel, the deliciousness of aspiration funds], *Modus Aceh*, 19 March 2009; 'Gubernur minta dana kerjanya Rp 68 m tak diaudit BPK' [Governor requests his working funds of Rp 68 billion not be audited by BPK], *Serambi Indonesia*, 1 June 2009.

tor. In 2012 they totalled almost Rp 543 billion ($54 million), an average of Rp 7.8 billion per legislator, with the highest allocation of Rp 18 billion going to the powerful Partai Aceh figure Adnan Beuransyah.[24] In theory the funds are supposed to support small-scale community development and infrastructure programs in legislators' home constituencies, though a great deal is also provided as direct subsidies (*dana hibah*) to religious and educational institutions, cooperatives, KPA branches and the like. But according to preliminary analysis by the Aceh branch of the Movement against Corruption (Gerakan Anti Korupsi, GeRAK), as much as 50 per cent of the funds may in fact be lost to corruption, with some designated recipients receiving only a fraction of the allocated funds, other recipient organizations being altogether fictitious and some of the grants going to activities that are already funded through the regular development budget.[25] Most district legislatures have copied the province and implemented similar programs, though on a smaller scale.

GAM leaders have also been able to use their political authority to extract resources from many sectors of the economy. One avenue, especially important in the early years of peace, was to obtain projects in the construction sector. Using their newfound political influence, their territorial control in rural areas and the muscle power of their followers, many local KPA commanders were able to gain contracts from both the provincial and district governments to build roads, irrigation channels, bridges and other small-scale infrastructure. While a few of them became successful contractors as a result, most were unable to develop sustainable businesses, instead simply skimming off fees from the projects they had won and then handing them on to more established contractors (Aspinall 2009a).

In the mining sector, a similar process is under way. There has been a veritable boom in mining in the province since security conditions improved, mostly involving small and medium-scale operations extracting a variety of minerals, including iron ore, manganese and gold. In a few districts, former GAM combatants have been directly involved in establishing and running some of these enterprises, but more often they play the role of facilitators and security providers, taking fees for helping companies to secure licences from local governments, and guaranteeing them smooth operations in the field.

Similar dynamics are visible throughout the Aceh economy. In areas where the former combatants are politically powerful, we can find KPA

24 In presenting these figures I am relying on a compilation and spreadsheet prepared by an anti-corruption NGO, GeRAK.
25 Interview with Askhalani, Coordinator of GeRAK Aceh, 12 June 2013. See also Gunawan (2013).

commanders, Partai Aceh politicians and their business and political allies involved in land deals, plantations and the issuing of licences for all manner of business activities. The extraction of projects, rents, licences and fees happens at all levels, involving core leaders of the movement at the provincial level right down to the smallest *sagoe* (the lowest level in the GAM/KPA command structure), where local leaders will try to monopolize, or at least extract fees from, whatever small-scale development projects are occurring in their villages.

In many ways the situation described here is an outgrowth of the dynamic of predation that first became entrenched during the conflict years, when GAM fighters used to skim money off construction projects, Indonesian security forces levied fees on local citizens and businesses, and local politicians created fictitious projects in the knowledge that nobody would venture out to violent areas to check if the funds were being used for their allocated purposes (McGibbon 2004: 29–30; Aspinall 2009b: 178–91). This dynamic has been consolidated during peacetime, with dramatic effect. Movement supporters have been able to extract enough resources to be able to distribute them downward through their networks, and thus construct a powerful political machine in the form of a Partai Aceh–KPA amalgam. Partly as a result, this machine has assumed a position of local political dominance without rival in contemporary Indonesia. In no other province do we see a single party dominating provincial and district legislatures and executive governments to such a degree, let alone possessing an effective paramilitary arm and apparatus of control that stretches down into the villages. No less striking has been the enrichment of a whole layer of former GAM commanders and leaders – a phenomenon that is a popular topic of cynical conversation wherever one travels in Aceh, and which is everywhere visible in the fancy houses, cars, second and third wives, and other symbols of wealth now possessed by many former insurgents.

It is little exaggeration to say that a new layer of predatory rulers has been consolidated in the province. This dynamic is the key to the success of the peace process. Many former combatants have a powerful material interest in maintaining the current arrangements, no matter how disappointed they may be with elements of the autonomy package that applies in Aceh.

19.5 CONCLUSION

From early on in the peace process, Indonesian national leaders believed that convincing GAM fighters to give up their armed struggle and agree to Aceh remaining part of Indonesia would require a concerted attempt to address the economic marginalization they believed was a key driver of the conflict. Early attempts to arrive at a peace deal thus involved promises of both large-scale development projects for Aceh and programs promoting economic reintegration of former combatants, as well as more crude attempts to buy off individual leaders (Aspinall 2005: 16–17). It is hard to avoid the impression that this effort has been massively successful. By opening the spigots of political and economic participation for the former rebels, the government has effectively integrated them into the patronage-based networks that are an important underpinning of national political and economic life in Indonesia. Conceding political control to the former rebels was a bold and even risky move, but (so far at least) the national government has ceded relatively little else that is new in terms of additional political and economic autonomy for Aceh. This approach has been effective in securing the peace so far; most former rebels are too busy pursuing their political and economic advancement to seriously consider a return to armed conflict.

Nevertheless, it is hard to avoid the conclusion that there is a deep, underlying fragility to this outcome. Many features of the old Acehnese nationalist ideology espoused by GAM – an ideology that saw Aceh and Indonesia as incompatible entities, and that positioned Aceh as an eternal victim of manipulation and exploitation by Jakarta – have not been challenged, and have even been reinforced by the current dynamics. Certainly, Partai Aceh and KPA members at all levels espouse a view of Aceh's historical relationship with Indonesia that has changed little since the conflict years. Most talk about the need to maintain a strict dividing line between Indonesia and Aceh, rather than being interested in promoting integration; some mutter quietly about their continued commitment to the independence goal. At the same time, the enrichment of a layer of former nationalist leaders has inevitably led to competition, jealousy and conflict at the grassroots of the movement, sometimes expressed violently.[26]

So far, the buy-in to the new political dispensation by the most senior former leaders of GAM, and their successful construction of a powerful political machine able to discipline the grassroots, has forestalled the emergence of powerful splinter groups promoting renewed violence. The central government has also taken care to prevent conflicts with the Aceh government and Partai Aceh from escalating dangerously – for example, by delaying elections in 2011 while still insisting that independent candidates would be allowed to stand, or by taking steps to de-escalate tensions around the flag in mid-2013. Even so, many of the underlying sources of the Aceh conflict remain unresolved.

---

26 See Anderson (2013) for a recent analysis.

REFERENCES

Anderson, B. (2013) 'Gangster, ideologue, martyr: the posthumous reinvention of Teungku Badruddin and the nature of the Free Aceh Movement', *Conflict, Security & Development*, 13(1): 31–56.

Aspinall, E. (2005) 'The Helsinki agreement: a more promising basis for peace in Aceh', Policy Studies No. 20, East-West Centre, Washington DC.

Aspinall, E. (2007a) 'From Islamism to nationalism in Aceh, Indonesia', *Nations and Nationalism*, 13(2): 245–63.

Aspinall, E. (2007b) 'Guerillas in power', *Inside Indonesia*, 90(October–December).

Aspinall, E. (2009a) 'Combatants to contractors: the political economy of peace in Aceh', *Indonesia*, 87: 1–34.

Aspinall, E. (2009b) *Islam and Nation: Separatist Rebellion in Aceh, Indonesia*, Stanford University Press, Stanford.

Aspinall, E. (2011) 'Aceh's no win election', *Inside Indonesia*, 106(October–December).

Aspinall, E. (2012) 'Special autonomy, lines of authority and access to resources', in E. Aspinall, B. Hillman and P. McCawley (authors) *Governance and Capacity Building in Post-crisis Aceh*, United Nations Development Program and Australian National University Enterprise, Jakarta, Aceh and Canberra.

Aspinall, E. and H. Crouch (2003) *The Aceh Peace Process: Why It Failed*, East West Center, Washington DC.

Aspinall, E., B. Hillman and P. McCawley (2012) 'Governance and capacity building in post-crisis Aceh', report prepared by the Australian National University Enterprise for the United Nations Development Programme, Jakarta.

Awaludin, H. (2008) *Damai di Aceh: Catatan Perdamaian RI-GAM di Helsinki* [Peace in Aceh: Notes from the RI–GAM Peace [Negotiations] in Helsinki], Centre for Strategic and International Studies, Jakarta.

Barter, S.J. (2011) 'The free Aceh elections? The 2009 legislative contests in Aceh', *Indonesia*, 91: 113–30.

Clark, S. and B. Palmer (2008) *Peaceful Pilkada, Dubious Democracy: Aceh's Post-conflict Elections and Their Implications*, Indonesian Social Development Paper No. 11, World Bank, Jakarta.

Gunawan, R. (2013) 'Terindikasi bermasalah, GeRAK sorot dana aspirasi dewan' [Signs of problems, GeRAK focuses on council aspiration funds], *Aceh Online*, 13 March.

Hamid, A.F. (2006) *Jalan Damai Nanggroe Endatu: Catatan Seorang Wakil Rakyat Aceh* [The Road to Peace for the Land of the Ancestors: Notes of a Representative of the People of Aceh], Penerbit Suara Bebas, Jakarta.

Husain, F. (2007) *To See the Unseen: Kisah di Balik Damai di Aceh* [To See the Unseen: The Story behind Peace in Aceh], Health & Hospital Indonesia, Jakarta.

ICG (International Crisis Group) (2006) 'Aceh: now for the hard part', Asia Briefing No. 48, ICG, Jakarta/Brussels, 29 March.

ICG (International Crisis Group) (2007) 'Indonesia: how GAM won in Aceh', Asia Briefing No. 61, ICG, Jakarta/Brussels, 22 March.

ICG (International Crisis Group) (2013) 'Indonesia: tensions over Aceh's flag', Asia Crisis Briefing No. 139, ICG, Jakarta/Brussels, 7 May.

Kingsbury, D. (2006) *Peace in Aceh: A Personal Account of the Helsinki Peace Process*, Equinox Publishing, Jakarta.

May, B. (2006) 'Law on the Governing of Aceh: a brief review and assessment', Powerpoint presentation, available online.

May, B. (2008) 'The Law on the Governing of Aceh: the way forward or a source of conflicts?', *Accord*, 20: 42–5.

McGibbon, R. (2004) *Secessionist Challenges in Aceh and Papua: Is Special Autonomy the Solution?* East West Center, Washington DC.

Miller, M.A. (2006) 'What's special about special autonomy in Indonesia?', in A. Reid (ed.) *Verandah of Violence: The Background to the Aceh Problem*, Singapore University Press, Singapore.

MSR (Multistakeholder Review) (2010) *Multistakeholder Review of Post-conflict Programming in Aceh*, MSR, Jakarta and Aceh.

Palmer, B. (2010) 'Services rendered: peace, patronage and post-conflict elections in Aceh', in E. Aspinall and M. Mietzner (eds) *Problems of Democratisation in Indonesia: Elections, Institutions and Society*, Institute of Southeast Asian Studies, Singapore.

Pemerintah Aceh (2010) 'Implementasi MOU Helsinki dan UUPA: bidang regulasi dan non-regulasi' [Implementation of the Helsinki MOU and the Law on the Governing of Aceh: regulatory and non-regulatory matters], Powerpoint presentation, December.

Stange, G. and R. Patock (2010) 'From rebels to rulers and legislators: the political transformation of the Free Aceh Movement (GAM) in Indonesia', *Journal of Current Southeast Asian Affairs*, 29(1): 95–120.

20 Aceh's economy: prospects for revival after disaster and war

Peter McCawley

20.1 INTRODUCTION

Aceh has a troubled history (Box 20.1). During much of the last century, and notably during the three decades to 2005, local conditions across much of the province were hardly conducive to sustained economic growth and development. Although the development process proceeded apace across most of the rest of Indonesia, throughout much of this period broadly based development in Aceh was slow. Today, widespread poverty is still a major problem in many parts of Aceh and the challenges to be faced of promoting growth remain daunting.

In order to consider options for a development strategy during the period ahead, this chapter will first survey trends in Aceh during the past decade (section 20.2). It will then outline the key development challenges facing Aceh today, focusing first on the impact of the aid program and the 2005 Helsinki peace agreement, and then on the policy issues that need to be considered to promote development (sections 20.3–20.7). Finally, it will set out some of the main points of a development strategy for Aceh (section 20.8).[1]

---

1 This chapter draws on the extended discussion of development challenges in Aceh set out in a study prepared for the United Nations Development Programme (UNDP) by Aspinall, Hillman and McCawley (2012). See Dawood and Sjafrizal (1989) for an earlier, valuable survey of economic developments in Aceh in the 1970s and 1980s.

BOX 20.1 CHRONOLOGY OF EVENTS AFFECTING ACEH

1945   Indonesian independence.

1976   4 December: Hasan di Tiro declares independence for Aceh and forms the Free Aceh Movement (GAM).

1981   Zaini Abdullah (the current governor of Aceh) leaves Indonesia to live in exile in Sweden, where he stays for over 20 years.

1989   August: President Suharto declares a Military Operations Area in Aceh, usually referred to as the Daerah Operasi Militer (DOM) policy. The policy remains in force until 1998.

1998   August: DOM status is withdrawn three months after President Suharto resigns.

1999   National government legislates the initial *reformasi*-era laws on decentralization.

2001   March: Following continuing armed clashes in Aceh, the Indonesian cabinet declares GAM to be a 'separatist movement'.

2002   During 2002 and 2003, under President Megawati Sukarnoputri, the central government pursues efforts to establish arrangements with GAM for special autonomy for Aceh within the Unitary State of the Republic of Indonesia. Agreement cannot be reached, however.

2003   19 May: President Megawati imposes martial law in Aceh and declares a military emergency.

2004   National government legislates further *reformasi*-era laws on decentralization.

2004   26 December: Tsunami mega-disaster occurs, with an estimated death toll in Aceh of 167,000.

2005   January 15: Foreign Minister Hassan Wirajuda announces that the Indonesian government will resume peace talks with GAM.

2005   15 August: MOU signed in Helsinki.

2006   Law 11/2006 on the Governing of Aceh promulgated.
               11 December: Gubernatorial elections held in Aceh.

2007   8 February: Irwandi Yusuf sworn in as governor of Aceh for the five-year period from 2007 to 2012.

2012   25 June: Zaini Abdullah sworn in as governor of Aceh for the five-year period from 2012 to 2017.

2013   Matters of the provincial flag and emblem arise, posing difficulties for Aceh/national government relations.

20.2   DEVELOPMENTS SINCE 2000

The past decade has been a tumultuous period for Aceh. In order to consider both the opportunities and the challenges that Aceh is facing today, it is necessary to consider the difficult situation in the province in the period after the turn of the century, and then the recent history of transformation since 2005.

In the first few years of the post-Suharto period, during the transition to the *reformasi* (reform) era, there was much political change across Indonesia and considerable political upheaval in Jakarta as several presidents came and went in quick succession. There was turmoil in Aceh too, but of a different kind. In the early 1990s the central government had initiated military operations against the separatist Free Aceh Movement (Gerakan Aceh Merdeka, GAM) and around 12,000 troops had been deployed to the province. Clashes between the Indonesian military and GAM were common, with frequent allegations of human rights breaches on both sides. Orderly governance in the province was barely possible. In many areas local development was badly held back.

Then, in the immediate post-Suharto period after 1998, the leadership of GAM became emboldened and the level of tension in Aceh rose markedly, especially in some of the more densely settled areas along the eastern coast.[2] In May 2003, President Megawati Sukarnoputri imposed martial law in Aceh and the central government launched a military offensive. As a result, in the period up to December 2004 when the tsunami struck, over 40,000 soldiers and police officers were engaged in operations against GAM.

The mega-disaster of the great Asian tsunami of 26 December 2004 effectively ended the period of open military hostilities between the central government and GAM. But the long period of conflict reflected deeply held views about the way that Aceh should be developed. The numerous issues that had underpinned the conflict – political, religious, social and economic – remained to be addressed.

The sustained tensions that these issues give rise to in current policy affairs is evident in various ways. For one thing, across Acehnese society there is a continuing deep suspicion and resentment of the central government, and of any institution (such as the Indonesian military or international oil and gas companies) that is seen as having close connections with Jakarta. Also, although Aceh is relatively peaceful for the time being, GAM supporters continue to maintain strong influence in

---

2   A useful survey is provided in the Wikipedia reference for 'Insurgency in Aceh' at https://en.wikipedia.org/wiki/Insurgency_in_Aceh.

the province. Talk of full independence from Indonesia may have been set aside, but the long period of conflict has left a determination among GAM leaders to continue to press for greater autonomy from Jakarta.

The continuing – perhaps even growing – importance of GAM can be seen in the key roles that individuals with connections to the organization have had in the province, both in the past and currently. Two of the most well-known figures with close GAM links are the former governor, Irwandi Yusuf (who held the position from 2007 to 2012), and the current governor, Zaini Abdullah. Numerous other senior figures in the province are associated with GAM and support its aspirations for the future of the province.

Within this context, it should perhaps be noted that the goals and expectations of many members of the Acehnese elite have, for many decades, been ambitious ones. The gap between expectations, on the one hand, and the reality of what changes can reasonably be hoped for, on the other, appears to be large. Until that gap can be narrowed, it seems likely that there will continue to be much discontent in Aceh.

It is against this background that the two key events of the December 2004 tsunami mega-disaster and the peace settlement for Aceh agreed in Helsinki in 2005 together mark a turning point in the recent history of the province. The first event took the lives of perhaps 170,000 people. The disaster quickly led to the design and delivery of a large relief and reconstruction program in Aceh generally estimated at around $7.5 billion over five years.[3] The second event brought an end to the longstanding regional conflict across the province that had held back development for over two decades (World Bank 2008: 16). The peace settlement greatly facilitated efforts to strengthen the processes of orderly governance in Aceh.

Looking back over the post-tsunami recovery period to the end of 2010, it is difficult to disentangle the long-term effects of the large aid program on the one hand and of the 2005 peace settlement on the other. But difficult though the task may be, it is important to consider the interrelationship between the two. For one thing, these two remarkable events are important case studies. Both have generated a large international literature that attempts to distil lessons that may be useful in comparable situations in other parts of the world. For another thing, the longer-term implications of the two events continue to affect events in Aceh today and are relevant in considering a development strategy for the province in the period ahead.

---

3   A detailed overview of the first two years of the post-tsunami aid program in Aceh can be found in Nazara and Resosudarmo (2010).

Figure 20.1   Stages of response in Aceh following the tsunami

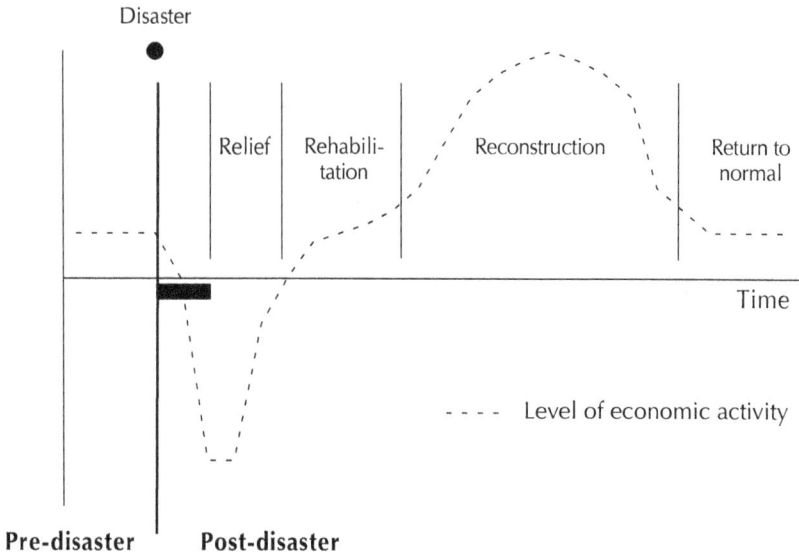

Source: Jayasuriya and McCawley (2010: 25).

20.3   AID TO ACEH

The overall post-tsunami aid program to Aceh, consisting of both international assistance and, importantly, a very large domestic Indonesian involvement, was a remarkable effort (Jayasuriya and McCawley 2010). The program began soon after the tsunami and was composed of a myriad of individual aid programs of varying effectiveness delivered over the next five years until around 2010. During this period, the activities of both Indonesian agencies and international donor agencies passed through a number of phases (Figure 20.1). Three main aspects of this aid program had important long-term implications for growth and governance in Aceh.

First, to a significant degree the economic effects of the aid program came to dominate the formal sector of the non-oil economy in Aceh for the five years following the tsunami. There was, not surprisingly, a surge in both financial and real flows of goods and services into the province, and especially into the tsunami-affected areas near Banda Aceh and along the west coast. This surge – which in some localized areas was very large relative to the size of the local economy – brought both benefits and challenges. Some of the assistance provided much needed physical assets such as food and clothing, medicines, fishing boats, computers to assist with administration and so on. But just as important in terms of the economic impact on the local economy was the dramatic call on resources (both local and imported) generated by the remarkable increase in financial spending through aid programs.

A sharp increase in demand for local resources following a disaster can generate significant strains. This is what happened in various areas in Aceh – especially the disaster-affected areas – following the tsunami. In effect, shock followed shock. First, there was the trauma and shock of the natural disaster itself. Soon after, there was the economic and administrative shock of dealing with the demands arising from the response of well-meaning aid agencies to the disaster.

In Aceh the second shock led, not surprisingly, to 'Dutch disease' challenges for the local economy. This is an economic phenomenon that arises when there is a sudden, sharp increase in financial flows into a region. In essence, there is a local boom. The Dutch disease phenomenon increases demand for local human and physical resources; depending on the supply response, this is likely to stimulate increased employment, cause localized inflation and often lead to an inflow of goods from nearby regions and perhaps imports from overseas.

There were various manifestations of the Dutch disease phenomenon in Aceh. One of the earliest was a jump in prices for hotel rooms, and for the limited supply of well-furnished housing and offices, as the sudden influx of large numbers of aid workers led to a steep increase in demand. There was also a sudden, urgent need for well-trained Indonesian staff with appropriate skills, so local wages for skilled labour tended to increase quite quickly. Later in 2005, and into the next few years as a major construction boom got under way, prices for inputs into construction activities tended to rise as well. Some of these inputs were tradable and could be purchased from other parts of Indonesia, such as the neighbouring province of North Sumatra, but others (such as land) were not tradable and thus local prices tended to rise.

A second consequence of the large aid program was that, in effect, three parallel systems of administration were operating in Aceh during the five-year period from 2005 to 2009. First, there was the usual Indonesian structure of central (*pusat*), provincial and district/municipality (*kabupaten/kota*) governance arrangements. The normal governance link between Jakarta and Banda Aceh had been disrupted somewhat in 2004 when former governor Abdullah Puteh was forced to resign following corruption charges. He was replaced in early 2005 by acting governor Mustafa Abubakar, who administered the province until newly elected governor Irwandi Yusuf took office for the five-year period from 2007 to 2012.

However, administrative arrangements became more complicated in early 2005, shortly after the tsunami, when the central government established the Aceh-Nias Rehabilitation and Reconstruction Agency (Badan Rehabilitasi dan Rekonstruksi, BRR). BRR was formed to oversee much of the administration of the post-tsunami aid program and for some years became almost a parallel administration in Aceh.

The multitude of organizations making up the international donor community active in Aceh in the post-tsunami period made up yet a third layer of administration. Nominally, these organizations were accountable to the Indonesian central government, the provincial government and BRR, but in practice they often operated with a considerable degree of independence.

While officials in the different systems tried their best to coordinate activities, some problems of setting objectives and implementing programs were inevitable (Nazara and Resosudarmo 2010: 115). The three different systems were often, to some extent, working towards different political and governance goals. To complicate matters, their internal administrative procedures were rather different. One result of this situation was that governance arrangements within the province of Aceh did not really converge towards the arrangements that prevailed in most other provinces until 2010. And even when BRR and most international donors had ceased work in Aceh, some difficult post-tsunami issues, such as the vexed and complex one of arranging the transfer of valuable post-tsunami assets, needed further attention.

Another result of the complicated governance arrangements in the province in the period up to 2010 was that the difficult task of designing a program to implement the provisions of the 2005 Helsinki memorandum of understanding (MOU) was, in effect, postponed. Like many agreements of its kind, the Helsinki MOU was a compromise document that left a range of items on which there was disagreement to be resolved at some later time. It is likely that, on one side, the central government hoped that GAM supporters would be prepared to drop some of their demands over time, while on the other side, the GAM delegates believed that further gains might be possible once they had been able to strengthen their position in Aceh.

A third consequence of the presence of the large aid program was to concentrate the attention of many senior policy makers on the challenges of reconstruction in the disaster-affected areas of Aceh. This was, of course, understandable. However, it meant that, over time, communities in other parts of Aceh, such as the poorer districts in southwest Aceh (including Nagan Raya, Southwest Aceh, South Aceh and Aceh Singkil) felt increasingly neglected. A lot of money seemed to be being spent in places like Banda Aceh. Poor communities in other areas increasingly began to wonder why the much vaunted bonanza of international aid brought them so little benefit.

In addition to these considerations, a major policy issue that remains unresolved relates to the 'linking relief, rehabilitation and development' (LRRD) process. Debates about LRRD have received much attention in the international disaster literature in recent years. The central issue relates both to the timing of the delivery of assistance and to the broad goal of aid programs following a disaster: should money be spent quickly so as to provide fast relief, or should an important underlying goal be the promotion of long-term development? The different views on these issues are important because they are reflected in the design and delivery of aid programs after disasters.

The issue of the long-term sustainability of activities supported by aid programs following mega-disasters such as the 2004 Asian tsunami was addressed in a major report released in early 2009 (Brusset et al. 2009). The promotion of the broad sustainability of activities supported by humanitarian aid programs following disasters is not an issue that the international aid community has learned to deal with especially well. It is true that the global aid community has given much attention to challenges of sustainability in the context of environmental issues. However, it has found it much harder to ensure that international aid activities, including humanitarian aid activities following disasters, are sustainable in the broad sense of remaining viable once donor support stops.

By late 2009, Aceh had entered the transition to a return-to-normal phase. Commenting on the need for a 'post-tsunami paradigm', the Banda Aceh daily, *Serambi Indonesia*, summarized some of the main concerns as follows:

> ... [S]tudies of post-disaster reconstruction are marked by the speed of infrastructure development in Aceh. But there is no guarantee that things will get better, or become more peaceful, or that there will be prosperity. The reality is that large amounts of funds have flowed into Aceh but have not reached out to touch basic social and real needs, especially for those who are economically, politically, socially and legally vulnerable. Good roads and luxurious buildings can exist alongside people who are still living in barracks, suffering from bad nutrition, and not getting health and education services – and this is both a bad precedent as well as an indicator that development in Aceh is still below what it should be. Furthermore, there are certain groups who aim to create disturbances in Aceh and who are irresponsible, discriminative, and who form 'organized gangs' with the potential to do damage in Aceh ('Mengubah paradigma pascatsunami' [Changing the post-tsunami paradigm], *Serambi Indonesia*, 26 December 2009).

Senior policy makers in Aceh in 2010 were well aware of the fact that the past benefits from the tsunami reconstruction and rehabilitation process would not be sufficient to overcome the wide range of social and development challenges in the province. What was less clear was how to design a viable post-tsunami development strategy.

20.4   THE 2005 HELSINKI PEACE AGREEMENT

The other key event in the recent history of the province was the signing of the 2005 Helsinki peace accord. Earlier attempts to broker an agreement between GAM and the central government had failed, and in 2003 the security situation had deteriorated sharply once again (Box 20.1). But following the dreadful event of the tsunami there was a renewed determination on both sides – arguably for a range of different reasons – to try once more to reach agreement.

In mid-January, less than four weeks after the tsunami, Indonesian foreign minister Hassan Wirajuda announced that the Indonesian government would resume talks with GAM representatives. Events moved quickly. Within two weeks, talks between delegations from both sides began in Helsinki in Finland. The negotiations were difficult and threatened to break down on several occasions. But eventually an acceptable compromise was reached and a peace agreement was signed in Helsinki on 15 August 2005.

Three aspects of the peace agreement were central to the restoration of medium-term stability and growth in Aceh. First, it was agreed that fighting would stop, that GAM would demobilize and that it would surrender all arms and explosives it possessed. Second, key arrangements were put in place to allow for the political participation of 'Aceh-based political parties' across the province. This opened the way for GAM to become an accepted, active political organization in Aceh. Third, it was agreed that a new Law on the Governing of Aceh would be promulgated to provide significantly increased authority to key leaders and stakeholders in Aceh.[4]

These three elements of the Helsinki MOU, along with other supporting parts of the agreement, provided acceptable political room for both GAM and the central government to cease hostilities. It is true that the MOU left important matters of disagreement to be settled in later discussions. But these unresolved issues notwithstanding, the Helsinki agreement represented a turning point in ending the longstanding regional conflict in Aceh (Aspinall 2005).

As many senior GAM supporters in Aceh still see things in 2013, some of the main central promises set out in the Helsinki MOU have not been

---

4   This was achieved in 2006 with the passage of Law 11/2006 on the Governing of Aceh.

met. One of the main reasons for this is that, for various reasons, GAM supporters were not in a position to press for the further implementation of the provisions of the MOU until the main post-tsunami assistance effort had ended. After that, the tussle for influence within GAM between supporters of Governor Irwandi Yusuf and followers of traditional GAM figures such as Zaini Abdullah served to further divert the attention of supporters from the issue of implementation of the Helsinki MOU. It was only when Abdullah defeated Yusuf for the governorship of Aceh in 2012 that GAM judged that the time was right to return, after a period of seven years, to a political program of renewing pressure on the central government to implement key parts of the agreement.

20.5   STOCKTAKE OF THE ECONOMY

Economic analysis of the overall performance of the Acehnese economy in recent years is complicated by the fact that the regional economy is marked by two distinct forms of dualism. The first is the sectoral dualism reflected in the difference between the resource-rich oil and gas part of the economy (concentrated particularly around the Lhokseumawe area in the district of North Aceh) and the non-oil and gas sector. The second is the urban–rural dualism reflected in the different levels of development in the better-off urban areas (especially Banda Aceh) and in the other parts of the province that do not have oil and gas resources.

The sectoral dualism of the Achenese economy is clearly evident in gross regional product (GRP) data. At the broadest level, total GRP (including oil and gas) has fluctuated markedly since 2000 (Figure 20.2). Moreover, average annual real growth over the 12-year period from 2000 to 2011 was *negative* 0.7 per cent (Table 20.1). Clearly, in overall terms, the Acehnese economy has performed very poorly during the past decade.

But a second view of the regional economy that focuses on non-oil and gas activities is just as useful. Production operations in the oil and gas sector are mainly enclave activities that have few direct linkages with the rest of the regional economy. When they are excluded from the regional economic statistics, a rather different picture emerges. Economic growth in the non-oil and gas sector has fluctuated markedly since 2000, but not nearly as sharply as in the oil and gas sector (Table 20.1). The main characteristics of the growth pattern in the non-oil sector since 2000 are, first, positive though somewhat disappointing growth (of around 4 per cent on average over the 12-year period), and second, a boom of sorts in 2006 and 2007, presumably reflecting the stimulus following the post-tsunami aid and reconstruction effort.

Figure 20.2   Real economic growth in Aceh, including and excluding oil and gas, 2000–11

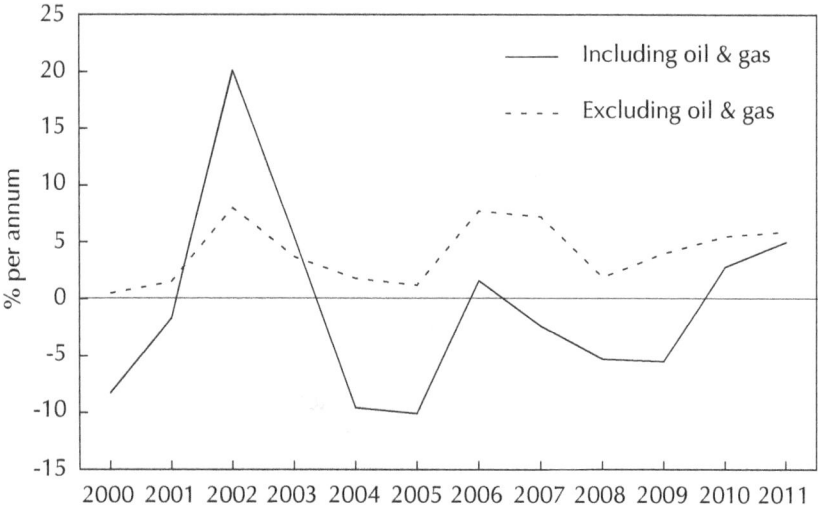

Source: BPS and BPPA (various years).

In reviewing the current state of the Acehnese economy, it is also helpful to survey recent patterns of economic growth in the province at the sectoral level. These indicate marked variations in growth patterns. The steady downward trend in oil and gas output shows up in the sector's sharp negative contributions to overall growth in the province (Table 20.1). In contrast, the non-oil sectors of the economy show stronger signs of growth. Not surprisingly, the impact of the tsunami is reflected in output in several of the main sectors in 2005. In the agriculture, utilities, construction and finance sectors, growth was held back in the immediate wake of the tsunami. There was then strong growth in several key sectors in 2006 and 2007 as spending on rehabilitation and reconstruction began to gather pace. The construction sector expanded by a remarkable 48 per cent in 2006 and another 14 per cent in 2007. There were also marked increases in output in several other sectors (trade and hotels, and transport and communications) resulting from the large increases in aid spending.

The net result of these differences in growth rates in different parts of the Acehnese economy was that the structure of the economy changed dramatically during the 12-year period from 2000 to 2011. The contribution of the oil and gas sector to GRP fell sharply from over 40 per cent in 2000 to under 20 per cent in 2011. Within the non-oil and gas sector,

Table 20.1 Real economic growth in Aceh, 2000–11 (% p.a.)

	2000	2001	2002	2003	2004	2005	2006	2007	2008	2009	2010	2011	Average
Agriculture	1.5	-3.2	2.1	3.3	6.0	-3.9	1.5	3.6	0.8	2.6	5.0	5.6	2.1
Oil & gas	-21.6	-5.4	34.8	7.3	-20.3	-23.8	-7.3	-19.9	-23.1	-36.6	-11.7	-0.6	-10.7
Manufacturing	-11.3	-31.3	61.6	1.6	-37.3	-5.1	1.1	8.5	3.6	4.5	6.4	5.9	0.7
Trade, hotels & restaurants	-1.1	11.3	2.2	2.5	-2.7	6.6	7.4	1.7	4.6	4.9	6.4	6.8	4.2
Other services	5.0	11.8	7.5	6.1	12.4	4.3	21.7	5.2	1.1	4.7	5.2	5.6	7.6
Total (including oil & gas)	**-8.3**	**-1.7**	**20.1**	**5.5**	**-9.6**	**-10.1**	**1.6**	**-2.4**	**-5.3**	**-5.5**	**2.8**	**5.0**	**-0.7**
Total (excluding oil & gas)	**0.5**	**1.5**	**8.0**	**3.7**	**1.8**	**1.2**	**7.7**	**7.2**	**1.9**	**4.0**	**5.5**	**5.9**	**4.1**

Source: BPS and BPPA (various years).

the shares of agriculture and the tiny non-oil manufacturing sector also fell slightly, while the services sector, broadly defined, expanded (Figure 20.3).

In summary, the broad trends evident in the recent data on economic growth across the province are the following.

- Overall growth in the non-extractive economic sectors has been significant but not high since 2000 – on average, about 4 per cent per annum.
- In the oil and gas sector, large and continuing reductions in output have markedly affected the overall provincial growth rate.
- Tsunami spending provided a significant boost to activity in the non-oil and gas sector, especially in 2006–07. However, just as the initial burst of tsunami spending stimulated growth through a positive economic multiplier effect, so the winding down of activities appears to have contributed to a slower growth rate through a negative multiplier effect.
- Economic activity appears to have accelerated in 2010–11; nevertheless, economic growth in Aceh has remained significantly below the average growth rate for the overall Indonesian economy.

Looking ahead, a key priority for economic policy makers in Aceh is to accelerate growth in the non-oil sector. To do this, they will need, on the one hand, to adjust development programs to deal with the impact of the sharply declining contribution from the oil and gas sector, and, on the other hand, to build on the various physical and institutional assets that now exist in the province following the significant boost to development provided by the post-tsunami assistance programs.

20.6   ISSUES OF SIZE

In reviewing the structural aspects of the provincial economy and in thinking about economic policy, it is useful to take note of absolute magnitudes (Table 20.2). In monetary terms, bearing in mind that the population of the province is around 4.5 million, the economic magnitudes being discussed are not large. Total GRP in 2011, including the oil and gas sector, was around Rp 86 trillion (approximately $8.6 billion). GRP excluding oil and gas was around Rp 72 trillion ($7.2 billion).

These magnitudes are important. First, Aceh is one of the so-called resource-rich provinces of Indonesia, with both the advantages and challenges that this brings. One of the main advantages is the expanded flows of natural resource revenues available to Aceh. One of the main

Figure 20.3 Sectoral shares of gross regional product in Aceh, including and excluding oil and gas, 2000–11

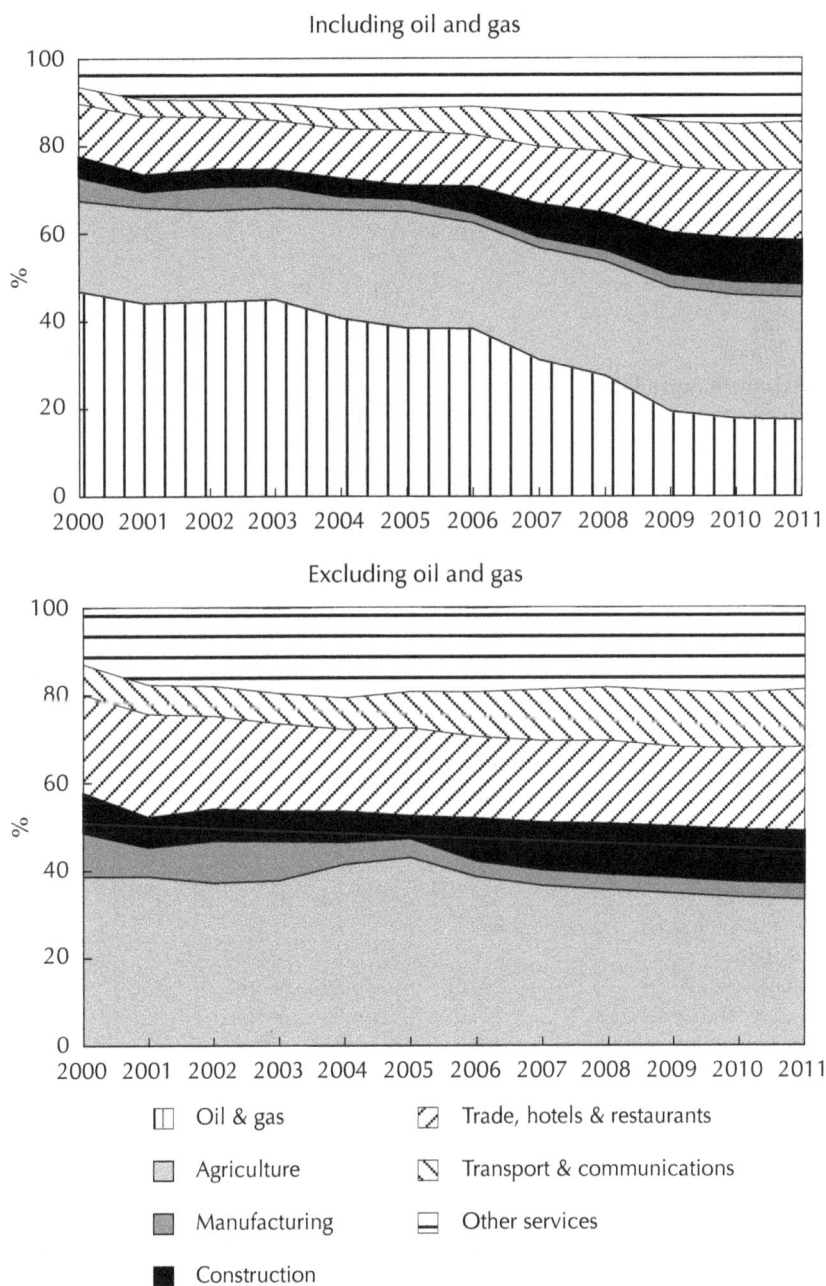

Including oil and gas

Excluding oil and gas

⊞ Oil & gas	▨ Trade, hotels & restaurants
▨ Agriculture	◺ Transport & communications
▨ Manufacturing	⊟ Other services
■ Construction	

Source: BPS and BPPA (various years).

Table 20.2   Selected key facts: Aceh and Indonesia

	Year	Unit	Aceh	Indonesia
Population				
Total	2010	million	4.5	237.6
Population density	2010	per km²	77	124
GDP & income per capita				
GDP	2010	$	7.8	642
Rp per year per capita	2010	Rp thousand	17,223	27,030
$ per year per capita	2010	$	1,722	2,703
Government				
Provinces	2011	no.	1	33
Districts	2011	no.	23	497
Subdistricts	2011	no.	287	6,747
Government expenditure				
Aceh province	2009	Rp trillion	9.8	
		$ million	980	
Aceh districts	2009	Rp trillion	10.4	
		$ million	1,040	
Indonesia	2010	Rp trillion		1,042
		$ million		104,000
Economic structure				
Workforce				
Agriculture	2010	%	46	40
Manufacturing	2010	%	5	13
Construction	2010	%	6	5
Trade, hotels & restaurants	2010	%	18	21
Transport & communications	2010	%	4	5
Other services	2010	%	21	15
Total	2010	%	100	100
Minimum wage				
Rp per month	2011	Rp thousand	1,350	989
$ per month	2011	$	135	99
Education				
Primary schools	2010	per million people	858	696
Junior secondary schools	2010	per million people	267	185
Senior secondary schools	2010	per million people	87	45
Health				
General hospitals	2009	per million people	9	6
Public health clinics	2009	per million people	69	37
Poverty				
Urban	2010	% poor	13.7	9.2
Rural	2010	% poor	21.9	15.7
Total	2010	% poor	19.6	12.5

Source: BPS (2011), *Statistik Indonesia.*

disadvantages is the pressures arising from the Dutch Disease phenomenon, including, importantly, a loss of economic competitiveness when compared with other provinces in Indonesia, especially the nearby province of North Sumatra, which is generally better endowed with facilities (such as the main port of Medan).

A second aspect of the magnitudes is that, in economic terms, the Acehnese economy is small. Some comparisons provide context. The Acehnese economy in total is somewhat less than 2 per cent of the Indonesian economy, and much smaller than the neighbouring economies of Malaysia, Thailand and Singapore. Obviously, the differing population sizes need to be borne in mind. However, even allowing for the relative sizes of populations, the differences are striking.

Size has a number of significant policy implications. Most individual production units (farms, firms and equivalent units) in Aceh are, in economic terms, very small indeed. The Establishment Census, which collects data on non-agricultural firms in Aceh, reports that in 2006 approximately 750,000 people were employed in almost 370,000 enterprises across the province. Several things are striking about this situation. First, the overwhelming majority of enterprises were really micro-enterprises, employing just one or two people. Only a few firms had over 10 employees. This structural feature of the Acehnese economy is very significant, because production units of this kind are quite unable to achieve modern economies of scale. Second, most enterprises (over 90 per cent) reported that they had no legal status. In effect, the great bulk of enterprises were operating in the informal sector with little direct contact with the formal institutions of the state. Third, the majority of people were active in just two areas: trading and manufacturing. In the former sector, the operation of small-scale stalls and shops was presumably the main activity, while the supply of manufacturing services, such as the repair of cars and motorcycles and the manufacture of simple metal-based products, was included in the latter category.

The policy response towards this phenomenon of smallness needs to be two-fold. On the one hand, appropriate packages of support (credit, infrastructure, marketing arrangements) need to be designed to fit the special needs of micro-entrepreneurs, especially female entrepreneurs. On the other hand, policies are needed to encourage the development of larger firms, because it is unrealistic to imagine that an economy composed almost entirely of micro-firms can compete successfully with the larger firms that exist in nearby economies such as North Sumatra (Medan), Malaysia and Singapore.

Another aspect of size is reflected in provincial government expenditures across Indonesia. As noted earlier, because Aceh is one of the resource-rich provinces, its provincial revenues benefit from the tax revenues received from the resource sector. This allowed the provincial government of Aceh to maintain a level of total budgetary expenditure in 2011 of around $800 million, or around $175 per person per annum.

Three aspects of this level of provincial expenditure need to be noted. One is that it is relatively high by Indonesian standards. For example, in 2011 the average level of per capita expenditure by provincial governments in Java (excluding the special case of Jakarta) was a remarkably low $24 per capita.

Second, although high by Indonesian standards, the level of expenditure in Aceh is extremely low by international standards, and severely limits the level of services that can be provided to the community. Similar levels of government in rich OECD countries (in provinces, or province-like, jurisdictions) often maintain levels of annual spending of around $6,000–8,000 per capita. Thus, whether the level of spending by the Aceh provincial government is seen as high or low depends entirely upon the benchmark that one chooses to use as a measuring rod.

A third aspect to note is that although the main focus of this chapter is on the processes of government at the provincial level, expenditure at the district (*kabupaten/kota*) level is important as well. In Aceh, total expenditures at the district level in 2011 (of around $1.2 billion) were about 50 per cent more than spending at the provincial level ($800 million). For Indonesia as a whole, expenditures at the district level in 2011 (of almost $40 billion) were roughly three times the total amount of expenditures controlled by provincial governments ($13 billion). The clear implication of this situation is that many of the challenges of provincial budget management are just as relevant for budget management at the district level in Aceh.

20.7 THE PROBLEM: LOOKING AHEAD

Looking ahead, from the point of view of governance and capacity building in Aceh, there appear to be two fundamental challenges that need to be addressed. The first is to promote economic growth, especially in a way that creates jobs and supports income-earning activities in small-scale activities. The second is to convert government financial revenues obtained from the resource sector and other revenue areas into public goods (roads, water supplies, electricity, health, education) that supply services of tangible benefit to the majority of the population. More specifically, it is useful to consider four strategic issues that require immediate attention: widespread poverty, and the associated need to promote development; rural policy; the role of the provincial government; and the proliferation (*pemekaran*) of local governments across the province.

Poverty

Various surveys have drawn attention to the enduring problem of poverty across Aceh. The World Bank's (2008) *Aceh Poverty Assessment* discusses trends in detail, as do numerous other studies prepared during the past few years (Cosgrave 2009a, 2009b; BPS, Government of Aceh and UNDP 2010). The key findings of the different surveys may be summarized as follows.

First, the 2004 tsunami caused huge economic damage as well as enormous personal and psychological loss in the affected areas; the province-wide impacts, however, were more limited. The largest damages and losses were generally concentrated in the areas directly affected by the disaster. Although province-wide measured poverty increased slightly after the tsunami, the statistical increase in poverty was rather short-lived. Among other things, the provision of relief, rehabilitation and reconstruction aid, in many different ways, appears to have been effective in helping alleviate the expected impact of the tsunami on poverty.

Second, setting the effects of the tsunami aside, widespread poverty has been a major problem in Aceh for decades. Largely because of the effects of conflict across the province, which have, among other things, greatly hampered rural development, Aceh has had poverty levels well above those seen in most other regions in Indonesia in recent decades (BPS, Government of Aceh and UNDP 2010). The high levels of poverty, especially in rural areas, are closely correlated with low or negative overall economic growth across the province. Although the main reason for slow growth was the longstanding conflict affecting the province, structural economic issues (connected especially with the large oil and gas reserves on Aceh's east coast) also appear to have affected the pattern of economic development. One central challenge in the immediate future, therefore, will be to promote economic expansion in ways that help to sustain social stability and peace in the province.

Third, poverty in Aceh (using conservative poverty levels) is especially marked in rural areas. In 2012, over 20 per cent of rural households were living below the poverty line (Table 20.3). Bearing in mind that the rural poverty line was approximately Rp 308,000 ($31) per person per month – which is significantly below the widely used international poverty line of $1.25 per day – it is clear that rural poverty is widespread in Aceh. Non-income characteristics associated with high poverty are the ones that are common in many developing countries, such as large households, low education levels, a high proportion of female-headed households and a high share of households predominantly dependent on agriculture. Issues affecting women – including access to assets (land, housing and other assets), pressures of household maintenance and care of children, opportunities to earn income and protection against

500   *Peter McCawley*

Table 20.3   Poverty in Aceh, March 2012[a]

	Number of poor (thousand)	Poor as share of total population (%)	Monthly poverty line	
			Rp thousand	$
Aceh				
Rural poor	737	22	308	31
Urban poor	172	13	350	35
Total poor	909	19		
Total population	**4,600**			
Indonesia				
Rural poor	18,400	15	229	23
Urban poor	10,650	9	267	27
Total poor	29,230	12		
Total population	**241,180**			

a   Data are approximate. Total population data and poverty data are from different surveys, so some totals do not match exactly.
Source: BPS (2012), *Statistik Indonesia.*

violence – became particularly important in the post-tsunami period. All these issues had important implications for household incomes (IDLO and UNDP 2007; BPS, Government of Aceh and UNDP 2010).

Rural policy

Rural policy is a second strategic issue that needs attention. Given the patterns of poverty across the province, pro-poor development programs during the return-to-normal period will need to focus on promoting growth in both agricultural and non-agricultural activities in rural areas. One main step will be to implement programs at the province-wide level to promote overall economic growth (World Bank 2009). In recent years, the Indonesian government has aimed for a national growth rate of around 6.5 per cent per annum.[5] It would seem that similar rates of

5 Details of the economic growth targets for the period to 2014 are set out in the National Medium Term Development Plan for 2010–2014 (Rencana Pembangunan Jangka Menengah Nasional 2010–2014), released in February 2010. A useful summary may be found at World Bank (2010). See also the growth targets set out in the Masterplan for the Acceleration and Expansion of Indonesia's Economic Development 2011–2025 (MP3EI).

growth at the provincial level in Aceh will be needed to make significant inroads into poverty.[6] However, it is also necessary to recall that different patterns of economic growth have different impacts on the overall level of poverty. Economic growth that has a higher poverty elasticity is more beneficial to the poor. But a significant share of the overall measured economic growth in Aceh during the past decade or so has been of a capital-intensive nature in enclave activities in the oil and gas sector. In general, economic growth of this type often fails to have regional spread effects that benefit the poor. This appears to have been the case in Aceh. Indeed, the 'enclave development' pattern of growth in the province was identified as a challenge for policy makers over 20 years ago, when Dawood and Sjafrizal (1989: 122) noted that 'The challenge for the provincial government is to harness the indirect effects of the [oil and gas] boom to develop the potential for the rest of the economy'. This is a challenge that still needs to be addressed by policy makers in Aceh.

To make inroads into poverty, especially in rural areas, a second main policy step is to find ways of encouraging development that are pro-poor. In particular, an increasing emphasis on development in rural areas is needed during the return-to-normal period to address concerns that some aspects of the post-tsunami assistance have been too urban-oriented. Measures would appear to be needed on both the supply and demand sides of local rural economies in Aceh. On the supply side, programs to increase the productivity of farmers would help to increase output. But it is very discouraging for farmers to put effort into increasing production only to find that it is difficult to sell their goods. Thus, on the demand side, programs to improve access to markets are also needed. Improving rural infrastructure (roads, markets, village infrastructure) would help improve access to markets for farmers as well as create jobs and stimulate local economies. Indeed, it was measures along these lines that Dawood and Sjafrizal (1989: 122) identified two decades ago to promote development in Aceh:

> [T]o ensure efficient resource allocation and exploitation of the province's abundant natural resources, continuing massive investments in infrastructure – particularly roads – are required. All the major agricultural subsectors have considerable potential if the current transport bottlenecks can be removed. … [I]n conjunction with these investments, there needs to be an expansion in agricultural extension programmes in fisheries, forestry, livestock, non-rice food crops, and selected estate crops. These measures will provide the 'unity of the dual economy' and will be important in restoring Aceh to its position as one of the most prosperous and progressive regions in Indonesia.

---

6 Sulaiman (2009) provides some details of steps taken by Governor Mustafa Abubakar during 2006 to promote economic growth in Aceh in the period following the tsunami.

Looking ahead, these recommendations for infrastructure investment and other supply-side measures to boost productivity seem just as appropriate today as when they were set out in the late 1980s. But other steps should also be taken to promote rural development, including programs to improve access to markets for rural producers, and targeted measures to reach the poor in rural areas.

Role of the provincial government

A third area of strategic focus relates to the relationship between the provincial government and the wider community. The political and social environment in Indonesia in 2013 is very different to that which prevailed during the Suharto New Order period. Indonesia is now widely recognized as one of the most democratic countries in Asia.

The shift towards a much more contestable political model at the national level has been reflected in changes at the local level as well. It is now quite common across Indonesia for the decisions of political leaders at both the provincial and district levels of government to be discussed vigorously by regional media (such as the daily newspaper, *Serambi Indonesia*, in Aceh) and by civil society groups. To give just one example of the way that issues are discussed in this open and contestable environment, in December 2009 a *Serambi Indonesia* columnist levelled a series of criticisms at the Aceh provincial government (Nivada 2009). The article detailed concerns regarding the administration of the Agency for the Peaceful Reintegration of Aceh (Badan Reintegrasi Damai Aceh); the work of the Committee for the Acceleration of Neglected Areas of Aceh; the activities of the Sabang Area Management Agency; the credit issues of the Regional Development Bank of Aceh; the moratorium on illegal logging; and the suggestions of increasing corruption in Aceh.

Considered in their entirety, the comments seemed to suggest incompetent administration within the provincial government. Whether this was true in the case of the particular examples mentioned is undoubtedly open to question. More generally, however, what is notable in the current environment of public discourse in Aceh is a perceived freedom on the part of civil society actors to criticize governments, as well as a willingness on the part of governments to respond to such criticisms.

Another aspect of the vigorous public policy dialogue taking place in Aceh is that discussions focus on both the formulation and implementation of policy. Some commentators press for better and clearer policies in such areas as post-tsunami policy development and government management. Others are more concerned with down-to-earth issues such as perceived shortcomings in service delivery in sectors such as health, education, basic transport, and law and order.

Proliferation of local governments

The fourth strategic issue requiring attention is the proliferation of subnational governments. In recent years, there has been a remarkable increase in the number of regional government units in Indonesia at both the provincial and district levels through the splitting of existing regions. This process has become known as *pemekaran*, literally meaning 'blossoming'. In historical terms, there was a marked phenomenon of *pemekaran* during the 1950s, especially the latter part of the decade.[7] The process slowed somewhat during the 1960s, and then largely stopped during the long 28-year period from 1971 to 1998 comprising the main part of the New Order period. But following the surge in support for decentralization that occurred after the main decentralization laws were passed in 1999, the process of *pemekaran* led to a jump in the total number of large regional units (provinces and districts) from around 330 in 1998 to over 520 a decade later.

Although widely seen as a welcome change at the end of the Suharto era, the process of *pemekaran* has become increasingly controversial.[8] It has presented important challenges for the government of Aceh, where 11 of the existing 21 district governments have been formed since 2000, and the number of subdistricts (*kecamatan*) increased from 243 in 2006 to 276 just two years later. The formation of so many new administrative units reflects strong local political pressures from political actors and communities who believe they will be advantaged by *pemekaran*. In February 2010, for example, demonstrations in the capital of South Aceh, Tapaktuan, obliged the district head to agree to put a proposal to the local assembly proposing the further fragmentation of the district through the formation of new subdistricts.[9]

In Aceh, as elsewhere across Indonesia, *pemekaran* has led to new demands of various kinds, affecting both the dynamics of provincial politics as well as administrative and financial arrangements. Moreover, the capacity of the administrative units varies widely.[10] Importantly, the

---

7   See UNDP (2009: 5) for details on the historical background of the tension between centralistic tendencies and pressures for decentralization in Indonesia.

8   See, for example, the critical comments by a spokesperson for the Indonesian Human Rights Committee for Social Justice reported in the article 'Pemekaran wilayah: jumlah kota di Indonesia meningkat 57 persen lebih' [Regional *pemekaran*: total number of municipalities in Indonesia jumps by over 57 per cent], *Kompas*, 12 October 2011.

9   'Ribuan warga tuntut pemekaran kecamatan' [Thousands demand the creation of subdistricts], *Serambi*, 27 February 2010.

10   For a useful survey of financial management performance at the district level in Aceh in mid-2006, see World Bank (2007).

establishment of each new regional unit automatically leads to the establishment of a regional assembly with a full set of political players.

This, in turn, has led to new social, financial and political debates at both the local and provincial levels. As a study by USAID–DRSP (2009: 17) has observed: 'The creation of new minorities within the new regions also holds the potential for conflict, and raises the possibility of subsequent claims for new regions or reconfiguration of regions'.

20.8   DEVELOPMENT STRATEGY FOR ACEH

At the broadest level, Aceh currently faces a daunting array of development challenges at the human, physical, and government and capacity-building levels. But now, perhaps for the first time in almost 40 years, leaders in Aceh appear to have a relatively free hand to support local economic and social reform in an environment largely free of conflict. The new governor, Zaini Abdullah, was able to win a clear mandate in the 2012 elections. Now, at this early point in his term, he is in a relatively strong position to promote change. In principle, the opportunities open to the local elite to promote effective governance are the most promising they have been since the mid-1970s.

A useful survey of the main human development challenges in Aceh can be found in the 2010 *Provincial Human Development Report* for the province (BPS, Government of Aceh and UNDP 2010). It is clear that a comprehensive development strategy for Aceh needs to set out programs for reform across numerous sectors. But in broad terms, and considering the limited resources of governments in Aceh, it would seem appropriate for both the provincial and district governments to focus on two main priorities in the period ahead: promoting economic growth, and reforming the role of government.

Promoting economic growth

A provincial development strategy for Aceh for the next five years might focus on two areas in particular. The first is to promote economic growth in ways that are pro-job and that support income-earning activities in small-scale informal-sector activities, especially in rural areas. The second is to convert government financial resources obtained from the resource sector as well as other revenue areas into public goods that supply much needed services such as roads, water supplies, electricity, health and education.

The promotion of economic growth, in turn, implies a focus on increasing the level of investment in the private and public sectors. An effective strategy will need both to set goals and to discuss, in detail, how those goals are to be achieved.

Rural development in particular needs to be a central part of Aceh's provincial development strategy. A package of measures focusing on both the supply side and the demand side would be appropriate. A set of possible approaches to rural development might include improved infrastructure, promotion of productivity at the farm level, provision of key social services and support for the development of the private sector.

The effective mobilization and use of financial resources, especially to create public goods to be supplied to the majority of the population, should also be a central part of the provincial development strategy. Management of provincial public finances currently presents a major problem for the government of Aceh. Steps to improve the situation are urgently needed.

Reforming the role of government

Surveys of public opinion suggest that the Acehnese community looks to the government to provide peace and prosperity, and for the efficient delivery of basic public goods such as health, education, infrastructure services (water and electricity) and support for agricultural and business development. For their part, in numerous public documents and statements, governments in Aceh have committed themselves in principle to improving the supply of public services. Arguably, then, since the policy commitment is clear, the effective *implementation* of policy, rather than the more detailed *definition* of policy, is now the main priority for the effective delivery of good government in Aceh.

But the capacity of governments to deliver what is expected of them is often limited. Governments everywhere, including in Aceh, have strengths to draw on but also face challenges of implementation. For governments in Aceh to become more effective, they need to define their roles carefully. In particular, in view of their quite limited capacities, they need to decide which services will be provided directly by government agencies, and which will be supplied indirectly by relying on service providers in the private sector. In each case, the role of the government and government agencies is very different.

Looking to the future, it would seem inevitable that Aceh's provincial and district governments will need to aim to strengthen *both* the private sector across the province *and* the internal capacity of government to regulate, and to strengthen, local markets. Reform in this direction will require improved skills within government to foster the private sector, while also providing an appropriate regulatory environment for the private sector to expand.

In broad terms, an approach of this sort suggests that moving towards a more performance-based model of government in Aceh would have substantial advantages. A strengthening of mechanisms of 'exit' and 'voice' would be consistent with this strategy and would help empower the citizens of Aceh to participate fully in the development of Acehnese society.

REFERENCES

Aspinall, E. (2005) 'The Helsinki agreement: a more promising basis for peace in Aceh', Policy Studies No. 20, East-West Centre, Washington DC.

Aspinall, E., B. Hillman and P. McCawley (2012) 'Governance and capacity building in post-crisis Aceh', report prepared by the Australian National University Enterprise for the United Nations Development Programme, Jakarta.

BPS (Badan Pusat Statistik) (various years) *Statistik Indonesia* [Indonesian Statistics], BPS, Jakarta.

BPS (Badan Pusat Statistik) and BPPA (Badan Perencanaan Pembangunan Aceh) (various years) *Aceh dalam Angka* [Aceh in Figures], BPS, Banda Aceh.

BPS (Badan Pusat Statistik), Government of Aceh and UNDP (United Nations Development Programme) (2010) *Provincial Human Development Report Aceh 2010*, UNDP, Jakarta.

Brusset, E. et al. (2009) *A Ripple in Development? Long Term Perspectives on the Response to the Indian Ocean Tsunami 2004*, Swedish International Development Cooperation Agency (SIDA), Sweden.

Cosgrave, J. et al. (2009a) *Summary Report. A Ripple in Development?* Swedish International Development Cooperation Agency (SIDA), Sweden.

Cosgrave, J. et al. (2009b) *A Ripple in Development? Document Review*, Swedish International Development Cooperation Agency (SIDA), Sweden.

Dawood, D. and Sjafrizal (1989) 'Aceh: the LNG boom and enclave development', in H. Hill *Unity and Diversity: Regional Economic Development in Indonesia since 1970*, Oxford University Press, Singapore.

IDLO (International Development Law Organization) and UNDP (United Nations Development Programme) (2007) *Perempuan Aceh di Hadapan Hukum Setelah Konflik dan Tsunami Berlalu: Laporan Case Study* [Acehnese Women in the Fact of the Law after Conflict and the Tsunami: Case Study Report], IDLO and UNDP, Aceh.

Jayasuriya, S. and P. McCawley (2010) (eds) *The Asian Tsunami: Aid and Reconstruction after a Disaster*, Asian Development Bank Institute and Edward Elgar Publishing, Cheltenham and Massachusetts.

Nazara, S. and B.P. Resosudarmo (2010) 'Indonesia: the first two years after the tsunami', in S. Jayasuriya and P. McCawley (eds) *The Asian Tsunami: Aid and Reconstruction after a Disaster*, Asian Development Bank Institute and Edward Elgar Publishing, Cheltenham and Massachusetts.

Nivada, A. (2009) 'Refleksi tiga tahun kinerja gubernur kita' [Reflections on the performance of our governor over three years], *Serambi Indonesia*, 28 December.

Sulaiman, D. (2009) 'Percepatan pembangunan ekonomi' [Accelerating economic development], in R. Mukri and Mujiyanto (eds) *Berani Tidak Popular: Mustafa*

Abubakar Memimpin Aceh masa Transisi [Brave Is Not Popular: Mustafa Abubakar Leads Aceh during the Period of Transition], Jakarta, Sinar Harapan.

UNDP (United Nations Development Programme) (2009) 'The missing link: the province and its role in Indonesia's decentralisation', Policy Issues Paper, UNDP, Jakarta, May.

USAID–DRSP (United States Agency for International Development–Democratic Reform Support Program) (2009) *Decentralization 2009: Stock Taking on Indonesia's Recent Decentralization Reforms. Update 2009: Summary Report*, USAID–DRSP, Jakarta, July.

World Bank (2007) *Public Financial Management in Aceh: Measuring Financial Management Performance in Aceh's Local Governments*, World Bank, Jakarta.

World Bank (2008) *Aceh Poverty Assessment 2008: The Impact of the Conflict, the Tsunami and Reconstruction on Poverty in Aceh*, World Bank, Jakarta.

World Bank (2009) 'Aceh economic update: May 2009', World Bank, Jakarta.

World Bank (2010) 'Indonesia economic quarterly: building momentum', World Bank, Jakarta, March.

Author index

Subject index

INDONESIA UPDATE SERIES

1989
Indonesia Assessment 1988 (Regional Development)
edited by Hal Hill and Jamie Mackie

1990
Indonesia Assessment 1990 (Ownership)
edited by Hal Hill and Terry Hull

1991
Indonesia Assessment 1991 (Education)
edited by Hal Hill

1992
Indonesia Assessment 1992 (Political Perspectives)
edited by Harold Crouch

1993
Indonesia Assessment 1993 (Labour)
edited by Chris Manning and Joan Hardjono

1994
Indonesia Assessment 1994: Finance as a Key Sector in Indonesia's Development
edited by Ross McLeod

1996
Indonesia Assessment 1995: Development in Eastern Indonesia
edited by Colin Barlow and Joan Hardjono

1997
Indonesia Assessment: Population and Human Resources
edited by Gavin W. Jones and Terence H. Hull

1998
Indonesia's Technological Challenge
edited by Hal Hill and Thee Kian Wie

1999
Post-Soeharto Indonesia: Renewal or Chaos?
edited by Geoff Forrester

2000
Indonesia in Transition: Social Aspects of Reformasi and Crisis
edited by Chris Manning and Peter van Diermen

2001
Indonesia Today: Challenges of History
edited by Grayson J. Lloyd and Shannon L. Smith

2002
Women in Indonesia: Gender, Equity and Development
edited by Kathryn Robinson and Sharon Bessell

2003
Local Power and Politics in Indonesia: Decentralisation and Democratisation
edited by Edward Aspinall and Greg Fealy

2004
Business in Indonesia: New Challenges, Old Problems
edited by M. Chatib Basri and Pierre van der Eng

2005
The Politics and Economics of Indonesia's Natural Resources
edited by Budy P. Resosudarmo

2006
Different Societies, Shared Futures: Australia, Indonesia and the Region
edited by John Monfries

2007
Indonesia: Democracy and the Promise of Good Governance
edited by Ross H. McLeod and Andrew MacIntyre

2008
Expressing Islam: Religious Life and Politics in Indonesia
edited by Greg Fealy and Sally White

2009
Indonesia beyond the Water's Edge: Managing an Archipelagic State
edited by Robert Cribb and Michele Ford

2010
Problems of Democratisation in Indonesia: Elections, Institutions and Society
edited by Edward Aspinall and Marcus Mietzner

2011
Employment, Living Standards and Poverty in Contemporary Indonesia
edited by Chris Manning and Sudarno Sumarto

2012
Indonesia Rising: The Repositioning of Asia's Third Giant
edited by Anthony Reid

2013
Education in Indonesia
edited by Daniel Suryadarma and Gavin W. Jones

2014
Regional Dynamics in a Decentralized Indonesia
edited by Hal Hill

www.ingramcontent.com/pod-product-compliance
Lightning Source LLC
Chambersburg PA
CBHW050226270326
41914CB00003BA/590